HEALTH SECURITY
AND GOVERNANCE

Critical Concepts in Military, Strategic, and Security Studies

HEALTH SECURITY AND GOVERNANCE

Critical Concepts in Military, Strategic, and Security Studies

Edited by
Nicholas Thomas

Volume I
Health Security and Foreign Policy Challenges

Routledge
Taylor & Francis Group

LONDON AND NEW YORK

First published 2013
by Routledge
2 Park Square, Milton Park, Abingdon, Oxon OX14 4RN

Simultaneously published in the USA and Canada
by Routledge
711 Third Avenue, New York, NY 10017

Routledge is an imprint of the Taylor & Francis Group, an informa business

British Library Cataloguing in Publication Data
A catalogue record for this book is available from the British Library

Library of Congress Cataloging in Publication Data
Health security and governance : critical concepts in military, strategic, and security
studies / edited by Nicholas Thomas.
     p. ; cm. – (Critical concepts in military, strategic, and security studies)
  Includes bibliographical references and index.
  ISBN 978-0-415-67104-0 (set : alk. paper) – ISBN 978-0-415-67105-7 (v. 1 : alk. paper) –
ISBN 978-0-415-67107-1 (v. 2 : alk. paper) – ISBN 978-0-415-67108-8 (v. 3 : alk. paper) –
ISBN 978-0-415-67109-5 (v. 4 : alk. paper)
  I. Thomas, Nicholas, 1970– II. Series: Critical concepts in military, strategic,
and security studies.
  [DNLM: 1. Health Policy. 2. Communicable Diseases, Emerging. 3. Human Rights.
4. Security Measures. 5. World Health. WA 530.1]
  LC classification not assigned
  362.1–dc23
                                                                              2011051203

ISBN: 978-0-415-67104-0 (Set)
ISBN: 978-0-415-67105-7 (Volume I)

Typeset in 10/12pt Times NR MT
by Graphicraft Limited, Hong Kong

Publisher's Note
References within each chapter are as they appear in the original complete work

Printed and bound in Great Britain by the MPG Books Group

To Tanya,
for all her love and support

CONTENTS

CONTENTS

VOLUME II INFECTIOUS DISEASES AND SECURITY

CONTENTS

CONTENTS

CONTENTS

VOLUME III   GLOBAL HEALTH GOVERNANCE – POLITICS, INSTITUTIONS AND ETHICS

CONTENTS

CONTENTS

CONTENTS

VOLUME IV   RIGHTS, LIBERTIES AND LAWS

CONTENTS

ACKNOWLEDGEMENTS

The publishers would like to thank the following for permission to reprint their material:

Council of Foreign Relations for permission to reprint Laurie Garrett, 'The Return of Infectious Disease', *Foreign Affairs*, (Vol. 71, No. 1, January/ February, 1996), pp. 66–79.

Oxford University Press for permission to reprint William Aldis, 'Health Security as a Public Health Concept: a Critical Analysis', *Health Policy and Planning*, (Vol. 23, 2008), pp. 369–375.

Oxford University Press for permission to reprint Steven J. Hoffman, 'The Evolution, Etiology and Eventualities of the Global Health Security Regime', *Health Policy and Planning*, (Vol. 25, No. 6, 2010), pp. 510–22.

Taylor & Francis for permission to reprint Paula Gutlove and Gordon Thompson. 'Human Security: Expanding the Scope of Public Health', *Medicine, Conflict & Survival*, (Vol. 19, No. 1, 2003), pp. 17–34.

Ashgate Publishing for permission to reprint David P. Fidler, 'A Pathology of Public Health Securitism: Approaching Pandemics as Security Threats', in Cooper, Andrew F., Kirton, John J. and Schrecker, Ted (eds.) *Governing Global Health: Challenge, Response, Innovation*, (Aldershot: Ashgate Publishing Ltd., 2007), pp. 41–63.

Lynne Rienner Publishers for permission to reprint Gro Harlem Brundtland, 'Global Health and International Security', *Global Governance*, (Vol. 9, No. 4, 2003), pp. 417–423.

Wiley for permission to reprint Sara E. Davies, 'Securitizing Infectious Disease', *International Affairs*, (Vol. 84, No. 2, 2008), pp. 295–313.

Taylor & Francis for permission to reprint David L. Heymann, 'The Evolving Infectious Disease Threat: Implications for National and Global Security', *Journal of Human Development*, (Vol. 4, No. 2, 2003), pp. 191–207.

Taylor & Francis for permission to reprint Susan Peterson, 'Epidemic Disease and National Security', *Security Studies*, (Vol. 12, No. 2, 2002), pp. 43–81.

Sage for permission to reprint Sandra J. Maclean, 'Microbes, Mad Cows and Militaries: Exploring the Links between Health and Security', *Security Dialogue*, (Vol. 39, No. 5, 2008), pp. 475–94.

Oxford University Press for permission to reprint Harley Feldbaum, Kelley Lee and Joshua Michaud, 'Global Health and Foreign Policy', *Epidemiologic Reviews*, (Vol. 32, No. 1, 2010), pp. 82–92.

Cambridge University Press for permission to reprint Colin McInnes and Kelley Lee, 'Health, Security and Foreign Policy', *Review of International Studies*, (Vol. 32, No. 1, 2006), pp. 5–23.

British Medical Journal for permission to reprint Nicholas Banatvala and Anthony B. Zwi, 'Conflict and Health: Public Health and Humanitarian Interventions: Developing the Evidence Base', *British Medical Journal*, (Vol. 321, No. 7253, 2000), pp. 101–5.

University of Bradford for permission to reprint John Grundy, Peter Leslie Annear, Seema Mihrshahi, 'Balancing National Security with Human Security – A Call for Comprehensive Pre-Event Public Health Analysis of War and Defence Policy', *Journal of Peace, Conflict and Development*, (No. 12, May 2008), 17 pp.

Cambridge University Press for permission to reprint Frederick M. Burkle, Jr., 'Future Humanitarian Crises: Challenges for Practice, Policy, and Public Health', *Prehospital and Disaster Medicine*, (Vol. 25, No. 3, May–June, 2010), pp. 191–9.

Annual Reviews for permission to reprint M. J. Toole and R. J. Waldman. 'The Public Health Aspects of Complex Emergencies and Refugee Situations', *Annual Review of Public Health*, (No. 18, 1997), pp. 283–312.

Elsevier for permission to reprint M. A. Connolly, M. Gayer, M. J. Ryan, P. Salama, P. Spiegel, D. L. Heymann. 'Communicable Diseases in Complex Emergencies: Impact and Challenges', *The Lancet*, (Vol. 364, 27 November, 2004), pp. 1974–83.

Elsevier for permission to reprint Stephen C. Waring and Bruce J. Brown. 'The Threat of Communicable Diseases Following Natural Disasters: A Public Health Response', *Disaster Management & Response*, (Vol. 3, No. 2, April–June 2005), pp. 41–7.

Disclaimer

Chronological table of reprinted articles and chapters

Date	Author	Article/chapter	Reference	Vol.	Chap.
1987	Andrew Green	The role of non-governmental organizations and the private sector in the provision of health care in developing countries	*International Journal of Health Planning and Management*, 2:1, 37–58	III	86
1994	Lucy Gilson, Priti Dave Sen, Shirin Mohammed and Phare Mujinja	The potential of health sector non-governmental organizations: policy options	*Health Policy and Planning*, 9:1, 14–24	III	88
1994	Jonathan M. Mann, Lawrence Gostin, Sofia Gruskin, Troyen Bremman, Zita Lazzarini and Harvey V. Fineberg	Health and human rights	*Health and Human Rights*, 1:1, 6–23	IV	100
1995	Christer Jönsson and Peter Söderholm	IGO–NGO relations and HIV/AIDS: innovation or stalemate?	*Third World Quarterly*, 16:3, 459–76	III	89
1995	Mary E. Wilson	Travel and the emergence of infectious diseases	*Emerging Infectious Diseases*, 1:2, 39–46	III	93
1996	Jack C. Chow	Health and international security	*Washington Quarterly*, 16:2, 63–77	I	11
1996	Laurie Garrett	The return of infectious disease	*Foreign Affairs*, 75:1, 66–79	I	1
1997	Ilona Kickbusch	New players for a new era: responding to the global public health challenges	*Journal of Public Health Medicine*, 19:2, 171–8	III	56
1997	M. J. Toole and R. J. Waldman	The public health aspects of complex emergencies and refugee situations	*Annual Review of Public Health*, 18, 283–312	I	22
1998	Derek Yach and Douglas Bettcher	The globalization of public health, I: threats and opportunities	*American Journal of Public Health*, 88:5, 735–44	III	59
1999	Andrew T. Price-Smith	Ghosts of Kigali: infectious disease and global stability at the turn of the century	*International Journal*, 54:3, 426–42	I	2

Chronological table continued

Date	Author	Article/chapter	Reference	Vol.	Chap.
1999	Brigit Toebes	Towards an improved understanding of the international human right to health	Human Rights Quarterly, 21:3, 661–79	IV	101
2000	Nicholas Banatvala and Anthony B. Zwi	Conflict and health: public health and humanitarian interventions: developing the evidence base	British Medical Journal, 321:7253, 101–5	I	19
2000	K. Buse and G. Walt	Global public–private partnerships: part II – what are the health issues for global governance?	Bulletin of the World Health Organization, 78:5, 699–709	III	69
2000	Kent Buse and Gill Walt	Role conflict? The World Bank and the world's health	Social Science Medicine, 50:2, 177–9	III	65
2000	Kelley Lee and Richard Dodgson	Globalization and cholera: implications for global governance	Global Governance, 6:2, 213–36	III	57
2001	Joseph Barbera, Anthony Macintyre, Larry Gostin, Tom Inglesby, Tara O'Toole, Craig DeAtley, Kevin Tonat and Marci Layton	Large-scale quarantine following biological terrorism in the United States: scientific examination, logistic and legal limits, and possible consequences	Journal of the American Medical Association, 286:21, 2711–7	IV	111
2001	Roy Widdus	Public–private partnerships for health: their main targets, their diversity, and their future directions	Bulletin of the World Health Organization, 79:8, 713–20	III	68
2002	Richard Dodgson, Kelley Lee and Nick Drager	Global Health Governance: A Conceptual Review	Discussion Paper 1, Geneva: World Health Organization and London School of Hygiene and Tropical Medicine, 27 pp.	III	55
2002	Tony Evans	A human right to health?	Third World Quarterly, 23:2, 197–215	IV	99
2002	Susan Peterson	Epidemic disease and national security	Security Studies, 12:2, 43–81	I	14

Chronological table continued

Date	Author	Article/chapter	Reference	Vol.	Chap.
2004	Máire A. Connolly, Michelle Gayer, Michael J. Ryan, Peter Salama, Paul Spiegel and David L. Heymann	Communicable diseases in complex emergencies: impact and challenges	*Lancet*, 364, 1974–83	I	23
2004	Melissa Curley and Nicholas Thomas	Human security and public health in Southeast Asia: the SARS outbreak	*Australian Journal of International Affairs*, 58:1, 17–32	II	33
2004	Mark J. DeHaven, Irby B. Hunter, Laura Wilder, James W. Walton and Jarett Berry	Health programs in faith-based organizations: are they effective?	*American Journal of Public Health*, 94:6, 1030–6	III	90
2004	A. J. McMichael	Environmental and social influences on emerging infectious diseases: past, present and future	*Philosophical Transactions of the Royal Society of London B Biological Science*, 359:1447, 1049–58	III	94
2004	Marc L. Ostfield	Bioterrorism as a foreign policy issue	*SAIS Review*, 24:1, 131–46	II	49
2004	Simon Shen	The "SARS Diplomacy" of Beijing and Taipei: competition between the Chinese and non-Chinese orbits	*Asian Perspectives*, 28:1, 45–65	II	35
2004	Alexandra Minna Stern and Howard Markel	International efforts to control infectious diseases, 1851 to the present	*Journal of the American Medical Association*, 292:12, 1474–9	III	53
2004	Allyn L. Taylor	Governing the globalization of public health	*Journal of Law, Medicine & Ethics*, 32:3, 500–8	III	58
2004	Caroline Thomas and Martin Weber	The politics of global health governance: whatever happened to "Health for all by the year 2000"?	*Global Governance*, 10:2, 187–205	III	60

Year	Author(s)	Title	Publication	Part	Page
2004	Robin A. Weiss and Anthony J. McMichael	Social and environmental risk factors in the emergence of infectious diseases	Nature Medicine, 10:12, S70–S76	III	92
2005	Daniele Archibugi and Kim Bizzarri	The global governance of communicable diseases: the case for vaccine R&D	Law & Policy, 27:1, 33–51	III	67
2005	Mely Caballero-Anthony	SARS in Asia: crisis, vulnerabilities, and regional responses	Asian Survey, 45:3, 475–95	II	34
2005	David P. Fidler	Health as foreign policy: between principle and power	Whitehead Journal of Diplomacy and International Relations, 6, 179–94	I	16
2005	Laurie Garrett	The next pandemic?	Foreign Affairs, 84:4, 3–23	II	37
2005	Jennifer Prah Ruger	The changing role of the World Bank in global health	American Journal of Public Health, 95:1, 60–70	III	66
2005	Andreas Schloenhardt	Keeping the ill out: immigration issues in Asia concerning the exclusion of infectious diseases	Hong Kong Law Journal, 35:2, 445–80	IV	115
2005	Stephen C. Waring and Bruce J. Brown	The threat of communicable diseases following natural disasters: a public health response	Disaster Management & Response, 3:2, 41–7	I	24
2006	Michael G. Baker and David P. Fidler	Global public health surveillance under new International Health Regulations	Emerging Infectious Diseases, 12:7, 1058–65	III	79
2006	Theodore M. Brown, Marcos Cueto and Elizabeth Fee	The World Health Organization and the transition from "international" to "global" public health	American Journal of Public Health, 96:1, 62–72	III	83
2006	Jon Cohen	The new world of global health	Science, 311:5758, 162–7	III	64
2006	Stefan Elbe	Should HIV/AIDS be securitized? The ethical dilemmas of linking HIV/AIDS and security	International Studies Quarterly, 50:1, 119–44	II	29
2006	Mark Harrison	Disease, diplomacy and international commerce: the origins of international sanitary regulation in the nineteenth century	Journal of Global History, 1:2, 197–217	III	54

Chronological table continued

Date	Author	Article/chapter	Reference	Vol.	Chap.
2006	Colin McInnes and Kelley Lee	Health, security and foreign policy	Review of International Studies, 32:1, 5–23	I	18
2006	Susan Okie	Global health—the Gates–Buffett effect	New England Journal of Medicine, 355:11, 1084–8	III	91
2006	Julian Palmore	A clear and present danger to international security: Highly Pathogenic Avian Influenza	Defense & Security Analysis, 22:2, 111–21	II	38
2006	Ann Swidler	Syncretism and subversion in AIDS governance: how locals cope with global demands	International Affairs, 82:2, 269–84	II	32
2006	Nicholas Thomas	The regionalization of Avian influenza in East Asia: responding to the next pandemic(?)	Asian Survey, 46:6, 917–36	II	39
2006	B. Vallat, J. Pinto and A. Schudel	International organisations and their role in helping to protect the worldwide community against natural and intentional biological disasters	Revue Scientifique et Technique, 25:1, 163–72	III	82
2007	Augustine D. Asante and Anthony B. Zwi	Public-private partnerships and global health equity: prospects and challenges	Indian Journal of Medical Ethics, 4:4, 176–80	III	70
2007	Cécile M. Bensimon and Ross E. G. Upshur	Evidence and effectiveness in decisionmaking for quarantine	American Journal of Public Health, Supplement 1, 97:S1, S44–S48	IV	110
2007	Philippe Calain	Exploring the international arena of global public health surveillance	Health Policy and Planning, 22, 2–12	III	80
2007	Richard Coker, Marianna Thomas, Karen Lock and Robyn Martin	Detention and the evolving threat of tuberculosis: evidence, ethics, and law	Journal of Law, Medicine & Ethics, 35:4, 609–15	IV	109

Year	Author(s)	Title	Publication		
2007	Timothy John Downs and Heidi Jane Larson	Achieving millennium development goals for health: building understanding, trust and capacity to respond	*Health Policy*, 83, 144–61	III	61
2007	David P. Fidler	A pathology of public health securitism: approaching pandemics as security threats	Andrew F. Cooper, John J. Kirton and Ted Schrecker (eds) *Governing Global Health: Challenge, Response, Innovation*, Aldershot: Ashgate, pp. 41–63	I	7
2007	David P. Fidler, Lawrence O. Gostin and Howard Markel	Through the quarantine looking glass: drug resistant tuberculosis and public health governance, law, and ethics	*Journal of Law, Medicine & Ethics*, (Winter), 616–28	IV	114
2007	Pieter Fourie	The relationship between the AIDS pandemic and state fragility	*Global Change, Peace & Security*, 19:3, 281–300	II	30
2007	Lance Gable	The proliferation of human rights in global health governance	*Journal of Law, Medicine & Ethics* (Winter), 534–44	IV	102
2007	Alexander Kelle	Securitization of international public health: implications for global health governance and the biological weapons prohibition regime	*Global Governance*, 13:2, 217–35	II	51
2007	Elizabeth M. Prescott	The politics of disease: governance and emerging infections	*Global Health Governance*, 1:1, 1–8	III	75
2007	Guénaël Rodier, Allison L. Greenspan, James M. Hughes and David L. Heymann	Global public health security	*Emerging Infectious Diseases*, 13:10, 1447–52	I	8
2007	Jessica L. Sturtevant, Aranka Anema and John S. Brownstein	The new International Health Regulations: considerations for global health surveillance	*Disaster Medicine and Public Health Preparedness*, 1:1, 117–21	III	81
2008	William Aldis	Health security as a public health concept: a critical analysis	*Health Policy and Planning*, 23, 369–75	I	4

Chronological table continued

Date	Author	Article/chapter	Reference	Vol.	Chap.
2008	Sara E. Davies	Securitizing infectious disease	*International Affairs*, 84:2, 295–313	I	12
2008	Cathal Doyle and Preeti Patel	Civil society organisations and global health initiatives: problems of legitimacy	*Social Science & Medicine*, 66:9, 1928–38	III	87
2008	Amy L. Fairchild, Ronald Bayer and James Colgrove	Privacy, democracy and the politics of disease surveillance	*Public Health Ethics*, 1:1, 30–8	IV	113
2008	John Grundy, Peter Leslie Annear and Seema Mihrshahi	Balancing national security with human security – a call for comprehensive pre-event public health analysis of war and defence policy	*Journal of Peace, Conflict and Development*, 12, 17 pp.	I	20
2008	Sandra J. Maclean	Microbes, mad cows and militaries: exploring the links between health and security	*Security Dialogue*, 39:5, 475–94	I	15
2008	Gregory J. Moran, David A. Talan and Fredrick M. Abrahamian	Biological terrorism	*Infectious Disease Clinics of North America*, 22:1, 148–87	II	50
2008	Roxanna Sjöstedt	Exploring the construction of threats: the securitization of HIV/AIDS in Russia	*Security Dialogue*, 39:1, 7–29	II	26
2008	Michael A. Stoto	Public health surveillance in the twenty-first century: achieving population health goals while protecting individuals' privacy and confidentiality	*Georgetown Law Journal*, 96:2, 703–19	IV	112
2008/ 2009	Devi Sridhar, Sanjeev Khagram and Tikki Pang	Are existing governance structures equipped to deal with today's global health challenges – towards systematic coherence in scaling up	*Global Health Governance*, 2:2, 1–25	III	84
2009	Tim Anderson	HIV/AIDS in Cuba: a rights-based analysis	*Health and Human Rights*, 11:1, 93–104	IV	105

Chronological table continued

Date	Author	Article/chapter	Reference	Vol.	Chap.
2009	Nirmala Ravishankar, Paul Gubbins, Rebecca J. Cooley, Katherine Leach-Kemon, Catherine M. Michaud, Dean T. Jamison and Christopher J. L. Murray	Financing of global health: tracking development assistance for health from 1990 to 2007	*Lancet*, 373:9681, 2113–24	III	71
2009	F. Sim and P. Mackie	The State's role and health – swine flu as a case study	*Public Health*, 123:8, 521–2	II	43
2009	Frank L. Smith	WHO governs? Limited global governance by the World Health Organization during the SARS outbreak	*Social Alternatives*, 28:2, 9–12	II	36
2010	Frederick M. Burkle, Jr.	Future humanitarian crises: challenges for practice, policy, and public health	*Prehospital and Disaster Medicine*, 25:3, 191–9	I	21
2010	Stefan Elbe	Haggling over viruses: the downside risks of securitizing infectious disease	*Health Policy and Planning*, 25:6, 476–85	III	76
2010	Christian Enemark	The role of the Biological Weapons Convention in disease surveillance and response	*Health Policy and Planning*, 25:6, 486–94	II	52
2010	Harley Feldbaum, Kelley Lee and Joshua Michaud	Global health and foreign policy	*Epidemiologic Reviews*, 32:1, 82–92	I	17
2010	Antoine Flahault and Patrick Zylberman	Influenza pandemics: past, present and future challenges	*Public Health Reviews*, 32:1, 319–40	II	41
2010	Nathan Ford, Alexandra Calmy and Samia Hurst	When to start antiretroviral therapy in resource-limited settings: a human rights analysis	*BMC International Health and Human Rights*, 10:6, 9 pp.	IV	104

Year	Authors	Title	Source	Part	Page
2010	Karen M. Hilyard, Vicki S. Freimuth, Donald Musa, Supriya Kumar and Sandra Crouse Quinn	The vagaries of public support for government actions in case of a pandemic	*Health Affairs*, 29:12, 2294–301	II	45
2010	Steven J. Hoffman	The evolution, etiology and eventualities of the global health security regime	*Health Policy and Planning*, 25: 510–22	I	5
2010	Colin McInnes and Simon Rushton	HIV, AIDS and security: where are we now?	*International Affairs*, 86:1, 225–45	II	28
2010	Simon Rushton	AIDS and international security in the United Nations system	*Health Policy and Planning*, 25:6, 495–504	III	77
2010	Nicole A. Szlezák, Barry R. Bloom, Dean T. Jamison, Gerald T. Keusch, Catherine M. Michaud, Suerie Moon and William C. Clark	The global health system: actors, norms, and expectations in transition	*PLoS Medicine*, 7:1, e1000183.	IV	95
2010	Matthew Thompson and Carl Heneghan	Antivirals for pandemic influenza: a triumph of policy over evidence?	*Trends in Pharmacological Sciences*, 31:9, 391–3	II	44
2010	Kumanan Wilson, John S. Brownstein and David P. Fidler	Strengthening the International Health Regulations: lessons from the H1N1 pandemic	*Health Policy and Planning*, 25:6, 505–10	II	47
2011	Melissa G. Curley and Jonathan Herington	The securitisation of avian influenza: international discourses and domestic politics in Asia	*Review of International Studies*, 37, 141–66	II	40
2011	Andrew Harmer	Understanding change in global health policy: ideas, discourse and networks	*Global Public Health*, 6:7, 703–18	IV	98

PREFACE

The existential threat to humanity posed by infectious diseases is a re-occurring fact of modern life. Understanding how such threats are securitized and how the response strategies are governed is critical to comprehending just how serious these diseases are to the functionality of states and to the well-being of their peoples. This is not simply a biomedical issue but one that draws in political scientists, international relations analysts, cultural affairs specialists, lawyers and ethicists – to name but a few. Drawing in all these different perspectives is problematic. They each have their own disciplinary methods for evaluating actions and cases, sometimes to the exclusion of other fields.

The inspiration for these volumes arose out of a long-running project on health security, which began in early 2003 when SARS emerged in Hong Kong. All we knew initially was that there was a bad form of the flu going around. As the weeks went on it was clear that not only was SARS a lot worse than the flu but that the best efforts of the doctors, nurses and virologists needed to be placed alongside legal, social, political and economic considerations if the virus was to be beaten. Since then, the editor has been involved in various workshops and conferences that have explored these issues. By drawing together both security theories as well as governance approaches, it is hoped that a deeper appreciation of the complexity of infectious disease outbreaks can be gained.

These volumes would not have been possible without the outstanding people at Routledge. Dominic Shryane and Maria Barrow, in particular, provided exceptional advice and support that enabled this series to be realized. As well, those whose works appear in this series should also be acknowledged for their excellent scholarship. The better we know how to respond to the threat of infectious diseases, the more prepared we can be.

INTRODUCTION
Securitizing Health

Catherine Lo Yuk Ping[1] and Nicholas Thomas[2]

Whether naturally occurring or intentionally inflicted, microbial agents can cause illness, disability, and death in individuals while disrupting entire populations, economies, and governments. In the highly interconnected and readily traversed 'global village' of our time, one nation's problem soon becomes every nation's problem as geographical and political boundaries offer trivial impediments to such threats.[3]

The end of the Cold War – and with it the demise of superpower conflict predicated on military strength – opened an intellectual and policy space for the consideration of threats of a non-military nature. In 1994, the United Nations Development Programme released its annual report entitled *New Dimensions of Human Security*. Although directed towards a development studies audience, the report was quickly co-opted by security studies policy-makers and scholars as a landmark document that established the initial parameters for the then nascent field of non-traditional security research. Among the seven fields of human security identified in the report was that of health security.

The 1994 report identified health security as encompassing infectious diseases in the developing world as well as lifestyle diseases in the developed world. It suggested that common vulnerabilities in both worlds included an unequal distribution of resources to combat disease as well as unequal access to health services. Where these insecurities overlapped were the sites of greatest health insecurity – with higher rates of infant mortality, the easier spread of infectious diseases and lower life expectancies. However, while the 1994 report created a set of baseline parameters for non-traditional security in general, and health security in particular, it only identified issues. A notable gap in the report is any understanding as to how these health challenges become to be identified as security threats. Put simply, in policy terms how is it possible to tell that 'X' is truly a threat? What are the indicators for a health challenge becoming a threat and, once it is identified as such, what are the appropriate responses?

Into this gap stepped the Copenhagen School (Buzan, Wæver and de Wilde) who suggested that the course of threat identification – the process by which 'X' became 'securitized' – could be broken down into several phases.[4] The first phase of securitization requires an actor to identify an existential threat to their existence. This identification is declaratory in nature (a speech act). This is followed by the acceptance of the issue by a target audience (usually civil society) who are convinced of its existential threat potential. With this acceptance comes a third phase shift whereby an emergency (extra-budgetary) reallocation of resources is made to combat the threat. Once the threat is successfully resolved, the issue is de-securitized to an extent that – if still present – it simply becomes part of the general policy environment with a re-allocation of resources back to earlier priorities.

However, what the Copenhagen School does not address is the politics of a disease threat. In conceptualizing a rational-actor model – where policy-makers logically respond to threats because they threaten human existence – the securitization model ignores real-world situations where securitizing actors – for domestic reasons – can deliberately choose not to securitize an existential health threat or may securitize the threat via a speech act but choose not to allocate emergency resources to resolve it. The model – located within a state structure – is also vague as to how it can be applied in inter-national organizations or across state borders. In identifying and resolving health threats, understanding the rationales of these different actors towards emergency health responses is critical. This requires an understanding of governance models. Given that, as Pierre suggested, governance requires 'sustaining co-ordination and coherence among a wide variety of actors with different purposes and objectives such as political actors and institutions, corporate interests, civil society, and transnational organizations'[5] such a perspective provides an applied lens through which observers can more accurately map the full range of interactions in a health emergency. As the papers in these four volumes demonstrate, the process of securitizing health threats (such as diseases) is frequently shaped by non-medical considerations; so understanding such governance interactions becomes essential.

This introduction will be organized as follows: it starts with a discussion of the history of diseases and securitization of health before moving on to review the externalization of health threats as a matter of foreign policy. This is designed to set the stage not only for the chapters that follow in this volume but also as an overarching theme across all four volumes. These volumes suggest that – in terms of health security and especially those aspects related to infectious diseases – there is an urgent need to externalize internal policy actions and to internalize external policy responses if these threats are to be successfully resolved. In other words, the borderless nature of these diseases requires a borderless policy environment. Prior to concluding, this volume analyses a case where traditional security meets health security – in the form of conflicts and their health implications.

Securitization and health

> The scale and geographical scope of the HIV/AIDS pandemic has only two parallels in recorded history: the 1918 flu pandemic and the Black Death in the fourteenth century.[6]

Prior to the early nineteenth century, no one knew that diseases were caused by microbes as they were invisible to the naked eye.[7] Lacking a plausible explanation, people often viewed disease as a type of punishment inflicted by the gods.[8] Marcus Terentius Varro (116 BC – 27 BC), a Roman writer, in his work entitled 'de Re Rustica', was the first person to anticipate the presence of invisible tiny living organisms: 'precautions must also be taken in the neighborhood of swamps, both for the reasons given, and because there are bred certain minute creatures which cannot be seen by the eyes, which float in the air and enter the body through the mouth and nose and there cause serious diseases'.[9] However, it took more than 1,500 years for this first hypothesis to be recognized after technology allowed people to see these minute creatures through a microscope.[10] This scientific breakthrough led to a deeper understanding of the continuous evolutionary struggle that is fought between human beings and microbes.

Microbes have also played a salient role in numerous past wars and war-like events in human history. As Smallman-Raynor and Cliff put it, 'war epidemics have decimated the fighting strength of armies, caused the suspension and cancellation of military operations, and have brought havoc to the civil populations of belligerent and non-belligerent states alike'.[11] In other words, human casualties of war – including both military and civilian populations – may arise not only as a result of enemy weapons but also as a result of the spread of diseases. The killing power of an infectious disease is even greater than that of physical weapons when a disease reaches a society with no previous exposure to it (a *virgin soil* infection).[12]

In the post-Cold War period, the discussion of infectious diseases has expanded from a traditional focus on war-related epidemics to non-traditional security studies, through both the human security and securitization schools. These linkages between health and security have created a greater sense of policy urgency in responding to diseases and other health threats. Amongst all the infectious diseases to span the globe, it is widely accepted that HIV/AIDS, for which there is still no cure, continues to present the most existential threat to human existence.[13] As Richard Feacham, the director of the Global Fund to Fight AIDS, Tuberculosis and Malaria, has stated 'HIV/AIDS is the greatest disaster in human history.'[14] HIV/AIDS was officially declared to be a security issue in the 2000 UN Security Council Resolution 1308, which found that HIV/AIDS would pose a risk to stability and security if it was left unchecked.[15] This initial declaration has been most recently followed up with the identification of H1N1 (swine flu) as the first pandemic of the new century; although strong arguments were made for both SARS and HPAI H5N1 (highly pathogenic avian influenza) to be likewise identified.

Microbes and people

It is time to close the book on infectious diseases, and declare the war against pestilence won.[16]

Microbes include bacteria, viruses, parasites and fungi. However, bacterium or viruses cause most infectious or contagious diseases.[17] All viruses and many bacteria are parasites – they cannot survive on their own without a plant or animal host that provides shelter and nourishment. They access their host via similar means, such as the air, water, bodily fluids or food. Yet they have different functions once inside the host body. Bacteria release chemical poisons that kill human cells, producing symptoms of illness that may end up destroying the host body. Viruses attack the host by altering the genetic material – DNA – in the nucleus of the host cell, forcing the cell to be a manufacturing plant to make more viruses via cell replication. The virus then spreads, infecting more cells and challenging the survival of the host.[18]

Responding to bacterial and viral infections, white blood cells will marshal the antibodies and other cells in the immune system to fight against the pathogen.[19] Despite this immune response, the infected individuals will still usually suffer considerable illness or even death. Those that survive can recover naturally and develop an immunity that protects them from the same pathogen.[20] Vaccines are also developed in this 'nature's proof of concept' – that the body could mount an effective immune response against a live pathogen.[21]

History reveals that numerous 'battles' have been fought between human beings and microbes from ancient times to the present; people usually achieved triumphs by developing natural immunity as well as vaccines to those diseases despite the loss of millions of human lives. However, human beings cannot claim to have achieved a complete triumph over these microscopic organisms. Based on the list released by the National Institute of Allergy and Infectious Diseases (NIAID), there are sixteen types of pathogens that have been newly recognized in the last two decades, five re-emergent pathogens, plus over forty potential bioterrorism agents.[22] Microbes will not just surrender themselves to the human immune system and vaccines. Following a Darwinian model, they continuously undergo natural genetic variations and re-combinations to form new strains of pathogens to adapt to adverse environments. Since the human immune system cannot recognize immediately these altered antigens, such as Swine Influenza A H1N1 in 2009, individuals exposed to the pathogens become ill.

Human behaviour also plays a significant role in the re-emergence of the diseases. Modern medical practice – coined as one of the disease multipliers by Caballero-Anthony[23] – particularly the increased and sometimes improper use of antimicrobial drugs and pesticides, has led to development of some resistant pathogens, such as the methicillin-resistant staphylococcus aureus (MRSA), also known as a 'superbug', Tamiflu-resistant H1N1[24] and the multidrug resistant colon bacillus that is found in livestock in Hong Kong. Owing to the success in developing penicillin and related medicines, which can eradicate the microbes within a comparatively shorter time than the human natural immune response, antibiotics have been widely used globally for a variety of illnesses, and indiscriminately used by medical practitioners and self-medicated patients.[25] Without proper instruction as to the use of antibiotics, microbes can be exposed to a level of medicine that is not enough to kill them, allowing them to become powerful drug-resistant bacteria.[26] For instance, certain strains of the bacterium named *Enterococcus faecium* (*E. faecium*) have proved resistant to over one hundred antibiotics that scientists have produced to date.[27]

On top of the improper usage of antibiotics, the decrease in compliance with vaccination policies has also led to the re-emergence of several 'ancient diseases', such as pertussis and measles, which had previously been brought under control by human immunity and specific vaccines. Low vaccination rates among populations led to the re-emergence of pertussis and measles in Japan and the United States in 1979 and 1989, during which time 13,000 and 55,000 people were infected respectively.[28] However, a more devastating problem is that some individuals and organizations have made use of deadly pathogens such as smallpox and anthrax as bio-weapons, since the vast majority of the civilian population nowadays does not possess immunity to these 'extinct' pathogens.[29] An example that illustrates this point is the case of the anthrax letters sent via the US Postal Service in 2001, which infected twenty-two people, killing five (discussed in more detail in the next volume).[30]

Above all, the current problems of newly emerging and re-emerging diseases, plus the bioterrorism threat, have led to a dramatic shift in the human response to diseases – from a solely medical perspective to a security discourse.

Health–security linkages

The health–security linkage is not a novel concept. It was explicitly pro-nounced that 'the health of all peoples is fundamental to the attainment of peace and security' in the constitution of the World Health Organization (WHO) back in 1946.[31] Yet, this linkage did not facilitate an immediate shift towards an emergency mode to deal with diseases. This weak linkage was maintained after the Cold War until the human security discourse emerged with the release of the 1994 UN Development Programme (UNDP) report. Among seven aspects of human security mentioned in Chapter 2, four aspects are directly related to human health – health security, food security, environ-mental security and personal security[32] – signifying the relative importance of health-related security within the human security discourse.

All the papers in these volumes support the core assertion that health challenges – whether from infectious diseases or biohazards – represent a clear and distinct form of security threat; one that requires extraordinary measures or special organizations to properly address. This is a finding that has been recognized elsewhere by a range of other social and medical sciences scholars. Pirages and Runci commented that, 'Viruses, bacteria, and various kinds of plants and animals have never respected national borders . . . Now there is growing concern over the impact of increasing globalization on the potential development and spread of new and resurgent diseases across increasingly porous borders.'[33] Works by Garrett and Oldstone have charted the various types of diseases to which Pirages and Runci refer;[34] those that have crossed national borders in the past and present, as well as the types of state-society responses that have accompanied each outbreak. In the virology and biomedical fields there is a large and rich literature on these diseases and their impact on the well-being of peoples.[35]

Narrowing the field of research down to security studies there are a smaller number of publications that link the threat of infectious diseases with national or human security and well-being. As Fidler noted, 'prior to the 1990s, infectious disease control, of whatever variety, *was* a neglected aspect of international relations'.[36] Altman demonstrated how political and social structures inhibit responses to the threat of HIV/AIDS.[37] A conclusion that was echoed by Whitman *et al.*, who focused on the political factors that inhibit responses to infectious disease outbreaks, clearly showing how the modern international political system – with its preoccupation on sovereignty – inhibits transnational responses to such outbreaks.[38] Without a more flexible system, virulent pathogens will be able to transcend national boundaries far more easily than could be the case. In Asia, where many societies have cultural reservations towards diseased persons and where most states are loath to relinquish or pool their sovereignty to achieve common policy objectives, these conclusions have particular resonance.

McMurray and Smith sought to consider the impact of globalization on the health and well-being of societies as they move up the economic development ladder and become more enmeshed in global processes of trade and human interaction.[39] Drawing on three case studies the authors showed how globalization is eroding state borders and thereby creating new transnational health challenges. As Price-Smith illustrated, these challenges can have a profound impact on the stability and prosperity of states.[40] Brower and Chalk extended the work on the threats of infectious diseases, with specific reference to HIV/AIDS and public policy responses by United States government agencies.[41] What these studies show is the need to develop strong linkages between sub-state, state and international agencies when addressing the security threat posed by infectious diseases and other biohazards.

This finding was backed up by Caballero-Anthony in her exploration of the link between securitization and public health goods.[42] Caballero-Anthony suggested that by applying a securitization approach to preventing infectious disease outbreaks, securitizing actors would have a greater capacity both within and across countries to deal with pandemic consequences. Enemark in his study on natural plagues and biological weapons noted that 'the health threats most suitable for securitization are outbreaks of infectious diseases – specifically those that inspire a level of dread disproportionate to their ability to cause illness and death – whether arising as a result of a natural process or human agency'.[43] Looking at a similar period, Fidler concluded that, 'The linking of public health and national security thus raises deeper theoretical issues and controversies about world politics in the global era.'[44] The need to raise these 'deeper theoretical issues' in the context of securitization theory is a gap in the securitization literature that the papers in this volume seek to address.

Globally, Chan, Støre and Kouchner have observed that 'pandemics, emerging diseases and bioterrorism are readily understood as direct threats to national and global security'.[45] Davies placed these responses particularly within the last two decades, noting that during the 1990s, 'awareness of the threat that infectious disease outbreaks could pose to their citizens' health and to their countries' economic and political stability encouraged western governments to develop responses in national security terms'.[46] As a result, 'health challenges now feature in national security strategies, appear regularly on the agenda of meetings of leading economic powers, affect the bilateral and regional political relationships between developed and developing countries, and influence strategies for United Nations reform. Although health has long been a foreign policy concern, such prominence is historically unprecedented.'[47]

Prioritizing health and security

Apart from the emergence of the conceptual framework of health threats within security, there are other developments that have escalated the health–security linkage. These include the destructive impact of emerging and re-emerging infectious diseases and the bioterrorism threat as well as the devastating political, social and economic impact on the developing world,[48] in conjunction with a rising awareness about the deepening vulnerabilities of populations in rich and poor countries caused by the global spread of diseases.[49] In response to these issues, attempts have been made by various scholars and analysts to securitize health in an effort to reprioritize policies and practices to yield greater efficiencies or to develop alternative response structures.[50]

Despite numerous theoretical inputs, there is no coherent voice as to whether or not the logic of securitization is the best way forward with respect to public health problems. As Orbinski asked, 'Is global health simply a security concern . . . Or is global health best conceptualised as pursuing equity, justice, and fairness, and as fundamentally considering public health measures and access to health care and healthcare technologies, such as drugs, as a basic human entitlement?'[51] Without doubt, it is salient to protect the fundamental values of health provision. To link health to security, however, does not imply the ignorance of these basic values. On the contrary, while the linkage is keeping the core value embedded in public health, it is at the same time strengthening the idea through security-related strategies and tactics, which is the fundamental value of public health security.[52]

In particular, the notion of public health security can improve the priority of public health issues on the government agenda. Indeed, despite the growing prevalence of global health threats, many countries still persist in according health a generally lower priority than the threat posed by infectious diseases would otherwise warrant. This phenomenon is even more apparent in many developing countries, where resources are scarce and developmental challenges abound, as indicated in Table 1. Based on Table 1, China spent 1.9 per cent and 2.0 per cent of GDP on education and military respectively, but only 1.8 per cent on health in 2004; India spent 3.8 per cent and 2.8 per cent of GDP on education and military respectively, but merely 0.9 per cent on public health.

Moreover, public health expenditure in the developing countries is comparatively much lower than in the developed ones. This argument is well illustrated in the table, which shows that developed countries (Norway, Germany, Canada and Japan) allocated over 6 per cent of GDP to health, while health expenditure in some developing countries (Bangladesh, India, Azerbaijan and Pakistan) was below 1 per cent. As argued by Curley and Thomas, 'the security of state resides in the security of the individual'.[53] Obviously the current public health expenditure in developing countries is problematic as the lack of fiscal support and domestic policy ranking creates an environment conducive to the spread of infectious diseases, which poses a significant threat to the human and national security of the affected state and other countries around the globe.

By linking public health security with that of health governance, issues that are prone to threaten the overall health of society will be securitized, resulting in 'alternative, potentially more effective, response mechanisms'.[54] From the *2008 Global Burden of Disease* and also the *2009 Global Risks Report*, it is apparent that chronic and infectious diseases remain the top two causes of death,[55] even as infectious diseases dominate the agendas of states and international organizations.[56]

Health security and foreign policy

Indeed, the transnational dimension of diseases now requires states to accord health a place on the external policy agenda in addition to its place in domestic policy rankings. As McInnes and Lee observed 'Health issues have been creeping up foreign and security policy agendas for some time.'[57] Huang suggests that the starting point for this creep was the 1980s, when 'events and developments in the political and epidemiological world – globalization, the rise of infectious disease, and the end of the Cold War – highlighted the importance of health as a key element of development and security policy'.[58] While Huang is correct in his timeframe, the implications and modalities of this creep only became the subject of significant academic and policy concerns

Table 1 Priorities in public spending on health, education and military.

Countries	Public expenditure on health (% of GDP) in 2004	Public expenditure on education (% of GDP) from 2002–2005	Military expenditure (% of GDP) in 2005
Developed countries			
Iceland	8.3	8.1	0.0
France	8.2	5.9	2.5
Germany	8.2	4.6	1.4
Norway	8.1	7.7	1.7
Austria	7.8	5.5	0.9
United Kingdom	7.0	5.4	2.7
United States	6.9	5.9	4.1
Canada	6.8	5.2	1.1
Australia	6.5	4.7	1.8
Japan	6.3	3.6	1.0
Developing countries			
Brazil	4.8	4.4	1.6
Russian Federation	3.7	3.6	4.1
Iran (Islamic Republic of)	3.2	4.7	5.8
Saudi Arabia	2.5	6.8	8.2
Thailand	2.3	4.2	1.1
Malaysia	2.2	6.2	2.4
Peru	1.9	2.4	1.4
China	1.8	1.9	2.0
Morocco	1.7	6.7	4.5
Georgia	1.5	2.9	3.5
Philippines	1.4	2.7	0.9
Singapore	1.3	3.7	4.7
Indonesia	1.0	0.9	1.2
India	0.9	3.8	2.8
Azerbaijan	0.9	2.5	2.5
Bangladesh	0.9	2.5	1.0
Pakistan	0.4	2.3	3.5

Source: All data in the table are extracted from 'Table 19: Priority in Public Spending', *Human Development Report 2007/2008*, *UNDP*, <http://hdr.undp.org/en/media/HDR_20072008_EN_Complete.pdf>, Accessed 6 March 2012, pp. 294–297.

after the turn of the century; when the rapid spread of SARS focused attention on the potential threat of epidemics in a globalized world.

Fidler identified three perspectives on health as a part of the foreign policy toolkit: foreign policy as health, health and foreign policy, and health as foreign policy. The first perspective argues 'that foreign policy now pursues, and should in the future pursue, health as an end in itself'.[59] The second perspective argues that health has evolved to 'become another issue with which

9

traditional approaches to foreign policy grapple'.[60] The final perspective is an intermediate position between the poles of the first two perspectives, where 'the health-foreign policy interaction involves a dynamic between science and politics that reflects an interdependence or mutual dependence, when health and foreign policy mix'.[61]

Feldbaum, Lee and Michaud explored Fidler's three perspectives further in an effort to reach a more definitive answer than that earlier offered. Their framework yields little support for Fidler's first perspective. However, Feldbaum *et al.* found that health has now joined the foreign policy agenda (if only intermittently). As the authors observed, 'global health has affected the practice of foreign policy on occasions when global health and foreign-policy interests align'.[62] Interestingly, when it comes to any form of 'interdependence or mutual dependence', the authors concluded that it is the responsibility of public health practitioners to push their issues rather than for members of both communities to better understand the needs and issues of the other. As the papers in this volume make clear, a mutual understanding between public health and foreign policy practitioners is essential – not just when responding to existential health threats but, more critically, in developing preventative health strategies that minimize such insecurities arising in the first place.

It is, however, inappropriate to identify just these two communities as being necessary to alleviating transarchical health threats. As the literature on human security makes clear, existential health insecurities may arise as secondary (or tertiary) consequences from other challenges, such as environmental threats or irregular migration flows. As a consequence, a need arises for multiple policy inputs to address such complex threats. Moreover, the resolution of such foreign health threats requires the participation of more actors than just health practitioners and foreign policy officials. As Bowers and Chalk made clear, given that health threats arise through a multitude of channels they require an equally complex array of actors to resolve them: both within and from without the state.[63] This multi-level governance model of health threats is expanded upon in the following three volumes.

Health and conflict

Beyond such non-traditional and foreign policy concerns lies an intersection of health and traditional security interests in the form of conflicts. As noted earlier, disease-related deaths in conflict zones have long been recognized: both for military as well as for civilian casualties. Florence Nightingale's experiences during the Crimean War in the 1850s highlighted the impact unhygienic conditions could have on survival rates in the conflict zone but it was not until the First World War that the global significance of disease and war became truly apparent. This war proved to be a perfect breeding ground for the Spanish flu pandemic – in terms of the unhygienic conditions observed earlier in the Crimea but also in terms of the globalized movement of military personnel.

The unsanitary battlefield conditions combined with the presence of non-European troops served to spread the flu throughout Europe and around the world. Without the presence of so many international participants and without the transport systems to move them around the world it is questionable as to whether the Spanish flu would have reached a pandemic level.

Of course, in the last thirty years there has been a decline in the interstate warfare that characterized the preceding centuries. Such large-scale conflicts – fought by armies across sovereign borders – have been replaced by intrastate conflicts between groups within states. Frequently these conflicts occur in the developing world, where access to social services (particularly health) is already compromised. Thus, when the conflict does break out, the population is placed at a greater risk of infectious and non-communicable diseases than was the case previously. As Toole and Waldman highlighted, even though the death toll for military deaths in armed conflicts is in the tens of thousands, the civilian death toll from these conflicts is in the millions. Beyond those killed in the fighting, the majority of deaths arise from the destruction of public health infrastructure and the displacement of local populations – both of which lead to a greater exposure to diseases. As Toole and Waldman noted in the case of the Goma refugee camps in Eastern Zaire, 'more than 90% of the estimated 50,000 deaths in the first month after the refugee influx were caused by either watery or bloody diarrhea'.[64] The impact of infectious diseases on the mortality rates of conflict zones is supported by Burkle who reported that 'In an early 2010 report, nearly 80% of the already 300,000 conflict-related deaths in Darfur were due to preventable infectious diseases, not violence. In a 2001 Congo study, this figure was 90%.'[65] All of which suggests that even as diseases are themselves securitized, reducing the secondary role diseases play in traditional security events is an important step in reducing the mortality rate of the overall conflict. Moreover, such disease outbreaks hold the potential to overshadow the original conflict in terms of the threat to human security.

These findings for conflicts and diseases are echoed by Connolly *et al.* with respect to complex emergencies. In their study the authors observed that 'Communicable diseases, alone or in combination with malnutrition, account for most deaths in complex emergencies.'[66] While this is not overly surprising given the extreme dislocations and disorder that accompany such emergencies, it does strongly support the need for interventions that are able to address secondary effects as well as the primary causes of the conflict. In such situations 'Morbidity from communicable diseases and psychological distress is common . . . The damage and breakdown of infrastructure increases exposure to diseases and diminishes opportunities for health.'[67] As Connolly *et al.* go on to detail, this is particularly pressing where there is an overlapping epidemic that can go unresolved or even spread amidst the emergency. In traditional cases this was seen with the Spanish flu pandemic and the First World War. In terms of complex emergencies this concern was evident in the case of displaced persons moving from Namibia and Zaire (countries with high HIV/ AIDS infection rates) to Angola (which had a low infection rate).[68]

In addition to infectious disease related deaths from conflicts, there is an increasing awareness of the public health threats posed by natural disasters. To a large extent the threat vectors from such events mirror those from conflicts and complex emergencies. However, for both of the previous categories there is a build-up to the threat, whereas with natural disasters there is a need to respond immediately – to alleviate the medical threat as well as to redirect policy resources. Due to the nature of these events, even public health capacities in developed states can be overwhelmed and higher rates of infectious diseases observed. As was seen after Hurricane Katrina in 2005, not only was disease control and surveillance in the United Stated disrupted but there were outbreaks of MRSA, diarrhoea and respiratory diseases as a result of the disaster. Similar disease outbreaks were seen after the 2004 Boxing Day tsunami, but rapid response coordination by multiple agencies prevented the outbreaks from worsening. As Dr Nabarro (then Head of WHO's Crisis Management Team) stated 'If we saw an outbreak, we would send in teams, helicopters and vaccines to sort things out . . . So disease outbreaks were common, but they didn't turn into epidemics . . . It's the first time I've seen the international community organise itself so well . . . But it's very important that people realise that it could have been amazingly terrible.'[69] The importance of such coordination is supported by Waring and Brown who concluded that, 'Any emergency response designed to mitigate adverse health effects resulting from natural disasters requires a multidisciplinary approach that employs a broad range of expertise to help minimize exposure to known health threats while identifying and attending to those in need of immediate treatment.'[70]

All of these cases (conflicts, complex emergencies and natural disasters) argue for the pre-existence of robust public health systems. Such systems cannot afford to be monolithic. They need to be flexible, with the capacity to act against threats that can emerge rapidly from a variety of sources. This need suggests a pluralist health order is necessary to ensure greater health security. As the next volume demonstrates, in the case of infectious diseases or related health threats, there is a clear demand for health systems that can coordinate multiple actors – within and across state borders – efficiently. When states chose to limit the actors involved in responding to infectious disease outbreaks they also limit their ability to resolve disease outbreaks, allowing the disease to cause greater harm and became a more serious threat than would have otherwise been the case.

Structure of this collection

In sum, the threat posed by diseases to the security of states and the well-being of their peoples has long been recognized. Yet by the mid-twentieth century, this war was considered won and the medical world turned to other concerns. Less than two decades later HIV/AIDS was identified and soon spread around the world, borne on the deepening patterns of globalization between peoples and commerce.

Although hopes were high that a cure would soon be found, more than a quarter of a century later HIV/AIDS remains a deadly threat to the international community. During the same period a host of new infectious diseases have emerged. SARS, H5N1 and H1N1 together represent the next phase in health insecurities, where ecological intrusions, modernization and globalization collide to give rise to zoonotic diseases able to reach around the world, diseases whose pandemic potential holds the power to wreck economies, divide societies and threaten the viability of states.

To properly understand the threat posed by these – and future – emerging infectious diseases it is necessary to cross disciplinary divides and focus on a complex set of perspectives. Infectious diseases are not simply medical issues. They are formed within the health practices of the host communities and are shaped by the policies and laws of the state. So, to understand, address and resolve them requires an equally comprehensive approach, encompassing the methods by which a medical concern becomes a threat and the forms these threats take, the types of diseases that generate such insecurities as well as the policy, legal and ethical considerations that shape the securitization responses.

To this end, the first of the four volumes explores the concept of health security before moving on to look at how health has transcended domestic borders to become a key foreign policy issue, and then how diseases become securitized. This volume concludes with a case study of health within conflict situations. With this umbrella, the second volume reviews the linkages between disease and security (covering the main infectious diseases of HIV/AIDS, SARS, H5N1 and H1N1). It then considers a key case study – bioterrorism – that lies at the nexus of these two issues. The third volume analyses the issue of health governance at both the local and the global levels to better understand how such policy structures and actors shape the responses to health threats. The fourth volume examines the over-arching legal and ethical frameworks that shape the health security and governance responses to threats of infectious diseases. It is intended that all four volumes (and their respective articles) can be read as stand-alone pieces but – when taken together – these volumes illuminate the complexity that characterizes the governance of health insecurities.

Notes

1 Ms Catherine Lo Yuk Ping is a Ph.D. candidate in the Centre of Asian Studies at the University of Hong Kong. Her thesis compares the Chinese and Indian securitization of HIV/AIDS.

2 Dr Nicholas Thomas is an Associate Professor in the Department of Asian and International Studies at City University of Hong Kong.

3 Mark Smolinski, Margaret Hamburg and Joshua Lederman (eds) *Microbial Threats to Health: Emergence, Detection, and Response*, Washington: National Academies Press, 2003, p. xvii.

4 Barry Buzan, Ole Wæver and Jaap de Wilde, *Security: A New Framework for Analysis*, Boulder, Col.: Lynne Rienner, 1998.

5 Jon Pierre, 'Introduction: understanding governance', in Jon Pierre, *Debating Governance: Authority, Steering, and Democracy*, New York: Oxford University Press, 2000, pp. 1–10, at p. 4.

6 L. Garrett, *HIV and National Security: Where are the Links?*, New York: Council on Foreign Relations, 2005, p. 9.

7 M. P. Friedlandler, *Outbreak: Disease Detectives At Work*, Minneapolis: Lerner, 2000, p. 16.

8 Diseases such as 'plague of Athens' (430–427 BC), smallpox in Japan (735–37), and Black Death in Europe (1346–50) were understood as punishment of the gods. See J. N. Hays, *Epidemics and Pandemics: Their Impacts on Human History*, Santa Barbara, Calif.: ABC-Clio, 2005, for more examples.

9 M. T. Varro, *de Re Rustica*, Loeb Classical Library, London: Heinemann, 1934, p. 210.

10 Friedlandler, *Outbreak*, pp. 31–3.

11 M. R. Smallman-Raynor and A. D. Cliff, *War Epidemics: An Historical Geography of Infectious Diseases in Military Conflict and Civil Strife, 1850–2000*, New York: Oxford University Press, 2004, p. 4.

12 Hays, *Epidemics and Pandemics*, preface, p. x.

13 L. C. Chen and V. Narasimhan, 'Health and human security: pointing a way forward', Paper presented to the Commission on Human Security, Stockholm, 9 June (United Nations Trust for Human Security, 2002), p. 3.

14 Quoted in T. Hultman, 'Africa: film industry spokesman and software entrepreneur join forces to fight HIV/Aids', Allafrica.com, 6 June 2004, at http://allafrica.com/stories/200406060139.html.

15 See UN Security Council Resolution 1308.

16 W. H. Stewart, *A Mandate for State Action*, presented at the Association of State and Territorial Health Officers, Washington DC, 1967.

17 J. C. Giblin, *When Plague Strikes: The Black Death, Smallpox, AIDS*, New York: HarperCollins, 1995, p. 4; Friedlandler, *Outbreak*, p. 27.

18 Friedlandler, *Outbreak*, p. 30; M. Drexler, *Secret Agents: The Menace of Emerging Infections*, Washington DC: Joseph Henry, 2002, p. 9.

19 Drexler, *Secret Agents*, p. 9.

20 A. Fanci, 'Fanci: why there is no AIDS vaccine', *msnbc.com*, 31 March 2009, at http://www.msnbc.msn.com/id/29898087/ (retrieved 15 April 2009).

21 Ibid.

22 See 'List of emerging and re-emerging diseases', National Institute of Allergy and Infectious Diseases, National Institutes of Health (updated 9 November 2011), at http://www.niaid.nih.gov/topics/emerging/Pages/list.aspx (retrieved 29 November 2011).

23 M. Caballero-Anthony, 'Combating infectious diseases in East Asia: securitization and global public goods for health and human security', *Journal of International Affairs* 59(2) (2006): 105–27, at 110.

24 'Treatment resistant swine flu detected in US', AFP, 3 August 2009, at http://www.google.com/hostednews/afp/article/ALeqM5hsS3W74VB3XpDzfh8qD-7Cmq0J0g> (retrieved 9 September 2009).

25 M. Shnayerson and M. J. Plotkin, *The Killers Within: The Deadly Rise of Drug-Resistant Bacteria*, Boston: Little, Brown, 2002, p. 35.
26 Ibid.
27 Ibid., p. 5.
28 'Understanding vaccines', National Institute of Allergy and Infectious Diseases, National Institutes of Health, January 2008, at http://www3.niaid.nih.gov/topics/vaccines/PDF/undvacc.pdf (retrieved 10 September 2009), p. 5.
29 'Emerging and re-emerging infectious diseases: introduction and goals', *National Institute of Allergy and Infectious Diseases, National Institutes of Health* (March 10, 2010), <http://www.niaid.nih.gov/topics/emerging/pages/introduction.aspx>, Accessed March 6, 2012.
30 T. Murphy, and N. Whitty, 'Is human rights prepared? Risk, rights and public health emergencies', *Medical Law Review* 17(2) (2009): 219–44, at 222.
31 Constitution of the World Health Organization. It was adopted by the International Health Conference held in New York from 19 June to 22 July 1946, signed on 22 July 1946 by the representatives of 61 States and entered into force on 7 April 1948 (see http://www.who.int/governance/eb/who_constitution_en.pdf, retrieved 18 September 2009).
32 See L. Thiesmeyer, 'Gender, public health, and human security policy in Asia', United Nations: Division for the Advancement of Women (DAW), 2005. Food security is related to the readiness of accessible food and effectiveness in distribution of food. Environmental security refers to the protection of the environment from deforestation and erosion, desertification, pollution and also the maintainability of sustainable development. Personal security is attained when one is free from threats from the state (torture), other states (war), other groups of people (ethnic tension) and other individuals or gangs (street crime). In particular, for women, it refers to freedom from threats of domestic violence and rape; for children, freedom from threats of child abuse; for oneself, to be free from drug use and suicide.
33 Dennis Pirages and Paul Runci, 'Ecological interdependence and the spread of infectious disease', in Maryann Cusimano (ed.) *Beyond Sovereignty: Issues for a Global Agenda*, New York: St. Martin's Press, 2000, pp. 173–94, at p. 176.
34 Laurie Garrett, *The Coming Plague: Newly Emerging Diseases in a World Out of Balance*, New York: Penguin, 1995; Michael Oldstone, *Viruses, Plagues & History*, Oxford: Oxford University Press, 1998.
35 Bernard Vallat, 'Emerging and re-emerging zoonoses', *World Organisation for Animal Health*, Editorial, November 2004, at http://www.oie.int/eng/Edito/en_edito_nov04.htm; T. M. Tumpey, D. L. Suarez, L. E. L. Perkins, D. A. Senne, J. G. Lee, Y. J. Lee, I. P. Mo, H. W. Sung and D. E. Swayne, 'Characterization of a highly pathogenic H5N1 avian influenza: a virus isolated from duck meat', *Journal of Virology* 76(12) (2002): 6344–55; Ian Brown, 'The pig as an intermediate host for influenza A viruses between birds and humans', *International Congress Series* 1219 (2001): 173–8; Y. Guan, K. F. Shortridge, S. Krauss, P. H. Li, Y. Kawaoka and R. G. Webster, 'Emergence of avian H1N1 influenza viruses in pigs in China', *Journal of Virology* 70(11) (1996): 8041–6; E. C. J. Claas, Y. Kawaoka, J. C. de Jong, N. Masurel and R. G. Webster, 'Infection of children with avian-human reassortant influenza virus from pigs in Europe', *Virology* 204(1) (1994): 453–7; and Y. K. Choi, T. D. Nguyen, H. Ozaki, R. Webby, P. Puthavathana, C. Buranathal, A. Chaisingh, P. Auewarakul, N. Hanh, S. Ma, P. Hui, Y. Huan, M. Peiris and R. G. Webster, 'Studies of H5N1 influenza virus infection of pigs by using viruses isolated in Vietnam and Thailand in 2004', *Journal of Virology* 79(16) (2005): 10821–5.

36 David P. Fidler, 'Germs, governance, and global public health in the wake of SARS', *Journal of Clinical Investigation* 113(6) (2004): 799–804, at p. 800.
37 Dennis Altman, 'AIDS and security', *International Relations* 17(4) (2003): 417–27.
38 Jim Whitman (ed.) *The Politics of Emerging and Resurgent Infectious Diseases*, New York: St. Martin's Press, 2000.
39 C. McMurray and R. Smith (2001), *Diseases of Globalization: Socio-economic Transitions and Health*, London: Earthscan, 2001.
40 Andrew T. Price-Smith, *The Health of Nations*, Cambridge, Mass.: MIT Press, 2002.
41 Jennifer Brower and Peter Chalk, *The Global Threat of New and Reemerging Infectious Diseases*, Santa Monica, Calif.: Rand, 2003.
42 Mely Caballero-Anthony, 'Combating infectious diseases in East Asia: securitization and global public goods for health and human security', *Journal of International Affairs* 52(2) (2006): 105–27.
43 C. Enemark, *Disease and Security: Natural Plagues and Biological Weapons in East Asia*, London: Routledge, 2007, p .8.
44 David P. Fidler, 'Public health and national security in the global age: infectious diseases, bioterrorism, and *realpolitik*', *The George Washington International Law Review* 35 (2003): 787–856 (Chapter 48 in Volume II).
45 Margaret Chan, J. G. Støre and B. Kouchner, 'Foreign policy and global public health: working together towards common goals', *Bulletin of the World Health Organization* 86(7) (2008): 497–576, at 498.
46 Sara Davies, 'Securitizing infectious disease', *International Affairs* 84(2) (2008): 295–313, at 298 (Chapter 12 in Volume I).
47 David P. Fidler and N. Draeger, 'Health and foreign policy', *Bulletin of the World Health Organization* 84(9) (2006): 687.
48 David P. Fidler, 'A pathology of public health securitism: approaching pandemics as security threats', in A. F. Cooper, J. J. Kirton and T. Schrecker (eds) *Governing Global Health: Challenge, Response, Innovation*, Aldershot: Ashgate, 2007, pp. 41–66, at p. 42 (Chapter 7 in this volume).
49 Colin McInnes and Kelley Lee, 'Health, security and foreign policy', *Review of International Studies*, 32(1) (2006): 5–23, at 16 (Chapter 18 in this volume).
50 Fidler, 'Pathology of public health securitism', p. 42.
51 J. Orbinski, 'Global health, social movements, and governance', in A. F. Cooper, J. J. Kirton and T. Schrecker (eds) *Governing Global Health: Challenge, Response, Innovation*, Aldershot: Ashgate, 2007), pp. 29–40, at p. 30.
52 Fidler, 'Pathology of public health securitism', p. 44.
53 Melissa Curley and Nicholas Thomas, 'Human security and public health in Southeast Asia: the SARS outbreak', *Australian Journal of International Affairs* 58(1) (2004): 17–32, at 17 (Chapter 33 in Volume II).
54 Davies, 'Securitising infectious disease', p. 296.
55 See *Global Burden of Disease: 2004 Update*, World Health Organization, 2008, p. 8; *2009 Global Risks Report*, World Economic Forum, 2009, p. 6.
56 See Caballero-Anthony, 'Combating infectious diseases in East Asia'.
57 McInnes and Lee, 'Health, security and foreign policy', p. 10.
58 Y. Z. Huang, 'Pursuing health as foreign policy: the case of China', *Indiana Journal of Global Legal Studies* 17(1) (2010): 105–46 .
59 David P. Fidler, 'Health as foreign policy: between principle and power', *Whitehead Journal of Diplomacy and International Relations* 6 (Summer/Fall 2005): 179–94, at 183 (Chapter 16 in this volume).
60 Ibid, p. 184.
61 Ibid, p. 185.

62 Harley Feldbaum, Kelley Lee and Joshua Michaud, 'Global health and foreign policy', *Epidemiologic Reviews* 32(1) (2010): 82–92, at 88 (Chapter 17 in this volume).

63 J. Bowers and P. Chalk, *The Global Threat of New and Reemerging Infectious Disease: Reconciling US National Security and Public Health Policy*, Santa Monica, Calif.: Rand, 2003.

64 M. J. Toole and R. J. Waldman, 'The public health aspects of complex emergencies and refugee situations', *Annual Review of Public Health* 18 (1997): 283–312, at 292 (Chapter 22 in this volume).

65 Frederick M. Burkle, Jr., 'Future humanitarian crises: challenges for practice, policy, and public health', *Prehospital and Disaster Medicine* 25(3) (2010): 191–9, at 192 (Chapter 21 in this volume).

66 Máire A. Connolly, Michelle Gayer, Michael J. Ryan, Peter Salama, Peter Spiegel and David L. Heymann, 'Communicable diseases in complex emergencies: impact and challenges', *Lancet* 364 (2004): 1974–1983, at 1974 (Chapter 23 in this volume).

67 Nicholas Banatvala and Anthony B. Zwi, 'Conflict and health: public health and humanitarian interventions: developing the evidence base', *British Medical Journal* 321(7253) (2000): 101–5, at 101 (Chapter 19 in this volume).

68 Connolly *et al.*, 'Communicable diseases', p. 1977.

69 C. Ryan, 'How tsunami diseases were curbed', *BBC News*, 22 March 2005.

70 Stephen C. Waring and Bruce J. Brown, 'The threat of communicable diseases following natural disasters: a public health response', *Disaster Management & Response* 3(2) (2005): 41–7, at 46 (Chapter 24 in this volume).

Part 1

HEALTH AND SECURITY: CONCEPTS AND PARAMETERS

1

THE RETURN OF
INFECTIOUS DISEASE

Laurie Garrett

Source: *Foreign Affairs*, 75:1 (1996), 66–79.

The post-antibiotic era

Since World War II, public health strategy has focused on the eradication of microbes. Using powerful medical weaponry developed during the post-war period—antibiotics, antimalarials, and vaccines—political and scientific leaders in the United States and around the world pursued a military-style campaign to obliterate viral, bacterial, and parasitic enemies. The goal was nothing less than pushing humanity through what was termed the "health transition," leaving the age of infectious disease permanently behind. By the turn of the century, it was thought, most of the world's population would live long lives ended only by the "chronics"—cancer, heart disease, and Alzheimer's.

The optimism culminated in 1978 when the member states of the United Nations signed the "Health for All, 2000" accord. The agreement set ambitious goals for the eradication of disease, predicting that even the poorest nations would undergo a health transition before the millennium, with life expectancies rising markedly. It was certainly reasonable in 1978 to take a rosy view of Homo sapiens' ancient struggle with the microbes; antibiotics, pesticides, chloroquine and other powerful antimicrobials, vaccines, and striking improvements in water treatment and food preparation technologies had provided what seemed an imposing armamentarium. The year before, the World Health Organization (WHO) had announced that the last known case of smallpox had been tracked down in Ethiopia and cured.

The grandiose optimism rested on two false assumptions: that microbes were biologically stationary targets and that diseases could be geographically sequestered. Each contributed to the smug sense of immunity from infectious diseases that characterized health professionals in North America and Europe.

Anything but stationary, microbes and the insects, rodents, and other animals that transmit them are in a constant state of biological flux and evolution. Darwin noted that certain genetic mutations allow plants and animals to better adapt to environmental conditions and so produce more offspring; this process of natural selection, he argued, was the mechanism of evolution. Less than a decade after the U.S. military first supplied penicillin to its field physicians in the Pacific theater, geneticist Joshua Lederberg demonstrated that natural selection was operating in the bacterial world. Strains of staphylococcus and streptococcus that happened to carry genes for resistance to the drugs arose and flourished where drug-susceptible strains had been driven out. Use of antibiotics was selecting for ever-more-resistant bugs.

More recently scientists have witnessed an alarming mechanism of microbial adaptation and change—one less dependent on random inherited genetic advantage. The genetic blueprints of some microbes contain DNA and RNA codes that command mutation under stress, offer escapes from antibiotics and other drugs, marshal collective behaviors conducive to group survival, and allow the microbes and their progeny to scour their environments for potentially useful genetic material. Such material is present in stable rings or pieces of DNA and RNA, known as plasmids and transposons, that move freely among microorganisms, even jumping between species of bacteria, fungi, and parasites. Some plasmids carry the genes for resistance to five or more different families of antibiotics, or dozens of individual drugs. Others confer greater powers of infectivity, virulence, resistance to disinfectants or chlorine, even such subtly important characteristics as the ability to tolerate higher temperatures or more acidic conditions. Microbes have appeared that can grow on a bar of soap, swim unabashed in bleach, and ignore doses of penicillin logarithmically larger than those effective in 1950.

In the microbial soup, then, is a vast, constantly changing lending library of genetic material that offers humanity's minute predators myriad ways to outmaneuver the drug arsenal. And the arsenal, large as it might seem, is limited. In 1994 the Food and Drug Administration licensed only three new antimicrobial drugs, two of them for the treatment of AIDS and none an antibacterial. Research and development has ground to a near halt now that the easy approaches to killing viruses, bacteria, fungi, and parasites—those that mimic the ways competing microbes kill one another in their endless tiny battles throughout the human gastrointestinal tract—have been exploited. Researchers have run out of ideas for countering many microbial scourges, and the lack of profitability has stifled the development of drugs to combat organisms that are currently found predominantly in poor countries. "The pipeline is dry. We really have a global crisis," James Hughes, director of the National Center for Infectious Diseases at the Centers for Disease Control and Prevention (CDC) in Atlanta, said recently.

Diseases without borders

During the 1960s, 1970s, and 1980s, the World Bank and the International Monetary Fund devised investment policies based on the assumption that economic modernization should come first and improved health would naturally follow. Today the World Bank recognizes that a nation in which more than ten percent of the working-age population is chronically ill cannot be expected to reach higher levels of development without investment in health infrastructure. Furthermore, the bank acknowledges that few societies spend health care dollars effectively for the poor, among whom the potential for the outbreak of infectious disease is greatest. Most of the achievements in infectious disease control have resulted from grand international efforts such as the expanded program for childhood immunization mounted by the U.N. Children's Emergency Fund and WHO's smallpox eradication drive. At the local level, particularly in politically unstable poor countries, few genuine successes can be cited.

Geographic sequestration was crucial in all postwar health planning, but diseases can no longer be expected to remain in their country or region of origin. Even before commercial air travel, swine flu in 1918–19 managed to circumnavigate the planet five times in 18 months, killing 22 million people, 500,000 in the United States. How many more victims could a similarly lethal strain of influenza claim in 1996, when some half a billion passengers will board airline flights?

Every day one million people cross an international border. One million a week travel between the industrial and developing worlds. And as people move, unwanted microbial hitchhikers tag along. In the nineteenth century most diseases and infections that travelers carried manifested themselves during the long sea voyages that were the primary means of covering great distances. Recognizing the symptoms, the authorities at ports of entry could quarantine contagious individuals or take other action. In the age of jet travel, however, a person incubating a disease such as Ebola can board a plane, travel 12,000 miles, pass unnoticed through customs and immigration, take a domestic carrier to a remote destination, and still not develop symptoms for several days, infecting many other people before his condition is noticeable.

Surveillance at airports has proved grossly inadequate and is often biologically irrational, given that incubation periods for many incurable contagious diseases may exceed 21 days. And when a recent traveler's symptoms become apparent, days or weeks after his journey, the task of identifying fellow passengers, locating them, and bringing them to the authorities for medical examination is costly and sometimes impossible. The British and U.S. governments both spent millions of dollars in 1976 trying to track down 522 people exposed during a flight from Sierra Leone to Washington, D.C., to a Peace Corps volunteer infected with the Lassa virus, an organism that produces gruesome hemorrhagic disease in its victims. The U.S. government eventually tracked down 505 passengers, scattered over 21 states; British Airways and the British government located 95, some of whom were also on the U.S. list. None tested positive for the virus.

In the fall of 1994 the New York City Department of Health and the U.S. Immigration and Naturalization Service took steps to prevent plague-infected passengers from India from disembarking at New York's John F. Kennedy International Airport. All airport and federal personnel who had direct contact with passengers were trained to recognize symptoms of *Yersinia pestis* infection. Potential plague carriers were, if possible, to be identified while still on the tarmac, so fellow passengers could be examined. Of ten putative carriers identified in New York, only two were discovered at the airport; the majority had long since entered the community. Fortunately, none of the ten proved to have plague. Health authorities came away with the lesson that airport-based screening is expensive and does not work.

Humanity is on the move worldwide, fleeing impoverishment, religious and ethnic intolerance, and high-intensity localized warfare that targets civilians. People are abandoning their homes for new destinations on an unprecedented scale, both in terms of absolute numbers and as a percentage of population. In 1994 at least 110 million people immigrated, another 30 million moved from rural to urban areas within their own country, and 23 million more were displaced by war or social unrest, according to the U.N. High Commissioner for Refugees and the Worldwatch Institute. This human mobility affords microbes greatly increased opportunities for movement.

The city as vector

Population expansion raises the statistical probability that pathogens will be transmitted, whether from person to person or vector—insect, rodent, or other—to person. Human density is rising rapidly worldwide. Seven countries now have overall population densities exceeding 2,000 people per square mile, and 43 have densities greater than 500 people per square mile. (The U.S. average, by contrast, is 74.)

High density need not doom a nation to epidemics and unusual outbreaks of disease if sewage and water systems, housing, and public health provisions are adequate. The Netherlands, for example, with 1,180 people per square mile, ranks among the top 20 countries for good health and life expectancy. But the areas in which density is increasing most are not those capable of providing such infrastructural support. They are, rather, the poorest on earth. Even countries with low overall density may have cities that have become focuses for extraordinary overpopulation, from the point of view of public health. Some of these urban agglomerations have only one toilet for every 750 or more people.

Most people on the move around the world come to burgeoning metropolises like India's Surat (where pneumonic plague struck in 1994) and Zaire's Kikwit (site of the 1995 Ebola epidemic) that offer few fundamental amenities. These new centers of urbanization typically lack sewage systems, paved roads, housing, safe drinking water, medical facilities, and schools adequate to serve even the most affluent residents. They are squalid sites of destitution where hundreds of thousands live much as they would in poor villages, yet so jammed together as to ensure astronomical transmission rates for airborne, waterborne, sexually transmitted, and contact-transmission microbes.

But such centers are often only staging areas for the waves of impoverished people that are drawn there. The next stop is a megacity with a population of ten million or more. In the nineteenth century only two cities on earth— London and New York—even approached that size. Five years from now there will be 24 megacities, most in poor developing countries: São Paulo, Calcutta, Bombay, Istanbul, Bangkok, Tehran, Jakarta, Cairo, Mexico City, Karachi, and the like. There the woes of cities like Surat are magnified many times over. Yet even the developing world's megacities are way stations for those who most aggressively seek a better life. All paths ultimately lead these people—and the microbes they may carry—to the United States, Canada, and Western Europe.

Urbanization and global migration propel radical changes in human behavior as well as in the ecological relationship between microbes and humans. Almost invariably in large cities, sex industries arise and multiple-partner sex becomes more common, prompting rapid increases in sexually transmitted diseases. Black market access to antimicrobials is greater in urban centers, leading to overuse or outright misuse of the precious drugs and the emergence of resistant bacteria and parasites. Intravenous drug abusers' practice of sharing syringes is a ready vehicle for the transmission of microbes. Underfunded urban health facilities often become unhygienic centers for the dissemination of disease rather than its control.

The emblematic new disease

All these factors played out dramatically during the 1980s, allowing an obscure organism to amplify and spread to the point that WHO estimates it has infected a cumulative total of 30 million people and become endemic to every country in the world. Genetic studies of the human immunodeficiency virus that causes AIDS indicate that it is probably more than a century old, yet HIV infected perhaps less than .001 percent of the world population until the mid-1970s. Then the virus surged because of sweeping social changes: African urbanization; American and European intravenous drug use and homosexual bathhouse activity; the Uganda-Tanzania war of 1977–79, in which rape was used as a tool of ethnic cleansing; and the growth of the American blood products industry and the international marketing of its contaminated goods. Government denial and societal prejudice every-where in the world led to inappropriate public health interventions or plain inaction, further abetting HIV transmission and slowing research for treatment or a cure.

The estimated direct (medical) and indirect (loss of productive labor force and family-impact) costs of the disease are expected to top $500 billion by the year 2000, according to the Global AIDS Policy Coalition at Harvard University. The U.S. Agency for International Development predicts that by then some 11 percent of children under 15 in sub-Saharan Africa will be AIDS orphans, and that infant mortality will soar fivefold in some African and Asian nations, due to the loss of parental care among children orphaned by AIDS and its most common opportunistic infection, tuberculosis. Life expectancy in the African and Asian nations hit hardest by AIDS will plummet to an astonishing low of 25 years by 2010, the agency forecasts.

Medical experts now recognize that any microbe, including ones previously unknown to science, can take similar advantage of conditions in human society, going from isolated cases camouflaged by generally high levels of disease to become a global threat. Furthermore, old organisms, aided by man-kind's misuse of disinfectants and drugs, can take on new, more lethal forms.

A White House-appointed interagency working group on emerging and reemerging infectious diseases estimates that at least 29 previously unknown diseases have appeared since 1973 and 20 well-known ones have reemerged, often in new drug-resistant or deadlier forms. According to the group, total direct and indirect costs of infectious disease in the United States in 1993 were more than $120 billion; combined federal, state, and municipal govern-ment expenditures that year for infectious disease control were only $74.2 million (neither figure includes AIDS, other sexually transmitted diseases, or tuberculosis).

The real threat of biowarfare

The world was lucky in the September 1994 pneumonic plague epidemic in Surat. Independent studies in the United States, France, and Russia revealed that the bacterial strain that caused the outbreak was unusually weak, and although the precise figures for plague cases and deaths remain a matter of debate, the numbers certainly fall below 200. Yet the epidemic vividly illu-strated three crucial national security issues in disease emergence: human mobility, transparency, and tensions between states up to and including the threat of biological warfare.

When word got out that an airborne disease was loose in the city, some 500,000 residents of Surat boarded trains and within 48 hours dispersed to every corner of the subcontinent. Had the microbe that caused the plague been a virus or drug-resistant bacterium, the world would have witnessed an immediate Asian pandemic. As it was, the epidemic sparked a global panic that cost the Indian economy a minimum of $2 billion in lost sales and losses on the Bombay stock market, predominantly the result of international boycotts of Indian goods and travelers.

As the number of countries banning trade with India mounted that fall, the Hindi-language press insisted that there was no plague, accusing Pakistan of a smear campaign aimed at bringing India's economy to its knees. After international scientific investigations concluded that *Yersinia pestis* had indeed been the culprit in this bona fide epidemic, attention turned to the bacteria's origin. By last June several Indian scientists claimed to have evidence that the bacteria in Surat had been genetically engineered for biowarfare purposes. Though no credible evidence exists to support it, and Indian government authorities vigorously deny such claims, the charge is almost impossible to disprove, particularly in a region rife with military and political tensions of long standing.

Even when allegations of biological warfare are not flying, it is often exceedingly difficult to obtain accurate information about outbreaks of disease, particularly from countries dependent on foreign investment or tourism or both. Transparency is a common problem; though there is usually no suggestion of covert action or malevolent intent, many countries are reluctant to disclose complete information about contagious illness. For example, nearly every country initially denied or covered up the presence of the HIV virus within its borders. Even now, at least ten nations known to be in the midst of HIV epidemics refuse to cooperate with WHO, deliberately obfuscating incidence reports or declining to provide any statistics. Similarly, Egypt denies the existence of cholera bacteria in the Nile's waters; Saudi Arabia has asked WHO not to warn that travelers to Mecca may be bitten by mosquitoes carrying viruses that cause the new, superlethal dengue hemorrhagic fever; few countries report the appearance of antibiotic-resistant strains of deadly bacteria; and central authorities in Serbia recently rescinded an international epidemic alert when they learned that all the scientists WHO planned to send to the tense Kosovo region to halt a large outbreak of Crimean-Congo hemorrhagic fever were from the United States, a nation Serbia viewed with hostility.

The specter of biological warfare having raised its head, Brad Roberts of the Center for Strategic and International Studies is particularly concerned that the New Tier nations—developing states such as China, Iran, and Iraq that possess technological know-how but lack an organized civil society that might put some restraints on its use—might be tempted to employ bioweapons. The Federation of American Scientists has sought, so far in vain, a scientific solution to the acute weaknesses of verification and enforcement provisions in the 1972 Biological Weapons Convention, which most of the world's nations have signed.

That treaty's flaws, and the very real possibility of bioweapons use, stand in sharp focus today. Iraq's threat in 1990–91 to use biological weapons in the Persian Gulf conflict found allied forces in the region virtually power-less to respond: the weapons' existence was not verified in a timely manner, the only available countermeasure was a vaccine against one type of organism, and protective gear and equipment failed to stand up to windblown sand. Last June the U.N. Security Council concluded that Iraqi stocks of bioweaponry might have been replenished after the Gulf War settlement.

More alarming were the actions of the Aum Shinrikyo cult in Japan in early 1995. In addition to releasing toxic sarin gas in the Tokyo subway on March 18, cult members were preparing vast quantities of *Clostridium difficile* bacterial spores for terrorist use. Though rarely fatal, clostridium infections often worsen as a result of improper antibiotic use, and long bouts of bloody diarrhea can lead to dangerous colon inflammations. Clostridium was a good

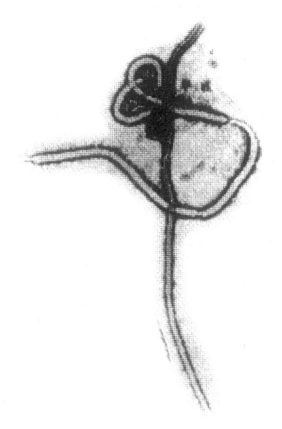

BETTMANN
The Ebola virus

28

choice for biological terrorism: the spores can survive for months and may be spread with any aerosol device, and even slight exposure can make vulnerable people (particularly children and the elderly) sick enough to cost a crowded society like Japan hundreds of millions of dollars for hospitalizations and lost productivity.

The U.S. Office of Technology Assessment has calculated what it would take to produce a spectacular terrorist bioweapon: 100 kilograms of a lethal sporulating organism such as anthrax spread over Washington, D.C., by a crop duster could cause well over two million deaths. Enough anthrax spores to kill five or six million people could be loaded into a taxi and pumped out its tailpipe as it meandered through Manhattan. Vulnerability to terrorist attacks, as well as to the natural emergence of disease, increase with population density.

A world at risk

A 1995 WHO survey of global capacity to identify and respond to threats from emerging disease reached troubling conclusions. Only six laboratories in the world, the study found, met security and safety standards that would make them suitable sites for research on the world's deadliest microbes, including those that cause Ebola, Marburg, and Lassa fever. Local political instability threatens to compromise the security of the two labs in Russia, and budget cuts threaten to do the same to the two in the United States (the army's facility at Fort Detrick and the CDC in Atlanta) and the one in Britain. In another survey, WHO sent samples of hantaviruses (such as Sin Nombre, which caused the 1993 outbreak in New Mexico) and organisms that cause dengue, yellow fever, malaria, and other diseases to the world's 35 leading disease-monitoring facilities. Only one—the CDC—correctly identified all the organisms; most got fewer than half right.

Convinced that newly emerging diseases, whether natural or engineered, could endanger national security, the CDC requested $125 million from Congress in 1994 to bolster what it termed a grossly inadequate system of surveillance and response; it received $7.3 million. After two years of inquiry by a panel of experts, the Institute of Medicine, a division of the National Academy of Sciences, declared the situation a crisis.

Today's reality is best reflected in New York City's battle with tuberculosis. Control of the W-strain of the disease—which first appeared in the city in 1991–92, is resistant to every available drug, and kills half its victims—has already cost more than $1 billion. Despite such spending, there were 3,000 TB cases in the city in 1994, some of which were the W-strain. According to the surgeon general's annual reports from the 1970s and 1980s, tuberculosis was supposed to be eradicated from the United States by 2000. During the Bush administration the CDC told state authorities they could safely lower their fiscal commitments to TB control because victory was imminent. Now

29

public health officials are fighting to get levels down to where they were in 1985—a far cry from elimination. New York's crisis is a result of both immigration pressure (some cases originated overseas) and the collapse of the local public health infrastructure.

National preparedness has further eroded over the past five years in the face of budgetary constraints. Just as WHO cannot intercede in an epidemic unless it receives an invitation from the afflicted country, the CDC may not enter a U.S. state without a request from the state government. The U.S. system rests on an increasingly shaky network of disease surveillance and response by states and territories. A 1992 survey for the CDC showed that 12 states had no one on staff to monitor microbial contamination of local food and water; 67 percent of the states and territories had less than one employee monitoring the food and water of every one million residents. And only a handful of states were monitoring hospitals for the appearance of unusual or drug-resistant microbes.

State capacity rests on county and municipal public health, and there too weaknesses are acute. In October, dengue hemorrhagic fever, which had been creeping steadily northward from Brazil over the past eight years, with devastating results, struck in Texas. Most Texas counties had slashed their mosquito control budgets and were ill prepared to combat the aggressive Tiger mosquitoes from Southeast Asia that carry the virus. In Los Angeles County that month, a $2 billion budget shortfall drove officials to close all but 10 of the 45 public health clinics and to attempt to sell four of the county's six public hospitals. Congress is contemplating enormous cuts in Medicare and Medicaid spending, which the American Public Health Association predicts would result in a widespread increase in infectious disease.

Prescriptions for national health

Bolstering research capacity, enhancing disease surveillance capabilities, revitalizing sagging basic public health systems, rationing powerful drugs to avoid the emergence of drug-resistant organisms, and improving infection control practices at hospitals are only stopgap measures. National security warrants bolder steps.

One priority is finding scientifically valid ways to use polymerase chain reaction (popularly known as DNA fingerprinting), field investigations, chemical and biological export records, and local legal instruments to track the development of new or reemergent lethal organisms, whether natural or bioweapons. The effort should focus not only on microbes directly dangerous to humans but on those that could pose major threats to crops or livestock.

Most emerging diseases are first detected by health providers working at the primary-care level. Currently there is no system, even in the United States, whereby the providers can notify relevant authorities and be assured that their alarm will be investigated promptly. In much of the world, the notifiers' reward is penalties levied against them, primarily because states want to hush up the problem. But Internet access is improving worldwide, and a small investment would give physicians an electronic highway to international health authorities that bypassed government roadblocks and obfuscation.

Only three diseases—cholera, plague, and yellow fever—are subject to international regulation, permitting U.N. and national authorities to interfere as necessary in the global traffic of goods and persons to stave off cross-border epidemics. The World Health Assembly, the legislative arm of WHO, recommended at its 1995 annual meeting in Geneva that the United Nations consider both expanding the list of regulated diseases and finding new ways to monitor the broad movement of disease. The Ebola outbreak in Kikwit demonstrated that a team of international scientists can be mobilized to swiftly contain a remote, localized epidemic caused by known nonairborne agents.

Were a major epidemic to imperil the United States, the Office of Emergency Preparedness and the National Disaster Medical System (part of the Department of Health and Human Services) would be at the helm. The office has 4,200 private-sector doctors and nurses throughout the 50 states who are at its disposal and committed to rapid mobilization in case of emergency. The system is sound but should be bolstered. Participants should be supplied with protective suits, respirators, mobile containment laboratories, and adequate local isolation facilities.

As for potential threats from biological weapons, the U.S. Department of Energy has identified serious lapses in Russian and Ukrainian compliance with the Biological Weapons Convention. Large stockpiles of bioweapons are believed to remain, and employees of the Soviet program for biological warfare are still on the state payroll. Arsenals are also thought to exist in other nations, although intelligence on this is weak. The location and destruction of such weapons is a critical priority. Meanwhile, scientists in the United States and Europe are identifying the genes in bacteria and viruses that code for virulence and modes of transmission. Better understanding of the genetic mechanisms will allow scientists to manipulate existing organisms, endowing them with dangerous capabilities. It would seem prudent for the United States and the international community to examine that potential now and consider options for the control of such research or its fruits.

To guard against the proliferation of blood-associated diseases, the blood and animal exports industries must be closely regulated, plasma donors must be screened for infections, and an internationally acceptable watchdog agency must be designated to monitor reports of the appearance of new forms of such diseases. The export of research animals played a role in a serious incident in Germany in which vaccine workers were infected with the Marburg virus and in an Ebola scare in Virginia in which imported monkeys died from the disease.

Nobel laureate Joshua Lederberg of Rockefeller University has characterized the solutions to the threat of disease emergence as multitudinous, largely straightforward and commonsensical, and international in scope; "the bad news," he says, "is they will cost money."

Budgets, particularly for health care, are being cut at all levels of government. Dustin Hoffman made more money last year playing a disease control scientist in the movie *Outbreak* than the combined annual budgets for the U.S. National Center for Infectious Diseases and the U.N. Programme on AIDS/HIV.

2

GHOSTS OF KIGALI

Infectious disease and global stability at the turn of the century

Andrew T. Price-Smith

Source: *International Journal*, 54:3 (1999), 426–42.

> Beyond the enormous suffering of individuals and families, South Africans are beginning to understand the cost [of HIV/AIDS] in every sphere of society, observing with growing dismay its impact on the efforts of our new democracy to achieve the goals of reconstruction and development.[1]

As the spectre of the Cold War and the traditional security threats associated with it recede into the past, international relations and national security analysts have begun to embrace concepts of human security and preventive defence, arguing that factors such as environmental degradation, resource scarcity, and overpopulation now pose more significant threats to global security. But another threat looms large on the horizon, namely the proliferation of emerging and re-emerging infections on a global scale. Indeed, the HIV pandemic is entrenched in subsaharan Africa and accelerating through eastern Europe and south and east Asia. Other widening pandemics include the re-emergence of such old scourges as tuberculosis, malaria, cholera, and dengue. New threats have also appeared in the form of hanta, ebola, legionella, and such antibiotic resistant organisms as vancomycin-resistant enterococci and methycillin-resistant staphylococcus aureas.

A primary purpose of international relations theory is to construct models that will assist in averting the premature loss of human life and productivity as a result of war. Indeed, as Thomas Hobbes claimed, it is the central function of the state to guarantee the physical safety of its citizens from both internal and external forms of predation.[2] However, traditional concepts of security usually ignored the greatest source of human misery and mortality, the microbial penumbra that surrounds our species. It is time to consider the additional form of ecological predation wherein the physical security and prosperity of a state's populace is directly threatened by the global phenomena of emerging and re-emerging infectious disease.[3]

Emerging and re-emerging infectious diseases (ERIDs) are significant obstacles to the political stability and economic development of seriously affected societies. Thus, the global resurgence of infectious disease presents a direct and significant long-term threat to international governance and prosperity.[4] Over the broad span of human history infectious disease has consistently accounted for the greatest proportion of human morbidity and mortality, easily surpassing war as the foremost threat to human life and prosperity. Historians have long argued that infectious disease has had a profound impact on the evolution and, at times, the dissolution of societal structures, governments, and empires.[5] Indeed, Robert Fogel argues that much of England's prosperity, if not the Industrial Revolution itself, resulted from the conquest of high morbidity and mortality in Britain during the late 18th and early 19th century,[6] largely because of significant advances in public health and in the increasingly equitable distribution of food. However, even in the era of modern medicine, states annually suffer much greater mortality and morbidity from infectious disease than from casualties incurred during inter- and intra-state military conflict.

According to the World Bank, of the 49,971,000 deaths recorded in 1990, infectious disease was responsible for 16,690,000 (34.4 per cent), while war accounted for 322,000 (0.64 per cent) or a ratio of 52:1.[7] Thus the relative destruction wrought by disease compared to deaths from military actions is significant. From the standpoint of human security, then, disease is a relatively greater threat to human well-being than war, and yet the subject is poorly understood within the general policy community.

Statistics gathered by the Harvard-based Global AIDS Policy Coalition show that in 1995 approximately 22 million people were infected with HIV/AIDS, and 4.7 million new infections occurred globally. Of the new infections, 2.5 million were in Southeast Asia and 1.9 million in subsaharan Africa; the industrialized world accounted for approximately 170,000 new cases.[8] The pace of the HIV/AIDS pandemic is accelerating: a total of 33.4 million people are now infected; there are 5.8 million new infections annually; and 2.5 million people died from HIV/AIDS related causes in 1998.[9] This translates into an increase in the global pace of infection of 24 per cent since 1995. In terms of the absolute magnitude of mortality, the HIV pandemic now rivals the greatest plagues in history, including the Black Death of Middle Ages Europe and the influenza pandemic of 1918, both of which killed over 20 million people. To date the HIV pandemic has resulted in the infection of 47 million, 14 million of whom died, and the contagion is spreading rapidly throughout south and Southeast Asia, eastern Europe, and Latin America.[10]

The heart of the HIV pandemic beats in subsaharan Africa where many states are now reporting HIV seroprevalence levels in excess of 10 per cent. Indeed, South Africa, Kenya, Uganda, Zambia, Namibia, Swaziland, Botswana, and Zimbabwe all have seroprevalence levels ranging from 10 to 25 per cent of the population.[11] Botswana, for example, has seen rates rise from 10 per cent in 1992 to 25.1 per cent in 1997 – an increase of 250 per cent over five years.[12] In South Africa total HIV infection levels rose from 1.4 million in 1995 to over 3 million in 1998,[13] or an increase of more than 200 per cent in 3 years. Some regions within these states have even higher infection levels. HIV prevalence in KwaZulu-Natal in South Africa has now reached 30 per cent, and Francistown in Botswana reports that 43 per cent of its citizens are infected.[14] Certain towns along the South African-Zimbabwe border claim astonishing rates of approximately 70 per cent.[15]

The pandemic is expanding into eastern Europe at an ever-increasing pace. A former Russian minister of health, Tatyana Dmitriyeva, has predicted that over one million Russians will be infected with HIV by 2000.[16] Ukraine has seen HIV incidence soar from a modest 44 cases in 1994 to an astonishing 110,000 cases as of mid-1998.[17] The epidemic is also spreading throughout India's vast population at a rapacious pace. Five years ago, HIV was practically unheard of in India; now almost 1 per cent of all pregnant women tested throughout the country are HIV positive.[18] By 1997 the epidemic was already firmly entrenched in some regions such as Nagaland along the Burmese border (7.8 per cent HIV seroprevalence) and nearby Manipur (over 10 per cent).[19] Indeed, with the exception of the developed world and certain states such as Uganda and Thailand which have seen some reduction in the rate of new infections, the HIV pandemic continues to expand at a truly alarming pace.

Other diseases once thought to be under control are reappearing as global scourges. Tuberculosis has been making such a steady comeback that the World Health Organization (WHO) declared it to be a global crisis in 1993. WHO estimates that '8.9 million people developed tuberculosis in 1995, bringing the global total of sufferers to about 22 million, of whom about 3 million will have died in the same space of time.' In the absence of increased effectiveness and availability of tuberculosis control measures, over 30 million tuberculosis deaths and more than 90 million new infections are forecast by the turn of the century. Furthermore, tuberculosis is making inroads into the industrialized nations, particularly Canada and the United States where it infects disadvantaged urban and incarcerated populations and then spreads throughout society. In the United States, reported cases of tuberculosis had declined from 84,300 in 1953 to 22,200 in 1984, a drop of approximately 4 per cent per annum. However, from 1985 to 1993, the number of cases increased by a cumulative 14 per cent, and the pace continues to accelerate.[20] Similarly, Zimbabwe has reported massive increases in incidence, from 5,000 cases in 1986 to 35,000 cases in 1997.[21] Murray Feschbach notes that the incidence in Russia, too, is increasing rapidly and, based on estimates provided by the Russian Ministry of the Interior, predicts that the result will be 1.75 million Russians deaths per year by 2000.[22]

Malaria also continues its relentless expansion into former regions of endemicity. For example, in 1989 it claimed 100 lives in Zimbabwe and debilitated many thousands; by 1997 the number had risen to 2,800 deaths, an astonishing rate of increase for a disease that was once thought to be under control.[23] Indeed, the best available estimates project that malaria currently claims 5,000 lives every day in Africa or some 1.8 million per year. Global estimates put the total annual death rate at upwards of 2.7 million and indicate that malaria debilitates as many as 500 million people every year.[24] Ellen Ruppel Shell claims that the global incidence of malaria has increased by approximately 400 per cent between 1992 and 1997 and notes that the disease has re-emerged in North America from urban centres in California to Michigan, from New York City to Toronto.[25]

Meanwhile familiar pathogens continue to exact their toll on humanity with relentless vigour. Acute lower respiratory infections are responsible for the death of nearly 4 million children annually, while diarrhoeal diseases such as adenovirus and rotavirus kill nearly 3 million infants every year. Viral hepatitis is another global scourge. A minimum of 350 million people are chronic carriers of the hepatitis B virus and an additional 100 million harbour the hepatitis C virus. According to WHO projections, at least 25 per cent of these carriers will die from related liver disease.[26] To make matters worse, many of the ten million new cases of cancer diagnosed in 1995 were caused by viruses, bacteria, and parasites. WHO calculates that 15 per cent of all new cancer cases (1.5 million) are the result of exposure to infectious agents, and this percentage will no doubt increase as our knowledge of both infectious disease and cancer advances.

New evidence is linking many other supposedly chronic or genetic diseases such as heart disease and multiple sclerosis to common infectious agents (chlamydia and herpes, respectively) which promote long-term disease processes within human hosts.[27] If certain conditions such as cancer, heart disease, and multiple sclerosis are indeed pathogen-induced, then the global burden of disease may be far greater than was previously thought.

While it is relatively easy to see that emerging and re-emerging infectious diseases are central agents of misery throughout the developing world, it is not often apparent that infection-induced mortality has been on the rise in the developed world as well. For example, the United States, which has enormous levels of state capacity, has seen a steady increase in mortality from infectious disease over the last two decades, from 15,360 deaths in 1979 to 77,128 ERID-induced deaths in 1995,[28] for a significant increase of 502 per cent.

Interdisciplinary models that combine the natural and social sciences require a fundamental reconceptualization of standard definitions of national interest and security. Constricting definitions that focus exclusively on the relative military capability of states are increasingly sterile in the face of the many global challenges of the post-cold war world. Threats to human welfare such as global environmental degradation, resource scarcity, and infectious disease present policy-makers with difficult dilemmas. Novel global collective action solutions are exceptionally difficult to achieve given the primacy of national sovereignty in an arena of international anarchy. In articulating the complex linkages between increasing disease prevalence and state capacity, some light can be shed on the association between the prevalence of infectious disease and growing poverty and political destabilization in regions such as sub-saharan Africa.

To begin with a specific definition: emerging infectious diseases are path-ogen-induced human illnesses which have increased in incidence, lethality, transmissibility, and/or have expanded their geographical range since 1973.[29] Re-emerging diseases are those pathogen-induced human illnesses that were previously controlled or were declining in range and/or incidence, but are now expanding – not just in range and incidence, but also in drug-resistance and increasing transmissibility and/or lethality. Pathogens are defined as viral, bacterial, parasitic, or proteinic organisms or agents that live in a parasitic and debilitating relationship with their human host.

Pathogenic microbes exist independently throughout the earth's biosphere, the vast majority of them in the zoonotic pool, outside of human ecology. In a very real way these pathogens are independent variables and are exogenous to the state because they are global phenomena (existing at the system level). They may cross over from the zoonotic reservoir into the human ecology at any time according to the principles of chaos. A classic example is falciparum malaria, which seems to have crossed over from various avian species to humans at some time within the last five thousand years. Because of the recent nature of the crossover, falciparum is far deadlier to humans than its cousin vivax, which has had a much longer time to adjust to its human hosts.

After pathogenic agents enter the human ecology (and become endogenized within human societies) their effects are magnified by intervening variables called 'disease amplifiers.' Examples of potent amplifiers are phenomena such as environmental degradation, warfare, climate change, the misuse of anti-biotics, changes in the speed of human transportation technologies, famine, natural disasters, and global trade,[30] all of which generate changes in viral traffic that result in ERIDs. Thus ERIDs are a product of the synergy between the independent variable (pathogens) and the intervening variables.

States and societies may at any point use adaptive resources to mitigate the effects of ERIDs on state capacity. But a state's ability to adapt is limited by several factors. First, the initial level of state capacity determines the scale of adaptive resources that can be mobilized to deal with the ERID problem. States with higher initial capacity have greater technical, financial, and social resources available to them to cope with crises. State adaptation is also affected by exogenous inputs of capital and social and technical ingenuity, courtesy of international organizations such as the WHO, the United Nations Children's Fund, and nongovernmental organizations (NGOs) such as the International Committee of the Red Cross. Adaptation may be compromised by certain outcomes generated by intervening variables, such as war, famine, and ecological destruction.

There is a logically positive association between state capacity and state adaptation because greater initial capacity means that there are more human, economic, and technical resources within the state to mobilize to deal with various crises. The lower the initial value of state capacity, the fewer the resources that can be mobilized to offset the crisis. This relationship operates in a reciprocal spiral: greater initial capacity leads to greater adaptive ability, which should in turn reduce the ERID-induced loss to state capacity. Thus states that have lower state capacity when ERIDs afflict them generally suffer much greater losses than states with high initial capacity. The only means by which states with lower state capacity can ameliorate the effects of ERID is through exogenous inputs which give them greater resources to mobilize and advance tactical knowledge to deal with the crisis.[31]

Intra-state effects of ERID

A brief explanation of the effects of ERID on state capacity, in the domains of economics and governance, is in order. The destructive effects of ERIDs reverberate throughout all levels of the economy from households and firms to sectors such as resource extraction, agriculture, insurance, and banking. When infected workers are debilitated or killed, the productivity of the workforce is reduced, particularly in labour-intensive sectors such as agriculture or mining.[32] Infectious disease imposes additional costs on the household in lost savings and in labour substitution, particularly in those units in the lower economic strata of society. Income inequalities between the lower and upper classes are thereby exacerbated. ERIDs also change household expenditure patterns as money earmarked for food, clothing, shelter, and so on is spent on medication instead. Thus ERIDs generate economic shocks to the household, changing savings and consumption patterns, eroding aggregate household wealth, and making significant labour substitution necessary. Rising levels of infectious disease also decrease incentives to invest in child education, as children spend more time working to support debilitated or bereaved family members. Nor is there much incentive to allocate resources to educate a child if that child is likely to die of some infection in the near future.[33] And when whole communities are affected, the problems are compounded.

Thus, the negative effects of an ERID on economic productivity include decreases in worker productivity, labour shortages and increased absenteeism, higher costs imposed on household units (particularly on the poor), reductions in per-capita income, reduced savings, capital flight, reductions in national gross domestic product, and increases in income inequalities within a society which may in turn generate increased governance problems. An ERID also impedes the settlement of marginal regions and the development of natural resources, negatively affects tourism, and results in the embargoing of infected goods. A prime example is the European Union's recent ban on all beef-related products from Britain, from foodstuffs to soaps to cosmetics, for fear of contamination with the bovine spongiform encephalopathy (BSE) prion (infected proteins) that causes Creutzfeld-Jacob disease in humans. All told, increasing disease prevalence poses a serious threat to the economic health of societies across the globe.

In the domain of governance, high levels of ERID incidence undermine the capacity of political leaders and their respective bureaucracies to govern effectively as the infection of government personnel results in the debilitation and death of skilled administrators who oversee the day-to-day operations of governance. For example, AIDS has resulted in a significant winnowing of educated and skilled workers from government, industry, and education in Tanzania. The destructive impact of ERID-induced mortality in capital-intensive institutions generates institutional fragility that will undermine the stability of nascent democratic societies. As the burden of disease on the population of a state increases, the resulting poverty and physical destruction visited on the populace will over time erode governmental legitimacy. Therefore, ERID-induced poverty, morbidity and mortality, migration, and psychological stresses wear upon the economic and social fabric of society and will contribute to repression and the collapse of democracy as a weakening state seeks to maintain order while the government's legitimacy erodes and as governmental institutions become increasingly fragile. This in turn poses problems for the United States and the administration of President Bill Clinton, whose strategy of 'engagement and enlargement' places a premium on establishing and strengthening democratic regimes on a global level.

The presence of ERIDs in military populations jeopardizes military readiness, international co-operation, national security, and the ability of a state to preserve its territorial integrity. At the intra-state level, ERIDs reduce force strength through the death or debilitation of military personnel, deplete the supply of healthy recruits, and generate costs that limit military budgets, all of which impairs a state's capacity to defend itself against a potential aggressor and limits a state's ability to project power for peacekeeping or coercive measures.

The adaptive capability of states depends on their current and future supply of technical and social ingenuity, on their domestic reservoirs of capacity, and on the contribution that outside actors make in the form of capital, goods, and technical assistance. Thomas Homer-Dixon's concept of ingenuity is a partial factor in the ability of states to adapt to crises. While the ingenuity model that he has constructed deals with the issue of economic development in a climate of resource scarcity and environmental degradation, the concept is useful in determining the capacity of a state to adapt in the face of significant challenges. Homer-Dixon argues that 'resource scarcity can simultaneously increase the requirement and impede the supply [of ingenuity], producing an "ingenuity gap" that may have critical consequences for adaptation and, in turn, social stability.'[34] Similarly, the negative economic and social effects of ERID can also increase the requirement for ingenuity while limiting its supply.[35] The lesson to be drawn from the ingenuity argument is that the longer we wait to address the problem of infectious disease, the greater the costs of generating the levels of ingenuity that will be required to resolve the problem.

Because of low initial levels of state capacity and ingenuity in the developing world, the global proliferation of infectious disease presents the greatest threat to the least developed societies. This has given rise to a disturbing tendency on the part of some Western scholars, policy-makers, and the media to see ERIDs as a threat to the populations only in those societies. But hubris and denial are shortsighted and bound to lead to significant downstream losses for developed societies as well. The natural world is of course infinitely complex and interdependent. As the human species continues to alter the global environment, that environment will produce corresponding responses, such as the continuing emergence of human pathogens. As we have seen from the emergence of AIDS, hepatitis, drug-resistant tuberculosis, and 'flesh eating disease,' the developed world remains vulnerable to the ravages of infection.[36]

The negative effects of ERIDs on state capacity at the unit level produce related pernicious outcomes at the systems level. Within the domain of economics, as an ERID produces a significant drag on the economies of affected countries, we may see chronic underdevelopment, which may in turn exert a net drag on global trade and impair global prosperity. In all likelihood, because of the nature of spiral dynamics inherent in the relationship between an ERID and state capacity, countries with low initial levels will suffer greater losses over time from an increasing prevalence of infectious disease within their populations. Because of the spiral effect, an ERID's negative influence on the economic development of states may exacerbate the economic divide between North and South. Furthermore, the negative effects of infectious disease are not confined to the developing world. At the systems level, trade goods from ERID-affected regions may be subject to international embargo (as was the case with British beef and BSE and with influenza-infected chickens in Hong Kong). As infectious agents continue to emerge and re-emerge, and as agricultural crops and animal stocks become increasingly infested, we should expect that (presumably infected) trade goods from affected states will be embargoed, tourism may decline, and economic damage will likely intensify.

One conclusion which can be drawn from the emergence of prion-induced Creutzfeld-Jacob, ebola, HIV, and plague is that people are extremely risk-averse when it comes to the emergence of new pathogens. The result may be paranoia, hysteria, and xenophobia that may impair rational decision-making in the foreign policy of an affected state. The epidemic of pneumonic plague (yersina pestis) in western India during the autumn of 1994 gives some idea of how the psychological effects of the outbreak of an infectious disease may affect both state capacity and an afflicted state's relations with its neighbours. The very rumour of plague in Surat prompted the frenetic exodus of over 300,000 refugees from the city who then carried the pestilence with them to Bombay, Calcutta, and as far as New Delhi.[37] Out of fear, Pakistan, Bangladesh, Nepal, and China rapidly closed their borders to both trade and travel from India. Some even restricted mail from the affected state: India had become an instant international pariah. As the plague spread, concern mounted, and international travel to and with India became increasingly restricted. On 22 September 1994, the Bombay stock exchange plunged and soon after many countries began to restrict imports from India, placing impounded goods in quarantine or turning them back altogether at the border.[38]

As the crisis deepened, the Indian army was called in to enforce a quarantine in the affected area. Doctors who had fled Surat were forced back to work under threat of legal prosecution by the government. In the aftermath of an epidemic that killed 56 people, the Indian government was notified by the Center for Disease Control in Atlanta that the yersina pestis bacillus was an unknown and presumably new strain. To Indian authorities this information was 'unusual,' and they promptly accused rebel militants (Ultras) of procuring the bacillus from a pathogen-manufacturing facility in Almaty, Kazakhstan, with the object of manufacturing an epidemic in India. As a result of paranoia on the part of Indian officials, the inquest into the epidemic was transferred from public health authorities to the Department of Defence.[39] Beyond the acrimony that the plague fostered between India and its Islamic neighbours, the economic toll has been estimated at a minimum of US$1 billion in lost revenue from exports and tourism.[40] While the loss may seem trivial, it dealt a serious blow to a developing economy and had negative repercussions throughout numerous sectors.

As the events in Surat and the current BSE scare in Europe show, infectious disease and the irrational behaviour that it generates may worsen relationships between states and/or cultures.[41] The recent panic in Britain over BSE or 'Mad Cow Disease' has resulted in the embargo of many beef-derived British products and dictated the cull of a significant proportion of Britain's beef stocks. BSE has frightened the British population as scientists talk about the possibility of thousands of Britons infected with a new variant of Creutzfeld-Jacob disease, and Britain's European partners have summarily banned the import of British beef in violation of Europen Community trade law.[42]

Increasing levels of ERID correlate with a decline in the state capacity of affected countries. The decline, coupled with an increase in pathogen-induced deprivation and increasing demands upon the state, is accompanied by an attendant increase in the incidence of chronic substate violence and state failure. State failure frequently produces chaos in affected regions, as neighbouring states seal their borders to prevent the massive influx of ERID-infected refugee populations. Adjacent states may also try to fill the power vacuum and seize valued territory from the collapsing state, prompting other proximate states to do the same, thereby exacerbating regional security dilemmas. As ERID incidence and lethality increase, deprivation will mount and state capacity will decline, which in turn will generate increasing levels of stress and demands upon government structures and undermine its legitimacy. Thus, ERID-induced stresses may combine with other environmental, demographic, and economic stressors to create riots, rebellions, and insurgencies. As the prevalence of ERID increases and the geographical range of pathogens expands, the number of failing states may rise, necessitating increased humanitarian intervention by United Nations security forces to maintain order in affected regions. As we have seen from its experiences in central and west Africa, the United Nations is unlikely to have a lasting effect in restoring order to areas where ERID incidence and lethality remain high.

Conclusions

The global resurgence of infectious disease has significant implications for state survival, stability, and prosperity, as well as ramifications for interstate relations. The premature death and debilitation of a significant proportion of a state's population erodes worker productivity and undermines state prosperity, induces high levels of psychological stress in the populace, fosters internal migration and emigration, threatens a state's ability both to defend itself and to project force, generates institutional fragility, and undermines the legitimacy of authority structures, thereby impairing the state's ability to govern effectively. While ERID acts as a stressor on state capacity, it simultaneously generates poverty and misery within the population which may result in deprivation conflicts, widespread insurrection, and governance problems.[43] At the global level, ERID-induced poverty generates a drag on both regional development and global prosperity. Disease-induced poverty and instability may exacerbate migration from the biologically onerous regions of the South to the prosperous and relatively benign regions of the North. Furthermore, as ERID-induced shortcomings in the realms of governance and defence impair state survival, the international community may be called on to intervene and restore order in affected states.

It is likely that plagues have contributed to the collapse of governance over the broad span of history: they hampered the Athenian war effort during the Peloponnesian war, contributed to the demise of Byzantine Rome and to the destruction of the feudal order in Europe, and were the primal force in the annihilation of the pre-Colombian societies in the Americas after their first contacts with Europeans.[44] This dynamic is not relegated to the annals of history but continues to affect state capacity in the modern era. Because of the negative association between infectious disease and state capacity, the global proliferation of emerging and re-emerging diseases (particularly HIV, tuberculosis, and malaria) is a threat to international economic development and global governance. The growing destabilization of subsaharan Africa is at least partly due to the exceptionally high ERID levels in the region, particularly HIV/AIDS and malaria. Indeed, extreme governance problems in the Democratic Republic of the Congo, Rwanda, Uganda, and Burundi are likely related to increasing ERID stresses on state capacity.

Based on the experience of subsaharan Africa, we can project that the continuing and rapid spread of HIV and other ERIDs in eastern Europe and south and west Asia will erode state capacity in those regions as well, generating widespread poverty and political instability in seriously affected nations. In particular, the proliferation of infectious diseases such as HIV and tuberculosis threatens the economic well-being and political stability of several key states in the world, notably Russia, Ukraine, India, South Africa, Thailand, perhaps China. To promote global stability and prosperity significant resources will have to be allocated to public health infrastructures within these countries, and public health will have to become a central component of foreign development assistance packages.

Global phenomena such as infectious diseases frequently act in concert with other global collective action problems, such as environmental degradation, resource scarcity, and overpopulation, to strain state capacity. This synergy between stressors of state capacity will increasingly destabilize seriously affected states and in some cases entire regions (such as subsaharan Africa). We will have to foster increased communication and co-operation between the global policy and medical communities and provide increased resources for surveillance, containment, and co-operative policy measures if we ever hope to check the global proliferation of emerging and re-emerging diseases. Above all, the gravity of these issues has to be brought to the attention of the heads of all governments, as the greatest weapon in stemming the global tide of infection is political will.

Tangible actions that governments should take include establishing a global disease surveillance system which incorporates the successful civil-society model of the ProMED network that currently monitors disease outbreaks. Governments should also collect 'health intelligence' so as to monitor the progression of diseases through the populations of states that either cannot provide accurate statistics on disease prevalence or refuse to do so for political reasons. Policy-makers should also take action to reduce the pace of global environmental degradation, curb the abuse of anti-microbial medications within their societies, and provide increased funding for research to develop vaccines and other anti-microbial agents.

Although the World Health Organization has been the principal actor in tracking disease emergence and proliferation, it faces several problems in dealing with these issues. Even though funding is increasingly diverted within the WHO to infectious surveillance, treatment, and control, these programmes are generally underfunded, understaffed, and less than effective in fighting ERIDs on so many fronts. Thus, greater resources should be given to the WHO to increase its capacity, and these funds should be specifically targeted to deal with the greatest current ERID threats (HIV, tuberculosis, and malaria). The United States and Japan are currently developing a policy framework for greater co-operation in checking the spread of ERIDs within and between their own territories. Furthermore, the G-7 states are exploring means by which they might collaborate to reduce the threat of emerging diseases to their populations. While these efforts have not produced any concrete results in the form of multilateral anti-contagion regimes, they are a step in the right direction. Given the will, policy-makers can orchestrate the required redistribution of fiscal resources, ingenuity, and technology to stem the rising tide of disease and thus help to promote global prosperity and stability.

Notes

Andrew Price-Smith would like to thank David Welch, Janice Gross Stein, Louis Pauly, Marc Levy, Mark Zacher, Stephen S. Morse, Nils-Petter Gleditsch, Franklyn Griffiths, Robert Matthews, Wesley Wark, David Fidler, Peter Gizewski, Laurie Garrett, Jim Whitman, Jay Keystone, Patrick Kelley, Peter Zoutis, Ann-Marie Kimball, Thomas Homer-Dixon, and Ron Deibert for their insightful comments and critiques.

1 Nelson Mandela, 'AIDS: facing up to the global threat,' Address to the World Economic Forum, Davos, 3 February 1997. http://www.us.unaids.org/highband/speeches/mandela.html, 2 (20 April 1997).

2 See Thomas Hobbes, *Leviathan*, ed C. B. Macpherson (Harmondsworth: Penguin 1968).

3 Until very recently the concept of microbial threats to human security had not been explored. Two recent works which begin to do so are Laurie Garret, 'The return of infectious disease,' *Foreign Affairs* 75 (January/February 1996), 66–79; and Dennis Pirages, 'Ecological security: micro-threats to human well-being,' paper presented at the International Studies Association, annual meeting, San Diego CA, April 1996.

4 Andrew T. Price-Smith, *Contagion and Chaos: Infectious Disease and its Effects on Global Security and Development*, CIS Working Paper no 1, 1998 (Toronto: Centre for International Studies, University of Toronto, January 1998).

5 See William H. McNeill, *Plagues and Peoples* (Toronto: Doubleday 1989); Alfred W. Crosby, *Ecological Imperialism: The Biological Expansion of Europe, 900–1900* (New York: Cambridge University Press 1994); Crosby, *The Colombian Exchange: Biological and Cultural Consequences of 1492* (Westport CT: Greenwood 1972); Sheldon Watts, *Epidemics and History: Disease, Power, and Imperialism* (New Haven CT: Yale University Press 1997); and Hans Zinsser, *Rats, Lice, and History* (New York: Little, Brown 1934).

6 See Robert W. Fogel, 'The conquest of high mortality and hunger in Europe and America: timing and mechanisms,' in David Landes, Patrice Higgonet, and Henry Rosovsky, eds, *Favorites of Fortune: Technology, Growth and Economic Development Since the Industrial Revolution* (Cambridge MA: Harvard University Press 1991); Fogel, 'Nutrition and the decline in mortality since 1700: some preliminary findings in long-term factors in American economic growth,' in Stanley L. Engerman and Robert E. Gallman, eds, *Conference on Research in Income and Wealth*, vol 41 (Chicago IL: University of Chicago Press 1986); and Fogel, *Economic Growth, Population Theory, and Physiology: The Bearing of Long-term*

Processes in the Making of Economic Policy, working paper no. 4638 (Cambridge MA: National Bureau of Economic Research, April 1994).

7 Statistics on the causes of global deaths in 1990 are derived from World Bank, *World Development Report 1993: Investing in Health* (New York: Oxford University Press 1993), 224–5.

8 Global AIDS Policy Coalition, Johnathan Mann, ed, *Status and Trends of the HIV/AIDS Pandemic as of January, 1906* (Cambridge MA: Harvard School of Public Health, François-Xavier Bagnoud Center for Health and Human Rights, 18 January 1996), 2.

9 See UNAIDS, *AIDS Epidemic Update: December 1998*, 2–3, at http://www.unaids.org/highband/document/epidemio/wadr98e.pdf.

10 *Ibid*, 3.

11 Namibia and Swaziland currently report HIV seroprevalence levels in excess of 20 per cent; Zimbabwe and Botswana have the dubious distinction of having infection levels of over 25 per cent of the total population. Individual country annual sero-prevalence statistics are available at http://www.unaids.org/highband.

12 Lawrence K. Altman, 'Parts of Africa showing HIV in 1 in 4 adults,' *New York Times*, 24 June 1998, A1.

13 Suzanne Daly, 'A post-apartheid agony: AIDS on the march,' *New York Times*, 23 July 1998, A1.

14 Donald McNeil, Jr, 'AIDS stalking Africa's struggling economies,' *New York Times*, 15 November 1998, A1.

15 André Picard, 'UN warns of alarming gap in prevention of AIDS,' *Globe and Mail* (Toronto), 24 June 1998, B4.

16 Cited in Murray Feschbach, 'Dead souls,' *Atlantic Monthly*, January 1999, 26.

17 'HIV rising in CIS countries,' *Globe and Mail*, 22 April 1998, A16.

18 Lawrence K. Altman, 'Dismaying experts, HIV infections soar,' *New York Times*, 24 November 1998, F7.

19 John Stackhouse, 'Nagaland choking in grip of AIDS,' *Globe and Mail*, 1 December 1997, A11.

20 *World Health Report 1996*, 27, 28.

21 Michael Specter, 'Doctors powerless as AIDS rakes Africa,' *New York Times*, 6 August 1998, A1.

22 Feschbach, 'Dead souls,' 27.

23 Specter, 'Doctors powerless as AIDS rakes Africa,' A1.

24 Ellen Ruppel Shell, 'Resurgence of a deadly disease,' *Atlantic Monthly*, August 1997, 47, 48.

25 *Ibid*, 45. Malaria's re-emergence as an endemically transmitted pathogen in Toronto has been verified by Kevin Kain of the Tropical Disease Unit, Toronto General Hospital. Comments made to the author, 30 October 1998.

26 *World Health Report 1996*, 2.

27 Note the evidence compiled by Paul Ewald, cited in Judith Hooper, 'A new germ theory,' *Atlantic Monthly*, February 1999, 41–53.

28 See http://cdc.gov/nchswww/fastats for this data.

29 1973 is a significant date. Up until the early 1970s, advances in public health contributed to the dramatic fall in infectious disease-induced morbidity and mortality on a global scale. Thus the prevalence of infectious disease reached its nadir circa 1973. In that year a new pathogen 'rotavirus' was recognized, the first of many new pathogenic agents which would emerge in the coming decades. Essentially, 1973 is the turning point in the 'health transition' where the curve of infectious disease incidence stops declining and begins to ascend. See Report of the National Science and Technology Committee, Committee on International

Science, Engineering, and Technology (CISET) Working Group on Emerging and Re-Emerging Infectious Diseases, *Global Microbial Threats in the 1990s* (Washington DC: White House), September 1995.

30 Stephen S. Morse, ed, *Emerging Viruses* (New York: Oxford University Press 1993).

31 This methodology (and the use of surrogate measures of disease prevalence such as infant mortality and life expectancy) can be found in Andrew T. Price-Smith, *Wilson's Bridge: A Consilient Methodology for the Analysis of Complex Biological-Political Relationships*, CIS Working Paper no 8, 1998 (Toronto: Centre for International Studies, University of Toronto, November 1998).

32 See Randall M. Packard, *White Plague, Black Labor: Tuberculosis and the Political Economy of Health and Disease in South Africa* (Berkeley: University of California Press 1989).

33 These hypothetical causal relationships are empirically confirmed via diachronic national and global correlations in Andrew T. Price-Smith, *Statistical Evidence of a Negative Association between Infectious Disease and State Capacity: 1951–1991*, CIS Working Paper no 1, 1999 (Toronto: Centre for International Studies, University of Toronto).

34 Thomas F. Homer-Dixon, 'The ingenuity gap: can poor countries adapt to resource scarcity?' *Population and Development Review 21* (September 1995), 589.

35 The determinants of adaptation are: the change in the requirements for adaptation – that is, how difficult the job is – and whether the necessary knowledge, adaptive strategies, and technologies can be supplied, when and where required and at the optimal time.

36 Note the significant penetration of developed societies by pathogens such as HIV, Hepatitis C and B, and our continuing vigilance against another lethal influenza pandemic.

37 'The old enemy,' *Economist*, 1 October 1994, 40.

38 Hamish MacDonald, 'Surat's revenge: India counts the mounting costs of poverty,' *Far Eastern Economic Review*, 13 October 1994, 76.

39 'Were Ultras responsible for Surat plague?' *Hindustan Times*, 9 July 1995.

40 'Was it the plague?' *Economist*, 19 November 1994, 38–40.

41 For an analysis of human reaction and aversion to risk, with the attendant irrational behaviour that results, see Roger E. Kasperson et al, *The Social Amplification of Risk: A Conceptual Framework* (Worcester MA: Center for Technology, Environment, and Development, Clark University, 1989).

42 As of 23 March 1996, France, Italy, Germany, and Belgium, among others, had banned British beef imports. John Darnton, 'France and Belgium ban British beef over cow disease,' *New York Times*, 22 March 1996, A4; David Wallen, 'European partners ban U.K. beef,' *Globe and Mail*, 22 March 1996, A1, A10.

43 For further literature on deprivation conflicts and state failure, see Jack Goldstone, *Revolution and Rebellion in the Early Modern Era* (Berkeley: University of California Press 1991); Thomas F. Homer-Dixon, 'On the threshold: environmental changes as causes of acute conflict' and 'Environmental scarcities and violent conflict: evidence from cases,' both in Sean M. Lynn-Jones and Steven E. Miller, eds, *Global Dangers: Changing Dimensions of International Security* (Cambridge MA: MIT Press 1995), 43–83, 144–82; Colin Kahl, 'Population growth, environmental degradation, and state-sponsored violence: The case of Kenya, 1991–93,' *International Security* 23 (autumn 1998), 80–119; Kalevi J. Holsti, *The State, War, and the State of War* (Cambridge: Cambridge University Press 1996); Ted Gurr, *Why Men Rebel* (Princeton: Princeton University Press

1970); and Edward Rice, *Wars of the Third Kind: Conflict in Underdeveloped Countries* (Berkeley: University of California Press 1988).

44 This conclusion is based on the negative empirical association between infectious disease and state capacity. The statistical evidence shows that the arguments of historians for linking plagues with the collapse of empires and societies are likely accurate. See, for example, Michael Oldstone, *Viruses, Plagues and History* (New York: Oxford University Press 1998).

3

HEALTH AND SECURITY IN HISTORICAL PERSPECTIVE

Simon Szreter

Source: Lincoln C. Chen, Jennifer Leaning and Vasant Narasimhan (eds) *Global Health Challenges for Human Security*, Cambridge, Mass.: Global Equity Initiative, 2003, pp. 31–52.

Health and security: twins recently parted

It is distinctly odd that such a primeval human concern as *security* should only recently be explicitly linked in the academic and policy literature with *health*, another of humanity's eternal preoccupations. This signifies nothing so much as the manner in which both the worlds of knowledge and of action may be divided by meaningless disciplinary fences and can be separated, instead of joined, by words. *Security* and *health* have been kept segregated from each other for several decades largely because they have each acted as major symbols for previously opposed — or at least mutually disinterested — sets of political interests, ideological dispositions, and networks of institutions. *Security* is undoubtedly long established as a key term in the lexicon of the defense establishment of most western liberal democracies, notably that of the U.S. *Health* has been adopted by many groups wishing to promote it in various contexts but most consistently in an academic or policy context by those studying and advocating public health.

However, the separate usage of these two terms in recent decades belies the fact that historically they have usually dwelled together. Sovereigns such as the French medieval kings swore in their coronation oaths to protect the frail and weak, widows and cripples. The power to afford such security was both symbol and justification of their divine right to rule. Successful generals, from the time of Alexander the Great, have long known that the effectiveness of their armies depends crucially on their health — summarized in Napoleon's celebrated dictum that an army "marches on its stomach." Naval surgeons and army doctors in the 18th century were important early exponents of the principles of preventive medicine and techniques of epidemiology (1). Much of the whole field of tropical (formerly imperial)

48

medicine developed from the joint interests of the military and the medical professions (2).

But in the general public's discourse, too, there was a time until not so long ago when the explicitly twinned themes of security and health of the populace dominated attention. A good example is the era of debate over National Efficiency during the decade of imperialist rivalry that led to the outbreak of World War I in 1914 (3). Indeed, in England, the successful turning of this discourse by the medically trained leaders of the public health movement (away from its social Darwinist formulation, toward a more environmentalist understanding of the poor health of the urban masses) paved the way for the British state's belated conversion to a range of Bismarckian, insurance-based welfare and social security provisions (4, 5). This trend led eventually in 1919 to the establishment of the British public health movement's dream of a national Ministry of Health (6). Thus, the historical omens are not unpropitious. When the public health movement is able to ally its arguments with profound concerns for national security, great progress can be made in mobilizing resources and creating new institutions to promote health and human security.

It was the even more direct subsequent military threat to Britain's human security, the fight against aerial bombardment on the home front in World War II, that provided the context for the formation of the Emergency Medical Service, the forerunner for the National Health Service (NHS) (7). Indeed, the close affinity between the promotion of the nation's health and its security was semantically fused in the celebrated wartime Beveridge Report on *Social Insurance and Allied Services*, the 1942 blueprint for the nation's future welfare state and the NHS. At its heart was Beveridge's Plan for Social Security:

> 'Social Security is defined as security for the individual, organized by the State, against risks to which the individual will remain exposed even when the condition of the society as a whole is as good as it can be made (8).'

Beveridge's plan for society's security consisted of several main elements: children's allowances; maintenance of full employment; national insurance and pensions; and, of course, a universal and free (at point of use) health service. There is, then, nothing new in the occurrence of periods of crisis, provoked by the perception of external threat to the nation's security, like the American public's shocked response to September 11, providing a galvanizing political opportunity for the promotion of ambitious new thinking about health, framed as an issue of national security. Indeed, when comparing the way in which the same vested interests — the insurance industry and the medical profession itself — were able to resist politicians' attempts to create a national health service in the U.S. in the 1940s while being unable to resist it in Britain, the absence in America of such a traumatic threat to citizens' personal security as the experience of the Nazi bombing campaign would seem to have been a politically decisive factor (9, 10).

Thus, although the words *security* and *health* have rarely appeared in public together during the last half-century, a little history reveals their secret: they are in fact — and always have been — twins. From an historical perspective, the interesting question is how the two terms could have remained apart for several decades recently in the academic and policy literature? There is, I believe, a revealing, somewhat paradoxical answer to this question. But before we can arrive at this answer, we must begin by establishing the historical correctness of a profoundly counterintuitive understanding of the relationship between economic growth, human security, and health.

Economic growth and the disruption of human security and health

Economic growth has always been, by definition, a process that transforms and challenges all dimensions of human security: of individuals, states, even businesses. The more generally held, superficially optimistic view of economic growth and the expansion of markets — as synonymous with opportunity and as the source of all our creature comforts — has led to a blind reverence for maximizing national economic growth rates among political leaders and electorates alike.

As Amartya Sen has cogently insisted, development is not equivalent to rising per capita GDP, but relates primarily to enhanced freedoms and dignity (11). These benefits *may* flow from economic growth, but to portray them as if they were essential and integral to the process itself is a dangerous untruth. The growth process guarantees no net benefits, least of all to the general society. The only statement that is true about the process of economic growth is that it is thoroughly disruptive. It is as full of insecurities as it is of opportunities or risks.

The potential for economic growth, trade, capital accumulation, market competition, and cost-cutting to be of genuine long-term benefit to the great majority, rather than merely to a few successful individual competitors, depends entirely on the manner in which peoples and their governments adapt: how they negotiate, fight over, and decide to manage, tax, and distribute the wealth created. This process constitutes the political and constitutional history of economic and social change. Without any recorded exception known to this author, all current, successful, leading western societies that industrialized before 1945 (most of them before 1914), suffered a painful and difficult learning experience in coming to terms with the insecurities and health threats of full commercialization and economic growth (12). They all experienced at some point in their growth trajectory the severe 'demographic footprint' of the 'four Ds' of economic growth: disruption, deprivation, disease, and death (13). In some of the worst cases, such as Britain, the disruption for an entire half century was so great for large proportions of the national population that insecure, marginal, and deprived sections (the urban proletariat, in particular children, women, and the Irish in the British case) died prematurely and from preventable infectious and sanitary diseases in such numbers as to depress the national average health measures for decade after decade (14).

The process of constitutional and political adaptation to the turbulent demands of living with economic growth, so as to minimize its accompanying disruption of security and health, has taken these 'successful' advanced economies centuries to achieve — literally. This situation seems to be an extremely poorly understood and distinctly undervalued lesson of history and one which has, incredibly, been ignored if not entirely forgotten during the last two decades, with the separation of health from security in the policy literature as symptomatic of this amnesia.

We are repeatedly told that we now live in a world where economic growth is occurring within the novel context of globalization. What does this mean for health and human security if history tells us that economic growth entails disruption? The only prudent conclusion is to expect health and security problems on a global scale, unless the difficult historical lessons of adaptation are heeded.

What is globalization, and what is new about it? There has rarely been a society in recorded human history where economic change has not occurred. However, there is no doubt that the rate of such change and the geographic scale of its effects began to increase substantially as a result of the intercontinental commercial, mercantile, and industrial revolutions of the 17th and 18th centuries. For all the hype about the novelty of globalization, economic growth is a phenomenon that has been continuously transforming social, political, and natural relationships almost everywhere, on a truly global scale, for at least the last two centuries (15).

There are, however, three truths about historical novelty in the period since 1989 underlying the 'g-hype.' Each of these is largely the consequence of the information-acceleration effects of satellite plus fiber-optic communications and computing technology, allied to previous political decisions, taken at the behest of the world's financial elites, to free up international capital and foreign exchange markets. The three truths are: firstly, the rate and volume of short-term financial flows has increased significantly; secondly, with the end of the Cold War, there is something more like a single global system of trade and finance than at any time since the gold standard era preceding the Great War and the Bolshevik Revolution; thirdly, the most articulate and influential citizens of the richest democracies in the world are more immediately, frequently, painfully, and worryingly aware of the truly global nature of their interdependence with the fate of all the rest of humanity than ever before.

The latter in particular encapsulates the most important single paradox of humanity's long-term love affair with the post-Enlightenment project of economic growth, world development, and progress. The promise of security and health has been a primary aim and justification of all the effort that humans have devoted to contriving their economic growth during the last several centuries. Freedom from the caprices and misfortunes of fate and nature has been a motivating dream for a populace that can manufacture its own secure food supply, shelter, and protection from disease, weather, and other species. However, as the doyen of Polish economic historians, Witold Kula, has astutely observed,

> 'The mastering of the forces of nature, the uncovering of its poten-
> tialities, the growing utilization of its wealth, all these do away with
> some manifestations of the dependence, but create new ones in their
> stead. . . . The more of nature's inherent potentialities man learns to
> bring to the surface, the more, by mastering her, he comes to depend
> on her (16).'

To this premise we can add that our capacity to 'master' nature ever more elaborately is based on an increasing specialization and division of labor on a global scale. Hence, we become ever more dependent for the maintenance of our way of life on wider circles and networks of our fellow humanity. The pursuit of personal wealth and the promise of material security through market exchange thus brings with it an ever-greater dependency on nature, technologies, and institutions, and on all those myriad humans contributing to the global market, from which we draw the means to our material security and enhanced life expectancies.

Economic growth — the process whereby these expanding markets for diverse goods and services are brought into exchange — is an intrinsically disruptive and destabilizing process of change. It works firstly by converting into commodities aspects of the material environment not previously perceived to have commercial value; secondly, by imaginatively creating the market for entirely new goods and services; and thirdly, by cutting the price of existing commodities. All of these activities, as can readily be appreciated, are fundamentally transformative and necessarily associated with psychological, social, ideological, and cultural change. These challenges create tides of disruption and insecurity, especially for workers or owners of assets who find that their labor or property has been devalued by the ever-changing commodity markets.

Thus, if we live now in an age of more rapid and global economic change than ever before in human history, it is crucial in any evaluation of the current prospects for health and human security, that we commence our analysis with the clear-eyed understanding that economic growth does not directly enhance human security, and in fact, systematically jeopardizes it for many if not most people at some point during their lives. Although the accumulation over generations of productive physical capital and the construction of all the associated human and social capital undoubtedly gives both individuals and societies the capacity to live healthier, longer, and more fulfilled lives, the process whereby this potential is realized can be an extremely rough ride for all concerned. Economic growth is intrinsically a process of creative destruction, as the two greatest historians of industrial capitalism — Karl Marx and Joseph Schumpeter — would readily agree, from quite opposed ideological positions.

Paul Farmer's revealing analysis of the 'structural violence' of inequality has shown that the commercial and ephemeral values of newsworthiness mean that crises, such as famines, may be the only health threats to the world's poor that gain adequate public attention in the free presses of the First World's liberal democracies (17, 18). Yet it is the 'silent crises' of preventable infectious diseases such as malaria and tuberculosis, killing millions every year, that are much more quantitatively important. They remain unknown, however, to western public opinion, partly because their perennial nature renders them unnewsworthy. They also constitute guilty secrets, since they are 'orphan diseases,' that the commercial pharmaceutical industry has neglected because there is little prospect of any payment from impoverished individuals or debt-ridden governments, who have in any case been ordered to slash their health budgets in the structural adjustment programs of the International Monetary Fund (IMF) (19).

In thinking about the historical relationship of economic growth to human health and security, it may be helpful to invoke another geological metaphor, that of the volcano. Living with rapid economic growth is like living on the fertile lava slopes of an active volcano. The volcanic energy is the force of economic growth. Like the market, the volcano is extremely prolific in producing an accumulation of useful matter, which continually alters the living environment, indeed the very landscape.

There is much inconvenience and need for adaptation when living in the shadow of the volcano. However, given time, the inhabitants know that these disruptive flows of lava will provide them the most fertile soil, enhancing their living standards over the generations. But in the shorter term, the volcano's mode of operation is always somewhat threatening and can occasionally be disastrous. Over a period of many centuries, those peoples who have been encamped longest on and around the volcano of rapid economic growth have slowly and painfully learned the best ways to minimize the personal and collective risks of living with the disruptive processes of economic transformation in their midst.

The problem appears to be that, since 1989, people have suffered a collective attack of euphoria-induced amnesia. They have beckoned all sorts of newcomers to the vicinity of the volcano and suggested that they take up residence as near as possible to the rim. Indeed, they have decamped and moved in that direction themselves, failing to recall why, over the previous centuries, they had adopted a less exposed and more protected location. Now they profess surprise when the newcomers show anger at getting burned in the volcano's frequent eruptions, fight among themselves for a less exposed position, and even try to enter the safer encampments of the well-established.

Learning to live with the volcano comprises the conflict-ridden history of the developed western societies during the last several centuries. To illustrate some of the conflicts and adaptations that have been necessary, a brief overview of certain aspects of British history since the 16th century is offered below. This example shows the importance for health and human security, under conditions of economic growth, of constitutional, legislative, and institutional change — all of it highly contested and closely fought in the political arena. Without these developments, the forces of economic growth would rapidly have extinguished themselves in a holocaust of infectious and sanitary diseases in Britain's industrial cities, which no amount of in-migration could have matched.

After literally centuries of painful social, political, and international conflict, and tragic levels of mortality, western liberal democracies had, by 1945, gradually and with many setbacks along the way, inched their way toward establishing a constitutional form that dealt tolerably well — safely and securely for all — with the vicissitudes of continuous economic growth. This form combined a social democracy with institutional and political pluralism, strong individual rights and protection in law, a free press, and a market economy carefully regulated and taxed so as substantially and widely to redistribute the wealth it generated through a welfare state (20).

Maintaining human security and health under conditions of economic growth: the lessons of British history

The constitutional changes required to adapt to economic growth while maintaining health and security comprise three related historical developments. Firstly, official registration of all individuals and acknowledgment of their rights to security and health, critically including respect for their diverse social, religious, and ethnic identities. Secondly, the formation by such diverse citizens of legally recognized civil associations and institutions to represent and campaign for their varied and changing interests. This notably includes elected local government, trade unions, professional and employers' associations, as well as a host of less directly political civic associations and, of course, an independent free press. Thirdly, the establishment of some form of welfare or social security state: the securing through the state of various forms of effective collective provision to ensure the promotion of citizens' aspirations for their own security and health.

In Britain, the evolution of these three essential provisions took centuries to accomplish and was disrupted by the process of industrialization. The inception in 1538 of the nationwide parochial registration of all births, deaths, and marriages by Henry VIII was a crucial step in creating a system to record and therefore recognize each individual's existence. By the end of the same century, the Elizabethan Poor Laws gave every person a right to claim sustenance from his or her community of settlement in times of hardship. Historians recognize these laws as having provided the institutional underpinning that ensured that the English (but not the Irish, where there was no such Poor Law) were the first nation in the world to cease to experience famine mortality (21, 22). Although in no way a voting democracy, the subjects of the British sovereign in the 17th and 18th centuries enjoyed advanced, state-guaranteed practical entitlements to security and health — functionings and capabilities in Amartya Sen's terminology — which facilitated the society's precocious economic development (11, 23).

However, in the absence of a democratic franchise to defend these privileges, individual rights were then rudely interrupted, paradoxically by the industrial revolution itself. The reason was very simple and has a parallel in virtually all of today's developing countries. Decades of extremely rapid and chaotic urban industrial growth through in-migration from the countryside produced a breakdown in the urban registration system by the late 18th century. As today in the shantytowns of India, Africa, or Latin America, many individuals were unknown to the authorities and had no recognized address.

Eventually, in 1836, Parliament legislated for a new civil registration system to keep full and accurate records of all births, deaths, and marriages in England and Wales, regardless of religion (Scotland and Ireland were granted such systems somewhat later). With the availability of this centrally collated registration data, the Victorian public health movement found its voice and began to publicize authoritatively the diseased state of the crowded cities and to explore and devise effective remedial policies (24).

But simultaneously in 1834, following the dictates of the then-new liberal ideology of the free market — the classical political economy of Adam Smith, Ricardo, and Malthus — the state radically curtailed its support for the poor, as has happened in many developing countries today under neo-liberal structural adjustment programs and also in the U.S. with welfare cuts. Access to sources of support in these circumstances became closely tied to membership in certain privileged groups, such as religious congregations, workingmen's mutual associations, or the paternalism of some large employers (25, 26, 27).

The subsequent period until 1914 was characterized by a gradual and conflict-ridden process of building up the second factor emphasized above: elected, representative, local government; trade unions; professional and employers' associations; and many other civil and voluntary organizations or forms of social capital. This process culminated in the beginning of a serious movement on the part of these institutions toward negotiation of the third element — collective provision of health and social security.

During the last three decades of the 19th century, the two rival munici-palities of Glasgow and Birmingham led a nationwide provincial revolution in government, finance, and social capital, which amounted to a wholly new, collectivist, and municipal (but not yet national) model of delivering social security and health to their crowded urban populations. This system included administering a massive range of municipal schemes of regulation of the urban environment and food supply, preventive and public health measures, welfare and social services, and even the education system and public hous-ing schemes (28, 29, 30). Interestingly, powerful businessmen heading leading international companies, such as Joseph Chamberlain in Birmingham — whose imagination was caught by the 'civic gospel's' promise to transform the lives of the poor — were integral to the practical success of this movement. It was a genuinely cross-class alliance, involving the electoral support of newly enfranchised working-class men, as well as the administrative and technical expertise of new and growing categories of public professionals, such as medical officers of health, and food and sanitary inspectors.

The longer-term product of the experience and momentum built up in this period was the British electorate's eventual acceptance after 1905 of the beginnings of collectivist, state-funded models of provision for health and social security (4, 5, 6). Following the further harsh learning experiences of two world wars, the fight for national survival, and the severe interwar crises of the international economic system, the ultimate result was the acceptance of the Keynesian principles of macroeconomic management and the Beve-ridge Plan for national social security of the 1940s (7, 8, 31).

Human security and health problems in less developed countries: historical reflections on an inverted mirror image

If there is one single foundational policy that the world's poorest states should be encouraged to undertake (and given financial grants to fund) in pursuit of their citizens' long-term health and security, it is to start at the democratic ground level by establishing a full and accurate registration and census enumeration of all their citizens from birth to death. This data must of course be protected (as it has been by strong confidentiality laws in the British case), so that it is used for public health and civil rights purposes only, and not for political surveillance and repression. But the possibility that it could be used for such negative purposes does not destroy its funda-mental value, provided this abuse can be avoided. Indeed, without the legally sanctioned capacity to prove one's identity, most positive legal and civil rights are worthless, while the individual's capacity to function economically is severely constrained to a local context or a network of familiars. Cor-respondingly, in a fast-changing economy, the capacity of central or local governments (or NGOs) to devote scarce resources to effective promotion of social security and health is extremely limited without accurate, locally precise intelligence, derived from individual-level data, on demographic trends and epidemiological patterns.

Registration and enumeration of individuals — to become officially acknowledged, legal persons — comprise a crucially necessary development to facilitate the integration of the poor into property markets, which also function on their behalf in the world's poorest countries. In his path-breaking analysis, Hernando de Soto identifies the failure of an appropriate formal property law system to develop in many countries, such as his native Peru, as a gross institutional disability preventing capital formation (32). This failure restricts the commercial usage to which all but the richest in society (who alone can afford the costs, bribes, and delays of the tortuous legal processes) can assign their assets — homes, land, businesses. For the rest, their inability to gain legal formal title to their assets means that these cannot be used as capital in the conventional economic sense, as a security to generate credit or funds for investment.

But de Soto's policy prescription is radically incomplete. He focuses on only one half of the problem of creating fixity and security of legal title, and omits the question of the legal personhood of agents themselves in many poor countries. As we have seen, from the 16th century onward in British history the two aspects worked together in the form of the common law's rules of property ownership and the Henrician parish register system — the nationwide registration through parishes of all births, deaths, and marriages — enabling British capital markets to develop sufficiently to drive the mercantile and industrial revolutions. The process was jeopardized by its own success but was then brought back into full working order with the creation in 1836 of the modern civil (secular) registration system.

When we consider today's less developed countries and continents — notably Latin America, Africa, and Southeast Asia — their histories since the 18th century (themselves very diverse of course) have been extremely different from Britain's when evaluated in these terms. The mercantile and industrial revolutions of western Europe affected and transformed these three other continental areas and their indigenous polities and peoples at least as much as they transformed Europe itself. But the relationship between the capital-accumulating European metropole and the southern and eastern trading partners was, as is well known, highly unequal. Many of the populations of these vast areas were subject to formal, colonial, or imperial domination or to practical dependency status (China) throughout much of the period from 1750 to 1945 or even until the 1960s. The main regional exceptions were the independent countries of Latin America. However, having precociously flung off their Spanish and Portuguese colonial rulers, most Latin American states fell prey to a vicious, nepotistic, post-colonial, neo-aristocratic elite who relied on primitive rather than industrial capital accumulation, often through slave-labor, to exploit their enormous continent's rich natural resources and agricultural potential.

Consequently, the three constitutional and institutional developments, identified above as crucial for societies faced with the challenges and disruptions of economic change to evolve the political capacity to pursue their own health and security agenda, never occurred in these three, continent-scale regions of underdevelopment. These crucial adjustments to law and the social relations between citizens and their government, taking decades or even centuries to negotiate in the histories of today's developed nations, were blocked at the source in Africa, large tracts of Asia, Latin America, and the Caribbean.

The possibility for such a set of changes to the constitution of social relations in a dependent or colonial society was inimical to the political requirements of the dominant colonial European political forces and the neocolonial plantation and ranch elites of Latin America. Individuals were not granted meaningful voting rights; they were permitted only carefully policed rights of civic association. The central state (the colonial government) mainly used local rulers or authorities as transmission mechanisms for its own centrally administered policies. Population registration was not primarily motivated to ensure a diverse citizenry's property rights or to devise the expense of effective public health measures, but was primarily a surveillance exercise for law and order purposes to keep the costs of policing under control. Hence in India the efficient registration of deaths was of much less pressing interest to the authorities than it was in England, where the relevant census official, William Farr, became the world's leading expert on the subject (33). In India, the geographical distribution of religions and castes was of much greater interest to the census authorities, especially following the trauma of the Indian mutiny in 1857, after which the British believed that specific Indian castes had to be watched carefully (34).

In the final analysis, the main goals of colonial rule were — and always have been — to benefit the colonizing country economically to the maximum. Europe's plutocratic class found it advantageous to exploit territories whose populace lacked the citizenship rights that their own middle and working classes increasingly enjoyed. Rates of profit and rent extraction could be highly lucrative in such unprotected labor markets. A convenient, evolutionary, racist ideology explained and justified the absence of civic rights for the colonized peoples (35). The governing interests of the imperial states firmly committed them to maintaining these dependent societies in a limbo of constitutional underdevelopment.

Thus, during the period from 1815 to 1945 in northwest Europe and those parts of the globe in which migrants from these states settled and suppressed the indigenous peoples (principally North America and Australia), citizenship/civil society/state relationships gradually evolved and adapted to the challenges of rapid economic growth in a manner that ultimately enabled human security and health to be preserved and maintained. But, through the direct and indirect influence of the formal and informal trading empires that these same states established throughout the globe, they simultaneously prevented virtually all other societies from adapting in similar ways to world economic growth.

When decolonization and independence came relatively suddenly in the two decades after 1945, world economic development did not stop to enable these societies — lacking a history of the development of state-recognized individual citizenship, civic associations, elected local self-government, and collective state provision — to catch up with a century and a half of missing adaptation. Their societies, having a long tutelage in dependence as the worst possible preparation, were immediately subjected to all the disruptions and demands of ongoing world economic growth.

In fact, in many ways, the period of tutelage was prolonged for most of these countries for a further three to four decades after 1945 because of the clientalist relationships eagerly sought by the two nuclear superpowers, the U.S. and the U.S.S.R. Thus the tendency, already marked under formal colonial regimes, for small, trusted (by the foreigners), subaltern elite groups and families to garner most of the power and economic resources, through their personal contacts at the very center of the state's administrative apparatus, was further emphasized in these initial decades of independence. At least this protracted period of Cold War clientage permitted the independent governments of many poor countries to enjoy a reasonably dependable flow of income. Although much went into private bank accounts, in most countries enough of it found its way into the state's investment programs so that roads, schools, and hospitals were built between the 1950s and the 1980s. And more importantly, precious human capital to staff the schools and hospitals was increasingly forthcoming, much of it initially trained through exchange programs set up by the nations of the rival liberal and socialist ideological blocs of the First and Second Worlds. There were also, of course, substantial helpful UNESCO educational and WHO-sponsored health programs during this period, such as the celebrated smallpox eradication program.

In calibrating the experience of many Third World countries in the 1945–1989 era against the historical model that has been set out here of the three constitutional developments that most First World countries achieved, and which, it is argued, are necessary to maintain security and health in the face of the disruptive challenges of economic growth, their most obvious weakness has been in the middle area of civic society: associations giving voice to groups — most importantly trade unions, representatives, elected local government — and bridging and linking social capital. Individual citizens certainly had a reasonable range of formal rights, including universal suffrage, in many of these newly independent states. There were also promising signs of collective provision by the state in terms of education, health, and social security. But now we see, given the tragic way in which many of these societies have buckled and some have virtually collapsed during the 1990s, how fragile and unviable formal individual rights and a relatively proactive central state are, without the vital range of middling civic institutions. These institutions took a long time to evolve, deepen, and multiply in the history of the west. They are important to making formal individual rights substantial and useful in practice and to giving the state and its resources the capacity for effective traction with the diverse, real society it both serves and guides.

The separation of security and health from 1975 to 2000: forgetting history

Tragically for the Third World and painfully for the socially excluded of the First World, the important historical lessons regarding the preservation of human security and health under conditions of rapid economic change have been progressively lost to the policymakers and leading opinion formers of the world's elite societies and global institutions during the 1980s and especially in the era of triumphalist 'free market fundamentalism' of the 1990s.

Historical developments — full citizenship rights, civil associations, a free press, and collective provision for human security and health — culminated in the mid-20th century with most of the advanced western liberal democracies assuming the form of pluralist societies with welfare states (20). This balanced pattern served the western democracies reasonably well for over a quarter century following the end of World War II, and also provided a helpful model for various client states in the Third World to emulate. Economic growth rates in both sets of states were consistently strongly positive, while rising average life expectancies confirmed that the fruits of such economic growth were being equitably distributed without undue disruption to the lives of the majority. But then, after a generation of relatively successful, well-adapted life on the slopes of the volcano (so successful that it has been referred to as the post-war 'golden age') (36), the inhabitants — or at least their political and ideological leaders — seem to have fallen into a fog of collective amnesia. They lost the plot.

The financial elite could no longer remember why they had agreed in the 1940s to set up an international system of strong currency controls and capital regulations, and could only see this system now as an encumbrance to their market-driven aspirations to earn greater profits from a larger, more globalized capital market. The libertarian right could no longer remember why, after the 1930s, they had agreed to provide generous collective welfare services. The intellectual left naively played into the hands of this New Right attack on the welfare state, since it now aspired to an unrealistic radical egalitarianism. It disparaged the welfare states for failing as yet to achieve equality, while ignoring the important evidence of the welfare state's effectiveness in dramatically reducing absolute poverty and health differentials between rich and poor in the space of a single generation (37). The Keynesian revolution's great policy gift to liberal market democracy of countercyclical government spending to maintain effective demand in the economy was subverted by lazy politicians into the practice of continuously increasing government spending to give the appearance of higher economic growth rates, figures which had come to assume a totemic electoral significance. In such an inflationary context, trade unions' and employers' negotiations were increasingly confrontational, leading to industrial strife between the two sides in many western democracies during the 1970s.

The ideological and political counterrevolution of the New Right was primarily an Anglo-Saxon initiative, whose main focus was the populist target of the supposedly bloated and inefficient high-taxing central state, aiming to reduce its welfare spending programs (the primary focus in the U.S.) and the range of publicly owned industries and services (mainly in the UK; there were almost none to privatize in the U.S.). It was an article of faith for the libertarian New Right that the world's ills were principally traceable to the overbearing and inefficient activities of unaccountable, bureaucratic central states, and that the general solution was to open up as much of the economy as possible and all spheres of life to the rigors of free market, commercial, competitive forces, incentives, and risk-takers.

After a generation of change since 1945, there was certainly much that needed reform and reinvigoration in the relationship between state, civic society, and citizenship in western liberal democracies by the 1970s. The prescriptions of the New Right offered partial diagnosis and a rather extreme form of medicine. The ensuing two decades have resulted in significant reforms along the lines advocated; however, considerable damage to human security and health also has been wreaked in these societies by the evangelical application of New Right ideology, resulting in sharply rising inequality and deepening poverty for the socially excluded in both developed and less developed countries.

In terms of the constitutional and civic underpinnings to ensure human security and health in a turbulent world of economic growth, it is arguable that the last thing the citizens of the poorest countries needed — emerging from centuries of dependence and decades of tutelage — was a generalized attack on the legitimacy of their state structures and nascent public goods and services. The neoliberal policies were originally devised in Chicago, Wall Street, and London by First World economists unhappy at the role played by a highly developed central state in their own economies. But these policies were soon applied as the 'Washington consensus' in many other contexts.

In developed western democracies, the ideologists of the New Right have had a fairer fight on their hands, facing a strong state and a well-developed range of civic associations able to argue for the continuing provision of collective services to ensure human security and health. Public services, so essential for the health and security of the poor, have been pruned but not eradicated. By contrast, in far too many ex-colonial countries, the IMF found that it could impose its strictures at will, through conditionality clauses to its loans, on relatively unconfident and young state bureaucracies and on civil societies lacking sufficient development in local government, trade unions, an independent press, or other civic associations capable of representing the poor and resisting the attack on their interests. In 1980, what all of these developing countries needed, and what was appropriate for the provisional state of development they had achieved by that point, was to expand and strengthen their nascent welfare states so as to boost significantly their nation's human and social capital. Instead, they received orders from Washington in the form of the structural adjustment programs to abandon the minimal welfare states they had begun to construct, and to open themselves up to western capitalism and trade.

It all looks very similar to these same countries' experiences under the European colonial powers before 1945. This is an era of U.S. neo-imperialism, backed by a similarly inhumane, rigid, self-righteous, and self-serving ideology and with the financial interests of the metropole as the principal beneficiaries. The evidence for this harsh judgment is found in Joseph Stiglitz's analysis of IMF policies in many countries. Stiglitz devastatingly observes that while using the justificatory rhetoric of promoting competition, in fact privatization was the goal most consistently pursued, which is not at all the same thing:

'Economic theory says that for markets to work well, there must be both competition and private property. . . . The IMF chose to emphasize privatization, giving short shrift to competition. The choice was perhaps not surprising: corporate and financial interests often oppose competition policies, for these policies restrict their ability to make profits (38).'

In order supposedly to boost the vigor and scope of free markets, the Washington consensus waged a messianic war throughout the 1990s on state capacity in the First World, on the Second World of the ex-Comecon transition countries, and on the Third World. This policy was based on an ahistorical and entirely sciolistic misunderstanding, which ignores the intimate relationship of interdependence between strong states and strong markets. For, as de Soto's historical reconstruction of the emergence of capital itself in the west demonstrates, only states strong enough to provide a universally available system of sanctions to guarantee individuals' legal titles to their diverse property holdings could provide the basis for markets in capital to develop, a theme that also emerges from the earlier Nobel prize winning work of D. C. North (39).

Without the state's capacity to guarantee the rule of law, interpersonal violence becomes commonplace, eroding the basis for public confidence, respect, and trust in others. Most societies are a diverse coalition of many kinds of 'others': strangers who learn to place a degree of trust in each other.

This basic level of trust in the street is crucial for the practical functioning of a democratic citizenship of equal rights. In turn, this trust provides the social groundwork for all civic associations and representative bodies to form. They negotiate the pluralist democracy that liberal market societies require if they are to avoid degenerating into oligarchic plutocracies (the characteristic flaw of the capitalist system, first analyzed by Marx, being its inherent tendency toward monopoly).

Thus we come back to the central paradox of human security — its inherently collective and social nature — all the more so in a globalized world trading economy. Human security is conditional, negotiated, and dependent on the maintenance through appropriate behavior of respectful relations with others. This insight is one of the central tenets of social capital theory, with emphasis on its importance for development (40).

However, there is a powerful bias within the western, liberal, methodological, individualist, reductive, analytical tradition of thought, toward simplistically equating security with individual autonomy and household autarchy. To strive for the illusion of personal control over one's own destiny — elevated by Woodrow Wilson at the Versailles Treaty of 1919 to the principle of an individual nation's self determination when applied to the field of international relations — has been a consuming obsession in the western consciousness and in recent international political history. History repeatedly confirms that these are fantastically dangerous and self-defeating delusions. To elevate 'my' security or 'our nation's' security to the status of an absolute value that I/we have an absolute and unconditional right to defend and promote as only I/we see fit, is all too close to denying all rights of negotiation to others. It is the disposition of Fascist states. It directly implies a relationship of distrust to others and must look, in the eyes of others, like a threat to their security. This is a fundamental error, since it fails to perceive the intrinsically relational nature of security, succinctly summarized by Meddings, Bettcher, and Ghafele in this volume: 'One cannot be secure if one's neighbor . . . is not secure (41).' This simple observation has profound implications.

Building faith in collective security in the face of the vicissitudes of disruptive economic growth is a difficult social and political accomplishment that the citizens of the advanced western liberal democracies gradually negotiated for themselves over a period of centuries, through a range of civil associations and in conjunction with their states, while simultaneously denying it to the supposedly inferior peoples of their imperial possessions. It requires simultaneously strong individual rights, upheld and rendered equal by a strong, redistributionist state, and strong civic institutions, including an independent free press. The strength of these three develops dialectically and unevenly, and the delicate balance between the three forces can unravel. If the state's legitimacy is brought into question, and its capacity to sustain individuals' equal rights is compromised, then citizens may rapidly turn from reliance on collective security and confidence in strangers in their society to more sect-like, defensive arrangements, reserving trust only for a carefully selected few. In social capital terms this scenario represents a retreat from a balance of bonding, bridging, and linking social capital to a predominance of bonding patterns only. This is certainly what happened in Britain's industrial cities during the first half of the 19th century; it also has been diagnosed as a current affliction of the U.S. during the last three decades (10, 42).

This trend is most unfortunate and ominous in the U.S., which is clearly the most powerful and influential state in today's globalized world. If American opinion leaders in this generation understand the pursuit of security as something most effectively achieved through finding and trusting only those recognizable as exactly like oneself (bonding social capital), while using the material technology available to create a supposedly impregnable homeland for oneself, then history indicates this approach is futile. Only the slow building of trust through negotiation of conflicts of interest with respected others and within agreed rules of law (including international law) can create any durable security between citizens or nations. The French Maginot line did not prevent German invasion in 1940, but the agreement of these two states and their citizens to participate in continual dialogue and negotiation through the European Union has now maintained peace between these two old enemies for the longest period in modern history.

History indicates that there are a number of critical issues to consider in pursuing strategies to promote human security and health in a globalized world in the 21st century. Firstly, a self-denying ordinance from the world's wealthiest nations and corporations will allow poor countries to develop their industries and economies at their own pace and follow their own domestic population's gradually rising demand levels for goods and services, rather than service the demand for a narrow range of goods that western consumers want at the lowest prices and for which the poor countries happen to have a comparative advantage (often little more than cheap labor costs because of the absence of unions and protective labor legislation). It is only in this gradual and organic manner that poor countries can build the all-important middle sector of civic institutions, which are necessarily intimately related to their capacity to develop a wide range of economic activities to supply their own needs.

Secondly, this means that the world's international organizations — such as the UN, WHO, ILO, World Bank, and even the IMF and WTO — must call for and work toward a new era of contingent protectionism. Despite its impeccable historical pedigree as the primary policy that the governments of the U.K., U.S., Germany, and Japan, for instance, each followed when it suited them to nurture their nascent industrial economies (43), the endorsement of any kind of protectionism will undoubtedly require a substantial alteration in the favorite assumptions of such important international bodies as the IMF and WTO. It should be noted that such contingent protectionism for poor countries will in fact have almost no aggregate negative impact whatsoever on international investment flows, for the simple reason that almost all such investment capital flows between developed nations only. It will, however, reduce the outlets for hot money gambling at the expense of the living standards of non-First World citizens, such as those in Argentina or Indonesia; and it will restrict the scope for highly profitable activity at the expense of poor countries' environments and labor forces, which many multinationals currently enjoy. These powerful vested interests cannot possibly be expected to change their practices without a protracted battle. Those who wish to promote global human security will necessarily come into conflict with these commercial interests, which are not acting in accordance with the ethics of human security.

Only the most developed economies with the most comprehensive social security protections in place should be exposed to the full competitive rigors of global free markets, since they alone have the constitutional and governmental machinery — their welfare states — to stand up to its disruptive effects. All the world's poorest societies should be granted general exemptions from free trade, with the restrictions gradually lifting as the constitutions and civic institutions of their societies (not simply their per capita GDPs) develop in strength and depth. This process is almost the opposite of the practical policies pursued throughout the 1990s by the WTO and especially the IMF, which have instead imposed open exposure to international capitalism and trade only on the poorest countries unable to resist the insistence on conditionality in return for life-saving loans. By contrast, the IMF remains impotent to force the richest countries, with their entrenched lobbying power of the producer interests, to drop their favored protections for large branches of the economy, such as agriculture in both Europe and the U.S.

The profound problems of the resistance to such desirable reforms of the vested interests of corporate and financial elites in the west bring us, thirdly, to the need for substantial constitutional changes. Individual voters and the rich inheritance of civic associations in western, liberal, pluralist democracies must push for anticorruption rules to better insulate their own political establishments and render their states more autonomous from the corroding and insidious influence of commercial interests and corporate entry into the processes of state policy formulation and execution. This problem is a mirror image to the one identified by the New Right philosophy of a generation ago, which decried all forms of government as sclerotic, inefficient, and intrinsically corrupt, and advocated reducing the role of the state or, where possible, running it more along the efficient, supposedly open, and competitive lines of the market. So successful has the New Right been in advancing the reach of the market that government in the U.S. and even in Britain has now become endemically prone to the market's own version of sclerosis: the corporate buying of influence (44, 45). The hubris of the business world, with no independent masters, no doubt also has contributed to the scale of the recent accounting scandals that have sent Wall Street into a bear market of distrust.

In the U.S., the far from impartial perspectives and vested interests of corporate America and Wall Street have become conflated with those of the

U.S. government, as exemplified by the current occupant of the White House, George W. Bush, and his Vice President. This is also true of the international institutions dominated by the U.S., notably the IMF, where Wall Street financiers have frequently held the top post and the U.S. has veto power over its policies. This situation looks dangerously like a plutocratic system, the antithesis of democracy. The IMF represents probably the single most important and egregious case for reform among the international institutions, since it is so patently undemocratic in its constitution and has by now accumulated an unenviable record of policy mistakes, indefensible because of their dogmatic invariability, in the countries that have so little voice at its table.

There is nothing new here. Such corporate and financial interests undoubtedly managed to influence to their own advantage, both at a strategic level and in more specific ways, the state policies of the British government in London when it was the dominant world trading power in the late 19th century, as the important examples of the Opium Wars, the Suez Canal, and public health policy in India each illustrate in their different ways (46, 47). It is vital that other powerful nation blocs, notably the E.U., use their independent bargaining power today to oppose and criticize the policies and strategies of the dominant power, the U.S., and those institutions that it most directly influences, wherever it is reasonable and just to do so. It is the only conceivable hope for keeping honest the distorting and myopic force of U.S. financial and corporate elites who, like the British in the 19th century, will continue relentlessly to advocate the grand principle of free trade that is so evidently in their own self-interest.

Today, there is a vital need for both security and health to be visualized and understood in thoroughly global terms. It has been noted that in the past whenever the cause of health could be strongly linked to that of national security, it paid dividends to the public health movement; enhanced collective resources were consequently mobilized. But we need now to find the correct forms of political rhetoric and the compelling arguments to ally health with a more genuinely global conception of human security. History indicates that this scaling up from the national collectivity to the global, and the building of institutions for the global citizenship and civic forms necessary to accompany such a political entity, is going to be a heroically difficult task. It will be crucial for a portion of the world's leading businessmen to become genuinely motivated with this challenge, in the manner in which Chamberlain and leading British industrialists became fired by the civic gospel from the 1870s. Whether such activism is possible now hangs in the balance. It is vitally important for the future ecological security of the planet that the American nation and its business elite not be encouraged to perceive the appropriate response to the threat posed by September 11th merely in national security terms. Instead, they need to learn to embrace positively the truth of the dependence of their own security and health on that of their neighbors in this small globe of ours.

References

1. Haines R., Shlomowitz R. Explaining the mortality decline in the eighteenth-century British slave trade. *Economic History Review* 2000;53:262–83.
2. Curtin P. D. *Death by migration: Europe's encounter with the tropical world.* Cambridge: Cambridge University Press; 1989.
3. Searle G. R. *The quest for national efficiency: a study in British politics and thought, 1899–1914.* Oxford: Clarendon Press; 1971.
4. Szreter S. *Fertility, class, and gender in Britain, 1860–1940.* Cambridge: Cambridge University Press; 1996, ch. 4.
5. Hennock E. P. *British social reform and German precedents: the case of social insurance, 1880–1914.* Oxford: Clarendon Press; 1987.
6. Hongisbaum F. *The struggle for the Ministry of Health, 1914–19.* London: G. Bell; 1970.
7. Titmuss R. *Problems of social policy.* London: HMSO; 1950.
8. Beveridge W. H. *Full employment in a free society.* London: George Allen and Unwin; 1944. p. 11.
9. Starr P. *The social transformation of American medicine.* New York: Basic Books; 1982. p. 280–9.
10. Szreter S. The state of social capital: bringing back in power, politics, and history. *Theory and Society* 2002;31:note 34.
11. Sen A. *Development as freedom.* Oxford: Oxford University Press; 1999.
12. Szreter S. The population health approach in historical perspective. *American Journal of Public Health* 2003; 93: 421–31.
13. Szreter S. Economic growth, disruption, deprivation, disease, and death: on the importance of the politics of public health for development. *Population and Development Review* 1997;23:693–728.
14. Szreter S., Mooney G. Urbanisation, mortality, and the standard of living debate: new estimates of the expectation of life at birth in nineteenth-century British cities. *Economic History Review* 1998;50:84–112.
15. Hopkins A. G., editor. *Globalization in world history.* London: Pimlico; 2002.
16. Kula W. *The problems and methods of economic history.* Szreter R., translator. Aldershot: Ashgate; 2001. p. 371–2.
17. Farmer P. Social inequalities and emerging infectious diseases. *Emerging Infectious Diseases* 1996;2:259–69.
18. Farmer P. *Infections and inequalities: the modern plagues.* Berkeley: University of California Press; 1999.
19. Trouiller P., et al. Drug development for neglected diseases: a deficient market and a public-health policy failure. *The Lancet* 2002;359:2188–94.
20. Esping-Andersen G. *The three worlds of welfare capitalism.* Cambridge: Polity Press; 1990.
21. Slack P. *The English poor law 1531–1782.* London: Macmillan; 1990.
22. Outhwaite R. B. *Dearth, public policy, and social disturbance in England, 1550–1800.* London: Macmillan; 1991, ch. 2.
23. Solar P. M. Poor relief and English economic development before the industrial revolution. *Economic History Review* 1995;48:1–22.
24. Szreter S. The G.R.O. and the public health movement 1837–1914. *Social History of Medicine* 1991;4:435–63.

25. Gilbert A. D. *Religion in Industrial Society: church, chapel, and social change 1740–1914*. London: Longman; 1976.
26. Roberts D. *Paternalism in early Victorian England*. London: Croom Helm; 1979.
27. Neave D. Friendly societies in Great Britain. In: van der Linden M., editor. *Social security mutualism*. New York: Peter Lang; 1996. p. 41–64.
28. Fraser W. H., Maver M., editors. *Glasgow volume II: 1830–1912*. Manchester: Manchester University Press; 1996, chs.10–12.
29. Hennock E. P. *Fit and proper persons*. Montreal: McGill-Queens' University Press; 1973.
30. Bell F., Millward R. Public health expenditures and mortality in England and Wales, 1870–1914. *Continuity and Change* 1998:13:1–29.
31. Addison P. *The road to 1945: British politics and the Second World War*. London: Cape; 1975.
32. de Soto H. *The mystery of capital*. New York: Basic Books; 2000.
33. Eyler J. M. *Victorian social medicine: the ideas and methods of William Farr*. Baltimore: Johns Hopkins University Press; 1979.
34. Cohn B. The census, social structure, and objectification in South Asia. In: Cohn B. S. *An anthropologist among the historians and other essays*. Oxford: Oxford University Press; 1987. p. 224–54.
35. Stocking G. W. *Victorian anthropology*. New York: The Free Press; 1987.
36. Marglin S., Schor J., editors. *The golden age of capitalism*. Oxford: Clarendon Press; 1990.
37. Szreter S. Health, class, place, and politics: social capital, opting in, and opting out of collective provision in nineteenth- and twentieth-century Britain. *Contemporary British History* 2002;26:27–57, table 1.
38. Stiglitz J. E. *Globalization and its discontents*. New York: Norton; 2002. p. 156.
39. North D. C. *Structure and change in economic history*. New York: Norton; 1981.
40. Woolcock M. Social capital and economic development: toward a theoretical synthesis and policy framework. *Theory and Society* 1998;27:151–208.
41. Meddings D. R., Bettcher D. W., Ghafele R. Violence and human security: policy linkages. In: Chen L., Leaning J., Narasimhan V., editors. *Global health challenges for human security*. Cambridge (MA): Global Equity Initiative, Asia Center, Faculty of Arts and Sciences, Harvard University; 2003.
42. Putnam R. D. *Bowling alone: the collapse and revival of American community*. New York: Simon and Schuster; 2000.
43. Chang H.-J. The real lesson for developing countries from the history of the developed world: freedom to choose. Available at: URL: http://www.historyandpolicy.org/main/policy-paper-09.html, accessed on 2003 May 30.
44. Boggs C. *The end of politics: corporate power and the decline of the public sphere*. New York: Guilford; 2000.
45. Monbiot G. *Captive state: the corporate takeover of Britain*. London: Macmillan; 2000.
46. Davis M. *Late Victorian holocausts: El Nino famines and the making of the Third World*. London: Verso; 2001.
47. Watts S. World trade and world disease. Available at: URL: http://www.historyandpolicy.org/main/policy-paper-07.html, accessed on 2003 May 30.

4

HEALTH SECURITY AS A PUBLIC HEALTH CONCEPT

A critical analysis

William Aldis

Source: *Health Policy and Planning*, 23 (2008), 369–75.

There is growing acceptance of the concept of health security. However, there are various and incompatible definitions, incomplete elaboration of the concept of health security in public health operational terms, and insufficient reconciliation of the health security concept with community-based primary health care. More important, there are major differences in understanding and use of the concept in different settings. Policymakers in industrialized countries emphasize protection of their populations especially against external threats, for example terrorism and pandemics; while health workers and policymakers in developing countries and within the United Nations system understand the term in a broader public health context. Indeed, the concept is used inconsistently within the UN agencies themselves, for example the World Health Organization's restrictive use of the term 'global health security'. Divergent understandings of 'health security' by WHO's member states, coupled with fears of hidden national security agendas, are leading to a breakdown of mechanisms for global co-operation such as the International Health Regulations. Some developing countries are beginning to doubt that internationally shared health surveillance data is used in their best interests. Resolution of these incompatible understandings is a global priority.

> **Key messages**
>
> - Although the concept of health security is becoming accepted in public health literature and practice, there is no agreement on scope and content.
> - Incompatible understanding of the concept between developed and developing countries sets the stage for breakdown in global cooperation.
> - Breakdown in cooperation on vital global activities such as disease surveillance could be avoided by sharing benefits of improved surveillance through global commitment to strengthen response capacity (health systems) in the most vulnerable countries.

Introduction

What is 'health security'? Despite the availability of a vast literature on 'human security', 'health security' and 'global public health security', there is no universally agreed definition. Widespread but inconsistent use of the term by global public health stakeholders with widely divergent perceptions, priorities and agendas has created confusion and mistrust. This paper explores the origins—and more important, some of the consequences—of that confusion, which is leading to breakdown of communication and collaboration on several important global public health initiatives, such as global communicable disease surveillance under the World Health Organization's International Health Regulations (IHRs). There is significant and growing opposition to the use of a 'security' justification for global health cooperation, particularly on the part of some developing countries. This opposition has not so far been recognized or understood by many academicians and policy-makers in western countries.

This paper also proposes some steps to relieve the present state of confusion, and to assure continuing global cooperation. These measures must begin by reaching consensus between various stakeholders on the meaning and implications of 'health security'. Reaching consensus on what is meant by 'health security' and 'global public health security', while necessary, will not be easy, because hidden national security agendas will have to be brought out into the open.

Because problems around the concept of 'health security' occur at the intersection of several fields or disciplines which do not share a common theoretical approach or academic methodology, it is difficult to proceed from any unified theoretical approach, however useful this might be as a guide to further study of these complex issues. Diverse players in the 'health security' game include practitioners in the fields of security studies, foreign policy and international relations, development theory and practice of United Nations (UN) agencies and others, and in health development in developing countries themselves. Even within the UN system, there appear to be significant differences in understanding and application of the concept of 'health security', for example between the United Nations Development Programme (UNDP) and the World Health Organization (WHO).

Given the fact that it is words and meanings which are in doubt here, perhaps further research should employ the tools of socio-linguistics: what are the origins and consequences of a word or concept being used by different 'speech communities' (in this case, the different stakeholders in global public health), and how can these different usages, and the confusions that result, be resolved? Whatever approach is taken, progress is needed soon. Considering the many rapidly evolving global health problems before us, we have no margin for error and no time to waste.

Methods

A literature review identified approximately 300 publications relevant to human security, health security, global health security and related topics. These were located through online literature searches, non-governmental organization (NGO) and agency websites, and consultation with colleagues. This review was supplemented by an internet search using a commercial search engine in order to develop a simple frequency analysis of usage of the term 'health security', and also by interviews with key informants. Interviews were particularly helpful in recovering information from settings such as drafting committees of the World Health Assembly for which no written record was available. Confirmation through second sources was obtained whenever possible. The analysis was strengthened by direct participation of the author in some of the policy-related events, although information from this participation was not used as a source for any of the factual findings contained in this paper.

Findings

Human security, health security, health and security, global public health security

In 1994 the UNDP published its annual Human Development Report, titled *New Dimensions of Human Security* (UNDP 1994). Although numerous commissions and national groups have issued reports on human security, the UNDP report has been particularly influential. The report describes human security in terms of security of individuals as well as nation-states, and as a platform for sustainable development. As only one of many attempts to define human security (also see, for example, Nef 1999; Reed and Tehranian

1999; Thomas 1999; Axworthy 2001), the UNDP Human Development Report identified seven categories of threats to human security: economic, food scarcity, health, environment, personal, community and political. This report began the process of linking health concerns to human security, a process which many writers have taken forward (Chen *et al.* 2003).

In May 2003, the Commission on Human Security submitted a report titled *Human Security Now* to the Secretary General of the United Nations (Commission on Human Security 2003). This report described human security as complementary to state security, but with emphasis on human rights and human development. Of the ten policy recommendations of the Commission, one referred to health: 'according higher priority to ensuring universal access to basic health care'. Soon after the submission of the Commission's report, a Human Security Unit was established in the UN Office for Coordination of Humanitarian Affairs (OCHA), which gave human security an organizational base within the United Nations.

The preamble of the 1946 constitution of the WHO refers to '. . . happiness, harmonious relations and *security* of all peoples'. The constitution states that 'the health of all peoples is fundamental to the attainment of peace and *security*' (WHO 2005a). As used here, 'security' seems to refer to 'health and security' (the contribution that health makes to global security) rather than to 'health security' (securing health itself). However, a potentially useful distinction between 'health and security' and 'health security' has not been developed in the literature, with some authors using the terms interchangeably.

In 2001, the World Health Assembly's Resolution 54.14 'Global health security: epidemic alert and response' linked the health security concept to a global strategy for prevention of movement of communicable diseases across national borders. This resolution supported the revision of the IHRs, and was the first step in associating 'global health security' with IHR compliance. This was taken forward in 2007, when health security was selected as the theme of the World Health Day and of the annual World Health Report (WHR), titled *A Safer Future: Global Public Health Security in the 21st Century* (WHO 2007a). Significantly, this report addresses only 'global public health security', which is defined as '. . . the activities required . . . to minimize vulnerability to acute public health events that endanger the collective health of populations living across geographic regions and international boundaries'. The report makes a distinction between 'global public health security' and 'individual security', which will be addressed in a subsequent report. Thus the 2007 WHR focuses only on 'specific issues that threaten the health of people internationally', with emphasis almost exclusively on global compliance with the revised IHRs, which came into force in June 2007. WHO went further to link health security to communicable disease control when it re-named its Communicable Disease Cluster as 'Health Security and Environment'. While these relatively restrictive uses of the terms 'global public health security' and 'health security' provide clarity and focus, they exclude many other global public health concerns (e.g. maternal mortality reduction, child survival, nutrition), and seem to deviate from a broader interpretation of the concept shared by other UN agencies (UNDP 1994; UNICEF 1998). WHO has not fully addressed the larger questions on the definition, scope and implementation of 'health security' (Lancet 2007). Security for whom? Security for which values? How much security? Security from what threats? Security by what means? (Baldwin 1997).

Recurrent themes

Stimulated by the work of UNDP, the Commission on Human Security and others, an extensive and rapidly expanding literature on human security and health security has emerged. This literature is extraordinarily diverse, reflecting a lack of common definition and understanding of 'security', 'human security', 'health security', 'health and security', 'individual health security' and 'global public health security' (Paris 2001). However, despite surprising and substantial divergences in the views and understandings of different authors on the scope and content of human security and health security, the literature does contain recurrent themes. Some of these recurrent themes are:

1 *Protection against threats*: These threats are described from many different viewpoints. In the UNDP's 1994 Human Development Report and many publications which followed, human security is distinguished from the previous state-centred concept of security. This understanding of human security includes protection of vulnerable people against hunger, disease and repression; poverty reduction; and 'empowerment' of people. Other writers, however, emphasize threats to populations as a whole, such as emerging pandemic-prone communicable diseases such as SARS and avian influenza. Many recent publications emphasize bio-terrorism (Greenberg 2002; Gursky 2004; Aginam 2005) and indeed, in some national legislation, the concept of health security and protection from bio-terrorism seem almost interchangeable (United States House of Representatives 2002).

2 *Emergence of new global conditions for which existing approaches are inadequate*: These include the challenge of providing medical aid and humanitarian intervention in 'failed states', in which conflicts within rather than between states have replaced the dynamic of superpower competition of the Cold War. Some observers have raised concerns that intervention in these situations may be motivated more by the security interests of intervening states than by humanitarian (including health) concerns (McInnes 2004). In these cases, pre-emptive intervention in particular, especially if military forces are involved, is open to criticism that the principles of neutrality, impartiality, independence and universality

which usually guide humanitarian interventions will not be respected (Patel *et al.* 2004). It is at this point of intersection between classical security concerns (peacekeeping, maintenance of law and order) and humanitarian operations where lack of common understanding of the term 'health security' is especially problematic.

3   *Engagement of new actors, including military establishments*: Although concerns have been raised by a minority of observers and by NGOs (Knudsen 2001; Bristol 2006), there is increased (and in some cases routine) involvement of military units in public health interventions. An example is the involvement of foreign militaries in the response to the 2005 Asian tsunami disaster. While this assistance was welcome, low-altitude surveillance flights over areas such as the politically sensitive Aceh region of Indonesia by foreign armed forces were a potential source of concern. Other examples of foreign military presence under the justi-fication of public health assistance are the US Naval Medical Research Units (NAMRU) laboratories in Cairo, Jakarta and Lima. When avian influenza was first detected in Egypt in 2002, national authorities were dependent on the CAIRO NAMRU-3 lab for sub-typing of the virus as H5N1 (Meleigy 2007). This type of arrangement has been described as 'dual usage' for public health and military purposes (Chen 2004). While some observers support and encourage this kind of assist-ance and recommend that it be accelerated (Chretien 2006), there is obviously a potential for conflict of interest (Fidler 2005). In another example of military cooperation overseas, the US Department of Defense collaborates with national authorities to receive data from more than 260 sites in 56 countries, including weekly internet-based reporting from civilian hospitals in 18 provinces and 6 army hospitals in a single south-east Asian country (Sanchez 2006). Taking this one step further, it has been proposed that 'since the health services are now in the front line . . . they could legitimately request support from government defence and security budgets' (Health Protection Agency 2001). If support of this kind is accepted by multilateral international agencies, it could certainly raise questions concerning their neutrality and independence (Calain 2007a). A senior WHO official agrees with the suggestion to fund public health activities from security budgets, and suggests that governments create 'a special body to address both public health and national security . . . to get these two sectors working together' (WHO 2007b).

4   *Linkage to foreign policy interests*: There is increasing acceptance that health is a legitimate foreign policy concern (Katz and Singer 2007). In 1999, the United Nations Security Council considered a health problem for the first time, declaring HIV/AIDS a national security threat. The scope of foreign policy health concerns has since been expanded to include problems of trans-border spread of other communicable diseases and protection of the poor and those living in failed states (Ingram 2005;

Amorim *et al.* 2007; Fidler 2007). It is hoped that donor countries can be persuaded that it is in their foreign policy interest to provide increased development aid (Smith 2002). However, the trend to link foreign policy interests to health problems has been criticized on the grounds that it may result in injecting great power politics and narrow national security interests into health and humanitarian matters (Farmer 1999; McInnes and Lee 2006), as well as on more theoretical grounds by the security studies community (Elbe 2005). There is no consensus on the role and limitations of foreign policy in public health and health security, and the subject has been described as 'divided politically and fragmented analytically' (Feldbaum and Lee 2004).

Uncritical insertion of military and foreign policy (political) interests into the arena of global public health is problematic. Much of the literature makes simplistic assumptions about natural harmony between 'health security', 'global public health security', national security and foreign policy. Other observers take a more cautious view:

> Global health is a humanitarian endeavour that seeks to improve the world's health including the most vulnerable peoples, while national security works to protect the interests of people within a given state . . . While there is potential to expand global health activities through partnership with the security and foreign policy communities, treating global health issues as national security threats may focus attention disproportionately on countries or diseases which pose security threats to wealthy nations, rather than on the greatest threats to global health. The global health community should carefully scrutinize areas where global health and national security interests overlap.
>
> (Feldbaum *et al.* 2006)

Convergence of public health and bio-defence

The 1995 sarin gas attack in the Tokyo subway system by the terrorist group Aum Shinrikyo and the 2001 mailing of weaponized anthrax spores through the US postal system sensitized policymakers in industrialized countries to the vulnerability of their populations to chemical and bio-weapons, and more important, brought about a convergence of national bio-defence programmes with existing disease control activities. The harmonization of programmes for security from disease with bio-defence, while superficially a positive development, does have profound implications which have not been fully explored (Kelle 2007). This process has been described as a 'securitization' of public health or 'drafting of public health to fight terror' (Gursky 2004). In some countries, the role of public health services is increasingly seen as provision

of defence against bio-terrorism (Jolly and Ray 2007); with increasing investment for this purpose displacing usual public health functions, such as routine immunization, screening and health promotion (Staiti *et al.* 2003).

Growing concerns of developing countries

Developing countries are increasingly suspicious of global health initiatives
justified on grounds of 'global health security'. The 2005 revision of WHO's
IHRs set off several highly contentious late night drafting sessions, with one
western country arguing for broad powers for international collective action,
including early entry into the territory of affected countries without their
invitation, in the event that a member state's actions to control an epidemic
were felt to be inadequate to prevent international spread. This introduction of
the concept of preemption into the IHR was rejected by the majority of countries.

A more specific rejection of the 'global health security' rationale came in
November 2007, at WHO's Intergovernmental Meeting on Influenza Viruses
and Benefit Sharing. This meeting attempted to resolve the crisis that followed Indonesia's refusal to share virus isolates from human cases of H5N1
influenza A infection (avian influenza), on the grounds that Indonesia was
unlikely to receive any benefits including vaccines or technology transfer
(Enserink 2007). During a long and heated debate, Portugal, then president
of the European Union, attempted to introduce the term 'global health
security' into a draft statement. Portugal stated that 'global health security'
should prevail over other laws. This was vigorously opposed by Indonesia,
Brazil, Thailand and India; with Brazil stating that it was not committed to
working under the security concept. The meeting ended with no agreement
(Shashikant 2007).[1]

Member states' concerns about 'health security' were carried forward into
the meeting of WHO's Executive Board in early 2008. In a discussion on
implementation of the IHRs, the concept of 'global health security' was challenged by Brazil, with the claim that there was no clear meaning of the
term and it enjoyed no consensus among members of the World Health
Assembly. Brazil further noted that the word 'security' did not appear anywhere in the revised IHRs, yet had been introduced in the WHO secretariat's
report to the Executive Board, in which IHR was described as an 'important
instrument for ensuring that the goal of international public health security
is fully met'. The representative of Brazil stated that it 'had no idea what
the goal of international health security' was. The US then intervened to
provide its interpretation of 'global health security', and Brazil suggested
that member states should work on a definition of the term (Tayob 2008).

So far, these debates have done nothing to clarify the definition of 'health
security'. A search of the term using an internet search engine confirms an
alarming lack of agreement on the meaning and scope of the concept. Of
the first 100 citations found on the search, 44 referred only to bio-terrorism

or trans-border spread of disease, 36 referred to effects of rising health care costs and health insurance in developed countries, 2 referred only to HIV/AIDS, 10 referred to unrelated matters (e.g. electronic home protection systems), and only 7 referred to 'health security' in the sense intended by the UNDP.

Discussion

Distortion of 'global public health'?

Taken together, the introduction of a threat protection mentality, foreign policy agendas, military interests and bioterrorism concerns into global public health, under the concept of global public health security, have subtly altered our understanding of global public health. A re-assignment of policy priorities and re-allocation of resources is underway (Staiti *et al.* 2003; Feldbaum *et al.* 2006), without sufficient clarity on definitions or intent (particularly surrounding the concept of 'security'), and without consensus of the global community (Shashikant 2008). Developing countries are unlikely to accept a 'global health security' justification for international agreements which are not perceived to benefit all countries. This is well demonstrated by the reactions of WHO member states Brazil, India, Thailand and Indonesia in recent WHO negotiations cited above (Shashikant 2008). The increasing use of foreign military forces in international disaster response further complicates the situation.

Relationship of 'health security' to existing public health approaches

A good beginning point in assessing the proper role of the 'health security' concept in today's global public health is to put it into the context of established understandings and approaches. Is the emphasis placed on protection against threats consistent with pre-existing public health approaches, such as those based on primary health care, and district health systems? Perhaps because the health security concept originated outside the public health community, very little attention has been given to its added value with respect to existing public health concepts. Does health security supplement, replace or conflict with existing approaches?

The main difficulty in analysing the place of the health security concept in relation to existing public health approaches is the problem of inconsistency in definition and understanding of the concept, as described above. For those who understand health security as it is presented in UNDP's 1994 Human Development Report, the concept is not incompatible with a primary health care approach, emphasizing community involvement, self-sufficiency and protection of vulnerable groups such as pregnant women and the poor. But if health security is defined exclusively in terms of protection of national populations against external threats such as bio-terrorism, the concept becomes disengaged from usual public health epidemiologic approaches, which measure and respond to differential levels of risk and disease burden within populations. These contradictions are well understood by opinion leaders on human and health security (Jolly and Ray 2007), but remain unresolved. To the extent that it is not responsive to the particular needs of the most vulnerable, the theoretical and operational underpinnings of 'health security' (and more important, the benefits to individuals, families and communities, especially in poor countries) remain obscure.

Even if a people-centred understanding of human security and health security is universally accepted (certainly not now the case), questions remain as to the operational implications at the individual and community level. Can existing approaches of primary health care and district health systems be 'co-opted' to deliver the protection and empowerment envisioned for health security? There is a technical basis for this, at least for the communicable disease surveillance element of 'health security'. Community-based outbreak surveillance as part of an integrated disease surveillance and response system is already established in many countries, and is proving to be a valuable tool for early detection and response (WHO 1998). But these systems perform best, and are most sustainable, when they are part of a comprehensive public health system (WHO 2005b). Are international partners and donors willing to fund all of the core functions now being provided by these systems? If not, health security will evolve as a parallel and competing initiative at country level.

A deeper question is the incompatibility of a threat protection mentality implied in some interpretations of 'health security' with the more optimistic emphasis on community-based self reliance which characterizes pre-existing public health concepts such as primary health care. The first priority stated in the UN document *Human Security Now*—protection—implies a primary role of outside helpers, with perhaps a passive role of communities and individuals themselves. This distinction may seem obscure, but differing underlying attitudes can affect the acceptability of a social initiative. Is the threat protection approach which seems to be embedded in the health security concept part of a more general divide between a 'fear-driven' foreign policy approach which has emerged in some countries (Stabile and Rentschler 2005), while a more optimistic attitude is gaining strength in others (Moisi 2007)?

Future directions: a danger of breakdown in global cooperation?

We have shown that there is insufficient global consensus on the meaning of 'health security' and on the scope and intent of national and global programmes designed to ensure it. This lack of agreement has already contributed to the failure of a major international negotiation, the Intergovernmental Meeting on Influenza Viruses and Benefit Sharing in November 2007. This failure could expose us to a global avian-derived human influenza pandemic. International cooperation on implementation and enforcement of the recently revised IHRs is equally at risk, as developing countries become aware that in some cases unconditional open sharing of surveillance data may not be in their national interests (Calain 2007b). Strengthening of surveillance for epidemic-prone diseases brings little benefit to any country which lacks the public health infrastructure necessary for an effective response. In Laos, for example, there have been at least four donor-supported surveillance initiatives (ASEAN Disease Surveillance Network, US Navy EWORS, Rockefeller Foundation funded Mekong Basin Disease Surveillance Project, and the JICA Global Surveillance Network). Although these initiatives do include support for response, there is not sufficient investment in basic health services in Laos to ensure that response is sustainable and sufficiently broad-based to deal with a variety of potential threats. Surveillance data, while of great value in providing early warning to other countries of possible international spread of disease, may be of little practical value to the country originating the data (Calain 2007b). Disaster response, including containment of disease outbreaks, begins with local and national response based on a viable health system (Watts 2005) followed only days or weeks later by international support (Ungchusak *et al.* 2007).

Conclusions

Ambiguity and confusion surround the concept of 'health security'. This has caused damage to international relationships, and is likely to lead to more serious problems in the future. The global public health community must work toward a common understanding of the concept, starting with acceptance that there is a problem. While this might seem obvious from the evidence presented above, it is not evident to many stakeholders, and an open exchange of views is urgently needed, particularly between stakeholders in developing countries, industrialized countries, the humanitarian community, and military organizations. Late night accusations which pop up during drafting sessions at the World Health Assembly are symptoms of deeper mistrust, and it is necessary to move towards a more open and constructive dialogue, perhaps through consensus conferences sponsored by WHO in cooperation with several of the many existing bodies which have a stake in the 'health security' concept. Reaching consensus on what is meant by 'health security' and 'global public health security', while necessary, will not be easy: hidden national security agendas will have to be brought out into the open.

Beyond achieving clarity and openness on the definition of health security, what concrete steps must be taken to reassure developing countries that international health cooperation based on a security concept is in their national interest? In the important case of international surveillance under the IHRs, it is obvious that surveillance data is useful only to those countries with a sufficient response capacity. We need a collective global commitment to build up sustainable response. This cannot be limited to outbreak containment alone, but must be built into strengthened health systems.

The WHO has stated unequivocally that 'functioning health systems are the bedrock of health security' (WHO 2007c), but it remains to be seen whether development partners, including donors in developed countries, are prepared to make the technical and financial commitments for development of health systems which are necessary to ensure that poor countries benefit from timely and open sharing of information in accordance with the global health security concept. The cost of these commitments should not be under-estimated; it is much more expensive to develop and maintain a national health system than to introduce national communicable disease surveillance and outbreak containment alone. But failure to do this may result in breakdown of health security for rich and poor alike.

Acknowledgements

The author is a staff member of the World Health Organization. The author alone is responsible for the views expressed in this publication and they do not necessarily represent the decisions, policy or views of the World Health Organization.

Endnote

1 Even before the November 2007 Intergovernmental Meeting, public health officials in Indonesia had serious concerns about the security implications of H5N1 virus sharing. In 2006, Indonesian officials saw reports in the media that Indonesian H5N1 viral sequences submitted earlier to WHO had been submitted to the Los Alamos National Laboratory in the US. This was distressing because this is understood to be a national security, not a public health, facility. The Laboratory's website clearly states that 'The mission of Los Alamos National Laboratory is national security' (Los Alamos National Laboratory 2008). Indonesian Minister of Health Siti Fadilah Supari later commented that 'Whether they used it to make vaccine or develop chemical weapon, would depend on the need and the interest of the US government'. She was critical of the lack of transparency of the process: 'In a transparent mechanism, anybody has the right to know where the viruses go, what process they are undergoing, and who processes them' (Supari 2008).

References

Aginam O. 2005. Bio-terrorism, human security and public health: can international law bring them together in an age of globalization? *Medicine and Law* **24**: 455–62.
Amorim C., Douste-Blazy P., Wirayuda H. *et al.* 2007. Oslo Ministerial Declaration—global health: a pressing foreign policy issue of our time. *The Lancet* **369**: 1373–8.

Axworthy L. 2001. Human security and global governance: putting people first. *Global Governance* **7**: 19–23.

Baldwin D. 1997. The concept of security. *Review of International Studies* **23**: 12–18.

Bristol N. 2006. Military incursions into aid work anger humanitarian groups. *The Lancet* **267**: 384–86.

Calain P. 2007a. Exploring the global arena of global public health surveillance. *Health Policy and Planning* **22**: 2–12.

Calain P. 2007b. From the field side of the binoculars: a different view on global public health surveillance. *Health Policy and Planning* **22**: 13–20.

Chen L. C., Leaning J., Narasimhan V. (eds). 2003. *Global health challenges for human security*. Cambridge, MA: Harvard University Press.

Chen L. C. 2004. Health as a human security priority for the 21st century. Paper for Human Security Track III, Helsinki Process. Online at: http://www.helsinkiprocess.fi/netcomm/ImgLib/24/89/LCHelsinkiPaper12%5B1%5D.6.04.pdf, accessed 3 September 2007.

Chretien J. P., Gaydos J. C., Malone J. L., Blazes D. L. 2006. Global network could avert pandemics. *Nature* **440**: 25–26.

Commission on Human Security. 2003. *Human security now: protecting and empowering people*. New York: United Nations.

Elbe S. 2005. AIDS, security, biopolitics. *International Relations* **19**: 403–19.

Enserink M. 2007. Avian influenza. Indonesia earns flu accord at World Health Assembly. *Science* **316**: 1108.

Farmer P. 1999. *Infections and inequalities: the modern plagues*. Berkeley, CA: University of California Press.

Feldbaum H., Lee K. 2004. Public health and security. In: Ingram A. (ed.). *Health, foreign policy and security: towards a conceptual framework for research and policy*. London: The Nuffield Trust.

Feldbaum H., Patel P., Sondorp E., Lee K. 2006. Global health and national security: the need for critical engagement. *Medicine, Conflict and Survival* **22**: 192–98.

Fidler D. P. 2005. Health as foreign policy: between principle and power. *Whitehead Journal of Diplomacy and International Relations* **6**: 179–94.

Fidler D. P. 2007. Reflections on the revolution in health and foreign policy. *Bulletin of the World Health Organization* **85**: 243–44.

Greenberg D. S. 2002. USA expands homeland health security. *The Lancet* **359**: 237.

Gursky E. A. 2004. Drafted to fight terror. U.S. public health on the front lines of biological defense. Arlington, VA: Analytic Services, Inc. (ANSER). Online at: http://www.homelandsecurity.org/bulletin/drafted_gursky.pdf, accessed 3 September 2007.

Health Protection Agency. 2001. The World Health Organization Global Outbreak Alert and Response Network – what can Europe learn from this example? *CDR Weekly* **11**: 6.

Ingram A. 2005. The new geopolitics of disease: between global health and global security. *Geopolitics* **10**: 522–45.

Jolly R., Ray D. P. 2007. National human development reports and the human security framework: a review of analysis and experience. New York: United Nations Development Programme. Online at: http://hdr.undp.org/docs/network/hdr_net/NHDRs_and_the_Human_Security_Framework_Final_Draft.doc, accessed 3 September 2007.

Katz R., Singer D. A. 2007. Health and security in foreign policy. *Bulletin of the World Health Organization* **85**: 233–34.

Kelle A. 2007. Securitization of international public health – implications for global health governance and the biological weapons prohibition regime. *Global Governance: A Review of Multilateralism and International Organizations* **13**: 217–35.

Knudsen O. V. 2001. Post-Copenhagen security studies: desecuritizing securitization. *Security Dialogue* **32**: 355–68.

Lancet editorial. 2007. WHO fails to address health security. *The Lancet* **370**: 714.

Los Alamos National Laboratory. 2008. Online at: http://www.lanl.gov/natlsecurity/, accessed 2 February 2008.

McInnes C. 2004. Health and foreign policy. In: Ingram A. (ed.). *Health, foreign policy and security: towards a conceptual framework for research and policy*. London: The Nuffield Trust.

McInnes C., Lee K. 2006. Health, security and foreign policy. *Review of International Studies* **32**: 5–23.

Meleigy M. 2007. Navy labs play public health role. *Bulletin of the World Health Organization* **85**: 165–66.

Moisi D. 2007. The clash of emotions. *Foreign Affairs* **86**: 8–12.

Nef J. 1999. *Human security and mutual vulnerability: the global political economy of development and underdevelopment (2nd edition)*. Ottawa: International Development Research Centre.

Paris R. 2001. Human security: paradigm shift or hot air? *International Security* **26**: 87–102.

Patel P., Lee K., Williams O. 2004. Health, development and security. In: Ingram A. (ed.). *Health, foreign policy and security: towards a conceptual framework for research and policy*. London: The Nuffield Trust.

Reed L., Tehranian M. 1999. Evolving security regimes. In: Tehranian M. (ed.). *Worlds apart: human security and global governance*. London: I.B. Tauris.

Sanchez J. L. 2006. DoD Global Emerging Infections Surveillance & Response System (DoD-GEIS) Global Influenza Surveillance Efforts. Presentation to Committee for the Assessment of DoD-GEIS Influenza Surveillance and Response Programs, Board of Global Health, Institute of Medicine, National Academy of Sciences, USA. 19 December 2006. Online at: http://72.14.235.104/search?q=cache:qTqhJN_17iAJ:wwv.eis.fhp.osd.mil/GEIS/Surveillance Activities/IOM/IOM_PDFS/Sanchez%2520DoDGEIS_Influenza_Surveillance.pdf +Navy+EWORS+Laos&hl=en&ct=clnk&cd=2, accessed 3 September 2007.

Shashikant S. 2007. WHO meeting on avian flu virus ends with draft documents. TWN information service on health issues. Geneva: Third World Network. Online at: http://www.twnside.org.sg/title2/health.info/twnhealthinfo041107.htm, accessed 5 December 2007.

Smith R. 2002. A time for global health. *British Medical Journal* **325**: 54–55.

Stabile C. A., Rentschler C. 2005. States of insecurity and the gendered politics of fear. *NWSA Journal* **17**: vii–xxv.

Staiti A. B., Katz A., Hoadley J. F. 2003. Has bioterrorism preparedness improved public health? Issue Brief no. 65. Washington, DC: Centre for Studying Health System Change.

Supari S. 2008. *It's time for the world to change*. Jakarta: PT Sulaksana Watinsa Indonesia.

Tayob R. 2008. WHO board debates 'global health security', climate, IPRs. TWN information service on health issues. Geneva: Third World Network. Online at: http://www.twnside.org.sg/title2/health.info/2008/twnhealthinfo010108.htm, accessed 2 February 2008.

Thomas C. 1999. Introduction. In: Thomas C., Wilkin P. (eds). *Globalization, human security and the African experience*. Boulder, CO: Lynne Rienner.

UNDP. 1994. *Human Development Report*. Oxford: Oxford University Press.

United States House of Representatives. 2002. Public Health Security and Bio-terrorism Response Act 2002 Jun 12 HR 3448. Online at: http://www.fas.org/sgp/congress/2001/hr3448.html, accessed 3 September 2007.

Ungchusak K., Chunsuttiwat S., Braden C. R. *et al.* 2007. The need for global planned mobilization of essential medicine: lessons learned from a massive Thai botulism outbreak. *Bulletin of the World Health Organization* **85**: 238–40.

UNICEF. 1998. *The State of the World's Children*. Oxford: Oxford University Press.

Watts J. 2005. Thailand shows the world it can cope alone. *The Lancet* **365**: 284.

WHO. 1998. *Integrated disease surveillance in the African region: a regional strategy for communicable diseases, 1999–2003*. Harare: WHO Regional Office for Africa.

WHO. 2005a. *Basic Documents (forty-fifth edition)*. Geneva: World Health Organization.

WHO. 2005b. *Asia-Pacific strategy for emerging diseases*. New Delhi: WHO Regional Office for South-East Asia.

WHO. 2007a. *World Health Report 2007: a safer future: global public health security in the 21ˢᵗ century*. Geneva: World Health Organization.

WHO. 2007b. New rules on international public health security. *Bulletin of the World Health Organization* **85**: 421–500.

WHO. 2007c. High-level debate tackled need for improved international health security. Online at: http://www.who.int/world-health-day/2007/activities/global_event/en/index.html, accessed 3 September 2007.

5

THE EVOLUTION, ETIOLOGY AND EVENTUALITIES OF THE GLOBAL HEALTH SECURITY REGIME

Steven J. Hoffman

Source: *Health Policy and Planning*, 25: (2010), 510–22.

Background   Attention to global health security governance is more important now than ever before. Scientists predict that a possible influenza pandemic could affect 1.5 billion people, cause up to 150 million deaths and leave US$3 trillion in economic damages. A public health emergency in one country is now only hours away from affecting many others.

Methods   Using regime analysis from political science, the principles, norms, rules and decision-making procedures by which states govern health security are examined in the historical context of their punctuated evolution. This methodology illuminates the catalytic agents of change, distributional consequences and possible future orders that can help to better inform progress in this area.

Findings   Four periods of global health security governance are identified. The first is characterized by unilateral quarantine regulations (1377–1851), the second by multiple sanitary conferences (1851–92), the third by several international sanitary conventions and international health organizations (1892–1946) and the fourth by the hegemonic leadership of the World Health Organization (1946–????). This final regime, like others before it, is challenged by globalization (e.g. limitations of the new International Health Regulations), changing diplomacy (e.g. proliferation of global health security organizations), new tools (e.g. global health law, human rights and health diplomacy) and shock-activated vulnerabilities (e.g. bioterrorism and avian/swine influenza). This understanding, in turn, allows us to appreciate the impact of this evolving regime on class, race and gender, as well as to consider four possible future configurations of power, including greater authority for the World Health Organization, a concert of powers, developing countries and civil society organizations.

Conclusions This regime analysis allows us to understand the evolution, etiology and eventualities of the global health security regime, which is essential for national and international health policymakers, practitioners and academics to know where and how to act effectively in preparation for tomorrow's challenges.

Key messages

- The principles, norms, rules and decision-making procedures by which states govern health security have evolved synchronously over time in four separate phases as responses to globalization, changing diplomacy, new tools and shock-activated vulnerabilities.
- Contemporary manifestations of these four catalytic agents of change and the distributional consequences of the current regime on class, race and gender point to the emergence of a new period of global health security governance to replace the existing one.
- Challenges to the current regime are likely to result in one or a combination of several possible configurations of power involving the World Health Organization, a concert of powers, states and/or civil society organizations, each of which carry significant implications.
- Regime analysis shows that the existing architecture for global health security is likely in transition, which should encourage national and international health policymakers, practitioners and academics to plan now in order to effectively prepare for it.

Introduction

Attention to the global governance of health security is more important now than ever before. Three million people travel by airplane each day and goods are shipped worldwide at unprecedented volume and speed. The World Health Organization (WHO) estimates that a public health emergency in one country is only a few hours away from affecting another. And the consequences are staggering. The fallout from Severe Acute Respiratory Syndrome (SARS) in 2003 revealed just how devastating a breakdown in health security can be, halting all travel to affected areas, causing severe economic hardship and prompting total international isolation. The current influenza A(H1N1) pandemic highlights that no city or region is immune from such calamity no matter how healthy or wealthy their populations may be. Scientists predict that a future influenza pandemic could be much worse, affecting 1.5 billion people (WHO 2007c), causing up to 150 million deaths (United Nations 2005) and leaving US$3 trillion in economic damages (Gale 2008).[1] This terrifying reality has catalyzed renewed global interest in the health security mechanisms that national governments and international organizations predict will be necessary to contain 'inevitable' pandemics of the future (WHO 2004; World Bank 2006).

Recent academic publications and discussions in the World Health Assembly have demonstrated that there is no consensus on the meaning of 'health security' among researchers and policymakers (Aldis 2008). For the purposes of this analysis, global health security is defined narrowly as the collection of preventative and response activities that minimize the vulnerability of populations to communicable disease transmission across geographical, national or regional boundaries (WHO 2007c). It is distinguished from the related 'health protection' and 'human security' concepts by its focus on protecting *entire populations*, rather than individuals, from threats of global proportion that can spread menacingly irrespective of established natural or political borders. The term 'global health security regime', therefore, can be defined as the implicit or explicit principles, norms, rules and decision-making procedures (Krasner 1983) by which international actors (including both states and civil society organizations) aim to protect their constituencies from the transmission of diseases from one area to another.

A review of historical analyses shows that the global governance of health security has not remained constant. Indeed, the nature, extent and understanding of threats to health security, as well as the international approach to mitigating them, have all evolved synchronously in punctuated equilibrium. The dramatic changes witnessed by the world over the last century mirror those that were seen over the several hundred years that preceded it. The global response to health security threats transformed accordingly. Understanding the evolution and etiology of each successive period of global health security governance will help us to predict possible configurations of power that may eventually arise. This understanding, ultimately, will better enable us to prepare for them.

This paper will first propose four periods of global heath security governance by which the major causes of regime change can be distilled. Consideration will then be given to contemporary manifestations of these catalytic agents of change and whether we are currently witnessing the emergence of a new regime. The distributional consequences of the current health security regime will be evaluated and four potential future orders will be explored. Understanding the role that WHO, the G8/G20, developing countries and civil society organizations may have to play in the future is necessary to know where and how to effectively prepare for and respond to such eventualities.

Evolution of the global health security regime

International approaches to governing health security can be divided into four stages based on the core principles, norms, rules and decision-making procedures that prevailed at those times on a global scale (see Table 1). The first regime (1377–1851) is characterized by the invocation of unilateral quarantine regulations by many European ports and extends back to the bubonic plague of the 14th century. At this time there were limited mechanisms for international cooperation (Allen 1950), few international travelers, uncertainty regarding the cause of disease (Howard-Jones 1950), strong views on state sovereignty and exclusive territoriality—which included the right to unilaterally impose restrictions on others—and the perspective that Europe must be protected from 'foreign' diseases (Aginam 2004). Having proved ineffective, costly and susceptible to abuse (Harrison 2006), unilateralist approaches to communicable disease control were replaced with a second regime (1851–92) of nascent international dialogue and security harmonization via a series of International Sanitary Conferences. While encouraged to collaborate by fear of cholera pandemics, the outcomes of the first six gatherings were limited due to contradictory medical testimony, disagreement on disease etiology and overriding commercial interests (Howard-Jones 1975; Cooper 1989). These meetings, however, fostered the creation of a common vocabulary with which countries could communicate and achieve agreement in the health arena (Bynum 1993; Fidler 2001; Stern and Merkel 2004) and implicitly demonstrate recognition for the importance of tackling communicable diseases from a global perspective—a marked departure from previous approaches.

The third global health security regime (1892–1946) moved the early sanitary conferences forward with a new sense of institutionalized coordination structured by several international legal conventions and three intergovernmental organizations: the Pan-American Sanitary Bureau (1902), Office International d'Hygiène Publique (1907) and the League of Nations' Health Organization (1923) (Cooper 1989). The contagion theory of disease prevailed despite the plethora of 'incidental interests' (*The Lancet* 1892) and formal diplomacy advanced concurrently with communication and transportation technology. World War II and the collapse of the League of Nations, however, catalyzed transition to the fourth global health security regime (1946–????), which engendered a time of internationalism, multilateralism and universalism, whereby global health security was facilitated collectively through WHO as a single and comprehensive health agency. Today the organization has 193 member states (WHO 2010a) and a secretariat of 8000 staff spread across 147 country offices, six regional offices and one headquarters (WHO 2010b).

Table 1 Evolution of the global health security regime.

Regime	Description	Key characteristics				Agents of continuity
		Principles	*Norms*	*Rules*	*Procedures*	
I	Unilateral quarantine regime (1377–1851)	• Disease causation unknown • Population as power • Europe vulnerable to 'foreign' diseases	• Limited international cooperation • State sovereignty	• Quarantine by land and sea (ad-hoc and uncoordinated)	• Extremely limited • Sanitary councils (e.g. Alexandria, Constantinople and Tangier)	• Uncertainty of disease etiology • No alternative to quarantine was known or available • Political utility
II	Nascent sanitary conference regime (1851–92)	• Contagiousness of only certain diseases • Europe vulnerable to 'foreign' diseases	• Nascent international cooperation • State involvement in health issues • State sovereignty	• Quarantine by land and sea (ad-hoc and uncoordinated)	• Conference diplomacy	• Uncertainty of disease etiology • Potential harm of new rules to commercial interests
III	Institutionalized Sanitary Coordination Regime (1892–1946)	• Broad acceptance of germ theory • Self-interest for disease eradication everywhere • Europe vulnerable to 'foreign' diseases	• Institutionalized international cooperation • State sovereignty	• International sanitary conventions	• Multiple international organizations • Conference diplomacy	• Existence of three international health agencies • Success in coming to agreement on the International Sanitary Conventions
IV	Hegemonic health cooperation regime (1946–????)	• Universal adoption of germ theory • Health for all • Right to health • Link between health and security	• Institutionalized international cooperation • State centricity • State responsibility for health	• International Health Regulations • Resolutions of the World Health Assembly	• WHO • World Health Assembly	• Near-universal state participation • New International Health Regulations • WHO's early successes

Notes: 'Principles' are defined as beliefs of fact, causation and rectitude. 'Norms' are standards of behavior defined in terms of rights and obligations. 'Rules' are defined as specific prescriptions or proscriptions for action, and 'decision-making procedures' are prevailing practices for making and implementing collective choice (Krasner 1983).

Despite its increasingly expansive mandate (Garrett 1996), communicable diseases remains its core activity and the disproportionate focus of its budget (Stuckler *et al.* 2008). WHO has become a global hub for health security—albeit with questionable moral authority and effectiveness.

The history and evolution of global health security highlight several agents of continuity. These include entrenched political power, scientific uncertainty, limited options and the desire to both maximize sovereignty and promote national commercial interests. For example, the lack of alternatives to quarantine in the first period, the uncertainty of disease etiology and importance of commercial interests in the second, the existence of three international health agencies in the third, and the near-universal state-based membership of WHO in the fourth period have all been highly influential in deterring transformation (see Table 1).

The primary causes of regime change are equally clear. First, globalization and the sheer volume of trade, travel and tourism has made national borders ever more porous (Yach and Bettcher 1998a, 1998b; WHO 2007c). As a result, states face progressively more dangerous threats to their population's health security (Lee and Dodgson 2000), far greater incentives to collaborate on public health issues (Gostin and Archer 2007) and mere hours to prepare for pandemics (Dr Margaret Chan, personal communication, 4 July 2008). This has encouraged states to restrain their power, set binding commitments and relinquish some control to multilateral institutions. Second, innovations for increasingly institutionalized mechanisms of multilateral dialogue, like conference diplomacy (early 19th century), international organizations (late 19th century) and the United Nations (1945) (Ikenberry 2001), have enabled increasingly cooperative stages of global communicable disease control. Contemporary examples include the proliferation of civil society organizations, complex government networks (Slaughter 2004) and powerful multilateral forums like the G8, G20 and APEC. Third, medical knowledge has facilitated greater and more sophisticated tools for governments to coordinate their health security efforts, with global action historically dependent upon scientific consensus. Finally, each regime transition has always been accompanied by a shocking event that highlights a particularly devastating vulnerability. Whether bubonic plague, epidemics of cholera or World War II, catalytic triggers—often in the form of a cataclysmic incident—have brought states together and made international collaboration politically advantageous (see Table 2).

Existential challenges and the emergence of a new global health security regime

Contemporary manifestations of these catalytic agents of change and other developments over the past decade have collectively challenged the existing global health security regime such that a new one may be emerging (or may indeed have already emerged). Moving from a position of unquestioned

Table 2 Etiology of the global health security regime.

Regime change	Turning point (event/year)	Key catalytic agents of change			Shocking events
		Globalization	Diplomacy	New tools	
» I	Quarantine regulations in Ragusa (1377)	• Maritime trade	• Limited diplomacy	• Limited medical knowledge	• Bubonic plague in Europe
I » II	1st International Sanitary Conference (1851)	• Expansion of trade • International travel • Porous national borders	• Formalized diplomacy • Conference diplomacy • International consciousness	• Some recognition for disease contagiousness • Continued debate on disease etiology	• Cholera epidemics in Europe • Failure of congress system and rise of conference diplomacy
II » III	1st International Sanitary Convention (1892)	• Further expansion of international trade • New communication technologies (e.g. telegraph) and modes of transportation	• Conference diplomacy • International laws and organizations	• Dominance of contagionist school • Disease pathogenesis	• Cholera pandemic • Intense fear of epidemics coming to Europe via Suez Canal
III » IV	Ratification of the WHO's Constitution (1946)	• Further expansion of international trade • More advanced communication technologies • Faster transportation	• Intense multilateralism and internationalism • United Nations System • Decline of colonialism and trustee system • Failure of International Sanitary Covenants	• Capacity to detect, treat and prevent most diseases • Health as a state of physical, mental and social well-being	• World War II • Collapse of the League of Nations • Creation of the United Nations System
IV » V	Unknown (????)	• Proliferation of global health security organizations • Instant communication technologies • Increasing volume and speed of air, land and sea transportation	• Less confidence in the United Nations System • Proliferation of international fora (e.g. G8/G20, World Bank, Global Fund) • Renewed interest in global health law, human rights and health diplomacy	• Scientific revolution in medicine & technology • Recognition of health's social determinants • Relative simplicity of launching bioterrorist attacks	• Tokyo's sarin gas attacks (1995)? • Terrorist attacks of September 11 (2001)? • Global Health Security Initiative (2001)? • SARS (2003)? • International Health Regulations (2005)? • H1N1 pandemic (2009)?

Notes: The key catalytic agents of change for each period of the global health security regime are highlighted and categorized according to their respective time of transition. The typology of change agents (i.e. globalization, diplomacy, new tools and shocking events) was developed in this paper based on a historical

---

Box 1. Applying a hegemonic transition framework to predict the World Health Organization's possible decline in the governance of global health security

The World Health Organization became a hegemonic health security power in 1948 by supplying world governance capabilities and generating demand for such governance by offering system-level solutions to system-level problems. It fostered systemic expansion in the global health security field by leading its structural reorganization (e.g. revision of the International Health Regulations in 1951, 1969 and 2005) and its activities served as a model for emulation (e.g. World Bank, Gates Foundation, Médecins San Frontières). This, in turn, ironically worked to undermine the organization's hegemony itself. As competition in the health security field increases along with the volume and density of the system, a hegemonic crisis may ensue (or may already have commenced). Such a crisis is typically characterized by three processes: (1) intensification of inter-enterprise competition (e.g. proliferation of civil society organizations); (2) escalation of social conflicts (e.g. between developed and developing countries); and (3) interstitial emergence of new configurations of power (e.g. the G7's Global Health Security Initiative). While this self-reinforcing crisis is eventually supposed to lead to a total hegemonic breakdown, it is also said to facilitate evolution with the emergence of a new hegemony that has greater concentration of organizational capabilities and a higher system volume and dynamic density to organize (Arrighi and Silver 1999).

Notes: This framework, originally designed to predict the rise and fall of state superpowers, is applied to the World Health Organization's current dominance in the global health security field to provide further evidence that a regime change may be forthcoming in the near future.

dominance 60 years ago to an environment in which it is heavily criticized (Brown *et al.* 2006; Lee *et al.* 1996; UK House of Lords Select Committee on Intergovernmental Organisations 2008), it is clear that WHO lacks the authority and resources commensurate with its vast responsibilities. It is unable to coordinate all global communicable disease control activities (Gostin 2009; Ruger and Yach 2009) and has been criticized as 'bureaucratic', 'complex' and 'outdated' (Godlee 1994; Peabody 1995; Stern and Merkel 2004). Even its independence and impartiality are threatened (Calain 2007a). Applying a traditional political science analysis of hegemonic transitions to this field also reveals that the elements may be in place for a new global health security power to emerge (Box 1) (Arrighi and Silver 1999). Insights from political economy and the recent global financial crisis point to a similar conclusion (MacLean *et al.* 2009).

Globalization and the limitations of the new International Health Regulations

Despite the optimism surrounding their recent ratification, WHO's new International Health Regulations (2005) have been subjected to just as much criticism as praise. There is no doubt that the new agreement includes several significant improvements from its 1969 predecessor: it increases the number of diseases for which the rules apply; expands the variety of events for which WHO must be notified; allows the organization to investigate, assess and declare public health emergencies of international concern and issue formal recommendations; requires the appointment of national health security focal points who liaise with WHO; requires states to develop their own capacity for disease surveillance, response and border control; obliges developed countries to assist developing countries in achieving these core public health capacities; and permits WHO to accept surveillance information from non-state sources (WHO 1969; WHO 2005; Fidler and Gostin 2006; Baker and Forsyth 2007; McDougall and Wilson 2007). Each of these provisions challenges the traditional Westphalian bargain of exclusive state authority in international affairs and empowers WHO as an independent global actor.

However, the new regulations also contain no legal enforcement mechanism (Sturtevant *et al.* 2007), rely upon peer pressure and public knowledge for compliance (Wise 2008), emphasize surveillance to the exclusion of other essential elements (*The Lancet* 2004), remain difficult to implement in federated countries (Wilson *et al.* 2006; Wilson *et al.* 2008a; Wilson *et al.* 2009), provide opportunities for the politicization of epidemic responses (Suk 2007), depend upon national governments' acquiescence to new global health responsibilities (Merianosa and Peiris 2005), fail to specify how national governments are actually supposed to collaborate with one another (Bhattacharya 2007), narrowly define health security (*The Lancet* 2007), and rely upon surveillance networks in developing countries which may not be functioning optimally (Wilson *et al.* 2008b). Indeed, the very effectiveness of the International Health Regulations in preventing deadly epidemics and responding to outbreaks, their *raison d'être*, has been called into question.

Yet in addition to the structural weaknesses of the new rules, ambiguity has led to divisions between developed and developing countries. Indonesia, for example, refused to share H5N1 virus samples in February 2007 because it doubted that it would ever benefit from such scientific collaboration, particularly in the desired form of technology transfers or vaccine provision (Enserink 2007). Supported by most of the developing world, Indonesia demanded guaranteed access to future vaccines for poorer states that carry a disproportionate burden of the relevant disease, and justified these demands by invoking the principles of sovereignty over biological materials, transparency of the global health system, and equity between developed and developing countries (Sedyaningsih *et al.* 2008). While viral sharing eventually resumed following a WHO-brokered provisional compromise (WHO 2007b), this ongoing dispute highlights the fact that ambiguity and political considerations continue to challenge the regulations' real-world implementation and effectiveness. It also highlights the existing divisions between developed and developing countries, which no doubt serve as a destabilizing force. Indeed, deliberations at subsequent WHO meetings have shown that there is not even consensus among states for the conceptualization of virus sharing as a health security issue (Aldis 2008).

Changing diplomacy and the proliferation of global health security organizations

The past decade has also witnessed challenges to the entire United Nations (UN) System (of which WHO is part) and the emergence of several new players involved in coordinating, funding and implementing global communicable disease control activities. The optimistic expectations for global cooperation and an end to international conflict via the UN have given way to criticism of this diplomatic system, assumption by civil society of increasingly important roles, greater violence and more emergency health situations. Recognized contemporary challenges to the UN include widespread cultural diffusion resulting in higher expectations, detachment from multilateralism by developed countries, self-interest defined in domestic terms, memories of recent failures (e.g. to contain the global HIV/AIDS pandemic) and greater attention on relieving conflict than promoting well-being. In terms of its financial importance, a mere US$5 billion was disbursed through the UN System in 1996 as compared with the approximately US$55 billion that was given by national bilateral aid agencies (Walt 1998). This trend applies equally to development assistance for health, which in 2007 was channeled in much larger sums through bilateral development agencies (US$7.4 billion) and non-governmental organizations (US$4.5 billion) than through all the UN's various agencies, funds and programmes combined (US$3.1 billion) (Institute for Health Metrics and Evaluation 2009).

Today there are also numerous players involved in global communicable disease control, including other multilateral organizations (e.g. Joint United Nations Programme on HIV/AIDS, World Bank, World Trade Organization, United Nations Children's Fund, United Nations Population Fund and European Community), philanthropic foundations (e.g. Gates Foundation, Kellogg Foundation and Rockefeller Foundation), international partnerhips (e.g. GAVI Alliance, International Health Partnership, Stop TB Partnership, Roll Back Malaria Partnership and Global Fund to Fight AIDS, Tuberculosis and Malaria), national development agencies (e.g. Canadian International Development Agency, Swedish International Development Agency and UK Department for International Development) and civil society organizations (e.g. Red Cross, World Medical Association, International Society for Infectious Diseases and Médecins San Frontières). Some of them were even created as a direct response to dissatisfaction with WHO's leadership (Fox 1995). Public–private partnerships have also increasingly been seen as essential mechanisms for achieving global health security goals (Buse and Walt 2000a, 2000b; Buse and Waxman 2001; Widdus 2001; Yamey 2002; Kickbusch 2005; Cohen 2006), and the central importance of sub-national actors, including national institutes of public health and academic health centres, has also been recognized (Leggat and Tse 2003; Rodier *et al.* 2007). Finally, the emerging 'Health 8' (i.e. Gates Foundation, GAVI Alliance, Global Fund, UNAIDS, UNFPA, UNICEF, WHO and World Bank) (WHO 2007a; Silberschmidt *et al.* 2008) and the G7's Global Health Security Initiative (which also includes the European Union and Mexico) (GHSI Secretariat 2009) offer alternative sources of 'networked governance' for the global health security regime (Fidler and Gostin 2008). This proliferation of health security initiatives, indeed, has meant that WHO is merely one of many major global health security organizations in an increasingly crowded field.

New tools and renewed focus on global health law, human rights and health diplomacy

The framework within which states cooperate on public health issues has also recently been challenged. With the recent revision of the International Health Regulations and ratification of the WHO Framework Convention on Tobacco Control (WHO 2003b), many commentators have highlighted the utility of public international law as a mechanism for better structuring global health diplomacy during this time of increasing interdependence (Taylor 2002, 2004; Gostin 2005). A Framework Convention on Global Health has been proposed (Gostin 2007, 2008) and the proliferation of human rights discourse in the health field recognized (Gable 2007). While WHO has frequently been cited as a natural champion for this new legalistic approach to global health, there is also recognition that international health lawmaking would be neither workable nor desirable under the auspices of a single international agency (Taylor 2002). As the importance of health rises dramatically in the hierarchy of foreign policy objectives (Drager and Fidler 2007; Fidler 2007; Horton 2007; Støre 2007), there is also the possibility that more traditional forums of power will seek to expand their authority to include this increasingly vital domain.

94

Shock-activated vulnerabilities and new threats
to health security

Finally, several recent focusing events have further raised doubts as to WHO's current capacity to address new threats to health security. For example, international concern for bioterrorism was exacerbated by each of the 1995 sarin gas attacks on Tokyo's subway system, the terrorist attacks of 11 September 2001 and the anthrax attacks in the United States throughout the autumn of 2001. The episode of SARS in 2003 and the H1N1 pandemic in 2009 further heightened awareness of the steep consequences of global pandemics (WHO 2003a; Gostin 2009), and the recent emergence and pro-liferation of extremely drug-resistant microbes has demonstrated the need for new techniques and strategies.

While WHO's central role in the new International Health Regulations points to its continued hegemony over health security, these catalytic agents of change highlight the challenges that face the organization in maintaining this position of dominance. A fifth global health security regime appears to be emerging.

Distributional consequences of the current global health security regime

The future of global health security governance, however, will not only be shaped by the identified catalytic agents of change but also by the prevailing regime's distributional consequences. The dominant principles, norms, rules and decision-making procedures of each period carry costs and benefits for different groups of people and states based on various factors. Understanding these consequences can present opportunities to mitigate or promote them by informing future evolution in the regime.

First, as much as bacteria and viruses are largely ignorant of social divisions, disease invariably leads to disproportional repercussions for people in poverty, women and racial groups that already face discrimination. For example, many of the feared communicable diseases can be treated with existing medical knowledge, except that poorer people may not be able to afford treatment, take time off work to recuperate properly or find family members to take care of them. Women, similarly, are often isolated in many countries, benefit from fewer societal protections, encounter longer delays in accessing health services (Karim *et al.* 2007), suffer from gender stereotyping (Cook and Cusack 2009) and can face greater exposure to diseases from their traditional responsibility of caring for those who are sick. People who experience racial discrimination may also face artificial barriers to treatment, difficulty in accessing health services and greater stigma.

However, this inequitable burden of disease may not be alleviated pro-portionally depending on the way in which the world chooses to govern health security. A key element of early regimes, for example, was the belief that Europe had to be protected from the 'foreign' diseases of the developing world. This isolationist approach is most likely rooted in unfortunate beliefs of race-based hierarchies, the dirtiness of tropical disease and developing countries being a reservoir for illness (Aginam 2004). This approach to global health security strictly divides developed and developing countries into opposing camps, a stratification that was likely further entrenched by the latter's exclusion from global health decision-making. On one hand, this situation may be improving over time. Certain redistributional consequences, for example, are likely to emerge as the health security interests of wealthier countries increasingly align with the social and economic goals of less developed countries. Yet on the other hand, the incentive for the world's most powerful nations to continue asserting their influence and challenge developing countries' internal sovereignty remains substantial, especially given that global health security governance now operates in a sphere of action beyond the territoriality of any individual country (Kickbusch and de Leeuw 1999). One could even argue that wealthier countries to this day retain complete control over this area due to their significant political influence in multilateral forums and their financial capacity to support (or deny support to) their preferred global projects, including disease surveillance and pandemic preparedness (Calain 2007b). Indonesia's decision to withhold H5N1 virus samples in 2007 highlights this perceived power imbalance.

This historical convergence of health and traditional security interests has also led to far greater institutionalization and concern for the global health security regime (as compared with other public health issues) such that it has often dominated the global health agenda. This has led to a general 'securitization' of public health more broadly defined, which in turn carries wide-ranging consequences (Peterson 2002; Calain 2007a; Kelle 2007). Public health initiatives, for example, are increasingly being justified solely as defensive measures against the threat of epidemics or biological terrorism (Gursky 2004; Jolly and Ray 2006; United States Commission on the Prevention of Weapons of Mass Destruction 2008). While this focus may have resulted in greater investments by national governments in their health security, it has come at the expense of other traditional public health programmes, including screening, chronic diseases and health promotion (Staiti et al. 2003; Aldis 2008). Similarly, at the global level, the framing of health as a security issue has likewise been quite effective in rallying wealthy countries to guard against this common threat for all through enhanced bilateral aid. However, this development has also served to prioritize resources for certain communicable diseases to the detriment of all other health issues—often to the point of extreme disproportionality compared with the burden that is faced (Shiffman 2006). For example, infectious diseases receive 86% of WHO's budget for the Western Pacific but only account for 14% of the region's mortality. Non-communicable diseases, in contrast, earn a mere 13% of the budget and injury prevention only 1% even though they represent 75% and 10% of all deaths in the region respectively (Stuckler *et al.* 2008). The opportunity cost of this imbalance must be devastating.

Yet additional implications of the global health security regime's securitization of public health are foreseeable. Other consequences may include the further disempowerment of women (who are often sidelined in male-dominated security decision-making) (Cohn 1993), diminished compatibility with global development goals (which usually emphasize community empowerment rather than threat management), distortion of national health priorities (Biesma *et al.* 2009) and conflicts with local cultures (which may reject the biomedical approach to disease control). Recent debates in high-level WHO meetings reveal the growing opposition to this sweeping securitization of public health (Bhattacharya 2007), especially among policymakers from developing countries who may be suspicious of their wealthier neighbours' intentions (Aldis 2008).

Considering possible future configurations of power

The evolutionary history of the global health security regime points to several future configurations of power in this area (see Table 3). While four possible orders will be considered separately to facilitate the analysis, the future will likely feature a combination of various elements from each moving in tandem based on the way global health politics evolve.

Greater authority for the World Health Organization

If states believe that global health security requires centralized leadership and fulfilment of WHO's core functions (Ruger and Yach 2009), they may decide to delegate (or WHO may wrest) more control and financial resources to the UN organization to create, administer and enforce stronger global health security regulations. Specific gaps in WHO's capabilities are highlighted by the current H1N1 pandemic and include its limited ability to monitor and enforce rules, facilitate capacity building in developing countries and demand the sharing of virus samples (Gostin 2009). States may also decide to implement proposals for more democratic, accountable and transparent WHO decision-making processes that empower and welcome the participation of other influential global health actors (Silberschmidt *et al.* 2008). Giving greater authority to WHO would yield the advantages and disadvantages of building upon an existing institution, having a single coordinating agency and using an inclusive framework with near-universal participation. However, it relies upon WHO's ability to harness these new powers to better govern the global health security regime, states' willingness to entrust further decision-making authority to the multilateral organization, and continued confidence and legitimacy in the UN system.

Table 3 Eventualities of the global health security regime.

Future order	Contingent causes	Key characteristics	Catalytic factors	Consequences
Greater authority for WHO	• Current authority of WHO is inadequate for its responsibility of governing global health security • Decline of WHO's dominance in health security field • States are best suited to govern the global health security field • UN ideal for cooperation • WHO can harness new powers to better govern health security	• States delegate more control over both global and domestic health security to WHO • Greater financial resources for WHO's health security and other activities • Enforcement mechanism developed for the International Health Regulations • WHO restored as unquestionable leader of global health security	• Advantages of a universal mechanism for directing global health activities • Legitimacy of and respect for the UN system • Desire to build upon existing institutions • Recognized need for a single coordinating body for global health security	• Central coordinating body for global health security • Decline of omnipotent state power over public health issues • Continued cooperation through the UN, with all of its benefits and challenges • Universal participation in global health security governance
Dominance by a concert of powers	• WHO proves unable to effectively regulate communicable disease transmission • Cooperation through UN has failed or is not ideal for this field • Global health security best governed by smaller group of very powerful states	• A concert of powers like the G8 assumes leadership of global health security • Greater role for leading economic powers • Concert uses vast economic resources to achieve universal participation • Compels compliance using its substantial influence	• Diminished credibility of International Health Regulations and WHO • Decline of UN-style multilateralism • Concert recognizes national security and public health to be inherently connected • Practical efficiency of fewer decision-makers	• Concert recognized as health security leader • Further securitization of global health issues • Exclusive participation in global health security governance • Diminished role for WHO as a multilateral and universal forum

Global rebalancing among states	• Global health inequalities between developed and developing countries • Perceived control of WHO by developed countries via its budget • Growing frustration among developing and emerging nations • Desire for universal compliance in health security sphere among developed countries	• Either WHO is restructured or a new global health security organization is created that more equitably represents the views, concerns and needs of all countries • Focus on transfer of resources and expertise on health security from developed to developing countries	• Recognized need for global health equity among developed country policymakers • Health for all as a global responsibility • Recognized duty in politics, law and ethics to assist poorer states • Greater influence in health security demanded by developing and emerging countries	• Reorientation of communicable disease control to focus on developing and emerging country needs • Greater influence for developing and emerging countries in global health security governance • More resources devoted to global health activities • Increased transfers to developing countries
Civil society leadership	• WHO and national governments fail to effectively govern global health security • Loss of confidence in state-based systems of global governance (e.g. UN) • Proliferation and greater credibility for powerful civil society organizations	• Civil society organizations assume leadership of global health security field • Decentralized governance • Diffused leadership among many decision-makers • Greater number of policy pathways • Significant influence among funders of civil society organizations	• Expansion of resources in the civil society sector • Unwillingness of states to effectively collaborate or provide sufficient resources for global health security • Public–private partnerships • Declining trust in national governments and UN • Reliance on civil society for disease surveillance data	• Faster decision-making processes and innovation-catalyzing decentralized governance • Greater variability in governance and accountability of health security decision-makers • Less influence for countries with small populations • Diminished role for WHO

Notes: The contingent causes, key characteristics, catalytic factors and consequences of four possible future orders of global health security governance.

Dominance by a concert of powers

Alternatively, a powerful group of actors with world governance capabilities may challenge WHO's current dominance and provide new solutions for governing global health security. Members of the G8/G20 or Health 8, for example, may collectively have the capacity to assume leadership in this area through networked governance (Fidler and Gostin 2008), and may be more effective in making the necessarily difficult decisions and coercing others to follow them. Indeed, the G8 has already demonstrated such interest through unprecedented engagement with global health policy at their recent 2008 Hokkaido Toyako Summit in Japan (Reich and Takemi 2009). A decision by the G8 to assert further control in this area could perhaps stem from democratic chauvinism or the inherent interdependence of security and health (Gursky 2004; Jolly and Ray 2006). Indeed, national self-interest has already encouraged wealthier countries to support the public health architecture of their poorer neighbours based on the notion that the health security of every country depends on the ability to prevent and respond to communicable diseases in each of them (Gostin and Archer 2007; Hein 2007; United Nations 2007; National Intelligence Council 2008; UK Government 2008; Institute of Medicine 2009). Dominance by a concert of powers like the G8/G20, however, presumes that states would have lost confidence in UN-facilitated multilateralism and that a concert of powers is capable and desirous of using its collective economic resources and political influence to compel adherence to their health security decisions. It also assumes that this concert will not repeat the G8's commitment–compliance gap (Labonte and Schrecker 2004), which indeed has improved since 1996 (Kirton *et al.* 2007; Kirton and Guebert 2009), as disenfranchised states would otherwise be less likely to cooperate.

While tying communicable disease control to the G8's more traditional areas of governance (e.g. peace, security and economic prosperity) could yield greater financial aid for developing countries, it could also be the ultimate demonstration that global health has become subservient to the national security interests of the world's most powerful states (Staiti *et al.* 2003; Aldis 2008). Divisions among developed, developing and emerging states may also be further exacerbated.

Global rebalancing with greater influence for developing and emerging countries

A third possibility is that WHO could be restructured, a new global health organization created, or an existing organization (like the Global Fund or Health 8) empowered to more equitably represent the views, concerns and aspirations of developing and emerging countries in health decision-making. Indeed, frustrated by developed countries' stranglehold on WHO via its policy of zero-nominal budget growth and conditional voluntary contributions, developing and emerging countries may demand a new approach to global health security governance in which they have greater influence. They may also demand greater transfers of resources, technology and expertise—all of which have recently been advocated for by international health organizations (Lazcano-Ponce *et al.* 2005). Alternatively, this future order could arise from recognition among policymakers in developed countries that health for all people is a global responsibility such that they have a duty to provide assistance to poorer states. Such a duty could be found in international law (e.g. International Health Regulations, Universal Declaration of Human Rights, International Covenant on Economic, Social and Cultural Rights), political commitments (e.g. UN Millennium Declaration, G8 Communiqués, Doha Declaration on the TRIPS Agreement and Public Health) or ethical frameworks (i.e. developing countries have great need, developed countries have the ability to help and the public supports such assistance) (Gostin and Archer 2007). It could alternatively be part of a 'new global social contract for health' (Fidler 2007) or recognition for communicable disease control as a 'global public good' (Smith *et al.* 2004).

Greater influence for leaders in developing and emerging states may not only help them meet their development and equity goals but also work in the national security interests of developed countries (Bond 2008). Since bacteria and viruses are oblivious to state sovereignty, the historical dichotomization of the Global North and South may even have left much of the world 'multilaterally defenseless' against the threat they pose (Aginam 2004). Further, as the Indonesian virus-sharing incident demonstrates, wealthier countries may have to encourage compliance with the new International Health Regulations by conceding political decision-making power, offering greater financial support and promising equal access to future vaccines and treatments. The rise of Brazil, China, India and other growing powers may make such concessions by today's ruling states even more necessary and likely in the future.

Leadership of civil society organizations

Finally, civil society may assume leadership of preparing for and responding to a future crisis in this area. Such groups may be able to access greater financial resources, invoke faster decision-making processes, better align themselves with national health priorities, and benefit from their innovation-catalyzing decentralized governance structures. Indeed, their extensive contributions to global health policymaking have already been widely recognized in the academic literature (Lee and Dodgson 2000; Dodgson *et al.* 2002; Hein and Kohlmorgen 2009). This future order could possibly come about from the continuing proliferation and expansion of these organizations, trends towards greater utilization of public–private partnerships, and increasing reliance on this sector for disease surveillance data. However, this possible Balkanization of global health security governance would feature greater variability in the accountability of health security decision-makers, unclear responsibility and priority-setting (Kickbusch 2000, 2005), less influence for countries with small populations and a diminished role for WHO. It would also result in significantly more influence for the funders of civil society organizations as well as other wealthy entities—including for-profit corporations—that have the resources to engage in their own health security activities. Further adverse implications may emerge if many different actors launch independent initiatives with limited coordination or start competing for funds, media attention and legitimacy (Kickbusch 2005; Garrett 2007).

Conclusion

Understanding the evolution, etiology and possible eventualities of the global health security regime is crucial for all national and international health policymakers, practitioners and academics alike to know where and how they must act to effectively prepare for tomorrow's most pressing challenges. This paper highlights four of many possible future configurations of power based on a multiplicity of contingent causes that may emerge, with recognition that the future will likely feature a web of elements from each depending on the dynamics of global health politics. Their characteristics and consequences urge renewed debate on the most effective and equitable global health security governance arrangements possible.

Several questions nevertheless remain unanswered. For example, there is still great uncertainty as to the effectiveness of the new International Health Regulations and the capacity of states to comply with them. The impact that additional well-funded civil society organizations will have on the regime also remains unknown, as does the possible influence that greater recognition for the 'right to health' will have to bear. A final question is whether the world is adequately prepared for the next global pandemic, or if another episode Like SARS or H1N1 is needed to achieve the crucial changes. Further analysis is necessary.

Conflict of interest

The author was employed by the World Health Organization at the time that this study was conducted.

Acknowledgements

Thank you to John Kirton, Chris McDougall and Cliff van der Linden for their comments and suggestions on earlier versions of this paper.

Endnote

1 An internal World Bank report obtained by Bloomberg indicates that a possible influenza pandemic could cost up to US$3 trillion.

References

Aldis W. 2008. Health security as a public health concept: a critical analysis. *Health Policy and Planning* **23**: 369–75.

Allen C. E. 1950. World health and world politics. *International Organization* **4**: 27–43.

Aginam O. 2004. Between isolationism and mutual vulnerability: a South-North perspective on global governance of epidemics in an age of globalization. *Temple Law Review* **77**: 297–312.

Arrighi G., Silver B. 1999. Hegemonic transitions: past and present. *Political Power and Social Theory* **13**: 239–75.

Baker M. G., Forsyth A. M. 2007. The new International Health Regulations: a revolutionary change in global health security. *New Zealand Medical Journal* **120**: e1–8.

Bhattacharya D. 2007. An exploration of conceptual and temporal fallacies in international health law and promotion of global public health preparedness. *Journal of Law, Medicine and Ethics* **35**: 588–98.

Biesma R. G., Brugha R., Harmer A. *et al.* 2009. The effects of global health initiatives on country health systems: a review of the evidence from HIV/AIDS control. *Health Policy and Planning* **24**: 239–52.

Bond K. 2008. Health security or health diplomacy? Moving beyond semantic analysis to strengthen health systems and global cooperation. *Health Policy and Planning* **23**: 376–8.

Brown T. M., Cueto M., Fee E. 2006. The World Health Organization and the transition from 'international' to 'global' public health. *American Journal of Public Health* **96**: 62–72.

Buse K., Walt G. 2000a. Global public–private partnerships: part I – a new development in health? *Bulletin of the World Health Organization* **78**: 549–61.

Buse K., Walt G. 2000b. Global public–private health partnerships: part II – what are the issues for global governance? *Bulletin of the World Health Organization* **78**: 699–709.

Buse K., Waxman A. 2001. Public–private health partnerships: a strategy for WHO. *Bulletin of the World Health Organization* **79**: 748–54.

Bynum B. F. 1993. Policing hearts of darkness: aspects of the international sanitary conferences. *History and Philosophy of the Life Sciences* **15**: 421–34.

Calain P. 2007a. Exploring the international arena of global public health surveillance. *Health Policy and Planning* **22**: 2–12.

Calain P. 2007b. From the field side of the binoculars: a different view on global public health surveillance. *Health Policy and Planning* **22**: 13–20.

Cohen J. 2006. The new world of global health. *Science* **311**: 162–7.

Cohn C. 1993. Wars, wimps and women: talking gender and thinking war. In: Cooke M., Woollacott A. (eds). *Gendering War Talk*. Princeton, NJ: Princeton University Press, pp. 227–46.

Cook R. J., Cusack S. 2009. *Gender Stereotyping: Transnational Legal Perspectives*. Philadelphia, PA: University of Pennsylvania Press.

Cooper R. N. 1989. International cooperation in public health as a prologue to macroeconomic cooperation. In: Cooper R. N., Eichengreen B., Henning C. R., Holtham G., Putnam R. D. (eds). *Can Nations Agree? Issues in International Economic Cooperation.* Washington, DC: Brookings Institution, pp. 193–210.

Drager N., Fidler D. P. 2007. Foreign policy, trade and health: at the cutting edge of global health diplomacy. *Bulletin of the World Health Organization* **85**: 162.

Dodgson R., Lee K., Drager N. 2002. *Global Health Governance: A Conceptual Review.* Discussion Paper No. 1. London and Geneva: London School of Hygiene & Tropical Medicine and World Health Organization. Online at: http://whqlibdoc.who.int/publications/2002/a85727_eng.pdf, accessed 5 September 2009.

Enserink M. 2007. Avian influenza: Indonesia earns flu accord at World Health Assembly. *Science* **316**: 1108.

Fidler D. P. 2001. The globalization of public health: the first 100 years of international health diplomacy. *Bulletin of the World Health Organization* **79**: 842–9.

Fidler D. P. 2007. Reflections on the revolution in health and foreign policy. *Bulletin of the World Health Organization* **85**: 161–244.

Fidler D. P., Gostin L. O. 2006. The new International Health Regulations: an historic development for international law and public health. *Journal of Law, Medicine and Ethics* **34**: 85–94.

Fidler D. P., Gostin L. O. 2008. Globalizing governance: toward a global biosecurity concert. *Biosecurity in the Global Age: Biological Weapons, Public Health, and the Rule of Law.* Palo Alto, CA: Stanford University Press, pp. 219–56.

Fox R. 1995. Medical humanitarianism and human rights: reflections on Doctors Without Borders and Doctors of the World. *Social Science and Medicine* **41**: 1607–16.

Gable L. 2007. The proliferation of human rights in global health governance. *Journal of Law, Medicine and Ethics* **35**: 534–44.

Gale J. 17 October 2008. Flu pandemic may cost world economy up to $3 trillion. *Bloomberg.* Online at: http://www.bloomberg.com/apps/news?pid=20601202&sid=ashmCPWATNwU&refer=healthcare, accessed 26 November 2008.

Garrett L. 1996. The return of infectious disease. *Foreign Affairs* **75**: 66–79.

Garrett L. 2007. The challenge of global health. *Foreign Affairs* **86**: 14–38.

GHSI Secretariat. 2009. *Global Health Security Initiative Background.* Online at: http://www.ghsi.ca/english/background.asp, accessed 1 April 2009.

Godlee F. 1994. The World Health Organization: WHO in crisis. *British Medical Journal* **309**: 1424–8.

Gostin L. O. 2005. World health law: toward a new conception of global health governance for the 21st century. *Yale Journal of Health Policy, Law and Ethics* **5**: 413–24.

Gostin L. O. 2007. A proposal for a Framework Convention on Global Health. *Journal of International Economic Law* **10**: 989–1008.

Gostin L. O. 2008. Meeting basic survival needs of the world's least healthy people: toward a Framework Convention on Global Health. *Georgetown Law Journal* **96**: 331–92.

Gostin L. O. 2009. Influenza A(H1N1) and pandemic preparedness under the rule of international law. *Journal of the American Medical Association* **301**: 2376–8.

Gostin L. O., Archer R. 2007. The duty of states to assist other states in need: ethics, human rights, and international law. *Journal of Law, Medicine and Ethics* **35**: 526–13.

Gursky E. A. 2004. Drafted to Fight Terror: U.S. Public Health on the Front Lines of Biological Defense. Arlington, VA: Analytic Services Inc. Online at: http://www.homelandsecurity.org/bulletin/drafted_gursky.pdf, accessed 3 December 2008.

Harrison M. 2006. Disease, diplomacy and international commerce: the origins of international sanitary regulation in the nineteenth century. *Journal of Global History* 1: 197–217.

Hein W. 2007. *Global Health: A Policy Field of Underestimated Importance*. Berlin: Friedrich-Ebert-Stiftung. Online at: http://www.chathamhouse.org.uk/files/13660_100309hein3.pdf, accessed 5 September 2009.

Hein W., Kohlmorgen L. 2009. Transnational norm-building in global health: the important role of non-state actors in post-Westphalian politics. In: MacLean S. J., Brown S. A., Fourie P. (eds). *Health for Some: The Political Economy of Global Health Governance*. New York: Palgrave Macmillan, pp. 87–104.

Horton R. 2007. Health as an instrument of foreign policy. *The Lancet* 369: 806–7.

Howard-Jones N. 1950. Origins of international health work. *British Medical Journal* 12: 1032–7.

Howard-Jones N. 1975. *The Scientific Background of the International Sanitary Conferences, 1851–1938*. Geneva: World Health Organization.

Ikenberry G. J. 2001. *After Victory: Institutions, Strategic Restraint, and the Rebuilding of Order After Major Wars*. Princeton, NJ: Princeton University Press.

Institute for Health Metrics and Evaluation. 2009. *Financing Global Health 2009: Tracking Development Assistance for Health*. Seattle, WA: University of Washington. Online at: http://www.healthmetricsandevaluation.org/print/reports/2009/financing/financing_global_health_report_full_IHME_0709.pdf, accessed 1 March 2010.

Institute of Medicine. 2009. *The U.S. Commitment to Global Health: Recommendations for the Public and Private Sectors*. Washington, DC: National Academies Press.

Jolly R., Ray D. B. 2006. *National Human Development Reports and the Human Security Framework: A Review of Analysis and Experience*. New York: United Nations Development Programme. Available at http://www.bvsde.paho.org/bvsacd/cd32/jolly.pdf, accessed 3 December 2008.

Karim F., Islam M. A., Chowdhury A. M. R., Johansson E., Diwan V. K. 2007. Gender differences in delays in diagnosis and treatment of tuberculosis. *Health Policy and Planning* 22: 329–34.

Kelle A. 2007. Securitization of international public health: implications for global health governance and the biological weapons prohibition regime. *Global Governance* 13: 217–35.

Kickbusch I. 2000. The development of international health policies: accountability intact? *Social Science and Medicine* 51: 979–89.

Kickbusch I. 2005. Action on global health: addressing global health governance challenges. *Public Health* 119: 969–73.

Kickbusch I., de Leeuw E. 1999. Global public health: revisiting healthy public policy at the global level. *Health Promotion International* 14: 285–8.

Kirton J. J., Guebert J. 2009. Health accountability: the G8's compliance record from 1975 to 2009. Toronto: G8 Research Group, University of Toronto. Online at: http://www.g8.utoronto.ca/scholar/kirton-guebert-health-091228.pdf, accessed 1 March 2010.

Kirton J. J., Roudev N., Sunderland L. 2007. Making G8 leaders deliver: an analysis of compliance and health commitments, 1996–2006. *Bulletin of the World Health Organization* 85: 192–9.

Krasner S. D. 1983. Structural causes and regime consequences: regimes as interven-ing variables. In: Krasner S. D. (ed.). *International Regimes*. Ithaca, NY: Cornell University Press.

Labonte R., Schrecker T. 2004. Committed to health for all? How the G7/8 rate. *Social Science and Medicine* **59**: 1661–76.

The Lancet. 1892. Editorial: The Venice Sanitary Conference. *The Lancet* **139**: 95.

The Lancet. 2004. Editorial: Public-health preparedness requires more than surveillance. *The Lancet* **364**: 1639–40.

The Lancet. 2007. Editorial: WHO fails to address health security. *The Lancet* **370**: 714.

Lazcano-Ponce E., Allen B., González C. C. 2005. The contribution of international agencies to the control of communicable diseases. *Archives of Medical Research* **36**: 731–8.

Lee K., Collinson S., Walt G., Gilson L. 1996. Who should be doing what in international health: a confusion of mandates in the United Nations? *British Medical Journal* **312**: 302–27.

Lee K., Dodgson R. 2000. Globalization and cholera: implications for global governance. *Global Governance* **6**: 213–36.

Leggat S. G., Tse N. 2003. The role of teaching and research hospitals in improving global health (in a globalized world). *Healthcare Papers* **4**: 34–38.

MacLean S. J., Brown S. A., Fourie P. 2009. *Health for Some: The Political Economy of Global Health Governance*. New York: Palgrave Macmillan.

McDougall C. W., Wilson K. 2007. Canada's obligations to global public health security under the revised International Health Regulations. *Health Law Review* **16**: 25–32.

Merianosa A., Peiris M. 2005. International Health Regulations (2005). *The Lancet* **366**: 1249–51.

National Intelligence Council. 2008. Intelligence Community Assessment 2008-10D. *Strategic Implications of Global Health*. Washington, DC: Office of the Director of National Intelligence. Online at: http://www.dni.gov/nic/PDF_GIF_otherprod/ICA_Global_Health_2008.pdf, accessed 5 September 2009.

Peabody J. W. 1995. An organizational analysis of the World Health Organization: narrowing the gap between promise and performance. *Social Science and Medicine* **40**: 731–42.

Peterson S. 2002. Epidemic disease and national security. *Security Studies* **12**: 43–81.

Reich M., Takemi K. 2009. G8 and strengthening of health systems: follow-up to the Toyako Summit. *The Lancet* **373**: 508–15.

Rodier G., Greenspan A. L., Hughes J. M., Heymann D. L. 2007. Global public health security. *Emerging Infectious Diseases* **13**: 1447–52.

Ruger J. P., Yach D. 2009. The global role of the World Health Organization. *Global Health Governance* **2**: 1–11. Online at: http://ghgj.org/ruger2.2rolewho.htm, accessed 5 September 2009.

Sedyaningsih E. R., Isfandari S., Soendoro T., Supari S. F. 2008. Towards mutual trust, transparency and equity in virus sharing mechanism: the avian influenza case of Indonesia. *Annals of the Academy of Medicine of Singapore* **37**: 482–8. Online at: http://www.annals.edu.sg/PDE/37VolNo6Jun2008/V37N6p482.pdf, accessed 5 September 2009.

Slaughter A. M. 2004. *A New World Order*. Princeton, NJ: Princeton University Press.

Sharpe W. R. 1947. The new World Health Organization. *American Journal of International Law* **41**: 509–30.

Shiffman J. 2006. Donor funding priorities for communicable disease control in the developing world. *Health Policy and Planning* **21**: 411–20.

Silberschmidt G., Matheson D., Kickbusch I. 2008. Creating a Committee C of the World Health Assembly. *The Lancet* **371**: 1483–6.

Smith R. D., Woodward D., Acharya A., Beaglehole R., Drager N. 2004. Communicable disease control: a 'global public good' perspective. *Health Policy and Planning* **19**: 271–8.

Staiti A. B., Katz A., Hoadley J. F. 2003. *Issue Brief No. 65: Has Bioterrorism Preparedness Improved Public Health?*. Washington, DC: Centre for Studying Health System Change. Online at: http://www.hschange.com/content/588/588.pdf, accessed 3 December 2008.

Stern A. M., Merkel H. 2004. International efforts to control infectious diseases, 1851 to the present. *Journal of the American Medical Association* **292**: 1474–9.

Støre J. G. 2007. Health is a foreign policy concern. *Bulletin of the World Health Organization* **85**: 167–8.

Stuckler D., King L., Robinson H., McKee M. 2008. WHO's budgetary allocations and burden of disease: a comparative analysis. *The Lancet* **372**: 1563–9.

Sturtevant J. L., Anema A., Brownstein J. S. 2007. The new International Health Regulations: considerations for global public health surveillance. *Disaster Medicine and Public Health Preparedness* **1**: 117–21.

Suk J. E. 2007. Sound science and the new International Health Regulations. *Global Health Governance* **1**: 1–4.

Taylor A. L. 2002. Global governance, international health law and WHO: looking towards the future. *Bulletin of the World Health Organization* **80**: 975–80.

Taylor A. L. 2004. Governing the globalization of public health. *Journal of Law, Medicine and Ethics* **32**: 500–8.

UK Government. 2008. *Health is Global: A UK Government Strategy 2008–13*. Online at: http://www.dh.gov.uk/en/Publicationsandstatistics/Publications/Publications-PolicyAndGuidance/DH_088702, accessed 15 January 2009.

UK House of Lords Select Committee on Intergovernmental Organisations. 2008. *Diseases Know No Frontiers: How Effective Are Intergovernmental Organisations in Controlling their Spread?*. London: Authority of the House of Lords. Online at: http://www.publications.parliament.uk/pa/ld200708/ldselect/ldintergov/143/143.pdf, accessed 15 January 2009.

United Nations. 2005. Press Release: Press conference by UN System Senior Coordinator for Avian, Human Influenza. 29 September. Online at: http://www.un.org/News/briefings/docs/2005/050929_Nabarro.doc.htm, accessed 26 November 2008.

United Nations. 2007. Press Release: Secretary-General commends 'Foreign Policy and Global Health Initiative' for use of diplomacy to secure better health for all at programme's launch. 27 September. Online at: http://www.un.org/News/Press/docs/2007/sgsm11190.doc.htm, accessed 5 September 2009.

United States Commission on the Prevention of Weapons of Mass Destruction Proliferation and Terrorism. 2008. *World at Risk: The Report of the Commission on the Prevention of WMD Proliferation and Terrorism*. New York: Random House Inc., p. 38. Online at: http://www.preventwmd.gov/report/, accessed 17 September 2009.

Walt G. 1998. Globalisation of international health. *The Lancet* **351**: 434–7.

Widdus R. 2001. Public-private partnerships for health. *Bulletin of the World Health Organization* **79**: 713–20.

Wise J. 2008. UK steps up its global health security. *The Lancet Infectious Diseases* **8**: 350.

Williams G. 1988a. WHO: reaching out to all. *World Health Forum* **9**: 185–99.

Williams G. 1988b. WHO: the days of the mass campaigns. *World Health Forum* **9**: 7–23.

Wilson K., Fidler D. P., McDougall C. W., Lazar H. 2009. Establishing public health security in a postwar Iraq: constitutional obstacles and lessons for other federalizing states. *Journal of Health Politics, Policy and Law* **34**: 381–99.

Wilson K., McDougall C., Fidler D. P., Lazar H. 2008a. Strategies for implementing the new International Health Regulations in federal countries. *Bulletin of the World Health Organization* **86**: 215–20.

Wilson K., McDougall C., Upshur R. 2006. The new International Health Regulations and the federalism dilemma. *PLoS Medicine* **3**: e1.

Wilson K., Tigerstrom B., McDougall C. 2008b. Protecting global health security through the International Health Regulations: requirements and challenges. *Canadian Medical Association Journal* **179**: 44–8.

World Bank. 2006. *Global Development Finance: The Development Potential of Surging Capital Flows*. Washington, DC: World Bank.

World Health Organization. 1969. *International Health Regulations (1969)*. Geneva: World Health Organization. Online at: http://whqlibdoc.who.int/publications/1983/9241580070.pdf, accessed 15 October 2008.

World Health Organization. 2003a. Chapter 5: SARS: Lessons from a new disease. *World Health Report 2003: Shaping the Future*. Geneva: World Health Organization, pp. 71–82.

World Health Organization. 2003b. *WHO Framework Convention on Tobacco Control*. Geneva: World Health Organization. Online at: http://www.who.int/tobacco/framework/WHO_FCTC_english.pdf, accessed 2 November 2008.

World Health Organization. 2004. World is ill-prepared for 'inevitable' flu pandemic. *Bulletin of the World Health Organization* **82**: 317–8.

World Health Organization. 2006. *International Health Regulations (2005)*. Geneva: World Health Organization. Online at: http://www.who.int/csr/ihr/en/, accessed 15 October 2008.

World Health Organization. 2007a. Informal meeting of global health leaders. Online at: http://www.who.int/dg/reports/31072007/en/index.html, accessed 1 April 2009.

World Health Organization. 2007b. Press Release: Indonesia to resume sharing H5N1 avian influenza virus samples following a WHO meeting in Jakarta. Online at: http://www.who.int/mediacentre/news/releases/2007/pr09/en/index.html, accessed 15 December 2008.

World Health Organization. 2007c. *World Health Report 2007: A Safer Future: Global Public Health Security in the 21st Century*. Geneva: World Health Organization.

World Health Organization. 2010a. Countries. Online at: http://www.who.int/countries/en/, accessed 1 March 2010.

World Health Organization. 2010b. WHO – Its People and Offices. Online at: http://www.who.int/about/structure/en/index.html, accessed 1 March 2010.

Yach D., Bettcher D. 1998a. The globalization of public health, I: threats and opportunities. *American Journal of Public Health* **88**: 735–8.

Yach D., Bettcher D. 1998b. The globalization of public health, II: the convergence of self-interest and altruism. *American Journal of Public Health* **88**: 738–44.

Yamey G. 2002. Why does the world still need WHO? *British Medical Journal* **325**: 1294–8.

6

HUMAN SECURITY

Expanding the scope of public health

Paula Gutlove and Gordon Thompson

Source: *Medicine, Conflict & Survival*, 19:1 (2003), 17–34.

Abstract

Human security is an evolving principle for organizing human-itarian endeavours in the tradition of public health. It places the welfare of people at the core of programmes and policies, is community oriented and preventive, and recognizes the mutual vulnerability of all people and the growing global inter-dependence that mark the current era. Health is a crucial domain of human security, providing a context within which to build partnerships across disciplines, sectors and agencies. These principles have been demonstrated in field programmes in which health-care delivery featuring multi-sectoral co-operation across conflict lines has been used to enhance human security. Such programmes can be a model for collaborative action, and can create the sustainable community infrastructure that is essential for human security.

Introduction

In an increasingly interdependent world, nations and peoples must think afresh about how we manage our joint activities, advance our shared interests, and confront our common threats. No shift in the way we think or act is more critical than that of putting people at the centre of everything we do. That is the essence of human security. That is something that all people — in rich and poor countries alike, in civil society or the precincts of officialdom — can agree on. And it is something that, with political will, can be placed at the heart of the work of the UN — our work to create security where it has been lost, where it is under threat, or where it has never existed.

Kofi Annan[1]

In his statement the United Nations Secretary-General offers the concept of 'human security' as an organizing principle that can be placed at the heart of the work of the UN. Many other world leaders have endorsed the concept with similar enthusiasm. Human security has been part of the discourse of diplomacy and international humanitarian work for only a decade, still has varying interpretations and has not yet entered public discourse. Nevertheless, this concept offers particular promise as a framework for debating and acting upon humanity's shared interests and mutual vulnerabilities.

Supporters of the concept argue that human security will broaden the scope of policy debates and create new opportunities for addressing humanitarian concerns. Others argue that it is simply a re-packaging of old ideas. However, even the critics agree that the lives of millions of people are plagued by insecurity, and that future events could undermine the security of many more people. Similarly, there is now broad agreement that security concerns should not be framed solely in terms of the interests of states or of powerful non-state actors. The concept of human security thus deserves careful attention. At present, there is no competing principle for comprehensively addressing humanitarian needs.

Public health has always been guided by a broad vision of human needs. For example, one of the pioneers of public health, the 19th-Century German pathologist Rudolf Virchow, fought for recognition of medicine as a social science. Virchow also called upon physicians to be the "apostles of peace and reconciliation".[2a] Human security offers a framework for applying this vision to contemporary needs, thereby creating new opportunities to expand the scope of public health. A human-security framework recognises humanity's global interdependence and mutual vulnerability to a range of old and new threats. Proven principles of public health can, with some expansion of their traditional scope of application, make major contributions to mitigating these threats.

This paper begins with a broad discussion of human security, addressing contemporary threats to individuals and societies, evolution and definition of the concept of human security, and application of the concept to practical programmes. It then focusses on the role of health as a crucial domain of human security, describes the benefits that can arise if public health activities are pursued within the context of human security, and offers a comprehensive strategy for enhancing health within a human-security framework.

Present and potential threats to individuals and societies

Millions of people around the world live in conditions of chronic insecurity, mostly because they are poor. As the World Bank has said:

> Poor people live without fundamental freedoms of action and choice
> that the better-off take for granted. They often lack adequate food

and shelter, education and health, deprivations that keep them from leading the kind of life that everyone values. They also face extreme vulnerability to ill health, economic dislocation, and natural disasters. And they are often exposed to ill treatment by institutions of the state and society and are powerless to influence key decisions affecting their lives. These are all dimensions of poverty.[2]

The effect of poverty on health is readily apparent from global data. For example, the mortality rate of children under five years of age is 120 per 1,000 or greater for the 40 per cent of the world's people who reside in low-income countries, 35–39 per 1,000 for the 45 per cent in middle-income countries and 6 per 1,000 for the 15 per cent in high-income countries.[3]

Although the populations of richer countries enjoy better health than those of poorer countries, they are potentially susceptible to infectious diseases, which account for a quarter to a third of deaths worldwide and could spread rapidly in the modern era. About 2 million people cross international borders each day, including about one million who pass between developed and developing countries each week. As a result of this interchange and the high level of international trade, no population can be completely shielded from infection. In the United States, annual deaths from infectious disease have doubled to 170,000 after reaching a historic low in 1980. Epidemics of new diseases or drug-resistant forms of familiar diseases could dramatically accelerate this trend. Such epidemics are especially likely to begin in populations that suffer from poverty, social breakdown and insecurity.[4] Richer populations therefore have a direct interest in ensuring that poorer populations enjoy basic health security.

Linked with the threat of infectious disease is the threat of bioterrorism. Many nations and sub-national groups now have the capability to prepare and disseminate pathogenic microbes, and this capability will become even more widespread in the future. The propensity of a group to apply this capability for a malicious purpose will be influenced by a variety of factors, one of which will be the group's perception of social injustice. While it would be foolish to attribute the entire threat of bioterrorism to social injustice, it would be equally foolish to ignore the potential for poverty, insecurity and injustice to motivate terrorists or provide a rationale for their actions.

Moreover, social justice can improve a society's capability to defend itself against bioterrorism. For example, it has become clear that the US government's ability to detect and respond to disease outbreaks at home is handicapped by two forms of social injustice: more than 40 million US citizens lack health insurance, and the numerous illegal immigrants are denied access to federally-funded medical clinics.[5] The limited contact of these populations with the health-care system could allow an undetected epidemic to begin within their ranks.

Violent conflict has always been a threat to the security of individuals and societies. Recently, violent conflict has tended to occur in lower-income countries, but higher-income countries are not exempt, as residents of the former

Yugoslavia discovered in the 1990s. Wherever violent conflict occurs, it has significant direct and indirect costs.[6] Collateral impacts — including economic dislocation and the degradation of public health infrastructure — remain evident for years after violence has ceased.

The ultimate level of violent conflict is nuclear war, a potential catastrophe that is, for most people, difficult to imagine. However, the threat is real, and it can be analysed. The consequences of a global nuclear war were examined in a special issue of *Ambio* in 1982:

> In such a war no nation on earth will remain undamaged. The industrialized societies of the Northern Hemisphere will be totally destroyed, and hundreds of millions of people will die, either directly or from the delayed effects of radiation. Even greater numbers may ultimately perish there and in Third World countries as a result of the collapse of their societies and of the international exchange of food, fertilizers, fuel and economic aid. The environmental support system on which man is dependent will suffer massive damage.[7]

These findings illustrate the interdependence and mutual vulnerability of all people, both rich and poor, in the modern world. However, political leaders sometimes seem unaware of the extent of our interdependence and mutual vulnerability, and of factors including economic inequality, poverty, political grievances, nationalism, environmental degradation and the weakening of international institutions that could destabilise the present international order. Military strategists, who are obliged to consider a range of contingencies, have considered factors of this kind and concluded that the future will not necessarily be benign.[8]

Over the coming decades, human society will be vulnerable to a variety of threats that are complex, inter-related and potentially additive, leaving but a short window of opportunity to reverse trends and improve the quality of human life. The Stockholm Environment Institute (SEI) has identified a range of scenarios for the future of the world over the coming decades, and has studied the policies and actions that will tend to make each scenario come true, concluding:

> In the critical years ahead, if destabilizing social, political and environmental stresses are addressed, the dream of a culturally rich, inclusive and sustainable world civilization becomes plausible. If they are not, the nightmare of an impoverished, mean and destructive future looms. The rapidity of the planetary transition increases the urgency for vision and action lest we cross thresholds that irreversibly reduce options — a climate discontinuity, locking-in to unsustainable technological choices, and the loss of cultural and biological diversity.[9]

Thorough, objective consideration of potential threats to individuals and societies is needed for a productive discussion of human security. Careful analyses, such as that by SEI, show clearly that the security of the world's people is, ultimately, indivisible. We all share a fragile ecosystem and a range of vulnerabilities, including potential susceptibility to new types of infectious disease. None of us can be fully secure unless all of us have at least some minimal level of security.

Evolution and interpretation of the concept of human security

There is an extensive literature on human security, including documents that review the evolution and interpretation of the concept.[10–12] Authors agree that human security refers to the security of people as individuals or in small communities, in contrast with security concepts that focus on the security of nations or other large entities. This is not a totally new concept:

> While the term 'human security' may be of recent origin, the ideas that underpin the concept are far from new. For more than a century — at least since the founding of the International Committee of the Red Cross in the 1860s — a doctrine based on the security of people has been gathering momentum. Core elements of this doctrine were formalized in the 1940s in the UN Charter, the Universal Declaration of Human Rights, and the Geneva Conventions.[13]

During the 1980s, these ideas were further developed through debates that centred on disarmament issues. One strand of thinking about human security can be traced to a debate about 'common security' that occurred during the final decade of the Cold War.[14] Common security offered an alternative vision to the Cold War confrontation, a vision in which nations co-operated to prevent conflict and to enhance the well-being of humanity. This vision found expression at the governmental level in the work of the Conference on Security and Co-operation in Europe (CSCE), which addressed issues ranging from multilateral arms control to human rights. The vision also nurtured a wide variety of non-governmental initiatives. For example, health professionals worked through the International Physicians for the Prevention of Nuclear War (IPPNW), not only to end the East-West nuclear confrontation but also to promote humanitarian objectives such as improved health care in poorer nations.[15]

The concept of human security became widely known through the United Nations Development Programme (UNDP) Human Development Reports of 1993 and 1994. The 1994 report is said to be the first document to provide a comprehensive definition of human security.[16] The concept was described as the security of persons in seven domains: economic security (assured basic income); food security (physical and economic access to food); health security (relative freedom from disease and infection); environmental security (access

113

to sanitary water supply, clean air and a non-degraded land system); personal security (security from physical violence and threats); community security (security of cultural identity); and political security (protection of basic human rights and freedoms). Chronic and acute threats to security were recognized. Human security was identified as a universal need, in recognition of the inter-dependence of people in the modern world. The preventive aspect of human security was emphasised, and a distinction was drawn between human development — which is about widening people's economic choices — and human security — which is about people being able to exercise these choices safely and freely.

The UNDP definition has not been universally employed, as illustrated by the differing interpretations of human security that have been used by the governments of Canada and Japan, which both support human-security initiatives. Canada says:

> A wide range of old and new threats can be considered challenges to human security; these range from epidemic diseases to natural dis-asters, from environmental change to economic upheavals. Through its foreign policy, Canada has chosen to focus its human security agenda on promoting safety for people by protecting them from threats of violence. We have chosen this focus because we believe this is where the concept of human security has the greatest value added — where it complements existing international agendas already focussed on promoting national security, human rights and human development.[17]

Japan has adopted a broader focus for its work on human security, based on an interpretation somewhat like that of UNDP:

> Japan emphasizes 'Human Security' from the perspective of streng-thening efforts to cope with threats to human lives, livelihoods and dignity [such] as poverty, environmental degradation, illicit drugs, transnational organized crime, infectious diseases such as HIV/AIDS, the outflow of refugees and anti-personnel land mines, and has taken various initiatives in this context.[18]

To some extent, differing views on human security reflect differing views on related issues of international policy. For example, the personal-security domain of human security is linked to the potentially controversial issue of 'humanitarian intervention' in the affairs of states.[19] However, differing per-ceptions of the utility or 'value added' of human security also play a powerful role in influencing the decision of an actor — such as a government — to emphasise one or another domain of human security.

Ultimately, as illustrated by the Canadian and Japanese positions, there is broad consensus that human security has multiple domains, but less consensus about applying the concept. At any given time, a particular actor will choose to emphasise some domains of human security more than others.

Towards an operational definition of human security

A decision by a government or other actor to emphasise a particular domain of human security will reflect the answers to at least three questions. First, is there an existing agenda for debate and a framework for implementing practical actions? Second, will application of the human security concept provide added value? Third, can this actor make a significant contribution? Affirmative answers will encourage the actor to proceed.

These questions could be framed and answered in the absence of consensus on an operational definition of human security. However, such a consensus would facilitate the questioning process and the implementing of practical actions. A consensual definition would help to ensure that actions taken by multiple actors, across multiple domains, are synergistic. Recent analysis provides a framework that could, over time, yield an appropriate definition. This framework brings together two ideas.

The first idea is that the objective of human security should be to provide a 'vital core' or minimal set of conditions of life.[20] There is a clear implication that a person lacking these conditions deserves assistance. People whose conditions of life are above the minimal level may live in comparatively undeveloped circumstances. However, they have a basic level of security that allows them to plan and work for a better future for themselves, their families and their communities. Their progress in this respect can be described as human development. Human security, defined in this manner, is a necessary, although not sufficient, precondition for human development.

The second idea is that the minimal set of conditions for a secure life can be specified by setting thresholds in each of a number of selected domains of human security. A person is said to be secure if her conditions of life, in every domain, are above the threshold value. Conversely, falling below the threshold in any domain places the person in a state of insecurity. With this formulation, there is no need for weights to be assigned to the domains. Analysts with WHO have identified five domains of human security: income; health; education; political freedom; and democracy. For each domain, they have identified indicators that are widely used by entities such as the World Bank and UN agencies. For each indicator, a threshold value can be chosen.[12]

In combination, these two ideas provide a framework for discussions that could lead to a consensual, operational definition of human security. During these discussions, a variety of domains, indicators and thresholds could be considered. Ultimately, there could be a consensus to adopt the seven domains articulated by UNDP, or the five domains proposed by the WHO analysts, or some other set of domains. For each domain, it would be necessary to reach consensus on indicators that are measurable, consistent over time, and appropriate for worldwide application. Before the chosen domains and indicators could be employed operationally, there would need to be consensus on an initial set of thresholds. Over time, assuming that the state of human security improves, the thresholds could be raised.

Efforts to develop a consensual definition of human security should be accompanied by comparable efforts to develop a consensual analytic framework for the application of human security. In view of the preventive aspect of human security, this framework must support forward-looking assessments of potential threats to human security. The framework must also support the planning, implementation and evaluation of actions that are taken to preserve human security. These actions will typically involve multiple actors, working across multiple domains.

Applying the concept of human security to practical programmes

The concept of human security will demonstrate its utility when it is used to guide the planning and implementation of practical programmes of action. As a general rule these programmes will continue a pre-existing strand of activity, and must be consistent with existing strategies for humanitarian work. A notable strategy of this kind is the set of Millennium Development Goals through which the UN system is operationalising the development goals set forth in the UN Millennium Declaration of September 2000.[21]

Human security must, if it is to be a useful concept, bring added value. This can occur in at least four ways. First, human security can provide a clear and compelling objective for humanitarian work. Second, human security has a preventive aspect, which can stimulate forward-looking contingency planning. Third, human security emphasises global interdependence and can therefore mobilise additional resources and new partnerships. Fourth, human security addresses interacting threats in multiple domains and can therefore stimulate holistic, comprehensive threat assessment and programme planning.

The fourth of these points can be illustrated by the interacting threats that must be considered in connection with the health domain of human security. For example, poor economic conditions, social injustice or bad governance can undermine health care and promote political or criminal violence. Violence can have adverse effects on health, either directly or through collateral effects such as economic dislocation, food shortages or degradation of the infrastructure for public health. Adverse effects on health can have adverse implications for the economy. The potential for a downward spiral in the conditions of life is obvious. Such a spiral can be difficult to arrest or reverse.

Planning and implementing a holistic, preventive response in each relevant situation will require new mechanisms for co-operation among actors. To facilitate this enhanced co-operation, and to ensure that the lessons of experience are rapidly incorporated into programmes, new mechanisms of information exchange, organisational learning and programme evaluation will be needed. Meeting these requirements will demand additional resources. Thus, new investments will be needed to capture the value that can be added by applying the concept of human security. However, these investments could be repaid many times over through enhanced effectiveness of programmes and the mobilisation of new resources.

Health: a crucial domain of human security

As pointed out above, practical programmes that are guided by the concept of human security will generally continue a pre-existing strand of activity. This will certainly be true in the health sector, in which there is a rich body of experience and active planning of new programmes. A notable example of current planning is the action agenda that has been set forth by the WHO Commission on Macroeconomics and Health (CMH).[3] This action agenda, which complements the Millennium Development Goals, focuses on the health needs of the general population in low-income countries and the poor in middle-income countries. The financing plan for the action agenda involves a substantial increase in donor commitments above the $7 billion available in 2001, to $27 billion in 2007 and $38 billion in 2015, and calls for increased local expenditures on health. These recommendations are predicated on the practical necessity of pursuing social justice, both within and between nations.

The concept of human security can bring added value to the CMH action agenda, in at least three ways. First, the human-security perspective can be used to mobilise new resources to support the action agenda. Second, the human-security perspective can catalyse new partnerships that recognise global interdependence and complement the action agenda; the linked threats of infectious disease and bioterrorism provide one context for such partnerships. Third, the human-security perspective can link the CMH action agenda with programmes that address related objectives — such as the prevention of violent conflict — and can thereby enhance the effectiveness of both strands of effort.

The potential for new partnerships that address the mutual threat of infectious disease — to developed and developing countries alike — was evident from discussions at a March 2002 conference on human security, held at American University in Washington, DC:

> US National Institutes of Health senior researcher Samir Khleif . . . said the continuing prevalence of easily preventable diseases in developing countries demonstrates the huge disparities between developed and developing countries and has 'tremendous' implications for the security of North-South relations. . . .
>
> 'Investing in global health is an investment in national security,' said Khleif, noting that no country is completely isolated from the diseases of the poor because of the effects of globalization, more

mobile populations and migration patterns. Citing the United States as an example, Khleif said that 40 per cent of cases of tuberculosis have originated with immigrants and that the US was unable to prevent the trans-Atlantic importation of the West Nile virus. 'You can't stop TB at the border,' he said.[22]

Another illustration of the potential for new partnerships is concern about the threat of smallpox as an instrument of bioterrorism. For example, the WHO Regional Committee for the Eastern Mediterranean has requested the Regional Director to plan a strategic stock of smallpox vaccine for the region.[23] The US government has issued guidelines whereby the entire US population can be vaccinated against smallpox within a five-day period. In view of the potential for rapid spread of infectious disease in the modern world, such actions should be part of a broader effort to develop a global strategy that addresses the linked threats of infectious disease and bioterrorism. This strategy would recognise the interdependence and mutual vulnerability of all people, accept social justice as a global security measure, and catalyse a wide range of new partnerships.

There is experience with international collaboration to control infectious diseases. Nations have been willing to co-operate to a remarkable degree, and to accept the authority of international organisations, because they recognise their mutual vulnerability. WHO campaigns to address polio, malaria and TB in south-east Asia illustrate this cooperation.[24]

As noted, one way in which the human-security perspective can add value is by linking the CMH action agenda — whose focus is health — with programmes that address related objectives — such as the prevention of violent conflict, the improvement of governance, or economic development. Human security provides a perspective that can link such efforts to their mutual benefit. For example, violent conflict and bad governance are severe constraints on the effectiveness of health interventions, which are difficult to address,[25] and programmes for the peaceful management of conflict and the promotion of social reconstruction can be successfully integrated with health interventions.[26,27] Thus, the potential exists for mutually-beneficial linkages between health programmes and other programmes.

Experience in integrating conflict management with health care is of particular interest in the context of health and human security. In situations of conflict, shared health concerns can create neutral fora for discussion and collaboration. Furthermore, health issues can provide a useful platform to address fundamental obstacles to peace, such as discrimination, polarisation and the manipulation of information. Health-care delivery programmes that feature co-operation between health professionals from different sides of a conflict can be a model for collaborative action, helping to create the sustainable community infrastructure that is essential for enduring peace. Relevant programmes could include inoculation campaigns and public health education.[26]

Health bridges for peace

Much of the experience in integrating conflict management with health care has been conducted under the rubric 'Health Bridges for Peace'. This experience provides an important illustration of the benefit of pursuing health and social justice within the context of human security.

Health professionals have a special role to play in healing violence-ravaged communities and enhancing a society's potential for human security.[28] They have an intimate association with the people who have suffered mentally and physically from armed conflicts, are well-educated, and have stature and access to a wide range of community groups. They can create a 'bridge of peace' between conflicting communities, whereby delivery of health care can become a common objective and a reason for continued co-operation. They can assist reconciliation after the trauma of war, through a healing process that restores relationships at individual and community levels.

In a post-conflict community, the health sector often receives international and NGO assistance, thereby providing options for communication, transport, technology transfer, and educational support that are otherwise unavailable.[29] In complex emergencies there is often a paralysis of the state, whereas health professionals can facilitate the development of sustainable institutions that deliver health care while addressing issues of social justice and human security. International medical organisations have experience in building bridges between medical communities in developing and developed countries, North and South, East and West.

Delivery of health care has been the basis for significant co-operation between parties divided by violence, as has been documented by the War and Health Program of McMaster University.[29] UNICEF has pioneered the promotion of humanitarian cease-fires for paediatric immunisations, and the brokering of 'corridors of peace' to allow the transport of medical supplies.[30] WHO has demonstrated the potential for health to be a unifying influence through research/action programmes, sustained inoculation campaigns and health-education programmes in conflict-torn areas.[31,32] In discussing the connection between health and peace, MacQueen et al. argue that 'there is a need for a new discipline of 'peace through health' that studies both the downward spiral of war and disease and the positive symbiosis of peace and health.'[33]

The Institute for Resource and Security Studies (IRSS) has sought to increase the potential for the health community to enhance human security by promoting the integration of health care with conflict management in selected conflict and post-conflict situations. IRSS's experience shows that social reconstruction, the healing of inter-communal relationships, and the transformation of violence-habituated systems can be significantly enhanced by training and assistance in the concepts and skills of conflict management. In this context, the term 'inter-communal' refers to the class of racial, ethnic, religious, and ideological conflicts that involve differences between communities of people, rather than individuals or governments, regardless of whether those communities exist within or across international borders. The field of conflict management encompasses efforts to prevent violent conflict, to mediate existing conflict, and to reconcile communities in the aftermath of violent conflict. Conflict management processes that address the underlying causes of conflict and provide sustainable structures for adaptive social change can transform the ways in which groups and societies deal with differences. This transformation, away from dealing with differences through violence and destruction, and toward constructive, co-operative interaction, is essential to sustainable peace, social justice and human security.

In 1996, IRSS launched the Health Bridges for Peace (HBP) project to help health-care professionals realise their potential to heal violence-ravaged individuals and communities. The project's purpose is to utilise a shared concern, the restoration of public health, as a vehicle to convene and train health-care professionals in conflict management and community-reconciliation techniques. Once these professionals are trained, they are assisted in designing and implementing inter-communal activities that integrate community reconciliation and conflict prevention into health-care delivery. The first HBP field programme was initiated in 1997 in the former Yugoslavia, and the second in the North Caucasus in November 1998.

The programme in former Yugoslavia helped to launch the Medical Network for Social Reconstruction in the former Yugoslavia (the Medical Network). This is a network of health-care professionals, drawn from all parts of the former Yugoslavia, dedicated to facilitating healing and recovery processes that promote individual and community health and empowerment and the prevention of future conflicts in this region. It is founded upon two major beliefs:

> Violent conflict and war are the ultimate threat to public health; and the health community has a unique and crucial role to play in promoting a healthy society, by mending the physical and psychological wounds of individuals and communities, by rebuilding structures for public health care, and by creating bridges for community reconstruction and social reconciliation.

The Medical Network convenes conferences and engages in health-care delivery and social-reconstruction activities. It has convened nine international HBP conferences and more than thirty workshops and seminars. More than four hundred physicians, psychologists, government officials, administrators and academicians from all parts of the former Yugoslavia have participated in its conferences, seminars and meetings, exhibiting a high level of inter-ethnic co-operation. It has promoted professional exchange, training and joint humanitarian-assistance projects in a variety of areas, including: war-trauma recovery; special issues in refugee medicine; social reconstruction in co-operation with other professional groups (police, teachers, social workers);

health care for the war-injured physically challenged; and special issues of war-affected children.

Training is recognised within the Medical Network as one of the most effective ways to bring together professionals from divided communities. Training programmes have been developed and taught by Medical Network members in co-operation with international experts. The training of physicians from Bosnia, Serbia and Croatia has provided a context for co-operation and the renewal of relationships. Many training programmes have involved the training of trainers, and mixed-ethnic teams of trainers have been developed.

One of the first co-operative projects of the Network was the development of a training programme for psychosocial assistance to promote trauma recovery. This is closely related to peacebuilding efforts; both are ultimately about developing or restoring healthy human relationships. Trauma recovery implies the decrease of loneliness, mood improvement, a sense of inner peace, a decrease in isolation, anger and bitterness, and a decrease in feelings of animosity and hatred toward others; it can only take place in the context of relationships. Recovery cannot occur in isolation because it is necessary to heal the psychological faculties that were damaged by the trauma, and this healing can only occur through relationships with other people.

Trauma-recovery training has both content and relational dimensions. The content of the training changes as the context evolves from basic trauma treatment to large-scale social reconstruction. The relational dimension also evolves, as trainers, caregivers and their clients all need sustainable support structures that can develop as their roles evolve. Trauma healing must, therefore, be integrated into a programme of psychosocial assistance that seeks to strengthen the remaining healthy resources within individuals, families and communities, and helps new resources evolve. In turn, psychosocial efforts must be synergistic with related humanitarian and democracy-building efforts in a region. In this way, trauma recovery can lead to an integrated process of rebuilding the social infrastructure of a violence-ravaged society while promoting reintegration, resettlement and retraining.

Building a community-based psychosocial assistance programme will open the way for the development of the NGO sector, and can lead to the development of new, community-based organisations. The Medical Network has found it valuable to mobilise large numbers of volunteers for these organisations. In all post-war situations there is widespread poverty, under-utilisation of human resources, and a lack of state-supported health services. In response, health professionals can promote volunteer action, training and empowering individuals and groups to engage in (unpaid) public-service and social-reconstruction activities. Volunteers, collaborating with the health professionals, can significantly improve the quality of life of persons with medical and psychosocial problems. Through voluntary work the values and practice of solidarity and of mutual help, regardless of religious, national or other attributes, are reinforced and promoted. In the period 1999–2002,

Medical Network psychosocial-assistance programmes have incorporated an estimated 4,000 volunteers from all parts of former Yugoslavia into social-reconstruction efforts that enhance human security in the region.

The Medical Network has reached out to physicians from other war-devastated areas. In April 1998, physicians from Chechnya were guests at a Medical Network conference in Sarajevo. Later that year, IRSS convened a meeting in the North Caucasus that brought together Chechen, Ingush, North Ossetian and Russian health professionals for conflict-management training and guidance in developing collaborative public-heath activities. From this meeting the Medical Alliance for Peace through Health in the North Caucasus (Medical Alliance) was born. Its planned co-operative public health projects, to be assisted by WHO, include: a regional network on tuberculosis control; co-operative centres for psycho-social rehabilitation; a North Caucasus inter-regional training centre for the prevention of drug addiction; and a co-operative programme for prosthetic assistance to amputees in the North Caucasus.

HBP field programmes have provided new hopes and possibilities to numerous indigenous health professionals. Many of them were in despair, and had all but given up their medical practice in the face of human and physical destruction. The HBP project has given them new opportunities, a new vision and a new role. It has demonstrated the potential of healing and collaborative action, and has built bridges between colleagues who thought they could never again work together. HBP has expanded the mission of international agency field staff and has sparked great excitement, both in the field and at headquarters.

The impact of HBP is not limited geographically to the former Yugoslavia and the North Caucasus. Health professionals from many other conflict areas (including other parts of Europe, Central Asia, South America and the Middle East) are interested in learning from, and emulating, the HBP programmes. International health and humanitarian assistance agencies have participated in IRSS's programmes or developed health-bridges programmes of their own. Some of these agencies are contracting with, or collaborating with, Medical Network personnel for trauma-recovery and peacebuilding work. At the policy level, IRSS is working with international organisations to develop policies and programmes whereby humanitarian assistance can be synergistic with the building of a healthy civil society, the enhancement of social justice and human security, and the creation of a culture of peace.

Pursuing public health within a human-security framework

Clearly, health is a crucial domain of human security, and a human-security approach rooted in international consensus can bring added value to existing policies and programmes. Thus, the world would benefit from a comprehensive strategy for enhancing public health within a human-security framework.

An effective strategy will operate through existing institutions and promote collaboration by: national governments; international agencies; private foundations;

academic institutions; professional groups; citizen organisations; and businesses, including pharmaceutical companies. Collaboration of this kind has become increasingly frequent in the modern era, but must be more intensive and must engage additional actors. It is especially important that people and institutions whose focus has been on national defence and security find a common purpose with their counterparts whose focus is health, social justice, and human security.

There needs to be a consensual definition of human security and an analytic and operational framework for the application of human security, which must support forward-looking assessments of potential threats to security and the development of plans to respond to these threats. The lessons of experience must be rapidly incorporated into programmes. This will require new mechanisms for information exchange, organisational learning and programme evaluation. These activities must proceed in a decentralised manner without any over-arching authority. There is no organisation that possesses such authority and, in any event, the pursuit of social justice requires broad-based collaboration.

Given the multiple tasks that must be performed, and the diversity of actors involved, there must be some division of labour. We propose four synergistic strands of effort to refine and implement the overall strategy: policy development; specific programme opportunities; research, training and technical collaboration; and outreach and promotion.

Work on *policy development* should be informed by experience in the field, to ensure that policies have an empirical basis. Policy decisions should be iterative, so that changes can be made as lessons are learned from experience. Also, policies must account for the evolving interests of the many actors involved. These are demanding requirements.

A wide variety of *specific programme opportunities* are available. Much work will be required to identify, select, plan and implement programmes that respond to these opportunities. The geographic scope of these pro-grammes will range from the local to the global. Each programme should follow a structured-learning model, whereby the outcomes of actions are monitored and documented, and implementation is adjusted accordingly. Findings from this experience should be widely shared, to inform policy development and other strands of effort.

Research, training and technical collaboration are inter-related. A major focus of the research effort should be on learning from experience, whether at the policy level or through work on the ground. This would be accom-plished by designing structured-learning evaluation models for policy and programme initiatives, and by independently observing these initiatives. The training effort would include building human capacities for research and for implementation of human-security programmes. Training would give special attention to development of the leadership and management skills that are required when working with diverse actors, in multi-sectoral contexts, to achieve shared goals. Developing these skills would be one of the most significant value-added contributions that a human-security approach would make. The technical collaboration effort would involve the creation of professional relationships among researchers, managers, trainers and practitioners, world-wide. This effort would benefit from the establishment of an inter-university network for research and training on health, social justice and human security.

In the *outreach and promotion* strand of effort, work would be undertaken to establish and maintain relationships with relevant actors, including those who are not directly involved in human-security initiatives. One purpose of these relationships would be to propagate knowledge about human-security initiatives and their accomplishments, the second would be to obtain knowledge and other resources, including financial support.

References

1. Annan K. Foreword. In: McRae R., Hubert D., eds. *Human Security and the New Diplomacy: Protecting People, Promoting Peace.* Montreal: McGill-Queen's University Press, 2001.
2. World Bank. *World Development Report 2000–2001: Attacking Poverty.* New York: Oxford University Press, 2001: 1.
2a. Jenssen C. *Medicine Against War: An Historical Review of the Anti-War Activities of Physicians.* In: Taipale I., et al., editors. *War or Health? A Reader.* Helsinki, Finland: Physicians for Social Responsibility, 2001: 9.
3. Commission on Macroeconomics and Health. *Macroeconomics and Health: Investing in Health for Economic Development, Executive Summary.* Geneva: World Health Organization 2001: 2.
4. National Intelligence Council. The Global Infectious Disease Threat and Its Implications for the United States. Jan 2000. Available from URL: http://www.cia.gov/cia/publications/nie/report/nie99–17d.html.
5. Wynia M. K., Lawrence G. The bioterrorist threat and access to health care. *Science* 2002; **296**: 1613.
6. Cranna M., ed. *The True Cost of Conflict.* New York: New Press, 1994.
7. Advisory Group Conclusions, In: special issue: *Nuclear War: The Aftermath. Ambio* 1982, 11: 162.
8. Kugler, R. L. *Toward a Dangerous World: U.S. National Strategy for the Coming Turbulence.* Santa Monica CA: RAND, National Defense Research Institute, 1995.
9. Raskin P., Banuri T., Gallopin G., *et al. Great Transition: The Promise and Lure of the Times Ahead.* Boston MA: Stockholm Environment Institute, 2002: 11.
10. Acharya A. Human Security. *International Journal* Summer 2001: 442–460.
11. Edson S. *Human Security: An Extended and Annotated International Bibliography.* Cambridge, UK: Centre for History and Economics, King's College, 2001.
12. King G., Murray C. J. L. Rethinking Human Security. *Political Science Quarterly* 2001–02; 116: 585–610.
13. Department of Foreign Affairs and International Trade. *Human Security: Safety for People in a Changing World.* Ottawa, Ontario: Department of Foreign Affairs and International Trade, 1999: 3.
14. Independent Commission on Disarmament and Security Issues. *Common Security: A Blueprint for Survival.* New York: Simon and Schuster, 1982.

15. International Physicians for the Prevention of Nuclear War. *Maintain Life on Earth: Documentation of the Sixth World Congress of IPPNW*. Neckarsulm and Munich: Jungjohann Verlagsgesellschaft, 1987.

16. United Nations Development Program. *Human Development Report 1994: New Dimensions of Human Security*. New York: Oxford University Press, 1994.

17. Department of Foreign Affairs and International Trade. *Freedom from Fear: Canada's Foreign Policy for Human Security*. Ottawa, Ontario: Department of Foreign Affairs and International Trade, 2000: 3.

18. The Ministry of Foreign Affairs of Japan. *2000 Diplomatic Bluebook*. 2000: Chapter II, Section 3. Available from URL: http://www.mofa.go.jp/policy/other/bluebook/2000

19. International Commission on Intervention and State Sovereignty. *The Responsibility to Protect*. Ottawa: International Development Research Centre, 2001.

20. Alkire S. Conceptual Framework for Human Security. 16 Feb 2002. Available from URL: http://www.humansecurity-chs.org/doc/frame.html

21. United Nations General Assembly. *Resolution 55/2, United Nations Millennium Declaration*. New York: 18 Sept 2000.

22. Hartmann S. Human security: conference stresses links between health, security. *UN Wire* March 2002.

23. WHO Regional Committee for the Eastern Mediterranean. *Resolution Em/Rc48/R.2, Regarding the Annual Report of the Regional Director for the Year 2000 and Progress Reports*, 2001 Oct: para. 15.3.

24. Shiffman J. Orchestrating collaboration among contending states: the World Health Organization and infectious disease control in southeast Asia. In: Montgomery J. D. and Glazer N., eds. *Sovereignty under Challenge*. New Brunswick NJ: Transaction Publishers, 2002: 143–163.

25. Jha P., Mills A., Hanson K., *et al.* Improving the health of the global poor. *Science* 2002; 295: 2036–9.

26. Gutlove P. Health as a bridge to peace: the role of health professionals in conflict management and community reconciliation. *Violence and Health: Proceedings of a WHO Global Symposium*. Kobe: World Health Organization, 2000.

27. Hotez P. Vaccine diplomacy. *Foreign Policy*, May/June 2001: 68–69.

28. Gutlove P. Health Bridges for Peace: integrating health care and community reconciliation. *Med Confl Surviv* 1998; 14: 6–23.

29. War and Health Program of McMaster University. *A Health to Peace Handbook*. Hamilton, Ontario: McMaster University, 1996: 5.

30. Peters M. A. Shots of vaccine instead of shots of artillery. In: *A Health to Peace Handbook*. Hamilton, Ontario: McMaster University, 1996: 11.

31. World Health Organization. *Health in Social Development*. Position Paper. Copenhagen: WHO, 1995.

32. Swartz S. Local support for peace through health. In: *A Health to Peace Handbook*. Hamilton, Ontario: McMaster University, 1996: 35–42.

33. MacQueen G., Santa-Barbara J., Neufeld V., Yusuf S., Horton R. Health and Peace: time for a new discipline. *Lancet* 2001; 357: 1460–1.

7

A PATHOLOGY OF PUBLIC HEALTH SECURITISM: APPROACHING PANDEMICS AS SECURITY THREATS

David P. Fidler

Source: Andrew F. Cooper, John J. Kirton and Ted Schrecker (eds) *Governing Global Health: Challenge, Response, Innovation*, Aldershot: Ashgate, 2007, pp. 41–63.

One of the most interesting and controversial features of the discourse on public health governance in the past decade concerns the proliferation of attempts to approach public health problems as security threats. These diverse efforts have formed part of the process that experts call the securitisation of public health. The securitisation process has raised many challenging issues and questions, including disagreements over the prudence of the governance strategy of securitising public health. Is the securitisation paradigm the best way forward with respect to pandemic preparedness and response?

Public health governance has now entered a post-securitisation phase. Viewing public health through the lens of security has become an integral aspect of public health governance in the 21st century. In short, securitisation has happened, and analysis should direct its attention to sorting out the implications of this sea change in public health governance. Entering into the post-securitisation phase means that the policy belief that public health can be improved by framing and approaching problems through security-related tactics and strategies has become a leading driver of public health governance.

The emergence and intensifying strength of this belief in 'public health securitism' represents a significant change for public health governance nationally and internationally. The coming of age of this belief in the power of linking public health and security adds a new element to thinking about the structure and dynamics of public health governance. Given its significance, it is important to deepen our understanding of this phenomenon and its implications for the future.

This chapter presents a pathology of public health securitism in order to outline the causes, processes, and consequences of this seminal development for the world of public health policy. This pathology reveals that the securitisation of public health has some unfinished business. Although the belief in the need to connect public health to concepts of security is strong, it has not been characterised by analytical rigour. A leading challenge in the post-securitisation phase is to strengthen the analytical content of public health securitism. This chapter reviews possible ways to bring clarity and stability to thinking about the relationship between public health and security. These approaches share the objective of providing a way to determine what public health threats are security issues and thus deserve the policy priority such a designation creates.

The chapter also examines three pandemics through the focus provided by analysing the different ways of defining how public health and security relate to each other. These pandemics are the continuing HIV/AIDS pandemic, mounting fears about pandemic influenza, and the growing global spread of tobacco-related diseases. These case studies shed light on how approaching pandemics as security threats illustrates the current and future importance of public health securitism for public health governance.

Public health governance's post-securitisation phase

As a policy matter, thinking about public health in terms of security is a recent phenomenon, emerging only since the mid 1990s. Public health and security concepts were linked earlier. The preamble of the constitution of the World Health Organization (WHO) proclaimed in 1946 that 'the health of all peoples is fundamental to the attainment of peace and security' (WHO 1994). Such earlier linkages did not, however, feature in the manner in which either national or international governance on public health developed in the post-World War II period.

The securitisation phase for public health governance began in the mid 1990s in response to three major developments: heightened fears about the proliferation of bioweapons, especially among terrorist groups; the continued global spread of HIV/AIDS and the pandemic's increasingly devastating political, economic, and social implications in the developing world; and growing awareness about deepening vulnerabilities of populations in rich and poor countries caused by the globalised spread of disease risks, be they pathogens, products, or pollutants. These developments stimulated analysts to begin to frame public health problems as security threats.

These attempts to securitise public health concerns attracted attention, as new paradigms tend to do. A significant literature developed as more people participated in the debate. Indeed, the securitisation debate remains lively. However, the securitisation process is now over. Efforts to approach public health challenges through security concepts have prevailed in a way that constitutes a transformative development for public health governance.

127

The most compelling evidence that the securitisation of public health has occurred, and now constitutes part of the public health governance landscape, can be found in the diverse ways security concepts have been used to draw attention to public health problems. The use of security as a trope has become ubiquitous in how experts frame public health governance. The prominence of security concepts in debates about public health threats and governance is historically unprecedented.

Academic literature and policy advocacy on security and public health include arguments that elevate the importance of public health with respect to the security of individuals, the nation-state, the international system of states, and the global community. The concept of human security holds that individuals are the proper subject matter for thinking about security (United Nations Development Programme [UNDP] 1994), and those interested in human security have attempted to integrate the threat that diseases pose to individuals and their communities into the human security approach (Commission on Human Security 2003).

More traditional notions of security focus on the nation-state and concern themselves with threats to national security (Princeton Project on National Security 2005). In this realm, too, public health has frequently appeared, in connection both with the threat posed by weapons of mass destruction (WMD), particularly bioweapons, and with the damage to a state's material power that naturally occurring communicable diseases could inflict (United States 2002; Fidler 2003). Public health problems have also been framed as indirect threats to national security, as illustrated by analysis that points to the ability of HIV/AIDS to contribute to the destabilisation of 'countries of strategic concern' to the United States (Eberstadt 2002; Garrett 2005).

A broader, but still traditional, perspective on security concerns international security, or the security relationships that exist among sovereign states. Although questions of war and armed conflict have dominated the study of international security, public health has appeared increasingly frequently on the international security agenda. The United Nations Security Council (UNSC) has, for example, twice addressed the HIV/AIDS pandemic as a threat to international peace and security (UNSC 2000, 2005). Proposals for UN reform have included recommendations that the UNSC use its mandate to maintain international peace and security in cases involving overwhelming outbreaks of communicable diseases (UN 2004, 2005).

Still more expansive concepts of security, such as those that focus on the security of the community of states and non-state actors, or global society, also incorporate public health considerations. The WHO (2001) described its efforts to improve global communicable disease surveillance and response capabilities as the pursuit of 'global health security'. The UN secretary general and the high-level panel he appointed to advise him on UN reform placed improving national and global public health at the centre of a new vision for collective security, a vision that went beyond the state-centric perspective that dominated the UN's post-World War II activities (UN 2004; UNSC 2005). The extent to which public health is central to this vision of 'comprehensive collective security' is remarkable in both the annals of public health and UN thinking on collective security.

To be sure, these diverse perspectives on what security means do not reveal consensus on the meaning of security or what the appropriate level of analysis is for security policy. What is common among these different, often antagonistic frameworks is that they all have made efforts to address public health problems. These activities across such a broad range of security outlooks demonstrate an increasing awareness about the political and governance importance of public health not seen in previous decades of security discourse. More importantly, these activities reveal a strong belief in a two-sided policy relationship: public health can be improved through a security focus, and security can be enhanced by incorporating public health concerns.

The strength of the policy belief in public health securitism across the range of security concepts has made such securitisation a permanent feature of public health governance in the 21st century. Arguments may still rage about whether it is good or bad for public health governance. But securitisation has happened at every conceivable level of security and public health analysis, even some not mentioned above (for example, the concept of ecological security) (Pirages 1997).

Some may doubt the sincerity of some efforts to connect public health and security, such as the cynical playing of the 'security card' by public health officials and advocates desperate for more political attention and economic resources. The deeper the cynicism the stronger the argument about the triumph of public health securitism becomes. Such cynicism reflects a coldly calculated decision that public health can be improved by appealing to security concepts and considerations. Similarly, some may find novel concepts, such as human security, hopelessly naive. However, the deep commitment to human security by many communities, and their integration of public health into this commitment, provides evidence of the power of the belief that security-related thinking can improve public health (Commission on Human Security 2003). When the United States Central Intelligence Agency and human rights advocates both agree that security needs mandate improvements in public health nationally and internationally, something interesting and perhaps profound has taken place (Fidler 2004).

Paradigm aggregation: public health securitism and public health governance

The emergence of public health securitism has produced paradigm aggregation rather than a paradigm shift. Post-securitisation public health governance involves three frameworks that converge to produce the political, economic, and moral context in which public health policy operates. The sea change that public

129

health securitism represents is best viewed in light of security considerations entering into a governance context previously oriented by concerns involving economic considerations and aspirations grounded in concepts of human dignity.

As historians of international health diplomacy have made clear, international cooperation on public health originated in the concerns of the European great powers with the economic burdens their trade and commerce suffered through the application of disparate, uncoordinated, and often irrational national quarantine systems (Goodman 1971; Howard-Jones 1950, 1975). The threat of the international spread of communicable diseases was thus constructed predominantly as a threat to the economic opportunities that trade and commerce provided states. This template dominated how states approached international health cooperation in the first century of such cooperation.

The focus of international health efforts slowly drifted away from national economic self-interest as humanitarian concerns about health in other countries gradually emerged prior to World War II. The establishment of the WHO in 1948 accelerated this trend because the organisation directed most of its energies toward trying to improve public health in developing countries (Pannenborg 1979). Animating this concern with health conditions in poor countries was the vision for health proclaimed in the preamble of the WHO constitution (WHO 1994). The idea that the enjoyment of the highest attainable standard of health was a fundamental human right was central to this vision.

The humanitarian and rights-based framework taking shape through WHO activities was connected to efforts in development being pushed by developing countries in the aftermath of decolonisation. The Declaration of Alma-Ata in 1978, which launched the Health for All by the Year 2000 initiative, captured the convergence of humanitarianism, the right to health, and the new thinking on development (International Conference on Primary Health Care 1978). The declaration reaffirmed the right to health, asserted that health inequalities between developed and developing countries were unacceptable, and linked health for all to the economic and social development strategies found in the so-called New International Economic Order (NIEO).

The emergence of linkages between security and public health since 1995 adds yet another governance template to the economic-based and human dignity-based frameworks that prevailed in earlier periods. Some concerns expressed about the securitisation of public health involved fears that security-based attitudes are eclipsing or subordinating the human dignity template that prevailed in international health governance from the WHO's establishment. As explored below, the securitisation process does create tensions with the human dignity agenda; but this process has not been a zero-sum game among the economic, human dignity, and security templates of public health governance.

Without question, security-based arguments have contributed to a new emphasis on the material self-interests of states with respect to public health governance. These arguments resonate with the original governance template for international health cooperation that reflected the economic concerns of the great powers. The security-related perspectives also help highlight the increasing economic costs that countries face from the globalisation of disease, especially with respect to their export interests. With disease rising as a threat to the state's material power and well-being, states have started to engage public health governance with more intensity.

Human dignity has not, however, dropped off the agenda. The securitisation process has included security concepts, especially human security, that conceive of security more broadly than the traditional narrow emphasis on the material power and interests of states. In addition, one of the dominant themes of the securitisation process has been that international cooperation and the national and global involvement of non-state actors are essential in public health governance to achieve security, whether the concept of security in question is narrow or broad. The commonalities of the strategies required to engage in successful public health governance in the early 21st century allow the economic, human dignity, and security templates to coexist, held together by the epidemiological requirements of addressing diseases effectively in an intensely globalising environment.

Pathology of public health securitism

Understanding that public health securitism has taken public health governance into a post-securitisation phase is important, but it is not sufficient for comprehending the seminal nature of this change in attitudes, strategies, and tactics concerning public health governance. This section provides a pathology of public health securitism, or an exploration of the causes, processes, and consequences of this important development in public health governance.[1] This brief examination supports the belief that security-based arguments have utility for public health policy.

Causes

The rise of public health securitism has many causes. But cutting across these causes is the realisation that the danger presented by diseases to states, peoples, and individuals has increased in the last decades of the 20th century and early stages of the 21st century. The *Oxford English Dictionary* defines security as 'the condition of being protected from or not exposed to danger'. The trend toward using security-based thinking and concepts in a time of increasing disease danger makes sense, at a basic level. The key to understanding the causes of public health securitism involves the scrutiny of the reasons why diseases are more dangerous in the early part of the 21st century than they were in the post-World War II period.

Analyses of communicable disease emergence provide insight into the increasing dangers these diseases present. In its well-known report, the U.S. Institute of Medicine's Committee on Microbial Threats to Health in the

Table 1 Factors in the Emergence of Communicable Diseases.

1	Microbial adaptation and change
2	Human susceptibility to infection
3	Climate and weather
4	Changing ecosystems
5	Human demographics and behaviour
6	Economic development and land use
7	International travel and commerce
8	Technology and industry
9	Breakdown of public health measures
10	Poverty and social inequality
11	War and famine
12	Lack of political will
13	Intent to harm (e.g., bioterrorism)

Source: Smolinski, Hamburg, and Lederberg (2003).

21st Century identified 13 factors that produce microbial dangers for the U.S. and other countries (see Table 1) (Smolinski, Hamburg, and Lederberg 2003). Similarly, public health experts argue that dramatic changes in patterns of product consumption, stimulated by the globalisation of trade and lifestyle choices, significantly increase risks to health, as evidenced by growing pandemics of chronic diseases related to tobacco use and obesity (Beaglehole and Yach 2003).

Increasing risks and dangers from diseases arise in an environment in which public health governance has proved ill equipped to respond. The turn to security-based arguments involves the perception that the human dignity and economic templates that prevailed in earlier historical periods are insufficient bases, on their own, for the kind of robust governance required in the early 21st century. With disease dangers rising, the rallying cries of the right to health and Health For All no longer carry the weight they previously did. Framing disease dangers in terms of security has proven to be attractive across political and ideological spectrums as an approach that can motivate states and communities to strengthen national and global public health.

Processes

In order to understand how the belief that security-related arguments could provide policy traction for public health governance developed as rapidly and strongly it is necessary to look at various processes through which this transformation occurred. These processes can be divided into practical, tactical, and strategic categories. At the practical level, many people concerned about growing disease dangers in a context of weak to non-existent public health capabilities used every argument available to raise policy attention about this governance challenge. Thus, security-based arguments were intermingled with economic rationales and appeals to humanitarian impulses in a melange that reflected a call for urgent action rather than a desire for theoretical coherency.

At the tactical level, there have been modifications made to accommodate public health concerns in traditional security concepts and practices. Thinking on U.S. national security attempted to graft public health into its priorities. This grafting process involved two aspects. First, the traditional Cold War definition of national security as security against the military power and potential military violence from other states began to look anachronistic when the U.S. felt threatened by potential violence from non-state actors, notably terrorists. Although national security was still defined in terms of threats of exogenous violence, the range of potential actors that could pose a security threat expanded in light of the terrorist threat. Part of that terrorist threat involved the possible use of bioweapons against the U.S., a threat that came to pass with the anthrax attacks of October 2001. This threat against the U.S. meant that the quality of public health systems in the U.S. and in other countries grew in national security importance.

Second, the post-Cold War period also encouraged policy makers and policy thinkers to question the narrow perspective on U.S. national security that prevailed during the long conflict with the Soviet Union. This questioning involved experts analysing whether U.S. national security policy should consider transnational phenomena, such as environmental degradation and communicable diseases, as threats to the material power, interests, and well-being of the United States. Part of this approach posited whether naturally occurring communicable diseases could directly cause such material damage to the U.S. as to be a threat akin to a violent attack. Another facet of this outlook focussed on how transnational phenomena might present indirect national security problems for the United States. Could, for example, environmental degradation or communicable diseases contribute to the violent destabilisation of important countries or regions and thus damage U.S. interests and power overseas?

At the strategic level, the process involved fundamentally rethinking the concept of security. Here, the rapid development of human security as a rival to the traditional, state-centric perspectives on security is the most important innovation. Human security's focus on the individual as the core subject of security policy opened more space in security thinking for public health issues. The tactical process described above allowed public health to have some national security significance, but the centre of policy attention remained the security of the nation-state in terms of its material power. Human security challenged the assumptions of the traditional national security template and thus created greater possibilities for states and the international community to consider public health more seriously as a security issue.

These practical, tactical, and strategic processes do not mesh into each other to produce a harmonised process that generated public health securitism. Each individually contributed to the politics that has gradually led to public health securitism's emergence. The messiness of the processes is one reason why public health governance faces some unfinished business in its post-securitisation phase.

Consequences

The last element of the pathology of public health securitism concerns its consequences. One consequence has already been highlighted — the aggregation of templates informing public health governance. This aggregation is not without competition and friction. The increased dangers that diseases present have reconnected the security and economic self-interests of states with public health governance. This reality has created tension with the governance template focussed on human dignity, with its concerns about the right to health and equitable social and economic development.

At one level, these tensions merely indicate that public health governance is returning to normality in international relations. Most issues involving international politics and foreign policy experience friction between interest-based approaches and value-based approaches. Public health governance after World War II witnessed the withering of great power interest in international disease control and prevention largely because these states enjoyed steadily improving national public health outcomes. International health activities devolved to the 'low politics' of 'mere humanitarianism' in international relations, allowing the human dignity template to appear dominant in the ethos of international health cooperation. The securitisation of public health has made what appeared to be a fundamental transformation look more like a transitory mirage.

The consequences of the securitisation of public health are not, however, exclusively about the potential fragmentation of public health governance into a rivalry between interests and values. The epidemiological requirements of addressing mounting disease dangers do not change according to whether an interest-based approach or a value-based perspective dominates. Surveillance remains critical under the framework of either public health securitism or human dignity. Vaccines and antibiotics do not change their physiological effects depending on whether the impetus behind their use is based on security or rights. Thus the nature of public health governance allows a degree of convergence between interest-centric and value-centric perspectives on solutions to disease dangers.

This convergence of interests and values forces both sides of the debate to think about public health security in depth. Thinking of disease threats as security dangers requires understanding not only disease-specific epidemiology but also the broader determinants of disease dangers. Public health securitism does not, by definition, imply that concern with the social determinants of health is jettisoned because security becomes an organising policy framework. Seeing diseases as security dangers actually forces interest-based approaches to appreciate the depth of the policy needs required to address disease dangers.

Where public health securitism has its greatest consequences for public health governance is in the area of priority setting. The attractiveness of security-related arguments flows from the priority policy attention that security threats are perceived to receive. The process of securitisation was a process of prioritisation in public health governance. This dynamic helps explain why virtually everybody has jumped on the security bandwagon since 1995. Like the various processes that produced public health securitism, the bandwagoning did not represent a coherent sorting out of priorities but rather a pluralistic endeavour that privileged security arguments without producing policy coherency on prioritisation.

A theme in the untidy bandwagoning process concerns priority setting between communicable and non-communicable diseases. Security-based arguments tend to cluster around communicable diseases. National security concerns identified bioweapons as the threat, especially those that might use contagious pathogens. The international security discourse has also centred on communicable diseases, as illustrated by the UNSC's work on HIV/AIDS. Initiatives informed by the concept of human security have gravitated toward communicable disease dangers, as evidenced by the focus on communicable disease problems in the Millennium Development Goals (MDGs) (WHO 2006a).

Public health securitism need not be restricted to communicable disease problems. Rather, the securitisation of public health governance makes it more difficult to elevate many non-communicable disease problems. The nature of some of the leading problems, such as tobacco-related diseases and obesity, makes the effort to use security-based arguments more difficult both in a conceptual sense and in terms of common sense. A similar difficulty arises with respect to tobacco-related and obesity-related diseases and the human rights framework because the spread of such non-communicable diseases requires, in most cases, voluntary participation in behaviour that is bad for one's own immediate health and the health of others. The difficulties experienced within the security and human rights frameworks perhaps explain the efforts made to cast non-communicable diseases as material burdens on the economic interests of countries and corporations.

Unfinished business: toward greater analytical rigour in the relationship between security and public health

Thus the dawn of the post-securitisation phase for public health governance does not mean that public health securitism has produced a clear and coherent consensus on the relationship between security and public health. Public health securitism has proved to be a powerful but promiscuous idea that will not disappear any time soon from the landscape of public health governance. The pathology of public health securitism points to some unfinished business, especially with respect to bringing more analytical clarity to the identification of security problems within public health governance.

There are four different ways to bring order to the process of identifying what public health problems pose security threats. Each of these frameworks shares the common goal of providing parameters for deciding what public health concerns should be labelled security threats and given the policy priority such threats require. These four contribute to more rigorous analysis of the security-public health relationship.

Bioweapons framework

Traditional notions of security have been based on the violence paradigm — the threat of exogenous violence against the state, its military power, or its people (Princeton Project on National Security 2005). The violence paradigm continues to have significant power because 1) threats of violence clearly fall within any definition of security and 2) states have to remain vigilant against potential violent threats. The bioweapons framework maintains that securitisation of public health should only involve public health's relationship to the identification of, and responses to, bioweapons threats. This approach produces a very narrow perspective because it rejects treating, for example, naturally occurring communicable diseases as security concerns.

The legitimacy of the bioweapons framework depends on the appropriateness of relying on the violence paradigm as the exclusive basis for thinking about security nationally or internationally. This framework is parsimonious and provides clear direction in terms of how public health governance should be securitised. Although some actions taken to improve security against bioweapons violence have general public health benefits (such as surveillance), these positive externalities for public health governance are not the intended security objective.

The bioweapons framework is unlikely to carry the day in the post-securitisation phase of public health governance. It recommends a drastic retrenchment in public health securitism that essentially throws every other perspective on security off the securitisation bandwagon. More fundamentally, this perspective rejects the broader thrust of the securitisation of public health governance — that disease dangers of multiple varieties have emerged that threaten individuals, populations, the state, and the international community. The 'back to the future' approach counselled by the bioweapons framework does not respond to the globalisation of disease threats that public health governance must address.

Communicable disease framework

A second approach involves limiting securitisation to communicable diseases. As noted earlier, the securitisation of public health governance has gravitated toward communicable diseases as the most prominent dangers to public health in the early 21st century. Limiting public health securitism to communicable diseases would also provide a bright-line rule for distinguishing what public health problems should be accorded security status. With such a limitation in place, securitising public health could focus on what communicable diseases are sufficiently dangerous to warrant heightened governance attention. Unlike the bioweapons framework, the communicable disease approach does not exclude looking at communicable disease problems through security perspectives that are broader than the violence paradigm.

The communicable disease framework may, however, be under-inclusive in terms of disease threats and over-inclusive in terms of concepts of security. The choice to exclude all non-communicable disease threats from public health securitisation neglects the acute dangers that can be posed by some such diseases. International legal regimes in trade and environmental protection have long recognised that pollutants and contaminants can pose extraordinary dangers to public health and should be prevented, protected against, and, if necessary, controlled. For example, states have used international law to address transboundary pollution generally and transboundary pollution caused by industrial or nuclear accidents specifically (Birnie and Boyle 2002). To leave these types of situations outside an understanding of public health's relationship with security appears arbitrary in light of all the diplomatic activity and international law devoted to dangerous non-communicable disease threats.

In terms of concepts of security, the communicable disease framework might be over-inclusive because the framework does not contain any parameters for determining which communicable disease problems deserve security status and which do not. Not all communicable diseases should be considered security threats. Some methodology is required for determining when a communicable disease becomes a security threat. The communicable disease framework does not provide this methodology. Without such a methodology, the concept of security could become little more than a rhetorical device used to bring more policy attention to a wide variety of communicable diseases.

Decision tree frameworks

A more sophisticated approach to bringing some conceptual order to the relationship between security and public health has appeared in decision tree frameworks. These break the question of a public health issue as a security threat into a series of factors that lead analysis to specific conclusions. Decision tree frameworks have appeared in the scholarship of Henry Feldbaum and Kelley Lee (2004) and of Colin McInnes (2004), as well as in the approach used by the WHO (2005) in the new International Health Regulations (IHR[2005]) adopted in May 2005.

The work of Feldbaum and Lee and of McInnes focusses on the need to improve analytical approaches to deciding what health problems are global health security issues. Figure 1 provides the Feldbaum-Lee decision tree, and

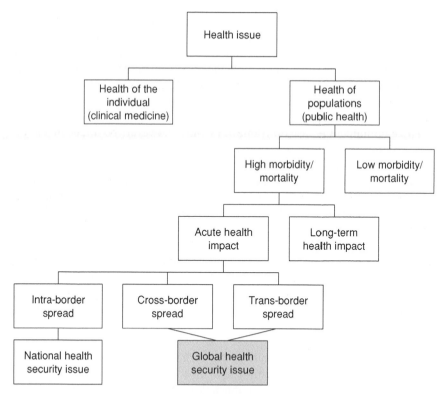

Figure 1 Feldbaum-Lee Decision Tree for Defining a Global Health Security Issue.
Source: Feldbaum and Lee (2004, 25).

Figure 2 provides the McInnes decision tree. Both construct a way to determine whether a health issue is a risk to the individual national security threat or is a global health security issue. The decision trees allow their analytical frameworks to be applied to bioweapons, communicable diseases, or non-communicable diseases. Unlike the communicable disease framework, the decision trees include a methodology for deciding whether a given problem is a security threat and what type of security threat it represents.

In the IHR(2005), a decision instrument guides states parties in determining what disease events may constitute a 'public health emergency of international concern' for the purposes of notifying the WHO (see Figure 3). Public health emergencies of international concern are not defined in the IHR(2005) as security threats, but the concept of a public health emergency of international concern is not far removed from identifying dangerous disease events as security problems. According to the WHO, for example, the IHR(2005) is a core component of its strategy to improve global health security (Fidler 2005). Like the academic decision trees, the IHR(2005) decision instrument

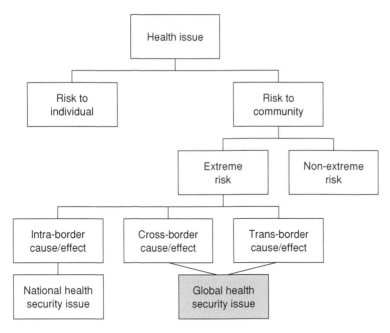

Figure 2 McInnes Decision Tree for Defining a Global Health Security Issue.
Source: McInnes (2004, 55).

applies to communicable and non-communicable disease events (whether intentionally caused, accidental, or naturally occurring) and thus avoids the under-inclusiveness of the bioweapons and communicable disease frameworks.

These decision tree approaches share the common elements of identifying acute health risks that cause, or have the potential to cause, high levels of morbidity and mortality as either security threats or public health emergencies of international concern. The Feldbaum-Lee decision tree expressly lays out these factors as securitisation criteria. The IHR(2005) is concerned with emergency situations, which clearly includes acute, high-impact disease events. The McInnes decision tree centres on extreme events, which appear to be defined as acute disease risks that post a threat of significant death and illness.

If adopted as the key variables for securitising public health problems, the acute and high morbidity and mortality factors eliminate most non-communicable diseases that cause high levels of morbidity and mortality through chronic but not acute disease. For example, radioactive pollution from a nuclear reactor accident, such as Chernobyl, could not be defined as a security issue because the potential high morbidity and mortality would, beyond the immediate accident site, develop chronically over years rather than acutely over days. Feldbaum and Lee (2004) argue, however, that tobacco-related diseases are acute threats that cause significant morbidity and mortality. They also argue that childhood obesity does not become securitised because

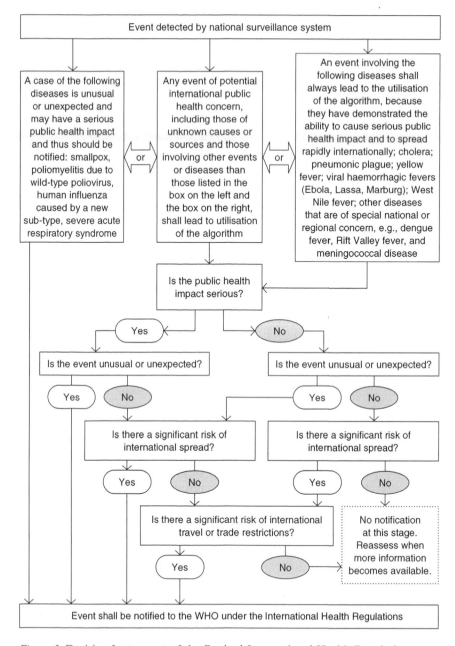

Figure 3 Decision Instrument of the Revised International Health Regulations.
Source: WHO (2005, 45).

it is not an acute health risk. Both tobacco-related and obesity-related diseases are chronic not acute health risks, as those concepts are understood by epidemiologists. Why tobacco but not obesity gets included in the Feldbaum-Lee securitisation process is not clear.

The common approach discernable from the decision trees raises questions about what constitutes an acute threat. From an epidemiological perspective, some communicable diseases, such as HIV/AIDS and tuberculosis (TB), damage health over lengthy periods of time, more akin to a chronic disease than an acute infection, such as influenza, severe acute respiratory syndrome (SARS), or haemorrhagic fever viruses (such as Ebola and Marburg). HIV/AIDS produces high levels of morbidity and mortality but not through physiological means that fit the traditional notion of an acute infection. In fact, the non-acute nature of HIV infection is part of what has made AIDS such a global public health problem.

Loosening the acute factor to open up securitisation to more non-communicable disease problems and to address infections that are chronic may, however, produce a one-branch decision tree that securitises public health problems that generate high levels of morbidity and mortality. Such a move risks equating security with public health rather than creating a framework for prioritising some public health problems as security threats.

Epidemiological elasticity approach

Another approach to identifying which public health problems constitute security issues involves assessing the level of danger posed by health risks by determining the propensity of the risks to spread and cause damage in human populations, or the epidemiological elasticity (epi-elasticity) of a public health threat. A public health risk would have a high epi-elasticity if the risk demonstrates mobility within human populations and creates adverse material impact for societies. Public health risks that exhibit high epi-elasticity would be candidates for security consideration.

Assessing the mobility of a public health risk would involve determining the means of transmission of the risk (for example, pathogen, pest, product, or pollutant), the speed with which the risk moves in human populations, and the geographical reach of the risk's mobility. The decision tree approaches showed interest in whether health risks were mobile, as illustrated by the attention paid to whether a risk was capable of cross-border, trans-border, or intra-border spread. But the spread capability of a risk only served to distinguish whether the risk was a national security issue or a global health security issue in the Feldbaum-Lee and McInnes decision trees. Mobility was not, therefore, a factor in deciding whether a risk was a security concern. The epi-elasticity approach makes mobility a central securitisation factor.

Assessing the material impact of a public health risk would involve determining the morbidity and mortality, the economic costs, and other adverse material effects (for instance, reduction in military capabilities, fear generated in societies) actually or potentially caused by the risk. The idea is to calculate the damage the risk poses to societies. The decision trees were interested in limited aspects of material damage, namely whether a risk threatened high or low morbidity and mortality. The Feldbaum-Lee decision tree does not accommodate a low morbidity or mortality risk that otherwise causes, or threatens to cause, enormous material damage to affected countries, such as a limited bioweapons attack with a non-contagious pathogen. The McInnes decision tree might accommodate such a risk within the concept of an extreme risk, but without a more precise definition of extreme, such accommodation is guesswork. The epi-elasticity approach expressly broadens the impact analysis in securitisation beyond morbidity and mortality statistics to include other forms of material damage to populations.

Assessments of a public health risk's mobility and potential for material damage will involve consideration of other important factors. One such factor is the means of response available to be brought to bear against the risk, such as surveillance and intervention capabilities. The existence or non-existence of public health infrastructure can affect the mobility of a public health risk and the material damage it can inflict on a population. For example, a population universally vaccinated against a highly mobile, contagious pathogen will not, in all likelihood, suffer high morbidity and mortality from that pathogen's spread. The vaccine — the means of response — has a material impact on the epi-elasticity of the pathogen's overall risk to public health.

Another factor that flows into both mobility and material impact is the mutability of the public health risk, or its ability or potential to change, or be changed, as it enters human populations or in response to intervention efforts. The most obvious example of the importance of mutability is the development of antimicrobial resistance in communicable pathogens, such as malaria and TB, which make resistant microbes more dangerous public health risks because the propensity to spread and to cause damage is enhanced. The mutability factor is not, however, limited to communicable diseases. The routes by which non-communicable disease vectors affect human populations can change, or be changed, in response to public health interventions. Raising taxes and increasing regulatory burdens on tobacco and alcohol, for example, may produce an increase in smuggling and other forms of illicit trade.

The epi-elasticity approach is not a decision tree because the assessment of the mobility and material impact factors produces an objective picture of the level of danger the public health risk poses. Concluding that a risk has a high epi-elasticity does not mean that it is automatically a security problem. The epi-elasticity approach leaves open a margin of discretion in the secur-itisation process because, as McInnes (2004) argued, how security is defined in most situations involves both objective and subjective considerations. This outcome is really no different from the definitional choices that have to be made in the decision tree approaches, such as whether a public health risk is acute or extreme. However, the epi-elasticity approach's focus on mobility and material damage provides a more robust methodology for using empirical data to aid the determination through the securitisation process of what public health problems should be prioritised as security threats.

Three pandemics: HIV/AIDS, pandemic influenza, and tobacco-related diseases

The rise of public health concern about pandemics provides an interesting lens through which to look at public health securitism, its pathology, and its unfinished business. The three pandemics involving HIV/AIDS, influenza, and tobacco-related diseases provide rich case studies for analysing the belief that public health can be improved through the use of security-based policies. Collectively, the developments related to these pandemics support the argument that public health governance has entered a post-securitisation phase. Public health securitism appears with respect to the policy discourse on each pandemic, illustrating the power of this policy belief today in public health and other circles. The pandemics also help illustrate the various parts of the pathology of public health securitism and underscore the importance of greater analytical rigour in the relationship between security and public health.

Pandemics and public health securitism

The ubiquity of thinking about public health problems in terms of security that has developed since 1995 owes much to the re-emergence of pandemic and potentially pandemic diseases. The threat of global disease as a public health concern diminished during the post-World War II period, particularly with respect to developed countries that dramatically reduced their vulnerability to communicable diseases. In addition, for much of this period, increased morbidity and mortality caused by non-communicable diseases remained largely a rich country concern and thus did not have global implications.

The re-emergence of pandemic potential for communicable diseases and the emergence of pandemic possibilities for non-communicable diseases since 1995 are directly connected to the fundamental cause behind the rise of public health securitism — the awareness that the dangers presented by diseases have significantly increased from the local to the global level. Pandemics are not, by definition, dangerous because whether a disease is dangerous involves other considerations. But pandemics can be dangerous, and mounting concerns about the dangers to public health posed by pandemics involving HIV/AIDS, influenza, and tobacco-related diseases have stimulated policy to gravitate toward security-based arguments as a strategy to motivate public health governance on these global disease threats.

The pandemic threat has acted as a counterweight to the bioweapons threat's tendency to produce narrow conceptions of the relationship between security and public health. But for the threat of pandemic communicable diseases, it is unlikely that the U.S. would have been willing to move the security–public health relationship beyond bioweapons. The grim progress of the HIV/AIDS pandemic and the emergence of conditions conducive to communicable disease pandemics have contributed to shattering the complacency many developed countries exhibited toward public health in the post-World War II period.

The rise of pandemic threats also supported the use of different kinds of security arguments in discourse about how to deal with these dangers. Pandemics provided a background against which concepts of national, international, and human security could be advanced and debated. The HIV/AIDS pandemic proved particularly powerful in attracting diverse security-related arguments in policy and academic debates about how to respond to this crisis. The continued use of these types of arguments in the frenzy of interest around avian influenza and its potential to trigger a global pandemic has reinforced the prominence of security-based thinking with respect to pandemic disease.

These observations suggest that the emergence and threat of pandemics have materially contributed to the securitisation of public health governance. This development is cold comfort because it means that diseases have emerged as global dangers for which past governance frameworks have proved inadequate. The security approach prioritises pandemic preparedness and response over other public health needs and aspirations.

Securitisation claims and the three pandemics

The growth in the threat posed by pandemics generally also raises issues explored above concerning the identification of public health threats as security problems. Are the HIV/AIDS pandemic, the feared influenza pandemic, and the pandemic of tobacco-related diseases all security threats? The hardest to analyse in response to this question is the pandemic of tobacco-related diseases. Experts have frequently securitised the HIV/AIDS pandemic and the anticipated influenza pandemic. Security-based arguments are not as frequently made with respect to the global spread of tobacco-related diseases. As already argued, part of the unfinished business of public health securitism involves the development of greater analytical rigour in the relationship between security and public health. Application of the various frameworks described earlier to the three pandemics at issue here underscores the need for such rigour.

Clearly, none of these three pandemics ranks as a security threat under the bioweapons framework because none involves the intentional use of disease as a weapon. This conclusion merely reinforces the under-inclusiveness and narrowness of the bioweapons approach to the securitisation of public health problems. The communicable disease framework would cover HIV/AIDS and pandemic influenza but not the pandemic of tobacco-related diseases. Given the actual and anticipated scale of the death and illness caused globally by tobacco consumption, the exclusion of this pandemic entirely on the basis that it involves non-communicable diseases does not seem analytically justifiable.

The various decision tree approaches produce important questions that cast some doubt on their utility. Although the IHR(2005) clearly applies to events involving sources of non-communicable diseases, no one has argued that the concept of a public health emergency of international concern would apply in any context to the continued spread of HIV/AIDS or tobacco-related diseases.[2] Such continued spread of these established pandemics would not be considered unusual or unexpected within the meaning of the IHR(2005). This situation might change with respect to HIV/AIDS if, for example, multi-drug resistant strains of HIV/AIDS began circulating globally, thus significantly imperilling the efficacy of antiretroviral treatment (ART) efforts.

Under the Feldbaum-Lee and McInnes decision trees, pandemic influenza would be the only pandemic of the three under consideration here to merit clear security status. For HIV/AIDS to be securitised under these decision trees, it would have to be considered either an acute disease (Feldbaum and Lee 2004) or an extreme disease event (McInnes 2004). As mentioned earlier, whether HIV/AIDS is an acute infection is questionable. The problem faced by the 'acute health impact' factor in the Feldbaum-Lee decision tree is stretching 'acute' to cover both pandemic influenza and HIV/AIDS, which stand at opposite ends of acuteness in epidemiological terms. Feldbaum and Lee stretch the concept further, in fact, in arguing that tobacco-related diseases should be securitised, which must mean Feldbaum and Lee think they have acute health impact; this again strains epidemiological credulity.

In terms of the McInnes decision tree, HIV/AIDS and tobacco-related diseases would have to be perceived to be extreme health risks to be securitised pandemics. Aggregate morbidity and mortality statistics are not sufficient to achieve extreme status because, under that approach, tobacco-related diseases would be more extreme as a health risk than HIV/AIDS. The heavy securitisation of the HIV/AIDS pandemic and the lack of security-related claims for tobacco-related diseases reinforce this conclusion.

The McInnes decision tree, furthermore, seems to exclude tobacco-related diseases as security threats altogether because it is hard to argue that their spread over the course of decades constitutes an extreme health risk in the same way as pandemic influenza. As with the concept of acute in the Feldbaum-Lee decision tree, the McInnes decision tree raises the question of whether the term 'extreme' needs to be defined more objectively. Both decision trees easily accommodate pandemic influenza, but they both have difficulty with HIV/AIDS, even though it is an intensively securitised pandemic.

In contrast to the awkward application of the decision trees to the HIV/AIDS and tobacco-related disease pandemics, the epi-elasticity approach assesses the level of danger presented by public health risks according to their respective propensities to spread and cause damage to human populations and societies. The mobility and material impact factors apply equally to all three pandemics, so the epi-elasticity approach does not exclude any pandemic for not satisfying a decision tree factor. This approach assesses the level of danger each of the pandemics presents, and policy makers can more objectively assess whether each pandemic poses a sufficient danger to warrant securitisation at the national or global level.

An epi-elasticity analysis of the three pandemics would lead to the conclusion that pandemic influenza would have the highest epi-elasticity and thus be the most dangerous public health risk of the three. This outcome means that pandemic influenza's combined mobility and material impact factors exceed those of HIV/AIDS and tobacco-related diseases. The next highest epi-elasticity would belong to HIV/AIDS, with tobacco-related diseases being third in terms of the level of danger posed to public health.

In terms of the mobility factor, pandemic influenza would exhibit mobility greater than the mobility of HIV or tobacco products. As an airborne virus, pandemic influenza's means of transmission is more efficient than that of HIV or tobacco products. Pandemic influenza would also have very high mobility because of the speed of virus transmission between humans and the potential of the virus to reach every corner of the earth very rapidly. HIV and tobacco products have also demonstrated impressive mobility locally, regionally, and globally in their respective spread and penetration of human populations.

In terms of material impact, pandemic influenza again would threaten to damage populations and societies on a scale and speed that HIV/AIDS and tobacco-related diseases could not currently generate. Projections about the impact of pandemic influenza often discuss the scale of morbidity and mortality, the economic harm, and the political and social disruption pandemic influenza could cause in both rich and poor countries (Russell 2005). The global hand-wringing about the lack of preparedness for pandemic influenza demonstrates that an adequate means of response is currently lacking. Prospects for mitigating the material impact of pandemic influenza are, at present, not good.

As between HIV/AIDS and tobacco-related diseases. HIV/AIDS is more dangerous in terms of its material impact in populations and societies. The morbidity and mortality and economic costs created by tobacco-related diseases are enormous in terms of aggregate numbers (WHO 2006b). But no one has argued that tobacco's material impact on societies has the potential to destabilise entire countries, decimate political elites and productive-age labour forces, harm peacekeeping efforts, and create legions of orphans, as HIV/AIDS is now doing in sub-Saharan Africa (Garrett 2005). Nor does contracting a tobacco-related disease involve the economic, social, and psychological costs associated historically with the stigma of HIV/AIDS.

There is also the ability of HIV to mutate in ways that may render existing ART ineffective and defeat attempts to create a vaccine. The means of response available for preventing tobacco-related diseases is, on the whole, easier and cheaper than HIV/AIDS prevention and control strategies. Thus the overall propensity of HIV/AIDS to cause material damage to a population is greater than that of tobacco.

This rough attempt to establish the level of danger these three pandemics respectively pose correlates with the way securitisation processes have unfolded. The epi-elasticity analysis supports the securitisation of pandemic influenza and HIV/AIDS because their combined mobility and material impact factors make them more dangerous risks than tobacco-related diseases. Thus pandemic influenza and HIV/AIDS deserve the public health governance priority that securitisation processes have accorded them as dangerous threats.

Although the epi-elasticity analysis does not rank tobacco-related diseases as a security threat, this approach acknowledges the possibility that a non-communicable disease could represent such a threat because of its mobility and material impact on the health of populations. In fact, the epi-elasticity of tobacco-related diseases may be higher than some communicable diseases, which helps underscore the emphasis that public health authorities nationally and globally have been placing on the importance of more vigorous action against tobacco consumption.

Conclusion

With respect to the war on terrorism, some have expressed the hope that one day terrorism will again be treated as a law enforcement problem rather than a threat to national security. Some in public health may long for the day when disease risks are again treated as public health problems rather than security threats. Desecuritisation would signal that the disease dangers that stimulated linkages between security and public health had been reduced. Ironically, the only way to desecuritise public health might be to increase political interest and policy attention on public health through securitisation. This reasoning supports this chapter's emphasis on the strength of securitism in public health governance today and the continuing importance of this policy belief in the future.

The pathology of public health securitism outlined in this chapter also highlights another reason why securitisation will not fade away any time soon as a feature of public health governance. Securitisation of public health has provided for convergences of narrow and broad conceptions of security and of interest-based and value-based approaches to health and security. In other words, the securitisation of public health creates a two-way street conceptually because it not only brings security into public health but also causes public health to inform security. The basis for a much deeper and broader governance transformation is now under construction in the post-securitisation phase of public health governance.

Notes

1 'Pathology' means the science of the causes and effects of diseases, especially the laboratory examination of blood and tissue samples for diagnostic or forensic purposes. The term is used very deliberately here. In the laboratory, a pathologist might determine that a health condition is benign or malevolent; pathology does not mean that something is sick. Many believe that the frequency of the use of security concepts marks a new 'condition' in the global health body politic that requires examination of its causes, effects, and consequences.
2 The IHR(2005) expressly applies to any new human influenza strain (WHO 2005).

References

Beaglehole, Robert and Derek Yach (2003). 'Globalisation and the Prevention and Control of Non-Communicable Disease: The Neglected Chronic Diseases of Adults'. *Lancet*, vol. 362, pp. 903–908.

Birnie, Patricia W. and Alan E. Boyle (2002). *International Law and the Environment*, 2nd ed. (Oxford: Oxford University Press).

Commission on Human Security (2003). 'Human Security Now: The Final Report of the Commission on Human Security'. New York. <www.humansecurity-chs.org/finalreport/English/FinalReport.pdf> (September 2006).

Eberstadt, Nicholas (2002). 'The Future of AIDS'. *Foreign Affairs*, vol. 81, no. 6, pp. 22–45. <www.foreignaffairs.org/20021101faessay9990/nicholas-eberstadt/the-future-of-aids.html> (September 2006).

Feldbaum, Henry and Kelley Lee (2004). 'Public Health and Security'. In A. Ingram, ed., *Health, Foreign Policy, and Security: Towards a Conceptual Framework for Research and Policy*, pp. 19–28 (London: Nuffield Trust).

Fidler, David P. (2003). 'Public Health and National Security in the Global Age: Infectious Diseases, Bioterrorism, and Realpolitik'. *George Washington International Law Review*, vol. 35, pp. 788–856.

Fidler, David P. (2004). 'Caught between Paradise and Power: Public Health, Pathogenic Threats, and the Axis of Illness'. *McGeorge Law Review*, vol. 35, pp. 45–104.

Fidler, David P. (2005). 'From International Sanitary Conventions to Global Health Security: The New International Health Regulations'. *Chinese Journal of International Law*, vol. 4, no. 2, pp. 325–392.

Garrett, Laurie (2005). 'HIV and National Security: Where Are the Links?' Council on Foreign Relations, New York. <www.cfr.org/content/publications/attachments/HIV_National_Security.pdf> (September 2006).

Goodman, Neville M. (1971). *International Health Organizations and Their Work*, 2nd ed. (Edinburgh: Churchill Livingstone).

Howard-Jones, Norman (1950). 'Origins of International Health Work'. *British Medical Journal*, vol. 1, no. 4661, pp. 1032–1037.

Howard-Jones, Norman (1975). *The Scientific Background of the International Sanitary Conferences, 1851–1938* (Geneva: World Health Organization).

International Conference on Primary Health Care (1978). 'Declaration of Alma-Ata'. 12 September. Alma-Ata, Kazakhstan. <www.euro.who.int/AboutWHO/Policy/20010827_1> (September 2006).

McInnes, Colin (2004). 'Health and Foreign Policy'. In A. Ingram, ed., *Health, Foreign Policy, and Security: Towards a Conceptual Framework for Research and Policy*, pp. 29–42 (London: Nuffield Trust).

Pannenborg, Charles O. (1979). *A New International Health Order: An Inquiry into the International Relations of World Health and Medical Care* (Alphen aan den Rijn, Netherlands: Sijthoff and Noordhoff).

Pirages, Dennis (1997). 'Ecological Theory and International Relations'. *Indiana Journal of Global Legal Studies*, vol. 5, no. 1, pp. 53–63.

Princeton Project on National Security (2005). 'Report of the Working Group on State Security and Transnational Threats'. Woodrow Wilson School of Public and International Affairs, Princeton. <www.wws.princeton.edu/ppns/conferences/reports/fall/SSTT.pdf> (September 2006).

Russell, Sabin (2005). 'Bird Flu Capable of Causing "Incalculable" Misery: 100-Nation Meeting Focuses on Plans to Contain Outbreak'. *San Francisco Chronicle*, 8 November. <sfgate.com/egi-bin/article.cgi?f–/c/a/2005/11/08/MNGGAFKKU51.DTL&type–science> (September 2006).

Smolinski, Mark S., Margaret A. Hamburg, and Joshua Lederberg, eds. (2003). *Microbial Threats to Health: Emergence, Detection, and Response* (Washington DC: National Academies Press).

United Nations (2004). 'A More Secure World: Our Shared Responsibility'. Report of the Secretary General's High-Level Panel on Threats, Challenges, and Change. New York. <www.un.org/secureworld> (September 2006).

United Nations (2005). 'In Larger Freedom: Towards Security, Development, and Human Rights for All'. Report of the Secretary General of the United Nations for Decision by Heads of State and Government in September 2005. New York. <www.un.org/largerfreedom> (September 2006).

United Nations Development Programme (1994). *Human Development Report* (New York: United Nations Development Programme).

United Nations Security Council (2000). 'Resolution 1308 (2000) on the Responsibility of the Security Council in the Maintenance of International Peace and Security: HIV/AIDS and International Peacekeeping Operations'. <daccess-ods.un.org/access.nsf/Get?Open&DS–S/RES/1308%20(2000)&Lang–E&Area–UNDOC> (September 2006).

United Nations Security Council (2005). 'Security Council Presidential Statement Recognizes "Significant Progress" Addressing HIV/AIDS among Peacekeepers, But Says Many Challenges Remain'. Press release SC/8450, 18 July, New York. <www.un.org/News/Press/docs/2005/sc8450.doc.htm> (September 2006).

United States (2002). 'The National Security Strategy of the United States of America'. Washington DC. <www.whitehouse.gov/nse/nss.html> (September 2006).

World Health Organization (1994). 'Constitution of the World Health Organization'. Geneva. <www.who.int/about/en » WHO Constitution> (September 2006).

World Health Organization (2001). 'Global Health Security: Epidemic Alert and Response'. World Health Assembly Resolution WHA54.14, 21 May, Geneva. <ftp.who.int/gb/pdf_files/WHA54/ea54r14.pdf> (September 2006).

8

GLOBAL PUBLIC HEALTH SECURITY

Guénaël Rodier, Allison L. Greenspan, James M. Hughes and David L. Heymann

Source: *Emerging Infectious Diseases*, 13:10 (2007), 1447–52.

"When the world is collectively at risk, defense becomes a shared responsibility of all nations."
—Dr. Margaret Chan, Director General, World Health Organization; World Health Day 2007

The framework of the newly revised International Health Regulations is a key driver in the effort to strengthen global public health security. Unanimously agreed upon by the World Health Assembly on May 23, 2005, the regulations are the result of experience gained and lessons learned during the past 30 years. This global legal framework includes a commitment from the World Health Organization (WHO) and from each WHO member state to improve capacity for disease prevention, detection, and response. It provides standards for addressing national public health threats that have the potential to become global emergencies. Its success will rely on the capacity and performance of national public health systems, anchored by strong national public health institutes (NPHIs). The new International Association of National Public Health Institutes aims to strengthen and invigorate existing NPHIs, to create new NPHIs where none exist, and to provide funded grants to support NPHI development priorities.

In the wake of the 2003 outbreak of severe acute respiratory syndrome (SARS), preparedness for public health emergencies was propelled into worldwide consciousness. The appearance and rapid international spread of SARS demonstrated to all—including global leaders, ministers of health, prime ministers, and heads of state—how an infectious disease can rapidly cross borders and deliver health threats and economic blows on an unimaginable scale (*1,2*). Since then, the entrenchment of highly pathogenic avian influenza virus (H5N1) in poultry flocks of Asian countries, and the spread of the virus across Europe and into Africa, has put the world on high alert for an influenza pandemic and affirmed the urgency of strengthening public health systems and capacity worldwide (*3,4*).

Compounding the challenges of threats to public health security from new and reemerging infectious diseases and the concerns about intentional dissemination of chemical or biological substances are the challenges of ensuring individual health security. These latter challenges include the unfinished agenda of broadening access to the drugs, vaccines, and other interventions needed to control endemic diseases such as malaria, acute lower respiratory tract infections, diarrheal diseases, measles, and tuberculosis, as well as to address the ongoing problems of HIV/AIDS, neglected tropical diseases, humanitarian emergencies, and global environmental changes.

The scale, range, and complexity of these modern challenges to health security call for new approaches of comparable dimension and strength. Protecting the world from transnational health threats demands a global public health perspective and investment in global public health infrastructure. The theme of this year's World Health Day and the World Health Report 2007 is "Global public health security—the need to reduce the vulnerability of people around the world to new, acute, or rapidly spreading risks to health, particularly those that cross international borders" (*5*). With a call to all nations to "invest in health, and build a safer future," the World Health Organization (WHO) emphasizes the need for collaboration among nations to increase our collective capacity and infrastructure to respond to potential international health emergencies and other public health risks. As recent events have shown, global public health security is a complex, costly, and information-intense undertaking that requires strong national public health leadership and infrastructure, cross-border collaboration, capacity to identify problems rapidly and design real-time evidence-based solutions, well-trained and well-equipped workforces, well-functioning laboratories and service-delivery systems, capacity to sustain interventions, and ability to respond to unexpected events (*5,6*). Investment in these elements will strengthen not only global public health security but also the infrastructure needed to help broaden access to healthcare services and improve individual health outcomes, which would help break the cycles of poverty and political instability and thus contribute to national economic development and achievement of the Millennium Development Goals (*7*).

A key driver in the effort to strengthen global public health security is the framework of the newly revised International Health Regulations (IHR [2005]) (*8*), the legally binding global agreement designed to build and strengthen national alert and response systems. Unanimously agreed upon by the World Health Assembly on May 23, 2005, the regulations are the result of experience gained and lessons learned about global public health security over the past 30 years. This global legal framework constitutes a "major development in the use of international law for public health purposes" (9). It includes a commitment from WHO and from each of its 193 member states to improve capacity for disease prevention, detection, and response and provides ground rules to address national public health threats that have the potential to become global emergencies. The adoption of the new regulations ended a 10-year process of revision, stimulated by the pneumonic plague outbreak in India in 1994 (10) and the Ebola hemorrhagic fever outbreak in the former Zaire in 1995 (11). The revised regulations have now entered into force for all WHO member states.

New times, new requirements

The revised regulations reflect a growing understanding that the best way to prevent the global spread of diseases is to detect and contain them while they are still local. WHO member states have obligations to rapidly assess and alert the global community about potential disease threats as well as to prevent and control the spread of disease inside and beyond their borders. Compared with the previous regulations, adopted in 1969 (12), IHR (2005) expands the scope of internationally reportable diseases and events, provides criteria for identifying novel epidemic events, and specifies conditions for involvement of the international community in outbreak responses. The revision includes the following 5 substantive changes.

Expanded scope

The previous regulations applied to only 3 infectious diseases: cholera, plague, and yellow fever. IHR (2005) reflects shifting concepts about disease control, shaped by recent and impending disease threats and the experiences of the past 2 decades in detecting and responding to disease outbreaks. The emergence and reemergence of a cascade of infectious diseases fueled by globalization and international travel (13), the threat of biological terrorism, and novel environmental threats (14) have spotlighted the need for heightened vigilance and increased capacity to recognize and manage public health risks and emergencies. The appearance and rapid international spread of SARS and the pandemic potential of circulating avian influenza (H5N1) strains—with their combined health and economic effects—confirmed the inapplicability of the 1969 IHR to most emerging and reemerging infectious diseases.

The revised regulations replace the previous disease-specific framework with one built on timely notification of all events that might constitute a public health emergency of international concern, taking into account the context in which an event occurs (*15*). The advantage of this approach is its applicability to existing threats as well as to those that are new and unforeseen. The regulations also recognize the existence of threats to public health outside the infectious disease context, such as those associated with natural disasters, industrial or chemical accidents, and other environmental changes, which might cross international borders.

Decision instrument and notification

Expanding the scope of the IHR beyond reporting of 3 diseases to reporting of any public health emergency of international concern required an algorithm to assist in identification of such events. The resulting decision instrument (see [*8*], Annex 2, p. 43) identifies a limited set of criteria for use by member states for fulfilling the obligation to determine whether an event occurring within their territory might constitute a public health emergency of international concern and therefore require formal notification to WHO within 24 hours of assessment. Essentially, the events that must be reported are those that fulfill at least 2 of the following criteria:

- Is the public health impact of the event serious?
- Is the event unusual or unexpected?
- Is there a significant risk of international spread?
- Is there a significant risk of international trade or travel restriction?

To facilitate the use of the decision instrument, which requires some judgment to answer each of the questions, Annex 2 of the Regulations provides specific examples of events that might constitute a public health emergency of international concern. In addition to this broad scope for notification, IHR (2005) includes a list of diseases for which a single case must be reported to WHO immediately, regardless of the context in which the disease occurs. This list includes smallpox, poliomyelitis due to wild-type poliovirus, human influenza caused by a new subtype, or SARS. In addition, an event involving certain other diseases (e.g., cholera, pneumonic plague, yellow fever, viral hemorrhagic fevers) calls for a careful evaluation using the decision instrument to determine whether notification is indicated. The need for recognition of specific diseases requires adequate diagnostic laboratory capacity.

After an event is reported, only the Director General of WHO can determine whether the event formally constitutes a public health emergency of international concern. However, the Director General shall first consult with the affected state party and hear the view of the emergency committee. This committee, composed of experts from the newly established IHR roster of experts, is specifically set up to review a reported event and provide advice to the Director General on whether an event constitutes a public health emergency of international concern and whether a temporary recommendation must be issued. On request, WHO will be able to provide technical support to affected countries, including the mobilization of the Global Outbreak Alert and Response Network.

Focal and contact points

A third innovation under IHR (2005) is the requirement for member states to designate "national IHR focal points" as the operational link for notification and reporting to WHO and for WHO to name corresponding "IHR contact points." Effective communication between these 2 organizational entities will be central to the rapid management of a possible public health emergency of international concern. IHR focal points, or their designees, are required by IHR (2005) to be accessible at all times.

National core surveillance and response capacities

Experiences during the past several years have shown that public health emergencies expose the weaknesses and vulnerabilities of national and subnational public health infrastructure. The fourth change calls for member states to develop, strengthen, and maintain core capacities to 1) detect, assess, notify, and report disease events, and 2) respond promptly and effectively to public health risks and public health emergencies of international concern. State parties are required to complete a capacity assessment within 2 years of the revised IHR entering into force and, after this assessment, to develop public health infrastructure and human resources that ensure full compliance within 5 years of the IHR entering into force. This assessment must lead to the development of national action plans to meet the core capacity requirements that Annex 1 of the Regulations specifies for different levels (i.e., local community or primary, intermediate, and national public health response) as well as designated airports, ports, and ground crossings. For these national points of entry, IHR (2005) also introduces special provisions for travelers, including the obligation to treat them with respect for their dignity, human rights, and fundamental freedom.

WHO support

WHO is required to assist all member states in fulfilling the new obligations. On request, WHO will collaborate with countries to evaluate their public health capacities and facilitate technical cooperation, logistical support, and mobilization of financial resources for strengthening capacity in surveillance and response. Countries will build on existing national or regional strategies such as the Asia Pacific Strategy for Emerging Diseases in WHO's Southeast

Asia and Western Pacific Regions (*16*) and the Integrated Disease Surveillance and Response strategy in the African Region (*17*). In many countries, national action plans can also build on the influenza pandemic preparedness plans developed with WHO's guidance. Specific WHO guidelines and initiatives, particularly in the areas of external quality assessment for laboratories, data gathering and analysis at the health district level, and the central and coordination functions of national public health institutes, are being developed. WHO's Lyon Office for National Epidemic Preparedness and Response is specifically dedicated to supporting countries in meeting the core national capacity requirements of IHR (2005).

Under IHR (2005), new powers for WHO include an information-gathering responsibility that is not limited solely to official state notifications or consultations but covers all available scientific evidence and other relevant information. WHO can consult nonofficial reports and require countries to collaborate with a request for verification. WHO is also empowered to recommend and coordinate measures that will help contain the international spread of disease, including public health actions at ports, airports, and land borders, and on means of transportation that involve international travel.

Critical role of national public health institutes

Because weak national public health capabilities undermine efforts to strengthen global public health security, IHR (2005) imposes substantial responsibilities on countries to improve public health capacity and infrastructure. However, despite the broad new goals included in IHR (2005), improvements in global public health security will depend on what member states are actually able to do. Success will rely on the capacity and performance of national public health systems (*15*), anchored by strong national public health institutes (NPHIs). Low-resource countries, which are particularly vulnerable to emerging threats, will be particularly challenged by the IHR (2005) requirements and the need to ensure an appropriate and coordinated public health response to health emergencies.

Many countries have been well served by centralizing their public health expertise and activities within 1 institution or network of institutions that provides leadership and coordination for public health (*18;* unpub. data). Examples include the US Centers for Disease Control and Prevention, the National Public Health Institute of Finland, and the Chinese Center for Disease Control and Prevention. These NPHIs are usually governmental or quasi-governmental agencies with a central focus and organizational structure that allow coordination of national public health service delivery and ensure a country's ability to detect, investigate, and respond to public health emergencies. The core functions of an NPHI have been defined (unpub. data) and include evaluation and analysis of health status; public health surveillance, problem investigation, and control of risks and threats to public health; and public health research.

Given the scope and range of their activities, NPHIs are a vital asset to health development and security and will have a critically important role in implementing IHR (2005), whether as national focal points or as operational partners in fulfilling the requirements of the regulations. Unfortunately, however, many countries still either have no NPHIs or have institutes with severely limited capacities and capabilities relative to the need. Even in countries with strong NPHIs, unpredictable and rapidly evolving health threats can quickly overwhelm capacity and inhibit a timely and complete response.

A new organization, the International Association of National Public Health Institutes (IANPHI, www.ianphi.org), was created to address these gaps through the enhancement and proliferation of NPHIs throughout the world. Founded in 2006 by 39 NPHI directors who recognized the importance of strong national public health capacity and the mutual benefits of shared information, experience, and expertise, IANPHI aims to be a catalyst for sustained improvements in public health capacity and infrastructure globally. With the partnership of WHO and funding first from the Rockefeller Foundation and now from the Bill and Melinda Gates Foundation, the organization focuses on strengthening public health capacity in low-resource countries by strengthening NPHIs and on providing tools and a context that will support all NPHIs. IANPHI is also a professional association for NPHI directors; it fosters leadership development and advocacy for public health and collaborates with WHO.

Since early 2006, the founding members have continued to expand the network and put their shared vision into practice. IANPHI is managed by an executive board and a secretariat located both in Finland and in the United States. With nearly 50 current members and an ambitious agenda for collaboration, service, and growth, IANPHI is committed to a vision of a robust and fully integrated global network of NPHIs equipped to address critical public health challenges. Its mission is to strengthen and reinvigorate existing NPHIs, create new NPHIs where none exist, and provide funded grants to support NPHI capacity development priorities.

IANPHI achieves its service mission through a 3-part approach of advocacy, technical assistance, and linkages. IANPHI advocates for NPHI development and proliferation through partnerships with key global health organizations, such as WHO. Through these partnerships, IANPHI ensures that NPHIs are considered in major global public health initiatives and that public health and the work of NPHIs are included in efforts to strengthen health systems.

Assistance to NPHIs in low-resource countries is provided through 3 grant programs. A short-term technical assistance program helps countries quickly resolve priority gaps in NPHI capability and infrastructure. A medium-term capacity-building program helps NPHIs address high-priority needs for up to 3 years. IANPHI's long-term grant program, the most intensive of the assistance efforts, will help create NPHIs in low-resource countries that cur-

156

rently lack a central public health focus. With funding from a $20 million grant from the Bill and Melinda Gates Foundation, the organization is committed to implementing 60 NPHI development projects by 2011.

As of June 2007, IANPHI had awarded technical assistance grants to public health institutes in 5 nations. The new awards include 3 short-term grants to NPHIs in Thailand, Uganda, and Iran to support training and infrastructure development. A medium-term grant to the Nigerian Institute of Medical Research will support sustainable improvements in disease surveillance, outbreak investigation, and emergency preparedness and strengthen linkages with other groups working to advance public health in the country; special focus will be on public health laboratory capacity building and integration of surveillance, epidemiology, and laboratory programs. Colombia's Institutos Nacional de Salud was awarded a medium-term grant to establish a pilot chronic disease study site to generate, collect, and disseminate chronic disease data by using multiple mechanisms. The activities are designed to yield a sustainable network of surveillance and research sites to guide national-level public health decision making.

The cornerstone of the IANPHI approach is a peer-assistance model for NPHI strengthening and enhancement, with an emphasis on countries without NPHIs or with NPHIs in their early stages. Experts from IANPHI member institutes provide technical assistance and project support targeted at critical NPHI needs. Teams are guided by the Framework for the Creation and Development of NPHIs (www.ian-phi.org/?action=arkisto&RYH MA=47&ID=&valittu=8), a product of IANPHI in partnership with WHO. The Framework provides a working definition of an NPHI and suggests a process for creating or enhancing an institute. By defining the critical characteristics of an NPHI, IANPHI hopes to bring specificity to the organization's vision, align efforts to assist low-resource countries in building NPHIs, and provide benchmarks and resources to help any country assess and improve the functioning of its NPHI. To that end, IANPHI has also developed an NPHI toolkit (www.sph.emory.edu/IANPHI), which provides access to a variety of Web-based information resources for countries, NPHIs, and IAN-PHI peer-assistance teams to use as they work to assess, develop, and improve NPHIs and build public health capacity around the world.

Through strategies to define and develop core public health functions and to share expertise, IANPHI helps NPHIs sharpen their focus and raise standards of performance. IANPHI also links NPHIs through annual meetings, regional events, leadership development activities, research seed grants, and communication outlets including a website, newsletter, and listserv. By fostering an international community of public health leadership, IANPHI helps NPHIs gain the benefits of shared information, experience, and expertise to address public health threats and opportunities. Through its grant program and other activities, IANPHI aims to help national governments develop organizational infrastructures to devise and implement comprehensive public health priorities, meet global public health goals, develop workforce capacity, effectively absorb donor funds, address emerging threats, and improve the health of their populations (*18*).

Conclusions

In today's global environment, every country confronts similar challenges in keeping its population healthy and preventing the cross-border spread of disease. SARS demonstrated this dramatically in 2003, and the ongoing challenges posed by avian influenza have focused attention on the need for global pandemic influenza preparedness. Polio has reemerged in countries that had virtually eradicated it, while HIV/AIDS and other diseases continue to threaten the stability of communities around the world. Recent examples of emerging and reemerging diseases of global significance are the resurgence of dengue in tropical and subtropical areas of the world; the spread and establishment of Japanese encephalitis and West Nile viruses in new habitats and environments; and the reoccurrence and spread of chikungunya virus in India, East Africa, and several Indian Ocean islands (*19,20*). As life expectancy increases worldwide, issues related to noncommunicable conditions are also becoming increasingly common to all. By working within the collaborative framework provided by IHR (2005), countries can benefit through improved national and international surveillance; improved systems for rapid detection of and response to public health emergencies; standardized rules for evaluation, control, and resolution of urgent events; and mechanisms to increase national and local public health security.

Nonetheless, the success of IHR (2005) and other global public health initiatives such as the Millennium Development Goals depends on strong national public health systems with competent, well-trained staff and well-equipped facilities. By targeting the core of public health systems, especially in low-resource countries that currently lag behind in public health capacity and infrastructure, IANPHI will play a key role in improving the capacity of countries to effectively detect, investigate, and respond to public health emergencies. The result will be better control of endemic diseases such as HIV/AIDS, acute lower respiratory tract infections, diarrheal diseases, measles, tuberculosis, malaria, and the neglected tropical diseases. These efforts will strengthen the practice of public health worldwide, yield global public health benefits of disease control and prevention, and ultimately accelerate social and economic development in the poorest countries of the world and progress toward achieving the Millenium Development Goals.

References

1. Heymann D. L. The international response to the outbreak of SARS in 2003. Philos Trans R Soc Lond B Biol Sci. 2004;359:1127–9.

2. Heymann D. L. SARS and emerging diseases: a challenge to place global solidarity above national sovereignty. Ann Acad Med Singapore. 2006;35:350–3.
3. Parry J. Ten years of fighting bird flu. Bull World Health Organ. 2007;85:3–4.
4. Webster R. G., Govorkova E. A. H5N1 influenza—continuing evolution and spread. N Engl J Med. 2006;355:2174–7.
5. World Health Organization. Invest in health, build a safer future World Health Day 2007 issues paper. Geneva: The Organization; 2007. [cited 2007 Jul 31] Available from http://www.who.int/world-health-day/2007/issues_paper/en/index.html
6. Andrus J. K., Vicari A., Tambini G., Periago M. R. The global inter-relatedness of disease control. Lancet Infect Dis. 2007;7:176.
7. United Nations. UN Millennium Development Goals. [cited 2007 Jul 1]. Available from http://www.un.org/millenniumgoals
8. World Health Organization. Revision of the International Health Regulations, WHA 58.3. [cited 2007 Jul 31]. Available from http://www.who.int/gb/ebwha/pdf_files/wha58/wha58_3-en.pdf
9. Baker M. G., Fidler D. P. Global public health surveillance under the new international health regulations. Emerg Infect Dis. 2006;7:1058–65.
10. Centers for Disease Control and Prevention. Human plague—India, 1994. MMWR Morb Mortal Wkly Rep. 1994;43:689–91.
11. Khan A. S., Tshioko F. K., Heymann D. L., Le Guenno B., Nabeth P., Kerstiëns B., et al. The reemergence of Ebola hemorrhagic fever, Democratic Republic of the Congo, 1995. J Infect Dis. 1999;179(Suppl 1):S76–86.
12. World Health Organization. International Health Regulations (1969). 3rd ed. Geneva: The Organization; 1983. [cited 2007 Aug 20]. Available from http://whqlibdoc.who.int/publications/1983/9241580070.pdf
13. Morens D. M., Folkers G. K., Fauci A. S. The challenge of emerging and re-emerging infectious diseases. Nature. 2004;430:242–9.
14. Knobler S. L., Mahmoud A. A. F., Pray L. A., editors. Biological threats and terrorism: assessing the science and response capabilities. Washington: Institute of Medicine; 2002.
15. Rodier G., Hardiman M., Plotkin B., Ganter B. Implementing the International Health Regulations (2005) in Europe. Euro Surveill. 2006;11:208–11.
16. World Health Organization. Asia-Pacific strategy for emerging diseases. 2005. [cited 2007 Jul 31]. Available from http://www.wpro.who.int/nr/rdonlyres/fceebb9d-21bb-4a16-8530-756f99efdb67/0/asia_pacific.pdf
17. World Health Organization. Integrated disease surveillance in the African region: a regional strategy for communicable diseases, 1999–2003. 1998. [cited 2007 Aug 20]. Available from http://www.afro.who.int/csr/ids/publications/ids.pdf
18. Koplan J. P., Puska P., Jousilahti P., Cahill K., Huttunen J., and National Public Health Institute Partners. Improving the world's health through national public health institutes. Bull World Health Organ. 2005;83:154–7.
19. Mackenzie J. S., Gubler D. J., Petersen L. R. Emerging flaviviruses: the spread and resurgence of Japanese encephalitis, West Nile and dengue viruses. Nat Med. 2004;10(Suppl):S98–109.
20. Mavalankar D., Shastri P., Raman P. Chikungunya epidemic in India: a major public health disaster. Lancet Infect Dis. 2007;7:306–7.

9

HEALTH AS A GLOBAL SECURITY CHALLENGE

Jonathan Ban

Source: *Seton Hall Journal of Diplomacy and International Relations*, 4:2 (2003), 19–28.

I. Introduction

As threats to security evolve, we are forced to reexamine our notions of security to determine their current contribution, to discard what is no longer relevant, and to search for new approaches to what still may be uncertain threats but very real challenges. One relatively novel but rapidly expanding paradigm examines the overlap of health and security issues. While it is clear that health issues often intersect with security issues, not all health challenges represent security concerns. In fact, health challenges are rarely immediate threats to national security. Therefore, to lend clarity to what constitutes the nexus of health and security, we must deepen our conceptual and analytical approaches to such problems. This article aims to contribute to this objective by not only arguing for the inclusion of health challenges in our changing conceptions of security, but also by offering two analytical approaches for advancing "health and security" as a paradigm. First, characterizing threats posed by health and security challenges as either *direct* or *indirect* will help clarify whether the problem is an immediate or tangential concern for security planners. Second, elaborating a *risk-based approach* to health and security challenges will provide a framework that characterizes the degree to which health concerns represent threats to security. By identifying health and security challenges as direct or indirect threats and by evaluating the level of risk associated with these threats, we begin to elaborate on an analytical framework that will help policymakers and analysts better understand the nexus of health and security. Ultimately, this will lead to improved policy responses to novel challenges.

II. Changing conceptions of security

The concept of security has evolved over time so that today it encompasses many different things. Traditional conceptions of "national security" are concerned with the well-being of the state, relative power between states, the pursuit of national interests, and ultimately efforts by states to protect their borders from invasion. This notion of security is primarily concerned with military affairs and interstate conflict. The concept of "international security" explicitly acknowledges that the security of one state is connected with the security of other states. International security tends to focus on transnational dynamics, such as how actions taken by one state have an impact on the security of other states or the role of international organizations. "Global security" extends the security agenda in scale and includes social development, environmental protection, public health, human rights, and other issues considered to be inalienable prerequisites of security. "Human security" shifts the focus towards the individual and community levels and takes a more holistic approach to security by not only encompassing the concepts mentioned above, but also incorporating a notion of "physical" security of the individual or his or her freedom from injury, violence, sickness, poverty, or psychological harm. "Ecological security" may be the most far reaching of all because it looks at not only human populations on a global scale, but also the macro and micro natural environments in which they live.[1]

While many analysts see the need to expand the definition of security to encompass nontraditional national and international security problems such as health challenges, others resist incorporating novel threats into their notions of security for fear of spreading our national security focus and resources too thin. The health and security debate has at times met resistance from the traditional national security community who argued that casting security in such terms dilutes the concept to an unmanageable degree. Skeptics of an expanded notion of security, therefore, argue that because everything can be related to national security in some way, systematic parameters must be created in order to establish what constitutes a national security challenge. Meanwhile, many in the public health community are also uneasy about viewing public health problems in security terms, fearing that framing the issues in such a way would offer a skewed perspective on what are in actuality public health, ecological, humanitarian, and developmental issues. These diverse approaches to security raise a question: What constitutes security as we enter the new millennium?

Each of these conceptions of security is useful for examining the changing dynamics, unique challenges, and nontraditional and uncertain threats, including those posed by health challenges. Therefore, to the degree to which they have implications for national security they should be more fully considered. This is not to say that all health challenges constitute national security concerns; they do not. It also does not suggest that health concerns with security implications are the most important national security threats of the day, but the growing sense of urgency that surrounds many of the intersections between health and security have become increasingly apparent in recent years. For these reasons, such pressing health challenges warrant more attention from the national security community than they currently receive.

III. Health and security: degrees of risk

Former United Nations Secretary-General, Boutros Boutros-Ghali, in his 1992 report, *Agenda for Peace*, points out that our evolving conceptions of security in the post-cold war era must include "new risks for stability," noting that "drought and disease can decimate no less mercilessly than the weapons of war."[2] At the nexus of health and security lie many poignant examples of "new risks to stability"—the growing threat of biological weapons, the potential destabilization of much of Africa from HIV/AIDS, the negative impact of naturally occurring infectious diseases on military and peacekeeping operations, the migration and proliferation of emerging and reemerging infectious diseases to non-endemic areas—that produce a strong case for including health concerns in the national security debate. The question is not *whether* some health challenges generate risks that have implications for security, but rather, *to what degree* do various health challenges pose risks that have security implications? The link between health and security should not be seen as a single point of intersection. Instead, it should be regarded as a continuum that encompasses a variety of risks ranging from high-risk bio-logical weapon contingencies that are clearly security concerns to low-risk health issues with little relevance for security. When we examine the degree of risk generated by a health issue in relation to other health and security topics, it becomes clear that some health issues are far more important in terms of security than are others.

To understand the degree of security risk that various health challenges create, we can distinguish health challenges as direct threats to national secur-ity in the traditional sense or as indirect factors that contribute to emerging national security threats.[3] Greater risk would be associated with direct threats than indirect threats. For example, direct security threats might involve risks related to more traditional aspects of security such as biological weapon attacks, attacks on medical personnel, facilities, and supplies by combatants in a conflict, and the declining health status of military personnel, peacekeepers, or deployed contingencies due to infectious diseases. Each of these challenges has direct implications for traditional national security considerations.

Indirect security threats might involve risks embedded in a broader definition of security such as global health emergencies caused by communic-able diseases. Examples include severe acute respiratory syndrome (SARS), the potentially destabilizing social, political, or economic impact of HIV/AIDS, or a growing AIDS orphan population that could potentially turn to criminal, insurgent, or terrorist activity. While these challenges carry less risk than direct threats, they have the potential to impact national and international security and should not be excluded from traditional national security considerations.

Characterizing the nexus of health and security in terms of degrees of risk provides greater analytical clarity. A risk-based approach weeds out low-risk health challenges that are not appropriately viewed through the lens of security and clarifies the "hard" security issues in light of the high-risk health challenges that directly impact security. Moreover, the risk-based method identifies shifting health and social dynamics that could generate, in the future, increasing levels of risk to security. Using such an approach, we begin to distinguish the high-risk challenges from the medium- and low-risk challenges that lie at the intersection of health and security.

IV. Health and security: the "big" issues

The ways in which health and security interact are numerous, but not all of these interactions warrant examination in the context of security. To comprehend the nature of the health and security relationship, we must start by asking: What are the "big" issues? As we survey the health and security landscape, several critical issues stand out.

First, among infectious disease threats to both military and civilian populations, biological weapons have emerged as the most salient. Over the last decade, biological weapons took on a new level of importance for the United States after revelations in the 1990s by the United Nations Special Commission that in Iraq, Saddam Hussein had one of the world's most advanced biological weapon programs, including large amounts of anthrax. It was this and other discoveries, like Dr. Ken Alibek's (former Deputy Director of the Soviet biological weapons agency Biopreparat) description of the Russian biological program, which made the United States realize that the security risk associated with biological weapons was higher than anticipated. September 11th and the subsequent anthrax mail attacks illustrate how much the security landscape has changed both generally and at the intersection of health and security. Not only are non-state actors challenging the rights of states to monopolize the use of violence, but also they are doing so with weapons of mass destruction and indiscriminate violence, resorting to the use of disease against their adversaries. The risks related to biological weapons no longer lie solely at the juncture of colliding military forces. Biological weapons threaten political leaders and civil servants in their workplaces. Civilians are threatened in their own homes by a routine postal delivery. No longer is the battle reserved solely for the battlefield, and no longer is military might the only appropriate response. Biological weapons are now being used to attack us at the most personal level by targeting the health of individuals, communities, and societies. As such, the health of the individual is now vulnerable to deliberate attack, and security has come to encompass to some degree the protection of the individual citizen from these risks. The anthrax mailings, though a relatively small-scale occasion of biological weapon use, are a poignant example of the high-risk national security challenges located at the intersection of health and security.

Second, naturally occurring infectious disease outbreaks represent a direct threat to military operations. In 1987, Brigadier General Ognibene noted in the journal *Military Medicine*:

> *Disease is woven intricately into the fabric of war. The story of one cannot be told without the other and yet, each succeeding generation of history, soldier and scholar alike, seems destined to repeat the errors of history and fail to perceive the impact of disease.*[4]

In fact, naturally occurring infectious disease outbreaks, rather than fire-power, are often responsible for more casualties in warfare. During the U.S. Civil War, for example, twice as many soldiers died of disease than were killed in combat.[5] More recently, some contingencies of the United Nations Mission in Sierra Leone reported an excess of 30 percent of troops bedridden with malaria in any given month, a significant drag on the performance of the operation.[6] Likewise, of the 225 U.S. Marine Corps service members who were in Liberia in August 2003, fifty were hospitalized with malaria.[7]

Infectious diseases also impact predeployment force readiness. Throughout Africa, the armed forces and security apparatuses are particularly afflicted by HIV/AIDS with prevalence rates typically, and often drastically, higher than in the general population. For example, in 1999, the HIV prevalence rate in Nigeria's military is estimated to be 10 to 20 percent, in Tanzania 15 to 30 percent, and in Angola 40 to 60 percent whereas prevalence rates in the adult civilian populations were estimated to be 5.06 percent, 8.09 percent, and 2.78 percent, respectively.[8] These developments affect manpower resources and preparedness in military and police forces and may reduce the effectiveness and capability of these security apparatuses to maintain order domestically and abroad. Furthermore, faced with enormous HIV/AIDS challenges in their national militaries, major African troop-contributing countries are becoming reluctant to offer soldiers for peacekeeping missions given the strain HIV/AIDS is placing on the readiness of their national militaries. Moreover, many host countries are reluctant to accept HIV-positive peace-keepers because of the risks related to the spread of the disease to local populations. Despite the enormous impact that infectious diseases have on force readiness, on the effectiveness of military operations, and on regional peacekeeping capabilities, military planners rarely give the risks posed by such health challenges sufficient attention.

Third, infectious diseases also represent an indirect threat to security as major killers of civilian populations. Smallpox alone is estimated to have killed 300 million people in the twentieth century, about three times as many people that died in wars during the same time period. Today, infectious diseases—

HIV/AIDS, tuberculosis, malaria, and many others—continue to ravish the developing world. Of these, HIV/AIDS exemplifies the burden of disease because of its devastating impact, primarily in Africa. An estimated 20 million people have died globally since HIV/AIDS was reported in 1981, and 29.4 million are estimated to be living with the disease in sub-Saharan Africa as of 2002.[9] Countries such as Botswana, Zimbabwe, and Swaziland are witnessing prevalence rates in the 15 to 49 age group of 38.8 percent, 33.7 percent, and 33.4 percent, respectively.[10] With such a large percentage of these countries' populations sick and dying, economic productivity is drained through labor shortages and heightened absenteeism. National resources are redirected from critical needs such as education and infrastructure development to health care spending. Furthermore, economic development is impeded because the epidemic discourages capital investment, and gross national product decreases as HIV prevalence rates rise.[11] Poor health also reduces individual and family resources by diminishing savings and imposing higher health care costs. Left unabated, HIV/AIDS will not only continue to destroy the social fabric of communities in Africa, but also roll back economic development and impede democratic transition. Furthermore, HIV/AIDS will erode the capacity of governments to provide basic human services, place enormous strain on already fragile institutions, and with other pressures, potentially spark violence and state instability.

Although the HIV/AIDS pandemic does not directly threaten security in the way that HIV/AIDS impacts military populations, should HIV/AIDS contribute to factors that result in instability, there would be serious security implications for the directly impacted countries and for regional and international security. While it is difficult for the national security community to calculate the security risks associated with such a scenario, some degree of risk, however uncertain, does exist. Failure to consider the potentially serious health and security implications of HIV/AIDS on social stability would be shortsighted.

Fourth, HIV/AIDS is negatively impacting social stability and the security sectors in Africa while simultaneously creating a huge orphan cohort as parents succumb to the disease. AIDS orphans, approximately 13 million currently in Africa, are expected to double by 2010 and are estimated to grow to 40 million by 2020.[12] Lacking family support and guidance and educational and economic opportunities and ostracized socially, many AIDS orphans will be forced to turn to crime or prostitution to survive. Already, many orphans are feared to have been recruited into paramilitary and terrorist organizations that offer attractive incentives such as food, shelter, and a sense of purpose. Should the involvement of AIDS orphans in illicit activities increase as their numbers grow, many national security sectors in Africa will be hard pressed to effectively control growing criminal or insurgent elements of society. While presently AIDS orphans represent an indirect and relatively low security risk, should AIDS orphans become involved in illicit activities, the threat to security may become increasingly direct.

Fifth, in addition to the potential risk of infectious diseases contributing to instability in the developing world, globalization has increased the vulnerability of the developed world to infectious disease outbreaks originating abroad. An outbreak of SARS in China is only a plane ride away from Washington, D.C., London, or Tokyo and can no longer be viewed as a local event. The emergence and global proliferation of SARS illustrates the risks associated with the global spread of infectious disease.[13] Yet, we must be careful not to characterize all outbreaks of infectious diseases as security issues. Communicable diseases such as SARS represent a much higher risk of developing into a national or international security threat than other infectious diseases such as West Nile Virus or monkey pox. Even SARS, despite the relatively high level of risk associated with the outbreak and its declaration as a health emergency by the World Health Organization, did not reach proportions that would constitute a threat to national security. While SARS represented a public health crisis requiring the rapid implementation of emergency public health measures to contain and control the outbreak, it is difficult to argue that the national security of China, Canada, or the United States at any point was in serious jeopardy. This is not to say that infectious disease outbreaks cannot become security concerns. Without aggressive measures to control the outbreak, SARS could (and still may) develop into a security threat. In addition, most infectious disease experts agree that the emergence of a virulent strain of influenza could unleash a *pandemic* that would certainly constitute a global health crisis and possibly an international security crisis. Likewise, discovery of a *single case* of smallpox would be viewed as a public health, national, and international security crisis. The key point to highlight is that SARS, influenza, smallpox, monkey pox, West Nile Virus and other infectious diseases each have different levels of risk associated with them. While some outbreaks could potentially represent security concerns, not all emerging and reemerging infectious diseases carry the same level of risk. This must be kept in mind as we think about infectious diseases in the context of security.

Finally, many of the HIV prevalence trends seen in Africa a decade ago are now emerging in what is being called the "Next Wave" countries of China, Russia, and India.[14] If these trends are not halted and prevalence rates continue to climb, the "Next Wave" countries will completely transform the demographics of the HIV/AIDS pandemic in terms of the sheer numbers infected and the geographic distribution of the pandemic. India and China are countries with enormous populations and double-digit prevalence rates in these countries would translate into hundreds of millions of HIV-positive persons. Despite the explosive potential of HIV/AIDS in these countries, and the benefit of hindsight regarding the pandemic in Africa, it is difficult to calculate the degree of risk, in terms of public health and security, associated with the "Next Wave" countries.

If the past is any indication of the future, national security calculations are likely to be a primary catalyst for action in the "Next Wave" states. The experience in Africa over the past decade is instructive. Throughout the 1990s, the public health, humanitarian, and developmental communities warned of an impending HIV/AIDS tragedy in Africa and called for a stronger response by national governments and the international community to stem the spread of the disease. Although these warnings were heeded to some degree, it was not until January 2000 that the international community truly took notice when the United Nations Security Council convened a meeting to discuss AIDS. This was the first time that a health issue was considered by the UN body with primary responsibility for international peace and security. A National Intelligence Council report, *The Global Infectious Disease Threat and its Implications for the United States*, published in January 2000 corresponded with the Security Council meeting and with the Clinton administration's April 2000 announcement that it had formally designated AIDS as a threat to U.S. national security. These steps firmly established the linkage between HIV/AIDS and security, drew a great deal of attention in the international community to what had previously been a widely overlooked characterization of the HIV/AIDS challenge, and mobilized both political and financial capital to address the problem. We should not overlook that national and international security concerns were a primary driver behind the current response to HIV/AIDS and are likely to be a central factor in how the international community responds to epidemics in the "Next Wave" countries.

V. Conclusion

At a time when our conceptions of security are evolving rapidly, we must look hard at our answers to the question: What constitutes security? Although the debate remains divided on whether to include health issues in the security debate, clearly health and security challenges are intersecting with greater frequency and intensity. Some health and security challenges represent direct threats to security in its traditional context, while others remain indirect and uncertain threats. Given this uncertainty and ambiguity, much more work is needed to bring analytical clarity to the health and security paradigm. The first step toward developing an analytical framework is to elaborate on the specific characteristics that emerge from the health and security paradigm, which produces particular risks. By creating and applying a standard risk-based methodology, analysts and policymakers alike will have a tool to assess the nature of such problems and thereby fashion better responses to them.

Notes

1 Dennis Pirages, "Ecological Theory and International Relations," in Charles W. Kegley, Jr. and Eugene R. Wittkopf, eds., *The Global Agenda: Issues and Perspectives*, 5th ed. (New York: McGraw–Hill, 1998).

2 Report of the Secretary-General Boutros Boutros-Ghali, "An Agenda for Peace: Preventive Diplomacy, Peacemaking, and Peacekeeping," A/47/277-S/2411, January 31, 1992, p. 3. Also available online at www.un.org/Docs/SG/agpeace.html.

3 Andrew Price-Smith, *The Health of Nations: Infectious Diseases, Environmental Change, and Their Effects on National Security and Development* (Cambridge, MA: MIT Press, 2002). See Price-Smith for a discussion of the direct and indirect impact of health issues in terms of relative deprivation and on a state's capacity to govern.

4 Andre J Ognibene, "Medical and Infectious Diseases in the Theater of Operations," *Military Medicine*, vol. 52, no. 1, 1987, p. 14.

5 James McPherson, *Battle Cry of Freedom: The Civil War Era* (New York: Oxford University Press, 1988), p. 485.

6 Jonathan Ban, *Health, Security, and U.S. Global Leadership*, Health and Security Series, Special Report No. 2. (Washington, DC: Chemical and Biological Arms Control Institute, December 2001), p. 45.

7 Amir Attaran, "Malaria, The Terrorist's Friend," *The New York Times*, September 25, 2003.

8 Stefan Elbe, "Strategic Implications of HIV/AIDS," *The Adelphi Papers*, vol. 357, no. 1, July 2003 (London: International Institute for Strategic Studies), p. 18.

9 UNAIDS. *Fact Sheet: HIV/AIDS in Sub-Saharan Africa*, January 9, 2003, accessed September 23, 2003 at: http://www.unaids.org/html/pub/Publications/FactSheets03/FS_AIDS_in_Africa_2003_en_doc.htm.

10 UNAIDS. *Report on the Global HIV/AIDS Pandemic* (Geneva, July 2002), p. 190.

11 WHO. *Macroeconomics and Health: Investing in Health for Economic Development*, Report of the Commission on Macroeconomics and Health, December 20, 2001, pp. 22–23, 47, 103, 108.

12 USAID, UNAIDS, UNICEF, *Children on the Brink 2002: A Joint Report on Orphan Estimates and Program Strategies*, July 2002. The 2020 Figure is from Phiri, Stanley and Webb, "The Impact of HIV/AIDS on Orphans and Program and Policy Responses," in Giovanni Andrea Cornia, ed, *AIDS, Public Policy and Child Well-Being*, chapter 15 (New York: UNICEF, June 2002), http://www.unicef-icdc.org/research/ESP/aids/chapter15.pdf (accessed September 23, 2002).

13 For a review of the SARS outbreak see Elizabeth M. Prescott, "SARS: A Warning," *Survival*, vol. 45, no. 3, Autumn 2003, pp. 207–225.

14 National Intelligence Council, *The Next Wave of HIV/AIDS: Nigeria, Ethiopia, Russia, India, and China*, ICA 2002–04 D, September 2002.

10

GLOBAL HEALTH AND INTERNATIONAL SECURITY

Gro Harlem Brundtland

Source: *Global Governance*, 9:4 (2003), 417–23.

Historically in the West, disease was often seen as an impediment to exploration and a challenge to winning a war. Cholera and other diseases killed at least three times more soldiers in the Crimean War than did the actual conflict. Malaria, measles, mumps, smallpox, and typhoid felled more combatants than did bullets in the American Civil War. And the Panama Canal went over schedule became of "tropical" diseases—then unknown, untreatable, and often fatal.

Today, in an interconnected world, bacteria and viruses travel almost as fast as e-mail and financial flows. Globalization has connected Bujumbura to Bombay and Bangkok to Boston. There are no health sanctuaries. No impregnable walls exist between a world that is healthy, well-fed, and well-off and another that is sick, malnourished, and impoverished. Globalization has shrunk distances, broken down old barriers, and linked people. Problems halfway around the world become everyone's problem. Like a stone thrown on the waters, a difficult social or economic situation in one community can ripple and reverberate around the world.

Now, there are solutions for those diseases that plagued early explorers, soldiers, and colonists. We know how to prevent and treat malaria. There are vaccines for yellow fever and treatments for tuberculosis (TB). Although travelers from industrialized nations diligently take antimalarials and update vaccinations when visiting developing countries, the people living there do not have access to these precautions. Three thousand African children die each day from malaria. They die of vaccine-preventable diseases, like measles, by the hundreds of thousands, and millions of people are dying every year from HIV/AIDS (human immunodeficiency virus/acquired immunodeficiency syndrome).

Today, we cannot view health solely as an issue of how many people get ill and how many recover, of who lives and who dies. We must look at why.

169

And we should broaden debate to accept that health is an underlying determinant of development, security, and global stability. We must consider the impact of armed conflict and, perhaps more importantly, the silent march of diseases that devastate populations over time—these are the stones that cause the largest ripples, and the ones that go unnoticed until it is too late.

Twenty years ago, HIV was a specter, all but invisible on the horizon. It was considered a disease that affected specific minorities—gay men and intravenous drug users. Science was slow to respond. The world took more notice with the realization that HIV knew no borders. Given the right vector, it could infect anyone—man, woman, gay, straight, healthy, and hemophiliac. By 1990, wealthy countries were screening blood donors and teaching children how to protect themselves. Condom use increased and incidence declined. Then antiretrovirals were made available to those who could afford them. HIV diminished as an urgent public health problem in rich countries.

In 2003, more than 42 million people are HIV positive, with 30 million living in sub-Saharan Africa. Many are dying and many have died. These people are mothers and fathers, nurses and other health professionals, teachers, civil servants, miners, and soldiers. They are leaving a huge social and professional gap, which presents an imminent threat to countries struggling to develop. Those who remain are orphans, penniless grandmothers caring for their children's children, and family members and communities who are frightened, hurt, and stigmatized. Health systems are stretched well beyond their often frail capacities. We will see the effects of this tragedy for decades to come.

A number of political, economic, and social factors have combined to create a situation in which more than 12 million people in southern Africa have been affected by famine. No sudden event has caused the crisis. Rather, it comes as the result of a long process of underinvestment in human resources. This practice of denial and neglect has been exacerbated by the AIDS pandemic that, for example, has reversed much of the tremendous progress that Botswana had achieved and is becoming a burden in South Africa, Zimbabwe, Zambia, and Malawi. We see a downward spiral, weakening countries that can least afford it. We must address the underlying causes of famine, disease, and human suffering and arrest the decline before we are forced to deal with the ultimate consequences. HIV is encroaching in other areas—China, India, and the Central Asian republics. We simply cannot stand on the sidelines and watch another HIV crisis unfold before our eyes with the economic, social, and political devastation it will bring.

The explosion of conflict immediately brings to light the links between health and security—soldiers and civilians wounded and displaced by war. The medium-term impact is felt when people are uprooted and forced to live in camps with little sanitation or health services, schools are disrupted, and food is scarce. In Liberia, hundreds are suffering from cholera because there is not enough clean drinking water. In Iraq, insecurity makes it difficult for health workers to care for patients. In the Democratic Republic of Congo

(DRC), more than 3 million people have died, but many others are traumatized and plagued by diseases that attack, kill, and debilitate. The impact of conflicts is compounded when people spill across borders or flee their homes, professionals emigrate, and health and education systems crumble.

In the spring of 2003, however, a different kind of outbreak captured the public's attention, often garnering more column inches than the war in Iraq. Severe acute respiratory syndrome (SARS) put the world on high alert and elicited unprecedented international cooperation to stop a disease that hurt markets, tourism, and trade. Hospitals, even in the most well-developed countries with the most advanced health systems, confronted problems.

One infected person staying at an international hotel put the world at risk. Unlike other diseases, SARS was undiagnosable, untreatable, and fatal for one in every six people that contracted the disease. The response to SARS was global public health at its best. Scientists put aside their competition and shared their research and study results. Doctors from around the world gathered in virtual conferences to share advice. Public health authorities from every region flew to Geneva to share their success and failures with the 192 member states at the World Health Assembly. In just four short months, we identified a new disease and contained a global outbreak that could have become a global catastrophe.

The sudden shock made us all stand up and pay attention. Governments were committed, resources made available, people alerted, health workers given tools for action, and information resources shared. In short, there was global mobilization to fight a global threat. As a result, we are less likely to find ourselves ten years down the road with a SARS epidemic in the countries that can least afford it. In today's connected societies, there was no choice but to act. It was impossible to hide SARS in a world with the Internet and e-mail, or to pretend it did not exist or was contained.

What are the lessons learned? Investment in people and in enhanced international cooperation, for health as for many other arenas, are prerequisites for security. We must go back to the slow creep of disease—who is affected, and why? Malaria, TB, HIV, measles, diarrheal diseases, and respiratory infections are treatable but are hurting people in the poorest countries, where stagnant economies, social unrest, and the threat of civil war force the deterioration of health and education systems.

The numbers are not small. Between 1990 and 2000, the human development index declined in nearly thirty countries.[1] More than one-fifth of the world's population are unable to meet their daily subsistence requirements. Almost one-third of all children are undernourished. In many countries, increasing social inequality means that the poorest people have seen little or none of the benefits of economic growth. The average African household consumes 20 percent less today than it did twenty-five years ago.

A world where a billion people are deprived, insecure, and vulnerable is an unsafe world. The functional separation between domestic and international health problems is losing its usefulness as people and goods travel across continents. More than 2 million people cross international borders every day (about one-tenth of humanity each year) and more than 1 million travel from developing to industrialized countries each week.

We also know that in places where people feel powerless and watch as much of the rest of the world gets richer, hatred can be channeled in devastating ways. A giant construction site where the World Trade Center used to be reminds us of a world of conflict, a world divided. It exposes a new awareness of our vulnerability. We must counter the manipulation of despair. We should seek to engage even more strongly with countries in crisis, to promote the values of democracy and social justice.

We cannot afford to have large neglected areas where the population is left to fend for itself against diseases. Ebola, for example, with a 90 percent fatality rate when left untreated has so far been contained because it has been confined to small villages. Health systems, like that of Uganda, have done a fine job in isolating patients and restricting its spread. They were able to do this with the help of international specialists from the World Health Organization (WHO) and the Centers for Disease Control, in part because of the favorable security situation in the area of the outbreak.

What if an outbreak takes place in a devastated central African country? What if the security situation becomes so bad that we can not send international experts to assist in containing the outbreak? What if infected people start fleeing into cities, to neighboring countries, and eventually out of the region? The most recent Ebola outbreak almost resulted in such a nightmare scenario by spreading from the Congo into the neighboring DRC.

There are also places where the provision of health is a bridge for peace. Polio eradication has brought entire regions together. In sixteen countries across West Africa, warring factions laid down their weapons and picked up a vaccine vial as some 60 million children were protected against polio in less than one week.

In May 2003, the world came together in the largest demonstration of unity for health when 192 countries adopted the Framework Convention on Tobacco Control.[2] Implementation of this first truly international health treaty will lead to bans on tobacco advertising, price increases for tobacco products, efforts to control smuggling, and the creation of more smoke-free places. Developing countries, in particular, fought to have the convention adopted to help reverse the current trend, which if left unchecked would kill 10 million people annually by 2020. Such foresight and cooperation—for health, development, and global security—contributes to the creation of a global public good.

The health treaty is not the only answer. For diseases themselves, solutions include treatment for HIV and TB and preventive tools against measles, polio, and whooping cough. But what is the most effective method for getting these resources to those who need them most? The answer is investment in people.

As the eighteen leading economists and health experts who formed my Commission on Macroeconomics and Health have argued, disease impedes development and weakens societies.[3] Malaria alone cost Africa's combined gross domestic product about U.S.$100 billion, which could have been much less if that disease had been tackled thirty years ago when effective control measures first became available. The commission has presented a definitive argument for the need to invest in health as a prerequisite for economic development and an important part of any development strategy.

The commissioners concluded that health systems spending $10 or $12 per capita on health are not able to provide even the most basic health services. Their report calls for a six-fold increase in health expenditures for the developing world with a focus on a few key diseases and issues: AIDS, TB, malaria, children's diseases, and maternity conditions. As many as 8 million lives could be saved each year with a six-fold return on the investment in terms of economic growth if we managed to channel enough resources into health for the poorest countries to achieve the UN Millennium Development Goals.

Increased competitiveness in a global marketplace will not provide enough opportunities for poor countries to move out of poverty. The idea that international financial assistance should be limited to supporting free-market reforms and democracy is fortunately being challenged. But even among those of us who believe that overseas development assistance (ODA) is a crucial part of any attempt to create a better and more secure world, strict prioritizing of aid has become a matter of necessity. After a decade of shrinking resources, donors increasingly emphasize measurable results.

I am a strong proponent of this approach. We need to direct aid into activities that give concrete outcomes if we are to build momentum for development assistance. Key donors have made commitments to raise, not lower, their levels of ODA, and humanitarian aid and development assistance have helped reduce suffering and increase security. Through the Global Alliance for Vaccines and Immunization; the Global Fund to Fight AIDS, TB and Malaria; and a number of other alliances and partnerships, we have developed new tools. The common denominator is that these initiatives respond to countries' own priorities, process funds rapidly, reward results, and are transparent.

We see the devastating changes that disease brings to our world, but we also see that foresight, investment, and cooperation can make a difference. HIV has been with us for three decades, and its impact on societies and economies is well known. By contrast, the global effort to contain SARS with determination and speed limited the impact to thousands, not hundreds of thousands, of cases. We still face threats from the environment and from human manipulation of the natural world. We have already had one anthrax scare, and each of us has probably considered the threat of bioterrorism. SARS jumped from nature to humans—a rare occurrence requiring perfect conditions. But bioterrorism, while far from a simple undertaking, is controlled by people not nature.

The tools for countering these threats are in fact the same. Boosting capacity for surveillance is essential to detecting all diseases. Our experience with SARS exposed weaknesses in this vital function. Globally, we must strengthen disease surveillance and control. SARS was a warning and now we must take this opportunity to rebuild our public health protections.

We need more public health specialists who can tell us from where a disease emanated and to where it is liable to spread. But we can only find disease when we have the tools to look for it. Disease surveillance and response systems are critical, in conjunction with strong national, regional, and global linkages in reporting. Governments also need to invest more in infection control.

At the 2003 World Health Assembly, member states adopted a resolution that would revise and strengthen international health regulations. It hinges on putting a system in place to find, report, and stop infectious diseases. Depending on the threat, this will require continued international cooperation—a system in which all parties recognize that any disease, whether it is affecting rich or poor, will touch everyone at some point.

Commitment, foresight, investment, and cooperation are required. And for the next outbreak of SARS, or some even more infectious and deadlier illness, we may have very little time. Ultimately, improving people's lives remains the bottom line. The way that we work together to address current crises and prevent future ones will determine whether we succeed or fail in our efforts to advance global development, growth, security, and peace.

Notes

Gro Harlem Brundtland was director-general of the World Health Organization from 1998–2003, and is the former prime minister of Norway. This essay is based on a talk given in July 2003 at the Geneva Centre for Security Policy.

1 United Nations Development Program, *Human Development Report 2002* (New York: Oxford University Press, 2002), pp. 149–156.
2 The final text of the convention is available online at www.who.int/tobacco/fctc/text/final/en/.
3 World Health Organization, *Macroeconomics and Health: Investing in Health for Economic Development*, Report of the Commission on Macroeconomics and Health (WHO: Geneva, 2001). Text is available online at www.cmhealth.org/.

11

HEALTH AND INTERNATIONAL SECURITY

Jack C. Chow

Source: *Washington Quarterly*, 16:2 (1996), 63–77.

A fundamental national security obligation of governments is providing and assuring the safety and well-being of their citizens. To the extent authorities lapse in these duties, unmitigated health burdens will add to discontent, conflict, and desire for political change. Accordingly, examining the nexus between conflict, disease, and instability, and challenging assumptions that medical and human rights emergencies are isolated and self-limiting, would establish global health in a strategic context for the security interests of the United States in the post-cold war era. The goal of this article is to make such an examination.

A world besieged by disease

In terms of disease, the earth remains a dangerous, unstable habitat. Early in this century, a great influenza pandemic killed nearly 20 million people worldwide, 500,000 in the United States alone.[1] Today, in spite of antibiotics and vaccines, myriads of infectious and chronic diseases ravage continents and countries with impunity, afflicting millions and evading containment.

The global extent of disease is staggering. According to the World Health Organization (WHO), more than 2 billion people are seriously ill at any one time with diseases that account for over 50 million deaths annually.[2] Malaria alone infects up to 500 million people each year while tuberculosis (TB) scourges 1.9 billion people, or one-third of the world's population, and kills 3 million people annually.[3] At present rates, by the year 2005, 2 billion people will be infected by TB, a prospect that triggered WHO's 1993 declaration of a "global tuberculosis emergency." In sub-Saharan Africa, diseases striking children—diarrhea, parasites, and respiratory illnesses—cause such high rates of mortality that the median age of death in the region is a mere 5 years, compared to nearly 75 years in advanced countries.[4]

175

Political instability and disease often reinforce each other. Once dormant, cholera has struck several continents, often in tandem with armed conflict or large-scale upheaval. Disease heightened political competition among ethnic rivals during the Rwandan crisis. As throngs of refugees crowded into camps in neighboring Zaire and Tanzania, the wretched conditions erupted into a fury of cholera, dysentery, and other highly communicable diseases. The United Nations (UN) urged the refugees to return home to halt rampant propagation of disease and to encourage restoration of order in Rwanda. Hutu authorities in the camps, however, openly discouraged repatriation to deny the Tutsis their claim to rule.[5] Hutu refugees were caught between enduring the squalor of the camps or returning to Rwanda, where they risked death under Tutsi rule.

Adding to the world's burden of illness is the threat of "new and reemerging diseases" caused by microorganisms that have previously been quiescent or have arisen renewed by mutation. Outbreaks by these pathogens are striking with frightening and deadly frequency. In recent years, the emergence of legionnaires' disease, Lyme disease, AIDS, drug-resistant tuberculosis, gonorrhea, and malaria, and the reappearance of previously suppressed entities such as plague, cholera, hanta virus, and "flesh eating" variants of streptococcus, have defied the medical armamentarium. The most recent outbreak of Ebola virus in Zaire, which incited emergency measures by U.S. and international health authorities, demonstrates the pathogens' power to wreak sudden havoc.

With rapid population growth, industrialization, integrated markets, international travel, and environmental changes, new patterns of interactions between man and reservoirs of disease-causing microorganisms will instigate opportunities for rogue pathogens to affect regional stability. The 1994 plague outbreak in India, for example, had an impact far beyond its epidemiological boundaries. The ensuing panic resulted in abrupt shutdowns of major industries, including aviation, exports, and tourism, as stigmatization of products fanned irrational fears of contamination. The outbreak cost India's economy nearly $2 billion.[6]

AIDS

Over the past decade, the explosive emergence of the human immunodeficiency virus (HIV) has propelled AIDS to the forefront of global concerns. No other disease has equaled AIDS in dominating policies and commanding societal fears. From its beginning, the unrelenting propagation of HIV has come to signify the failure of medical and political systems alike to contain an international health emergency.

As AIDS accelerates, its political dimension is emerging as a major destabilizing factor. HIV's infiltration into the middle class, ruling elites, and military personnel of developing countries poses unique threats to security. In these countries, government officials risk recrimination should their actions be perceived as having helped spread the disease. HIV within military ranks diminishes morale and readiness. Furthermore, rumors among and perceptions by local populations that peacekeeping troops from other countries harbor the virus could complicate deployments. Even wealthy countries are not immune to the destabilizing political impact of AIDS. HIV blood testing scandals in Germany, France, and Switzerland have resulted in national uproars and compelled the dismissal or prosecution of government and other officials.

Eastern Europe, Russia, and the newly independent states of the former Soviet Union are especially vulnerable to AIDS. With rampant poverty, drug use, prostitution, weakened law enforcement, and a freer interchange of people, accelerated HIV infection rates in the region are almost certain unless strong preventive measures are undertaken. Also worrisome are the fear-mongering and ostracization that exacerbate social tensions and even arouse nationalistic passions. Fearing an influx of HIV carriers from outside, Russia imposed new HIV-testing requirements upon long-term foreign residents.[7] Should HIV reach uncontrollable levels there and in other struggling democracies, economic and political reforms could be derailed not only by the consumption of money and the death of individuals, but by further restrictions on liberties as well.

Drugs

Reducing drug abuse and its subversive impact upon governments remains vital to global security. The addictive power of illicit substances over the human body and behavior drives a multibillion dollar illegal drug industry that exploits the habits of millions of individuals. The protection and perpetuation of drug profits have engendered efforts by traffickers to attain and wield political influence. The rampant bribery, intimidation, and corruption of local and national officials throughout Latin America, Southeast Asia, and the Middle East are well known.

Newly arising narcopolitical empires pose direct threats in regions important to U.S. interests. Failing economies and weakened governments are prime targets for drug infiltration and subversion. With the dissolution of the former Soviet Union into smaller, poorer states with lax law enforcement, drug traffickers have quickly established new distribution channels. Through bribery and intimidation, many rings operate freely with the protection and consent of authorities. The government of oil-rich Nigeria, rife with corruption, was cited by the United States as notoriously abetting trafficking in spite of both entreaties and warnings.[8]

The easy profitability of drugs confounds efforts to sustain democratic institutions and legitimate economies. Refugees from fighting and political turmoil in the Middle East, the Balkans, and Southeast Asia often resort to trafficking for survival. Guerrillas in Peru and Afghanistan bankrolled military operations and undermined authorities with narcotics profits. Economic hardship in key regional states like Mexico and Turkey is swelling the ranks of the impoverished who may resort to the drug trade, further compounding the adverse impact of failed national policies.

Collapsing health infrastructures

Sustaining health requires dedicated systems of delivery for services and treatment. In turn, adequate medical infrastructures with trained professionals, facilities, and financing require a stable political economy to provide both resources and public support. When economies and governments fail, or are chronically enfeebled, health systems rapidly falter, leaving populations more prone to illness and weakening economic and social stability.

With dilapidated economies, the nations of the former Soviet Union are deprived of the resources necessary to sustain public health. With growing numbers of impoverished, malnourished, and undertreated people but no money for medical countermeasures, these states have been wracked by quickly proliferating outbreaks of disease: cases of diphtheria alone skyrocketed from nearly 600 in 1989 to almost 40,000 in 1994. From Russia, diphtheria has already spread outward to 12 of the 13 former Soviet republics.[9] More inhabitants of conflict-stricken states, such as Georgia, Chechnya, and Armenia, suffer from illness as armed conflict and political chaos perpetuate disease-propagating conditions.

Debilitated health systems worsen the impact on health of environmental degradation and rapid population growth. As pollutants and overcrowding proliferate, countries are faced with insidious threats that freely traverse national boundaries without the resources to combat them. Tightened assistance budgets among donor entities further restrict what these countries can do.

Humanitarian warfare

That wars inflict a terrible toll upon civilians is an all too familiar reality. Depiction in the media of the plight of refugees, the starving, and the besieged conveys the impression that such sufferings are unintended by-products of war. What has emerged, however, is that combatants are increasingly willing to deliberately control or destabilize populations as a means to achieve their war aims.

"Humanitarian" warfare—aggression through the control and the denial of vital human needs—now complements or even substitutes for direct force. In many conflicts, starvation and privation are primary weapons, reminiscent of wars of premodern eras. Having learned that denying resources can yield substantial leverage for less risk and cost than armed conflict, warring parties unflinchingly subvert civil order as strategic doctrine. No more than a token force at a chokepoint is needed to be effective: marauding bands of soldiers in Bosnia have halted entire food convoys from reaching destitute towns.

War by starvation

Amid scarcity, the political and strategic value of food outweighs its nutritional content. In times of extreme privation, power accrues to those with access to stable supplies. In famine-racked sub-Saharan Africa, the struggle to control food defined war strategy. As outside aid either increased or diminished power among rivals, the availability and distribution of relief were subject to manipulation. Partisans bitterly and openly disputed efforts to aid populations under enemy control for fear that the food would strengthen armies rather than civilians. Prime Minister Sadiq al-Mahdi of Sudan forthrightly told UNICEF relief officials: "Your food is killing my soldiers."[10]

Food and aid have intrinsic political value. In their battle for independence from Ethiopia, Eritrean rebels asserted their authority by setting conditions for the arrival and distribution of aid. Aid was used to discriminate against targeted ethnic groups. In Sudan, food delivered to a government-controlled town was diverted away from refugee Dinka tribesmen whose loyalties were suspect in Khartoum. In Somalia, Operation Restore Hope and its premise as a purely humanitarian mission were immediately undermined by the Somali warlords' struggle for advantage. Somali strongman Mohamed Farah Aideed publicly "welcomed" the intervention, calculating that an ostensible alignment with the United States would strengthen his standing against his rivals. An Aideed rival also claimed alliance with the United States and used this as a pretext to attack his own opponents on the Americans' supposed behalf.

Open subversion of assistance mocked the donors' intention that aid should be free of politicization. Donors risked entanglement in local disputes when providing relief and fending off manipulation. During Ethiopia's famine wars, assistance routed through the Eritrean rebels bolstered their claims to governance, thereby incurring attacks on aid by the regime of Mengistu Haile Mariam. But aid entrusted to Mengistu risked diversion of food to his own forces. Although the United States diversified delivery channels to reduce dependency on either side, it could not prevent the use of food as leverage. After capturing a key port, the Eritreans threatened to block shipments and starve Mengistu-controlled populations in retaliation for the government's own acts of deprivation. Faced with the prospect of mass starvation from the standoff, President George Bush and Soviet leader Mikhail Gorbachev declared a bilateral effort to open the port. Defiant, the rebels continued to block shipments and demanded that the city be officially recognized as Eritrean.

Countertactics, such as the withholding of aid as a means of applying pressure, may actually extend or prolong suffering. In Somalia, the Bush administration felt compelled to withhold aid to the Aideed-controlled city of Bardera, despite the desperate situation there, to avoid strengthening Aideed's authority beyond that of his rivals.

Keeping people alive when others want them to starve politicizes assistance because help is perceived as potentially threatening. As aiding the besieged narrows disparities in power, relief itself becomes inherently political in nature, instigating a struggle for control. With up to 800 million people in the world suffering from some degree of protein-energy malnutrition—many in regions with endemic conflicts—and because food sustains civilian and soldier alike, the calculated use of starvation to win conflicts seems destined to grow.

War by privation

In Bosnia, human deprivation characterized the country's ethnic war. Deliberate cutoffs of food, water, medicine, and heat indelibly marked the war as a campaign of terror against civilians. With no ethnic group possessing sufficient strength to attain outright military victory, systematic blockade of enclaves was used as an efficient if deadly method in capturing territory or extracting concessions. Negotiations to reach besieged pockets consumed both time and political capital as numerous hard-won agreements securing convoy routes were capriciously nullified by military field commanders.

The propaganda wars of the factions compounded the suffering. Forces purportedly fired at their own cities to direct blame against their enemy and thus elicit outside sympathy. When Serb forces threatened Bihac, the town's women and children were sequestered, ostensibly to prevent panic by defending soldiers fleeing with their families, but also to draw media attention to Serb attacks. The desire for victimization required participants; allowing civilians to escape would have dissipated sympathetic media coverage.

The degree to which roles for peacekeepers attempting to ameliorate privation has become conflicted is embodied in the UN's reluctant agreement to enforce the Serbian siege at Sarajevo and sustain a tenuous cease-fire. During the winter of 1992, the Serbs cut off utilities, fuel, and even water chlorination. Faced with imminent disaster, UN forces struck an expedient but morally difficult bargain with the Serbs—refugees would not be allowed to flee the city in exchange for Serb permission for relief flights to land. To the Serbs, to hold a population captive was more important than allowing it to escape to areas where Serbs had no control. The Sarajevo airport symbolized a painful duality of neutralized peacekeeping: as UN soldiers captured fleeing Sarajevans at the tarmac's edge, UN cargo planes landed only yards away bearing the food to sustain the would-be refugees in their captivity.

Dependency does not always entail acquiescence; aid recipients can exert substantial reverse leverage upon donors. In the winter of 1993, in a stunning act of brinkmanship, Sarajevo officials rejected UN shipments to protest the paucity of aid to other Muslim enclaves and castigated the UN's inability to force supplies past Serb obstructions. Sarajevo's hunger strike prompted the UN high commissioner for refugees, Sadako Ogata, to push aid into besieged enclaves, only to find the Serbs implacably opposed. Frustrated, Ogata then suspended all UN efforts, blaming political manipulation by the combatants.[11] The tumultuous decision making brought renewed pressure on the UN, whose secretary general, Boutros Boutros-Ghali, overruled Ogata and ordered operations to resume. The incident underscored the dependence of donors upon the consent of recipients. The Sarajevans, by spurning aid, even as an act of desperate expediency, momentarily deprived the aid effort of an implied mandate from victims that they wanted such help. Without consent, undertaking major rescue efforts with the accompanying risk to lives becomes politically infeasible.

When confronted by this war of privation with all its attendant risks, the United States and Europe balked at direct, full-scale intervention, preferring a risk-dispersing policy of collective and retractable engagement through the North Atlantic Treaty Organization. The allies at first hoped that alleviating privation on humanitarian grounds would facilitate diplomatic bargaining. But the Bosnian factions, as has happened elsewhere, saw subverting such assistance as advancing their own agendas.

Forced displacement

Mass flight, when compounded with war's catastrophic effects, breeds destabilization because existing authority is confused and dissolved. The Bosnian cauldron of warring ethnic groups fostered mass expulsion as a means of acquiring territory or settling historical enmities. Croatia's military strategy in capturing the Serb-held Krajina territory employed selective targeting of key towns to bring out a wave of refugees that stood in the way of Serb resistance. The flood of Croatian Serbs into Bosnia transformed the region's political calculus by bolstering Croatian Serb strength against Bosnian Muslims and Croats while causing fissures in Serbia's own military and political leadership.

The unleashing of refugees has been central to diplomatic strategies directed against the United States in other cases too. Fidel Castro's boatlifts in 1980 and 1994 sought to burden the United States with thousands of unwanted individuals and to force reconsideration of American economic sanctions. The economic and social strains from the influx polarized Florida's electorate, propelling domestic concerns directly into foreign policy. Citing Castro's attempt to discharge his own economic and political troubles onto America, the Clinton administration altered long-standing U.S. policy and sequestered intercepted refugees. The eventual deal, which allowed those already sequestered to immigrate but forcibly repatriated future boat escapees, defused the crisis without compromising the U.S. embargo. Nonetheless, Castro's maneuvers, although unsuccessful in relieving economic sanctions, forced Washington to change an immigration policy of high domestic sensitivity.

Even the very threat of a refugee crisis may provoke either hesitation or resolve as aversion to political entanglement clashes with the desire to save lives. The horrors of Rwanda were a telling example of this tension. Chastened by Somalia, the Clinton administration initially sought to avoid direct involvement. President Clinton declared that the United States could not "solve every such outburst of civil strife or militant nationalism simply by sending in our forces."[12]

Within days, however, as the human dimensions of the slaughter and the chaotic exodus unfolded, the administration relented and dispatched a small U.S. force to provide limited aid. The toll of human suffering thus proved great enough to override enunciated policy in a region of no strategic consequence to the United States.

"Safety zones" or "safe havens" created for humanitarian purposes can become dangerous sanctuaries. The French safety zone in Rwanda induced such massive numbers of people to converge on it that relief efforts were overwhelmed. Further moves to curtail or control these flows, such as Zaire's intermittent closure of its borders, only exacerbated panic. When France withdrew from its zone, the feared loss of protection instigated additional flight to the Zaire border. Humanitarian enclaves may blur national boundaries and even weaken authority to the point where conflict is created, rather than averted. Camps along the Thai–Myanmar border set up to protect refugees from Myanmar were frequently raided by the Myanmar military to forcibly repatriate their inhabitants. The U.S.-enforced "no-fly" protection zone over northern Iraq, while shielding the Kurds from Baghdad, may have inadvertently also sheltered the infiltration of Turkish rebel groups that led to Turkey's subsequent armed incursion into the area.

Exploiting disaster

Major natural disasters are prominent destabilizing events with consequences for both health and political stability. Public health is endangered when delivery systems for food, water, and medical supplies are disrupted or destroyed. But disasters also expose the political vulnerabilities of governments. Constituents see their government's responsiveness as a primary test of its competence. Abrupt, extensive destruction shatters organized functions and operations, forcing leaders to reassemble their own authority. Political rivals may then seize on public perceptions of inadequacies or delays to press for change.

Recent history is replete with the political aftershocks of disasters. The 1972 earthquake in Nicaragua and the Somoza government's mishandling of relief spurred the popular discontent that fueled the rise to power of the Sandinistas. The 1985 Mexico City earthquake and the government's tepid response cost the ruling Partido Revolucionario Institucional (PRI) substantial support. Sensing discontent arising in part from the quake, opposition groups arose to challenge Carlos Salinas de Gortari, the PRI presidential nominee, who barely won election. The devastating 1988 earthquake in Armenia so stressed a Soviet economy already tottering from the Chernobyl nuclear reactor disaster that Soviet leader Gorbachev reversed long-standing policy and permitted foreign assistance. Public anger over the Japanese government's slow response to the 1995 Kobe earthquake kindled widespread criticism of Prime Minister Tomiichi Murayama from opposition parties, and government agencies blamed each other for inadequacies in the rescue efforts.

The withholding of emergency help has been used to apply political pressure. When a hurricane struck Nicaragua in 1988, the Reagan administration chose not to provide aid, citing concerns that the ruling Sandinistas could not be trusted to distribute aid to its intended recipients.[13] The large losses from the hurricane added to the Sandinistas' portfolio of economic problems, and the United States had no desire to ease their new burdens. Meanwhile, anti-Sandinista groups accused Sandinista leader Daniel Ortega of using the crisis to rally political support for his flagging regime. Cuba's offer of troops to assist relief efforts prompted opposition claims that Castro was making a disguised attempt to reinforce Sandinista rule.

Even expeditious responses may not always be welcome. In 1990, when the United States provided aid after a powerful earthquake struck the Philippines, American efficiency cast an unfavorable light on the Aquino government's sluggish responses. Assistance from abroad fueled local criticism of the Philippines' continued dependency on the United States. This perception complicated ongoing negotiations over the Clark air and Subic Bay naval bases. Ironically, later volcanic eruptions shut down both facilities, diminished their already depreciated post-cold war value, and ultimately hastened the U.S. departure from the bases. When the United States provided military logistical assistance to Bangladesh in 1991 following a cyclone that killed over 100,000 people, the Indian government made known its displeasure at the presence of American forces in the region, asserting that the U.S. efforts displaced those of nongovernmental organizations. New Delhi perceived humanitarian efforts that helped a rival as threatening to its own political interests.

Strategy versus charity

Countering humanitarian warfare and the burdens of global disease presents new, profound challenges to security. In struggling to define its role in these crises, the United States confronts the tension between wanting to help and wanting to avoid the inherent risks involved in reimposing order. Protecting and sustaining large populations is risky, expensive, and open-ended, and containing chaotic events requires large-scale force and forthright commitment. Meanwhile, the Pentagon worries that humanitarian diversions will reduce military readiness; Congress pushes cuts in foreign aid and advocates retrenching U.S. international obligations; and the administration contends with articulating policy in the face of proliferating disasters.

The debate on intervention reveals the fundamental ambivalence for the United States of undertaking large-scale, open-ended humanitarian operations, especially when there is substantial risk to life. This tension might be characterized as a conflict between strategy, or the pursuit of national interests, and charity, the delivery of help on an egalitarian basis. Without a clear rationale, the altruistic tradition of the American people is a tenuous license for action; public support for U.S. relief efforts in Somalia evaporated when

American troops were killed, compelling the end of U.S. and UN efforts. In contrast, when the Rwandan slaughters swelled into hundreds of thousands of deaths, overriding humanitarian concerns superseded that country's lack of geopolitical value to the United States and compelled it to take action.

Toward strategic humanitarianism

The emergence of disaster and disease as threats to global stability, coupled with the reality of limited resources and wavering political support, requires the United States to rank its priorities about where, when, and how to intervene, and for whom. The problem is to define the basis of such a policy. A purely strategic basis of intervention would exclude future Rwandas and Somalias, whereas a charitable basis alone would embroil the United States in nearly every conflict of consequence.

In today's rapidly evolving and uncertain geopolitical landscape, U.S. foreign policy interests might be well served by adopting a principle of strategic humanitarianism: a linkage of U.S. assistance with achieving U.S. national aims in the international system. Charity and strategy should be brought together in support of a world order more congruent with American values.

In deciding the necessity or even desirability of unilateral action during health or humanitarian crises, the following criteria would need to be considered:

Threat to U.S. geopolitical or diplomatic interests Challenges that threaten nations or peoples of strategic importance to the United States ought to command the highest attention of policymakers. The Eurasian landmass and the Middle East are prime areas of concern. American protection of Iraqi Kurds from Saddam Hussein's persecution, for example, served not only humanitarian objectives but also the strategic U.S. interest in impeding Baghdad's political and military recuperation after the Persian Gulf War.

Morality and values The United States rightly prides itself on being a nation that supports democratic principles and is responsive to humanitarian needs. The "CNN era," however, has saturated the public with depictions of crises of such vividness and frequency as to heighten overall awareness of global human suffering but weaken support for unilateral intervention in any subsequent crisis. To sustain support for strategic humanitarianism, the nation would be well served, through public dialogue and well-articulated leadership, by the identification of those values that the United States would be willing to defend on either a universal or selective basis. Indeed, humanitarian intervention may be embarked upon in special situations to fulfill a national sense of duty to humanity.

Magnitude of disaster The United States has an abiding interest in averting large-scale disasters that affect great numbers of people or large swaths of land. Genocide and global disease pandemics are among those calamities

184

that should warrant U.S. concern because they degrade other U.S. national interests, such as political stability in key regions, and, in the case of genocide, violate deeply held moral values. Of central importance is gauging the danger that an incident will escalate into ever more death and destruction. Predicting how, when, and why nascent conflicts mutate into the future Rwandas or Bosnias is essential if the United States is to accurately determine what national interests, if any, are at stake in a given situation and what actions, if any, may be needed to protect them.

Risks and costs   Miscalculating the price of intervention—lives lost, dollars spent, or political capital consumed—can gravely undermine political support for action. Policy limited to attaining discrete objectives has the strongest likelihood of success, thereby sustaining its political viability. When the United States feels pressure to intervene in areas where it has no clear geopolitical interests at stake, such as Rwanda or Somalia, it should avoid getting involved except when there are compelling moral reasons to do so or when it can identify limited, tangible, and attainable outcomes that can be pursued within the realm of politically tolerable risk. As Americans learned from Somalia, intervention can add risk disproportionate to the minimal stakes involved. Should, however, another major disaster befall a key ally like Mexico, whose importance is much greater to the United States, the large U.S. political and economic interests at stake would warrant much stronger responses.

To implement an effective policy of strategic humanitarianism, the following actions might be taken:

Establish a "U.S. humanitarian command"   This entity, composed of specialized military as well as civilian medical and logistical units, would support an array of humanitarian activities, such as coordinating the efforts of private relief groups or clearing land mines to protect civilians following wars. Once activated to pursue unilateral objectives, the command could respond quickly to crises with sufficient resources to be successful. Such a command would make possible the development of a wider array of options integrating both strategic and moral considerations.

Expand national intelligence capabilities   Strengthening the ability of the United States, through improved technical means or new analytical frameworks, to gather information and assess threatening health situations would enhance decision making at a stage early enough to consider preventive action. Gauging the intentions of parties that could exploit distressing conditions or undertake humanitarian warfare, and estimating the success of U.S. action under certain circumstances will be essential to politico-military risk assessment.

Sustain multilateral capabilities for humanitarian response and for disease abatement   It is in the interest of the United States to support international institutions and activities that engage the world community in sharing the risks and responsibilities of averting global health threats and ending humanitarian warfare, especially in areas or situations with reduced geopolitical stakes for the United States. Ensuring sufficient global capacity would reduce U.S. involvement outside a defined sphere of limits. A multilateral agenda might include imposing tough sanctions against the exploitation of basic human needs or refurbishing institutions such as the WHO to make them less bureaucratic and more engaged in combating disease. Furthermore, a dialogue, perhaps initiated by a world summit on global health and humanitarian assistance, might be established to seek a working consensus.

Global health and the national interest

Unlike other transnational threats, health has never been defined as an element of national and international security. The nature of the global health crisis—diffuse, costly, long term, with uncertain outcomes—eludes traditional diplomatic-military approaches. Contemporary security institutions remain reliant upon force-based intervention in protecting U.S. interests abroad. The security community ought to recognize that government failure to meet basic needs is a frequent cause of strife and that, in some nations, citizens judge the effectiveness and even the legitimacy of their government by its ability to promote health.

The extent of disease both in the United States and abroad is symptomatic of the world's collective failure to support viable, stable economies and governing authorities. AIDS is a prominent example of how just one disease has put entire generations at risk for social strife, and yet more important, for premature death. To the degree that illness and instability together breed further disorder, facilitate discontent, and engender warfare, any future consideration of international security as it affects American interests must consider health-based threats.

The reality of global interdependency subjects the United States to the repercussions of disorder from distant quarters. Conversely, prudent engagement by the United States in addressing key health-related problems would not only benefit the international community but U.S. citizens as well. As the world is engulfed by turmoil, the United States is now reconsidering its international commitments. Although the United States cannot be expected to solve all the world's problems, the value of its engagement to avert future health disasters such as the AIDS pandemic is readily apparent.

Such an engagement will only be successful if it has a base of domestic support. The recent profusion of disasters has sensitized the public to the destabilizing impact of large-scale destruction. Marshaling that understanding to confront global calamities will require enlightened and assertive leadership. The question remains whether Americans have the will to invest the proverbial ounce of prevention that will spare them the expensive pounds of curing disorder.

Notes

The views in this article are those of the author only. He expresses appreciation to Robert Blackwill of Harvard University for reviewing the manuscript and offering helpful comments.

1 Institute of Medicine, *Emerging Infections—Microbial Threats to Health in the United States* (Washington, D.C.: National Academy Press, 1992), Summary, p. 1.

2 David Brown, "Infection Is World's No. 1 Cause of Death," *Washington Post*, May 2, 1995.

3 World Health Organization World Wide Web reference page (http://www.who.ch/whois/malinfo/2-repest.html).

4 World Bank, *World Development Report 1993, Investing in Health* (New York, N.Y.: Oxford University Press, 1993).

5 Jonathan C. Randal, "New Rwandan Regime, Ousted Hutus Vie for Refugees," *Washington Post*, July 26, 1994; Raymond Bonner, "Wisdom of Sending Rwandans Home Divides Officials," *New York Times*, July 29, 1994.

6 *India Today*, October 31, 1994.

7 Alessandra Stanley, "Russian AIDS Law Requires Testing for Most Foreigners," *New York Times*, April 4, 1995.

8 Elaine Sciolino, "State Department Report Labels Nigeria Major Trafficker of Drugs to U.S.," *New York Times*, April 5, 1994.

9 Centers for Disease Control and Prevention, *Morbidity and Mortality Weekly Report*, March 17, 1995.

10 Editorial, "A Killing Silence in the Sudan," *New York Times*, January 17, 1989.

11 David B. Ottaway, "Three Warring Factions Are Accused of Mixing Relief with Politics," *Washington Post*, February 18, 1993.

12 The White House, President Clinton's Address to the U.S. Naval Academy, May 25, 1994.

13 Julie Johnson, "U.S. Rules Out Nicaragua Storm Aid," *New York Times*, October 25, 1988.

Part 2

SECURITIZING HEALTH

12

SECURITIZING INFECTIOUS DISEASE

Sara E. Davies*

Source: *International Affairs*, 84:2 (2008), 295–313.

Approximately 14.7 million people die each year from known and preventable infectious diseases.[1] Respiratory infection, AIDS, diarrhoeal diseases, tuberculosis (TB) and malaria were the five leading causes of mortality from infectious disease between 2002 and 2006.[2] At the same time, the possibility of a pandemic influenza represents one of the most serious threats to global health because it is one of the few infections that could be transmitted easily and to which all populations would be equally susceptible.[3] In addition to all of this, there are a number of neglected infectious diseases such as guinea worm disease, schistosomiasis, leprosy, Buruli ulcer, cholera, dengue, dengue haemorrhagic fever, measles and human rabies, all of which cause painful debilitating side-effects and/or death, but receive little budgetary support for research or prevention.[4]

In this article I will trace how the international community—in particular, western states and the World Health Organization (WHO)—have combined forces to construct infectious disease as an existential security threat that requires new rules and behaviours for its effective containment. The outcome of this has been the development of international health cooperation mechanisms that place western fears of an outbreak reaching them above the prevention of such outbreaks in the first place. In turn, the desire of the WHO to assert its authority in the project of disease surveillance and containment has led it to develop global health mechanisms that primarily prioritizes the protection of western states from disease contagion.

The WHO has a history of seeking to dominate health agendas, and on previous occasions its own health agenda has been dominated by that of its main donor states.[5] What is important about the political relationship between the WHO and developed states in this case is that the WHO has been a primary actor in constructing the emerging discourse of infectious disease securitization, and western states in particular have been quick to engage with this discourse. Developing states have been noticeable in this process only by their absence as key actors. Nevertheless, the notification and verification of an infectious disease outbreak relies upon its confirmation by the state,[6] and there has been a collective failure, first, to deal with the possibility that a state or group of states may reject the discourse of securitization and withhold cooperation and second, that the affected state may not be aware of the outbreak. As Checkel argues, the mechanisms by which norms are internalized may result in states acting in very different ways to the same phenomenon.[7] The result could be that the WHO becomes locked into one social construction of infectious disease that crowds out alternative, potentially more effective, response mechanisms.

As has been argued elsewhere, the problem with securitizing infectious disease is that securitization locks agents into the logic of defining a referent object and an external threat source.[8] Security, as Buzan et al. argue, can be best defined as a 'self-referential practice, because it is in this practice that the issue become a *security issue*—not necessarily because a real existential threat exists but becauses the issue is presented as such a threat'.[9] Therefore, while the WHO ostensibly seeks to fulfil its mandate by securitizing the health of all, states inevitably seek to secure the health of their citizens. The result has been that the WHO has ended up running a global surveillance system that prioritizes western states' concerns. This has occurred, I argue, largely because of the WHO's interest in retaining an authoritative role in the area of global health governance. The conundrum is that in capitulating to western concerns, the WHO may have actually compromised its moral authority and the potential for cooperation with developing states affected by outbreaks.[10]

This article will proceed in three sections. The first section will chart the increased awareness of western states during the 1990s that infectious diseases posed a potential threat to their citizens' health. This increased awareness led to the emergence of infectious diseases as an item on national security agendas. The securitization of infectious disease led western states to increase their support for surveillance and response measures. This created a dilemma for the WHO, because individual acts to securitize disease by individual states posed a potential challenge to the global organization's authority on these matters.

This analysis leads into the second section of the article, which explores the WHO's securitization of infectious disease. This occurred at the same time that securitization by western states was increasing. The rationale for the WHO was that increased awareness of the problem would raise the profile of infectious diseases in general, demonstrate the threat that infectious disease could pose to both developing *and* developed states, and thus prevent western states from creating their own independent national surveillance mechanisms for infectious diseases. I trace how the combination of the WHO's motives led to their argument that the best response to the threat of infectious disease was the creation of the Global Outbreak and Alert Response Network (GOARN), which would manage disease outbreak and alerts at the international level under the WHO's auspices. GOARN has been promoted as the pinnacle of the WHO's authority in global health governance.[11] However, I suggest that it may also represent a demonstration of the WHO's attempt to retain its authority and privileged position in the global response to infectious disease.

In the third section of the article I explain why the WHO was so concerned with setting up a surveillance mechanism that retained western interest and support. I suggest that Barnett and Finnemore's work on the constitutive relationship between international organizations and states helps to explain the impact that the securitization of infectious disease has had on the organization and mandate of the WHO.[12] I argue that the widespread assumption that the development of GOARN has been the product of the successful securitization of infectious disease, which will in turn improve compliance with the WHO's new mechanism for global health governance, is flawed. The main problem is that the causes of non-compliance have not been adequately addressed by these new measures. This, I argue, is because the rationale dominating GOARN's construction has largely related to preserving the WHO's authority in surveillance of and response to infectious disease, and maintaining the support of western states by allaying their fears of epidemics reaching their shores.

The securitization of infectious disease by western states

By the late 1970s there was some confidence among public health officials that the risk of infectious disease had decreased. It was widely believed that new treatments, vaccines and knowledge of microbes would lead to the eradication of infectious disease as a major cause of death.[13] Just a decade later, however, this optimism had proved to be ill-founded. The outbreak and spread of HIV/AIDS, followed by the resurgence of stronger microbe-resistant pathogens, such as malaria, TB, meningitis and dengue fever, were compounded by the fear that bioterrorists might use deadly pathogens as a weapon of war.[14] Since the late 1980s new infectious pathogens have been discovered at the rate of one per year.[15] Serious infectious disease discoveries in the past decade have included Lassa and Marburg haemorrahagic fevers in Africa, variants of Creutzfeldt–Jakob disease in Europe, meningococcal meningitis W135, Nipah virus in Malaysia and the West Nile virus in the Americas.[16] In addition, the recent outbreak of severe acute respiratory syndrome (SARS) and the threat of a pandemic arising from the H5N1 strain of avian influenza have led to the argument that the world cannot escape a potential epidemic influenza that could kill anywhere between 2 million and 12 million people.[17] These developments have all served to increase calls for infectious diseases to be targeted as threats to national security.[18]

These developments did not go unnoticed in the West. During the 1990s, awareness of the threat that infectious disease outbreaks could pose to their citizens' health and to their countries' economic and political stability encouraged western governments to develop responses in national security terms. Acute awareness that western states were not immune to this threat was raised by outbreaks of West Nile virus and drug-resistant infectious diseases, such as TB, measles and meningitis, in the United States and Britain, as well as the outbreak of SARS in Canada. In the rest of this section I will briefly demonstrate how infectious disease was increasingly framed as a security threat in the United States, Australia, Canada and Europe up to the turn of the century, and how each of these states, and the European Union, has increasingly seen containment at the source as the primary response required.

The United States has been a keen participant in disease surveillance and response since the mid-1990s.[19] The United States Department of Defense (US DoD) has had overseas infectious disease research laboratories located in over 20 countries for nearly ten years. The Global Emerging Infectious Surveillance and Response System (DoD-GEIS) mobile laboratories were set up for the purpose of 'responding to outbreaks of epidemic, endemic and emergent diseases',[20] and their location in the DoD, as opposed to the United States Agency for International Development (USAID) or Centre for Disease Control (CDC) demonstrates how seriously the United States views the response to infectious disease as a key national security strategy. Further evidence of American urgency in containing infectious disease outbreaks was demonstrated by its providing complete funding for GOARN's Strategic Health Operations Centre (SHOC) at WHO headquarters to monitor and report on disease outbreaks.[21]

Fidler suggests that there are three reasons for America's increasingly securitized response to infectious disease. The first is the threat of bioterrorism.[22] Even before the anthrax attacks in the United States in late 2001, the US government had been warned of the threat posed by the deliberate release of pathogens into cities via subways or cinemas, or dispersed by turbine engines, water or sewerage ducts.[23] As early as 1996 President Clinton identified the need to bolster US biodefence capabilities, resulting in the DoD's development of the GEIS mobile units.[24] The US also increased its financial contributions to multilateral infectious disease surveillance operations, committing itself, for example, to the G7 plus Mexico 'Ottawa plan for improving health security', signatories to which agreed to 'strengthen global surveillance and outbreak response' to prepare for biological terrorist attacks.[25]

Second, Fidler argues that the US government started to connect the continuous evolution of naturally occurring infectious diseases with globalization, coming to the view that such interconnectedness between poor and wealthy travellers increased the risk of infection spreading across the globe.[26]

Within the United States, public health systems were encountering infectious diseases that they either had thought eradicated or had not seen before: West Nile encephalitis, new strains of measles, multi-drug-resistant tuberculosis, malaria and cyclosporiasis have been diagnosed in the United States as having arrived through water and food either imported or brought in by travellers from overseas.[27] A report for the US Institute of Medicine argued that the United States needed to enhance the 'global capacity for response to infectious disease threats, focusing in particular on threats in the developing world', and take a 'leadership role in . . . a system of surveillance for global infectious disease'.[28]

Finally, Fidler suggests that the US government realized that infectious disease epidemics in foreign countries could threaten US national interests. For example, HIV/AIDS has been increasingly linked to future state failure and regional instability in the developing world because of the high risk it poses to soldiers and skilled citizens.[29] More than 50 million people worldwide have been infected with the human immunodeficiency virus (HIV) since it was first identified in the United States in 1981.[30] Today, the disease kills over 4 million people a year, with women and girls at higher risk of infection than boys and men.[31] In a 1998 paper entitled 'Reducing the threat of infectious diseases', USAID asserted that the 'capacity of all nations to recognize, prevent, and respond to the threat of emerging and re-emerging infectious diseases is the critical foundation for an effective global response'.[32] Waiting for the outbreak to arrive and then responding is the last resort, it argued. The first line of defence is the application of 'prevention, treatment and control programs', before the disease reaches US shores.[33] Containment, then, was what USAID recommended as the best defence, to be effected by developing a strong infectious disease surveillance capacity. The crucial factor, argued USAID, was improved coordination between international health organizations and a willingness by states to report serious outbreaks of infectious diseases.[34]

Among policy-makers in Australia, Canada and the EU, McInnes and Lee have noted a similar realization of the perceived need to plan for infectious disease outbreaks, whether naturally occurring or caused by bioterrorism.[35] The emerging consensus has been that any such outbreak would constitute a threat to national security, and thus support for global health security has become a stronger feature in national and EU policy.[36]

In Australia, particularly since the outbreak of SARS and the re-emergence of H5N1 avian flu in 2003, defence strategists, academics, economists and politicians have all warned of the dire potential consequences if the government does not prepare at the federal level for a pandemic.[37] For example, the Australian Treasury has stated that an outbreak of pandemic influenza could cause a 'recession about half the size of the Great Depression'.[38] The websites of both the Australian Attorney General's Department and the Department of Industry, Tourism and Resources have links to pages on 'Being prepared for an influenza pandemic', stating the steps that individuals, companies and hospitals should take in preparing themselves against the 'threat of an outbreak'.[39] Alan Dupont has drawn up hypothetical models that indicate at which point the number of soldiers dying from AIDS constitutes a national security threat to Australia in a region destabilized by the ravages of AIDS.[40] The federal government also recently conducted a hypothetical infectious disease outbreak emergency, in which a 'contaminator' arrived at an Australian airport from an overseas destination and spread an undiagnosed infectious disease throughout the wider community on arrival.[41]

In 1997, the Canadian government set up an electronic surveillance system entitled Global Public Health Information Network (GPHIN), which the WHO uses to this day as part of GOARN.[42] The Canadian government also hosted the first G7 plus Mexico ministerial meeting which led to the Ottowa Plan, referred to above, and the Global Health Security Initiative in November 2001.[43] In 2002—the same year that GOARN was introduced—it met in London with representatives of Japan, Mexico, the United States and states from the EU, as well as the WHO, to 'strengthen coordinated responses to improve health security'.[44] With the spread of SARS to Toronto in 2003, Ottawa's view of how infectious disease can undermine an economy unless earlier surveillance mechanisms are supported changed from recognition of a hypothetical scenario to a reality.[45] The Canadian government was estimated to have lost $3 million in the two weeks after SARS was first identified in a Toronto hospital. According to McInnes and Lee, SARS 'demonstrated how policy responses to emerging and re-emerging infectious diseases (ERIDs) can elicit a "garrison mentality" in an effort to prevent the spread of infection. Stricter border controls and attempts to regulate migration have been key features in state responses to the spread of infectious disease.'[46] For Canada, SARS also demonstrated that relative geographical isolation was not a strong enough defence in the face of an epidemic.

Finally, the EU has also sought to boost its shared health responsibilities through treaties and public health surveillance.[47] Since 2000 the WHO European Region has been discussing the need for strengthened surveillance of infectious diseases so that member states 'have the capacity to detect and respond to epidemics in a timely manner; and to collect the minimum data necessary for action linked to control measures'.[48] The EU, like the United States, Australia and Canada, has referred to its public health strategy as a security response, aimed at creating a 'network for the epidemiological surveillance and control of communicable diseases in the European Union . . . A programme of preparedness and response capacity in the event of attacks involving biological and chemical agents.'[49] The EU has also created an equivalent of the US CDC: the European Centre for Disease Prevention and Control, based in Sweden, which monitors the incidence of infectious disease across Europe. Some EU members, such as the United Kingdom, have also been referring to the risk of disease outbreak in national government policy statements. The British Foreign Office, for example, released a strategy paper in 2003 that described the spread of disease as 'an ill-effect of globalization and a risk to peace and development'.[50]

Western countries' awareness of the threat that an infectious disease epidemic could pose to their citizens and economic stability has elicited support among governments for a global strategy to contain infectious disease outbreaks. What this section has sought to demonstrate is that the risk of infectious disease outbreaks has been increasingly portrayed as a threat that western states must take steps to alleviate in the areas of foreign, economic and security policy.[51] At the same time, as the next section will demonstrate, while western states were portraying the risk of infectious disease outbreaks as a threat to national security, the WHO was seeking to assert itself as the pivotal organization for meeting these growing concerns.

The WHO: a coordinated response

The identification of infectious disease as a matter of national security policy presented the WHO with two possibilities. The first, advocated by the WHO itself, was that existing infectious disease regulations needed reform to ensure that international cooperation with the new global health surveillance network would be forthcoming.[52] The second possibility came from western states, as they started to associate infectious disease outbreaks with security threats. Western countries' awareness of infectious disease and its potential threat to their citizens prompted their interest in a system that would guarantee protection at their borders but could also operate as an effective alert and response, or containment, system in the affected region. As this section will demonstrate, the WHO worked very hard to situate itself as the best institution for managing both options—the reform of regulations concerning epidemic outbreaks and the development of the surveillance system.

Reform of the existing International Health Regulations (IHR) was agreed to by 191 World Health Assembly (WHA) member states in May 1995. The IHR embodied the WHO's mandate for managing the response to an outbreak of one of the three infectious diseases that fall under the IHR mandate (cholera, yellow fever and plague). Upon becoming aware of an outbreak, a state is to notify the WHO, which then sets in place notification procedures to alert neighbouring states, along with quarantine and travel restrictions for the affected state. However, at the 1995 WHA the WHO argued that the existing IHR could not adequately address newly emerging public health emergencies.[53]

Specifically, the WHO listed five key constraints on the implementation of the IHR. First, the regulations were limited in their coverage (applying only to cholera, yellow fever and plague), and by the 1990s the WHO had to respond to deadly outbreaks of other diseases to which the regulations did not apply. Second, the IHR, and in turn the WHO, depended entirely on the affected government notifying the WHO of an outbreak, and this, the WHO argued, was not always occurring. Third, there was nothing in the IHR to specify how the WHO and the affected country were to collaborate and cooperate in the containment of the disease. The fourth problem was a lack of incentives to encourage compliance. There was nothing the WHO could do to encourage countries weighing the options of alerting the WHO and not doing so to report a disease outbreak. In fact, if a state thought it would not get caught, there were probably more benefits in many cases (in terms of trade and tourism) associated with keeping quiet than with reporting. Finally, there were no risk-reduction measures to prevent the spread of disease.[54] The response to disease outbreaks largely depended on what the affected country had the capacity to do, with neighbouring or trading partners conducting their own containment measures. The WHO argued that there needed to be an agreed 'checklist' of procedures that every state at risk had to take to reduce the likelihood of the disease spreading and a collective response by all states to contain outbreaks to prevent them from reaching epidemic proportions.[55]

The WHO's proposal for IHR reform, and the WHA's agreement to it, came only a year after a political and economic crisis during its response to an outbreak of the plague in India in 1994. The WHO struggled to contain the panic and economic disaster that ensued once the outbreak was confirmed. Alarm spread via international media reports. Trade and travel embargoes were placed on India, while the WHO was unable to contain what it saw as an overreaction to the outbreak under the existing IHR. India's consequent economic losses amounted to US$1.7 billion, and the WHO was concerned lest this calamity impact on other countries' future willingness to report disease outbreaks.[56] It has been argued that two lessons were learnt by the WHO from the experience in India in 1994.[57] The first is that states ought to be protected from the economic devastation that follows report of a disease outbreak; the second is that new measures, giving the WHO more precise and 'far-reaching' capabilities to manage the chain of events following a disease outbreak, might contain panic such as that which ensued in India.[58]

It has taken ten years to achieve the necessary international consensus to complete the task of revising the IHR.[59] In the meantime, the WHO argued that there was an increased need for global infectious disease surveillance due to a

> resurgence in awareness of infectious diseases . . . occurring in the
> context of an information revolution . . . the promulgation of unveri-
> fied and inaccurate information on disease outbreaks often results
> in an excessive reaction by both the media and politicians leading
> to panic and inappropriate responses. These responses can lead to
> unjustified disruption of travel and trade with affected countries,
> which may result in great economic loss.[60]

Since its mandate was established in 1948, the WHO has been entitled by states to conduct surveillance of disease outbreaks across the world.[61] In tandem with its call for the revision of the IHR, the WHO argued that there was also a need for a global surveillance network which could gather outbreak reports from across the world round the clock, seven days a week, in order to manage outbreak verification and response.[62] This led to the first global infectious disease surveillance system, the Global Public Health Information Network, being developed in Canada in 1997. The GPHIN is a web-based electronic system that scans the World Wide Web to identify suspected outbreaks of disease.[63] Between 2000 and 2002 the surveillance system was improved with the creation of GOARN, which had additional mechanisms for outbreak verification, alert and fieldwork response.[64] The GPHIN was upgraded to scan in four different languages, as opposed to its original capability of scanning in only English and French.[65] GOARN was intended to 'improve epidemic disease control by informing key public health professionals about confirmed and unconfirmed outbreaks of international public health importance'.[66]

The WHO had other 'outbreak alert' systems that informed health professionals about the outbreak of specific disease threats, such as FluNet for influenza, RabNet for rabies and DengueNet for Dengue.[67] The new outbreak verification system would not be merely a mechanism for surveillance of disease outbreak, but would function as a 'global safety net that protects other countries when one nation's surveillance and response systems fail'.[68] Through the GPHIN, the WHO was to be the first actor on the scene to manage the verification and reporting of disease outbreaks; it would have the chance to negotiate with the affected state and surrounding states (if need be) to prevent the spread of infection and thus to situate itself as the key authority in infectious disease control, in other words, in containing the 'threat'.[69]

The WHO argued that the need for GOARN was made even more apparent by the speed at which the SARS outbreak in 2003 spread to 27 countries in four months: 'inadequate surveillance and response capacity in a single country can endanger national populations and the public health security of the entire world. As long as national capacities are weak, international mechanisms for outbreak alert and response will be needed.'[70] GOARN, argues the WHO, is vital for effective international containment of infectious disease outbreaks.[71] Furthermore, Roth argues that there 'is no single institution or agency that has all the capacity to approach and tackle such emergencies. WHO is able to achieve the goals of its strategic approach by bringing partners together to focus and coordinate global responses.'[72]

High-profile outbreaks such as those of H5N1 avian influenza in humans and SARS, both occurring in 2003, helped secure support for the WHO's surveillance initiative.[73] Between 1997 and 2000 the WHO had also assisted in responding to outbreaks of Rift Valley fever in Kenya and Somalia, monkey pox and Marburg virus infection in the Democratic Republic of Congo (DRC), Ebola haemorrahagic fever in Gabon, relapsing fever in southern Sudan, influenza in Afghanistan and epidemic dysentery in Sierra Leone.[74] In the aftermath of the SARS outbreak, a former director general of WHO wrote that it had been a 'warning' and that 'we must take this opportunity to rebuild our public health protections . . . Disease surveillance and response systems are critical, in conjunction with strong national, regional, and global linkages in reporting.'[75] This sense of urgency is reflected in the fact that during the same period in which the WHO was developing GOARN—between 2000 and 2002—external funding for the surveillance project steadily increased, and indeed has risen by a higher percentage than the amount that was going to communicable disease control.[76] Thus it is not surprising that the momentum for the WHO's surveillance system occurred at the same time that these same states were increasingly linking infectious disease with national security.[77]

The WHO has also stated that it expects most of its activity to be located in developing countries: 'Many countries have recognized the renewed threat of outbreaks and have sought to strengthen their national surveillance and response capacities. In many other countries similar developments have been very slow due to lack of funds and competing priorities.'[78] The WHO argues that, given the disparity among countries in public health infrastructure, it makes sense to create an effective international response that deals first with the 'humanitarian needs of other countries that are affected by [the] outbreak'; it goes on to assert that 'it is clear that assisting other countries to deal with outbreak threats actually reduces the risks of international spread'.[79] Most disease outbreaks 'in developing countries are contributed by nations with complex emergencies'.[80] During the SARS outbreak, Heymann and Rodier claimed, many states were not quick enough in diagnosing outbreaks of the disease and containing it in time to prevent its international spread.[81] In acknowledgement of this failing, the member states of the WHA passed a resolution calling for 'increasing national capacity development for surveillance and response' and endorsed the ways in which GOARN obtained information about SARS and supported containment efforts.[82] A second resolution was then passed, encouraging GOARN to strengthen its surveillance capacity and support countries that were attempting to strengthen their own national containment efforts. Jones argues that the containment of SARS should be attributed to the fact that while the CDC in the United States was doing a good job in preventing an outbreak there, 'this job would have been orders of magnitude harder had it not been for the work done by WHO to man the outer defences'.[83]

However, a key factor in GOARN's work is that it is dependent on the affected state's verification of an outbreak and its granting permission for a WHO field-work response team to enter its territory.[84] The updated GPHIN system has the capability to locate over 20 reports a day of suspected outbreaks. On request by the affected state, GOARN's SHOC will respond to outbreaks with field teams, specialized protective equipment and medical supplies, as well as robust communications to keep in contact with both state officials and WHO headquarters.[85] The key phrase here is 'on request'. The WHO argues that this is another reason why its role in global health security is so crucial.[86] It contends that its international partnerships make it of maximal use in a situation where 'financial, political and institutional' restraints may inhibit cooperation in more specialized, regional surveillance mechanisms.[87] In addition, WHO representatives argue not only that the WHO's 'coordinated response mechanism' can 'mobilize the appropriate resources that are necessary to contain the outbreak' but that the WHO 'has an international mandate [and this] provides an element of neutrality'.[88]

The principal justification for the establishment of a surveillance system was that 'as long as national capacities are weak, international mechanisms for outbreak alert and response will be needed as a global safety net that protects other countries when one nation's surveillance and response systems fail'.[89] The WHO has argued that a combination of security interests, recognition of common cause and concern for image will encourage states to cooperate: 'countries will comply because of a sense of global solidarity in the face of a common threat, but also they will comply because they prefer to maintain a good image and look responsible'.[90]

The WHO worked hard during the 1990s to create awareness among governments of the threat that infectious disease posed to humanity by encouraging changes to the IHR and promoting a surveillance system that could alert the affected state and surrounding states to an outbreak of disease—essentially, a containment mechanism. Its success, first in getting states to acquiesce in revised IHR that sought to provide stronger incentives for state compliance and create a wider base for their application, and second in creating a surveillance system capable of locating an outbreak no matter where it occurred, has prompted the WHO to herald a new era in global health governance.[91]

Previous analysis suggests that the willingness of western states (especially) to place primary responsibility for surveillance in the hands of the WHO represents a trust in the WHO's authority in the area of global health security.[92] But, as the discussion above has shown, the securitization of infectious disease has been accomplished by both western states and the WHO. Therefore, the assumption that these states have relinquished their attempt to control the infectious disease agenda needs further investigation. As the next section demonstrates, the WHO's authority in infectious disease control has been strengthened partly because it suited the interests of western states to allow this to happen. While there has been a transfer of power that demonstrates the WHO's authority in disease management, this development also reveals a choice by western states to *defer* to the authority of the WHO because it has been able to present itself as best placed to respond to the infectious disease threat. However, has this relationship with the West compromised the WHO's authority? Will its authority be recognized by relevant states when the WHO seeks verification of disease outbreaks and compliance from the host state in disease containment measures?

The third and final section of the article will assess the possible benefits that arise for the WHO and western states from the securitization of infectious disease. It will be argued that the perceived benefits were twofold. First, placing the responsibility for containing the threat into the hands of the WHO would benefit western states. The WHO is promoted as a 'neutral actor',[93] and thus, ostensibly, one likely to achieve greater access to potentially hostile states without being labelled as having the same interests as powerful sovereign actors. Western states thus benefit by being 'guarded' from infectious diseases by an international agency. The second benefit is for the WHO itself. The WHO's authoritative role, and thus normative power, is strengthened by the introduction of stricter surveillance and response measures that promotes its authority and position as a key player in global health governance.

Why undertake infectious disease surveillance?

As demonstrated above, there have been substantial moves by governments to securitize health, identifying threats to health as threats to national security. However, since 2003 concerns have been raised about the consequences of securitizing health, especially infectious disease.[94] The primary concern has been that the securitization of infectious disease leads to its being viewed as a threat only when those doing the securitizing—in this case, western states— actually feel threatened. When these states feel the threat to them has abated, their support and interest wane, leaving those who remain under threat potentially deprived of the assistance they need.[95] Even the WHO has repeatedly warned that states should not attempt to conduct their own surveillance and border control measures against the threat of infectious disease, but should instead support the WHO in providing a global surveillance programme.[96] However, whether a surveillance response to infectious disease is the best response, and whether it accurately reflects the threat of infectious disease compared to other global health concerns (primarily poverty), continues to be widely debated.[97]

In this final section, I want to step aside from both the advocates of and the dissenters from the health securitization movement and take a slightly different angle. I argue that the WHO's initiative to create a global health governance response to infectious disease via revised IHR and GOARN does, whether intentionally or not, favour western states' interests. The policy priority of western states in response to infectious disease has been to safeguard *their* citizens by supporting the development of a surveillance system that aims to prevent epidemics from reaching their borders. This concern enabled the WHO to situate itself in a position of authority in global health governance.[98] Western states have, in turn, permitted the WHO to occupy this authoritative role because in doing so they could pass responsibility on to the international body and avoid allegations of imperial overstretch by entrusting oversight power to a 'neutral actor'.

McInnes and Lee argue that 'over the past decade, health has once more become defined in terms of risk from selected infectious diseases, and has re-emerged as an issue in foreign and security policy circles'.[99] The WHO also noted that an increased 'awareness of infectious diseases' occurred near the end of the twentieth century.[100] Its director general, Gro Harlem Brundtland, later went on to insist that it was imperative this awareness should not lead to states isolating themselves from the global effort at reducing the threat of infectious diseases: investment in people and in 'enhanced international cooperation, for health as for many other arenas, are prerequisites for security'.[101] Furthermore, she argued, 'a world where a billion people are deprived, insecure, and vulnerable is an unsafe world. The functional separation between domestic and international health problems is losing its usefulness.'[102] Recall that the WHO argues that its mandate puts it in 'a unique position to coordinate infectious disease surveillance and response'.[103] Thus there was a definitive move to establish the WHO's role in the global response to the potential threat of an infectious disease epidemic.

At this moment, writes Fidler, we see the sustainability of a 'post-Westphalian public health governance dramatically ushered in'.[104] States have realized that their traditional reliance on international governance—regulation between states to manage threats of infectious disease—no longer works. The WHO argues that states have recognized that its 'primary role' is to 'maintain global health security through its global surveillance and response activities';[105] and that while the WHO has no enforcement mechanism, states will comply, for the various reasons noted above to do with self-interest, common interest and public image. Thus the WHO, charged with monitoring state compliance, is in a position to manipulate the international perception of states on the basis of their cooperation with its regime. According to Fidler, SARS was the catalyst that led to the WHO's increase in power, forcing states such as America, Britain and China to accept that there needed to be a 'reallocation of power above and below the sovereign state'.[106] According to this view, the Westphalian rules which preoccupied responses to infectious disease in the past no longer applied.[107] In 2003 SARS and H5N1 led states to realize that they were not more powerful than an unidentified microbe which could empty cities, bring about devastating economic collapse and cause immense loss of life. This, argues Fidler, marked the beginning of the post-Westphalian era where governance involves states, intergovernmental organizations and non-state actors.[108] The WHO concurs with Fidler, stating that 'after SARS, it was clear to governments that the [IHR] rules needed to be updated'.[109]

Fidler, Lee and the WHO all argue that GOARN is the perfect example of global health governance working.[110] GOARN was instrumental in the identification of SARS, as it has been in tracing H5N1.[111] Also noteworthy is that GOARN's infectious disease surveillance in these situations did not rely solely on the cooperation of states: in the case of the SARS outbreak in China, it was the participation of non-state actors in locating reports of the disease on the internet that led to the WHO's being alerted to the outbreak. In addition, the WHO's authority in the post-Westphalian era was demonstrated by the unimpeded access it was able to achieve upon entering states; and, as the SARS crisis deepened, it was the WHO that issued travel warnings and managed outbreak response in a number of countries simultaneously.[112]

However, as I have shown above, the WHO's efforts were not conducted independently of state support. I explained in the first section of this article that western states have as strong a vested interest as the WHO in developing strong global surveillance of infectious disease. As Jones argued, the WHO manned the 'outer defenses' against SARS while allowing the US CDC, for example, to concentrate on domestic measures of defence.[113] The WHO's primary funding for GOARN has come largely from donations by western states, prominent among them the United States, Canada, Australia and the UK, and from the EU.[114] At the same time, the revision of the IHR could not have occurred without all the member states of the WHA consenting to it; the same is true of the WHA resolutions that have supported the strengthened surveillance capability of WHO's GOARN.[115] All of these states in their domestic policy have argued strongly for an enhanced international surveillance network; this is demonstrated by the fact that, of the 130 partners in GOARN, a large proportion of the facilities that assist the WHO are located in developed states. Therefore, the claim that the WHO has achieved post-Westphalian authority must be measured against the fact that its authority in surveillance is rooted overwhelmingly in the support and consent of states.

Therefore, what measure of authority has the WHO gained from GOARN? Barnett and Finnemore argue that international organizations seek to shape agendas and rules to build their institutional power in global politics.[116] In contrast to neo-realist and neo-liberal arguments which state that international organizations have the capacity to do only what states tell them to do, Barnett and Finnemore argue that international organizations not only have authority independently of states, but that in fact their normative agendas can at times dominate or even direct the purpose of states.[117] However, in challenging the post-Westphalian governance argument above, I question whether international organizations such as the WHO can ever conduct actions beyond member states' authority. One key answer to this question that Barnett and Finnemore presented involved the transfer of authority.[118] When states turn to international organizations to conduct tasks that they do not wish to do themselves, a measure of authority inevitably passes from state to institution. This creates, over time, a situation where international organizations' power grows as they come to control the agenda surrounding a specific area. With the transfer of authority from state to institution comes the accrual of normative power to the institution that controls the relevant information and functions as a recognized authority in its particular area.[119]

The WHO has had a long history of directing and managing the tasks of global health awareness, but at the same time its power to direct states to comply with the regulations concerning infectious disease outbreaks has been weak. However, it succeeded in revising the IHR as a result of the West's increased association of infectious disease with a security threat in combination with the WHO's assertion that it was the best authority to manage this concern. In turn, the transfer of responsibility for infectious disease control to the WHO has led to the management of infectious disease outbreak alerts through GOARN. The centralization of authority in the area of infectious disease has led to the WHO gaining authoritative power in that, through its response mechanisms, it can coerce states into complying with the threat of public exposure for non-compliance. Through GOARN, the WHO has the authority to control the release of information surrounding infectious disease outbreaks; but it also has the power to alert the international community when it is not receiving the affected states' cooperation.[120] Therefore, the WHO's authoritative power resides in its management of information about infectious disease.

The transfer of authority is represented by the WHO essentially acting out the agenda set out by developed states that cannot or do not wish to carry out the programme themselves. This has entrenched the WHO's authority in the global health agenda and increased its power to the point where it now presides over the global response to infectious disease outbreaks. The WHO has secured its position on the global stage as the key referent authority in global health security.[121]

However, has this securitization of infectious disease led to the 'breaking' of traditional international governance rules—where states had the primary role in the surveillance and response to infectious disease? On the one hand, the shift of responsibility following the delegation of authority to the WHO has given it the power to secure individuals against infectious disease. The WHO has the capability to locate outbreaks of disease, in some cases before public health officials in the state affected are aware of it themselves, and to take primary responsibility in containing the outbreak. We have seen this in the case of SARS and to a lesser degree with the global response to avian influenza, with Ebola haemorrhagic fever in Gabon, DRC and Uganda, with an unidentified influenza in Madagascar and Afghanistan, and with Rift Valley fever in Kenya and Somalia. The ability of the WHO to report on outbreaks and to alert states to infectious disease location in various parts of the world gives the organization authority and enables it to coerce states to comply with the procedures set out under GOARN. On the other hand, this authority has been *delegated*. While affirming the authoritative role that international organizations can assert in global politics, we must also remember that the WHO's power has been delegated by a particular set of states to serve their interests. The delegation of tasks by developed states to WHO indicates that the agenda of infectious disease has been placed on the WHO's shoulders by developed states which have chiefly in mind their own narrow interests.[122]

Conclusion

In this article I have demonstrated that western states have encouraged the disintegration of old international governance rules by delegating authority to the WHO in the area of infectious disease response. This delegation allays western states' concerns by strengthening their domestic borders against the spread of infectious disease epidemics and simultaneously serves the WHO's interests by increasing its authority in global health governance. The revision of the IHR and the development of GOARN have met the needs of western states, while providing authoritative power to the WHO. However, the obstacle of sovereignty has not been overcome. Attempts to verify outbreaks of disease are still dependent for their success on state cooperation. While the WHO relies on its ability to shame non-compliant states by public notification to compel state cooperation, it remains to be seen whether the fear of an epidemic will induce recalcitrant states to cooperate in the midst of an infectious disease outbreak. This is a concern that the WHO has acknowledged,[123] as has the UN Secretary General's High Level Panel on Threats, Challenges and Change for Collective Security, in stating that 'the security of the most affluent State can be held hostage to the ability of the poorest State to contain an emerging disease'.[124]

Why, after the securitization of infectious disease, might the WHO's authority in this area still not be strong enough to compel states to verify outbreaks? Largely because the authority that the WHO has sought has been conferred on it by a selected number of states. The WHO and western states have simultaneously securitized infectious disease, with the result that, while western states have been able to ensure that progress made in disease surveillance and response mechanisms primarily suit their national interests, the WHO has been able to increase its presence as a powerful authority in the prevention of infectious disease. However, the WHO's authority derives from its powers under GOARN—a surveillance mechanism that largely does what western states do not wish to be seen doing themselves, namely, forcing developing states to comply with infectious disease alerts. Thus a final note of caution needs to be sounded: in placing such emphasis on the WHO's capacity in this area we must not forget that its power comes not through policing, but only through emphasizing the consequences of states' non-compliance.

Notes

* I would like to thank the Faculty of Law, Queensland University of Technology, for providing seed funding to support this research project; Alex J. Bellamy for comments on the earlier draft of this article; the UQ Conflict on Security Research Group for allowing me to present a draft version of this article; and the reviewers for their very helpful remarks.

1 World Health Organization, *Global defence against the infectious disease threat* (Geneva, 2003), pp. 6, 18.

2 WHO, *Global defence*, p. 7; Ellen't Hoen, 'TRIPS, pharmaceutical patents, and access to essential medicines: a long way from Seattle to Doha', in Sofia Gruskin, Michael A. Grodin, George J. Annas and Stephen P. Marks, eds, *Perspectives on health and human rights* (New York: Routledge, 2005), p. 203.

3 'Editorial: public-health preparedness requires more than surveillance', *Lancet* 364: 9446, 2004, p. 1639; WHO, *The World Health Report 2007. A safer future: global public health security in the 21st century* (Geneva, 2007), p. 47.

4 WHO, *Global defence*; Paul Hunt, 'Neglected disease, social justice and human rights: some preliminary observations', Health and Human Rights working paper, no. 4 (Geneva: WHO, 2003).

5 Meri Koivusalo and Eeva Ollila, *Making a healthy world: agencies, actors and policies in international health* (London: Zed, 1997); People's Health Movement, Medact and Global Equity Gauge Alliance, *Global Health Watch 2005–2006: an alternative world health report* (London: Zed, 2005).

6 David L. Heymann, 'Evolving infectious disease threats to national and global security', in Lincoln Chen, Jennifer Leaning and Vasant Narasimhan, eds, *Global health challenges for human security* (Cambridge, MA: Harvard University Press, 2003), p. 114.

7 Jeffrey T. Checkel, 'The constructivist turn in international relations theory', *World Politics* 50: 2, 1998, pp. 324–48.

8 Obijiofor Aginam, 'Between isolationism and mutual vulnerability: a South–North perspective on global governance of epidemics in an age of globalization', *Temple Law Review* 77: 3, 2004, pp. 297–312; Colin McInnes and Kelley Lee, 'Health and security', *Tidsskriftet politik* 8: 1, 2005, pp. 33–44; Colin McInnes, 'Health, security and the risk society', Nuffield Trust Global Programme on Health, Foreign Policy and Security (London: Nuffield Trust, 2005); Colin McInnes and Kelley Lee, 'Health, security and foreign policy', *Review of International Studies* 32: 1, 2006, pp. 5–23; Barry Buzan, Ole Waever and Jaap de Wilde, *Security: a new framework for analysis* (Boulder, CO: Lynne Rienner, 1998).

9 Buzan et al., *Security*, p. 24.

10 Similar concerns, though with arguments slightly different from mine, are raised by Eric Mack and Philippe Calain: Eric Mack, 'The World Health Organization's new International Health Regulations: incursions on state sovereignty and ill-fated response to global health issues', *Chicago Journal of International Law* 7: 1, 2006, pp. 365–77; Philippe Calain, 'Exploring the international arena of global health surveillance', *Health Policy and Planning* 22: 1, 2007, pp. 2–12.

11 Thomas W. Grein, Kande-Bure O. Kamara, Guénaël Rodier, Aileen J. Plant, Patrick Bovier, Michael J. Ryan, Takaaki Ohyama and David L. Heymann, 'Rumors of disease in the global village: outbreak verification', *Emerging Infectious Diseases* 6: 2, 2000, pp. 97–102; Gro Harlem Brundtland, 'Global health and international security', *Global Governance* 9: 4, 2003, pp. 417–23; David Fidler, *SARS, governance and the globalization of disease* (New York: Palgrave Macmillan, 2004), pp. 163–70; William Burns, 'Openness is key', *Bulletin of the*

World Health Organization 84: 10, 2006, pp. 769–70; Calain, 'Exploring the international arena of global health surveillance'.

12 Michael Barnett and Martha Finnemore, *Rules for the world: international organizations in global politics* (Ithaca, NY: Cornell University Press, 2004).

13 WHO, *A framework for global outbreak alert and response*, WHO/CDS/CSR/2000.2 (Geneva: WHO Department of Communicable Disease Surveillance and Response, 2000), p. 1.

14 David Sanders and Mickey Chopra, 'Globalization and the challenge of health for all: a view from sub-Saharan Africa', in Kelley Lee, ed., *Health impacts of globalization: towards global governance* (Basingstoke: Palgrave Macmillan, 2003), p. 106.

15 Angela Merianos and Malik Peiris, 'International Health Regulations (2005)', *Lancet* 366: 9493, 2005, p. 1250.

16 Heymann, 'Evolving infectious disease threats', pp. 106–8.

17 WHO, 'Ten things you need to know about pandemic influenza', http://www.who.int/csr/disease/influenza/pandemic10things/en/index.html, accessed 2 Dec. 2006.

18 Jennifer Brower and Peter Chalk, *The global threat of new and reemerging infectious diseases: reconciling US national security and public health policy* (Arlington, CA: Rand, 2003); WHO, *Global defence*; David Fidler, 'Germs, governance, and global public health in the wake of SARS', *Journal of Clinical Investigation* 113: 6, 2004, pp. 799–804; Lawrence O. Gostin, 'Pandemic influenza: public health preparedness for the next global health emergency', *Journal of Law, Medicine and Ethics* 32: 44, 2004, pp. 565–73; Obijiofor Aginam, 'Globalization of infectious diseases, international law and the World Health Organization: opportunities for synergy in global governance of epidemics', *New England Journal of International and Comparative Law* 11: 1, 2005, pp. 59–74; WHO, *World Health Report 2007*.

19 David P. Fidler, David L. Heymann, Stephen M. Ostroff and Terry P. O'Brien, 'Emerging and reemerging infectious diseases: challenges for international, national and state law', *International Lawyer* 31: 3, 1997, pp. 773–99.

20 Jean-Paul Chrétien, David L. Blazes, Joel C. Gaydos, Sheryl A. Bedno, Rodney L. Coldren, Randall C. Culpepper, David J. Fyrauff, Kenneth C. Earhart, Moustafa M. Mansour, Jonathan S. Glass, Michael D. Lewis, Bonnie L. Smoak and Joseph L. Malone, 'Experience of a global laboratory network in responding to infectious disease epidemics', *Lancet Infectious Diseases* 6: 9, 2006, p. 538.

21 Burns, 'Openness is key', p. 769; David Fidler, 'Constitutional outlines', *Temple Law Review* 77: 2, 2004, pp. 247–90; Christian Enemark, 'Pandemic pending', *Australian Journal of International Affairs* 60: 1, 2006, pp. 43–9.

22 Fidler, 'Constitutional outlines'.

23 Brower and Chalk, *The global threat of new and reemerging infectious diseases*, pp. 10–12.

24 Enemark, 'Pandemic pending', pp. 55–6; Chrétien et al., 'Experience of a global laboratory network', p. 538.

25 WHO, *Global defence*, p. 17.

26 Fidler, 'Constitutional outlines'.

27 Mark S. Smolinski, Margaret A. Hamburg and Joshua Lederberg, eds, *Microbial threats to health: emergence, detection and response* (Washington DC: National Academies Press, 2003), p. 1.

28 Smolinski et al., *Microbial threats to health*, pp. 8–9.

29 For further reading on the link between HIV/AIDS and security, see Gwyn Prins, 'AIDS and global security', *International Affairs* 80: 5, 2004, pp. 931–52;

International Affairs 82; 2, 2006, a special issue on AIDS and security; Stefan Elbe, 'Should HIV/AIDS be securitized? The ethical dilemmas of linking HIV/AIDS and security', *International Studies Quarterly* 50: 1, 2006, pp. 119–44.

30 Kelley Lee and Anthony Zwi, 'A global political economy approach to AIDS: ideology, interests and implications', in Kelley Lee, ed., *Health impacts of globalization: towards global governance* (Basingstoke: Palgrave Macmillan, 2003), p. 14.

31 Gillian MacNoughton, 'Women's human rights related to health-care services in the context of HIV/AIDS', Health and Human Rights working paper no. 5 (Geneva: WHO, 2004), p. 5; Daniel Tarantola and Sofia Gruskin, 'Children confronting HIV/AIDS: charting the confluence of rights and health', in Sofia Gruskin, Michael A. Grodin, George J. Annas and Stephen P. Marks, eds, *Perspectives on health and human rights* (New York: Routledge, 2005), pp. 235–6.

32 USAID, *Reducing the threat of infectious diseases* (Washington DC, 1998), p. 1, http://www.usaid.gov/our_work/global_health/id/idstrategy.pdf, accessed 25 Jan. 2008.

33 USAID, *Reducing the threat of infectious diseases*, p. 2.

34 USAID, *Reducing the threat of infectious diseases*, pp. 3–5.

35 McInnes and Lee, 'Health, security and foreign policy'.

36 However, McInnes and Lee note that this increased interest has 'not supplanted more traditional concerns': McInnes and Lee, 'Health, security and foreign policy', p. 7.

37 Jong-Wha Lee and Warwick J. McKibbin, 'Globalization and disease: the case of SARS', Working Papers in International Economics no. 5.03 (Sydney: Lowry Institute for International Policy, 2003); Hugh White, 'More than a dose of flu', *The Age*, 12 Sept. 2005, http://www.theage.com.au/news/hugh-white/more-than-a-dose-of-flu/2005/09/11/112, accessed 16 Feb. 2006; Peter Hartcher and John Garnaut, 'Bird flu threatens misery for millions', *Sydney Morning Herald*, 16 Feb. 2006, http://www.smh.com.au/news/national/bird-flu-threatens-misery-for-millions/2006/02, accessed 16 Feb. 2006; Michael Richardson, 'Express delivery of H5N1 via migratory birds', *Australian Journal of International Affairs* 60: 1, 2006, pp. 51–8.

38 Hartcher and Garnaut, 'Bird flu threatens misery for millions'.

39 Australian Government, Department of Industry, Tourism and Resources, 'Being prepared for an influenza pandemic', http://www.industry.gov.au/pandemic-businesscontinuity/, accessed 3 Aug. 2006.

40 Alan Dupont, 'HIV/AIDS: a major international security issue', paper presented to Asia Pacific ministerial meeting 9–10 Oct. 2001, Australian Government Overseas Aid Program, http://www.ausaid.gov.au/publications/pdf/security.pdf, accessed 25 Jan. 2008.

41 Australian Government, Department of Health and Aging, 'Exercise Cumpston '06', http://www.health.gov.au/internet/wcms/publishing.nsf/Content/ohp-cumpston.htm, accessed 25 Jan. 2008

42 Grein et al., 'Rumors of disease in the global village', p. 99; Burns, 'Openness is key', p. 769.

43 Harley Feldbaum and Kelley Lee, 'Public health and security', in Alan Ingram, ed., 'Health, foreign policy and security: towards a conceptual framework for research and policy', UK Global Health Programme working paper no. 2 (London: Nuffield Trust, 2004), p. 23.

44 Kelley Lee and Colin McInnes, 'Health, foreign policy and security: a discussion paper', UK Global Health Programme working paper no. 1 (London: Nuffield Trust, 2003), p. 25.

45 Aginam, 'Between isolationism and mutual vulnerability', p. 208; Colin McInnes, 'Health and foreign policy', in Alan Ingram, ed., 'Health, foreign policy and security: towards a conceptual framework for research and policy', UK Global Health Programme working paper no. 2 (London: Nuffield Trust, 2004), pp. 30–5.

46 McInnes and Lee, 'Health, security and foreign policy', p. 9.

47 Lee and McInnes, 'Health, foreign policy and security', p. 20.

48 WHO, 'Consensus meeting on surveillance of infectious diseases', report on a WHO Meeting in Grottaferrata, Italy, 4–7 April 2000, EUR/00/5016367 (Copenhagen: WHO Regional Office for Europe, 2000), p. 1.

49 Fidler, 'Constitutional outlines', p. 256.

50 McInnes and Lee, 'Health, security and foreign policy', p. 7.

51 McInnes and Lee, 'Health, security and foreign policy', p. 12.

52 WHO, 'World Health Assembly adopts new International Health Regulations: new rules govern national and international response to disease outbreaks', WHO Mediacentre, 23 May 2005, http://www.who.int/mediacentre/news/releases/2005/pr_wha03/en/print.html, accessed 11 Jan. 2006; Burns, 'Openness is key'.

53 World Health Assembly, 'Revision and updating of the International Health Regulations', WHA48.7, 12 May 1995.

54 WHO, *Global crises—global solutions: managing public health emergencies of international concern through the revised International Health Regulations*, EUR/00/5016367 (Geneva: WHO Department of Communicable Disease Surveillance and Response, 2002), p. 3.

55 WHO, *Global crises—global solutions*, p. 3.

56 WHO, *Global defence*, p. 65.

57 WHO, 'Global outbreak alert and response', report of a WHO meeting in Geneva, Switzerland, 26–28 April 2000, WHO/CDS/CSR/2000.3 (Geneva: WHO Department of Communicable Disease Surveillance and Response, 2000), pp. 4, 21.

58 WHO, *Global defence*, pp. 64–6.

59 For further discussion on the IHR revision process, see WHO, 'Strengthening national capacities for epidemic preparedness and response in support to national implementation of IHR (2005)', report of a WHO meeting in Lyon, France, 2–5 May 2006, WHO/CDS/EPR/LYO/2006.4 (Lyon: WHO Lyon Office for National Epidemic Preparedness and Response, 2006); David P. Fidler and Lawrence O. Gostin, 'The new International Health Regulations: an historic development for international law and public health', *Journal of Law, Medicine and Ethics* 34: 1, 2006, pp. 85–94; Mack, 'The World Health Organization's new International Health Regulations'; Calain, 'Exploring the international arena of global health surveillance'.

60 WHO, 'A framework for global outbreak alert and response', WHO/CDS/CSR/2000.2 (Geneva: WHO Department of Communicable Disease Surveillance and Response, 2000), p. 2.

61 Julius Weinberg, 'Responding to the global challenge of infectious disease', in Martin McKee, Paul Garner and Robin Stott, eds, *International co-operation in health* (Oxford: Oxford University Press, 2001), p. 51.

62 WHO, 'Global outbreak alert and response', p. 23.

63 Burns, 'Openness is key', p. 769.

64 WHO, 'Global outbreak alert and response', p. 3.

65 Burns, 'Openness is key', p. 769.

66 Grein et al., 'Rumors of disease in the global village', p. 97.

67 WHO, 'A framework for global outbreak alert and response', p. 4.

68 David L. Heymann and Guénaël Rodier, 'Global surveillance, national surveillance, and SARS', *Emerging Infectious Diseases* 10: 2, 2004, p. 173.
69 WHO, 'A framework for global outbreak alert and response', p. 4.
70 Heymann and Rodier, 'Global surveillance, national surveillance, and SARS', p. 173.
71 WHO, 'Global outbreak and alert response network', http://www.who.int/csr/outbreaknetwork/en/, accessed 11 Feb. 2006.
72 Cathy Roth, 'Epidemic and pandemic alert and response', *Refugee Survey Quarterly* 25: 4, 2006, p. 101.
73 David Fidler, 'Germs, governance, and global public health in the wake of SARS', *Journal of Clinical Investigation* 113: 6, 2004, pp. 799–804; Roth, 'Epidemic and pandemic alert and response'.
74 WHO, 'A framework for global outbreak alert and response', p. 4.
75 Brundtland, 'Global health and international security', p. 422.
76 However, it should be noted that in a 2004 interview the director of WHO's Department of Communicable Disease Surveillance and Response (CSR), Guénaël Rodier, stated that while support for GOARN had not been a problem, financial assistance had been, because of the number of programmes competing for funds from western states, the key donors to WHO's budget. See Martin Enserink, 'A global fire brigade responds to disease outbreaks', *Science*, 303: 5664, 12 March 2004, p. 1606, www.sciencemag.org, accessed 25 Jan. 2008. This competition for funding is evident when contributions to surveillance are traced over a period of four years: there was an increase in the WHO 2002/2003 budget; then a decrease in the 2004/2005 budget, and then an increase in the 2006/2007 budget. See WHO, 'Proposed programme budget 2002–2003' (Geneva: WHO Executive Board, 2001), p. 13; WHO, 'Proposed programme budget 2004–2005' (Geneva: WHO Executive Board, 2003); WHO, 'Proposed programme budget 2006–2007' (Geneva: WHO Executive Board, 2005), p. 19, http://who.int/gb/e/e_pb2006/html, accessed 25 Jan. 2008. Competition within WHO for funding is further discussed in section E1 of People's Health Movement et al., *Global Health Watch 2005–2006*.
77 David Fidler argues that the United States has provided substantial financial support for improving global infectious disease surveillance as a 'means to increase national and homeland security against bioterrorism, not as a vehicle for improving global health. Any constructive health consequences for other countries that spill over from improved global surveillance represent a positive externality but are not the primary foreign policy objective.' See David P. Fidler, 'Health as a foreign policy: between principle and power', *Whitehead Journal of Diplomacy and International Relations* 6: 2, 2005, pp. 179–94.
78 WHO, 'Global outbreak alert and response', p. 3.
79 WHO, 'A framework for global outbreak alert and response', p. 4.
80 Grein et al., 'Rumors of disease in the global village', p. 102.
81 Heymann and Rodier, 'Global surveillance, national surveillance, and SARS', p. 174.
82 Heymann and Rodier, 'Global surveillance, national surveillance, and SARS', p. 174.
83 Bruce Jones, 'Bio-security, nonstate actors, and the need for global cooperation', *Ethics and International Affairs* 20: 2, 2006, pp. 225–28, accessed 25 Jan. 2008.
84 WHO, 'A framework for global outbreak alert and response', p. 6; WHO, 'Global outbreak alert and response', p. 14; *Lancet*, 'Editorial: public-health preparedness requires more than surveillance', pp. 1639–40.
85 Burns, 'Openness is key'; Roth, 'Epidemic and pandemic alert and response'.

86 WHA, 'Global health security: epidemic alert and response', A54/9, 2 April 2001.
87 WHO, 'A framework for global outbreak alert and response', p. 6.
88 WHO, 'Global outbreak alert and response', pp. 7, 27.
89 Heymann and Rodier, 'Global surveillance, national surveillance, and SARS', p. 173.
90 Burns, 'Openness is key', p. 770.
91 Kelley Lee, *Globalization and health: an introduction* (Basingstoke: Palgrave Macmillan, 2003), pp. 212–14; Nana K. Poku and Alan Whiteside, *Global health and governance: HIV/Aids*, 2003, pp. 1–7; David Fidler, *SARS, governance and the globalization of disease* (New York: Palgrave Macmillan, 2004), pp. 166–70; Aginam, 'Globalization of infectious diseases, international law and the World Health Organization'.
92 Lee, *Globalization and health*; Fidler, *SARS, governance and the globalization of disease*; Roth, 'Epidemic and pandemic alert and response'.
93 WHO, 'Global outbreak alert and response', pp. 7, 27.
94 Aginam, 'Between isolationism and mutual vulnerability'; Robert Beaglehole and Ruth Bonita, *Public health at the crossroads: achievements and prospects*, 2nd edn (Cambridge: Cambridge University Press, 2004), p. 276; Alan Ingram, 'Global leadership and global health: contending meta-narratives, divergent responses, fatal consequences', *International Relations* 19: 4, 2005, pp. 381–402; McInnes and Lee, 'Health, security and foreign policy'.
95 Aginam, 'Between isolationism and mutual vulnerability'; McInnes and Lee, 'Health, security and foreign policy'.
96 WHO, 'A framework for global outbreak alert and response'.
97 Ilona Kickbusch, 'Global health governance: some theoretical considerations on the new political space implications', in Kelley Lee, ed., *Health impacts of globalization: towards global governance* (Basingstoke: Palgrave Macmillan, 2003), pp. 192–203; Caroline Thomas and Martin Weber, 'The politics of global health governance: whatever happened to "health for all by the year 2000"?', *Global Governance* 10: 2, 2004, pp. 187–205; Ingram, 'Global leadership and global health'; Ruth Bonita and Colin D. Mathers, 'Global health status at the beginning of the twenty-first century', in Robert Beaglehole, ed., *Global public health: a new era* (Oxford: Oxford University Press, 2005).
98 Fidler, *SARS, governance and the globalization of disease*, p. 170.
99 McInnes and Lee, 'Health and security', p. 33.
100 WHO, 'A framework for global outbreak alert and response', pp. 1–2.
101 Brundtland, 'Global health and international security', p. 419.
102 Brundtland, 'Global health and international security', p. 420.
103 WHO, 'Global outbreak alert and response', p. 4.
104 Fidler, *SARS, governance and the globalization of disease*, p. 167.
105 Burns, 'Openness is key', p. 770.
106 Fidler, 'Constitutional outlines', p. 257.
107 Fidler, 'Constitutional outlines', pp. 258–9.
108 Fidler, *SARS, governance and the globalization of disease*; Fidler, 'Constitutional outlines'.
109 Burns, 'Openness is key', p. 770.
110 Lee, *Globalization and health*; Fidler, *SARS, governance and the globalization of disease*; Heymann, 'Evolving infectious disease threats to national and global security'; Roth, 'Epidemic and pandemic alert and response'.
111 Fidler, 'Constitutional outlines', p. 266; Roth, 'Epidemic and pandemic alert and response'.
112 David Fidler, 'From international sanitary conventions to global health security: the new International Health Regulations', *Chinese Journal of International Law*

4: 2, 2005, pp. 325–92; Roth, 'Epidemic and pandemic alert and response'; WHO, 'Global outbreak and alert response network', http://www.who.int/csr/outbreaknetwork/en/, accessed 11 Feb. 2006.

113 Jones, 'Bio-security, nonstate actors, and the need for global cooperation'.

114 Beaglehole and Bonita, *Public health at the crossroads*, p. 270.

115 Heymann and Rodier, 'Global surveillance, national surveillance, and SARS', p. 174; Burns, 'Openness is key', pp. 769–70.

116 Barnett and Finnemore, *Rules for the world*.

117 Barnett and Finnemore, *Rules for the world*.

118 Barnett and Finnemore, *Rules for the world*.

119 Barnett and Finnemore, *Rules for the world*, p. 34.

120 WHO, 'Global outbreak alert and response'; Burns, 'Openness is key'.

121 Barnett and Finnemore, *Rules for the world*, pp. 163–7; WHA, 'Global health security: epidemic alert and response'.

122 McInnes and Lee, 'Health, security and foreign policy'.

123 WHO, *Global crises—global solutions*; Burns, 'Openness is key'.

124 United Nations Secretariat, *A more secure world: our shared responsibility*, report of the Secretary General's High-Level Panel on Threats, Challenges and Change (New York: UN, 2004), p. 14.

13

THE EVOLVING INFECTIOUS DISEASE THREAT

Implications for national and global security

David L. Heymann

Source: *Journal of Human Development*, 4:2 (2003), 191–207.

Abstract

This paper discusses the ways in which the sharply increased danger of bio-terrorism has made infectious diseases a priority in defence and intelligence circles. Against this background, the author sets out a central principle of global public health security: a strengthened capacity to detect and contain naturally caused outbreaks is the only rational way to defend the world against the threat of a bio-terrorist attack. He then discusses the three trends that underscore this point: vulnerability of all nations to epidemics, the capacity of a disease such as AIDS to undermine government and society, and the way in which the determinants of national security have been re-defined in the post-Cold War era.

Introduction

The deliberate use of anthrax to incite terror, which quickly followed the events of September 11 2001 in the US, changed the profile of the infectious disease threat in a dramatic and definitive way. Prior to these events, the emergence of new diseases — and, most especially, the devastation caused by AIDS — had sharpened concern about the infectious disease threat as a disruptive and destabilizing force, and given it space in national security debates. The reality of bio-terrorism immediately raised the infectious disease threat to the level of a high-priority security imperative worthy of attention in defence and intelligence circles. In so doing, it also focused attention on several features of the infectious disease situation that make outbreaks — whatever their cause — an especially ominous threat. As smallpox again became a disease of greatest concern, both politicians and the public began to comprehend problems long familiar to public health professionals. These have ranged from silent incubation periods that allow pathogens to cross borders undetected and undeterred, through the finite nature of vaccine manufacturing capacity, to the simple fact that outbreaks have a potential for international spread that transcends the defences of any single country. Perhaps most important, this heightened concern has clearly identified a central principle of global public health security: strengthened capacity to detect and contain naturally caused outbreaks is the only rational way to defend the world against the threat of a bio-terrorist attack. If, for example, the world's public health community can respond to the needs that will arise when the next major shift in the influenza virus occurs — pandemic planning, addressing insufficient vaccine supplies, the need for antivirals to treat infected cases, and the surge capacity in health facilities to manage a major influx of patients — these accomplishments will show the way forward for better preparedness for bio-terrorism.

This principle has evolved in response to three concurrent trends. First, the highly publicized resurgence of the infectious disease threat illustrated the vulnerability of all nations to outbreaks and epidemics, often of new or unusual diseases. Second, the impact of AIDS on sub-Saharan Africa demonstrated the capacity of an emerging disease to destabilize a large geographical region in ways that undermine the very infrastructures needed for governance. Third, a reconsideration of the determinants of national security broadened the perception of what constitutes a security threat in the post-Cold War era, making space to accommodate infectious diseases — at least in their most internationally disruptive forms. Each of these trends is discussed in detail.

The resurgence of the infectious disease threat

During the past 30 years, the infectious disease threat has diverged considerably from previous patterns of epidemiology, drug susceptibility, geographical distribution, and severity (Lederberg et al., 1992). Such divergence arises from the naturally volatile behaviour of the microbial world, amplified by recent ecological and demographic trends. Continual evolution is the survival mechanism of the microbial world. Infectious disease agents readily and rapidly multiply, mutate, adapt to new hosts and environments, and evolve to resist drugs. This natural propensity to change has been greatly augmented by the pressures of a crowded, closely interconnected, and highly mobile world, which has given infectious agents unprecedented opportunities to exploit (Rodier et al., 2000).

The result has been an equally unprecedented emergence of new diseases, a resurgence of older diseases, and a spread of resistance to a growing number of mainstay antimicrobials (Heymann and Rodier, 2001). Vulnerability to these threats is now seen to be universal. As adversaries, microbial pathogens have particular advantages in terms of invisibility, mobility, adaptability, and silent incubation periods that render national borders meaningless. Infectious

215

agents, incubating in symptomless air travellers, can move between any two cities in the world within 36 hours and slip undetected past any border. They can also be transported over long distances by migratory birds. Disease vectors, concealed in cargoes or riding in the cabins or luggage holds of airplanes, can likewise enter new territories undetected and become endemic. Such theoretical vulnerability has been amply demonstrated in practice.

New diseases, which are poorly understood, difficult to treat, and often highly lethal, are emerging at the unprecedented rate of one per year (Woolhouse and Dye, 2001). Ebola haemorrhagic fever in Africa, hantavirus pulmonary syndrome in the US, and Nipah virus encephalitis in South-East Asia are just a few examples. Older diseases have re-emerged in dramatic ways. Cholera, now in its seventh pandemic, returned to Latin American in 1991 after an absence of almost a century. Within a year, 400000 cases and 4000 deaths were reported from 11 countries of the Americas (Tauxe *et al.*, 1995). Yellow fever is poised to cause massive urban epidemics in sub-Saharan Africa and Latin America. An urban outbreak in Côte d'Ivoire in 2001 necessitated the emergency immunization of 2.9 million persons in less than 2 weeks, depleting the international reserve of vaccine stocks (World Health Organization, 2003). Urban yellow fever promptly returned in 2002 in outbreaks in Senegal that again caused frantic efforts to secure sufficient emergency vaccine supplies (*Weekly Epidemiology Record*, 2002a). The 1998 epidemics of dengue and dengue haemorrhagic fever were unprecedented in geographical occurrence and numbers of cases, and the epidemics of 2002 have continued this alarming trend (World Health Organization, 2002a, 2003). A new strain of epidemic meningitis, W135, emerged in 2002, defying emergency preparedness in the form of stockpiled vaccines against conventional strains (*Weekly Epidemiology Record*, 2002b; World Health Organization, 2003). New and more severe strains of common food-borne pathogens, including *Escherichia coli* O157:H7, *Campylobacter*, and *Listeria monocytogenes*, have made the profile of food-borne diseases distinctly more sinister (Tauxe, 1997; World Health Organization, 2001a, 2002b). The invariably fatal variant Creutzfeldt-Jakob disease, first recognized in 1996 and probably transmitted to humans through beef, has added considerably to this concern (World Health Organization, 2002c). Year by year, the highly unstable influenza virus is a reminder of the ever-present threat of another lethal influenza pandemic (Bonn, 1997).

Disease vectors are equally resilient and adaptable. Some anopheline mosquito species that transmit malaria have developed resistance to virtually all major classes of insecticides. Others, such as the tsetse fly that transmits African sleeping sickness, have returned to areas where they had previously been well controlled. The *Aedes aegypti* mosquito that transmits both yellow fever and dengue, originally confined to tropical jungles, has adapted to breed in urban litter. The diseases carried by vectors have likewise spread to new continents or returned to former homes. Rift Valley fever is now firmly established on the Arabian peninsula. West Nile virus, first introduced on the East coast of the US in 1999, has now been detected in 43 states across the US and in five provinces of Canada as well (Gubler, 2001; Molyneux, 2001; Centers for Disease Control and Prevention, 2002).

The threat posed by drug resistance is particularly ominous and universal. Health care in all countries is now compromised by the shrinking number of effective first-line antimicrobials and the need to resort to more costly, and often more hazardous, alternative drugs, when available. Fuelled by co-infection with HIV, the return of tuberculosis as a global menace has been accompanied by the emergence of multidrug-resistant forms costing up to 100 times more to treat (World Health Organization, 2003). Malaria may soon be resistant worldwide to all currently available first-line drugs (World Health Organization, 2003). Drug resistance to common bacterial infections is now so pervasive that it raises the spectre of a post-antibiotic era in which many life-saving treatments and routine surgical procedures could become too risky to perform (World Health Organization, 2001b).

These developments have eroded past confidence that high standards of living and access to powerful medicines could insulate domestic populations from infectious disease threats abroad. They have also restored the historical significance of infectious diseases as a disruptive force — this time cast in a modern setting characterized by close interdependence of nations and instantaneous communications (Heymann, 2001a). Within affected countries, the disruptive potential of outbreaks and epidemics is expressed in ways ranging from public panic and population displacement to the interruption of routine functions that occurs when containment requires the emergency immunization of populations numbering in the millions. Disruption can also be measured in economic terms. Outbreaks are always expensive to contain. Affected countries can experience heavy additional burdens in the form of lost trade and tourism — estimated at US$2 billion during the 1994 outbreak of plague in India (Cash and Narasimham, 2002). At the global level, some of the most telling efforts to measure economic consequences, in terms of international relations and foreign affairs, have centred on determining what the AIDS epidemic in sub-Saharan Africa means for the economies of wealthy nations. At one extreme, the high mortality caused by this disease and the particular age group it affects have been interpreted as the cost to industrialized countries of lost export markets (Kassalow, 2001). At the other extreme, the economic costs of AIDS to the international community have been expressed in terms of the price of drugs and services needed to rescue a continent (World Health Organization, 2001c). The human suffering caused by this disease defies calculation in any terms.

AIDS: a clear threat to national security

Of all diseases, AIDS provides the most dramatic and disturbing example of the capacity of a previously unknown pathogen to rapidly spread throughout the world, establish endemicity, and cause social and economic upheaval on a scale that threatens to destabilize a large geographical area. Although the disease has a global distribution, its impact is overwhelmingly concentrated in sub-Saharan Africa, where approximately 3.5 million new infections occurred in 2001. This brings the total number of people living with HIV/AIDS in sub-Saharan Africa to 28.5 million, accounting for 71% of the global total. In sub-Saharan Africa, an estimated 9% of all inhabitants between the ages of 15 and 49 carry the virus. In one country, HIV prevalence among pregnant women in urban areas now stands at 44.9%. The region as a whole is home to an estimated 11 million AIDS orphans (UNAIDS, 2002).

Prior to the events of September and October 2001, AIDS already provided a strong case for considering infectious diseases as a security issue. At the most obvious level, any agent with such high rates of mortality — whether infectious or otherwise — that directly threatens to kill a significant proportion of a state's population constitutes a direct threat to state security (Price-Smith, 2002). In this respect, few would argue against the proposition that AIDS is a direct security threat to countries in sub-Saharan Africa. Recent analyses by experts in international security and foreign affairs have defined the nature of this threat in more explicit terms (Eberstadt, 2002; Elbe, 2002; Ostergard, 2002). In Africa, AIDS poses an immediate threat to the organization of many different societies as well as to the security of political institutions, the capacity of military operations, and the performance of the police force (Ostergard, 2002). Evidence from several sources indicates that AIDS has already begun to diminish the operational efficiency of many of Africa's armed forces while also escalating the social costs of ongoing wars to new levels (Elbe, 2002). Other immediate effects on state capacity include the loss of high-level government officials, an overwhelming of the health care system, and an erosion of traditional systems of social support (Ostergard, 2002). Studies of the long-term security impact predict a significant decline in the economic performance of many countries due to absenteeism, the loss of skilled workers, reduced foreign investment, increasing government expenditure on health care, higher insurance costs, and a paucity of teachers to train the next generation of workers (Morrison, 2002; Ostergard, 2002). More, not less, state failure and insecurity is projected, and this is expected to translate into new forms of transnational security threats (Morrison, 2002).

Changing perceptions of security

Efforts to understand the security implications of AIDS have taken place within the context of a reconsideration of what constitutes a security threat in the post-Cold War era.

In its traditional meaning, 'security' has long been a strictly national pursuit aimed at defending territorial integrity and ensuring state survival. It is intrinsically self-centred, focused on shielding state citizens from external danger in an international system ruled by anarchy (Burchill, 1996). Traditional approaches to the defence of national security are military functions: protecting borders, fighting wars, and deterring aggressors (Center for Strategic and International Studies, 2000; Ban, 2001).

Two events have challenged these traditional views. First, the end of the Cold War meant an end to security issues polarized by the ideological conflict and geopolitical interests of the superpowers, and kept on edge by the nuclear arms race. As old threats subsided, more attention focused on threats arising from civil unrest, internal conflicts, mass migration of refugees, and localized wars between neighbouring countries, particularly when these had the capacity to undermine state stability or contribute to state failure (Weiner, 1992; Kelley, 2000; Nichiporuk, 2000; Price-Smith, 2002). The absence of a bipolar power system magnified these threats considerably, as intervention to prop up a failing state of geopolitical strategic interest was no longer assured (Tickner, 1995; Cooper, 1996; Fidler, forthcoming). As a result, security issues became broader and more complex, and attention began to focus on ensuring the internal stability of states by addressing the root causes of unrest, conflict, and mass population movement rather than defending national borders against external aggressors (Holsti, 1996). In the wake of these changes, a number of factors — from environmental conditions to income, education, and health — were put forward as determinants of internal state stability and therefore of potential relevance to the evolving security debate (Ostergard, 2002).

In a second event, the forces of globalization demonstrated the porous nature of national borders and eroded traditional notions of state sovereignty. In a closely interconnected and interdependent world, the repercussions of adverse events abroad easily cross borders to intrude on state affairs in ways that cannot be averted through traditional military defences (Center for Strategic and International Studies, 2000). For example, in the world's tightly inter-related financial system, a crisis in a distant economy can rapidly spread to affect others (Homer-Dixon, 2001). Many other transnational threats — whether arising from environmental pollution or tobacco advertising — were recognized as having an effect on internal affairs that went beyond the control of strictly national actions. Emerging and epidemic-prone diseases qualified as a transnational threat for obvious reasons: they easily cross borders in ways that defy traditional defences and cannot be deterred by any state acting alone (Center for Strategic and International Studies, 2000). In the broadened debate, their disruptive potential gave them added weight as a possible security concern, although this potential differs considerably between industrialized and developing countries (Kelley, 2000; National Intelligence Council, 2000).

In industrialized countries, global pandemics such as influenza, where supplies of vaccines and antivirals are clearly insufficient, have the capacity to destabilize populations, and the panic that they incite could cause great social disruption. In developing countries, where economies are fragile and infrastructures weak, outbreaks and epidemics are far more directly disruptive. In these countries, the destabilizing effect of high-mortality endemic diseases, including malaria and tuberculosis as well as AIDS, is amplified by emerging and epidemic-prone diseases, as they disrupt routine control programmes and health services, often for extended periods, due to the extraordinary resources and logistics required for their control (Heymann and Rodier, 2001). For example, outbreaks of epidemic meningitis, which regularly occur in the African 'meningitis belt', disrupt normal social functions and bring routine health services to the brink of a standstill as containment depends on the emergency vaccination of all populations at risk (World Health Organization, 2003). The resurgence of African sleeping sickness, which is also a disease of livestock, has disrupted productive patterns of land use and jeopardized food security in remote rural areas (World Health Organization, 2003). Recent outbreaks of dengue in Latin America required the assistance of military forces, sometimes from neighbouring countries, for their containment. Outbreaks of new or unusual diseases can cause public panic to a degree that calls into question government's capacity to protect its population. In addition, the dramatic interruption of trade, travel, and tourism that can follow news of an outbreak places a further economic burden on impoverished countries with little capacity to absorb such shocks (Heymann and Rodier, 2001).

High priority on the security agenda?

Several recent events suggest that emerging and epidemic-prone diseases are being taken seriously as a threat to national and global security. In an unprecedented step, a US government-supported study concluded in 1995 that emerging and re-emerging infectious diseases, especially AIDS, constituted a national security threat and foreign policy challenge (CISET, 1995). In 1996, the US Department of Defense established the Global Emerging Infections Surveillance and Response System, based on a network of domestic and overseas military laboratories, as an explicit acknowledgement that emerging diseases can threaten military personnel and their families, can reduce medical readiness, and present a risk to US national security (DoD-GEIS, 2003). The threat posed by microbial agents to the security of the US was further acknowledged in 2000 by an equally unprecedented report from the US Central Intelligence Agency's National Intelligence Council (2000). Citing the 'staggering' and 'destabilizing' number of deaths caused by AIDS in sub-Saharan Africa, the report documented specific consequences in the form of diminished gross domestic product, reduced life expectancy, weakened military capacity, social fragmentation, and political destabilization. The report also addressed the growing threat posed by infectious diseases in general, and drew attention to the contributing roles of rapid urban growth, environmental degradation, and cross-border population movements (National Intelligence

Agency, 2000). A further acknowledgement that microbial 'foes' could threaten international peace and security came in 2000 when the UN Security Council, in its first consideration of a health issue, concluded that the AIDS pandemic had moved beyond a health crisis to become a threat to global security, the viability of states, and economic development (UN Security Council, 2000).

Although the creation in January 2002 of the Global Fund to Fight AIDS, Tuberculosis and Malaria gives cause for hope, the magnitude of the response falls far short of what is needed to rescue Africa and other areas from a humanitarian crisis of historic proportions (World Health Organization, 2001c; Feachem, 2003). In many ways Africa has become increasingly marginalized as a player in global economics and politics, with the possible exception of South Africa (Eberstadt, 2002). At the same time, the reality of the industrialized country response to Africa's AIDS crisis brings into question the extent to which AIDS and other emerging diseases — even if formally acknowledged to be a security threat — rank as an absolute priority in national security agendas.

The events of September and October 2001 changed this situation dramatically, as the prospect of bio-terrorism brought infectious disease agents into direct intersection with national security imperatives. It has also brought into sharp focus many of the difficult problems faced by public health on a daily basis. For example, the anthrax incident demonstrated the difficulty of quickly identifying an unfamiliar disease. This difficulty arises with almost all outbreaks, particularly in the developing world, that do not follow a predictable geographical or seasonal pattern. It also arises with the thousands of cases of imported malaria and other tropical diseases that occur each year in temperate countries having large international airports, which are frequently misdiagnosed. It also occurred following the unexpected arrival of West Nile virus in the Western hemisphere, where the disease was initially misdiagnosed as St Louis encephalitis and a full 3 weeks lapsed before the causative agent was correctly identified. The rapid determination of whether a disease might be deliberately caused is likewise notoriously difficult. Plague in India, dengue in Cuba, hantavirus in New Mexico, and West Nile virus in New York are just some examples of diseases initially considered to have a deliberate origin in the recent past.

Also in connection with the anthrax incident, the question of whether a country experiencing a public health emergency has the right to over-ride the patent of a vital drug, such as ciprofloxacin hydrochloride, has been vigorously debated, primarily within the context of the AIDS humanitarian crisis, since shortly after the Agreement on Trade-Related Aspects of International Property Rights was signed in 1994. Concerning the particular problems posed by the sudden demand for smallpox vaccine, the difficulty of quickly building an adequate vaccine reserve as preventive defence is experienced on a daily basis in efforts to contain outbreaks of epidemic meningitis and urban yellow fever, where the finite nature of vaccine manufacturing capacity frequently jeopardizes emergency containment operations (World Health Organization, 2003). In the case of yellow fever, the situation is a particularly disturbing example of the impact of poverty. Because of the expense, few high-risk countries practice routine childhood immunization against yellow fever, although this option is ten times more cost-effective and prevents more cases and deaths than emergency immunization campaigns (World Health Organization, 2003). Vaccine shortages have also, on occasion, threatened the effectiveness of National Immunization Days during the end stage of the drive to eradicate poliomyelitis. Nor is smallpox the only severe infectious disease for which no effective treatment exists. Dengue, yellow fever, Japanese encephalitis, rabies, and the Ebola, Marburg and Crimean-Congo haemorrhagic fevers are just some of the diseases of major public health importance that lack effective treatments. In this sense, some of the terror incited by the prospect of a bio-terrorist attack in industrialized countries is a constant feature of life in the many developing countries prone to outbreaks of these diseases.

As a final example, the question of how the world can best defend itself against the threat of a bio-terrorist attack has also been addressed in a series of practical actions that date back to at least 1997 (World Health Organization, 2002d). On September 5 2001, the US Senate Committee on Foreign Relations, at a hearing on 'The threat of bio-terrorism and the spread of infectious diseases', heard testimony explaining how systems set up to detect and contain naturally caused outbreaks provide global defence against the threat posed by bio-terrorism (Heymann, 2001b).

'Dual use' defence

Efforts to prevent the international spread of infectious diseases have a long history. In the fourteenth century, ships that were potential carriers of plague-infected rats were forcibly quarantined in the harbour of the city-state of Venice to prevent importation of plague (Howard-Jones, 1975). A series of international health agreements between the newly industrialized countries, elaborated during the nineteenth century, culminated in the adoption of the International Health Regulations in 1969 (World Health Organization, 2001d). The regulations are designed to maximize security against the international spread of infectious diseases while ensuring minimum impact on trade and travel. Administered by the World Health Organization (WHO), these are the only international regulations that require reporting of infectious diseases. At the same time, they provide norms and standards for airports and seaports designed to prevent the spread from public conveyances of rodents or insects that may be carrying infectious diseases, and describe best practices to be used to control the spread of these diseases once they have occurred.

The regulations are currently being revised to serve as an up-to-date framework for global surveillance and response in the twenty-first century. To support the revision process, the World Health Assembly has endorsed a series of resolutions aimed at ensuring a global surveillance and response system, operating in real time and under the framework of the International Health Regulations, that facilitates rapid disease detection and rational responses (World Health Organization, 1983, 1995a, 1995b, 1998). The WHO is also now authorized by the Health Assembly to utilize information sources other than official notifications submitted by governments (World Health Organization, 2001d).

The WHO has long argued that the most important defence against the infectious disease threat in all its forms is good intelligence and a rapid response. Intelligence is gleaned through highly sensitive global surveillance systems that keep the world alert to changes in the infectious disease situation. Routine surveillance systems for naturally occurring outbreaks enhance the capacity to detect and investigate those that may be deliberately caused, as the initial epidemiological and laboratory response techniques are the same. Adequate background data on the natural behaviour of known pathogens provide the epidemiological intelligence needed to recognize an unusual event and to determine whether suspicions of a deliberate cause should be investigated (Heymann and Rodier, 2001, World Health Organization, 2001e, 2002d). A global surveillance system, operating in real time, facilitates rapid and rational responses. It ensures that the necessary laboratory and epidemiological skills are kept sharp, since the call-out for natural outbreaks at the global level is almost daily. It provides a mechanism for sharing expertise, facilities, and staff. The performance of routine systems in detecting and containing naturally occurring outbreaks provides an indication of how well they would perform when coping with a deliberately caused outbreak, although the scale of a deliberately caused outbreak would probably be much larger. Strong public health systems are vital, as public health plays the initial and leading role in the response to a deliberately caused outbreak (Knobler *et al.*, 2002).

The mechanisms for global surveillance and response are in place and operational, on a daily basis, in the Global Outbreak Alert and Response Network (Heymann and Rodier, 2001). Under development since 1997, this overarching network interlinks electronically, in real time, 110 existing laboratory and disease reporting networks. Together, these networks possess much of the data, expertise, and skills needed to keep the international community constantly alert and ready to respond.

The network, which was formalized in April 2000, is supported by several new mechanisms and a customized artificial intelligence engine for real-time gathering of disease information. This tool, the Global Public Health Intelligence Network (GPHIN, 2002), maintained by Health Canada, heightens vigilance by continuously and systematically crawling websites, news wires, local online newspapers, public health e-mail services, and electronic discussion groups for rumours of outbreaks. In this way, the network is able to scan the world for informal news that gives cause for suspecting an unusual event. Apart from its comprehensive and systematic search capacity, the GPHIN has brought tremendous gains in time over traditional systems in which an alert is sounded only after case reports at the local level progressively filter to the national level and are then notified to the WHO. The network currently picks up — in real time — more than 40% of the outbreaks subsequently verified by the WHO. However, outbreaks of some diseases, including Ebola haemorrhagic fever, frequently occur in very remote rural areas that fall outside the reach of electronic communications, thus necessitating continued reliance on other sources, including reports from countries.

Additional sources of information linked together in the network include government and university centres, ministries of health, academic institutions, other United Nations agencies, networks of overseas military laboratories, and non-governmental organizations having a strong presence in epidemic-prone countries. Information from all these sources is assessed and verified on a daily basis. 'Suspected accidental or deliberate release' is one of six criteria used to determine whether an outbreak is of international concern, and is routinely considered (Heymann and Rodier, 2001).

Once international assistance is needed, as agreed upon in confidential pro-active consultation with the affected country and with experts in the network, electronic communications are used to coordinate prompt assistance. To this end, global databases of professionals with expertise in specific diseases or epidemiological techniques are maintained, together with non-governmental organizations present in countries and in a position to reach remote areas. Such mechanisms, which are further supported by a network of specialized national laboratories and institutes located throughout the world, help make the maximum use of expertise and resources — assets that are traditionally scarce for public health. Surge capacity, insufficient vaccine supplies, and expensive drugs are issues that must be dealt with on a regular basis in order to keep the world ready to respond — issues similar to those needed for preparedness for bio-terrorism. Chronic shortages of vaccines for epidemic meningitis and yellow fever are being addressed through international collaborative mechanisms, also involving manufacturers, that stockpile vaccine supplies and pre-position them in countries at greatest risk of epidemics. The highly unstable influenza virus is kept under close surveillance by a WHO network of 110 institutes and laboratories in 83 countries. The network determines the antigenic composition of each season's influenza vaccine and keeps close watch over conditions conducive to a pandemic.

From July 1998 to August 2001, the network verified 578 outbreaks in 132 countries, indicating the system's broad geographical coverage. The most frequently reported outbreaks were of cholera, meningitis, haemorrhagic fever, anthrax, and viral encephalitis. During this same period, the network launched effective international cooperative containment activities in many developing countries — Afghanistan, Bangladesh, Burkina Faso, Côte d'Ivoire, Egypt, Ethiopia, Kosovo, Sierra Leone, Sudan, Uganda, and Yemen, to name a few (Heymann and Rodier, 2001).

The work of co-ordinating large-scale international assistance, which involves many agencies from many nations, is facilitated by operational protocols that set out standardized procedures for the alert and verification process, communications, co-ordination of the response, emergency evacuation, research, monitoring, ownership of data and samples, and relations with the media. By setting out a chain of command and bringing order to the containment response, such protocols help protect against the very real risk that samples of a lethal pathogen might be collected for later provision to a terrorist group.

A rational response to a shared threat

The source of the evolving infectious disease threat is a microscopic adversary that changes and adapts with great speed and has the advantages of surprise on its side. The possibility that biological agents might be deliberately used to cause harm is yet another divergence of the infectious disease threat. Its capacity to incite terror builds on the fears aroused by the resurgence of naturally caused outbreaks and epidemics. Its significance as a security threat is readily appreciated in light of the well-documented ability of naturally caused infectious diseases to invade, surprise, and disrupt. The issues that require attention and resources — vaccine production, stockpiling of antibiotics, and protective clothing — are vital.

The dramatic change in the profile of infectious diseases, which followed the deliberate use of anthrax, has focused high-level attention on features of the infectious disease situation that make all outbreaks especially ominous events, often with international as well as local repercussions. The challenge is to manage this new threat in ways that do not compromise the response to natural outbreaks and epidemics, but rather strengthen the public health infrastructure, locally and globally, for managing both threats. Increasing vaccine manufacturing capacity to counter the bio-terrorism threat should also work in the long term to increase the supply of vaccines needed to control naturally occurring infectious diseases.

In the US, the initial response to the anthrax incident concentrated almost exclusively on the strengthening of domestic public health capacity, with very little attention given to the international dimensions of either the threat itself or the measures needed to ensure protection (Knobler et al., 2002). More recent developments indicate a growing awareness of the inadequacy of a strictly national response. They also indicate a growing willingness to view improved global capacity to detect and contain naturally caused outbreaks as the most rational — and the most reliably protective — way to defend nations, individually and collectively, against the threat of a bio-terrorist attack (Chyba, 2002).

In November 2001, a meeting of G7 + Mexico health ministers culminated in agreement on the *Ottawa Plan for Improving Health Security* (G7 Health Ministers, 2001). The plan acknowledged bio-terrorism as an international issue requiring international collaboration, and launched a series of collective efforts aimed at improving international preparedness and capacity to respond. Additional emergency preparedness and response plans and exercises have moved forward quickly. By the time of its third meeting, held in Mexico in December 2002, the concerns of the group had expanded to include plans for increasing the WHO emergency reserve of smallpox vaccine to manage cases of an outbreak occurring in any country lacking the resources to purchase and stockpile vaccine in advance. The meeting established a working group to address problems surrounding influenza and other epidemic-prone diseases, including insufficient vaccine supplies and preparedness planning for the management of massive numbers of patients. The meeting also launched a global collaborative network of high-security laboratories as a strategy for improving global capacity to rapidly and accurately diagnose diseases 'whether naturally or intentionally occurring'.

In another significant development, the proposed US *Global Pathogen Surveillance Act 2002* acknowledged the universal nature of the infectious disease threat and frankly admitted that 'domestic surveillance and monitoring, while absolutely essential, are not sufficient' to combat bio-terrorism or ensure adequate domestic preparedness. The Act singled out the role played by the Global Outbreak Alert and Response Network, and further noted the inability of developing countries 'to devote the necessary resources to build and maintain public health infrastructures', thus underscoring the need for foreign assistance. Finally, the Act treated natural and intentionally caused outbreaks as closely related threats and recognized that strengthened capacity to monitor, detect, and respond to infectious disease outbreaks would offer dual dividends in the form of better protection against both threats (US Senate, 2002).

The acceptance of the infectious disease threat as a high-level security imperative has been sudden, ushered in by an equally sudden and previously unthinkable event. Within a year, the repercussions of the anthrax incident have led to an unprecedented appreciation of problems that have long hindered efforts to improve the detection and containment of naturally occurring outbreaks. Although public health has struggled — with little success — for decades to have these problems acknowledged, it can take some satisfaction from the fact that its experiences and advice are now guiding the way forward in a joint public health and security policy endeavour. Recent developments provide encouraging evidence that political leaders have a better understanding of the issues facing public health and — above all — appreciate both the need to strengthen public health infrastructures and the universal benefits of doing so. Equally important is the understanding that strong national and international public health must be considered as elements of national security, and that increased funding for strengthening national and international public health must come from government sectors that go beyond health to include national security, defence, and international development aid. Only then can the world begin to move towards a degree of security that sees the volatile infectious disease threat matched by a stable, alert, and universal system of defence. The lasting benefits for the daily work of outbreak detection and control could be enormous for both industrialized and developing countries.

Infectious diseases and human security

This paper has largely focused on the threat to global health security posed by emerging and epidemic-prone diseases. It is also pointed out that other infectious diseases, such as AIDS, impose a constant and unacceptable burden on individuals and communities, and are a recognized impediment to the achievement of human health security. According to the latest WHO estimates, infectious diseases caused 14.7 million deaths in 2001, accounting for 26% of total global mortality. Most of these deaths could have been prevented through existing drugs and vaccines and simple access to food and drinking water free of faecal contamination (World Health Organization, 2003).

Three diseases — AIDS, tuberculosis, and malaria — continue to account for a large share (39%) of deaths attributed to infectious diseases. Total deaths from these three diseases amounted to 5.6 million in 2001. When deaths from diarrhoeal disease and respiratory infections (5.8 million) are added, these five diseases alone are responsible for approximately 78% of the total infectious disease burden.

Perhaps the most powerful acknowledgement that these diseases compromise human security and impede development is inclusion of the control of HIV/AIDS, malaria, and other diseases as one of the eight time-bound and measurable Millennium Development Goals (United Nations, 2000). These goals, along with the report in December 2001 of the Commission on Macroeconomics and Health, and the establishment in January 2002 of the Global Fund to Fight AIDS, Tuberculosis and Malaria, give health a higher place on the global development agenda and underscore its fundamental importance to human health security (World Health Organization, 2001c; Global Fund to Fight AIDS, Tuberculosis and Malaria, 2003).

Other signs indicate the willingness of the international community to take unprecedented steps to combat infectious diseases, especially those that disproportionately affect poor populations in remote areas of the developing world — the so-called 'neglected diseases'. In just the past few years, partnerships, often involving open-ended donations of high-quality drugs and strongly supported on the ground by non-governmental organizations, have formed to eliminate or control, by a specified date, seven severely disabling diseases of the poor: African sleeping sickness, Chagas disease, guinea worm disease, leprosy, lymphatic filariasis, onchocerciasis, and trachoma. Progress has been strong and results, especially when elimination or eradication targets are met, can be permanent. For lymphatic filariasis, which seriously disables an estimated 40 million people in 80 countries, the annual number of people treated has rapidly risen from 2.9 million (in 12 countries) in 2000, to 26 million (in 22 countries) in 2001, to 65 million (in 34 countries) in 2002.

Growing concern over the issue of global health security, the main focus of this paper, has resulted in heightened vigilance, better disease intelligence, and strengthened capacity to respond when outbreaks occur. Populations in all countries will benefit from this strengthening of basic public health functions. While this trend can be seen as anchored in the enlightened self-interest of nations, the commitment and energy now focused on other diseases that are endemic in the developing world and concentrated among the poor are good evidence that humanitarian concerns are likewise shaping the response to the infectious disease threat in all its dimensions.

References

Ban, J. (2001) *Health, Security, and US Global Leadership*, CBACI Health and Security Series, Special Report 2, Chemical and Biological Arms Control Institute, Washington, DC.

Bonn, D. (1997) 'Spared an Influenza Pandemic for Another Year?', *Lancet*, 349, p. 36.

Burchill, S. (1996) 'Realism and Neo-Realism', in S. Burchill and A. Linklater (Eds), *Theories of international relations*, Macmillan, London.

Cash, R. A. and Narasimham, V. (2002) 'Impediments to Global Surveillance of Infectious Diseases: Consequences of Open Reporting in a Global Economy', *Bulletin of the World Health Organization*, 78, pp. 1353–1367.

Center for Strategic and International Studies (2000) *Contagion and Conflict: Health as a Global Security Challenge*, a report of the Chemical and Biological Arms Control Institute and the CSIS International Security Program, Center for Strategic and International Studies, Washington, DC.

Centers for Disease Control and Prevention (2002) *West Nile Virus Update: Current Case Count* [www.cdc.gov/od/oc/media/wncount.htm].

Chyba, C. F. (2002) 'Toward Biological Security', *Foreign Affairs*, 81, pp. 122–136.

CISET (1995) *US National Science and Technology Council Committee on International Science, Engineering, and Technology (CISET) Working Group on Emerging and Re-emerging Infectious Diseases: Infectious diseases — A Global Health Threat*, CISET, Washington, DC.

Cooper, R. (1996) *The Post-Modern State and the World Order*, Demos, Los Angeles.

DoD-GEIS (2003) US Department of Defense Global Emerging Infections Surveillance and Response System [http://www.geis.ha.osd.mil/aboutGEIS.asp].

Eberstadt, N. (2002) 'The Future of AIDS: Grim Toll in India, China, and Russia', *Foreign Affairs*, 81, pp. 22–45.

Elbe, S. (2002) 'HIV/AIDS and the Changing Landscape of War in Africa', *International Security*, 27, pp. 1150–1177.

Feachem, R. G. A. (2003) 'AIDS hasn't Peaked Yet — and that's not the worst of it', *Washington Post*, 12 January.

Fidler, D. P. (forthcoming) 'Public Health and National Security in the Global Age: Infectious Diseases, Bioterrorism, and *Realpolitik*', *George Washington International Law Review*, 27 (in press).

G7 Health Ministers (2001) *Ottawa Plan for Improving Health Security*, statement of G7 Health Ministers' Meeting, 7 November, Ottawa [www.g7.utoronto.ca/g7/health/ottawa2001.html].

Global Fund to Fight AIDS, Tuberculosis and Malaria (xxxx) [http://www.globalfundatm.org/].

Gubler, D. J. (2001) 'Human Arbovirus Infections Worldwide', *Annals of the New York Academy of Sciences*, 951, pp. 13–24.

Health Canada (2002) *How Canadian initiatives are changing the face of health care*, Ottawa: Health Canada, 2002. http://www.hc-sc.gc.ca/ohih-bsi/pubs/succ/national_e.html

Heymann, D. L. (2001a) 'The fall and Rise of Infectious Diseases', *Georgetown Journal of International Affairs*, 11, pp. 7–14.

Heymann, D. L. (2001b) 'Strengthening Global Preparedness for Defense Against Infectious Disease Threats', statement for the Committee on Foreign Relations, United States Senate, *Hearing on the Threat of Bioterrorism and the Spread of Infectious Diseases*, 5 September [http://www.who.int/emc/pdfs/Senate — hearing.pdf].

Heymann, D. L. and Rodier, G. R. (2001) 'Hot Spots in a Wired World', *Lancet Infectious Diseases*, 1, pp. 345–353.

Holsti, K. J. (1996) *The State, War, and the State of War*, Cambridge University Press, Cambridge.

Homer-Dixon, T. (2001) 'Now Comes the Real Danger', *Toronto Globe and Mail*, 12 September.

Howard-Jones, N. (1975) *The Scientific background of the International Sanitary Conferences*, 1851–1938, World Health Organization, 2001d.

Kassalow, J. S. (2001) *Why Health is Important to US Foreign Policy*, Council on Foreign Relations and Milbank Memorial Fund, New York.

Kelley, P. W. (2000) 'Transnational Contagion and Global Security', *Military Review*, May–June, pp. 59–64.

Knobler, S. L., Mahmoud, A. A. F. and Pray, L. A. (Eds) (2002) *Biological Threats and Terrorism. Assessing the Science and Response Capabilities*, National Academy Press, Washington, DC.

Lederberg, J., Shope, R. E. and Oaks, S. C., Jr. (Eds) (1992) *Emerging Infections: Microbial Threats to Health in the United States*, National Academy Press, Washington, DC.

Molyneux, D. H. (2001) 'Vector-Borne Infections in the Tropics and Health Policy Issues in the Twenty-First Century', *Transactions of the Royal Society for Tropical Medicines and Hygiene*, 95, pp. 235–238.

Morrison, J. S. (2001) 'The African Pandemic hits Washington', *Washington Quarterly*, 24, pp. 197–209.

National Intelligence Council (2000) *The Global Infectious Disease Threat and its Implications for the United States* [www.cia.gov/cia/publications/nie/report/nie99-17d.html].

Nichiporuk, B. (2000) *The Security Dynamics of Demographic Factors*, RAND, Santa Monica, CA.

Ostergard, R. L., Jr. (2002) 'Politics in the Hot Zone: AIDS and National Security in Africa', *Third World Quarterly*, 23, pp. 333–350.

Price-Smith, A. T. (2002) *Pretoria's shadow: The HIV/AIDS Pandemic and National Security in South Africa*, CBACI Health and Security Series, Special Report 4, Chemical and Biological Arms Control Institute, Washington, DC.

Rodier, G. R., Ryan, M. J. and Heymann, D. L. (2000) 'Global Epidemiology of Infectious Diseases', in G. T. Strickland (Ed.), *Hunter's Tropical Medicine and Emerging Infectious Diseases*, 8th edition, WB Saunders Company, Philadelphia, PA.

Tauxe, R. V. (1997) 'Emerging Foodborne Diseases: An Evolving Public Health Challenge', *Emerging Infectious Diseases*, 3, pp. 425–434.

Tauxe, R. V., Mintz, E. D. and Quick, R. E. (1995) 'Epidemic Cholera in the New World: Translating Field Epidemiology into New Prevention Strategies', *Emerging Infectious Diseases*, 1, pp. 141–146.

Tickner, J. A. (1995) 'Re-Visioning Security', in K. Booth and S. Smith (Eds), *International Relations Theory Today*, Pennsylvania State University Press, University Park, PA.

UNAIDS (2002) *Report on the Global HIV/AIDS Epidemic*, July, UNAIDS, Geneva.

United Nations (2000) *United Nations Millennium Development Goals*, United Nations, New York [http://www.un.org/millenniumgoals/].

UN Security Council (2000) *Session on HIV/AIDS in Africa*, 10 January.

US Senate (2002) *Global Pathogen Surveillance Act of 2002* [http://thomas.loc.gov/cgi-bin/query/F?c107:5:./temp/~c1076twsgK:e369].

Weekly Epidemiology Record (2002a) 'Yellow Fever, Senegal (Update)', *Weekly Epidemiology Record*, 77, pp. 373–374.

Weekly Epidemiology Record (2002b) 'Urgent Call for Action on Meningitis in Africa — Vaccine Price and Shortage are Major Obstacles', *Weekly Epidemiology Record*, 77, pp. 330–331.

Weiner, M. (1992) 'Security, Stability and International Migration', *International Security*, 17, pp. 91–126.

Woolhouse, M. E. J. and Dye, C. (Eds) (2001) 'Population biology of Emerging and Re-Emerging Pathogens', *Philosophical Transactions of the Royal Society for Biological Sciences*, 356, pp. 981–982.

World Health Organization (1983) *International Health Regulations (1969)*, World Health Organization, Geneva.

World Health Organization (1998) *Revision of the International Health Regulations: Progress Report*, Report by the Director General, World Health Organization, Geneva (World Health Assembly document A51/8).

World Health Organization (1995a) *Revision and Updating of the International Health Regulations*, World Health Organization, Geneva (World Health Assembly resolution WHA48.7).

World Health Organization (1995b) *Communicable Disease Prevention and Control: New, Emerging, and Re-Emerging Infectious Diseases*, World Health Organization, Geneva (World Health Assembly resolution WHA48.13).

World Health Organization (2001a) *The Increasing Incidence of Human Campylobacteriosis*, report and proceedings of a WHO consultation of experts, World Health Organization, Geneva (document number WHO/CDS/CSR/APH 2001.7).

World Health Organization (2001b) *WHO Global Strategy for Containment of Antimicrobial Resistance*, World Health Organization, Geneva (document number WHO/CDS/CSR/DRS/2001.2).

World Health Organization (2001c) *Macroeconomics and Health: Investing in Health for Economic Development*, report of the Commission on Macroeconomics and Health by J. D. Sachs (Chairman), World Health Organization, Geneva.

World Health Organization (2001d) *Global Health Security: Epidemic Alert and Response*, World Health Organization, Geneva (World Health Assembly resolution WHA54.14).

World Health Organization (2001e) *Public Health Response to Biological and Chemical Weapons*, World Health Organization, Geneva [www.who.int/emc/book_2nd_edition.htm].

World Health Organization (2002a) *Dengue Prevention and Control*, report by the Secretariat, World Health Organization, Geneva (World Health Assembly document A55/19).

World Health Organization (2002b) *Emerging Foodborne Diseases*, WHO Fact Sheet 124, World Health Organization, Geneva.

World Health Organization (2002c) *Understanding the BSE Threat*, World Health Organization, Geneva (document number WHO/CDS/CSR/EPH/2002.6).

World Health Organization (2002d) *Preparedness for the Deliberate Use of Biological Agents: A Rational Approach to the Unthinkable*, World Health Organization, Geneva (document number WHO/CDS/CSR/EPH/2002.16).

World Health Organization (2003) *Global Defence Against the Infectious Disease Threat*, World Health Organization, Geneva.

14

EPIDEMIC DISEASE AND NATIONAL SECURITY

Susan Peterson

Source: *Security Studies*, 12:2 (2002), 43–81.

The United Nations Security Council's January 2000 meeting on AIDS marked the first time in the institution's history that it addressed a health issue. In his speech to the Security Council, then-vice president Al Gore called for a "new, more expansive definition" of security that includes emerging and reemerging infectious diseases (IDs) like acquired immune deficiency syndrome (AIDS).[1] That same month, a National Intelligence Estimate on the security implications of global infectious diseases concluded that "these diseases will endanger U.S. citizenry at home and abroad, threaten U.S. armed forces deployed overseas, and exacerbate social and political instability in key countries and regions in which the United States has significant interests."[2] Thirteen months later, Colin Powell, the Secretary of State for a new administration that initially had dismissed the link between health and security and eliminated the position of Special Advisor for International Health Affairs on the National Security Council, also described Africa's AIDS crisis as a U.S. national security concern.[3]

These pronouncements echo a decade of books and essays that warn of the dangers of IDs and call for "a fundamental reconceptualization of standard definitions of national and international security."[4] Nevertheless, the promise of systematic analysis of the link between IDs and security remains largely unfulfilled.[5] Most scholars and practitioners who explore the link between disease and security do so from within the "human security" tradition, which seeks to expand the concept of security beyond the state to include basic human needs like health. Their arguments remain at the margins of the security literature, however, because their appeal to human security does not resonate with more traditional approaches to national and international security, which focus on physical threats to the state. As Daniel Deudney writes, "Not all threats to life and property are threats to security. Disease, old age, crime and accidents routinely destroy life and property, but we do not think of them as 'national security' threats or even threats to 'security'. . . . If everything that causes a decline in human well-being is labeled a 'security' threat, the term loses any analytical usefulness and becomes a loose synonym of 'bad'."[6]

Historians should find such reasoning puzzling, since epidemic disease has shaped human history, generally, and military conflict, in particular.[7] Thucydides describes how, during the Peloponnesian Wars, disease demoralized the Athenian people, undermined the political leadership, and weakened the army, preventing it from achieving key military objectives.[8] More than 2,300 years later, the 1918 influenza epidemic killed 25 million people, including 500,000 Americans. The Spanish flu struck 294,000 allied troops in the fall of 1918 alone. Nearly 23,000 died, and the disease caused significant, if short-lived problems on both the allied and German sides.[9] It seems clear, in short, that catastrophic IDs like AIDS can and have threatened national security.

This article asks whether, when, and how epidemic disease endangers national security, rather than assuming that anything that undermines the nation's health automatically challenges its security. In what follows, first, I attempt to move beyond efforts to persuade nations and individuals to broaden their concept of security to include basic human needs, including freedom from disease, by investigating the two main causal mechanisms by which IDs can threaten *national* security: (1) IDs may contribute to violent conflict by altering the balance of power among states, fostering foreign policy conflicts, or creating economic and political instability; and (2) IDs can alter the outcome of international conflicts either deliberately, through the use of biological weapons or the targeting of public health, or inadvertently, by eroding military readiness.

Second, I briefly examine whether these processes threaten the national security of the United States and conclude that IDs do not challenge U.S. security as directly or to the extent that many scholars and practitioners currently claim. Certainly, there are important security elements and consequences of AIDS and other catastrophic infectious diseases. At the same time, however, these security implications are often limited relative to the other consequences of epidemic disease. The most direct disease threat to the United States today comes from its vulnerability to biological weapons attack. Because this threat is so apparent, it has been and will be possible, if far from simple, to mobilize public support to meet it. It will be significantly more difficult to rally Americans against two less direct, longer term threats—to the health of armed forces and, most significantly, to the social, economic, and political stability of certain key regions—especially Russia—that also challenge American security. Particularly in the aftermath of 9/11, perhaps the greatest indirect and long run threat that IDs like AIDS pose to U.S. security is their potential to undermine democratic transition and fuel anti-Americanism and terrorism. This connection, however, is a tenuous and distant one, and it will be relatively difficult to seek support for aid to countries ravaged by IDs on the basis of U.S. security concerns alone.

Third, I examine the question of whether it matters that scholars and policy officials make a rhetorical link between epidemic disease and national security if the empirical relationship between the two variables is weak. Numerous students of international health draw this connection to gain attention and resources to fight infectious disease. As P. W. Singer notes, "Conceptualizing AIDS as a security threat, thus is not just another exercise in expounding on the dangers of the disease. . . . [I]t strengthens the call for serious action against the menace of AIDS. It is not just a matter of altruism, but simple cold self-interest."[10] By overdrawing the link between ID and security, however, public health and human security advocates may sabotage their own attempts to motivate developed nations to fight AIDS in Africa and elsewhere. Students of global health might take a lesson from earlier analyses of the relationship between the environment and national security: Linking an urgent issue to security may raise awareness, but it likely also will hinder much of the cooperation that human security and public health advocates seek and that the disastrous humanitarian and development effects of IDs demand.[11] Appealing to the national interest of advanced industrialized states like the United States to justify a massive commitment to international disease control will likely fail, because the true security implications of IDs for the United States remain limited and indirect. Such a strategy then relieves westerners of any moral obligation to respond to health crises beyond their own national borders, unless or until those crises directly and immediately impact national security.

The article is divided into four sections. The first part examines the severity of the global ID problem today. The second part compares different definitions of security—human and national or international—by which to measure whether and to what extent epidemic disease threatens security. The third part examines the relationship between IDs and national security, defined as protection of the state from physical threats. The fourth part reviews the implications of the argument and revisits the issue of why it matters whether we view AIDS and other IDs as security threats or primarily as health and development challenges.

Catastrophic infectious disease in the modern world

Human history is replete with stories of epidemic infections. These epidemics tend to follow a cyclical pattern, since they often produce immunity in survivors, and the microbes must await a new generation of hosts to infect. Alternatively, the disease-causing microbes migrate to geographically distant and immunologically vulnerable populations, producing a pandemic, or global outbreak. In this sense, AIDS is just one more disease—albeit a very deadly one—in a long line of devastating IDs. Until the early twentieth century, plague, smallpox, influenza, and other scourges decimated human populations around the globe. Many in the West thought that technological progress had halted the spread of these diseases and that they had been replaced with a second generation of diseases—the so-called diseases of affluence—including heart disease, diabetes, and cancer. Yet IDs remain a significant and growing threat. Their "third wave" includes newly emerging threats like AIDS as well as reemerging threats like plague, cholera, and tuberculosis (TB).[12]

Despite unprecedented progress in disease control, IDs remain a major killer. In 1998, 13.3 of the 53.9 million deaths worldwide—or 25 percent of all deaths— resulted from IDs. These illnesses accounted for 45 percent of all deaths in Southeast Asia and Africa. In the hour it takes to read this article, more than 1,500 people worldwide will die of an ID; at least half will be under the age of five. To put these numbers in perspective, the World Health Organization (WHO) estimates that since 1945 three diseases alone—AIDS, TB, and malaria—have claimed 150 million lives, many times the approximately 23 million deaths from wars.[13]

As this last comparison suggests, a handful of diseases pose the greatest threat to human health. Almost 90 percent of all deaths and half of all premature deaths from IDs result from six diseases—AIDS, pneumonia, TB, diarrhoeal diseases, malaria, and measles.[14] AIDS is spreading the most quickly and with the most catastrophic consequences. At the end of 2002, more than 42 million people worldwide were living with AIDS or the human immunodeficiency virus (HIV) that causes it, according to the Joint United Nations Programme on HIV/AIDS (UNAIDS) and the WHO. More than 5 million people were newly infected in 2002 alone. Short of a cure in the very near future, they will join the 26 million who have died since the start of the epidemic. HIV discriminates in its choice of victims: 95 percent of all people living with the virus reside in the developing world, and more than 29 million live in sub-Saharan Africa. Four countries, all in southern Africa, have infection rates above 30 percent; in Botswana 38.8 percent of adults are HIV-positive.[15] In 1998, 200,000 Africans lost their lives to war, but more than 2 million died from AIDS.[16]

As devastating a disease as AIDS is, it is not the only pressing ID threat.[17] Each year, more than 275 million people contract malaria, and 1.5 million die from it. Three thousand people, three out of four of them children, die from the illness each day. Malaria remains largely a disease of the developing world, but a third major scourge more clearly threatens north and south alike: Like many other diseases once thought to be on the verge of eradication, TB now infects eight million people a year, killing one-and-a-half million. It kills even more people who are infected with HIV. Nearly one-third of the earth's total population has latent TB infections, but TB is only the most widespread disease making its deadly comeback. Recent years also have witnessed numerous outbreaks of cholera, anthrax, yellow fever, and plague. In addition to these known killers, new ones continue to emerge. At least 30 new diseases have been identified over the last several decades, including Lassa fever, Ebola hemorrhagic fever, Marburg virus, Legionnaires' disease, hantavirus pulmonary syndrome, Nipah virus, Hepatitis C, new variant Creutzfeldt-Jakob disease (the human disease believed to be linked to bovine spongiform encephalo-pathy or mad cow disease), and of course HIV/AIDS.[18]

Defining security: human security vs. national security

Different terms—"human security" and "national security"—reflect disparate definitions and referents of security, as well as conflicting assessments of the significance of and appropriate response to IDs. Scholars and practitioners within the first tradition view catastrophic IDs as security problems by definition, since they threaten the lives of large numbers of people, while national security analysts and scholars gauge the degree of threat these diseases pose to the territorial integrity and political independence of the state. Members of the two schools talk past each other at nearly every turn, stymieing any serious engagement over whether and how IDs threaten security.

Human security

Much of the recent surge in concern about IDs comes out of a desire to protect human security. This approach emphasizes the welfare of individuals or people collectively. As Roland Paris notes, "Human security is the latest in a long line of neologisms—including common security, global security, cooperative security, and comprehensive security—that encourage policymakers and scholars to think about international security as something more than the military defense of state interests and territory."[19] Most students of human security date the concept from 1994, when the United Nations Development Programme issued its annual *Human Development Report*, calling for

> ... another profound transition in thinking—from nuclear security to human security.
>
> The concept of security has for too long been interpreted narrowly: as security of territory from external aggression, or as protection of national interests in foreign policy or as global security from the threat of a nuclear holocaust. It has been related more to nation-states than to people. ... Forgotten were the legitimate concerns of ordinary people who sought security in their daily lives. For many of them, security symbolized protection from the threat of disease, hunger, unemployment, crime, social conflict, political repression and environmental hazards.[20]

Theoretically, the human security approach harkens back at least as far as Barry Buzan's distinction between individual and national security and his view of the state as a threat to individual security.[21] Rothschild traces the understanding of security as an individual good to the late Enlightenment period.[22] From these arguments, flow many contemporary analyses of so-called non-traditional security threats like epidemic disease.

Public health advocates and students of IDs often champion increased mobilization against diseases that threaten security in the broad sense of human well-being. Indeed, these arguments often invoke the concept of "health security."[23] Implicitly or explicitly, health security advocates view IDs as threats to human security because of the enormous loss of life they cause.[24] As Gore argued in his January 2000 UN speech, "the heart of the security agenda is protecting lives—and we now know that the number of people who will die of AIDS in the first decade of the 21st century will rival the number that died in all the wars in all the decades of the 20th century."[25]

Linking disease and security is a means of highlighting a dire problem, capturing scarce resources, and accelerating national, international, and transnational responses.[26] Peter Piot, executive director of UNAIDS, explains public health advocates' tendency to invoke the security term this way: "Whether we conceptualize AIDS as a health issue only or as a development and human security issue is not just an academic exercise. It defines how we respond to the epidemic, how much is allocated to combating it, and what sectors of government are involved in the response."[27] In short, "sometimes national security says it all."[28]

Sometimes, however, national security may say too much. The literature on environmental security suggests that arguments for linking security and disease have at least three flaws. First, they invite the question of whether *any* serious health, environmental, economic, or other problem automatically constitutes a security threat. They provide no guidance on how to make trade-offs among different security values, such as health and military defense, or between health security and other presumably nonsecurity values, such as conservation, environmental preservation, or economic development.[29] Second, that the study of IDs has remained on the fringes of the international relations field despite countless calls for the two areas to be joined suggests that the security community remains cool to the idea of human security.[30] From their positions on the margins, advocates of human security are unlikely to influence debates about national security. Unless a link is drawn between epidemic disease and national security, not human security, security elites will pay little attention. Third, it is not clear what is gained by linking epidemic disease and human security, rather than relying on public health, development, or humanitarian arguments.

Indeed, public health advocates' appeal to the high politics of security may have unwanted effects. It implies, first, that human health is less important than, and can be justified only in terms of its impact on, security. Moreover, these arguments contain an internal contradiction that may impede health cooperation. To paraphrase Deudney's claims about efforts to link the environment and security, human security advocates usually argue that it is necessary to challenge the utility of thinking in purely national terms if we are to deal effectively with issues like AIDS, but they then turn around and appeal to nationalism to achieve their goals.[31] Finally, equating health with security may imply that a national military response to public health crises is needed, when the goal of health for all might be served better by independent international, or transnational organizations.[32]

National security

If some public health advocates embrace the mantle of human security because they believe it will secure scarce resources for their cause, it stands to reason that national security would make an even more effective rallying cry. Indeed, a small group of practitioners and scholars addresses the impact of IDs on national security, more narrowly and conventionally defined.[33] Security, in this sense, refers to the preservation of the state—its territorial integrity, political institutions, and national sovereignty—from physical threats. This definition of national security is consistent with another common definition, "the study of the threat, use, and control of military force,"[34] although it also allows for nonmilitary or nontraditional threats to the state.[35] Physical threats to the state may emanate from either or both of two sources. Traditionally, the security field has focused on external threats largely because security studies developed in the United States, which has faced few serious internal threats. Area specialists and students of comparative politics, who may study military defense issues in nondemocratic or developing states, are more likely to concentrate on internal threats to governments and states.

Since the end of the cold war, numerous students of national and international security have sought to expand the boundaries of the field to include nontraditional threats like terrorism, civil war and ethnic conflict, economic threats, crime, drugs, cyberterrorism, and disease. What binds these disparate topics together and allows scholars to examine the security dimensions of each is that they can all threaten territorial integrity, national institutions, or sovereignty. "[T]he referent is still in many ways the state . . . although the [nature of the] challenge—and the response—may have changed."[36]

Most of the voices raised in support of expanding the concept of security to encompass IDs belong to the human security school, but a number also couch their arguments in more conventional national security rhetoric.[37] On 25 March 1998 U.S. ambassador Wendy R. Sherman told a Department of State Open Forum, "[Infectious diseases] endanger the health of Americans and our national security interests."[38] In a 1996 speech to the National Council for International Health, Gore similarly noted, "Today, guaranteeing national security means mote than just defending our borders at home and our values abroad or having the best-trained armed forces in the world. Now it also means defending our nation's health against all enemies, foreign and domestic."[39] A 1998 USAID report on the impact of AIDS on national militaries likewise concluded, "the HIV/AIDS pandemic now represents a direct threat . . . to national and international security and peace in many parts of the world."[40]

These claims avoid many of the problems of the human security school by considering how IDs threaten the state, but they often suffer from two other problems. First, as many public health advocates note, traditional security language has difficulty capturing the nature of a transnational threat like IDs. Health threats like catastrophic ID, however, need not be threats to national security to warrant decisive action. They only become security threats when they threaten the territory, institutions, or sovereignty of the state. Second, the causal relationships between ID and security remain ill-defined, mostly because proponents of this link, like their colleagues in the human security camp, often make the connection largely for rhetorical purposes.[41] Many link national security to human security without considering whether all threats to individuals necessarily threaten the security of states and whether those that do necessarily threaten all states. For example, the head of the Pan American Sanitary Bureau notes, "Attention to health and well-being, which goes beyond concern about the international spread of disease, will be key for ensuring the global security that is essential to the security of modern states."[42] The referent of security by the end of the sentence is the state, but it is not clear why the threat to the health and well-being of individuals—described at the beginning of the sentence—automatically translates into a threat to the physical security of the state. Section III addresses this issue by examining key causal relationships between epidemic disease and national security, defined as preservation of the state, its institutions, and sovereignty.

Catastrophic infectious disease and national security: the causal links

For the foreseeable future, IDs will continue to claim more lives than war and to jeopardize the security of many states. The relevant questions are what states and under what conditions. The heart of the link between IDs and national security concerns the effect of catastrophic disease on violent conflict.[43] IDs may be thought of as "war-starters" and "war-outcome determinants."[44] That is, they may threaten national security in either or both of two ways —by contributing to the outbreak of violent conflict or by deliberately or inadvertently influencing the outcome of conflict. Viewed in this way, IDs present a humanitarian problem of staggering proportions, but they do not always or automatically pose a security threat. For the United States and most western states, and with the exception of biological weapons, IDs pose only indirect and long-term threats, around which it will be difficult to mobilize public support.

Epidemic disease and the outbreak of military conflict

Catastrophic ID may contribute to the outbreak of military conflict within or between states, although it is relatively unlikely to be a war-starter on its own. In theory, there are at least three paths by which IDs may pro-voke war—by influencing the relative balance of power among adversaries, generating disputes between nations over appropriate health and human rights policies, and engendering domestic instability. In practice, the last of these presents the most significant threat, but only to some states. For the United States, ID-induced conflict poses only an indirect and long run security threat.

Balance of power

The first hypothesized relationship between disease and war holds that cata-strophic ID may alter the balance of power among competitors. Realist scholars of international politics maintain that shifts in the relative capabilities of states can precipitate war, particularly when national leaders perceive that the balance is shifting against them.[45] Some students of environmental security similarly suggest that severe environmental threats can disturb the international balance of power and increase the risk of military conflict, including preventive war.[46] A preventive war may be particularly likely during or following an ID outbreak if one nation remains relatively immune to the disease. One can imagine, for example, that the diminished size of native North American populations might have led Europeans to anticipate an easy victory in their attempt to conquer and settle the continent. The earliest European "discoverers" introduced epi-demic diseases that killed as many as 95 percent of North American Indians between 1492 and the late 1600s, when European settlers arrived in significant numbers.[47] There is little evidence, however, that these ID-induced power shifts played a role in the timing or outbreak of this or any other historical war of conquest. European conquerors did not know when they set out for the Americas that they carried deadly diseases that would prove more lethal than their swords.

This incentive for war is less likely to emerge in the contemporary inter-national system because of several differences between this and earlier periods. The major epidemics of our time strike entire regions, like sub-Saharan Africa, or strike simultaneously on different continents with little respect for national political boundaries. Partly, this is because high-speed travel and trade have exposed national populations to numerous epidemic diseases and conveyed immunity on diverse populations. Additionally, technological changes mean that the contemporary balance of power depends on numerous factors other than the size of a state's military or general population, factors like weapons of mass destruction, advanced aircraft, and missile technology. Unlike other diseases, moreover, AIDS kills all its victims rather than conferring immunity on survivors. Nearly all individuals, therefore, are equally vulnerable to the disease if they are exposed to it via the dominant routes of transmission—sexual activity, blood or blood product exchange, transmission from mother to child during pregnancy, or intravenous (IV) drug use that involves sharing contaminated needles. These reasons would suggest that ID outbreak is relatively unlikely to prompt a preventive war.

Unlike individuals, however, nations are not equally vulnerable. Differences in resources, state strength, the organization of society, and the relationship between state and society influence the way states respond to epidemics.[48] Weak, resource-poor states are particularly susceptible to AIDS and other IDs, which may undermine political and economic stability and social cohesion. Below, I discuss the likelihood that this process will produce civil conflict. It is unlikely, however, given the reasons already discussed, that it will produce a preventive war between states.

Foreign policy conflict

In theory, ID outbreaks may prompt disputes among states over appropriate policy responses in a number of areas, including freedom of movement for people and goods. Nineteenth-century leaders employed quarantine as their primary instrument of ID control. In the first decade of the AIDS epidemic, despite a half century of human rights advances, some people again viewed quarantine as a reasonable reaction to a frightening new scourge. Cuba instituted mandatory testing and compulsory isolation of its HIV-positive population in sanatoriums, and in 1987 the West German minister of the interior ordered border police to turn back any foreigner suspected of carry-ing HIV.[49] The United States, which continues to deny entry to HIV-positive immigrants and visitors, bowed to international pressure in the 1990s and allowed waivers for short-term trips to visit family, receive medical treatment, conduct business, or attend scientific or health conferences. Another foreign policy dispute revolves around the issue of intellectual property rights. Major pharmaceutical companies and the U.S. government advocate protection of patents on AIDS drugs and oppose the production in other countries of inexpensive, generic versions of these medications.[50]

Nevertheless, states are unlikely to come into conflict with other states over such health-related foreign policy disputes for at least two reasons. First, and somewhat paradoxically, disease theoretically may reduce the likelihood of such conflicts arising. As disease increases, a society may devote a greater proportion of national budgets and human resources to disease control. Some states already weakened by disease may not want to bear the additional costs of lost trade and military conflict and so may respond to epi-demics by turning inward to deal with this and related domestic issues.[51] Second, disease actually may facilitate international cooperation. In the nineteenth century, for instance, disparate national quarantines produced international collaboration, not military conflict. States recognized the trade benefits of standardizing quarantine policies and met regularly to hammer out regulations on disease prevention and control. The current dispute over AIDS therapies suggests a similar lesson: Pharmaceutical corporations negotiate with foreign governments and companies to make their medications available at significantly lower prices in developing than in developed countries, while preserving their patents. David Gordon argues that, in the long run, the ID threat will "further energize the international community and most countries to devote more attention and resources to improved ID surveillance, response, and control capacity."[52]

Social effects

The final hypothesized relationship between IDs and war suggests the greatest threat to national security: By causing severe economic, political, and social effects, epidemic disease can produce domestic instability, civil war, or civil-military conflict, or it may lead a state to lash out against another state. "There is a growing realization that national security depends in great measure on domestic stability, which is in turn heavily influenced by human development—embracing economic, environmental, health, and political concerns."[53]

In many states, particularly in sub-Saharan Africa, IDs like AIDS produce devastating consequences for all economic actors, from the household and firm to the industry and state.[54] At the household level, ID effects are dramatic: Income declines precipitously when bread-winners sicken and die, health care and burial costs mount, savings are depleted, surviving children leave school to work or care for sick relatives, food consumption drops, malnutrition and poverty worsen, and medical expenditures soar. UNDP estimates that AIDS lowers the income of affected households by 80 percent; food consumption drops 15–30 percent; and primary school enrollments decline 20–40 percent.[55] In Thailand, rural families affected by AIDS spend the equivalent of an average annual income on treatment during the last year of an AIDS patient's life, while in Nigeria subsistence farmers spend as much as 13 percent of their total household income on malaria treatment.[56]

Because AIDS is spread largely by sexual behavior, it strikes people in their economically most productive years, with ruinous consequences for numerous sectors of the economy. Agriculture may be hardest hit with the most catastrophic results, given its importance in the economies of most developing countries. A 2001 UN Food and Agriculture Organization study estimates that by year's end AIDS will have claimed 26 percent of the agricultural work force in the ten most affected African nations.[57] In Zimbabwe, for instance, the output of largely subsistence communal agriculture has dropped 50 percent in the last five years, leading some experts to warn of a food crisis in the near future.[58] Price-Smith notes that both demand- and supply-side shocks induced by IDs will compromise productivity in agriculture and other economic sectors, including education, mining, tourism, and health.[59]

Sectors dependent on skilled workers and professionals may be particularly hard hit. AIDS disproportionately attacks the middle and professional classes in a society—its teachers, scientists, technicians, and managers—and may prompt surviving elites to flee. Individual businesses bear much of the cost of AIDS in the form of lost work time and benefits. In South Africa, 7.2 percent of total salary costs involve AIDS expenses.[60] One Kenyan company reports a 500 percent increase in funeral expenses and 1,000 percent increase in the cost of health care between 1989 and 1997.[61] With life expectancy plummeting, many companies hire two or more workers for every one job.[62]

AIDS, and IDs more generally, crush national economies, which face labor shortages and diminished productivity. Life expectancy at birth has fallen to about 34 in Sierra Leone, 48 in South Africa, and 42 in Uganda.[63] The U.S. Bureau of the Census estimates that life expectancy in Botswana in 2010 without AIDS would have been neady 75; with AIDS it will be less than 30.[64] In Zimbabwe and Zambia, as well, life expectancy in 2010 will be half of what it would have been without AIDS—in Zimbabwe, 35 rather than 70, and in Zambia, 30 instead of 60.[65] By 2010, there will be 71 million fewer people in South Africa because of AIDS.[66] This decline is producing alarming demographic trends: Because AIDS most often strikes women in their child-bearing years and HIV may be transferred from a pregnant woman to her child *in utero*, mortality rates among children are soaring. In Kenya, child mortality has risen more than 20 percent since 1986 and now exceeds its level of more than two decades ago. Men and women in their 20s and 30s, a decade or more after they have become sexually active, are dying of AIDS at astonishing rates. Nearly 90 percent of all fifteen-year-old boys in Botswana will become HIV-infected at some point in their lives; the figure is more than 65 percent in South Africa and nearly 70 percent in Zimbabwe. There soon will be more adults in their 60s and 70s than in their 40s or 50s in these societies because of AIDS deaths.[67] The lost generation is the economically most productive segment of society and the one that in most countries supports the oldest, youngest, and most vulnerable members.

These trends are devastating the national economies of sub-Saharan Africa. In high prevalence countries, AIDS will cut GDP growth rates by 0.5 to 1.0 percent a year.[68] Channing Arndt and Jeffrey D. Lewis forecast that South African GDP will be 17 percent lower in 2010 with AIDS than it would have been without the disease, and an alternative measure that they call "non-health, non-food absorption" will be 22 percent lower. Even after accounting for AIDS-induced population decline, per capita GDP in South Africa will be 8 percent lower in 2010 with AIDS than without it.[69] These findings are consistent with John T. Cuddington's claims that AIDS may reduce Tanzania's GDP in 2010 by 15–25 percent compared to what it would have been without AIDS. Despite a population size that is 20 percent smaller than in a world without AIDS, per capita GDP is still projected to decline by as much as 10 percent.[70]

Not surprisingly, IDs promise dire social and political consequences. It has become commonplace to note that AIDS is producing a generation of orphans: As many as 11 percent of children in some African states had lost one or both parents by 1997, compared with about 2 percent before the AIDS era.[71]

This means that millions of children already have been orphaned, and that number will reach the tens of millions in the next decade. This generation—which is likely to be homeless, poor, hungry, uneducated, increasingly desperate, and decreasingly bound by social norms and laws—presents a challenge to political stability, particularly in societies where criminal opportunities and weapons are readily available.

> AIDS orphans are a vulnerable group, and may be recruited into military activities or into crime with promises of food, alcohol and drugs, as well as need for "family". In chilling words, a recent CIA report on the threat of HIV/AIDS to national security concluded that AIDS "... will produce a huge and impoverished orphan cohort unable to cope and vulnerable to exploitation and radicalization."[72]

One major foundation of any political system, education, is being devastated. More than one-third of children orphaned by AIDS drop out of school.[73] The disease also depletes the supply of teachers. In South Africa, as many as one-third of teachers are HIV positive. In Zambia, the number is 40 percent, and in Swaziland, 70 percent.[74] A recent World Bank study of Malawi asserts that roughly 40 percent of education personnel in that country will die from AIDS.[75] In the Central African Republic, 107 of 173 schools have closed recently because of a lack of teaching staff. As many teachers in that country died between 1996 and 1998 as retired. They died an average of ten years before the minimum retirement age of 52, and 85 percent of those who died were HIV positive.[76] Over all, Africa will lose ten percent of its educators to AIDS by 2005, setting the continent back a century in education levels.[77] AIDS erodes a state's technical and managerial capacity by incapacitating and killing government personnel at the same high rates at which it strikes other skilled workers and elites. In September 2000, Zimbabwe's president, Robert Mugabe, took the unusual step of announcing that AIDS had claimed three of his cabinet ministers and many traditional tribal chiefs.[78] In South Africa, the spokesman for Presidents Nelson Mandela and Thabo Mbeki died at age 36 of what is generally regarded to be an AIDS-related illness.[79] The human costs of AIDS reach every level of the polity. Eighty-six percent of all employee deaths at the Kenya Revenue authority in 1998 and 75 percent of all police deaths in 1996–98 were AIDS related.[80] More than one-fourth of South African police forces are probably now infected.[81] In Botswana, a lawyer relays his frustration with a legal system that cannot function properly because of the loss of court officials, and in Uganda political decentralization is hampered because AIDS has decimated local government in some regions.[82]

How might these political and economic effects produce violent conflict? Price-Smith offers two possible answers: Disease "magnif[ies] . . . both relative and absolute deprivation and . . . hasten[s] the erosion of state capacity in seriously affected societies. Thus, infectious disease may in fact contribute to societal destabilization and to chronic low-intensity intrastate, violence, and in extreme cases it may accelerate the processes that lead to state failure."[83] Disease heightens competition among social groups and elites for scarce resources. When the debilitating and deadly effects of IDs like AIDS are concentrated among a particular socio-economic, ethnic, racial, or geographic group, the potential for conflict escalates. In many parts of Africa today, AIDS strikes rural areas at higher rates than urban areas, or it hits certain provinces harder than others. If these trends persist in states where tribes or ethnic groups are heavily concentrated in particular regions or in rural rather than urban areas, AIDS almost certainly will interact with tribal, ethnic, or national differences and make political and military conflict more likely. Price-Smith argues, moreover, that "the potential for intra-elite violence is also increasingly probable and may carry grave political consequences, such as coups, the collapse of governance, and planned genocides."[84]

The likelihood that IDs will produce violent conflict by generating these social effects depends on at least three factors. Homer-Dixon and Price-Smith offer the first two.[85] First, other stressors like environmental degradation or scarcity may interact with and exacerbate IDs. Second, the strength of the state before the onset of epidemic disease strongly influences the extent to which IDs produce these social, political, and economic effects and thereby provoke military conflict. "There is a logically positive association between state capacity and state adaptation because greater initial capacity means that there are more human, economic, and technical resources within the state to mobilize to deal with various crises. . . . Thus states that have lower state capacity when IDs afflict them generally suffer much greater losses than states with high initial capacity."[86] The states of sub-Saharan Africa are doubly doomed: Lacking the state capacity to assemble an effective defense against IDs, they are then hit with epidemics that they lack the financial and technical resources to fight.

Third, whether AIDS or other IDs generate severe economic and political effects leading to violent conflict also may depend on prevailing beliefs about religion, society, and medicine. Populations judge their governments' responses to health crises according to their dominant social beliefs. In the nineteenth century, where and when the theory prevailed that disease was contagious, quarantine was the preferred policy response to disease outbreak. Where and when the idea prevailed that disease was acquired through bad air and filth, rather than contagion, people demanded sanitary reform instead.[87] Religious traditions, like Christianity and some forms of Buddhism, that explain human suffering and comfort survivors, may placate individuals and at least temporarily insulate governments against charges that they are not responsive to the health needs of their peoples.[88] In the Middle East and North Africa, social values in predominantly Islamic countries may limit the spread of HIV, but they also inhibit the prevention, reporting, and treating of sexually transmitted diseases, and they likely shield the government.[89]

Moral stigma may perform a similar function. Syphilis reached epidemic dimensions in the First World War, for example, because the stigma surrounding it led to poor medical management.[90] A similar shame continues to mark AIDS sufferers, leading many governments to delay and populations to tolerate inaction.

This provides yet another reason that IDs will continue to pose the most serious threat to developing states. With western industrialization came secularization and scientific advancement. In the 1980s, nonetheless, social beliefs posed a significant obstacle to AIDS control and prevention in some developed countries because of bias against the homosexual population, which suffered disproportionately from the disease. These prejudices, as well as prevailing beliefs about sexuality, continue to hinder progress in some segments of western society. The problem is likely to be even more serious in less developed states, where traditional customs like wife inheritance and genital mutilation spread AIDS directly and where the role of women and the stigma surrounding AIDS create intolerance and silence that allow the disease to spread unchecked. In a highly publicized case in December 1998, neighbors beat to death a volunteer for a South African AIDS organization for bringing shame on their community by publicly acknowledging that she was HIV-infected.[91] In June 2001, in a three-day special session on AIDS, the UN General Assembly passed a Declaration of Commitment, a global AIDS plan that includes specific goals and time frames. The final document explicitly addressed "harmful traditional and customary practices," but not before agreement was nearly scuttled and language about high risk populations was deleted because Islamic nations opposed wording that would obligate them to help gay men, one of the high risk groups.[92]

Not all the causal pathways identified in figure 1 threaten national security. There can be little doubt, however, that ID seriously threatens national security, traditionally defined, when large numbers of people die, national economies crumble, and social structures and political institutions weaken and fail, particularly when these factors generate violent conflict. Many sub-Saharan states that are resource-poor and institutionally weak face such threats unless other states, international institutions, or nongovernmental organizations (NGOs) provide significant financial, medical, and administrative assistance. That IDs

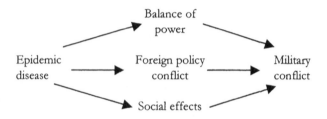

Figure 1 Epidemic Disease and Military Conflict.

threaten security in these states, however, does not necessarily or automatically compromise U.S. security.

U.S. national security

Indeed, none of the mechanisms illustrated in figure 1 immediately or directly threatens U.S. security. Large numbers of Americans die each year from IDs. In fact, the number of deaths from IDs in the United States doubled between 1980 and 1999.[93] These numbers, however, pale in comparison to those in sub-Saharan Africa and other regions, and they do not threaten the state in the way they do in other countries. As Price-Smith points out, "the United States has less to fear from the direct threat of infectious disease (or other environmentally induced health threats) to its population than do developing countries with much lower endogenous capacity."[94] This does not mean, of course, that the United States can afford to bury its head in the sand.

Epidemic disease may exacerbate domestic conflict in key states where vital U.S. interests are at stake. In Russia, for instance, HIV rates have risen dramatically in the past two years and are poised to explode. The 1999 infection rate in Moscow was three times that of all previous years combined.[95] In fact, AIDS is spreading more quickly in Russia than in any other country in the world. According to a 2002 National Intelligence Council (NIC) estimate, between one and two million Russians (or 1.3–2.5 percent of the adult population) is currently infected, and that number is expected to increase to 5–8 million (or 6–11 percent) by 2010.[96] Much of this increase is fueled by IV drug use, commercial sex, and, especially, the prison system, in which inmates may be held for up to two years before being charged and in which more than a million convicts are periodically released through amnesty programs. As Nicholas Eberstadt notes, "Russia's prison system, in other words, functions like a carburetor for HIV—pumping a highly concentrated variant of the infection back through the general population."[97]

In June 2001, Russia's first deputy minister of health, Gennadi Onish-chenko, called AIDS "a direct threat to the nation's security."[98] This may be true for several reasons. First, AIDS will exacerbate Russia's projected population decrease. In less than 25 years, it is estimated, Russia's population will decline by 12–13 million, even if the nation faces only a mild HIV/AIDS epidemic. In the face of the more severe epidemic now feared, that decline will reach 25 million, with a concurrent drop of 11 million in Russia's working-age population.[99] By 2050, it is estimated, the population of the "superpower" may plummet by as much as one-third to 95–100 million people.[100] The director of the Federal Research Center for AIDS Prevention in Moscow, Vadim Pokrovskii, sums up the problem this way: "In Africa, there are high birth rates, but in Russia the birth rate is low. If we have a rate of only three percent infected, population would fall by six percent. . . . In Russia, AIDS is scarier than in Africa. There the population is replaced. In Russia it will not be."[101]

Second, and closely related, AIDS is likely to cause severe economic problems. A recent World Bank study predicts that HIV/AIDS will reduce annual economic growth in Russia by one percent by 2020.[102] While Russia's GNP per person of working age could be expected to increase by 50 percent by 2025 without HIV/AIDS, the disease will significantly reduce worker output and decimate the working-age population. The result, Ebertadt projects, is that under even the mildest epidemic-scenario now predicted, Russia's future GNP will remain stagnant through 2025.[103]

Finally, these demographic and economic problems, combined with the disease's effect on military readiness, may undermine political stability in Russia. The chairman of the Defense Ministry's Medical Commission reports that 37 percent of all draft-age men in Russia cannot serve because of serious health problems. Fifty-five percent of those drafted can perform only limited duties because of poor health. In 2001, over 2,000 servicemen were dismissed from the Russian Army for being HIV-positive.[104] In the not too distant future, in short, AIDS could further erode Russia's ability to staff a conventional army and potentially lead Moscow to rely more on a deteriorating nuclear force to maintain its great power status.

China is in the early stages of a similar HIV/AIDS explosion. Reported infections were 67.4 percent higher in the first six months of 2001 than for the same period in 2000, and the rate of infection among Chinese drug users is ten times as high today as it was in 1995.[105] Seven of China's 22 provinces already are experiencing full-blown epidemics, while nine more face similar fates in the near future.[106] According to a recent United Nations study, current trends indicate that 20 million Chinese will be HIV-positive by 2010.[107] The problem is especially acute, because many Chinese blame their government for the AIDS crisis. Until recently, government officials have refused to acknowledge the epidemic publicly. More importantly, government actions helped spread AIDS throughout central China. There, government-owned or -operated blood collection centers paid poor farmers to donate blood. Blood of the same type was pooled and centrifuged to separate out the plasma. The leftover red blood cells then were pooled and reinjected into the donors, preventing anemia and allowing donors to give blood more frequently. Not surprisingly, there have been a growing number of protests against the government by farmers trying to publicize their plight.[108]

HIV/AIDS will have serious human and economic costs in China, but it is relatively unlikely to cause the kind of widespread disruption that could jeopardize China's regional status. The spreading epidemic could curtail the international investment that has helped fuel China's economic growth. As the recent NIC study notes, however, China has several things going for it that Russia does not. First, although domestic AIDS spending remains low, the Chinese government has recently taken great strides in acknowledging the extent of the epidemic, seeking assistance, and organizing a public health response. Second, the sheer size of China's population will mute the epidemic's impact. Even an infected population of fifteen million would represent just two percent of the adult population of China.[109]

Another nuclear-armed state, India, also faces a looming epidemic. Infection rates remain low—7 of 1,000 adults are HIV-positive. Five to eight million people in India currently live with the disease, however, and that number is expected to rise to 20–25 million (3–4 percent of the adult population) by 2010. In some areas of northeast India, more than 70 percent of the mostly male IV drug-using population is infected, suggesting that infection rates in the general population may soon soar.[110] Public awareness of AIDS remains low, but the Indian government responded relatively early to the epidemic, creating the National AIDS Control Organization in 1986, and India possesses a relatively strong public health infrastructure. As in China, moreover, the NIC estimates that the effects of India's epidemic will be lessened by being diffused among a large population.[111] For the present, significant unrest in Russia, India, or China remains a distant and remote possibility for American policy makers and the public, even though it is becoming increasingly obvious that Russia, in particular, faces a severe ID threat in the near future. If scholars and policy makers are to draw a credible link between ID and U.S. national security, it is here that they should look.

Nevertheless, the more immediate threat is to sub-Saharan Africa, and it is here that scholars and practitioners have focused their attention by arguing that U.S. security is linked to stability in Africa. In February 2001, Secretary of State Powell announced that the AIDS epidemic in Africa is a national security issue.[112] In May of the same year, Powell told South African students, "Africa matters to America," citing $30 billion in U.S.-African trade.[113] In the aftermath of the events of 9/11, the West in general and the United States in particular have a heightened security interest in Africa. Disease can contribute to instability and violence. Indeed, high infant mortality—which exists in sub-Saharan Africa largely because of IDs—is strongly correlated with the likelihood of state failure in partial democracies.[114] Failed states may breed anti-western sentiment and even terrorism.[115] Alternatively, they may influence domestic actors in the United States to pressure their government to intervene on humanitarian grounds. Once U.S. troops are committed, whether alone or as part of a multilateral force, U.S. security is clearly engaged.

These security concerns likely will not seem terribly compelling to Americans for at least three reasons. First, they may appear relatively remote possibilities, particularly at a time when the United States is dealing with immediate and direct security threats. Second, even if Americans think about the longer run, there are more obvious candidates for state-sponsored terrorism or state failure than the states of sub-Saharan Africa, particularly the Islamic states of the Middle East and North Africa. Third, regardless of current interest in Africa, that continent has never figured heavily in U.S. security and foreign policy calculations. Americans see few material or strategic interests at stake, particularly in sub-Saharan Africa. As Helen Epstein and Lincoln

Chen state, "In 1999, the UN Security Council declared AIDS in Africa an international security issue, because it further destabilizes already politically fragile African nations. How much, however, does this really matter to the West, particularly the United States? The postwar history of the West's relationship with Africa suggests that when millions of Africans die, or when African states collapse, Western leaders often look away."[116] Secretary Powell's own words confirm this. In February 2000, less than a year before assuming office, he said, "While Africa may be important, it doesn't fit into the national strategic interests, as far as I can see them."[117]

It seems obvious, in short, that epidemic disease can contribute to violent conflict, particularly by engendering domestic instability, and in that way can threaten the national security of affected states. At present, however, most ID-induced unrest poses at most an indirect and medium to long term threat to U.S. security, suggesting that a rhetorical linkage to national security may not be the most effective way of inspiring public and political support for AIDS-ravaged Africa. Russia, where IDS may pose the most immediate threat to U.S. interests, is receiving relatively little attention in discussions of disease threats to U.S. national security.

Epidemic disease as a determinant of war outcome

Even when disease plays little role in the outbreak of war, it can influence the course and outcome of military conflict. In theory, IDS can be "war-stoppers" or "war-outcome-determinants," contributing to one side's victory and another's defeat, depending on their differential impact on the adversaries. As figure 2 suggests, disease can influence the outcome of contemporary conflict in at least three ways: the deliberate dissemination of biological agents; the targeting by conventional means of public health; and the unintentional impact of epidemic disease on military readiness.

Biological weapons and disease

Biological warfare has been described as "public health in reverse" because of its potential to disperse deadly infectious agents.[118] Because biological

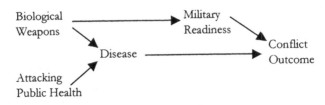

Figure 2 Disease and the Outcome of Military Conflict.

weapons potentially pose direct security threats to the United States and other countries, because they are not new threats, and because they fit more easily within traditional definitions of security, attempts to link disease and security in this way should resonate with the American public and policy makers.

Biological weapons are living organisms, most commonly self-replicating micro-organisms—including bacteria, viruses, fungi, and rickettsia—deliberately disseminated to cause disease and death in humans or animals.[119] Since 1972, 144 parties to the Biological Toxins and Weapons Convention have agreed not to develop, produce, stockpile, acquire, or retain biological weapons. At least eleven states nevertheless have some sort of biological weapons program. These efforts produce or are capable of producing numerous IDs. As Americans are all too aware, anti-human biological weapons agents include *bacillus anthracis* (anthrax), which produces fever, severe respiratory problems, shock, pneumonia, and death within days of exposure.[120] Anthrax is not a particularly effective agent, however, since it is not contagious and, in many cases, is susceptible to treatment. Smallpox is extremely contagious, by contrast, and spreads through the inhalation of virus droplets. It can incubate for more than 12 days before sickening its victims for up to several weeks with vomiting, lesions, fever, and in 35 percent of stricken people, death. In 1980, after the WHO announced that smallpox had been eradicated, stocks of the disease were destroyed and, officially, samples exist only in the Centers for Disease Control (CDC) in Atlanta and the State Centre for Research on Virology and Biotechnology in Siberia. For this reason, until very recently, there was no commercially available supply of smallpox vaccine.[121]

Anti-animal and plant pathogens also make potent biological weapons.[122] Diseases like Newcastle disease, bovine spongiform encephalopathy ("mad cow disease"), avian influenza, swine fevers, anthrax, brucellosis, and—among the most contagious and most costly—foot-and-mouth disease can disrupt cattle, hog, and poultry production. In the process, such agroterrorism can cause significant threats to the agricultural sector, disrupt trade and, in extreme cases, provoke famine. As Dorothy Preslar has noted, terrorism against agricultural targets may pose a greater threat than against human targets because it "[i]s not as repugnant to prevailing sensibilities; [c]annot easily be proved intentional . . . ; [c]an be instigated without violating international arms control agreements; [and w]ill incite neither a crushing military response nor [an] international man-hunt."[123] Crop diseases may be introduced to spread famine and disrupt the economy. Because they are highly sensitive to humidity, temperature, and sunlight and they cannot circulate airborne as far or as fast as many human and animal diseases, however, crop diseases would be more difficult to disseminate.[124]

Unlike nuclear and chemical weapons, biological agents are relatively simple and inexpensive to manufacture and easy to conceal. They can be made in facilities otherwise devoted to legitimate medical and pharmaceutical research at a fraction of the cost of other weapons. One government analyst has calculated that a penny's worth of anthrax is the equivalent in lethality of $1,500 of nuclear power.[125] It can be difficult to stabilize biological agents, but relatively easy to deliver them to their targets. They can be sprayed efficiently as respirable aerosols from a truck or small plane. Only ten grams of anthrax spores spread over one square mile would kill as many people as would a metric ton of sarin gas.[126] As Garrett notes, "Enough anthrax spores to kill five or six million people could be loaded into a taxi and pumped out its tailpipe as it meandered through Manhattan."[127]

Despite strong prohibitions against biological weapons and warfare, ID has been used as a weapon of war throughout history. Greek, Roman, and Persian armies tossed dead bodies in enemy wells to poison the water supply. In the fourteenth century, the Black Plague spread to Europe—where it ultimately claimed as much as one-third of the population—from what is now Ukraine, after Tartar soldiers catapulted their own plague victims over the fortress walls as weapons against their Italian foes.[128] The British employed smallpox in their fights against native Americans in the 1754–63 French and Indian War and against U.S. troops in the Revolutionary War.[129] During their southern campaign in the Revolutionary War, the British used infected African slaves, whom they had enticed to fight the Americans with the promise of freedom, as weapons of war.[130] During the Second World War, the Japanese Imperial Army's Unit 731 developed biological weapons to disperse anthrax, typhoid, cholera, plague, and at least a dozen other IDs and tested these weapons on Chinese civilians.[131] More recently, Stefan Elbe argues, African armies have used HIV/AIDS as a psychological, and perhaps even biological, weapon.[132]

Although the risk of biological warfare is modest, it remains one of the most significant and immediate security threats that disease poses for the West, particularly the United States.[133] These weapons pose two distinct challenges. First, a state's pursuit of biological weapons capabilities could provoke preventive war by other states fearful of that power. Concerns about Iraq's budding biological, chemical, and nuclear capabilities provoked the 1981 Israeli attack on an Iraqi nuclear reactor, helped fuel two wars against Iraq, and prompted the decade of inspections and air strikes between the two Persian Gulf Wars. Second, biological agents could be used as weapons of war or terrorism. State use remains relatively unlikely, however, given normative prohibitions against the use of biological weapons and the deadliness of other available weapons. Despite its extensive biological and chemical weapons program, for example, Iraq did not use these weapons during the 1991 Persian Gulf War and, as of this writing, has not used them in the current conflict. At present, moreover, most states lack the capability to launch a successful biological weapons attack. Non-state actors and some rogue states are more likely to use these weapons of the weak against a domestic population, government, or other target. Certainly, there is no shortage of states or terrorist groups with grievances to air, and these actors will care less, if at all, about international public opinion. That Osama bin Laden actively sought to acquire weapons of mass destruction supports Richard Falkenrath's claim that the rise of religious and anti-American terrorist groups will weaken the bias against causing mass fatalities and using nuclear, chemical, or biological weapons to do so.[134]

Biological weapons pose a substantial and direct threat to U.S. national security. On the one hand, the United States presents the most likely target for such terrorist attacks, even if the overall likelihood of such an attack remains small. On the other hand, key states that the United States considers strategically important might acquire, use, or become a target of biological weapons and indirectly threaten U.S. interests. The U.S. government recognized this potential, for example, when it designated $100 million to defuse the biological weapons threat from the former Soviet Union by converting former weapons facilities and employing scientists previously involved in the Soviet biological warfare program.[135]

Given the immediate and direct nature of the threat, and especially following the 2001 anthrax attacks, it should be relatively easy (compared with efforts to link economic instability in Africa to U.S. security) to link biological weapons to American national security in the public mind and therefore to mobilize domestic support for antiterrorist and counterterrorist activities. In 1998, President Clinton announced that he expected a biological or chemical attack within the next five years. The following year, R. James Woolsey, director of Central Intelligence under Clinton, described biological terrorism as the "single most dangerous threat to [U.S.] national security in the foreseeable future."[136] More recently, Secretary of Health and Human Services, Tommy Thompson, responded to the anthrax threats by announcing that "[p]ublic health is a national security issue."[137] Scholars may differ on the perceived likelihood of attack, but few would deny that disease—when used deliberately as a weapon of war—poses a significant threat to national security. Indeed, it has long been recognized as such and included in planning for war and homeland defense.

Targeting public health

Biological agents are not the only way to deliberately disseminate disease during war. Armed forces have often targeted civilians—and civilian health— as part of a deliberate military strategy, and the use of this tactic seems only to have risen since the end of the cold war. What Jack Chow calls "'humanitarian' warfare—aggression through the control and denial of vital human needs— now complements or even substitutes for direct force."[138] Two tactics of humanitarian warfare, in particular, link ID and national security. What Chow calls "war by starvation" emphasizes the political and strategic value of food. In Sudan, Somalia, and Ethiopia, soldiers and warlords have struggled to control the food supply as a means of increasing their military and political power. This deliberate use of starvation inevitably spreads IDs, given the link between malnutrition and disease. What Chow terms "war by privation" is somewhat broader and includes "deliberate cutoffs of food, water, medicine and heat."[139] In Sudan, for instance, government troops routinely target hospitals.[140] In Kosovo, Yugoslav president Slobodan Milosovec targeted medical care as far back as 1989–90 when he ordered the firing of thousands of Albanian professionals, closing 75 percent of all state-run medical facilities. This contributed to 170 epidemics between 1990 and 1998. In fighting in 1998, ethnic Albanians were prevented from receiving or forced to pay for medical care that ethnic Serbs received free, and numerous hospitals and out-patient clinics were deliberately destroyed. After the NATO bombing campaign began, government troops and paramilitary units destroyed 90 more country-based health care clinics run by the Mother Teresa Society. Providing medical assistance to members of the Kosovo Liberation Army was labeled terrorism, and doctors were harassed routinely for providing medical aid to people in areas of conflict.[141]

The United States determined that it had strategic interests in Kosovo worth fighting for, so Serbian engagement in war by privation influenced U.S. national security. When the United States becomes militarily involved for humanitarian reasons in areas with little or no strategic value, humanitarian warfare also may threaten its ability to meet its military objectives. In this case, however, the threat is an indirect one and one that is already captured in traditional considerations of military strategy and tactics.

Military readiness

Even when disease is not deliberately used, it can alter the evolution and outcome of military conflict by eroding military readiness and morale. As Jared Diamond notes, "All those military histories glorifying great generals oversimplify the ego-deflating truth: the winners of past wars were not always the armies with the best generals and weapons, but were often merely those bearing the nastiest germs to transmit to their enemies."[142] During the European conquest of the Americas, the conquistadors shared numerous lethal microbes with their native American foes, who had few or no deadly diseases to pass on to their conquerors. When Hernando Cortez and his men first attacked the Aztecs in Mexico in 1520, they left behind smallpox that wiped out half the Aztec population. Surviving Aztecs were further demoralized by their vulnerability to a disease that appeared harmless to the Europeans, and on their next attempt the Spanish succeeded in conquering the Aztec nation.[143] Spanish conquest of the Incan empire in South America followed a similar pattern: In 1532 Francisco Pizarro and his army of 168 Spaniards defeated the Incan army of 80,000. A devastating smallpox epidemic had killed the Incan emperor and his heir, producing a civil war that split the empire and allowed a handful of Europeans to defeat a large, but divided enemy.[144] In modern times, too, pandemic infections have affected the ability of military forces to prosecute and win a war. The German Army chief of staff in the First World War, General Erick Von Ludendorf, blamed Germany's loss of that war at least partly on the negative effects of the 1918 influenza epidemic on the morale of German troops.[145] In the Second World War, similarly, malaria caused more U.S. casualties in certain areas than did military action.[146] Throughout history, then, IDs have had a significant potential to decimate armies and alter military history.

Still, IDs' impact in the contemporary international system may be somewhat different. Unlike other diseases, AIDS has an incubation period of ten years or more, making it unlikely that it will produce significant casualties on the front lines of a war. It will still, however, deplete force strength in many states. On average, 20–40 percent of armed forces in sub-Saharan countries are HIV-positive, and in a few countries the rate is 60 percent or more. In Zimbabwe, it may be as high as 80 percent.[147] In high incidence countries, AIDS significantly erodes military readiness, directly threatening national security. Lyndy Heinecken chillingly describes the problem in sub-Saharan Africa:

> AIDS-related illnesses are now the leading cause of death in the army and police forces of these countries, accounting for more than 50% of inservice and post-service mortalities. In badly infected countries, AIDS patients occupy 75% of military hospital beds and the disease is responsible for more admissions than battlefield injuries. The high rate of HIV infection has meant that some African armies have been unable to deploy a full contingent, or even half of their troops, at short notice. . . . [In South Africa, because] participation in peace-support operations outside the country is voluntary, the S[outh] A[frican] N[ational] D[efence] F[orce] is grappling with the problem of how to ensure the availability of sufficiently suitable candidates for deployment at short notice. Even the use of members for internal crime prevention and border control, which subjects them to adverse conditions or stationing in areas where local infrastructure is limited, presents certain problems. Ordinary ailments, such as diarrhoea and the common cold, can be serious enough to require the hospitalization of an immune-compromised person, and, in some cases, can prove fatal if they are not treated immediately.[148]

Armed forces in severely affected states will be unable to recruit and train soldiers quickly enough to replace their sick and dying colleagues, the potential recruitment pool itself will dwindle, and officers corps will be decimated. Military budgets will be sapped, military blood supplies tainted, and organizational structures strained to accommodate unproductive soldiers.

HIV-infected armed forces also threaten civilians at home and abroad. Increased levels of sexual activity among military forces in wartime means that the military risk of becoming infected with HIV is as much as 100 times that of the civilian risk. It also means that members of the armed forces comprise a key means of transmitting the virus to the general population; with sex and transport workers, the military is considered one of the three core transmission groups in Africa.[149] For this reason, conflict-ridden states may become reluctant to accept peacekeepers from countries with high HIV rates.

Rather than contributing directly to military defeat in many countries, however, AIDS in the military is more likely to have longer term implications for national security. First, IDs theoretically could deter military action and impede access to strategic resources or areas. Tropical diseases erected a formidable, although obviously not insurmountable, obstacle to colonization in Africa, India, and Southeast Asia. French and later American efforts to open the Panama Canal, similarly, were stymied until U.S. mosquito control efforts effectively checked yellow fever and malaria. Second, in many countries AIDS already strains military medical systems and their budgets, and it only promises to divert further spending away from defense toward both military and civilian health. Third, AIDS in the military promises to have its greatest impact by eroding a government's control over its armed forces and further destabilizing the state. Terminally ill soldiers may have little incentive to defend their government, and their government may be in more need of defending as AIDS siphons funds from housing, education, police, and administration. Finally, high military HIV/AIDS rates could alter regional balances of power. Perhaps 40–50 percent of South Africa's soldiers are HIV-infected. Despite the disease's negative impact on South Africa's absolute power, Price-Smith notes, AIDS may increase that nation's power relative to its neighbors, Zimbabwe and Botswana, with potentially important regional consequences.[150]

AIDS poses obvious threats to the military forces of many countries, particularly in sub-Saharan Africa, but it does not present the same immediate security problems for the United States. The authors of a Reagan-era report on the effects of economic and demographic trends on security worried about the effects of the costs of AIDS research, education, and funding on the defense budget,[151] but a decade of relative prosperity generated budget surpluses instead. These surpluses have evaporated, but concerns about AIDS spending have not reappeared and are unlikely to do so for the foreseeable future, given the relatively low levels of HIV-infection in the United States. AIDS presents other challenges, including prevention education and measures to limit infection of U.S. soldiers and peacekeepers stationed abroad, particularly in high risk settings, and HIV transmission by these forces to the general population. These concerns could limit U.S. actions where American interests are at stake.[152]

AIDS' effects on the militaries of key states also could erode vital U.S. interests by undermining allies' military readiness or friends' and foes' political stability. As discussed above, Russia will be among the states hardest hit with potentially serious consequences for the international balance of power. IDs may not prevent the U.S. military from fighting and winning wars, in short, but they still impact U.S. national security. They do not, however, and for the foreseeable future will not, degrade security in the direct ways or to the extent that many health security advocates suggest.

Misstating the threat

At the start of the twenty-first century, human beings face what may be the worst plague in history, a disease so devastating that it has already surpassed in absolute terms the most notorious epidemics of earlier generations. In response, politicians, health professionals, and scholars plead with the West to recognize the threat this modern plague presents to human security. They attempt to persuade nations and individuals to broaden their thinking about security to encompass basic needs like health. From there, it is often only one small rhetorical step to the argument that AIDS and other IDs threaten national and international security. Intellectually, however, that step is much steeper. It must include a serious analysis of whether and how epidemic IDs challenge national security, more narrowly construed as the preservation of the state's territory, institutions, and sovereignty.

Using this definition, we see that epidemic disease outbreak can endanger national security. First, it may generate violent conflict by creating significant domestic economic and political instability. Second, epidemic disease historically has altered the outcome of international conflicts, and this remains possible today. Biological agents—including epidemic IDs—can be weapons of war and thereby directly and immediately threaten security. Combatants may deliberately target public health and spread disease to weaken and demoralize an enemy population. Or IDs can reduce military readiness in the hardest hit countries. For many states, particularly in sub-Saharan Africa, ID-induced civil unrest and declining military power directly threaten security, but these pose only long term threats to the United States. ID-induced instability in Russia may pose a less distant challenge to U.S. interests, but that threat has received scant attention to date. For other states, IDs spread by war may add another level to the security threats inherent in violent conflict but, again, this remains a distant threat to the United States. Only biological weapons pose a significant, immediate, and direct threat to the nation's security for the foreseeable future.

The most catastrophic contemporary disease and the first lethal pandemic disease in the lifetimes of most readers of this article, HIV/AIDS poses the greatest humanitarian crisis of this or perhaps any generation, but it does not now pose a significant security threat to most developed states. A humanitarian and even a security threat to southern Africa does not necessarily threaten other states' security unless southern Africa is of vital interest to them. So far, the United States has been wary of such arguments, choosing instead to rely on humanitarian justifications for its brief and often late incursions into places like Somalia and Rwanda. As the United States relies more on West African states like Nigeria and Angola for oil, the balance between humanitarian and security concerns may shift more toward the latter.[153] This still seems a distant likelihood, however, as the United States continues to focus its efforts on stabilizing its major source of imported oil, the Middle East.

Why should it matter whether policy makers and scholars overdraw the link between IDs and security? Security provides a relatively poor rationale for addressing health threats like AIDS. From a national security perspective, in fact, AIDS poses a far smaller threat to most states than it does from almost any other viewpoint, including health, human rights, economic and political development, and social and economic justice. It is not clear, moreover, that anything is gained by adopting the rhetoric of national security to address IDs.

Ironically, at least two things may be lost. First, the appeal to national security relieves states without major public health threats of any moral obligation to respond to health crises of monumental proportions in the developing world, since it suggests that only national security concerns can justify significant expenditures on disease control. Historically, narrow self-interest has not motivated a sustained commitment to international health cooperation. In the nineteenth century, when epidemic disease in less developed states provoked divergent national quarantine policies within Europe and endangered gains from trade, European states negotiated common quarantine standards and made significant strides in international disease control. By the mid-twentieth century, however, developed states had acquired powerful medical, pharmaceutical, and public health weapons to fight epidemic disease in their own countries and had lost interest in helping the developing world transition to better health. Narrow self-interest is no more likely to promote the sustained commitment that will be necessary to fight AIDS in Africa and elsewhere. Even in the shorter run, in fact, public opinion is more likely to support foreign aid that serves humanitarian than strategic ends. As David H. Lumsdaine notes about twentieth-century foreign aid practices, "The principle of help to those in great need implicit in the very idea of foreign aid led to steady modification of aid practices, which focused them more on the needs of the poor and moved them away from donor interests."[154]

Second, policymakers' and scholars' attempts to whip up support for ID control by making it a national security issue may generate security dilemmas. The more some states accept and attempt to paint epidemic disease as a security threat, the greater the chance that national disease-control and antiprolifera-tion policies aimed at biological weapons will arouse suspicion in other states. Paradoxically, international organizations and NGOs then may be called upon to play a greater role in global health efforts, as the purely national and bilateral efforts of states become increasingly suspect. In this regard, it may be more fruitful to view disease and health issues as concerns for U.S. foreign policy deserving of multilateral responses, rather than as narrow security threats requiring bilateral policy responses that may provoke suspicion.[155]

If well-intentioned people seek to rally support among western governments for anti-AIDS efforts in Africa, portraying disease as a security issue may be exactly the wrong strategy to employ. Rather, the world must face AIDS for what it is and will be for the foreseeable future—a health tragedy of unprecedented and staggering proportions that cries out for international and transnational humanitarian assistance, not for the garrisoning of states behind national boundaries and national security rhetoric.

Notes

The author thanks Dave Brown, Anthony DeVassy, Jason Fabricante, Joe MacAvoy, and Karen Willmer for research assistance, and the College of William and Mary for financial support. She also thanks Ben Frankel, Sean Lynn-Jones, Michael Tierney, several anonymous reviewers and, especially, Andrew Cortell, Jonathan Mercer, and Heather Scully for their careful readings and thoughtful comments.

1 The White House, Office of the Vice President, "Remarks prepared for delivery by Vice President Al Gore, United Nations Security Council Opening Session," 10 January 2000, www.whitehouse.gov/ONAP/pub/vp_sc2.html (8 July 2000). Since 1996, the Clinton administration had argued that "[e]merging infectious diseases present one of the most significant health and security challenges facing the global community." The White House, Office of Science and Technology Policy, "Fact Sheet: Addressing the Threat of Emerging Infectious Diseases," 12 June 1996, www.fas.org/irp/offdocs/pdd_ntsc7.htm (10 September 1999). The policy was announced in response to National Science and Technology Council, Committee on International Science, Engineering, and Technology, Working Group on Emerging and Re-emerging Infectious Diseases, "Global Microbial Threats in the 1990s," www.whitehouse.gov/WH/EOP/OSTP/CISET/html/ciset/html (10 September 1999). Also, see Al Gore, "Emerging Infections Threaten National and Global Security," www.state.gov/www/global/oes/health/task_force/article.htm (6 August 2001), reprinted from *American Society for Microbiology News* 62, no. 9 (1996): 448–49. Clinton's was not the first U.S. administration to explore the link between security and public health. In October 1988, a Department of Defense (DoD) working group had issued a report that, among other things, examined the effects of the Human Immunodeficiency Virus (HIV) that causes AIDS on U.S. security. The document is reprinted as "Economic and Demographic Trends and International Security: A U.S. Analysis," *Population and Development Review* (September 1989): 587–99.

2 National Intelligence Council (NIC), "The Global Infectious Disease Threat and Its Implications for the United States," NIE 99-17D, January 2000, www.cia.gov/publications/nie/report/nie99-17d.html (17 November 2000). David F. Gordon is the principal author of this document.

3 Jeffrey Sachs, "The Best Possible Investment in Africa," *New York Times*, 10 February 2001, A15.

4 Andrew T. Price-Smith, "Ghosts of Kigali: Infectious Disease and Global Stability at the Turn of the Century," *International Journal* 54, no. 3 (summer 1999): 432. Popular and academic works on IDs include Laurie Garrett, *Betrayal of Trust: The Collapse of Global Public Health* (New York: Hyperion, 2000); Laurie Garrett, *The Coming Plague: Newly Emerging Diseases in a World Out of Balance* (New

York: Farrar, Straus, and Giroux, 1994); David P. Fidler, *International Law and Infectious Diseases* (Oxford: Clarendon Press, 1999); David P. Fidler, "The Return of 'Microbialpolitik'," *Foreign Affairs* (January/February 2001): 80–81; Arno Karlen, *Man and Microbes: Disease and Plagues in History and Modern Times* (New York: G. P. Putnam's Sons, 1995); Andrew T. Price-Smith, *The Health of Nations: Infectious Disease, Environmental Change, and Their Effects on National Security and Development* (Cambridge: MIT Press, 2002); Richard Preston, *The Hot Zone* (New York: Random House, 1994); and Stephen Peter Rosen, "Strategic Implications of AIDS," *The National Interest*, no. 9 (fall 1987): 64–73.

5 A recent exception is P. W. Singer, "AIDS and International Security," *Survival* 44 no. 1 (spring 2002): 145–58.

6 Daniel Deudney, "The Case Against Linking Environmental Degradation and National Security," *Millennium* 19, no. 3 (1990), 463–64. Deudney makes this comment about attempts to link the environment and security. Also, see Marc A. Levy, "Is the Environment a National Security Issue?" *International Security* 20, no. 2 (fall 1995): 35–62.

7 See, esp., Frederick F. Cartwright, *Disease and History* (New York: Thomas Y. Crowell, 1972); Jared Diamond, *Guns, Germs, and Steel: The Fates of Human Societies* (New York: Norton, 1997); William H. McNeill, *Plagues and Peoples* (New York: Anchor Books, 1998); and Hans Zinsser, *Rats, Lice and History* (Boston: Little, Brown for the Atlantic Monthly Press, 1935).

8 Thucydides, *History of the Peloponnesian War*, trans. Rex Warner, rev. ed. (London: Penguin Books, 1972), 151–56 (Bk. 2, 47–55). The disease was probably smallpox. Zinsser, *Rats, Lice and History*, 119–27.

9 Alfred W. Crosby, *America's Forgotten Pandemic: The Influenza of 1918* (Cambridge: Cambridge University Press, 1989), 11, 157–66.

10 "AIDS and International Security," 158.

11 See Deudney, "Case Against Linking Environmental Degradation and National Security," 466–69. For a related argument about health, see Eoin O'Brien, "The Diplomatic Implications of Emerging Diseases," in *Preventive Diplomacy: Stopping Wars before They Start*, ed. Kevin M. Cahill (New York: Basic Books and the Center for International Health and Cooperation, 1996), 254.

12 "Can AIDS Be Stopped?" *New York Review of Books*, 14 March 2002, www.nybooks.com/articles/15188 (5 March 2002).

13 The figure is for wars from 1945 to 1993. World Health Organization, "Removing Obstacles to Healthy Development, Report on Infectious Diseases" (Geneva: WHO, 1999), graph 1, chap. 1, graph 22. Available online at www.who.int/infectious-disease-report/ (7 August 2001).

14 WHO, "Removing Obstacles," chap. 2.

15 UNAIDS and WHO, *AIDS Epidemic Update* (Geneva: UNAIDS, December 2002).

16 UNAIDS, *Report on the Global HIV/AIDS Epidemic* (Geneva: UNAIDS, June 2000), 21, available online at www.unaids.org/ (7 August 2001).

17 The following figures are from WHO, "Removing Obstacles," chap. 2, graph 37, and graph 31; Scott R. Lillibridge, "Emerging Infectious Disease: Threats to Global Security," in *Preventive Diplomacy: Stopping Wars before They Start*, rev. ed., ed. Kevin M. Cahill (New York: Routledge and Center for International Health and Cooperation, 2000), 293; and Hiroshi Nakajima, "Global Disease Threats and Doreign Policy," *The Brown Journal of World Affairs* 4, no. 1 (winter/spring 1997): 319–32.

18 Garrett, *Coming Plague*; WHO, "Removing Obstacles," chap. 10 and graph 32. In 1995, CISET identified twenty-nine new diseases that had emerged and twenty

that had reemerged since 1973. For extensive discussions of the emergence and reemergence of ID at this point in human history, see Laurie Garrett, "The Return of Infectious Disease," *Foreign Affairs* 75, no. 1 (January/February 1996): 66–79; NIC, "Global Infectious Disease Threat"; Nakajima, "Global Disease Threats"; and Price-Smith, *Health of Nations*, esp. chap. 5.

19 "Human Security: Paradigm Shift or Hot Air?" *International Security* 26, no. 2 (fall 2001): 87–102. Also, see Edward Newman, "Human Security and Con-structivism," *International Studies Perspectives* 2, no. 3 (August 2001): 239–51; Emma Rothschild, "What is Security?" *Daedalus* 124, no. 3 (summer 1995): 53–98; Mejid Tehranian, ed., *Worlds Apart: Human Security and Global Governance* (London: I. B. Tauris, 1999), esp. chap. 2; and Caroline Thomas and Peter Wilkins, eds., *Globalisation, Human Security, and the African Experience* (Boulder: Lynne Rienner, 1999), esp. chap. 1.

20 United Nations Development Programme, *Human Development Report 1994* (New York: Oxford University Press), 22.

21 Barry Buzan, *People, States & Fear: The National Security Problem in Inter-national Relations* (Chapel Hill: University of North Carolina Press, 1983), esp. chap. 1.

22 "What is Security?"

23 The first use of this term I find is in "International Health Security in the Modern World: The Sanitary Conventions and the World Health Organization," *Depart-ment of State Bulletin*, 16 November 1947, 953–58. For contemporary examples, see Lillibridge, "Emerging Infectious Disease"; and esp. Price-Smith, *Health of Nations*.

24 See Peter Piot, "Global AIDS Epidemic: Time to Turn the Tide," *Science* 288, 23 June 2000, 2176–78; Deniis Pirages, "Microsecurity: Disease Organisms and Human Well-Being," *Washington Quarterly* 18, no. 4 (fall 1995): 5–12; Price-Smith, "Ghosts of Kigali": and Laura Reed and Majid Tehranian, "Evolving Security Regimes," in Tehranian, *Worlds Apart*, 23–53.

25 "Remarks, United Nations Security Council Opening Session."

26 Rothschild outlines the ways different "principles of security" have been used to contest existing policies and influence the distribution of power and wealth. "What is Security?" 58–59.

27 Piot, "Global AIDS Epidemic," 2177. Also, see Peter Piot, "AIDS and human security," Statement by Peter Piot, UNAIDS Executive Director, United Nations University, Tokyo, Japan, 2 October 2001, www.unaids.org/whatsnewpercent5C-speechespercent5 Cengpercent5Cpiot021/00tokyo.htm (14 November 2001).

28 David E. Sanger, "Sometimes National Security Says It All," *New York Times*, Week in Review, 7 May 2000, 3.

29 Marc A. Levy makes this argument about environmental threats to security: "Is the Environment a National Security Issue?" 35–62. Also, see Paris, "Human Security," 94.

30 In fact, Deudney points out, the concept is not widely embraced outside certain progressive circles. "Case Against Linking Environmental Degradation and National Security," 469.

31 Deudney, "Case Against Linking Environmental Degradation and National Security," esp. 468. Also, see Levy, "Is the Environment a National Security Issue?" esp. 44–46.

32 On this point, see O'Brien, "Diplomatic Implications of Emerging Disease," 254.

33 I use the terms "national security" and "international security" interchangeably. The latter term largely replaced the former by the 1980s, but the content of the field remained much the same, the study of military threats to the state. See

David A. Baldwin, "Security Studies and the End of the Cold War," *World Politics* 48, no. 1 (October 1995): 125. Some students of security claim that "[t]raditional conceptions of 'national security' are concerned with the well-being of the state," whereas "[t]he concept of 'international security' explicitly acknowledges that the security of one state is connected with the security of others." Jonathan Ban, "Health, Security, and U.S. Global Leadership," Special Report 2, *Health and Security Series* (Chemical and Biological Arms Control Institute, 2001), 5. Also, see International Crisis Group, "HIV/AIDS as a Security Issue," ICG Report, Washington/Brussels, 19 June 2001. These definitions are not mutually exclusive, however, since the latter simply emphasizes a long recognized aspect of the former.

34 Stephen M. Walt, "The Renaissance of Security Studies," *International Studies Quarterly* 35, no. 2 (June 1991): 211–39. For other discussions, see Baldwin, "Security Studies"; Joseph S. Nye Jr. and Sean M. Lynn-Jones, "International Security Studies: A Report of a Conference on the State of the Field," *International Security* 12, no. 4 (spring 1988): 5–27; and Richard Smoke, "National Security Affairs," in *Handbook of Political Science*, vol. 8, *International Politics*, ed. Fred I. Greenstein and Nelson W. Polsby (Reading, Mass.: Addison-Wesley, 1975), 247–362.

35 In this sense, I combine Paris's "national security" and "redefined security" categories. "Human Security," 98.

36 Newman, "Human Security and Constructivism," 246. Newman includes this "new security" as a variant of human security. For post–cold war attempts to examine nontraditional threats to national security, see Thomas Homer-Dixon, *Environment, Scarcity and Violence* (Princeton: Princeton University Press, 1999); Ethan Kapstein, *The Political Economy of National Security: A global perspective* (Columbia: University of South Carolina Press, 1992); Jessica Tuchman Mathews, "Redefining Security," *Foreign Affairs* 68, no. 2 (spring 1989): 162–77; Norman Myers, "Environment and Security," *Foreign Policy*, no. 74 (spring 1989): 23–41; and Phil Williams and Stephen Black, "Transnational Threats: Drug Trafficking and Weapons Proliferation," *Contemporary Security Policy* 15, no. 1 (April 1994): 127–51.

37 For a work that does both, see International Crisis Group, "HIV/AIDS as a Security Issue."

38 Wendy R. Sherman, "Emerging Infectious Diseases Are a National Security Challenge to the United States," Remarks Before the Open Forum on Emerging Infectious Diseases, Department of State Open Forum, Washington, D.C., 25 March 1998, www.state.gov/www/policy_remarks/1998/980325_sherman_diseases.htm (6 August 2001).

39 Gore, "Emerging Infections Threaten National and Global Security."

40 USAID, "Military Populations" AIDS Briefs, 22 May 1998, www.usaid.gov/regions/afr/hhraa/aids_briefs/military.htm (14 August 2001). For other examples, see Sir George Alleyne, "Health and National Security", *Bulletin of the Pan-American Health Organization* 30, no. 2 (June 1996): 158–63; and WHO, "Removing Obstacles," graph 22.

41 Important, if partial, exceptions include Alleyne, "Health and National Security"; Garrett, "Return of Infectious Disease"; Price-Smith, "Ghosts of Kigali"; and Price-Smith, *Health of Nations*.

42 Alleyne, "Health and National Security," 162. Piot makes a similar point in "Global AIDS Epidemic," 2177.

43 Actually, the relationship between IDs and security is a reciprocal one, since the search for security through war, militarization, or defense spending can also influence the emergence and spread of ID. I discuss this in Susan Peterson, "The Forgotten Horseman of the Apocalypse: Epidemic Disease and National Security" (unpub. ms., 4 September 2001).

44 Donald Burke, Frederic D. Daniell, and John Lowe, "Berlin Seminar," *AIDS and Society: International Research and Policy Bulletin* 4 (July/August 1993), 4; United States, Department of State, "United States International Strategy on HIV/AIDS," July 1995, 40–41.

45 See especially Robert Gilpin, *War & Change in World Politics* (Cambridge: Cambridge University Press, 1981); and Stephen Van Evera, *Causes of War: Power and the Roots of Conflict* (Ithaca: Cornell University Press, 1999), esp. chap. 4.

46 David A. Wirth, "Climate Chaos," *Foreign Policy*, no. 74 (spring 1989): 10.

47 Diamond, *Guns, Germs, and Steel*, 78. Also see Donald Joralemon, "New World Depopulation and the Case of Disease," *Journal of Anthropological Research* 38, no. 1 (spring 1982): 108–27, reprinted in *Biological Consequences of European Expansion, 1450–1800*, ed. Kenneth F. Kiple and Stephen V. Beck (Aldershot, Hampshire: Ashgate, 1997), 71–90.

48 Homer-Dixon *Environment, Scarcity and Violence*; Price-Smith, *Health of Nations*.

49 On nineteenth century quarantine policy, see Neville M. Goodman, *International Health Organizations and Their Work* (Edinburgh: Churchill Livingstone, 1971), chaps. 2–3. On Cuba, see Marvin Leiner, *Sexual Politics in Cuba: Machismo, Homosexuality, and AIDS* (Boulder: Westview, 1994), chap. 5. The German example is from Rosen, "Strategic Implications," 72.

50 For example, see Carl Mortished, "AIDS Drugs Price War Threatens Big Firms," *Times* (London), 16 July 2001, Business section.

51 Thanks to Andrew Cortell for discussion of this issue. For the argument that multinational disease control efforts may reduce or prevent violent conflict, see Peter J. Hoetz, "Vaccine Diplomacy," *Foreign Policy* no. 124 (May/June 2001): 68–69; and Ban, "Health, Security, and U.S. Global Leadership," 9.

52 NIC, "Global Infectious Disease Threat," 28.

53 Alleyne, "Health and National Security," 159.

54 For efforts to examine disease effects on these different actors or levels of the economy, see Desmond Cohen, "The Economic Impact of the HIV Epidemic," Issues Paper No. 2 (UNDP HIV and Development Programme, 1992), www.undp. org/hiv/publications/issues/english/issue02e.htm (5 March 2002); Desmond Cohen, "Socio-Economic Causes and Consequences of the HIV Epidemic in Southern Africa: A Case Study of Namibia," Issues Paper no. 31 (UNDP HIV and Development Programme, 1998), www.undp.org/hiv/publications/issues/english/issue31e.htm (5 March 2002); ICG, "HIV/AIDS As a Security Issue," 9–14; Price-Smith, *Health of Nations*, chap. 3; Andrew T. Price-Smith, "Praetoria's Shadow: The HIV/AIDS Pandemic and National Security in South Africa," Special Report 4, *Health and Security Series* (Chemical and Biological Arms Control Institute; and UNDP, "HIV/AIDS Implications for Poverty Reduction," UNDP Policy Paper (Background Paper prepared for the United Nations Development Programme for the UN General Assembly Special Session on HIV/AIDS, 25–27 June 2001), available online at www.undp.org/hiv (7 August 2001).

55 "HIV/AIDS Implications for Poverty Reduction," 2.

56 UNAIDS, *Report on the Global HIV/AIDS Epidemic*, 27; WHO, "Removing Obstacles," chap. 3. When adults die from any cause in Zimbabwe, small farm output drops by approximately 45 percent, but when AIDS is the cause of death output declines by 61 percent. UNDP, "HIV/AIDS Implications for Poverty Reduction," 10.

57 Cited in ICG, "HIV/AIDS as a Security Issue," 11.

58 UNAIDS, *Report on the Global HIV/AIDS Epidemic*, 33.

59 *Health of Nations*, 91–103.

60 UNDP, "HIV/AIDS Implications for Poverty Reduction," 9.

61 UNAIDS, *Report on the Global HIV/AIDS Epidemic*, 33.

62 Robert E. Fritts, ret. ambassador, U.S. Department of State, personal conversation with author, November 2000.

63 World Health Organization, *The World Health Report 2000: Health Systems: Improving Performance* (Geneva: World Health Organization, 2000), 157–63; WHO, "Removing Obstacles," chap. 2.

64 Cited in UNDP, "HIV/AIDS Implications for Poverty Reductions," 8.

65 Cohen, "Socio-economic Causes and Consequences," 10.

66 UNDP, "HIV/AIDS Implications for Poverty Reductions," 7.

67 UNAIDS, *Report on the Global HIV/AIDS Epidemic*, 21–26.

68 Desmond Cohen, "The HIV Epidemic and Sustainable Human Development," Issues Paper no. 29 (UNDP HIV and Development Programme, 1998), www.undp.org/hiv/publications/issues/english/issue29e.htm (5 March 2002).

69 Channing Arndt and Jeffrey D. Lewis, "The Macro Implications of HIV/AIDS in South Africa," Africa Region Working Paper Series, no. 9 (World Bank, Africa Region Public Expenditures Effectiveness Project, November 2000). For further discussion of the national costs of malaria and AIDS, see Price-Smith, *Health of Nations*, 109–16.

70 "Modeling the Macroeconomic Effects of AIDS, with an Application to Tanzania," *The World Bank Economic Review* 7, no. 2 (1993): 173–89.

71 UNAIDS, *Report on the Global HIV/AIDS Epidemic*, 28.

72 UNDP, "HIV/AIDS Implications for Poverty Reductions," 12. HIV/AIDS already has been blamed for much of the recent violence in Zimbabwe, violence perpetrated by "alienated youths [who] form their own political organizations well beyond the boundaries of constitutional politics or democratic parties." "Another Nail in Zimbabwe's Coffin," *Africa News Service*, 5 December 2000, cited in Lyndy Heinecken, "Strategic Implications of HIV/AIDS in South Africa," *Conflict, Security & Development* 1, no. 1 (April 2001): 113.

73 UNDP, "HIV/AIDS Implications for Poverty Reductions," 9.

74 ICG, "HIV/AIDS as a Security Issue," 16.

75 This is in addition to the regular attrition through retirement, relocation, and death from other causes. Cited in Desmond Cohen, "The HIV Epidemic and the Education Sector in sub-Saharan Africa," Issues Paper no. 32 (UNDP HIV and Development Programme, 1999), www.undp.org/hiv/publications/issues/english/issue32e.htm (5 March 2002).

76 UNAIDS, *Report on the Global HIV/AIDS Epidemic*, 29.

77 ICG, "HIV/AIDS as a Security Issue," 16.

78 "Mugabe Announces that AIDS had Killed Ministers," Panafrican News Agency Wire Service, 7 September 2000.

79 Kurt Shillinger, "Mbeki Aide's Death Renews HIV Debate," *Boston Globe*, 31 October 2000, A8.

80 ICG, "HIV/AIDS as a Security Issue," 10, 14–15.

81 Price-Smith, "Praetoria's Shadow," 24.

82 Desmond Cohen, "Responding to the Socio-Economic Impact, of the HIV Epidemic in Sub-Saharan Africa: Why a Systems Approach is Needed" (UNDP HIV and Development Programme, March 1999), www.undp.org/hiv/publications/issues/english/issue34e.htm (5 March 2002).

83 *Health of Nations*, 121. Thomas Homer-Dixon makes a similar argument about environmental degradation. The social and economic effects of environmental stresses weaken the capacity of the state and its relationship to society, reducing its ability to respond creatively to environmental problems and heightening the possibility of violent conflict. Homer-Dixon, *Environment, Scarcity, and Violence*.

84 *Health of Nations*, 124.

85 See Homer-Dixon, *Environment, Scarcity, and Violence*; and Price-Smith, *Health of Nations*, esp. 121.
86 Price-Smith, "Ghosts of Kigali," 434.
87 See Goodman, *International Health Organizations and Their Work*, chap. 2.
88 McNeill argues that such religions developed in countries where disease was prevalent. *Plagues and Peoples*, 149–50.
89 NIC, "Global Infectious Disease Threat," 3–4.
90 McNeill, *Plagues and People*, 289.
91 UNICEF, *The Progress of Nations 1999* (New York: UNICEF, 1999), 17.
92 Jennifer Steinhauer, "U.N. Redefines AIDS as Political Issue and Peril to Poor," *New York Times*, 28 June 2001, A4.
93 Erica Barks-Ruggles, "The Globalization of Disease: When Congo Sneezes, Will California Get a Cold?" *Brookings Review* 19, no. 4 (fall 2001): 30–33.
94 Price-Smith, *Health of Nations*, 138.
95 UNAIDS, *Report on the Global HIV/AIDS Epidemic*, 18.
96 "The Next Wave of HIV/AIDS: Nigeria, Ethiopia, Russia, India, and China," ICA 2002-040, September 2002, 8. David F. Gordon is the principal author.
97 "The Future of AIDS," *Foreign Affairs* 81, no. 6 (November/ December 2002): 26. Also see NIC, "Next Wave," 11–12.
98 David E. Powell and Heidi A. Kostin, "Rapid Spread of AIDS in Russia Imperils a Generation," *Boston Globe*, 10 February 2002.
99 Eberstadt, "Future of AIDS," 37. Eighty-seven percent of new HIV infections in Russia occur among 15 to 30 year olds. Lisa McAdams, "Looming AIDS Crisis in Russia to Have Profound Impact on Society," Voice of America, 27 November 2002, available from Center for Defense Information, *Russia Weekly*, no. 233, www.cdi.or/russia/233-2-pr.cfm (29 January 2003).
100 Ban, "Health, Security, and U.S. Global Leadership," 35.
101 Peter Graff, "INTERVIEW—AIDS in Russia 'scarier than Africa' yet ignored," Reuters.
102 Cited in NIC, "Next Wave," 24.
103 "Future of AIDS," 40–41.
104 Powell and Kostin, "Rapid Spread of AIDS in Russia Imperils a Generation." Also, see NIC, "Global Infectious Disease Threat," 34; and David L. Heyman, Executive Director for Communicable Diseases World Health Organization, Statement before the Committee on International Relations, U.S. House of Representatives, 29 June 2000, www.who.int/infectious-disease-report/dlh-testimony/testmo.pdf (24 September 2001).
105 Elisabeth Rosenthal, "China Now Facing an AIDS Epidemic, a Top Aide Admits," *New York Times*, 24 August 2001, A10.
106 Bates Gill, Jennifer Chang, and Sarah Palmer, "China's HIV Crisis," *Foreign Affairs* 81, no. 2 (March/April 2002): 96–110; quote from 97.
107 Rosenthal, "China Now Facing an AIDS Epidemic." According to NIC estimates, 10–15 million (1.3–2 percent of Chinese adults) will be infected by 2010. "Next Wave," 8.
108 Rosenthal, "China Now Facing an AIDS Epidemic"; and Elisabeth Rosenthal, "Spread of AIDS in Rural China Ignites Protests," *New York Times*, 11 December 2001.
109 NIC, "Next Wave," 20, 24.
110 UNAIDS, Report on the global HIV/AIDS epidemic, 12–13; NIC, "Next Wave," 8.
111 "Next Wave," 24.
112 Sachs, "Best Possible Investment in Africa," A1.
113 "Powell: U.S. committed to Africa's economic growth," CNN.com, 25 May 2001, www.cnn.com/201/WORLD/africa/05/25/powell.speech/index.htm (4 February 2002).

For the text of Powell's speech, see Secretary Colin L. Powell, "Remarks at the University of Witwatersrand," Johannesburg, South Africa, u.s. Department of State, 25 May 2001, www.state.gov/secretary/rm/2001/3090.htm.

114 NIC, "Global Infectious Disease Threat," 32.

115 For a recent statement of this argument, see "Blair urges action on Africa," BBC News, 6 February 2002, news.bbc.co.uk/hi/english/uk_politics/newsid_1803000/1803567. stm. (6 February 2002).

116 "Can AIDS Be Stopped?"

117 Alex Duval Smith, "AIDS, Trade and War Top Powell's African Agenda," *The Independent* (London), 25 May 2001, 20.

118 Jonathan B. Tucker, "The Biological Weapons Threat," *Current History* 96, no. 609 (April 1997): 167.

119 They also may include nonliving, non-self-replicating agents that are either secreted by living organisms or synthetically produced to be similar to agents secreted by living organisms. See Malcolm Dando, *The New Biological Weapons: Threat, Proliferation, and Control* (Boulder: Lynne Rienner, 2001), esp. 18.

120 Information on the effects of anthrax and smallpox is taken from "Biological Weapons Agents," Chemical and Biological Weapons Nonproliferation Project, Henry L. Stimson Center, www.stimson.org/cwc/bwagent.htm (10 November 2000).

121 Fifteen million doses of the vaccine stored at the CDC were scheduled to be destroyed when the last remaining smallpox virus was destroyed. Routine civilian immunization against smallpox halted nearly two decades ago, and human immunity to the disease is thought to fade within 15 years of vaccination. After 9/11, the u.s. government ordered large quantities of smallpox vaccine for the first time in decades. More recently, the government confirmed that existing doses could be diluted safely and that a private company had unexpectedly found 70–90 million doses. Justin Gillis, "Smallpox Vaccine Supply Could Be Stretched," *Washington Post*, 29 March 2002, A10.

122 These diseases may also pose security threats when they occur naturally rather than secondary to a terrorist attack.

123 Dorothy B. Preslar, "The Role of Disease Surveillance in the Watch for Agro-terrorism or Economic Sabotage," November 2000, www.fas.org/ahead/bwconcerns/agro-terror. htm (16 April 2002).

124 Anne Kohnen, "Responding to the Threat of Agro-terrorism: Specific Recommendations for the United States Department of Agriculture," BCSIA Discussion Paper 2000-29, ESDP Discussion Paper 2004-04, John F. Kennedy School of Government, Harvard University, October 2000, 10.

125 Michael T. Osterholm and John Schwartz, *Living Terrors: What America Needs to Know to Survive the Coming Bioterrorist Catastrophe* (New York: Delacourt Press, 2000), 8.

126 Tucker, "Biological Weapons Threat," 168.

127 Garrett, "Return," 76.

128 Tucker, "Biological Weapons Threat," 169; J. M. Roberts, *History of the World* (New York: Oxford University Press, 1993), 413.

129 For example, see John Duffy, "Smallpox and the Indians in the American Colonies," *Bulletin of the History of Medicine* 25, no. 4 (1951): 340, reprinted in Kiple and Beck, *Biological Consequences of the European Expansion*, 249.

130 See Elizabeth A. Fenn, *Pox Americana: The Great Smallpox Epidemic of 1775–82* (New York: Hill and Wang, 2001).

131 See Peter Williams and David Wallace, *Unit 731: The Japanese Army's Secret of Secrets* (London: Hodder and Stoughton, 1989); Sheldon H. Harris, *Factories of*

Death: Japanese Biological Warfare, 1932–45, and the American Cover-Up (New York: Routledge, 1994); and Nicholas D. Kristof, "Unmasking Horror—A Special Report; Japan Confronting Gruesome War Atrocity," *New York Times,* 17 March 1995, A1.

132 "HIV/AIDS and the Changing Landscape of War in Africa," *International Security* 27, no. 2 (fall 2002): 167–71. Also, see Singer, "AIDS and International Security."

133 There have been 121 incidents involving the use of biological agents in the last four decades. Jeremy Laurance, "U.S. on Alert for Smallpox Terror Attack," *Independent on Sunday* (London), 22 April 2001, 2. In addition to extensive scientific, medical, and public health literatures on biological weapons, see Richard K. Betts, "The New Threat of Weapons of Mass Destruction," *Foreign Affairs* 77, no. 1 (January/February 1998): 26–41; Malcolm R. Dando, *Biological Warfare in the 21st Century: Biotechnology and the Proliferation of Biological Weapons* (London: Brassey's, 1994); Peter R. Lavoy, James J. Wirtz, and Scott D. Sagan, *Planning the Unthinkable: How New Powers Will Use Nuclear, Biological, and Chemical Weapons* (Ithaca: Cornell University Press, 2000); Joshua Lederberg, ed., *Biological Weapons: Limiting the Threat* (Cambridge: MIT Press, 1999); John D. Steinbruner, "Biological Weapons: A Plague Upon All Houses," *Foreign Policy,* no. 109 (Winter 1997–98): 85–113; Tucker, "Biological Weapons Threat."

134 Richard A. Falkenrath, "Confronting Nuclear, Biological and Chemical Terrorism," *Survival* 40, no. 3 (autumn 1998): 43–65.

135 See Michael Dobbs, "Soviet-Era Work on Bioweapons Still Worrisome: Stall in U.S. Dismantling Effort Could Pose Proliferation Threat," *Washington Post,* 12 September 2000, A1. For information on the Soviet Union's extensive biological warfare program, see Ken Alibek (with Stephen Handelman), *Biohazard: The Chilling True Story of the Largest Covert Weapons Program in the World* (New York: Delta/Random House, 1999).

136 Quoted in Contagion and Conflict: Health as a Global Security Challenge, A Report of the Chemical and Biological Arms Control Institute and the CSIS International Security Program (Washington, D.C.: Center for Strategic and International Studies, 2000), 37–38.

137 Sheryl Gay Stolberg, "Health Secretary Testifies About Germ Warfare Defenses," *New York Times,* 4 October 2001, B7.

138 "Health and International Security: U.S. Policy on World Health," *Washington Quarterly* 19, no. 2 (spring 1996): 63–77. The authors of the CSIS report, "Contagion and Conflict," call this "community warfare." See chap. 2.

139 Chow, "Health and International Security."

140 CSIS, "Contagion and Conflict," 29.

141 CSIS, "Contagion and Conflict," 30–31.

142 Diamond, *Guns, Germs, and Steel,* 197.

143 By 1618, Mexico's population had fallen from 20 million to 1.6 million. McNeill, *Plagues and Peoples,* 19–20; Diamond, *Guns, Germs, and Steel,* 210.

144 "If it had not been for the epidemic, the Spaniards would have faced a united Empire." Diamond, *Guns, Germs, and Steel,* 67–81, quoted at 77.

145 Crosby, *America's Forgotten Pandemic,* 27.

146 Agency for International Development, *Malaria: Meeting the Global Challenge* (Boston: Oelgeschlager, Gunn & Hain, 1985) 4.

147 Heinecken, "Strategic Implications of HIV/AIDS in South Africa," 109. Also, see Elbe, "HIV/AIDS and the Changing Landscape of War in Africa."

148 Heinecken, "Strategic Implications of HIV/AIDS in South Africa," 109–11. Also, see Price-Smith, "Praetoria's Shadow," 18–22.

149 USAID, "Military Populations"; Heinecken, "Strategic Implications of HIV/AIDS in South Africa," 109.

150 Price-Smith, "Praetoria's Shadow," 19, 31.

151 "Economic and Demographic Trends," 598.

152 In 2000, the Security Council adopted its first resolution on a health issue, asking member states to initiate AIDS testing and prevention programs among their peacekeeping forces.

153 On the projected impact of AIDS in Nigeria, see NIC, "Next Wave."

154 *Moral Vision in International Politics: The Foreign Aid Regime, 1949–1989* (Princeton: Princeton University Press, 1993), 5, 43, quoted at 5.

155 For a work that views disease as a foreign policy, rather than a security, concern, see Jordan S. Kassalow, "Why Health is Important to U.S. Foreign Policy," (New York: Council on Foreign Relations and Milbank Memorial Fund, 2001).

15

MICROBES, MAD COWS AND MILITARIES

Exploring the links between health and security

Sandra J. Maclean*

Source: *Security Dialogue*, 39:5 (2008), 475–94.

The 'securitization' of health has generated considerable debate. In public health, the debate focuses mainly on health effects. Although securitization may refocus attention and resources toward certain health issues, it may focus undue attention on a few issues or on the military aspects of issues to the detriment of a broad range of health issues and their human rights aspects. In international relations, the concern is the effect on security analysis and policy. While some welcome a broadening of the security agenda to include items such as health, others are concerned that analytical rigour and operational effectiveness are lost. This article argues that, normative concerns notwithstanding, securitizing is occurring as a result of perceived changes, associated with globalization, that are creating changes in the nature or degree of threats. But, in international relations, security is largely a social construction, as the Copenhagen School claims. Contemporary social struggles are ongoing around competitions to define security. The article argues that human security is a concept that has considerable relevance for understanding the nature of change that is producing new or intensified threats. It also offers conceptual space for analyzing what security is provided and for whom in the changing world order.

Introduction

Ominous threats of bioterrorism, pandemics of rapidly spreading infectious diseases and trade-related biocrises are features of the increasingly interconnected, globalizing world. In response, international relations scholars and practitioners have become notably more attentive to public health issues. Indeed, as one eminent scholar exclaimed, we are witnessing a 'political revolution ... in the area of health' (Fidler, 2005: 179). However, as with many political processes, the increasing politicization of global health is contentious. This is especially apparent in the area of health and security, where the growing securitization of certain health issues has generated considerable debate (Elbe, 2006; Feldbaum et al., 2006; Fidler, 2005; Owen & Roberts, 2005; Youde, 2005).

Discussion has settled into two related, but distinct, streams. The first involves a normative concern with the effect of securitization on health outcomes (much of the debate has been focused on HIV/AIDS, although the securitization trend also involves several emerging infectious diseases with global pandemic potential) (McInnes & Lee, 2006: 10). With respect to HIV/AIDS, one view holds that describing it as a security threat could help raise international awareness and generate more resources to combat the disease (Singer, 2002: 158). The opposing view is that a security framework is likely to divert attention toward militaries and intelligence organizations and away from the rights and needs of ordinary citizens who are living with HIV/AIDS (Elbe, 2006: 119; O'Manique, 2006; Peterson, 2002/03). Overall, the worry is that the securitization of health will direct attention toward a few specific (infectious) diseases and susceptible populations, while other health problems and vulnerable groups will be ignored (McInnes & Lee, 2006: 11).

The second consequential analytical debate regarding the securitization of health concerns the implications for security of broadening the concept beyond the traditionally held understanding of the term. Currently, security studies is a contested terrain (see, for example, Booth, 2005a). One of the areas of contestation has been the concept of 'human security', especially as this was articulated by the United Nations Development Programme in 1994. The UNDP's concept (reasserted by the UN Commission on Human Security in 2003), places humans rather than states as the primary security referent. According to the UNDP (1994: 22) definition, human-centric, as opposed to state-centric, security involves protection from a range of threats to human safety and welfare, including 'disease, hunger, unemployment, crime, social conflict, political repression and environmental hazards'. When humans are the central focus, the distinction between insecurity due to conflict and insecurity caused by other threats to human safety becomes less meaningful.

Devising policy agendas based on human security has gained in international acceptance over the past decade, but the idea has also provoked considerable criticism and debate (Smith, 2005). The main criticism levelled at the concept as it was articulated by the UNDP is that conceiving of security broadly to include non-traditional items of basic need and social welfare renders it analytically empty and/or policy-inoperable (MacFarlane, 2004: 369). If the shift from national security to human security is taken to mean that all and everything relate to human development and welfare, argue critics, it may ultimately turn out to be 'hot air' rather than an important 'paradigm shift' (Paris, 2001). One effort to resolve the intellectual impasse has been to retain the concept but restrict its meaning to 'freedom from fear' (personal safety), as opposed to the broader interpretation that also includes 'freedom from want' (economic well-being) (Krause, 2004; MacFarlane & Khong, 2006; Mack, 2002). However, some scholars reject efforts to narrow the meaning of the concept precisely because they view the connections between physical violence and social environment as integral as well as critical. As Caroline Thomas (2004: 353) asserts, the broader concept of human security not only exposes but also can serve as 'a bridge between the interconnected challenges confronting the world'. Moreover, the orthodox, narrow concept of security ignores structural violence. As Steve Smith (2004: 506) observes, while orthodox international relations theory privileges war as the central form of violence in international relations, 'by far the most violence on the planet is economic in origin'. Similarly, in the words of David Roberts (2008: 21):

> The emphasis on conventional security whilst millions die without good reason reflects the power relations threaded throughout international relations, between rich and poor, males and females, marginal and included, vulnerable and secure.

It appears that there is no imminent consensus on a singular conception of security in international relations. As Ken Booth (2005b: 21) asserts, 'conceptualizations of security are . . . the product of different understandings of what politics is and should be about'. The different approaches to security complicate debates on the securitization of health. But, too frequently, in the health and security literature that focuses on health outcomes there is insufficient critical engagement with alternative approaches to security. Instead, there is a tendency to discuss health as national, international, global and/or human security as though, first, there were agreement on what those terms mean and, second, they were concepts that are distinct and, if not necessarily always compatible, at least separate types of security that can and should be managed in different ways and sometimes by different agents (Elbe, 2006; Feldbaum et al., 2006). This article argues for more careful attention to the possibilities for a shift in paradigm that privileges human security as an alternative, rather than as an adjunct, to the traditional normative framework of security studies. It argues that the protection of security (national and/or human) in the contemporary global order requires placing the interests and needs of people as the central objective. Furthermore, rather than rendering security inoperable, a broad conception of security, as freedom from want as well as from fear, is a necessary starting point for exposing and elucidating the complex interconnections among social/community relations, governance actors/structures and policy outcomes. Health outcomes at population levels are largely socially determined, and thus contingent upon these complex interactions. Likewise, the securitization of health can be understood as a set of responses by security actors to social transformations in a changing global political economy.

The article begins by looking at health as security in historical context. While the securitization of health has occurred at other times in the past, there are unprecedented developments that account for the most recent trend toward securitization. The article argues that the security dimensions of these developments require human security as an analytical framework as well as a normative objective. A human security agenda should not be regarded either as separate from national, international or global security, or as traditional security with non-traditional items added to the list of threats. Rather, human security involves a rethinking and reordering of world politics that addresses the structural causes of human fear and want as fundamental sources of insecurity. Insights from the constructivist theory of the Copenhagen School of security studies are useful here in providing an explanation of possible paradigm change, although in distinguishing among different types of security, this school underplays the integrated nature of structurally caused insecurity. Moreover, the 'speech act' that the school identifies as the critical moment in naming 'what is security' overemphasizes the role of major official players of the traditional security regime, especially states, and underestimates the role that non-state actors and ordinary citizens are playing in contemporary reconceptualizations of security.

Health and security in historical context

The securitization of health is not a new phenomenon. The spread of infectious diseases during war has been recognized for centuries as a threat to security,[1] but it was in the mid-to-late 19th century that health became an important international relations/foreign policy issue. At this time, there was a significant increase in transnational transmission of infectious disease as the result of advances in trade and transportation associated with the Industrial Revolution. Quarantines were the preferred method of dealing with the transmission of infectious disease at the time. However, they became increasingly costly to industry, so business began to press governments to set common international standards for the quarantines (Brockington, 1985: 30). These pressures yielded the 1851 International Sanitary Conference in Paris, 'the first attempt at international governance on infectious disease'.[2] A number of conferences on sanitation and epidemics followed, from which emerged several international health conventions and institutions: the incipient framework of a liberal institutional structure for international health. The cornerstone of this system was created in 1920 with the formation of the League of Nations Health Organization (Brockington, 1985: 31).

The establishment of the United Nations in 1945 reaffirmed the liberal internationalist ideal of interstate cooperation. Within the UN system, the World Health Organization (WHO) replaced the League of Nations Health

Organization as the organ for cooperation in international health. The main focus of international health, under the leadership of WHO, was the control of infectious disease. Although some scholars are dismissive of the actual gains made (Zacher, 2007: 17–18), WHO claimed success in its mission, largely due to advances in monitoring disease as well as in the development and distribution of vaccines. As Gro Brundtland (1999: viii), then secretary general of WHO, wrote in 1999: 'Under WHO's leadership the world eradicated smallpox, one of the most devastating diseases of history, and today a substantial majority of the world's population faces relatively low risk from infectious disease of any sort'.

WHO's infectious disease control strategy relied heavily on biotechnological innovation and health experts, but WHO's adoption of the Alma-Ata Declaration in 1978 was an international health initiative that focused as much on the political and social as on biology and technology, if not more so (MacLean, 2007).[3] The primary health care model promoted by the Declaration was based on the idea that better health outcomes could be achieved through measures to provide basic public health, community involvement in health care and greater social equity. This was deemed to be true especially, but not only, for developing countries, many of which had gained their independence only after World War II and lacked resources to establish robust tertiary health care systems.

The Alma-Ata initiative has been viewed largely as a failure (see, for example, Thomas & Weber, 2004), but it did highlight the relevance of the social determinacy of health, an idea that is currently gaining attention in international health, notably evidenced in the launch of the UN Commission on the Social Determinants of Health.[4] Also, interestingly, the Alma-Ata Declaration alluded to a link between health and security by calling for a reduction in expenditures on armaments, with the resulting peace dividend being used to fund health. However, few in the security sector were listening. Although certain advances in international health were occurring under a framework informed by liberal institutionalism, the realist paradigm had emerged in the post-World War II period as the dominant paradigm of international relations. In realism, state interests are tied to the power that states are able to wield vis-à-vis other states.[5] Realists measure power primarily by military strength, though acknowledging that such strength reflects other capabilities, such as economic strength (Waltz, 1979: 192), geographical position or attributes (O'Sullivan, 1986; Sprout & Sprout, 1968), culture (see Bull, 1977: 33–35), etc. Health, then, may feature in this power-centric discourse, but only indirectly, to the extent that health problems that significantly debilitate the working population or are otherwise economically costly reduce national capabilities, creating a potential threat to national security. In the post-World War II world, infectious diseases were thought to be under control; at least, they posed little risk for the wealthy, leading powers that matter the most in realist theory (Waltz, 1979). Indeed, because of advances in Western medicine (Altman, 2006) and public health (Rosen, 1958), health issues in general came to be seen as less relevant as threats to national security. As a result, the realists who dominated security studies left the developments that were occurring in international health to specialists in the health field while they focussed mainly on military security (Fidler, 2005: 180). In this area, biological weaponry was the only health-related topic that provoked much security interest, and this was relatively insignificant compared to other security concerns.

The globalization of health and 'new' security threats

Bioterrorism

Over the past two decades, thinking on biological weapons has changed, and they are now regarded as an important threat to national security. Resort to bioweapons by combatants or terrorists to achieve their political objectives is considered more likely in the global era, because of rapid, widespread movements of people and materiel and because the 'new' wars of the contemporary period are characterized, among other attributes, by non-state combatants who are more likely to use unconventional tools of warfare (Kaldor, 2006; Duffield, 2001). Events supported this growing concern. For instance, the discovery of inadequate protection of biowarfare sites in Russia in the early 1990s alerted security experts to the possibility that terrorists might gain access to them in the political turmoil of the post-Soviet period (Fein, 1997). Anxiety grew also following the use of biological weapons by the Iraqi government against its own citizens in 1995 and by a Japanese cult in a subway attack the same year (Henderson, 1998). The terrorist attacks in the USA on 11 September 2001 confirmed the need for greater attention to 'new' war personnel and tactics, and bioterrorism was highlighted when the attacks were followed by several anthrax 'scares' (Corder, 2001). The surge of interest in bioterrorism generated responses in both security and public health sectors, and at both national and international levels (see, for example, Sandhu et al., 2003). The US government has been particularly alert to the threat and has responded in several ways – by passing the Bioterrorism Act in 2002,[6] by increasing funding to confront bioterrorism (US Department of Health & Human Services, 2006), and by establishing liaisons with various organizations to act in the case of biological weapons attack.[7]

Emerging infectious diseases

Infectious diseases also feature in the contemporary 'securitization of health' trend. In 1976, Ebola, a deadly and previously unknown disease, broke out in Zaire (now the Democratic Republic of the Congo). Spreading rapidly, it killed 88% of those infected (318 people in total). A second outbreak in

Zaire soon thereafter and the identification of other, similar 'hemorrhagic fever' viruses[8] raised alarm far beyond the locations of infection, including in Western societies. As Harold Varmus (1983) warned in the *New York Times*:

> Even some of the most exotic viruses (Hantaan, Ebola, Lassa, Junin, Machupo) have already appeared in this country [the USA], and there is no virus in the world more than a long plane flight away.

Perceptions of risk due to other deadly diseases were reinforced in the 1980s by the rapid worldwide spread of HIV/AIDS, first diagnosed early in that decade (Mann, 1989), and anxieties continued to grow with the knowledge that the international meat trade had contributed to the spread of Bovine Spongiform Encephalopathy (BSE or 'mad cow' disease), which is thought to cause Creutzfeldt-Jakob Disease, a fatal neurological disease in humans (WHO, 2002).[9] The short-lived but deadly epidemic of Severe Acute Respiratory Syndrome (SARS) in 2002–03, which was transmitted from Asia by air travel to several countries, highlighted just how fast disease can now spread to destinations far from the site where the disease first appears. The sharp reduction in business and leisure travel to SARS-affected locations also underscored just how costly epidemics are to countries in economic terms. Given the heightened awareness of risk due to infectious disease, considerable attention is being paid now to the possibility of a future pandemic of 'Avian Influenza', a disease that is expected to emerge from the transfer to humans of the A(H5N1) virus from birds infected during an epizootic epidemic.[10]

With the exception of HIV/AIDS, the mortality and morbidity rates associated with the newly emerging diseases have been low to date. However, by the early 1990s, health professionals were voicing concerns to governments about the major threat to health that these diseases pose (Lederberg, Shope & Oaks, 1992), and journalists were informing the public about actual and impending crises of infectious disease (Garrett, 1994; Preston, 1994). The complacency that had grown around international public health in the previous several decades (Garrett, 2000), along with the assumption that health specialists and technology could deal effectively, and essentially apolitically, with any new disease trends (Fidler, 2005: 180), gave way to a realization that health problems are increasingly transnational and can have major impacts on international relations and national competitiveness. This realization produced the *Revision of the International Health Regulations* (WHA, 2005) as the main international health response to emerging infectious diseases.[11] In the international security sector, the inclusion of infectious disease in the Report of the High-Level Panel on Threats, Challenges and Change (United Nations, 2004) furthered the process of securitization. Meanwhile, national policymakers were also becoming more alert to the national and international security implications of these diseases. A report on health and foreign policy in the UK (McInnes, 2005: 13) notes, for instance, that infectious disease linked with immigration now figures as a (domestic) security concern. However, among countries it is in the USA that the securitization of infectious disease is most advanced. The US Central Intelligence Agency includes infectious diseases among the growing list of security threats associated with globalization (Gannon, 2000), and the US Department of Defense states clearly that 'emerging infectious diseases are a significant threat to global and US national security'.[12]

HIV/AIDS

Among infectious diseases, HIV/AIDS has drawn the most attention regarding 'securitization' and therefore deserves special comment (Piot, 2005). Several possible links between HIV/AIDS and national security have been identified. Feldbaum, Lee & Patel (2006) list the three most frequently cited as: (i) the disease's ability to deplete military forces; (ii) its propensity to destabilize nations and contribute to state failure, especially in sub-Saharan Africa; and (iii) the impact a worsening pandemic will have on 'strategically important states of Russia, India, and China'. Also, in relation to military security, others have suggested that HIV/AIDS is spread effectively, and sometimes consciously as a weapon of war, by military personnel (Garrett, 2005; UN-AIDS, 1998; Obaid, 2007: 5). According to some recent analyses, the various links between HIV/AIDS and national security are not firmly established (de Waal, 2005; Whiteside, de Waal & Gebre-Tensae, 2006) and are based more on assumptions than on clear evidence. Studies by Whiteside, de Waal & Gebre-Tensae (2006) show that the HIV rates in sub-Saharan militaries are not as high as have been widely reported, and in fact are actually lower than in the general populations of some countries with high rates of infection. Differing views notwithstanding, a security discourse around the disease is by now well established in both national and international security sectors.

Convincing policymakers of the threat had taken some time, however, as well as considerable diplomatic effort on the part of several individuals (Behrman, 2004; Gellman, 2000; White House, 2002). Most notable in the public health field were the late Jonathan Mann (Director of WHO's Global Programme on AIDS from 1986 to 1990) and Peter Piot (currently UNAIDS Executive Director and Under Secretary-General of the United Nations), who voiced warnings about the dangers of HIV/AIDS throughout the 1980s and 1990s. Meanwhile, in political circles, US ambassador Richard Holbrooke and economist Jeffrey Sachs were major players in promoting a sense of urgency about the disease (Behrman, 2004). The efforts of these and other like-minded individuals were rewarded in January 2000 when a Special Session of the UN Security Council on HIV/AIDS was held. This session was unprecedented in identifying a health issue as a security problem, and in Ambassador Holbrooke's (2000) words:

276

This event symbolized something that many of us have believed for a long time – that AIDS is as destabilizing as any war; that in the post-Cold War world, international security is about more than guns and bombs and the balance of power between sovereign states.

Even with this international encouragement, however, national policy-makers were reticent to respond to the epidemic as a major security problem. Some attention was paid to the disease in the last days of the Clinton administration, and in the early days of the Bush administration US Secretary of State Colin Powell expressed concern about the disease as a 'national security problem (Behrman, 2004: 264), but it was not until 2003 that President Bush announced his Emergency Plan for AIDS relief (Behrman, 2004: 307).

Health as security, but what security and for whom?

Given the unevenness, both temporally and geographically, with which the securitization process has progressed and the continuing debates about its merit, David Fidler's (2007: 42) characterization of the present period as a post-securitization phase (that is, the securitization of public health is complete) is probably overstated (see, for example, Callabero-Anthony, 2006: 114). However, there is no doubt that certain health issues are now viewed as significant threats to security within mainstream security governance.[13] 'At one level', suggests Fidler (2007: 48), the increasing securitization of health issues may indicate 'that public health governance is returning to normality in international relations'. States are doing what they have traditionally done: health has habitually been regarded as a 'high politics' national security issue when an issue such as the international spread of disease has threatened a country's economic or military strength. Also, the focus of international organizations on the broader, human dimensions of international health has precedents in history: consideration for human rights and the social determinants of health has informed the governance agenda in international health at times in the past. The present period is exceptional, however, in that health as national security is increasingly juxtaposed with health as global and/or human security.

David Fidler (2007: 61) sees this as a convergence of 'narrow and broad conceptions of security and of interest-based and value-based approaches to health and security'. However, he allows that this convergence is not always harmonious; rather, health as security is often combined in 'antagonistic frameworks' (Fidler, 2007: 43). This is partly because, as Feldbaum et al. (2006: 196) observe, 'the global and humanitarian objectives of the [global] health field do not fit readily into the state-centred perspective of national security'. It is questionable whether the distinctions between pragmatic interests and humanitarian motivations are as stark as Feldbaum and his colleagues imply, given that global health is becoming a high-stakes business enterprise. Indeed, as recent debates on the world food crisis illustrate, human security concerns often clash with the interests of international business, which are supported by the nation-based international political system (Stokes, 2008). The clash was highlighted, for instance, by reporter Sam Urquhart (2008), who describes the reaction of Eric Holt-Gimenez, head of the NGO Food First, following an emergency meeting in early June of the Food and Agriculture Organization (FAO):

> Holt-Gimenez expects the Bank to 'prepare the field with its loans and conditions for the spread of industrial (GMO) seeds and inputs' – allowing corporations and the Bank itself to pose as 'saviours' through the spread of high-tech methods. Echoing [Naomi] Klein, he calls this 'Another fine case of "disaster capitalism" at work' as human misery prepares the ground for renewed capital accumulation, against the wishes it purports to serve.

Although food security has not (yet) been incorporated in the 'securitization of health' discourse, it is clearly a health issue that fundamentally challenges human security. And, the food crisis highlights that health is situated uncomfortably in 'antagonistic frameworks' not only because national security concerns tend to take precedence, but because security is at the centre of a political struggle currently being waged to decide the future of world order.

For the most part, the securitization of health literature has not directly engaged the fundamental issue of world system change in which health has become a meaningful security concern. From a public health perspective, scholars have focused mainly on normative questions about the effect of securitization on health outcomes. In international relations, questions have been more about the range of health issues that should be included in a security framework, or whether health (outside of bioterrorism) should be included at all. Those scholars who have attempted to bring these together tend to accept that the securitization of health is a *fait accompli*, albeit differing on whether it is an ongoing or completed process (McInnes & Lee, 2006; Fidler, 2007). The objective of these scholars now is to provide advice on fine-tuning current approaches to health security governance rather than questioning the underlying structures that are culpable in producing and/or exacerbating the insecurities (Fidler, 2007: 50–57).

Overall, in most of the health and security analyses, security is treated as an entity that can be evaluated empirically, even though, as scholars of the Copenhagen School of security studies have argued, security as an international relations concept is socially constructed.

In 2004, Ole Wæver (2004: 56) of the Copenhagen School suggested that, 'in the [post-World War II] period, security has a particular international-affairs meaning distinct from its everyday sense'. This meaning, although widely accepted in modern international relations, was not inevitable, he argued. Instead, security is a subjective concept. The act of securitization begins when a 'securitizing actor' (an authoritative figure in government, bureaucracy or civil society) identifies an existentialist threat to a referent object 'with an inherent right to survive'. A 'speech act' designates the threat to be deserving of extraordinary measures beyond those of 'normal polities'. If the targeted audience is convinced of the authenticity of the threat, the securitization act is successful (see also Wæver, 1995; Buzan, Wæver & de Wilde, 1998).

The Copenhagen School's securitization theory has advanced analysis appreciably by explaining *how* issues become securitized. It is less helpful, however, in exploring *why* the securitization process takes place and why particular (in this case, health) issues are selected for security consideration (Callabero-Anthony & Emmers, 2006: 5).[14] It is also questionable whose security is ultimately at stake in the Copenhagen School's approach. While the school has broadened the concept of security, moved away from the state as the sole referent object and allowed for non-state actors to be the 'securitizing actors', it is required that 'the actor has the position of authority to make the securitizing claim, that the alleged threats facilitate securitization, and that the securitizing speech act follows the grammar of security' (Smith, 2005: 34). According to critics, these criteria allow for the exclusion of certain, grave security issues, including women's security issues, that either do not have authoritative figures to proclaim their relevance in a speech act or else will be exacerbated by speaking out (Hansen, 2000). Also, in distinguishing among different types of security, the Copenhagen School relegates women's security concerns to the social security category, where they tend to be marginalized, since social security is not deemed to be as important as international and/or military security (Hudson, 2005).

Towards securitizing health as *Human* security

One could argue that the UNDP's delivery of the concept of human security in 1994 was a 'speech act' that advanced the idea of securitizing issues beyond traditionally held notions of what security entails. By the Copenhagen School's reasoning, this act requires an audience. In this case, the targeted audience was policymakers and academics in the established security realm and in international development. Several among this audience have accepted the idea, so the securitization process may be advancing; however, as many or more have rejected it, the securitization act remains incomplete. To the extent that human security is deemed to have been successfully advanced, it is often viewed as an adjunct to traditional security, or in reduced form as 'freedom from fear' rather than 'freedom from want' as well as fear. In the public health and security literature, human security often tends to be seen in the first way, as a category of security that has been added on to the traditional security framework (Fidler, 2007: 61; Feldbaum et al., 2006). In international relations, the advances usually cited with regard to human security, such as the 'Responsibility to Protect' norm, the Ottawa Process to ban landmines, etc., are remarkable in their challenge to orthodox security thinking, but the narrow version of human security that is applied does not move the discourse outside the military-security areas circumscribed by tradition.

Yet, it is the broader version of human security that radically challenges us to think about what and for whom is security, as well as how our security objectives, whether defined narrowly or broadly, are most effectively met. The concept of human security illustrates the linkages that exist among currently 'securitized' issues and exposes the need for interdisciplinary approaches to deal with these problems (Thomas, 2001). Compelling evidence from the discipline of public health shows that health outcomes at population levels are determined as much (and more after a certain basic level of welfare) by social conditions as by technological interventions (Wilkinson & Marmot, 1998). In other words, it is clear that health is determined by level of development. Meanwhile, it is now widely accepted that the good health of a population is a necessary condition for economic growth and development (Sachs, 2001). More controversial and speculative, but nevertheless sufficiently persuasive to warrant further research, are claims that lack of development contributes to conflict (Daudelin, 1999; Gannon, 2000). These complex associations are at the heart of the concept of human security, and although there is nothing inherent in traditional security theory that prohibits exploration of dependent variables that impact upon the particular security issue being assessed, human security underscores that these variables are not so easily analysed in separation, either from each other or from the underlying political economy that configures these associations.

Currently, treatments of heath and security rarely address these associations as an ontological unit (that is, as suprastructural phenomena of a particular global political economy); rather, they address them as interacting or mutually influential, but as distinct categories. The Copenhagen School supports this practice, insisting that security is separable as five distinct areas. Barry Buzan (2004: 370), for instance, argues that human security 'risks mixing up the quite different agendas of international security on the one hand, and social security and civil liberties on the other'. It is questionable, however, how different these agendas actually are. Political order has been the primary objective of the international security agenda, whereas social security and civil liberties are issues primarily of justice. Traditionally, international relations scholarship has recognized a tension between aspirations for justice and for order (Bull, 1977). In the post-World War II years, under the dominance of realism, it came to be taken for granted that order is a condition that is prior to justice and that a system based on the power struggles of self-interested, sovereign states is the most effective model for maximizing order. Yet, globalization has challenged the state's exclusionary position at the centre of world politics (Scholte, 2000), and various new conflicts suggest that neither order nor justice is a primary condition: while justice is unlikely to exist without order, disorder is likely to erupt in situations of prevailing injustice. Social security and civil liberties are integral to international security: the broad conception of human security allows us conceptual space to examine how these attributes are linked and to explore how international structures and practices impinge upon the lived experiences of ordinary people.

The concept of human security helps to bridge the traditionally assumed incommensurability of the concepts of order and justice in international relations. But, if human security is to serve as this bridge, it requires that the concept be defined as 'freedom from want' as well as 'freedom from fear'. In other words, security is to be understood as epiphenomenal to underlying structures of political economy. For security to be understood in this sense requires a shift in the unit of analysis of security away from the state to 'either humanity as a whole or the individual' (Smith, 2004: 504). It also requires awareness that policy and statecraft are not viewed as being pre-determined or preordained by immutable principles of state behaviour or by an international system that is an unchanging structural edifice. Instead, 'speech acts' can lead to the emergence of new norms and change in the direction of governance and behaviour. Finally, the mechanisms by which new normative frameworks emerge cannot be divorced from struggles of political economy (Smith, 2004). Traditional international relations theory assumes that national security takes precedence over security defined in any other terms; and, according to the rationale of defending national security, order trumps justice in an anarchical world order. Yet, not only is 'anarchy . . . what states make of it' (Wendt, 1992), but, with the emergence of networks that constitute 'governance without government' (Rosenau & Czempiel, 1992), the official international order is no longer (if it ever was) the only order that informs and guides the behaviours of important political and economic actors in the world (Ba & Hoffman, 2005).

In an era of political contestation and changes in governance structures, the broad conception of human security encompasses the range of threats and perceptions of threat that have emerged with the changing world order. The existing international system is currently being challenged to deal with these threats and is responding, in part, by expanding the number of issues that states and international organizations address within their security apparatuses. However, not surprisingly, there is considerable resistance to fundamental or radical changes in official security policy (and thinking). Existing norms often persist for some time despite challenges; institutional structures change only gradually; and scarce resources often mitigate possibilities for change. But, current threats to human life and livelihood, outside of traditional security purview, are creating momentum for realignment in security analysis and policy. Although the securitization literature has focused mainly on the degree to which issues have been securitized by national governments or international organizations, both academics and nongovernmental organizations are often at the forefront of the struggle to promote norms change in security (MacFarlane

& Khong, 2006: 3; Michael, 2002; Caballero-Anthony, 2006). Also, ordinary people, those upon whom the concept of human security is focused, are contributing to this change, sometimes assisted by NGOs or academics. An interesting observation of the last point is provided by Ian Smillie. In interviews conducted in post-conflict Sierra Leone, he found that many people viewed security in broad-based and integrated terms. The prevailing concern of people he interviewed was crime, and then the 'deeper underlying causes of crime – and ultimately of the war itself: the economy, poverty, youth unemployment, corruption and mismanagement' (Smillie, 2006: 27).

The point is not that anyone gets to decide what constitutes national or international security agendas: obviously, states and international organizations will continue to securitize certain issues, based on precedent, changing awareness or knowledge of threats, and the dominance of particular theories and security actors. However, how people perceive their security realities, as well as how those perceptions are received and by whom, can contribute to the development of a 'speech act' that will eventually lead to changes in how security is perceived by authoritative security actors. For many ordinary people in the world, issues addressed under the broad umbrella of human security are in critical need of the extraordinary attention currently afforded to conventional security concerns. These include several health-related, multifactorial, international issues not currently securitized, ranging from chronic diseases exacerbated by the international trade in tobacco to cross-border trafficking in drugs, structural violence that disproportionately affects women and children, and the food/energy crisis (MacLean & MacLean, 2006; McInnes & Lee, 2006; Hansen, 2000; Brown, 2004).

Conclusions

Much of the debate on the securitization of health has been normative: Will securitization improve health outcomes or not? Few examine the fundamental structural alterations in world order from which the global health threats emerge and that are fostering changes in social relations and theory revision in international relations/security. Many scholars in the security field have also neglected these critical issues, contributing to the debate on the securitization of health by questioning the wisdom of broadening the concept of security, citing loss of analytical rigour and inoperability as problems that will stem from broadening the concept, especially to incorporate the 'freedom from want' as well as the 'freedom from fear' component of the human security agenda.

Yet, the concept of human security has been particularly instructive not only in illuminating unexamined issues of structural violence, but also in highlighting that structurally based inequalities and inequities are at the core of many of the relevant issues of the conventional security agenda. Conceived broadly, human security is consistent with the post-Westphalian ontological shift away from the state as the central unit of analysis (Scholte, 2000). In placing people as the main security referent, it acknowledges the need to understand what this shift entails for protecting the rights and needs of people (which supposedly was the rationale for traditional national security: citizens give up their freedom to the state in exchange for protection). Regarding operational effectiveness, the broader concept challenges us to address the multiple, interacting aspects of security simultaneously: rather than privileging military security at the expense of the social conditions of insecurity, it suggests that bread is as relevant to international order as guns, if not more so.

Revising security agendas to address the needs of justice and order in a changing global era will be achieved through political struggle, as much as or more than through appeals to empirical information on relative risks. As the Copenhagen School has advised, securitization is a social process, requiring an authoritative actor performing a 'speech act' and an audience that is receptive to the change suggested. With regard to human security, the process of securitization is incomplete, but the idea has persisted and is being promoted in various forums by policymakers, academics, NGOs and ordinary people. The audience is expanding largely because the problems of human insecurity are in danger of becoming insurmountable unless dominant security actors begin to think and act in terms of the security of people.

Notes

* Sandra MacLean would like to thank three anonymous reviewers for their comments on an earlier draft of this article.

1 Health-related security concerns predate the construction of the modern, Westphalian state form. Price-Smith (2002: 10) notes that 'Thucydides's account of the eventual fall of Athens during the Peloponesian Wars pays particular attention to the devastating effect that "the plague" had on Athenian governance, and by extension, on the Athenian war effort'. Prior to this, fears about the security of political actors in the face of health threats was evident, with examples of 'cordons sanitaires' that date as far back as 630 CE, when armed guards were placed on the road between Provence and Cahers to block the movement of diseased travellers (Brockington, 1968: 169).

2 See 'History of WHO and International Cooperation in Public Health', available at http://www.who.or.jp/GENERAL/history_wkc.html (accessed 5 July 2006).

3 For the text of the Alma-Ata Declaration, see http://www.paho.org/English/DD/PIN/alma-ata_declaration.htm (accessed 7 June 2008).

4 See the Commission's website at http://www.who.int/social_determinants/en/ (accessed 9 June 2008).

5 While 'power' can be interpreted in several ways (for example, 'power to' affect some action or 'power with' others to gain strength or leverage that acting alone would not provide), in traditional international relations theory it is defined as 'power over', meaning the ability to cause others to do what they might not otherwise have done (see, for example, Waltz, 1979: 192).

6 For the text of the US Bioterrorism Act of 2002, see http://www.fda.gov/oc/bioterrorism/Bioact.html (accessed 3 September 2006).

7 See 'Bioterrorism Overview' at the website of the US Centers for Disease Control and Prevention (CDC), available at http://emergency.cdc.gov/bioterrorism/overview.asp (accessed 9 June 2008).

8 These diseases, which include Lassa Fever and Marburg and Congo-Crimean Hemorrhagic Fevers, are so-called because one of their common symptoms is generalized bleeding.

9 It was not only that traded products could carry infectious agents; it also became underscored that health was impacted by the complexities of modern trading practices: trade in beef from the UK where BSE was first located was soon restricted, but it was realized that the disease could be transferred by live cattle and feed sources that are also traded but not always as easily traceable as beef itself.

10 See 'Avian Influenza: Current H5N1 Situation' at the website of the US Centers for Disease Control and Prevention (CDC), available at http://www.cdc.gov/flu/avian/outbreaks/current.htm (accessed 28 August 2006).

11 See Fidler (2003) for a discussion of innovations in the international governance of infectious disease.

12 See 'What Are Emerging Infectious Diseases?', at the website of the US Department of Defense Global Emerging Infections Surveillance and Response System (DoD-GEIS), available at http://www.geis.fhp.osd.mil/aboutGEIS.asp (accessed 8 June 2008).

13 See, for example, the 'Oslo Ministerial Declaration', available at http://www.emb-norway.ca/policy/humanitarian/priority/Health.htm (accessed 29 June 2008); Brower & Chalk (2003).

14 See McInnes & Lee (2006) and Chalk (2006) for interesting discussions of the range of issues included within the securitization framework.

References

Altman, Lawrence, 2006. 'So Many Advances in Medicine, So Many Left To Come', *New York Times*, 26 December.

Ba, Alice D. & Matthew J. Hoffman, eds, 2005. *Contending Perspectives on Global Governance: Coherence, Contestation and World Order*. London & New York: Routledge.

Behrman, Greg, 2004. *The Invisible People: How the U.S. Has Slept Through the Global AIDS Pandemic, the Greatest Humanitarian Catastrophe of Our Time*. New York: Free Press.

Booth, Ken, ed., 2005a. *Critical Security Studies and World Politics*. Boulder, CO & London: Lynne Rienner.

Booth, Ken, 2005b. 'Introduction to Part I', in Ken Booth, ed., *Critical Security Studies and World Politics*. Boulder, CO & London: Lynne Rienner (21–25).

Brockington, Fraser, 1968. *World Health*, 2nd edn. Boston, MA: Little, Brown & Company.

Brockington, Fraser, 1985. *The Health of the Developing World*. Lewes: Book Guild.

Brower, Jennifer & Peter Chalk, 2003. *The Global Threat of New and Reemerging Infectious Disease: Reconciling the U.S. National Security and Public Health Policy*. Santa Monica, CA: RAND.

Brown, Lester, 2004. *Outgrowing the Earth: The Food Shortage Challenge in an Age of Falling Water Tables and Rising Temperatures*. Washington, DC: Earth Policy Institute.

Brundtland, Gro., 1999. 'Message from the Director-General', in *The World Health Report 1999: Making a Difference*. Geneva: WHO (vii–xix).

Bull, Hedley, 1977. *The Anarchical Society: A Study of Order in World Politics.* Houndsmill: Macmillan.

Buzan, Barry, 2004. 'A Reductionist, Idealistic Notion that Adds Little Analytical Value', *Security Dialogue* 35(3): 369–370.

Buzan, Barry; Ole Wæver & Jaap de Wilde, 1998. *Security: A New Framework for Analysis.* Boulder, CO: Lynne Rienner.

Callabero-Anthony, Mely, 2006. 'Combating Infectious Diseases in East Asia: Securitization and Global Public Goods for Health and Human Security', *Journal of International Affairs* 59(2): 105–127.

Callabero-Anthony, Mely & Ralf Emmers, 2006. 'Understanding the Dynamics of Non-Traditional Security', in Mely Caballero-Anthony, Ralf Emmers & Amitav Acharya, eds, *Non-Traditional Security in Asia: Dilemmas of Securitization.* Aldershot: Ashgate (1–12).

Chalk, Peter, 2006. 'Disease and the Complex Processes of Securitization in the Asia-Pacific', in Mely Caballero-Anthony, Ralf Emmers & Amitav Acharya, eds, *Non-Traditional Security in Asia: Dilemmas of Securitization.* Aldershot: Ashgate (112–135).

Corder, Mike, 2001. 'Anthrax Scares Sweep Countries', *Washington Post*, 15 October; available at http://www.library.ohiou.edu/indopubs/2001/10/15/0050.html (accessed 12 June 2008).

Daudelin, Jean, 1999. 'Conflict and Development: Exploring Links and Assessing Impacts', *Review, the North–South Institute Newsletter* 3(3): 1.

de Waal, Alex, 2005. 'Issue Paper 1: HIV/AIDS and the Military', paper presented at Expert Seminar and Policy Conference on 'AIDS, Security and Democracy', Clingendæl Institute, The Hague, 2–4 May; available at http://programs.ssrc.org/HIV/publications/hague2005/issue_paper1.pdf (accessed 29 August 2006).

Duffield, Mark R., 2001. *Global Governance and the New Wars: The Merging of Development and Security.* London: Zed.

Elbe, Stefan, 2006. 'Should HIV/AIDS Be Securitized? The Ethical Dilemma of Linking HIV/AIDS and Security', *International Studies Quarterly* 50(1): 119–144.

Fein, Esther, 1997. 'The Nation; The Shots Heard "Round the World"', *New York Times*, 21 December.

Feldbaum, Harley; Kelley Lee & Preeti Patel, 2006. 'The National Security Implications of HIV/AIDS', *PloS Medicine* 3(6): e171.

Feldbaum, Harley; Preeti Patel, Egbert Sondorp & Kelley Lee, 2006. 'Global Health and National Security: The Need for Critical Engagement', *Medicine, Conflict and Survival* 22(3): 192–198.

Fidler, David P., 2003. 'Emerging Trends in International Law Concerning Global Infectious Disease Control', *Emerging Infectious Diseases*, March; available at http://www.cdc.gov/ncidod/EID/vol9no3/02-0336.htm (accessed 5 July 2006).

Fidler, David P., 2005. 'Health as Foreign Policy: Between Principle and Power', *Whitehead Journal of Diplomacy and International Relations* 6(2): 179–194.

Fidler, David P., 2007. 'A Pathology of Public Health Securitism: Approaching Pandemics as Security Threats', in Andrew F. Cooper, John J. Kirton & Ted Schrecker, eds, *Governing Global Health: Challenge, Response, Innovation.* Aldershot: Ashgate (41–64).

Gannon, John C., 2000. 'The Global Infectious Disease Threat and Its Implications for the United States', NIE (National Intelligence Council) 99-17D, January 2000; available at www.odci.gov/cia/publications/nie/report/nie99-17d.html (accessed 16 June 2008).

Garrett, Laurie, 1994. *The Coming Plague: Newly Emerging Diseases in a World Out of Balance*. New York: Farrer.

Garrett, Laurie, 2000. *Betrayal of Trust: The Collapse of the Global Public Health System*. New York: Hyperion.

Garrett, Laurie, 2005. 'The Lessons of HIV/AIDS', *Foreign Affairs* 84(4): 54–61.

Gellman, Barton, 2000. 'The Belated Global Response to AIDS in Africa: World Shunned Signs of the Coming Plague', *Washington Post*, 5 July.

Hansen, Lene, 2000. 'The Little Mermaid's Silent Security Dilemma and the Absence of Gender in the Copenhagen School', *Millennium* 29(2): 285–306.

Henderson, D. A., 1998. 'Bioterrorism as a Public Health Threat', *Emerging Infectious Diseases* 4(3): 488–492.

Holbrooke, Richard C., 2000. 'Battling the AIDS Pandemic', *Global Issues* 5(2); available at http://usinfo.state.gov/journals/itgic/0700/ijge/gj02.htm (accessed 12 June 2008).

Hudson, Heidi, 2005. '"Doing" Security as Though Humans Matter: A Feminist Perspective on Gender and the Politics of Human Security', *Security Dialogue* 36(2): 155–174.

Kaldor, Mary, 2006. *New and Old Wars: Organized Violence in a Global Era*, 2nd edn. Cambridge: Polity.

Krause, Keith, 2004. 'A Key to a Powerful Agenda, If Properly Defined', *Security Dialogue* 35(3): 367–368.

Lederberg, Joshua; Robert E. Shope & Stanley C. Oaks, Jr., eds, 1992. *Emerging Infections: Microbial Threats to Health in the United States*. Washington, DC: National Academies Press.

MacFarlane, S. Neil, 2004. 'A Useful Concept That Risks Losing Its Political Salience', *Security Dialogue* 35(3): 368–369.

MacFarlane, S. Neil & Yuen Foong Khong, 2006. *Human Security and the UN: A Critical History*. Bloomington, IN & Indianapolis, IN: Indiana University Press.

McInnes, Colin, 2005. *Health and Foreign Policy in the UK: The Experience Since 1997*. London: Nuffield Trust.

McInnes, Colin & Kelly Lee, 2006. 'Health, Security and Foreign Policy', *Review of International Studies* 32(1): 5–23.

Mack, Andrew, 2002. 'Human Security in the New Millennium', *Work in Progress: A Review of the United Nations University* 16(3): 4–6.

MacLean, Sandra J., 2007. 'Health in Development', in Andrew McGrew & Nana K. Poku, eds, *Globalization, Development and Human Security*. Cambridge: Polity (132–151).

MacLean, Sandra J. & David R. MacLean, 2006. 'The Globalisation of Cardiovascular Disease: Seeking Answers in International Relations and Political Economy', paper presented at the Annual Meeting of the International Studies Association, San Diego, CA, 22–25 March.

Mann, Jonathan M., 1989. 'AIDS: A Worldwide Pandemic', in M. S. Gottlieb, D. J. Jeffries, D. Mildvan, A. J. Pinching & T. C. Quinn, eds, *Current Topics in AIDS, Vol. 2*. New York: John Wiley & Sons (1–10).

Michael, Sarah, 2002. 'The Role of NGOs in Human Security', paper prepared for the Commission on Human Security, Harvard University, Cambridge, MA; available at http://www.hks.harvard.edu/hauser/active_backup/PDF_XLS/workingpaper_12.pdf (accessed 14 June 2008).

Obaid, Thoraya Ahmed, 2007. 'Introduction' to edition on 'Sexual Violence: Weapon of War, Impediment to Peace', *Forced Migration Review* 27: 5–6; available at http://www.genderandaids.org/modules.php?name=News&file=article&sid=845 (accessed 14 June 2008).

O'Manique, Colleen, 2006. The "Securitisation" of HIV/AIDS in Sub-Saharan Africa: A Critical Feminist Lens', in Sandra J. MacLean, David R. Black & Timothy M. Shaw, eds, *A Decade of Human Security: Global Governance and the New Multilateralisms*. Aldershot: Ashgate (168–176).

O'Sullivan, Patrick, 1986. *Geopolitics*. New York: St. Martin's Press.

Owen, John Wyn & Olivia Roberts, 2005. 'Globalization, Health and Foreign Policy: Emerging Linkages and Interests', *Globalization and Health* 1(12); available at http://www.globalizationandhealth.com/content/pdf/1744-8603-1-12.pdf (accessed 30 June 2008).

Paris, Roland, 2001. 'Human Security: Paradigm Shift or Hot Air?', *International Security* 26(2): 87–102.

Peterson, Susan, 2002/03. 'Epidemic Disease and National Security', *Security Studies* 12(2): 43–81.

Piot, Peter, 2005. 'HIV/AIDS Is Exceptional', speech given at London School of Economics, 8 February; available at http://www.lse.ac.uk/collections/LSEPublicLecturesAndEvents/pdf/20050208-PiotAIDS2.pdf (accessed 14 June 2008).

Preston, Richard, 1994. *The Hot Zone: A Terrifying True Story*. New York: Anchor.

Price-Smith, Andrew T., 2002. *The Health of Nations: Infectious Disease, Environmental Change, and Their Effects on National Security and Development*. Cambridge, MA: MIT Press.

Roberts, David, 2008. 'The Science of Human Security: A Response from Political Science', *Medicine, Conflict and Survival* 24(1):16–22.

Rosen, George, 1958. *A History of Public Health*. New York: MD Publications.

Rosenau, James N. & Ernst-Otto Czempiel, eds, 1992. *Governance Without Government: Order and Change in World Politics*. Cambridge: Cambridge University Press.

Sachs, Jeffrey, 2001. *The Links of Public Health and Economic Development*. London: Office of Health Economics.

Sandhu, Hardeep S.; Christopher Thomas, Peter Nsubuga & Mark E. White, 2003. 'A Global Network for Early Warning and Response to Infectious Diseases and Bioterrorism: Applied Epidemiology and Training Programs, 2001', *American Journal of Public Health* 93(10): 1640–1642.

Scholte, Jan Aart, 2000. *Globalization: A Critical Introduction*. New York: St. Martin's.

Singer, Peter, 2002. 'AIDS and International Security', *Survival* 44(1): 145–158.

Smillie, Ian, 2006. 'Whose Security? Innovation and Responsibility, Perception and Reality', in Sandra J. MacLean, David R. Black & Timothy M. Shaw, eds, *A Decade of Human Security: Global Governance and the New Multilateralisms*. Aldershot: Ashgate (19–30).

Smith, Steve, 2004. 'Singing Our World Into Existence: International Relations Theory and September 11', *International Studies Quarterly* 48(3): 499–515.

Smith, Steve, 2005. 'The Contested Concept of Security', in Ken Booth, ed., *Security Studies and World Politics*. Boulder, CO: Lynne Rienner (27–62).

Sprout, Harold & Margaret Sprout, 1968. *An Ecological Paradigm for the Study of International Politics*. Princeton, NJ: Centre for International Studies.

Stokes, Bruce, 2008. 'Food Is Different', *National Journal Magazine*, 7 June; available at http://www.nationaljournal.com/njmagazine/cs_20080607_6060.php (accessed 14 June 2008).

Thomas, Caroline, 2001. 'Global Governance, Development and Human Security: Exploring the Links', *Third World Quarterly* 22(2): 159–175.

Thomas, Caroline, 2004. 'A Bridge Between the Interconnected Challenges Confronting the World', *Security Dialogue* 35(3): 353–354.

Thomas, Caroline & Martin Weber, 2004. 'The Politics of Global Health: Whatever Happened to "Health for All by the Year 2000"', *Global Governance* 10(2): 187–205.

UNAIDS, 1998. *AIDS and the Military*. Geneva: UNAIDS.

UN Commission on Human Security, 2003. *Human Security Now*. New York: United Nations.

United Nations, 2004. *A More Secure World: Our Shared Responsibility*, Report of the Secretary-General's High-Level Panel on Threats, Challenges and Change. New York: United Nations.

United Nations Development Programme (UNDP), 1994. *Human Development Report 1994*. New York & Oxford: Oxford University Press.

United Press International, 1983. 'Fevers Are Added to Quarantine List', reprinted in *New York Times*, 31 January.

Urquhart, Sam, 2008. 'Food Crisis, Which Crisis?, *COA News*, 5 June; available at http://coanews.org/article/2008/food-crisis-which-crisis (accessed 14 June 2008).

US Department of Health & Human Services (HHS), 2006. 'News Release: HHS Announces $1.2 Billion in Funding to States for Bioterrorism', 7 June; available at http://www.hhs.gov/news/press/2006pres/20060607.html (accessed 17 September 2006).

Varmus, Harold, 1983. 'No One Is Really Immune', *New York Times*, 18 April.

Waltz, Kenneth N., 1979. *Theory of International Politics*. Toronto: Random House.

Wæver, Ole, 1995. 'Securitization and Descuritization', in Ronnie Lipschutz, ed., *On Security*. New York: Columbia University Press (46–86).

Wæver, Ole, 2004. 'Peace and Security: Two Concepts and Their Relationship', in Stefano Guzzini & Dietrich Jung, eds, *Contemporary Security Analysis and Copenhagen Peace Research*. London: Routledge (53–65).

Wendt, Alexander, 1992. 'Anarchy Is What States Make of It: The Social Construction of Power Politics', *International Organization* 46(2): 391–425.

White House, 2002. *The National Security Strategy of the United States of America*. Washington, DC: White House; available at http://www.whitehouse.gov/nsc/nss.html.

Whiteside, Alan; Alex de Waal & Tsadkan Gebre-Tensae, 2006. 'AIDS, Security and the Military in Africa: A Sober Appraisal', *African Affairs* 105(419): 210–218.

Wilkinson, Richard G. & Michael Marmot, eds, 1998. *Social Determinants of Health: The Solid Facts*. Copenhagen: World Health Organization Regional Office for Europe.

World Health Assembly (WHA), 2005. *Revision of the International Health Regulations*, WHA 58.3, 23 May; available at http://www.who.int/csr/ihr/IHRWHA58_3-en.pdf (accessed 28 June 2008).

World Health Organization (WHO), 2002. 'Bovine Spongiform Encephalopathy'; available at http://www.who.int/mediacentre/factsheets/fs113/en/ (accessed 28 August 2006).

Youde, Jeremy, 2005. 'Enter the Fourth Horseman: Health Security and International Relations Theory', *Whitehead Journal of Diplomacy and International Relations* 6(1): 193–208.

Zacher, Mark W., 2007. 'The Transformation in Global Health Collaboration Since the 1990s', in Andrew F. Cooper, John J. Kirton & Ted Schrecker, eds, *Governing Global Health: Challenge, Response, Innovation*. Aldershot: Ashgate (15–27).

Part 3

FOREIGN POLICY AND HEALTH

16

HEALTH AS FOREIGN POLICY

Between principle and power

David P. Fidler

Source: *Whitehead Journal of Diplomacy and International Relations*, 6 (2005), 179–94.

Introduction

This article focuses on a political revolution—the political revolution that has occurred in the area of health as an issue in international relations.[1] In the last decade, events in the microbial and the political worlds have radically transformed health's place in world affairs. The nature and extent of foreign policy attention devoted to health today is historically unprecedented.

Recognizing that a political revolution concerning health has taken place is not, however, the same as understanding the revolution's nature or policy implications. At present, health's political revolution means different things to different people. Diversity of views, in the wake of such a dramatic trans- formation of health's place in international relations, is understandable and should be encouraged. Diverse opinions and approaches suggest, however, that this revolution's meaning remains enigmatic.

In this article, I probe this enigmatic change in the relationship between health, foreign policy, and international relations. The article pushes the mean- ing of this revolution analytically in order to better understand how health's relationship with foreign policy is developing. In addition, I ponder whether this political revolution reflects a transformation of foreign policy for the benefit of health, or a transformation of health for the benefit of foreign policy.

I begin by describing why the last decade has witnessed a political revolution in terms of how health relates to foreign policy and international relations. Having fleshed out this change, I explore three different ways to conceptualize health's new political importance. These frameworks may not entirely capture the complexity and nuance of health's rise as an issue in international relations, but they serve as useful analytical devices for scrutinizing what has happened and why it has happened.

With the frameworks described, the article analyzes which framework provides the most accurate account of health's new prominence in foreign policy and international politics. The best conceptualization of the health-foreign policy relationship most accurately captures the dynamic between science and politics found at the heart of this relationship. The science-politics dynamic in the health-foreign policy relationship is, however, unstable, and perhaps dangerously so. With this in mind, I suggest how the volatility in the relationship between health and foreign policy might be mitigated to produce a more sustainable foundation for the future.

The rise of health as a foreign policy issue

My analysis proceeds from the assertion that health has undergone a political revolution in the last decade. I need to provide some sense of this revolution and not ask the reader to take this assertion on faith. To begin, let me make clear that health has been an issue for foreign policy and international relations for a long time. International health cooperation began in the mid-19th century with the convening of the first International Sanitary Conference in Paris;[2] and, since that meeting, states have concluded many treaties, created international health organizations, and cooperated with non-governmental organizations on a diverse range of health issues, covering both communicable and non-communicable diseases.[3]

International health activity has, however, been an obscure and neglected area in the study of foreign policy and international relations. Those who dissect international politics have long considered health issues unimportant or uninteresting. Scholars now interested in global health have commented on how much health as a foreign policy and diplomatic concern has been neglected in the study of international relations.[4]

Sometimes the neglect of health has been considered a function of health's place in the so-called "low politics" of international relations. "High politics" involves issues of war and peace, competition for power, the dilemma of national security, and the fight for survival in anarchy. "Low politics" concerns international cooperation on economic, environmental, and social issues. The distinction between "high politics" and "low politics" has been prominent in debates in international relations theory. Realist scholars, such as John Mearsheimer have, for example, argued that the theory of institutionalism concentrates on economic and social issues while largely ignoring the central questions of security, war, and peace.[5]

The distinction between "high" and "low" politics in international relations is useful for this article's purposes because, even in the world of "low politics," health issues have also generally been neglected. Health has occupied an area we can perhaps call "really low politics." A major reason for health's status as "really low politics" is that international health activities were, by and large, considered technical, humanitarian, and non-political endeavors.

In fact, health's non-political status is what some people thought gave it political power.

This seemingly counter-intuitive idea explains the incorporation of international health endeavors in functionalist theories of international relations.[6] Functionalists argued that international cooperation in technical, non-political areas would create spillover effects, transforming the nature of overall political interaction between sovereign states, from one of competition for power to one of cooperation for human welfare.[7]

Health's political revolution represents health's escape from "really low politics" into a new situation in which health features prominently on many political agendas in international relations today. In short, health has ceased to be merely a technical, humanitarian, and non-political activity. Some examples help support this observation:

- Through the specific threat of bioterrorism, and the more general threat of terrorists using weapons of mass destruction, the quality of a nation's public health and health care systems has become a matter of national and homeland security concern,[8] producing in the United States significant increases in funding for biodefense[9] and further calls for biodefense activities the scale of which would dwarf that of the Manhattan Project.[10]

- In 2000, the United Nations (UN) Security Council, considered the HIV/AIDS epidemic in the developing world, especially sub-Saharan Africa, as a threat to international peace and security, marking the first time a health threat was discussed before the UN body mandated to maintain international peace and security.[11]

- The UN Secretary-General's High-Level Panel on Threats, Challenges and Change embedded threats from biological weapons, bioterrorism, infectious diseases, and social determinants of health (e.g., poverty and environmental degradation) as critical components of what it termed "comprehensive collective security."[12] The Panel even recommended that the UN Security Council intervene during epidemics to mandate greater compliance from states with needed public health responses and to support international action to assist in quarantine measures.[13]

- The United States, other developed countries, and experts from various disciplines have expressed concerns that the political, economic, and social devastation HIV/AIDS causes in some parts of the developing world would contribute materially to the failure of states, resulting in their becoming breeding grounds of civil disorder, regional instability, and global crime and terrorism.[14] The scale of the HIV/AIDS crisis prompted the United States to launch the President's Emergency Plan for AIDS Relief (PEPFAR), a $15 billion, five-year initiative in the global fight against HIV/AIDS.[15]

- The growing burdens created by epidemics of communicable and non-communicable diseases adversely affect the prospects for economic development in many developing countries and have led to calls for putting health protection and promotion at the heart of economic development strategies.[16]

- Health issues have risen significantly on the agenda of international trade, whether the issue is the impact of pharmaceutical patents on a developing-country's access to essential medicines;[17] the increasing threat to food safety posed by globalized trade in food products;[18] concerns about how liberalization of trade in health-related services would affect national health systems;[19] or fears about how epidemics (such as SARS and avian influenza) could seriously disrupt trade and commerce.[20]

- Foreign and international aid agendas also reveal the growth in the importance of health problems, as illustrated by the increases seen in international aid designated for addressing HIV/AIDS, tuberculosis, and malaria,[21] and the use of health as a criterion for the distribution of bilateral aid.[22]

- The importance of health-related concerns has increased in the human rights area. Health threats, whether from bioterrorism or HIV/AIDS, now significantly affect both civil and political rights (e.g., public health measures restricting freedom or movement)[23] and economic, social, and cultural rights (e.g., access to life-saving therapies as part of the right to health).[24] Documents as diverse as the Bush administration's *National Security Strategy for the United States* and reports from the UN special rapporteur on the right to health[25] provide indications of health's new human rights importance.

- Health issues have focused more policy attention on new actors in international relations, especially the participation of non-state actors in global health initiatives, most prominently various public-private partnerships that attempt to increase access to existing treatments or create new drugs and vaccines for communicable diseases.[26]

Many more examples could be mentioned, but these provide a sense of how events have transformed the relationship of health and foreign policy over the last decade. Moreover, the transformation is reciprocal in the sense that foreign policy more frequently has to grapple with health, and health more frequently has to grapple with foreign policy.

The new relationship between health and foreign policy: three perspectives

Two policy worlds, previously distant from one another, have collided, creating reverberations for both the pursuit of health and the conduct of foreign policy. I have participated in seminars and workshops, involving doctors, epidemiologists, academics, activists, and diplomats, at which this mélange of expertise has explored how to understand and handle this new

political reality. Discussions in these settings often reveal different interpretations of the new relationship between health and foreign policy. I now
sketch three distinct ways in which the new health-foreign policy linkage can
be conceptualized in order to provide the reader with a sense of the range
of possibilities the linkage generates.

Foreign policy as health

The first perspective—"foreign policy as health"—perceives health's rise in
international relations as transformative of foreign policy. In short, "foreign
policy as health" maintains that foreign policy now pursues, and should in
the future pursue, health as an end in itself. This perspective argues that
health affects so many political agendas that it has emerged as a transarchical
value—defined as a value that influences the substantive nature of hierarchical
politics within states and anarchical politics between states.

One way to capture this "foreign policy as health" position is to consider
how central health as a value is to the Millennium Development Goals
(MDGs) adopted in 2000 under the auspices of the United Nations.[27] The
MDGs establish a new framework for economic development in the 21st
century, and health is at this strategy's heart. Three of the eight MDGs are
specific health objectives: reducing child mortality, improving maternal health,
and reducing the burden of HIV/AIDS and other diseases. Four of the
remaining five MDGs concern key social determinants of health: poverty,
education, gender equality, and the environment. The eighth MDG, building
global partnerships, incorporates a specific health-related target of increasing
access to essential medicines in the developing world.

The "foreign policy as health" perspective emphasizes other features of
international relations that reinforce the recognition of health as an end in
itself for foreign policy action. The frequency with which health concerns
have cropped up in the realm of national and international security, whether
the issue is bioterrorism or damage to state capacity caused by communicable
diseases, suggests that the pursuit of health capabilities has become important
even for the highest of high politics.[28]

The "foreign policy as health" perspective contains a broad definition of
both "foreign policy" and "health." This perspective views "health" as more
than the mere absence of disease and embeds health into the broader social
and economic context of human activity. This expansive view of health
enlarges the scope of foreign policy beyond the traditional concerns with
military power and matters external to the nation's territory. In fact, the
expansive notion of health collapses foreign and domestic policy into a global
policy paradigm that more accurately reflects the reality of 21st century
human interdependence.

This perspective on health's rise on foreign policy agendas differs from
the old functionalist interpretation of international health cooperation.

Functionalism maintained international health activities constituted a technical, non-political area of cooperation with the potential to generate positive political externalities in other areas of international relations. The "foreign policy as health" conception rejects the idea that health is merely a technical, non-political activity and argues that health has become a pre-eminent *political value* for 21st century humanity. As such, health's potential to generate positive political spillover operates overtly rather than through functionalism's more obscure stealth dynamic.

Health and foreign policy

The second perspective on health's political revolution contrasts with the conception of foreign policy pursuing health as an end in itself. This alternative framework holds that health's rise on foreign policy agendas merely indicates that foreign policy is shaping health, not vice versa. This perspective—"health and foreign policy"—captures the essence of the argument: health has merely become another issue with which traditional approaches to foreign policy grapple. Health is no different from any other issue that foreign policy addresses, and foreign policy approaches health in the same manner it approaches other issues. Health does not transform thinking about foreign policy; rather, foreign policy transforms how we conceptualize health.

The "health and foreign policy" approach accepts that health issues have more frequently appeared as foreign policy challenges in the last ten to fifteen years. The reason for this change is not, however, the emergence of a transarchical health norm that states believe in and to which they adhere. To the contrary, health issues have become more prominent foreign policy issues because health-related threats to the material interests and capabilities of states have increased. When diseases threaten, or show the potential to threaten, national security, military capabilities, geopolitical or regional stability, national populations, economic power, and trade interests, foreign policy makers take notice. When diseases interfere with and frustrate a state's pursuit of its material interests, as frequently happened in the last decade in international trade, foreign policy bureaucracies respond. What drives responses is the threat posed to the material interests and capabilities of states, not a cosmopolitical consensus on health's intrinsic importance to 21st century humanity.

In fact, we might more accurately call the "health and foreign policy" perspective "only certain communicable diseases and foreign policy" because, by and large, only certain communicable disease problems, such as SARS, HIV/AIDS, or a killer influenza pandemic, cause serious perturbations requiring high-level foreign policy action. Thus, foreign policy's target is not "health" but mitigating risks and costs that certain infectious diseases create for foreign policy objectives, such as protecting national security and maintaining flows of international trade and commerce.

Further, the foreign policy task often has nothing to do with reducing disease burdens in other countries. For example, the foreign policy challenge faced by developed countries with respect to the controversy over the Agreement on Trade-Related Aspects of Intellectual Property Rights (TRIPS Agreement) of the World Trade Organization (WTO) and developing-country access to anti-retrovirals, was managing a tactical retreat on the scope of patent rights, not contributing to efforts to stem the galloping HIV/AIDS pandemic.

When improving health or health systems in foreign countries is an intended consequence of foreign policy action, the strategic objective is usually something other than health. For example, the United States' interest in improving global infectious disease surveillance views improved global surveillance as a means to increase national and homeland security against bioterrorism, not as a vehicle for improving global health.[29] Any constructive health consequences for other countries that spill over from improved global surveillance represent a positive externality but are not the primary foreign policy objective.

In contrast to the expansive definitions of "health" and "foreign policy" in the "foreign policy as health" perspective, "health and foreign policy" maintains a traditionally narrow understanding of foreign policy and adopts a limited conception of what health means for foreign policy purposes. Under the "health and foreign policy" perspective, health is merely a tool, an instrument of statecraft the value of which extends no farther than its utility in serving the material interests and capabilities of the state. In that regard, its function is no different from the functions of war, military power, economic wealth, and international institutions in the anarchical politics of international relations.

Health as foreign policy

The third framework stakes out a middle ground between the previous two perspectives and maintains that health's rise as an issue in world affairs creates a relationship between health and foreign policy under which neither completely transforms the other. I call this perspective "health as foreign policy." This conceptualization of the health-foreign policy interaction involves a dynamic between science and politics that reflects an interdependence, or mutual dependence, when health and foreign policy mix.

"Health as foreign policy" focuses on a different aspect of health from the other two perspectives because it concentrates on the science of health, or epidemiology.[30] The first framework, "foreign policy as health," concerns the ideology of health, while "health and foreign policy" emphasizes the power politics of health. Health as an endeavor is, however, deeply scientific. The science of health produces learning that applies within states or between states. Epidemiology produces, therefore, transarchical knowledge and information about health and threats to it.

Such transarchical knowledge creates scientific principles and imperatives that affect political action and governance. For example, epidemiology

297

stresses the critical nature of surveillance. Virtually everything else in public health hinges, for example, on knowing what diseases are affecting what parts of what population. Surveillance is not a function of ideology or politics, but a scientific principle and imperative that applies everywhere.

Epidemiology also develops scientific principles and imperatives in terms of how disease threats should be addressed. Scientifically, breaking the chain of transmission of a virulent airborne virus, such as SARS, requires interventions different from those required to reduce obesity-related diseases. Science drives both the identification of, and the interventions to be deployed against, threats to health.

Scientific principles and imperatives channel action on health in specific directions that neither ideology nor power politics can alter. Science's role in health undermines the ideology of health that informs the "foreign policy as health" perspective, and it challenges the "health and foreign policy" assumption that health functions no differently in international politics than other kinds of material interests and capabilities. Let me elaborate on these arguments.

The ideology of health contained in the "foreign policy as health" perspective assumes that the health of all peoples is interdependent and mutually vulnerable, giving rise to a context in which health serves as a common denominator for political action. Classical expressions of this notion appear in the preamble of the Constitution of the World Health Organization.[31] The preamble states, for example, that the health of all peoples is fundamental to the attainment of peace and security, and that the achievement of any state in the promotion and protection of health is of value to all.

These statements are empirically dubious, at best. To my knowledge, no correlation exists between a people's health status and its disposition for violence and war. The 20th century saw life expectancies rise in most regions of the world, yet that century was one of the most violent and bloodiest in human history. The assertion that health gains in one state are of value to all peoples in the world is also too sweeping to be taken seriously from an epidemiological point of view. One country's successful efforts to eradicate a highly transmissible disease may indeed benefit everyone else on the planet, but one country's success in reducing non-communicable diseases may have no epidemiological relevance at all to health in other countries. Levels of health interconnectedness and interdependence among populations in the world vary significantly, which creates a complex epidemiological reality that the ideology of health simplifies for political not scientific purposes.

Traditional foreign policy concerns with the preservation and promotion of a state's material national interests occupy the gap between epidemiology and ideology. The idea of "health" does not overcome the political dynamics created by states interacting in a condition of anarchy. Just as students of international relations have generally neglected health as an issue, health experts and advocates have shown little serious interest in understanding the problem anarchy poses for collective action among states.[32] Jumping from

298

epidemiology to ideology without appreciating the anarchy problem causes trouble for health advocates.

Likewise, science's role in health challenges the assumptions of the "health and foreign policy" perspective. This perspective plugged health into foreign policy as a fungible issue controlled by the laws of power politics. I have not yet seen a medical treatise, public health text, or Phase III clinical trial that indicates that the balance of power is an empirically valid strategy for dealing with disease threats to health. The "health as foreign policy" perspective encourages us to "speak science to power" rather than accept the proposition that, in the intersection of health and foreign policy, statesmen only think and act in terms of interest defined as power. Jumping from anarchy to power politics without appreciating epidemiology causes foreign policy on health issues problems.

Thus, the "health as foreign policy" perspective focuses on the science-politics dynamic at the heart of the health-foreign policy linkage. This dynamic contains scientific principles and imperatives that foreign policy cannot overlook, and anarchy/power considerations that health cannot ignore. "Health as foreign policy" provides a perspective on the health-foreign policy relationship that is more balanced conceptually than the other two frameworks explored above.

Between principle and power: health as foreign policy

Which, then, of these three perspectives—foreign policy as health, health and foreign policy, or health as foreign policy—most accurately describes the political revolution health has undergone as an issue in international relations? I argue that "health as foreign policy" provides the best perspective on health's political revolution, but selecting this perspective over "health and foreign policy" proves difficult for reasons examined below. These reasons also provide clues as to why "health as foreign policy" only precariously emerges as the perspective that best describes health's political revolution over the last decade.

Ideology without interests: foreign policy as health

The argument that health's political revolution means that foreign policy now pursues health as an end in itself, as a transarchical political value, is appealing at many different levels. It conceives of states and peoples commonly bound together through health and acting upon this common bond through global policy. This conceptualization also connects with long-standing beliefs and principles in international health, including the interdependence of the health of all peoples and the enjoyment of the highest standard of health attainable as a fundamental human right.[33]

The "foreign policy as health" perspective does not, however, accurately describe the relationship between health and foreign policy produced by the last decade's events. One need only reflect on the awful progression of the HIV/

AIDS pandemic to understand that states and peoples have not behaved as if their health is interdependent and that they share a common health bond. The Executive Director of UNAIDS stated that "the world stood by while AIDS overwhelmed sub-Saharan Africa."[34] The United Nations Special Envoy for AIDS in Africa has lashed out at countries for finding billions of dollars to fight terrorism but failing to provide adequate funds for fighting HIV/AIDS and called this situation a "double standard [that] is the grotesque obscenity of the modern world."[35]

The "foreign policy as health" perspective fails to describe health's political revolution for two reasons. First, the assumption that the health of countries and peoples is tightly interdependent, or mutually vulnerable, is overbroad from an epidemiological point of view. Mutual vulnerability exists with respect to some health threats, such as transmissible pathogens. SARS provided another reminder that epidemiological dependence is a reality with some health threats. Even with communicable diseases, "mutual vulnerability" might be overstating the epidemiological reality. Perhaps "variable vulnerability" would be more accurate in communicating the idea that some countries and peoples are more vulnerable than others to certain health threats. Malaria provides a good example of variable vulnerability because countries located in tropical regions are much more vulnerable to malaria than countries located in temperate climates.

Second, in a context of variable vulnerability, countries and peoples have different interests regarding health that are expressed through domestic and foreign policy. Divergent interests often appear in circumstances of variable vulnerability when health risks are connected with international trade. Developed and developing countries often have been at odds over health-related trade issues partly because health actions developing nations want to take conflicted with trade interests of developed states. Examples of these conflicts can be found in international infectious disease control, controversies over the WTO's TRIPS Agreement and General Agreement on Trade in Services, and global tobacco control. Behind such conflicts is the absence of mutual vulnerability to the health risk at issue.

The ideology of health has not eliminated material interests that states have in health-related contexts, and the "foreign policy as health" perspective seems unable to account conceptually for the conflict and controversies that arise when material interests on health held by different states clash. "Foreign policy as health" contains a version of the old "harmony of interests" doctrine in which health advocates assume that what is in the interests of world health is in the interests of each state. As in other contexts, reality deflates such "harmony of interests" assumptions when states interact.

Power play: health and foreign policy

The "health and foreign policy" perspective, with its emphasis on power and the material interests of states, is a strong candidate for the framework that best describes health's political revolution. Health's rise as a foreign policy issue in the last decade can, for example, be tracked against growing concerns of powerful states about health-related problems developing in the world of foreign policy. The great powers, such as the United States, have had to address health more frequently in their foreign policies because health problems have threatened, or complicated the satisfaction of, their material interests.

Further, the shape of international health activities today reflects how the great powers want health issues addressed. The United States' pursuit of national biodefense is more robust and better funded than any international initiative on any health problem, including the global nightmare of HIV/AIDS.[36] Frustrated with the WTO in its attempts to create high levels of patent protection for pharmaceutical products, the United States pursues this objective through regional and bilateral trade agreements.[37] SARS prompted an impressive global response because it threatened the health and trade interests of developed countries. Other than in connection with direct threats from chemical or radiological agents, non-communicable diseases do not register strongly in foreign policy calculations of developed states.

Thus, the "health and foreign policy" perspective presents a more plausible explanation of health's political revolution than "foreign policy as health." In fact, I am tempted to conclude that "health and foreign policy" is the most accurate account of what has happened to the relationship between health and foreign policy in the last decade. The reality of global health today can hardly be explained without reference to the impact that power has on the health-foreign policy relationship. "Health and foreign policy" provides the most robust explanation of that impact.

Two things temper the temptation to choose "health and foreign policy" as the explanation of choice. The first involves a reluctance to drain "health" of normative content and energy and subject it exclusively to the power play that exists among states in an anarchical political system. The second concerns the epidemiological short-sightedness of this perspective on health and foreign policy. "Health and foreign policy" also drains health of the insight provided by science.

Epidemiology identified the likelihood of a major HIV/AIDS epidemic in the developing world in the 1980s, with sub-Saharan Africa being particularly affected. The CIA even issued an intelligence estimate in 1987 that the impact of HIV/AIDS in sub-Sabaran Africa in the following decade would be severe.[38] Warnings largely went unheeded, however, in both the developing and developed worlds until the end of the 1990s when the magnitude of the public health disaster could no longer be ignored. What epidemiology foresaw, foreign policy ignored. The world is now in the midst of struggling to mitigate the costs of one of history's worst pandemics, with experts predicting the worst is still to come.[39] A foreign policy highly tuned to power politics but deaf to epidemiology is harmful to both foreign policy and health.

Epidemiology in the service of interests: health as foreign policy

My concerns with the "health and foreign policy" perspective lead me to prefer interpreting health's political revolution through the "health as foreign policy" approach. The science-politics dynamic at the heart of "health as foreign policy" establishes a context in which epidemiological evidence has to be marshaled for policy purposes through the lens of material interests. One striking thing about the last decade is the extent to which arguments for more foreign policy attention on health connected epidemiological evidence with adverse material consequences for states were relied upon rather than traditional concepts of health as a humanitarian or human rights issue. One document connecting health and U.S. foreign policy succinctly captured the emphasis on material self-interest when it identified the strategic objectives of U.S. engagement in global health as "protecting our people," "enhancing our economy," and "advancing our international interests."[40]

Use of the science-politics dynamic can be seen in the ways governments, international organizations, and non-state actors linked communicable disease problems to national and international security, international trade, economic development, national and regional stability, and the effectiveness of international aid. Similarly, a powerful tool in the new global strategy for tobacco control involved advocates tying the growth of tobacco-related diseases directly to significant economic costs that governments would have to bear if they did not improve tobacco control.[41] The interest shown in the concept of "global public goods for health" also illustrates the power of the science-politics dynamic because the "public goods" idea flows from economic theory not the ideology of health.[42]

Connecting epidemiology and material interests has proven traction in foreign policy contexts, and more traction than the concepts of "Health for All" and the human right to health. Perhaps we are witnessing a global health version of the famous Melian dialogue Thucydides recorded in his history of the Peloponnesian War.[43] In this dialogue, Athenian envoys come before the leaders of Melos to convince them to surrender or be destroyed by Athens. The Athenians and Melians agree to dispense with pleasing rhetoric and talk about material interests. In the science-politics dynamic, epidemiology is the envoy from Athens, nation-states are the interest-calculators of Melos, and the results of not adequately adjusting interests to epidemiology leads to adverse consequences for the state and unnecessary human suffering.

A dangerously unstable dynamic

Thinking about "health as foreign policy" also involves understanding that the science-politics dynamic is unstable, and perhaps dangerously so. This instability is worrying because it threatens to destroy a way in which the health-foreign policy relationship can be strengthened. The instability arises because the science-politics dynamic is not yet deeply grooved in either the health or foreign policy communities. Many health specialists and advocates remain leery of abandoning the ideology of health for a materialistic approach that compromises what they believe is special about health in human societies. Foreign policy experts remain skeptical about acting on the foresight of epidemiology in a world where short-term calculations of power and interest dominate state behavior. In the anarchical world of international politics, the shadow of the future does not extend very far, reducing a state's motivation to solve a problem today that can be left for tomorrow.

The dynamic is also unstable because matching epidemiology with material interests is not easy, and disputes about whether a health risk or problem requires foreign policy attention could occur. In these circumstances, the health concern may be ignored entirely or lumped in with other "merely humanitarian" issues that clutter the "low politics" of international relations. This scenario simply encourages matters to return to the status quo ante, with health and foreign policy specialists operating in separate worlds, neither of which captures the reality of the health-foreign policy relationship in the era of globalization.

Grooving health as foreign policy

Strategic construction of policy linkages between epidemiology and state interests can mitigate the instability present in the science-politics. Elsewhere I argued that today we are witnessing the emergence of "constitutional outlines" of public health's new world order.[44] These outlines are governance functions that are developing nationally and globally, and these functions provide channels through which the "health as foreign policy" approach can be more deeply grooved, reducing the volatility that threatens the science-politics dynamic.

These governance functions involve: (1) health and security; (2) health and commerce; (3) health preparedness and response; and (4) human rights scrutiny of health-related actions. Each function connects to strong interests held by states in the international system, and the functions provide pathways through which epidemiology can influence foreign policy. These functions reflect, in fact, how epidemiology has, in the last ten years, already affected foreign policy because they represent areas in which health's political revolution has been most apparent.

Connecting health problems with the pursuit of national and international security has been an unprecedented development in the health-foreign policy relationship, which has created new territory for the science-politics dynamic. The commerce-health linkage is old, but its long historical pedigree merely underscores how international commerce provides a fertile area for the science-politics dynamic. Health preparedness and response as an area for pursuing "health as foreign policy" directly connects epidemiology and material interests, because preparedness and response capabilities are essential for states to be able to manage health's intersections with security and trade. Another important feature of health's political revolution—human rights—can also be a tool for shaping political responses to health threats in epidemiologically and ethically appropriate ways that serve the national interest.

Systematically targeting security, commerce, preparedness and response, and human rights as ways to groove more deeply the science-politics dynamic is a formidable task that may require structural and procedural changes in how governments conduct foreign and health policy in the future. This observation supports the concern now being shown in international health circles about national "policy coordination and coherency" in areas in which health affects, and is affected by, foreign policy. Concerns about the impact of the new political importance of health on the U.S. Centers for Disease Control and Prevention illustrate, for example, the growing pains of melding science and politics together effectively.[45] Efforts to improve such coordination and coherency are, in essence, endeavors that support the prudence of the "health as foreign policy" strategy.

Conclusion

When asked about the French Revolution's impact, Chinese statesman Chou En-Lai said that it was too early to tell. Perhaps it is also too early to determine the ultimate direction and meaning of health's enigmatic political revolution. This article examined perspectives that interpret this revolution in different, sometimes antithetical ways. I also selected which perspective I believe not only best describes the political revolution but also offers the best prospects for mitigating the volatility seemingly inherent in the relationship between health and foreign policy.

Plotting a path between principle and power is risky, but in the context of health and foreign policy, it is empirically necessary and normatively appropriate. The goal of pursuing "health as foreign policy" is neither health for all nor the balance of power but rather the creation and sustenance of a constructive approach to the relationship of health and foreign policy that avoids being utopian, hegemonic, or irrelevant.

Notes

David P. Fidler is one of the world's leading experts on international law and public health, with an emphasis on infectious diseases. This article is based on the 2004 Maloy Lecture delivered by Professor Fidler at Georgetown University, October 5, 2004.

1 For more on this political revolution, see David P. Fidler, "Germs, Norms, and Power: Global Health's Political Revolution," *Law, Social Justice & Global Development*, 2004, no. 1, also available at www2.warwick.ac.uk/fac/soc/law/clj/ldg/2004_1/fidler/.

2 N. Howard-Jones, *The Scientific Background of the International Sanitary Conferences 1851–1938* (Geneva: World Health Organization, 1975).

3 Neville M. Goodman, *International Health Organizations and Their Work*, 2nd ed. (London: Churchill Livingstone, 1971), and David P. Fidler, *International Law and Public Health* (Ardsley, NY: Transnational Publishers, Inc., 2000).

4 Kelly Lee and Anthony Zwi, "A Global Political Economy Approach to AIDS: Ideology, Interests and Implications," in *Health Impacts of Globalisation: Towards Global Governance*, ed. K. Lee (Basingstoke: Palgrave, 2003), 13–32, and Ilona Kickbusch, "Global Health Governance: Some Theoretical Considerations on the New Political Space," in *Health Impacts of Globalisation: Towards Global Governance*, ed. K. Lee (Basingstoke: Palgrave, 2003), 192–203.

5 John J. Mearsheimer, "The False Promise of International Institutions," *International Security* 19, no. 3 (1994/95): 5–49.

6 Ernst Haas, *Beyond the Nation-State: Functionalism and International Organization* (Stanford: Stanford University Press, 1964), and Javed Siddiqi, *World Health and World Politics: The World Health Organization and the UN System* (Columbus: University of South Carolina Press, 1995), and Ulysses B. Panisett, *International Health Statecraft: Foreign Policy and Pubic Health in Peru's Cholera Epidemic* (Lanham, MD: University Press of America, 2000).

7 Haas, *Beyond the Nation State.*

8 *National Security Strategy for the United States* (Washington, D.C.: The White House, 2002).

9 U.S. Department of Health and Human Services, *HHS Factsheet: Biodefense Preparedness*, April 28, 2004, www.whitehouse.gov/news/releases/2004/04/print/20040428-4.html.

10 Ben Hirschler, "Call for New 'Manhattan Project' to Fight Bioterror," *Reuters New Service*, Jan. 27, 2005.

11 Dennis Altman, "Understanding HIV/AIDS as a Global Security Issue," in *Health Impacts of Globalisation: Towards Global Governance*, ed. K. Lee (Basingstoke: Palgrave, 2003), 33–46.

12 *Report of the UN Secretary-General's High-Level Panel on Threats, Challenges and Change—A More Secure World: A Shared Responsibility* (New York: United Nations, 2004).

13 *Ibid.* at paragraph 144.

14 *National Security Strategy of the United State*, and Andrew T. Price-Smith, *Pretoria's Shadow: The HIV/AIDS Pandemic and National Security in South Africa* (Washington, D.C.: Chemical and Biological Arms Control Institute, 2002), and Andrew T. Price-Smith and John L. Daly, *Downward Spiral: HIV/AIDS, State Capacity, and Political Conflict in Zimbabwe* (Washington, D.C.: United States Institute of Peace, 2004), and *The Human Security Challenges of HIV/AIDS and Other Communicable Diseases: Exploring Effective Regional and Global Responses* (New York: Asia Society, 2004).

15 White House, *Fact Sheet: The President's Emergency Plan for AIDS Relief*, January 29, 2003, www.whitehouse.gov/news/releases/2003/01/print/20030129-1.html.

16 Commission on Macroeconomics and Health, *Macroeconomics and Health: Investing in Health for Economic Development* (Geneva: World Health Organization, 2001).

17 Caroline Thomas, "Trade Policy, the Politics of Access to Drugs and Global Governance for Health," in *Health Impacts of Globalisation: Towards Global Governance*, ed. K. Lee (Basingstoke: Palgrave, 2003), 177–191.

18 World Health Organization and World Trade Organization, *WTO Agreements & Public Health—A Joint Study by the WHO and the WTO Secretariat* (Geneva: World Health Organization, 2002).

19 Nick Drager and David P. Fidler, *Managing Liberalization of Trade in Services from a Health Policy Perspective*, Trade and Health Notes No. 1, February 2004, www.who.int/trade/resource/en/GATSfoldout_c.pdf.

20 World Health Organization, *Global Defence Against the Infectious Disease Threat*, ed. M. K. Kindhauser (Geneva: World Health Organization, 2003).

21 Global Fund to Fight AIDS, Tuberculosis, and Malaria, at www.theglobalfund. org/cn/.

22 White House, *The Millennium Challenge Account*, www.whitehouse.gov/infcous/ developingnations/millennium.html.

23 Jason W. Sapsin et al., "SARS and International Legal Preparedness," *Temple Law Review* 77, no. 2 (2004): 155–174.

24 Africa Action, *Africa's Right to Health Campaign*, www.africaaction.org/campaign/ info.php.

25 The reports of the special rapporteur on the right to health can be accessed at www2.essex.ac.uk/human_rights_centre/rth/rapporteur.shtm.

26 *Global Defence Against the Infectious Disease Threat.*

27 Millennium Development Goals, at www.un.org/millenniumgoals/.

28 Chemical & Biological Arms Control Institute and CSIS, *Contagion and Conflict: Health as a Global Security Challenge* (Washington, D.C.: CBACT & CSIS, 2000), and Jonathan Ban, *Health, Security, and U.S. Global Leadership* (Washington, D.C.: Chemical & Biological Arms Control Institute, 2001), and Sue Petersen, "Epidemic Disease and National Security," *Security Studies* 12, no. 2 (2002): 43–81, and Jennifer Brower and Peter Chalk, *The Global Threat of New and Reemerging Infectious Diseases: Reconciling U.S. National Security and Public Health Policy* (Santa Monica: RAND, 2003), and Kurt M. Cambell and Philip Zelikow, *Biological Security & Public Health: In Search of a Global Treatment* (Washington, D.C.: Aspen Institute, 2003), and Jonathan Ban, "Health as a Global Security Challenge," *Seton Hall Journal of Diplomacy and International Relations* 4, no. 2 (2003): 19–27.

29 David P. Fidler, "Public Health and National Security in the Global Age: Infectious Diseases, Bioterrorism, and Realpolitik," *George Washington International Law Review* 35, no. 4 (2003): 787–856.

30 The *New Shorter Oxford English Dictionary* (p. 836) defines "epidemiology" as the "branch of medicine that deals with the incidence and transmission of disease in populations, esp. with the aim of controlling it; the aspects of a disease relating to its incidence and transmission."

31 Constitution of the World Health Organization, July 22, 1946, in World Health Organization, *Basic Documents*, 40th ed. (Geneva: World Health Organization, 1994), 1–18.

32 David P. Fidler, "Disease and Globalized Anarchy: Theoretical Perspectives on the Pursuit of Global Health," *Social Theory & Health* 1 (2003): 21–41.

33 Constitution of the World Health Organization, preamble.

34 Peter Piot, Keeping the Promise, Speech at the Opening Ceremony of the XIV International AIDS Conference in Barcelona, Spain (July 7, 2002), *quoted in* David P. Fidler, "Racism or *Realpolitik*? U.S. Foreign Policy and the HIV/AIDS Catastrophe in Sub-Saharan Africa," *Journal of Gender, Race & Justice* 7, no. 1 (2003): 97–146, at 97.

35 "AIDS Help for Africa 'Grotesque,'" *Toronto Star*, September 23, 2004.

36 *HHS Factsheet: Biodefense Preparedness* (reporting increase in biodefense spending in 2004 that was 17 times greater than in 2001).

37 For critical analysis, see Oxfam, *Robbing the Poor to Pay the Rich? How the United States Keep Medicines from the World's Poorest* (Oxfam Policy Briefing No. 56, November 2003).

38 Central Intelligence Agency, Sub-Saharan Africa: Implications of the AIDS Pandemic, SNIE 70/1-87 (June 1987).

39 Richard G. A. Feachem, "AIDS Hasn't Peaked Yet—And That's Not the Worst of It," *Washington Post*, January 12, 2003, at B03.

40 Institute of Medicine, *America's Vital Interest in Global Health* (Washington, D.C.: National Academy Press, 1997).

41 World Health Organization, "The World Health Organization Says That Tobacco is Bad Economics All Around," Press Release, May 31, 2004, www.who.int/mediacentre/news/releases/2004/pr36/cn/.

42 On global public goods for health, see Richard Smith et al., eds., *Global Public Goods for Health: Health Economic and Public Health Perspectives* (Oxford: Oxford University Press, 2003).

43 Thucydides, *History of the Peloponnesian War* (R. Warner, trans.) (New York: Penguin Books, 1954), 400–408.

44 David P. Fidler, "Constitutional Outlines of Public Health's 'New World Order,'" *Temple Law Review* 77, no. 2 (2004): 247–289.

45 Rob Stein, "Internal Dissension Grows as CDC Faces Big Threats to Public Health," *Washington Post*, March 6, 2005, at A09.

17

GLOBAL HEALTH AND
FOREIGN POLICY

Harley Feldbaum, Kelley Lee and Joshua Michaud

Source: *Epidemiologic Reviews*, 32:1 (2010), 82–92.

Health has long been intertwined with the foreign policies of states. In recent years, however, global health issues have risen to the highest levels of international politics and have become accepted as legitimate issues in foreign policy. This elevated political priority is in many ways a welcome development for proponents of global health, and it has resulted in increased funding for and attention to select global health issues. However, there has been less examination of the tensions that characterize the relationship between global health and foreign policy and of the potential effects of linking global health efforts with the foreign-policy interests of states. In this paper, the authors review the relationship between global health and foreign policy by examining the roles of health across 4 major components of foreign policy: aid, trade, diplomacy, and national security. For each of these aspects of foreign policy, the authors review current and historical issues and discuss how foreign-policy interests have aided or impeded global health efforts. The increasing relevance of global health to foreign policy holds both opportunities and dangers for global efforts to improve health.

Introduction

Global health issues have long been a concern for foreign-policy-makers. From sanitary cordons instituted to prevent plague from entering Croatia's Dalmatian Coast to the international sanitary conventions, which began in 1851, to the victories over malaria and yellow fever that permitted the construction of the strategic Panama Canal, health and disease have been intertwined with the pursuit of foreign-policy interests. However, over the last 2 decades, globalization has made global health more relevant across multiple aspects of foreign policy than ever before. Fidler calls this a "revolution" in the political status of global health, noting that "nothing in the prior history of national and international efforts on public health compares to the political status public health has reached today" (1, p. 45).

While the global health community has welcomed this elevated political priority, there has been less examination of why states incorporate global health into their foreign-policy agendas or what interests states pursue when they engage on global health issues. These questions, and the broader issue of understanding the relationship between global health and foreign policy, are the subject of this review.

Theoretical perspectives on global health and foreign policy

In an insightful examination of this subject, Fidler (2) suggests 3 possible interpretations of global health's rise onto foreign-policy agendas. The first interpretation argues that global health is an important objective of foreign policy in itself, and that "health has become a preeminent political value for 21st century humanity" (2, p. 183). This perspective concludes that global health can transform the state interests that have historically defined foreign policy. Echoing this position, Kickbusch et al. write that "foreign policy is now being driven substantially by health" (3, p. 971), and Horton suggests that health can move "foreign policy away from a debate about interests to one about global altruism" (4, p. 807).

Fidler's second perspective views global health as "merely a tool, an instrument of statecraft the value of which extends no farther than its utility in serving the material interests and capabilities of the state" (2, p. 185). Far from being transformational, global health is simply another issue that foreign-policy-makers weigh against other state interests. This perspective, based on the realist theory of international relations, explains the recent political prominence of global health as a result of the growing impact of disease upon traditional security concerns: "When diseases threaten, or show the potential to threaten, national security, military capabilities, geopolitical or regional stability, national populations, economic power, and trade interests, foreign policy makers take notice" (2, p. 184).

Fidler's final perspective sees the relationship between global health and foreign policy as an evolving dynamic between foreign-policy imperatives and the science of global health. This perspective does not discount that state interests drive foreign policy, but it recognizes that influence runs both ways, arguing: "Scientific principles . . . channel action on health in specific directions that neither ideology nor power politics can alter" (2, p. 186).

Methods and limitations

In this article, we examine the available literature on global health and foreign policy for evidence supporting 1 or more of these theoretical perspectives. We review published articles organized around 4 key dimensions in the relationship

309

between global health and foreign policy: aid, trade, diplomacy, and national security. Use of these 4 dimensions, modified from Fidler's hierarchy of foreign-policy governance functions (5), enables a detailed study of the relationship between global health and specific areas of foreign-policy practice.

A limitation of this paper is that stringent selection criteria for inclusion of published articles are not useful for addressing such interdisciplinary questions. An understanding of the relationship between global health and foreign policy benefits from examining papers across a broad range of public health, political science, and international relations literature and from incorporating case studies of interactions between global health and foreign policy that are difficult to target with search strategies. We conducted searches in numerous databases (PubMed, MEDLINE, Social Science Citation Index, JSTOR, EconLit, and Science Direct), selecting articles that either directly addressed the relationship between global health and foreign policy or were case studies of an interaction between global health and 1 or more of the 4 dimensions of foreign policy. Thus, this paper is not a comprehensive assessment of every published article related to this subject; rather, we seek to provide a review of key existing literature that illuminates the relationship and tensions between global health and the aid, trade, diplomacy, and national security aspects of foreign policy.

Aid and health

States engage in development assistance (including development assistance for health) for multiple reasons and with differing levels of commitment, but there is typically an explicit or implicit recognition of the value of such assistance to countries' foreign-policy objectives (6, 7). In 1961, when US President John F. Kennedy created the US Agency for International Development, he explicitly acknowledged the US security interest in providing aid to ward off the collapse of developing-country governments, which "would be disastrous to our national security, harmful to our comparative prosperity, and offensive to our conscience" (8). The United States and other countries continue to frame development aid in a foreign-policy context by linking aid to national security and economic interests (9, 10).

The foreign-policy rationale for aid has been clearly reflected in historical trends in development assistance. Since the end of World War II, large donor states have tended to focus bilateral and multilateral aid to support countries judged to be strategically linked to national security and economic interests (11–18). The basic institutional architecture for multilateral development aid—the World Bank, the International Monetary Fund, and the United Nations, along with specialized United Nations agencies such as the World Health Organization (WHO)—were created after World War II with the immediate goal of rebuilding and modernizing war-damaged societies and safeguarding the security of Western powers (19). Between the 1960s and the

1980s, aid from the United States and other Western countries "reflected anti-communist Cold War tensions" and focused on "containing Soviet influence in Latin America, Southeast Asia, and Africa" (20, p. 2). Promises of substantial US aid packages to Egypt and Israel facilitated their signing of the 1978 Camp David peace agreement, and since 1978 these 2 countries have ranked at the top of the list of recipients of US foreign assistance (21, 22). The top 6 recipients of US aid in 2008 were (in descending order) Israel, Afghanistan, Egypt, Jordan, Pakistan, and Iraq, indicating a clear preference for aiding strategically important partners instead of the poorest states (20).

Development assistance for health

Development assistance for health has generally followed the same trends as overall development assistance, but it is worthwhile to note 3 key, recent trends: the dramatic increase in funding, the growing number of actors and institutions, and the overwhelming focus on a single health condition, human immuno-deficiency virus (HIV)/acquired immunodeficiency syndrome (AIDS) (23, 24).

According to 1 estimate, development assistance for health increased 4-fold from 1990 to 2007, from $5.6 billion to $21.8 billion per year, with more than half of this increase coming after 2000 (25). This represents a change from previous decades, which were characterized by low, stagnant levels of health assistance (26). This increasing volume of aid comes from and is funneled through an ever more complex set of actors: In a 2008 article, McColl (27) estimated that there are more than 40 bilateral donors, 26 United Nations agencies, 20 global and regional funding mechanisms, and 90 distinct initiatives involved in development assistance for health.

Efforts to fight HIV/AIDS received most of the increased development assistance for health. International resources for HIV/AIDS grew from a relatively paltry $292 million in 1996 to over $10 billion in 2007, quadrupling from 2001 to 2007 alone (28, 29). While HIV/AIDS support drew just 5% of all development assistance for health in 1998, by 2007 it constituted 47% of all development assistance for health (30). This trend is likely to continue: The Obama administration's proposed global health budget dedicates fully 70% of US official development assistance for health to HIV/AIDS (31). It is worth noting that while the growth in US development assistance for health increased an impressive 208% between 2001 and 2007, it was eclipsed by the growth in aid for government/civil society/democratization efforts (often highly linked to foreign-policy objectives), which grew 260% during the same period (32).

Foreign policy links to development assistance for health trends

Foreign-policy considerations underlie much of the remarkable growth in development assistance for health, from rising concerns about the national security and economic implications of health disparities to the perception of health assistance as an important "soft power" tool, to shifting domestic political perceptions of global health issues (33, 34). In some cases, development assistance for health has been clearly and directly linked to national security. Since 2001, many donors have supported "health security" aid to reduce the threat of natural and intentional outbreaks of infectious diseases (35–37). For example, aid for international influenza surveillance and pandemic planning and response programs was virtually nonexistent prior to the emergence the H5N1 avian influenza virus, but with the growing perception that an influenza pandemic presents a direct security threat (38), more than $2 billion was provided to combat the disease between 2004 and 2008 (39).

Other development assistance for health efforts is linked in a more indirect fashion to foreign policy and national security goals. Iraq, for example, received the greatest share of health-related development assistance of any country in the North Africa/Middle East region during 2002–2004, reflecting US and European interests in using health as part of its effort to foster a stable, pro-Western government there (40). Still other development assistance for health programs has been justified on the basis of the relatively intangible benefits it provides, such as increased goodwill or trust-building. For instance, the US President's Emergency Plan for AIDS Relief has been touted as promoting positive views of the United States on the African continent (41, 42).

Foreign-policy extensions of domestic political priorities have also shaped development assistance for health. Perlman and Roy observed that "the orientation of [development assistance for health] had been heavily influenced by political changes in the United States and Great Britain" (7, p. 14). For example, during the conservative Thatcher (United Kingdom) and Reagan (United States) administrations, funding for family planning and social services was cut sharply to reflect these governments' priorities. The President's Emergency Plan for AIDS Relief, the largest bilateral health aid program ever, had origins rooted in US domestic politics, as President George W. Bush proposed the program partly in response to lobbying from his political base (43).

Foreign policy and development assistance for health

The character and amount of development assistance for health has major implications for the health of populations in poor countries, because external donor support can comprise a large percentage of their health spending (28, 44). This makes development assistance for health that is guided more by donor interests than by scientific evidence or the priorities of recipients a concern for global health proponents (45). While there is some evidence of increasing correlation between development assistance and recipient countries' overall burdens of disease (25), multiple studies demonstrate a continuing and significant disconnect between aid and the burden of health conditions, including maternal mortality (46) and malaria (47), and the disability-adjusted life years measure (48). However, even in cases where development assistance for health has been driven primarily by narrow foreign-policy concerns, health benefits can be realized; for example, US health aid for Egypt, an integral part of US Middle East policy, has helped the country achieve dramatic declines in child mortality (49). Thus, foreign policy's powerful influence on development assistance for health leaves many pressing global health battles underresourced but allows global health efforts that do align with foreign-policy interests to receive significant political support and funding.

Trade and health

The relationship between trade and health forms part of a long history of commercial exchange between human societies, dating from the 19th century BC through the extension of trade to India and China along the Silk Road and the expansion of trade by sea from the 15th century onward (50, 51). As trade has evolved in geographic reach, scale, mode, and type of commodity, so too have the human health implications. Most directly, the coming together of human populations through trade can spread communicable diseases, and commodities exchanged also have the potential to harm (e.g., tobacco) or promote (e.g., fruits and vegetables) health.

Since 1945, the world trading system has expanded rapidly. Built on the General Agreement on Tariffs and Trade (GATT) signed in 1947 and expanded through the creation of the World Trade Organization in 1995, the world trading system has grown from 23 member states to 153. Today, the World Trade Organization oversees the implementation of more than 20 trade agreements covering a vast range of trade matters, including agriculture, trade in services, and trade-related intellectual property rights. There is also a growing number of regional and bilateral trade agreements (52). With this growth has come tensions in the trade-and-health relationship due to frequent conflict between economic interests and global health goals (53). Here, we examine these tensions by reviewing trends in trade in health-related goods and services and the broader effects that traded goods and services can have on health and disease.

Trade of health-related goods and services

Trade in health-related goods, such as pharmaceutical agents, medicinal products, biologic agents, and medical or surgical equipment and appliances, has grown rapidly since the 1990s, notably in the Americas (54). While the GATT sets out rules to facilitate the trade of health-related goods, notably through tariff reductions and nondiscriminatory treatment, health-related goods are recognized as requiring specific provisions given the need for stringent quality standards. Insufficient regulation of blood products, for example, led to the inadvertent trade-facilitated transmission of HIV/AIDS and hepatitis C (55).

Another key issue in the trade of health-related goods is the health impact of standardizing patent rights under the Agreement on Trade-Related Intellectual

Property Rights (TRIPS). Given concerns that patent-protected drugs would be too expensive for the world's poor, the Declaration on the TRIPS Agreement and Public Health (known as the Doha Declaration) affirmed in 2001 the right of World Trade Organization member states to interpret and implement TRIPS in a manner that supports public health and, in particular, access to medicines (as permitted under GATT Article XX[b]) (56). A clarification in 2003 specified when countries can import drugs produced elsewhere under a mechanism known as "compulsory licensing" (57). Despite the World Trade Organization's claim that the Doha Declaration removed the "final patent obstacle to cheap drug imports" (58, p. 1), the limited capacity of developing states to actually implement the available flexibilities, especially given the stricter protections found in many bilateral and regional trade agreements (known as "TRIPS+" measures), demonstrates the power of economic interests over public health considerations (59). The WHO has convened an Intergovernmental Working Group on Public Health, Innovation and Intellectual Property Rights to seek an international agreement to balance innovation and access to medicines, but agreement has remained elusive and negotiations continue (60, 61).

Public health advocates argue that trade in goods with the potential to harm, such as arms, tobacco, and toxic and hazardous waste (known as "public bads"), should be restricted and that such goods should not be included in trade liberalization efforts (62, 63). However, such arguments have been successfully opposed by the industries behind such trade, often with the support of major governments, in order to protect their economic interests.

Countries also increasingly trade in health services, traditionally regarded as nontradable, as a result of advances in information and communication technologies, increased international mobility of service providers and patients, and growing participation by the private sector in health care (64). Under the World Trade Organization's General Agreement on Trade in Services, trade of health services is categorized under 4 modes: cross-border delivery of samples or services, consumption of health services abroad, establishment of health facilities by a foreign-based concern, and movement of health personnel across borders (65, 66). While the extent to which trade occurs varies across these modes, there is a general trend towards increased trade in health services (67, 68). There are potential opportunities arising from such trade, including efficiency, specialization and quality gains, public sector cost savings, expansion of service provision, export revenues and remittances, transfer of technology and skills, and increased patient choice. The risks concern distributive consequences for domestic patients and the possible "brain drain" of health professionals from resource-scarce countries (69).

Health impact of trade policies

There is a broad body of literature on the health effects of trade in non-health-related goods and services. Trade of food has received particular attention, especially with regard to issues such as access to an appropriate quantity (under- and overnutrition) and quality of food, factors that influence eating habits, and broader environmental issues (70). The regulatory framework for trade of food is focused on the World Trade Organization's Agreement on the Application of Sanitary and Phytosanitary Measures and the Codex Alimentarius Commission. Both, along with GATT Article XX(b), are concerned with preventing the spread of food-borne diseases while minimizing the required restrictions on trade, but application of restrictions is often controversial (71). For example, the appropriateness of trade restrictions on beef from countries affected by bovine spongiform encephalopathy, such as the United Kingdom, Canada, and the United States, on the grounds of protecting public health has been subject to ongoing dispute (72). Similar disputes over the public health risks of trade in poultry products (H5N1), apples (due to fire blight), and genetically modified organisms have highlighted the ongoing tensions between promoting trade and protecting health (73).

More broadly, unfair terms of trade and their contribution to health inequalities within and across countries has been the subject of scrutiny. The persistence of trade protectionism by many countries—in the form of agricultural subsidies, for instance—disadvantages low-income countries seeking economic growth through exports (74). Economic pressure and the desire to attract foreign direct investment sometimes engender poor occupational and environmental health regulations (75).

In summary, there has historically been friction between trade and health concerns, implying a need for greater coherence between trade and health policy (76–79). While countries have sometimes restricted trade to prevent the spread of disease, interactions between trade and health have generally been dominated by support for economic interests over health concerns and by a desire to minimize the impact of disease upon trade (80).

Diplomacy and health

Diplomacy is the art and practice of conducting international relations, and it "provides one instrument that international actors use to implement their foreign policy" (81, p. 318). Diplomacy has traditionally focused on dialogue and negotiating alliances, treaties, and other agreements. However, recent usage of the term "health diplomacy" has encompassed not only international agreements on health but also efforts to promote the role of global health in foreign policy, as well as the use of health interventions to support foreign-policy objectives.

International agreements and treaty-making

The origins of modern health diplomacy can be traced to 1851, when the first International Sanitary Conference met to discuss cooperation on cholera, plague, and yellow fever (82). Countries sought to meet after recognizing that the faster movement of people by rail and ship was facilitating the spread of disease and that uncoordinated, sometimes ineffectual, national quarantine policies interrupted trade and were causing discontent among merchants (82). With the founding of the WHO after World War II, prior sanitary agreements were folded into 1 set of regulations, the International Sanitary Conventions (later renamed the International Health Regulations (IHRs)). The new Conventions maintained the spirit of the previous negotiations in attempting to coordinate disease control measures while ensuring the least amount of interference with international trade.

During the final decades of the 20th century, it became clear to many member states that the IHRs were inadequate: The regulations covered only 3 diseases, countries were often noncompliant, and the WHO had limited flexibility to conduct outbreak surveillance and response (83, 84). Even with recognition of these weaknesses, attempted revisions of the IHRs stalled until the 2002–2003 epidemic of severe acute respiratory syndrome (SARS) (83). SARS demonstrated the direct and continuing threat that transnational disease epidemics pose to health and economic interests (85) and generated the political momentum necessary to complete the IHR revision process. In this case, a threat to state foreign-policy interests was critical to advancing diplomacy on global health.

However, in adopting the revised IHRs, countries gave the WHO a novel ability to intrude upon state interests, "privileg[ing] global health governance over state sovereignty" by allowing the use of surveillance reports from nongovernmental organizations and electronic surveillance systems (83, p. 90). Actions taken by certain countries during the SARS epidemic, especially China's attempts to conceal disease information, precipitated these new WHO powers to overcome selfish state interests. Despite this apparent victory of global health over narrow state interests, a number of countries and commentators have argued that the IHRs actually undervalue "equity between developed and developing nations" (86, p. 482) and risk fragmentation of poor countries' health systems and "national health priorities set up by developing countries" (87, p. 13). These objections center on the IHRs' primary focus on disease surveillance, which some argue may be of greater importance to wealthy countries seeking protection from new epidemics than for poor countries with large existing disease burdens (87). Thus, "the WHO's authority in infectious disease control has been strengthened partly because it suited the interests of Western states to allow this to happen" (88, p. 308). Whether the IHRs primarily benefit wealthy states seeking to avoid epidemics or can also address burdens of disease in poorer countries will depend upon the nature of future efforts to build surveillance and response capacity in support of the IHRs.

The second critical diplomatic agreement on health was the Framework Convention on Tobacco Control (FCTC). Approved by the World Health

Assembly in 2003, the FCTC represents the WHO's first-ever use of its authority to create a global health treaty to "reduce the growth and spread of the global tobacco epidemic" (89, p. 936). Unlike the IHRs, negotiation of the FCTC could not rely on the high political priority of such efforts. The WHO's Tobacco Free Initiative group gathered the extensive evidence that linked smoking to lung cancer, as well as studies on the negative economic impact caused by tobacco, which framed the treaty in terms of the economic self-interests of states (90). The WHO also highlighted proven interventions that reduce tobacco consumption and formed a fruitful partnership with an effective coalition of nongovernmental organizations called the Framework Convention Alliance (91).

While promoters of the treaty had ambitious goals and abundant scientific evidence to support stronger tobacco reduction policies, the treaty faced opposition from the governments of the United States, Japan, China, and Germany, all significant tobacco or tobacco-product producers, who succeeded in weakening the final text with flexibilities and optional language. Assunta and Chapman conclude that the "flexibility in the FCTC language offers an ostensible excuse for . . . parties to the Convention to avoid development of robust comprehensive tobacco control policies" (92, p. 755). There is also significant evidence that transnational tobacco companies sought to undermine the negotiations leading to the FCTC (93). Finally ratified in 2005, the FCTC sets out broad obligations for reducing both tobacco demand and tobacco production, but the weakened language of the treaty, continuing opposition from transnational tobacco companies (94), and different levels of commitment mean that enactment of FCTC measures is still highly variable across signatory countries.

As both the IHR and FCTC cases indicate, diplomatic health negotiations —even those viewed as triumphs of global health over foreign policy—are driven by state interests which can either facilitate or undermine global health objectives.

Foreign policy for global health

Spurred by the passage of the IHRs and the FCTC and the increasing political relevance of global health, a number of global health practitioners have advocated for and enacted policies seeking to apply diplomacy in the service of global health aims. The Oslo Ministerial Declaration, advanced by the ministers of foreign affairs of Brazil, France, Indonesia, Norway, Senegal, South Africa, and Thailand in 2006, declares that "health as a foreign policy issue needs a stronger strategic focus on the international agenda" and that these countries have agreed "to make health a point of departure and a defining lens that each of our countries will use to examine key elements of foreign policy and development strategies" (95, p. 1373; 96). Supporting this effort, the Director General of the WHO writes that "we need to embed the use of the health lens in foreign policy while we have this chance" but warns that this relationship requires "careful management for mutual benefit" (97, p. 498). The United Kingdom and Switzerland have enacted national strategies attempting to establish "policy coherence" between their global health and foreign policies (3, p. 971). A number of middle-income countries, including Brazil (98), Thailand (99), and Indonesia (86), also highlight global health in their diplomacy. Finally, Kaufmann and Feldbaum (100) note how diplomacy can be an essential tool for resolving global health crises of political origins, such as the 2003–2004 Nigerian boycott of poliomyelitis vaccine.

The instrumental use of health for foreign policy

Not all diplomacy on health seeks to achieve global health goals, and states are increasingly using health interventions to support ulterior foreign-policy objectives in efforts often termed "health diplomacy." One prominent example is the hospital ship tours of the US Naval Ships *Mercy* and *Comfort*, in which these US military assets deliver health, disaster, and humanitarian assistance to underserved countries. These missions work to improve health but are also driven by training needs and the intent to "win hearts and minds through the use of health interventions" (101, p. 3). Broader US investments in global health are also justified by foreign-policy interests; as a former US Senator stated, "You do not go to war with someone who has saved the life of your child" (42, p. 219). The United States is not alone in using health interventions to serve foreign-policy objectives; the Cuban health diplomacy program (102) and Chinese health cooperation in Africa (103) are other relevant examples. Other related attempts that utilize health as diplomatic outreach have been termed vaccine (104), science (105, 106), and disaster (107, 108) diplomacy. Such efforts have not been without criticism. Ingram observes that such efforts may ultimately be "self-defeating," as "it is precisely the fact that health professionals are not associated with the policies of states that gives them wider credibility" (109, p. 534).

In summary, diplomacy has been used to craft international agreements to improve global health, but state interests have been critical to either the success or obstruction of such agreements. The increasing use of health interventions by states in service of foreign-policy interests also confirms the strong role of such interests in diplomacy on global health, and will present the global health community with ethical and policy challenges.

National security and health

While a number of countries have integrated human security (with its focus on the safety and protection of individuals rather than states) into their foreign policies (110, 111), issues of national security remain atop the foreign-policy hierarchy (112). National security is a "contested concept" (113, p. 254) and has been defined both narrowly as "the study of the threat, use, and control of military force" (114, p. 212) and more broadly as an action or event that "threatens drastically to degrade the quality of life for the inhabitants of a state, or . . . threatens significantly to narrow the range of policy choices available to the government" (115, p. 133). Resistance to broadening the definition of national security to include public health or environmental issues has also been apparent. Deudney argues that "if everything that causes a decline in human well-being is labeled a 'security' threat, the term loses any analytical usefulness and becomes a loose synonym of 'bad'" (116, p. 448).

King writes that "although often characterized as an humanitarian activity, modern public health as practiced in the United States and other Western industrialized nations has long been associated with the needs of national security and international commerce" (117, p. 763). For example, the founding of the London School of Hygiene and Tropical Medicine by Sir Patrick Manson, medical advisor to the Colonial Office (118), was driven by the need to better understand tropical diseases to assure "the health of European soldiers, traders and settlers in hostile climates" (117, p. 765). Similarly, the US successes against malaria and yellow fever, which enabled the building of the Panama Canal, were driven by the desire to control this strategic and economically valuable passage (119, 120).

The close association between public health and national security was broken in the 20th century by decolonization, improved sanitation, and the introduction of vaccines and antibiotics, which together reduced the threat of disease to powerful countries and their interests (121), and by the specter of nuclear weapons, which came to dominate national security studies (114). However, by the 1990s, perceptions of increased vulnerability to infectious disease threats because of increased global interdependence brought infectious diseases back onto national security agendas. This was prominently expressed by the US Institute of Medicine: "[I]n the context of infectious diseases, there is nowhere in the world from which we are remote and no one from whom we are disconnected" (122, p. V).

Acute infectious disease threats and bioterrorism

Acute outbreaks of infectious diseases and the threat of bioterrorism have dominated recent national security discussions of global health, suggesting that global health issues gain political priority when they threaten state interests (33, 123). The SARS and H1N1 influenza A epidemics, the threat of H5N1 influenza A, and, to a lesser extent, the spread of extensively drug-resistant tuberculosis have threatened the citizens and economic interests of powerful countries and have been accepted as national security threats (124). Similarly, increasing knowledge about the extent of existing biological weapons programs (125), the rise of non-state terrorist actors, and the global dissemination of advances in biology (126) have driven many wealthy states to address bioterrorism as a serious threat to national security. The benefits of designating a global health issue a threat to national security include high levels of both political attention and funding (34).

However, the benefits of linking global health to national security have not come without criticism or costs. McInnes and Lee argue that the national security agenda on health has been narrowly framed and "dominated by the concerns of foreign and security policy, not of global public health" (33, p. 22), while Feldbaum et al. caution that the "global and humanitarian objectives of the health field do not fit readily into the state-centered perspective of national security" (127, p. 196). The costs of framing international cooperation on epidemic diseases in security terms are also becoming apparent. "Developing countries are increasingly suspicious of global health initiatives justified on the grounds of 'global health security'" (128, p. 372) because "the harvest of outbreak intelligence overseas is essentially geared to benefit wealthy nations" (87, p. 19). Controversy over sharing of H5N1 influenza A viral samples (86, 129) and within negotiations over the IHRs (87) are examples of developing countries' resistance to the concept of global health security.

The framing of the HIV/AIDS pandemic as a threat to national security, predominantly between 2000 and 2005, also provides insights into the costs and benefits of linking health issues to national security agendas. This linkage, which generated attention from the United Nations Security Council and the United Nations General Assembly, raised the political priority of HIV/AIDS, which contributed to efforts to establish the Global Fund to Fight AIDS, Tuberculosis and Malaria and increased the amount of development assistance for health on global AIDS, particularly in the United States (130, 131). However, much of the evidence used to frame the disease as a national security threat, including evidence on the prevalence of HIV among African militaries (132, 133) and its potential to cause instability in "next wave" states (134, p. 4; 135), has been shown to be inaccurate (136–140). Furthermore, linkage of the disease to national security agendas may have contributed to the possibly disproportionate focus on the pandemic in national aid budgets (141) and has been criticized (142) for its potential to push response to the disease "away from civil society toward state institutions such as the military and the intelligence community" (143, p. 122) or to push funding towards countries of strategic importance, rather than those most in need (127).

Health in conflicts

Health interventions are being used in complex and contradictory ways in conflict situations. The public health community has sought to implement "health as a bridge to peace," claiming that health interventions in "post-conflict societies can be specifically designed in such a way as to simultaneously have a positive effect upon the health of the population and contribute to the creation of a stable and lasting peace" (144, p. 96). Other practitioners have noted that cease-fires arranged for vaccine delivery (145, 146) and cooperative health projects between previously conflicting parties can provide beneficial and neutral forums for conflict resolution (147–150). However, critics say such efforts have "never yielded a tangible peace benefit" (151, p. 222) and have been driven more by "ideology" than evidence of effectiveness (152, p. 1020).

Militaries and nonstate actors alike are using health interventions to serve their political aims in conflict situations. In Iraq and Afghanistan, medical and veterinary civil-assistance programs are run by the US military "for supporting pacification, gathering local intelligence, or rewarding locals for their cooperation" (153, p. 69). On the other side, Burkle reports that the Iraqi insurgents fighting the US military "made controlling hospitals a priority because by owning the health and social services, the control of the people soon followed" (154, p. 31). In these cases, health interventions are not neutral or designed as a bridge to peace but are used to gain the support of, or control over, local populations through the offering or denial of health services.

Tension exists between public health and national security in part because "the landscape of political insecurity is not fully congruent with the landscape of need" (109, p. 539). Prioritization of health issues as national security threats can generate political attention and funding but can also result in actions directed toward addressing national security interests that may or may not coincide with public health needs.

Discussion

Evidence on the linkages between global health, aid, trade, diplomacy, and national security indicates that state action on health is often motivated by foreign-policy interests rather than a desire to promote health equity or achieve humanitarian benefits. These ulterior interests can be economic (protecting trade), diplomatic (preventing epidemics), strategic (preventing bioterrorism), or (often) combinations of these interests and are salient even in this new era of rising development aid for health and ground-breaking global health treaties. Conversely, little evidence supports the notion that "foreign policy is now being substantially driven by health" (3, p. 971). However, global health has affected the practice of foreign policy on occasions when global health and foreign-policy interests align, as the cases of SARS and the IHRs demonstrate.

While foreign-policy interests are likely to continue to determine state engagement on global health issues, self-serving motives for state action on health do not have to lead to poor outcomes, as evidenced by US aid for Egypt's leading to improved child health or the provision of medical relief by the US Naval Ship *Comfort* and Cuban medical professionals after the earthquake in Haiti. Whether we achieve further successes in global health or our efforts are undermined by the pursuit of traditional foreign-policy interests will depend upon the ability of public health practitioners to understand foreign-policy perspectives on health and promote global health interests in the world of high politics.

Acknowledgments

Author affiliations: Global Health and Foreign Policy Initiative, Paul H. Nitze School of Advanced International Studies, Johns Hopkins University, Washington, DC (Harley Feldbaum, Joshua Michaud); and Public and Environmental Health Research Unit, London School of Hygiene and Tropical Medicine, University of London, London, United Kingdom (Kelley Lee).

This paper was supported in part by the Bill and Melinda Gates Foundation (grant 40644) and by the European Commission under the Seventh Research Framework Programme (IDEAS grant 230489 GHG).

The funders played no role in study design, data collection, and analysis, the decision to publish, or preparation of the manuscript.

Conflict of interest: none declared.

Abbreviations

AIDS, acquired immune deficiency syndrome; FCTC, Framework Convention on Tobacco Control; GATT, General Agreement on Tariffs and Trade; HIV, human immunodeficiency virus; IHRs, International Health Regulations; SARS, severe acute respiratory syndrome; TRIPS, Agreement on Trade-Related Intellectual Property Rights; WHO, World Health Organization.

References

1. Fidler D. P. Caught between paradise and power: public health, pathogenic threats, and the axis of illness. *McGeorge Law Rev.* 2004;35(45):45–104.
2. Fidler D. P. Health as foreign policy: between principle and power. *Whitehead J Diplomacy Int Relat.* 2005;6(2):179–194.
3. Kickbusch I., Novotny T. E., Drager N., et al. Global health diplomacy: training across disciplines. *Bull World Health Organ.* 2007;85(12):971–973.
4. Horton R. Health as an instrument of foreign policy. *Lancet.* 2007;369(9564):806–807.
5. Fidler D. P. Health as foreign policy: harnessing globalization for health. *Health Promot Int.* 2006;21(suppl 1):51–58.
6. Lancaster C. *Foreign Aid: Diplomacy, Development, Domestic Politics.* Chicago, IL: University of Chicago Press; 2006.
7. Perlman D., Roy A. Health and development. In: Perlman D., Roy A., eds. *The Practice of International Health: A Case-based Orientation.* New York, NY: Oxford University Press; 2009:9–18.
8. US Agency for International Development. *USAID History.* Washington, DC: US Agency for International Development; 2009. (http://www.usaid.gov/about_usaid/usaidhist.html). (Accessed November 24, 2009).

9. The White House. *The National Security Strategy, March 2006*. Washington, DC: National Security Council; 2006. (http://georgewbush-whitehouse.archives. gov/nsc/nss/2006/). (Accessed November 23, 2009).

10. Alexander D. *Conflict, Fragile States and Security* [speech transcript]. London, United Kingdom: Department for International Development; 2009. (http:// www.dfid.gov.uk/Media-Room/Speeches-and-articles/2009/Conflict-fragile-states-and-security/). (Accessed November 24, 2009).

11. Barnebeck Andersen T., Hansen H., Markussen T. US politics and World Bank IDA-lending. *J Dev Stud*. 2006;42(5):772–794.

12. Alesina A., Dollar D. Who gives foreign aid to whom and why? *J Econ Growth*. 2000;5(1):33–63.

13. Frey B. S., Schneider F. Competing models of international lending activity. *J Dev Econ*. 1986;20(2):225–245.

14. Maizels A., Nissanke M. K. Motivations for aid to developing countries. *World Dev*. 1984;12(9):879–900.

15. Neumayer E. The determinants of aid allocation by regional multilateral development banks and United Nations agencies. *Int Stud Q*. 2003;47(1):101–122.

16. McKinley R. D., Little R. The US aid relationship: a test of the recipient need and the donor interest models. *Polit Stud*. 1979;27(20):236–250.

17. Thacker S. C. The high politics of IMF lending. *World Polit*. 1999;52(1):38–75.

18. Tsoutsoplides C. The determinants of the geographical allocation of EC aid to developing countries. *Appl Econ*. 1991;23(4):647–658.

19. International Development Association. *Aid Architecture: An Overview of the Main Trends in Official Development Assistance Flows. International Development Association Resource Mobilization (FRM), February 2007*. (IDA report no. 15). Washington, DC: International Development Association; 2007. (http://siteresources. worldbank.org/IDA/Resources/Seminar%20PDFs/73449-1172525976405/3492866-1172527584498/Aidarchitecture.pdf). (Accessed November 23, 2009).

20. Congressional Research Service. *Foreign Aid: An Introduction to U.S. Programs and Policy*. (CRS Report for Congress R40213). Washington, DC: US GPO; 2009.

21. Congressional Research Service. *U.S. Foreign Aid to Israel*. (CRS Report for Congress RL33222). Washington, DC: US GPO; 2008.

22. McMahon R. *Transforming U.S. Foreign Aid*. New York, NY: Council on Foreign Relations; 2007. (http://www.cfr.org/publication/13248/transforming_us_foreign_aid.html). (Accessed November 24, 2009).

23. McCoy D., Chand S., Sridhar D. Global health funding: how much, where it comes from and where it goes. *Health Policy Plan*. 2009;24(6):407–417.

24. Global Health Resource Tracking Working Group. *Following the Money: Towards Better Tracking of Global Health Resources*. Washington, DC: Center for Global Development; 2007. (http://www.cgdev.org/content/publications/detail/13711). (Accessed November 8, 2009).

25. Ravishankar N., Gubbins P., Cooley R. J., et al. Financing of global health: tracking development assistance for health from 1990 to 2007. *Lancet*. 2009;373(9681):2113–2124.

26. Organisation for Economic Co-operation and Development. *Measuring Aid to Health*. (OECD-Development Assistance Committee Report). Paris, France: Organisation for Economic Co-operation and Development, 2008. (http://www. oecd.org/dataoecd/20/46/41453717.pdf). (Accessed October 24, 2009).

27. McColl K. Europe told to deliver more aid for health. *Lancet*. 2008;371(9630):2072–2073.

28. Lieberman S., Gottret P., Yeh E., et al. International health financing and the response to AIDS. *J Acquir Immune Defic Syndr*. 2009;52(suppl 1):S38–S44.

29. Levine R., Oomman N. Global HIV/AIDS funding and health systems: searching for the win-win. *J Acquir Immune Defic Syndr*. 2009;52(suppl 1):S3–S5.

30. Shiffman J., Berlan D., Hafner T. Has aid for AIDS raised all health funding boats? *J Acquir Immune Defic Syndr*. 2009;52(suppl 1):S8–S12.

31. Dugger C. W. As donors focus on AIDS, child illnesses languish. *New York Times*. 2009;Oct 30:A10. (http://www.nytimes.com/2009/10/30/world/30child.html). (Accessed November 8, 2009).

32. Kates J., Lief E., Pearson J. *Donor Funding for Health in Low- & Middle-Income Countries, 2001–2007*. Menlo Park, CA: Kaiser Family Foundation; 2009. (http://www.kff.org/globalhealth/upload/7679-03.pdf). (Accessed November 8, 2009).

33. McInnes C., Lee K. Health, security and foreign policy. *Rev Int Stud*. 2006;32:5–23.

34. Katz R., Singer D. A. Health and security in foreign policy. *Bull World Health Organ*. 2007;85(3):233–234.

35. Global Health Security Initiative. *Health Ministers Take Action to Improve Health Security Globally*. Ottawa, Ontario, Canada: Global Health Security Initiative, 2001. (http://www.ghsi.ca/english/staternentOttawaNov2001.asp). (Accessed November 24, 2009).

36. Gannon J. C. *The Global Infectious Disease Threat and Its Implications for the United States*. (National Intelligence Estimate 99-17D). Langley, VA: National Intelligence Council; 2000. (http://www.fas.org/irp/threat/nie99-17d.htm). (Accessed November 24, 2009).

37. Esser D. E. More money, less cure: why global health assistance needs restructuring [electronic article]. Eth Int Aff. 2009;23(3):1. (http://www.cceia.org/resources/journal/23_3/essays/001). (Accessed on November 24, 2009).

38. United Kingdom Cabinet Office. *National Risk Register*. London, United Kingdom: Cabinet Office; 2008. (http://www.cabinetoffice.gov.uk/media/cabinetoffice/corp/assets/publications/reports/national_risk_register/national_risk_register.pdf). (Accessed November 24, 2009).

39. Scoones I., Forster P. *The International Response to Highly Pathogenic Avian Influenza: Science, Policy, and Politics*. (Working Paper 10). Brighton, United Kingdom: STEPS Centre; 2008.

40. Organisation for Economic Co-operation and Development. *Recent Trends in Official Development Assistance to Health*. Paris, France: Organisation for Economic Co-operation and Development; 2007. (http://www.oecd.org/dataoecd/1/11/37461859.pdf). (Accessed November 24, 2009).

41. Gerson M. One tool America needs [editorial]. *Washington Post*. 2007;Aug 1:A17. (http://www.washingtonpost.com/wp-dyn/content/article/2007/07/31/AR2007073101629.html) (Accessed November 24, 2009).

42. Frist W. H. Medicine as a currency for peace through global health diplomacy. *Yale Law Policy Rev*. 2007;26:209–228.

43. Burkhalter H. The politics of AIDS: engaging the conservative activist. *Foreign Aff*. 2004;83(1):8–14.

44. Sridhar D., Khagram S., Pang T. Are existing governance structures equipped to deal with today's global health challenges—towards systematic coherence in scaling up [electronic article]. *Glob Health Gov.* Fall 2008/Spring 2009;II(2):1–25.

45. Schieber G., Fleisher L., Gottret P. Getting real on health financing [electronic article]. *Finance Dev.* 2006;43(4). (http://www.imf.org/external/pubs/ft/fandd/2006/12/schieber.htm). (Accessed October 24, 2009).

46. Powell-Jackson T., Borghi J., Mueller D. H., et al. Countdown to 2015: tracking donor assistance to maternal, newborn, and child health. *Lancet.* 2006;368(9541):1077–1087.

47. Snow R. W., Guerra C. A., Mutheu J. J., et al. International funding for malaria control in relation to populations at risk of stable *Plasmodium falciparum* transmission [electronic article]. *PLoS Med.* 2008;5(7):e142.

48. Institute for Health Metrics and Evaluation. *Financing Global Health 2009: Tracking Development Assistance for Health.* Seattle, WA: Institute for Health Metrics and Evaluation; 2009. (http://www.healthmetricsandevaluation.org/print/reports/2009/financing/financing_global_health_report_overview_IHME_0709.pdf). (Accessed February 16, 2010).

49. Save the Children. *State of the World's Mothers 2007: Saving the Lives of Children Under 5.* Westport, CT: Save the Children; 2007. (http://www.savethechildren.org/jump.jsp?path=/publications/mothers/2007/SOWM-2007-final.pdf). (Accessed November 24, 2009).

50. Irwin D. A. *Against the Tide: An Intellectual History of Free Trade.* Princeton, NJ: Princeton University Press; 1996.

51. Packard R. *The Making of a Tropical Disease: A Short History of Malaria.* Baltimore, MD: Johns Hopkins University Press; 2007.

52. Jackson J. H. *The World Trading System, Law and Policy of International Economic Relations.* 2nd ed. Cambridge, MA: MIT Press; 1997:31–78.

53. Fidler D. P., Drager N., Lee K. Managing the pursuit of health and wealth: the key challenges. *Lancet.* 2009;373(9660):325–331.

54. Pan American Health Organization. *Data Base of Trade in Health Related Goods and Services in the Americas.* Washington, DC: Pan American Health Organization; 2003.

55. Seitz R., Heiden M., Nübling C. M., et al. The harmonization of the regulation of blood products: a European perspective. *Vox Sang.* 2008;94(4):267–276.

56. World Trade Organization. *Ministerial Declaration on the TRIPS Agreement and Public Health. Ministerial Conference, 4th Session, Doha, 9–14 November 2001.* (Publication WT/MIN(01)/DEC/1). Geneva, Switzerland: World Trade Organization; 2001.

57. World Trade Organization. *Implementation of Paragraph 6 of the Doha Declaration on the TRIPS Agreement and Public Health, Decision of 30 August 2003.* (Publication WT/L/540). Geneva, Switzerland: World Trade Organization; 2003.

58. World Trade Organization. *Decision Removes Final Patent Obstacle to Cheap Drug Imports.* (Press release, August 30, 2003). Geneva, Switzerland: World Trade Organization; 2003. (http://www.wto.org/english/news_e/pres03_e/pr350_e.htm) (Accessed November 23, 2009).

59. Bradford Kerry V., Lee K. TRIPS, the Doha declaration and paragraph 6 decision: what are the remaining steps for protecting access to medicines? [electronic article]. *Global Health.* 2007;3:3.

60. United Kingdom Department for International Development. *Increasing People's Access to Essential Medicines in Developing Countries: A Framework for Good Practice in the Pharmaceutical Industry*. London, United Kingdom: Department for International Development; 2005.

61. Higgins M. J., Graham S. J. Intellectual property. Balancing innovation and access: patent challenges tip the scales. *Science*. 2009;326(5951):370–371.

62. Shaffer E. R., Brenner J. E., Houston T. P. International trade agreements: a threat to tobacco control policy. *Tob Control*. 2005;14(suppl 2):ii19–ii25.

63. McKee M. Opium, tobacco and alcohol: the evolving legitimacy of international action. *Clin Med*. 2009;9(4):338–341.

64. Smith R. D. Foreign direct investment and trade in health services: a review of the literature. *Soc Sci Med*. 2004; 54(11):2313–2323.

65. Woodward D. The GATS and trade in health services: implications for health care in developing countries. *Rev Int Polit Econ*. 2005;12(3):511–534.

66. Chanda R. Trade in health services. *Bull World Health Organ*. 2002;80(2):158–163.

67. Adlung R., Carzaniga A. Health services under the General Agreement on Trade in Services. *Bull World Health Organ*. 2001;79(4):352–364.

68. Blouin C., Drager N., Smith R., eds. *International Trade in Health Services and the GATS: Current Issues and Debates*. Washington, DC: World Bank Publications; 2005.

69. Wibulpolprasert S., Pachanee C. A., Pitayarangsarit S., et al. International service trade and its implications for human resources for health: a case study of Thailand [electronic article]. *Hum Resour Health*. 2004;2(1):10.

70. Rayner G., Hawkes C., Lang T., et al. Trade liberalization and the diet transition: a public health response. *Health Promot Int*. 2006;21(suppl 1):67–74.

71. Goodman R. A. *Law in Public Health Practice*. New York, NY: Oxford University Press; 2003.

72. Wigle R., Weerahewa J., Bredahl M., et al. Impacts of BSE on world trade in cattle and beef: implications for the Canadian economy. *Can J Agric Econ*. 2007;55(4):535–549.

73. Zepeda C., Salman M., Ruppanner R. International trade, animal health and veterinary epidemiology: challenges and opportunities. *Prev Vet Med*. 2001;48(4):261–271.

74. Elinder L. S. Obesity, hunger, and agriculture: the damaging role of subsidies. *BMJ*. 2005;331(7528):1333–1336.

75. Shaffer E. R., Waitzkin H., Brenner J., et al. Global trade and public health. *Am J Public Health*. 2005;95(1):23–34.

76. Lee K., Sridhar D., Patel M. Bridging the divide: global governance of trade and health. *Lancet*. 2009;373(9661):416–422.

77. Blouin C., Heymann J., Drager N., eds. *Trade and Health: Towards Common Ground*. Montreal, Quebec, Canada: McGill University Press; 2007.

78. Bettcher D. W., Yach D., Guindon G. E. Global trade and health: key linkages and future challenges. *Bull World Health Organ*. 2000;78(4):521–534.

79. World Health Assembly. WHA59.26. International Trade and Health. In: *Resolutions*. (Resolutions and Decisions of the 59th World Health Assembly). Geneva, Switzerland: World Health Organization; 2006:37–38. (http://apps.who.int/gb/ebwha/pdf_files/WHA59-REC1/e/Resolutions-en.pdf). (Accessed November 23, 2009).

80. Lee K., Koivusalo M. Trade and health: is the health community ready for action? [electronic article]. *PLoS Med*. 2005;2(1):e8.

81. Diplomacy White B. In: Baylis J., Smith S., eds. *The Globalization of World Politics: An Introduction to International Relations.* New York, NY: Oxford University Press; 2001:317–330.

82. Fidler D. P. The globalization of public health: the first 100 years of international health policy. *Bull World Health Organ.* 2001;79(9):842–849.

83. Fidler D. P., Gostin L. O. The new International Health Regulations: an historic development for international law and public health. *J Law Med Ethics.* 2006;34(1):85–94.

84. Baker M. G., Forsyth A. M. The new International Health Regulations: a revolutionary change in global health security. *N Z Med J.* 2007;120(1267):U2872.

85. Keogh-Brown M. R., Smith R. D. The economic impact of SARS: how does the reality match the predictions? *Health Policy.* 2008;88(1):110–120.

86. Sedyaningsih E. R., Isfandari S., Soendoro T., et al. Towards mutual trust, transparency and equity in virus sharing mechanism: the avian influenza case of Indonesia. *Ann Acad Med Singapore.* 2008;37(6):482–488.

87. Calain P. From the field side of the binoculars: a different view on global public health surveillance. *Health Policy Plan.* 2007;22(1):13–20.

88. Davies S. E. Securitizing infectious disease. *Int Aff.* 2008;84(2):295–313.

89. Roemer R., Taylor A., Lariviere J. Origins of the WHO Framework Convention on Tobacco Control. *Am J Public Health.* 2005;95(6):936–938.

90. Peto R., Lopez A. D., Boreham J., et al. Mortality from tobacco in developed countries: indirect estimation from national vital statistics. *Lancet.* 1992;339(8804):1268–1278.

91. Warner K. E. The Framework Convention on Tobacco Control: opportunities and issues. *Salud Publica Mex.* 2008;50(suppl 3):S283–S291.

92. Assunta M., Chapman S. Health treaty dilution: a case study of Japan's influence on the language of the WHO Framework Convention on Tobacco Control. *J Epidemiol Community Health.* 2006;60(9):751–756.

93. Glantz S., Mamudu H. M., Hammond R. Tobacco industry attempts to counter the World Bank report *Curbing the Epidemic* and obstruct the WHO Framework Convention on Tobacco Control. *Soc Sci Med.* 2008;67(11):1690–1699.

94. Nakkash R., Lee K. The tobacco industry's thwarting of marketing restrictions and health warnings in Lebanon. *Tob Control.* 2009;18(4):310–316.

95. Oslo Ministerial Declaration—global health: a pressing foreign policy issue of our time. *Lancet.* 2007;369(9570):1373–1378.

96. United Nations General Assembly. *Resolution Adopted by the General Assembly. 63/33. Global Health and Foreign Policy.* New York, NY: United Nations; 2009. (http://www.who.int/entity/trade/events/UNGA_RESOLUTION_GHFP_63_33.pdf). (Accessed August 2, 2009).

97. Chan M., Støre J. G., Kouchner B. Foreign policy and global public health: working together towards common goals. *Bull World Health Organ.* 2008;86(7):498.

98. Gómez E. J. Brazil's blessing in disguise: how Lula turned an HIV crisis into a geopolitical opportunity. *Foreign Policy.* 2009;Jul 22. (http://www.foreignpolicy.com/articles/2009/07/22/brazils_blessing_in_disguise). (Accessed November 29, 2009).

99. Ford N., Wilson D., Costa Chaves G., et al. Sustaining access to antiretroviral therapy in the less-developed world: lessons from Brazil and Thailand. *AIDS.* 2007;21(suppl 4):S21–S29.

100. Kaufmann J. R., Feldbaum H. Diplomacy and the polio immunization boycott in Northern Nigeria. *Health Aff (Millwood).* 2009;28(4):1091–1101.

101. Vanderwagen W. Health diplomacy: winning hearts and minds through the use of health interventions. *Mil Med.* 2006;171(10 suppl 1):3–4.

102. Feinsilver J. M. Oil-for-doctors: Cuban medical diplomacy gets a little help from a Venezuelan friend. *Nueva Sociedad.* 2008;216:105–122.

103. Youde J. China's health diplomacy in Africa. *China Int J.* 2010;8(1):151–163.

104. Hotez P. Vaccine diplomacy: the multinational effort to eliminate disease might not only save lives but prevent conflict. *Foreign Policy.* 2001;May/Jun:68–69.

105. Fedoroff N. V. Science diplomacy in the 21st century. *Cell.* 2009;136(1):9–11.

106. Lord K. M., Turekian V. C. Science and society. Time for a new era of science diplomacy. *Science.* 2007;315(5813):769–770.

107. Yim E. S., Callaway D. W., Fares S., et al. Disaster diplomacy: current controversies and future prospects. *Prehosp Disaster Med.* 2009;24(4):291–293.

108. Kelman I. Hurricane Katrina disaster diplomacy. *Disasters.* 2007;31(3):288–309.

109. Ingram A. The new geopolitics of disease: between global health and global security. *Geopolitics.* 2005;10(3):522–545.

110. Takemi K., Jimba M., Ishii S., et al. Human security approach for global health. *Lancet.* 2008;372(9632):13–14.

111. King G., Murray C. J. L. Rethinking human security. *Polit Sci Q.* 2001–2002;116(4):585–610.

112. Buzan B., Waever O., de Wilde J. *Security: A New Framework for Analysis.* Boulder, CO: Lynne Rienner Publishers, Inc; 1998.

113. Baylis J. International and global security in the post-Cold War era. In: Baylis J., Smith S., eds. *The Globalization of World Politics: An Introduction to International Relations.* New York, NY: Oxford University Press; 2001:254–276.

114. Walt S. M. The renaissance of security studies. *Int Stud Q.* 1991;35(2):211–239.

115. Ullman R. H. Redefining security. *Int Secur.* 1983;8(1):129–153.

116. Deudney D. The case against linking environmental degradation and national security. *Millenn J Int Stud.* 1990;19(3):461–476.

117. King N. B. Security, disease, commerce: ideologies of post-colonial global health. *Soc Stud Sci.* 2002;35(5–6):763–789.

118. Cook G. C., Webb A. J. The Albert Dock Hospital, London: the original site (in 1899) of tropical medicine as a new discipline. *Acta Trop.* 2001;79(3):249–255.

119. Stern A. M. The Public Health Service in the Panama Canal: a forgotten chapter of U.S. public health. *Public Health Rep.* 2005;120(6):675–679.

120. Christie A. Medical conquest of the "big ditch." *South Med J.* 1978;71(6):717–723.

121. Fidler D. P. The return of 'microbialpolitik.' *Foreign Policy.* 2001;Jan/Feb:80–81.

122. Lederberg J., Shope R. E., Oaks S. C. Jr, eds. *Emerging Infections: Microbial Threats to Health in the United States.* Washington, DC: National Academy Press; 1992.

123. Maclean S. J. Microbes, mad cows and militaries: exploring the links between health and security. *Secur Dialogue.* 2008;39(5):475–494.

124. Monaghan K. *Strategic Implications of Global Health.* (Intelligence Community Assessment 2008-10D). Langley, VA: National Intelligence Council; 2008:56.

125. Henderson D. A. Bioterrorism as a public health threat. *Emerg Infect Dis.* 1998;4(3):488–492.

126. Koblentz G. Pathogens as weapons: the international security implications of biological warfare. *Int Secur.* 2003/04;28(3):84–122.

127. Feldbaum H., Patel P., Sondorp E., et al. Global health and national security: the need for critical engagement. *Med Confl Surviv.* 2006;22(3):192–198.

128. Aldis W. Health security as a public health concept: a critical analysis. *Health Policy Plan.* 2008;23(6):369–375.

129. Garrett L., Fidler D. P. Sharing H5N1 viruses to stop a global influenza pandemic [electronic article]. *PLoS Med.* 2007;4(11):e330.

130. Merson M. H. The HIV-AIDS pandemic at 25—the global response. *N Engl J Med.* 2006;354(23):2414–2417.

131. Morrison J. S. The African pandemic hits Washington. *Wash Q.* 2001;24(1):197–209.

132. United Nations Programme on HIV/AIDS. *AIDS and the Military: UNAIDS Point of View.* Geneva, Switzerland: United Nations Programme on HIV/AIDS; 1998.

133. Singer P. W. AIDS and international security. *Survival.* 2002;44(1):145–158.

134. National Intelligence Council. *The Next Wave of HIV/AIDS: Nigeria, Ethiopia, Russia, India, and China.* Langley, VA: National Intelligence Council; 2002.

135. Eberstadt N. The future of AIDS. *Foreign Aff.* 2002;81(6):22–45.

136. Whiteside A., De Waal A., Gebre-Tensae T. AIDS, security and the military in Africa: a sober appraisal. *Afr Aff.* 2006;105(419):210–218.

137. Chin J., Bennett A. Heterosexual HIV transmission dynamics: implications for prevention and control. *Int J STD AIDS.* 2007;18(8):509–513.

138. Garrett L. *HIV and National Security: Where Are the Links?* New York, NY: Council on Foreign Relations; 2005.

139. Feldbaum H., Lee K., Patel P. The national security implications of HIV/AIDS [electronic article]. *PLoS Med.* 2006;3(6):e171.

140. Mcinnes C. HIV/AIDS and security. *Int Aff.* 2006;82(2):315–326.

141. Shiffman J. Has donor prioritization of HIV/AIDS displaced aid for other health issues? *Health Policy Plan.* 2008;23(2):95–100.

142. Peterson S. Epidemic disease and national security. *Secur Stud.* 2002/3;12(2):43–81.

143. Elbe S. Should HIV/AIDS be securitized? The ethical dilemmas of linking HIV/AIDS and security. *Int Stud Q.* 2006;50(1):121–146.

144. Rushton S., McInnes C. The UK, health and peace-building: the mysterious disappearance of health as a bridge for peace. *Med Confl Surviv.* 2006;22(2):94–109.

145. de Quadros C. A., Epstein D. Health as a bridge for peace: PAHO's experience. *Lancet.* 2002;360(suppl 1):s25–s26.

146. Implementation of health initiatives during a cease-fire—Sudan, 1995. *MMWR Morb Mortal Wkly Rep.* 1995;44(23):433–436.

147. Blum N., Fee E. The St John Eye Hospital: a bridge for peace. *Am J Public Health.* 2009;99(1):32–33.

148. Santa Barbara J. Medicine as a bridge to peace. *Croat Med J.* 2004;45(1):109–110.

149. Sriharan A., Abdeen Z., Bojrab D., et al. Academic medicine as a bridge to peace: building Arab and Israeli cooperation. *Acad Med.* 2009;84(11):1488–1489.

150. Waterston T., Sullivan P., Hamilton P., et al. A health bridge to peace in the Middle East? *Lancet.* 2005;365(9458):473–474.

151. Thieren M. Health and foreign policy in question: the case of humanitarian action. *Bull World Health Organ.* 2007;85(3):218–224.

152. Vass A. Peace through health: this new movement needs evidence, not just ideology [editorial]. *BMJ.* 2001;323(7320):1020.

153. Baker J. Medical diplomacy in full-spectrum operations. *Mil Rev.* 2007;Sep–Oct:67–73.

154. Burkle F. M. Jr. Anatomy of an ambush: security risks facing international humanitarian assistance. *Disasters.* 2005;29(1):26–37.

18

HEALTH, SECURITY AND FOREIGN POLICY

Colin McInnes and Kelley Lee*

Source: *Review of International Studies*, 32:1 (2006), 5–23.

Abstract

Over the past decade, health has become an increasingly important international issue and one which has engaged the attention
of the foreign and security policy community. This article examines the emerging relationship between foreign and security
policy, and global public health. It argues that the agenda has
been dominated by two issues – the spread of selected infectious
diseases (including HIV/AIDS) and bio-terror. It argues that this
is a narrow framing of the agenda which could be broadened
to include a wider range of issues. We offer two examples: health
and internal instability, including the role of health in failing
states and in post-conflict reconstruction; and illicit activities.
We also argue that the relationship between global public health,
and foreign and security policy has prioritised the concerns of
the latter over the former – how selected health issues may
create risks for (inter)national security or economic growth.
Moreover the interests of the West are prominent on this
agenda, focusing (largely though not exclusively) on how health
risks in the developing world might impact upon the West. It
is less concerned with the promotion of global public health.

Health has risen markedly on the international agenda over the past decade.
Key to this increased prominence have been two issues: the emergence and
spread of infectious diseases such as HIV/AIDS, SARS and new drug-resistant
strains of TB; and the risk from biological weapons, especially bio-terrorism.[1]
There is of course nothing new about health as an international issue: infectious
diseases have never recognised state boundaries and systems of international

cooperation attempting to control their spread long pre-date the establishment of the World Health Organisation in 1948.[2] Moreover, there has long been humanitarian concern for international health development through the work of charitable foundations, nongovernmental organisations (NGOs), governments and multilateral organisations. What is different about recent attention to health issues is the apparently successful attempt to move health beyond the social policy and development agenda, into the realms of foreign and security policy.[3] In the United States for example, health issues (and most particularly HIV/AIDS) have been the focus of, or figured prominently in, a variety of foreign policy speeches from key members of the administration.[4] In 1999 the State Department cited the protection of human health as one of its strategic missions,[5] and in its Strategic Plan for Financial Years 2004–9 stated:

> The United States has a direct interest in safeguarding the health of Americans and in preventing the threats posed by diseases worldwide. Epidemic and endemic diseases can undermine economic growth and stability, and threaten the political security of nations, regions and the international community . . . emerging infectious diseases of epidemic or pandemic proportions . . . pose a serious threat to American citizens and the international community.[6]

In the UK, the FCO's 2003 strategy paper raised the spread of disease as an ill-effect of globalisation and a risk to peace and development,[7] although most of the attention to international health issues in Whitehall has traditionally come from the Department for International Development (DfID), whose White Paper on International Development also makes the links between globalisation and poor health.[8] In Australia, communicable disease is raised (albeit briefly) as a global challenge in its 2003 White Paper on foreign and trade policy,[9] while Foreign Minister Downer acknowledged that 'disease and global health issues certainly add to the uncertainty we face in the conduct of our foreign policy'.[10] One of the clearest statements in terms of making the link between health and foreign policy, however, came in the 2002 report of the Romanow Commission on *The Future of Health Care in Canada*. The report was critical that 'the broader area of health promotion is very much an afterthought in Canada's foreign policy' and argued that 'we have an opportunity to ensure that access to health care is not only part of our own domestic policy but also a prime objective of our foreign policy as well'. The report continued that 'Canada's health care system is not immune to international developments' and that Canada should use its international good standing to take a leadership role 'to help improve health and health care around the world'.[11] The recommendations of the Romanow Commission were not much evidenced by the Canadian government's subsequent consultation paper on foreign policy, although health issues did receive greater attention in the summary of responses to the paper.[12] However, Prime Minister Paul Martin supported the inclusion of health in efforts to organise a summit of Group of 20 (G20) leaders to address the global challenges from infectious diseases.

Health concerns are therefore beginning to emerge on the foreign and security policy agenda of Western states, although they have not supplanted more traditional concerns.[13] This policy shift can be most clearly observed in relation to biological weapons, where not only is disease (such as smallpox) considered a potential weapon, but public health systems are seen as part of the defence (even deterrent) against the use of such weapons.[14] More dramatic, however, in terms of global health impact has been the HIV/AIDS pandemic. In a little over two decades, the spread of the disease is such that UNAIDS estimates up to 44 million people are infected and that over 3 million died of AIDS in 2004 alone, of which 510,000 were children.[15] The scale of the catastrophe has, of course, prompted humanitarian concerns; but HIV/AIDS has also begun to be considered within a security context, particularly in relation to national and regional stability. This was highlighted by the 2000 UN Security Council special session on the HIV/AIDS threat to Africa and the subsequent Security Council Resolution 1308 which recognised 'that the HIV/AIDS pandemic, if unchecked, may pose a risk to stability and security'.[16] Concerns raised in the security context include the disproportionate HIV infection rate among security forces, the economic burden caused by the disease, increased social fragmentation, reluctance to send or receive peace-keepers due to the risk of infection, and even its use as a weapon of war, principally through rape.[17]

The spread of acute and potentially epidemic infections from the developing world more generally, including Ebola, West Nile virus and monkeypox, has also heightened concerns within the security community over risks to the health and economic well-being of citizens and communities in Western countries. Although the causal factors for the spread of such diseases are complex, globalisation, including increased population mobility, features prominently. The 2002–03 SARS outbreak is a good example of the extent and speed with which new diseases can spread. The disease began in southern China in November 2002 and began to spread internationally in February 2003. WHO issued global alerts on 12 and 15 March 2003, by which time the disease had already spread from China to Taiwan, Singapore, Vietnam and Canada. By the time the disease came under control in August 2003, 8,422 cases had been identified in 29 countries with 908 fatalities.[18] SARS also highlighted sensitivities to economic effects. Although the number of cases and deaths from the initial SARS outbreak was relatively small in comparison for instance with tuberculosis,[19] for the foreign policy community particular attention was paid to the considerable economic losses caused.[20] One estimate placed the losses at US$100 billion.[21] The macroeconomic effects of disease and poor health had already achieved attention, principally through the

WHO Commission on Macroeconomics and Health,[22] but SARS gave this a public and political prominence previously lacking. SARS also demonstrated how policy responses to emerging and re-emerging infectious diseases (ERIDs) can elicit a 'garrison mentality' in an effort to prevent the spread of infection. Stricter border controls and attempts to regulate migration have been key features in state responses to the spread of infectious disease, potentially disrupting the free movement of goods, people and services.[23]

This article presents two key arguments. First, the manner in which public health issues have begun to appear on foreign and security policy agendas reflects more the concerns of the latter than those of public health. The emphasis to date has been on public health as a foreign policy and security risk, rather than on how foreign and security policy can facilitate or hinder public health. Second, the agenda has been dominated by two issues, the spread of selected acute and potentially epidemic infections and the risk of bio-terror. Yet, from the perspective of seeing health as threats to foreign policy and security, there are other issues which could be of equal concern. This article identifies two such examples – illicit activities and internal state instability. The focus of this article therefore is on the issues which are, or which might appear, on this developing agenda. Our main argument is to critique the narrow framing of the agenda to privilege one set of concerns over another. In the Conclusion, however, we briefly open this up to identify some of the other questions raised by closer cooperation between the two policy communities.

Infectious disease: a new security risk?

Health issues have been creeping up foreign and security policy agendas for some time. Although this movement was accelerated by 9/11 and subsequent concerns over bio-terrorism, its origins lie with the attempt to develop a new security agenda in the aftermath of the Cold War, one focused on novel risks and areas of concern. In this context ERIDs, with their capacity to cross national borders, threaten the well-being of domestic populations, and undermine the economic and military capabilities of states, began to find a place as a security issue. In 2000 for example, the US National Intelligence Council identified a range of risks from the spread of infectious disease, including increased social fragmentation, economic decline, political polarisation and tension leading to the risk of instability.[24] Of particular concern though was HIV/AIDS. By the mid to late 1990s, amid evidence of failure to stem the spread of the disease, HIV/AIDS began to attract the keen attention of the security policy community, prompting US Secretary of State Colin Powell to declare that it 'now represents so great a threat to stability in Africa, Asia and Latin America that it needs to be regarded as a national security issue'.[25] Similarly, Richard Holbrooke, former US ambassador to the UN and Director of the Global Business Council on HIV/AIDS, described the disease as 'a direct threat to social, political and economic stability'.[26]

While HIV/AIDS has received particular focus, other acute infections of potentially epidemic proportions have also received attention. At the 54th World Health Assembly in May 2001, WHO urged member states to participate actively in improving epidemic alert and response measures to ensure 'global health security'.[27] A number of countries have already sought to strengthen disease surveillance and monitoring systems at the national and regional levels. For example, in 2000 the EU published an evaluation of arrangements for managing epidemiological emergencies involving more than one EU member state.[28] In the UK, the Department of Health commissioned an internal study of the public health implications of increased population mobility including infectious disease control.[29] Similar issues were raised in a study funded by The Nuffield Trust to review UK public health measures concerning population mobility and tobacco control in the context of growing transborder health risks.[30] Japan, Australia and the US have all reviewed their policies on border control in light of growing concerns of the perceived risk from certain infectious diseases.[31] In many cases, recommended policy responses have been focused on efforts to moderate perceived risks through control of population flows across borders or increased at-the-border screening. Examples include proposals for mandatory screening of all migrants in the UK for HIV/AIDS and in the US for tuberculosis.[32]

The increased attention to infectious disease as a 'new security risk' has largely been focused on selected infections that have the potential to move from the developing to industrialised world.[33] In 2002–03 SARS joined a list of such diseases which now includes West Nile virus, Ebola and monkeypox. However, by constructing the link between infectious disease and security in this manner, the global health agenda risks becoming inappropriately skewed in favour of the interests of certain populations over others. By any measure, notably data on the Global Burden of Disease, these infections have caused a relatively minor number of cases compared, for example, to diarrhoeal disease. The latter, due overwhelmingly to unsafe water supply, sanitation and hygiene in the developing world, causes 1.8 million deaths each year, with 90 per cent of these deaths being children.[34]

Perhaps ironically, some public health officials have been keen to emphasise the security implications of ERIDs as a means of pushing health higher on policy agendas, both domestically and internationally (including G8 Summits and the World Economic Forum). These initiatives have not always identified the risks involved in a securitising move and the result has been increased concern, not for shifting patterns of health and disease of world populations as a whole, but for selected infections that potentially threaten the privileged few.[35] This risks leading to a fortress mentality which seeks to control the transmission of infectious agents by regulating the flow of certain mobile populations, goods and services. For example, the Institute of Medicine proposed that the US introduce mandatory screening for tuberculosis (TB) of immigrants from high-prevalence countries, a proposal supported by the

Centers for Disease Control and Prevention (CDC). The policy also argued for provision of a permanent residence card (green card) to be linked to the completion of an approved course of preventive treatment.[36] As Coker and van Weezenbeek convincingly demonstrate, not only do such policies have dubious public health benefits (not least because of the number of migrants, legal and illegal, not covered by such a scheme) but it overestimates the risks involved.[37]

The concern over infectious diseases may therefore be understandable from a foreign and security policy perspective since they appear to pose risks to domestic populations, regional stability and economic growth. But this focus is problematic from a global public health perspective. Not only are the broader determinants of health underplayed (including poverty) but, from a global perspective, the health risks to populations in the industrialised world pall in comparison to those elsewhere. Moreover the focus on the spread of infectious disease obscures dangers from non-communicable diseases (including tobacco-related illnesses) which are related to foreign policy through international trade. In short, the attention given to the spread of infectious disease speaks more to the concerns of Western foreign (including economic) and security policy than it does for the concerns of global public health.

Bio-terrorism

In the aftermath of 9/11, much of the attention to the links between health and security policy has been focused on the perceived threats from biological weapons, most worryingly as wielded by terrorist organisations and/or 'rogue states' (what has been termed bio-terrorism).[38] Renewed concerns over biological weapons, however, had begun to emerge in the early to mid 1990s, supported by intelligence reports of a potential proliferation of materials to produce such weapons following the break-up of the Soviet Union.[39] Political and economic instability in the region, accompanied by growing lawlessness and the rise of organised criminal groups, raised fears that materials were being sold to terrorist organisations and 'rogue states' such as Iraq, Iran, Libya, Syria, Cuba, and North Korea.[40] While selective attacks using biological weapons have been carried out in the past, the increased potential for causing harm to mass populations and the relatively low cost of such weapons are believed to make the weapons especially attractive to such groups. The use of biological weapons by Iraq against its Kurdish population in 1988, suspicions that the same government was stockpiling anthrax, botulinum toxin, smallpox and other agents prior to the Gulf War of 1991–92, the attempt by followers of Rajneesh Bhagwan to spread salmonella in the US, and the attack on the Tokyo subway using sarin by the Aum Shinrikyo cult in 1995, all contributed to a heightened sense of awareness that 'non-traditional terrorists' were becoming better organised, some seeking access to biological weapons. Indeed, in an age of 'asymmetric warfare', fears began to be expressed that biological weapons could become a weapon of choice not only for terrorists but for states seeking an edge over the powerful in terms of conventional military weaponry.[41]

Even before 9/11 there was growing discussion between the public health and security communities among the G8 countries of the need to improve preparedness and response measures in the event of a major bio-terrorist attack. Within the public health community, the focus was on enhancing response and recovery from such an event, recognising that 'we will not be able to prevent every act of BW (biological weapon) terrorism'.[42] Indeed, arguing that 'the greatest payoff in fighting BW terrorism lies in improving our response to an incident', much effort was undertaken to anticipate strategic targets, improve surveillance,[43] draft contingency plans[44] stockpile vaccines and treatments, and train and inoculate health personnel.[45] Within the security policy community, efforts were made from 1994 to negotiate a legally binding instrument to strengthen the Biological and Toxin Weapons Convention (BWC) signed in 1972,[46] press rogue states to disarm, and improve intelligence on terrorist organisations.

The anthrax attacks following 9/11 brought into sudden focus the potential risks from terrorists wielding biological weapons. WHO encouraged countries to strengthen regional and global surveillance and response measures through the Global Outbreak Alert and Response Network,[47] and a series of meetings by the Global Health Security Group of the G8, formed in 2001, have been held to discuss global public health security.[48] Not least, in June 2002 US President George W. Bush signed the Public Health Security and Bio-terrorism Bill.[49] There was also a proliferation of public health literature on how to increase domestic measures to protect against, and respond to, various biological weapons. Other issues raised include clinical diagnosis and management,[50] and use of quarantine measures.[51] Diplomatic efforts were also made to achieve a more effective BWC.[52] However, there has been a clear tension between an internationally versus a domestically focused strategy. This is particularly apparent over vaccines. Although anthrax initially occupied popular attention after 9/11, fears of other infectious agents were soon raised. The US government had already ordered 40 million doses of smallpox vaccine in April 2001.[53] Following the anthrax attacks in September 2001, the US stepped up its stockpiling of the smallpox vaccine, joined by other countries including the UK.[54] Given this large scale purchasing, stocks worldwide were soon in short supply. Similarly, worldwide supplies of the antibiotic Cipro used to treat anthrax, rapidly became in short supply. This resulted in foreign policy tensions over hoarding of essential drugs by the US.[55]

The US and other Western states (including the UK,[56] Canada and Australia) have all increased their efforts to improve domestic capacity to respond to public health emergencies caused by bioterrorism.[57] Policy responses in the US have also seen priority given to traditional security measures, notably efforts to shore up 'at the border' controls and improve systems of intelligence intended to prevent a bio-terrorist attack. The focus on improving domestic capacity, however, added to criticism over the US government's decision to pull out of negotiations on the BWC, reinforces the sense that national measures were being prioritised over international cooperation. The public health community, in contrast, has focused on developing effective responses in the likelihood that biological weapons are used. These measures are divided between improving international surveillance and monitoring, and strengthening domestic public health systems. What is clear however is that bio-terrorism's presence on the international agenda is because of the security risk it represents to the West, not because of its significance as a health risk; and that although public health systems have been involved in devising methods to protect against attack, this is within a national security context where national interests are paramount, as seen by the stockpiling of drugs and the prioritising of domestic concerns.

Health, internal instability and failing states

Considerable attention has therefore focused on the links between health and foreign and security policy in the two areas of infectious disease and bio-terror. The attention devoted to these two issues, however, has suggested a rather narrow agenda with only limited points of contact between the policy communities. What we now attempt to do is to demonstrate how the agenda is somewhat broader than this and provide examples of two other policy areas where public health intersects with the foreign and security communities. The first of these is internal instability, where links have been made but not to the same extent or with the same priority as for bio-terrorism and infectious disease; the second, illicit trade, where the links remain relatively under-explored.

The problem of internal instability loomed high on the international agenda for much of the 1990s. A key concern was that internal instability could spill over into the international, threatening regional stability and international trade.[58] But the focus on internal instability and 'failed states' also reflected human rights concerns which transcended traditional ideas of state sovereignty.[59] Although the attention given to these problems has been overtaken by the 'war on terrorism', concern over internal instability and failed states continues. The Bush Administration's 2002 *National Security Strategy*, for example, argued that 'When violence erupts and states falter, the United States will work with friends and partners to alleviate suffering and restore stability', although subsequent paragraphs made clear its concern that such states might be linked with terrorism and that US actions in these circumstances were not necessarily divorced from the war on terror.[60] The UK's 2003 *Defence White Paper* similarly commented that 'Weak and failing states are an increasing problem for the stability of several regions especially on NATO's borders and in Africa', though it too made a link with international terrorism by commenting that such states 'can contain areas of ungoverned territory which provide potential havens and sources of support for terrorist groups'.[61] What is unclear is the extent to which poor health can contribute to internal instability,[62] and whether improved health and better health care provision can stabilise states, particularly in a post-conflict environment.

The argument that poor health can prove destabilising has two parts. The first is that poor health undermines the economic and social structures of the state. Not least, confidence in the state is reduced if it cannot provide a basic level of health care and protection against disease.[63] Poor health provision may contribute to social disorder by highlighting inequalities; but it may also present a government as ineffective regardless of whether it has the resources to deal with vital health issues. Poor health may also contribute to economic decline, fuelling discontent, by: forcing increased government spending on health as a percentage of GDP; reducing productivity due to worker absenteeism and the loss of skilled personnel; reducing investment (internal and external) because of a lack of business confidence; and by raising insurance costs for health provision.[64] The second part of the argument is that the tools of maintaining order, principally the security forces, are particularly vulnerable to sexually transmitted diseases (STDs) including HIV/ AIDS.[65] To what extent this second argument holds for poor health more generally is, however, uncertain. Prima facie it would seem reasonable to expect security forces to receive better health provision in these circumstances, simply because state survival might hinge on this. But the social world is rarely as clear-cut as this and, even when it is, the law of unintended consequences may operate (for example, better health care for security forces may reinforce images of inequality, thus fuelling discontent).

The reverse of the coin is that state failure can lead to deteriorating health through economic weaknesses, the collapse of state institutions including the public health infrastructure, and the breakdown of social order leading to violent conflict. External assistance to secure a failing state may therefore lead to positive health outcomes within that state. Failed states might also have regional health implications. Most obviously internal instability may lead to mass migration (as happened in Rwanda and Kosovo, for example), creating vectors for the spread of infectious disease. The breakdown of law and order may also provide a fertile ground for the development of organised crime leading to an increase in illicit trade, including trafficking in drugs, weapons smuggling and people. All of these may have regional (or even global) health implications. The problem of failed or failing states may have traditionally been seen as a foreign policy problem, but the health implications at a national, regional and global level should not be underestimated.

As an example to demonstrate the relationship between poor health and internal instability we use the results of the CIA's State Failure Task Force.[66] This study identifies three major variables in explaining state failure: (a) quality of life; (b) openness to trade; and (c) level of democracy. Health can contribute, directly and/or indirectly, to all of these. On quality of life, the study argues that the well-known linkage between infant mortality rates and the likelihood of conflict[67] is not a causal relationship; rather, high infant mortality rates indicate a poor quality of life, which in turn is a causal factor. In so doing the study appears to suggest that health is not itself directly a causal factor in state failure, but may be a contributory factor or indeed a reflection of imminent state failure. However, the study does not rigorously examine health in relation to the quality of life as a key variable. The second key variable, openness to trade, can also be affected by health conditions. The US National Intelligence Council for example estimated that infectious diseases would continue to disrupt trade and commerce on a regular basis throughout all regions of the world.[68] Examples of such disruptions include SARS, HIV/AIDS in South Africa, avian influenza in Asia, BSE and vCJD in the UK, plague in India, and cholera in Peru in the early 1990s. All of these threatened trade with and/or investment in states affected. Finally with regard to levels of democracy as a factor in state failure, the link with health is made explicitly in the 2002 US *National Security Strategy*. Here health is seen as part of the 'infrastructure of democracy'. The *Strategy* argues that health aid will only be effective if allied to good governance. The controversial implication of this is that health aid should be linked not to need – reflecting the humanitarian motives supposedly underpinning development aid – but to good governance and democratic reforms.[69] Health aid is therefore politicised in a manner which may disadvantage yet further those at greatest need. But as regards state stability, the assertion is clear: that democracy and good governance allow the effective transmission of aid, relieving health problems, but that corrupt or ineffective governance is wasteful of aid, leading to deteriorating health and increased social dissatisfaction.

The vicious cycle of poor health leading to conflict leading to worsened health may also be reversed. There is a growing body of work on how initiatives to improve health may be used to improve state stability, not least 'health as a bridge to peace' initiatives.[70] Examples include the work of WHO in Bosnia-Herzegovina[71] and in the Maluku Islands in Indonesia.[72] In Bosnia-Herzegovina there is anecdotal evidence that WHO and DfID programmes to rebuild the health system after the conflict assisted in overcoming separatist attitudes, reducing volatility and improving social cohesion. The negotiation of ceasefires to allow the delivery of humanitarian aid and immunisation programmes not only served as a respite from conflict, they acted as a confidence-building measure to allow negotiations for an end to the conflict.[73] On the other hand, WHO has recognised that health interventions which are based purely upon short-term considerations may have no effect upon peace-building, and may even prolong conflict.[74]

Although the idea of health as a bridge to peace is widely associated with WHO, the role of health in conflict prevention has been picked up elsewhere. The Bush administration for example has implicitly identified health as a weapon in the fight against terror.[75] Improved health systems may be used as part of nation-building and to reinforce democratic principles; denying medical aid through sanctions may also put regimes under pressure, forcing change. However both the principles and practice of the Bush administration have been challenged. Health for nation-building has not been particularly evidenced by US policies in Afghanistan and Iraq, while the effectiveness and morality of such sanctions have been questioned.[76] Further, a number have argued that improving health care during a conflict may also be counter-productive on two grounds: it delays reaching the breaking point where one or both sides decide that they must sue for peace; and medical aid may be diverted from civilians to the military, allowing the latter to fight on.[77]

Overall, the idea of health as a bridge for peace has attracted considerable attention. However, there is suspicion among some that it is 'ideology that is driving the movement at present'.[78] Critically, the evidentiary base appears slim and overly reliant on anecdotal evidence rather than rigorous and systematic empirical work.[79] Moreover, there has been little conceptual work done on key questions including: what works and why? What conditions are susceptible to such an approach? What level and form of health investment is required? When might it backfire and allow a conflict to continue? Can it be used to assist in ending conflicts, or just in post-conflict reconstruction? And can it be used to prevent conflict?

Health, globalisation and illicit activities

A second example of how the agenda might be broadened concerns illicit activities. A defining feature of globalisation is the increased flow of human social relations across territorially-based boundaries, notably the state. But alongside legal activities, globalisation has entailed a wide range of illicit activities. Indeed the undermining of the state's ability to control certain types of transborder flows, which circumvent state boundaries, has enabled such activities to flourish. By the mid-1990s organised crime was becoming a global network, with the groups involved closely linked by supply and demand chains beyond the reach of national authorities.[80] It is now estimated that organised crime generates US$750 billion annually, much of it 'washed' by complex financial transactions into the global economy. At least three[81] forms of illicit activity link health, foreign and security policy (see Table 1). First, the trafficking of illicit drugs has become a major challenge for both policy communities. Estimates of the total value of all sales of illicit psychoactive substances range from US$180 bn to US$300 bn. It is estimated that as much as US$122 bn annually is spent in the US and Europe on the three most popular drugs – heroin, cocaine and cannabis. Of this, as much as US$85 bn is laundered or invested in other enterprises, a sum larger than the GNP of three-quarters of the 207 economies in the world.[82] This makes illicit drug trafficking one of the biggest commercial activities in the world and a major source of ill health. Importantly, globalisation has fuelled a

Table 1 The foreign policy and health implications of illicit activities.

Illicit activity	Foreign policy implication	Health implication
Trafficking of illicit drugs	Revenues used to support organised criminal activity, terrorism	Increases and sustains widespread addiction to illicit drugs Increased morbidity and mortality from the use of illicit substances
Smuggling of people	Undermining of immigration policy Destabilisation of local community Financial burden on host country Lucrative source of earnings for organised crime	Health risks to undocumented migrants when being smuggled Increased risk of transmission of STDs from commercial sex workers
Smuggling of goods	Loss of revenue for national economy Revenues used to support organised criminal activity, terrorism	Increases supply of (e.g.) cheaper cigarettes Increases morbidity and mortality from tobacco-related diseases
Illegal weapons sales	Increased availability of weapons among terrorist organisations and civilian populations	Increased risk of injury or death from weapons

restructuring and growth of the illicit drug trade since the 1960s when there occurred a surge in demand in the US and Western Europe. The drug trade has increasingly become a transnational phenomenon, benefiting from global communications, transportation and financial systems (to launder proceeds).

Second, there has been a growing illegal trade in the smuggling and trafficking of people since the end of the Cold War. Definitions of undocumented migration vary and reliable data is difficult to obtain. Yet it is now widely believed that smuggling and trafficking of people is worth an estimated US$6 bn, making it more lucrative than the global trade in illicit weapons. The UN has estimated that four million men, women and children become victims of trafficking each year.[83] Some are captives taken as payment by mercenary armies. Some, especially young girls, are sold by their destitute families. Many are duped into slavery by fraudulent employment brokers who promise legitimate employment. In Europe, for example, there has been a significant increase since the mid-1990s in the trafficking of women from eastern Europe for forced prostitution. The trade is closely linked to organised criminal groups who are experienced at handling illicit drugs, weapons and other contraband.[84] In the US it has recently been estimated that 6 million out of a total 27 million foreign-born residents were believed to be 'illegal aliens', while Moscow is believed to have 400,000 undocumented foreign workers.[85] In the UK, high-profile cases of deaths of undocumented migrants hint at the degree of organised smuggling of migrants currently taking place across the English Channel.[86] The health implications of this growing trade arise from the risks to the health of the illegal migrants themselves, both during transit and at the point of destination where access to health care can be restricted. Illegal migrants may live in impoverished conditions, increasingly the risk of infections such as tuberculosis. They may engage voluntarily or otherwise in commercial sex work which increases the risk of contracting sexually-transmitted diseases. The neglected health needs of this population can, in turn, pose public health risks to the wider host community.[87]

Third, there has been an increase in the smuggling of contraband (including illegal weapons sales), some of which have direct health implications. Not the least of these is tobacco which causes an estimated 4.9 million deaths annually, a figure expected to rise to 10 m by 2030. The transborder problem of cigarette smuggling has become a major problem in the context of the globalisation of the tobacco industry, including a clear shift from traditional markets in North America and Western Europe to the developing world. Smuggling occurs when cigarettes manufactured legally are exported without domestic taxes, for sale abroad. These untaxed cigarettes are then illegally brought back into the producer country to be sold at a cheaper price on the black market. There is growing evidence that transnational tobacco companies are themselves implicated in smuggling operations, resulting in litigation and public investigations in the US, UK, Canada and elsewhere.[88] Smuggling enables tobacco companies to give international brands a local market presence and to undermine efforts by governments to raise cigarette taxes. It is estimated that one-third of the total number of cigarettes consumed worldwide are smuggled.[89] The scale of smuggling operations, the complex transborder networks of supply and distribution that exist, the central role of organised crime in such activities, the laundering of financial proceeds through the global financial system, and difficulties of national authorities in preventing such activities, make tobacco smuggling an issue that defies national boundaries.

The effective control of illicit activities such as these is in the shared interests of the health, foreign policy and security communities (see Table 1). The increased supply of illicit drugs,[90] greater availability of lower-priced (untaxed) cigarettes and alcohol, and public health risks to and from undocumented migrants have clear adverse impacts on health; the challenges of controlling illicit activities have been a long-standing source of foreign policy tensions; and the substantial funds earned from illicit activities have been found to support the activities of known terrorist organisations and organised criminal networks, creating serious security risks. So far such issues have remained outside emerging policy agendas, taxing the multiplicity of government ministries involved to work more closely together across sectors and internationally. Yet, with the continued acceleration of globalisation, it is likely that these issues will increase in significance.

As with health as a bridge to peace, the evidentiary base for understanding the impact of illicit activities on health, foreign policy and security remains slim. This is largely due to the difficulties of obtaining accurate and comprehensive data. Concerns about greater cooperation between the health and intelligence communities can also prevent the development of effective and appropriate policy measures, with medical professionals largely unwilling and unable to play a role in national security or law enforcement (for example, medical staff reporting of undocumented migrants seeking treatment). Nonetheless, there is growing research on health-related illicit activities based on interviews, survey data and documentary sources.[91] More detailed research on what are the trends in illicit activities, what populations are at risk, and how the health and security communities can work more coherently to address shared needs, is urgently needed.

Conclusion

This article has examined the manner in which the public health community has begun to develop a relationship with the foreign and security policy communities. Its focus has been on the issues which have begun to appear on this new agenda, and it has made two key arguments. The first is that the agenda has been dominated by the concerns of foreign and security policy, not of global public health. The relationship between the two policy communities tends to be unidirectional, namely how selected health issues may create risks for (inter)national security or economic growth, and how therefore they might be issues of concern to foreign and security policy. The agenda is not one of how foreign and security policy can promote global public health.[92] Australian Foreign Minister Alexander Downer's 2003 comment that global health could no longer be confined to health ministries, but must also be the concern of foreign ministries, implicitly suggests that what is driving this relationship are foreign policy concerns for protecting the national interest, not a concern for improving global public health.[93] Moreover the interests of the West are prominent on this agenda. Although this is not intended to dismiss humanitarian concerns in the West for health crises elsewhere, particularly HIV/AIDS, attention has generally focused on how health risks in the developing world might impact upon the West.

The second argument is that the agenda to date has been dominated by two issues: infectious diseases (including HIV/AIDS as a special case) and bio-terror. We argue that this is a narrow framing of the agenda and offer two examples of other issues which might be accorded greater attention. The first of these concerns the relationship between health and internal instability. Although this has received some limited attention it has failed to achieve particular prominence. This is despite continuing concerns in both the foreign and especially the security policy communities over internal instability, and the recognition in the public health community that internal instability is often detrimental to public health. The second, illicit activities, has received almost no attention despite very clear shared interests between public health and foreign and security policy on these issues.

This emerging relationship between public health, and foreign and security policy, however, raises a number of other questions beyond simply the manner in which the current agenda is framed. Although these wider questions are not the focus of this article, they are of broader concern to the issues raised here and it would therefore be remiss not to identify them. In particular we would highlight two questions. The first concerns the agenda itself and, in particular, the lack of conceptual clarity over what WHO and others term 'global health security'. The growing awareness of links between the various interested sectors has led to a series of meetings in recent years, regionally and internationally, and from the G8 to more locally based initiatives. These meetings have in turn led to initiatives such as the Global Fund, Millennium Development Goals and FCTC. The existence of some common ground, however, has obscured more fundamental differences stemming from the lack of a shared conceptual understanding of health and security. In particular there is a lack of clarity over two questions crucial to the framing of a future agenda: whose health and whose security is at risk; and what issues should be part of the global health security agenda (and which are not).[94]

Second, there remain unresolved questions over how the two sectors should cooperate and, indeed, whether such cooperation is in their mutual interest. Although some within the public health community have welcomed a closer relationship positively, in that it could give global health issues greater political prominence followed by more action and resources, others view this as problematic because of the skewing of the agenda. This emerging agenda leans inappropriately towards certain issues which, while important to the foreign and security policy communities, are not of highest priority for the public health agenda. Moreover, there are concerns over the role of medical personnel and other health professionals if this link is drawn more tightly. Specifically, could security or other political concerns impinge inappropriately upon the actions of health personnel? The tensions over reporting of undocumented migrants by health personnel is a good example. From the perspective of immigration policy or, given recent anti-terrorism concerns, security or law enforcement, health personnel may be required to report undocumented migrants. However, from a public health perspective, such actions not only politicise the role of health personnel, but are contrary to basic public health principles and good practice. Addressing these questions is beyond the scope of this article. Nevertheless, how they are answered is likely to have an effect upon which issues form part of the emerging agenda and which do not. This article suggests that this agenda so far is narrowly conceived, prioritising the foreign and security policies of Western countries. Without a broader understanding of the shared challenges facing the health, foreign policy and security communities, responses could ultimately be counter-productive to all concerned.

Notes

* This article draws on discussions held at meetings in Australia, Canada, the UK and the US at which the authors were participant observers. These include a Conference on Health as a Foreign Policy Issue held at Ditchley Park, England in March 2002; Symposium on Global Health and Foreign Affairs held by The Nuffield Trust in London in March 2003; a Trilateral Meeting on Global Health and Security hosted by RAND in Washington in April 2003; UK-Australia Seminar on Health and Foreign Policy hosted by the Commonwealth Government of Australia in Canberra in September 2003; Workshop on Rapid Assessment of the Economic Impact of Public Health Emergencies of International Concern held at the University of Toronto in January 2004; and Meeting on HIV/AIDS and Other Infectious Diseases, Project on the G20 Architecture in 2020, Costa Rica, 12–13 November 2004. We are grateful to participants at these meetings although the authors remain wholly responsible for the material in this article. Research for this article was made possible from funding from The Nuffield Trust and The Nuffield Health and Social Services Fund. We would like to thank John Wyn Owen and Alan Ingram for their support and assistance in this work.

1 Arguably a third important area where public health has impacted upon the international agenda has been tobacco control, not least the successful conclusion of the Framework Convention on Tobacco Control (FCTC). Tobacco-related diseases remain the single greatest cause of preventable deaths in the world. Tobacco sales have earned the industry record profits since the 1990s as companies have shifted their attention to the developing world, facilitated by trade liberalisation. The World Health Organisation under Gro Harlem Brundtland campaigned for comprehensive tobacco control measures worldwide, supported by the FCTC. Although the WHO presents this as a successful partnership between the public health and foreign policy communities, as Jeff Collin points out, this smacks somewhat of hagiography. The reality is that the public health community, particularly WHO, initiated and led this international effort. Working with the foreign policy community on tobacco control proved an uphill task at times. Working with them on infectious disease and bio-terror proved much easier. Jeff Collin, 'Tobacco Control', unpublished paper for The Nuffield Trust.

2 The beginnings of sustained international cooperation on health were the International Sanitary Conferences held during the nineteenth century. These originated in concerns over the risk to European states from the transmission of acute and epidemic infectious diseases from outside the continent. Given the potential of such diseases to spread rapidly across national borders and cause high rates of morbidity and mortality, as well as disrupt burgeoning trade routes, international cooperation was pursued to mitigate the risks involved. Institutions such as the Organisation International d'Hygiene Publique (OIHP) were therefore created to build surveillance and reporting systems to support such cooperation.

3 For example, the Millennium Development Goals agreed in 2000 set three out of eight goals, eight of the 18 targets and 18 of the 48 indicators as related directly to health; the UN Security Council session of January 2000 was devoted to the threat in Africa from HIV/AIDS; UN Security Council Resolution 1308 of July 2000 addressed the need to combat the spread of HIV/AIDS during peacekeeping operations; United Nations Special Session on HIV/AIDS held in June 2001 declared the disease a security issue; World Health Assembly Resolution 54.14

adopted in May 2001 on 'Global health security: epidemic alert and response' focused on revision of the International Health Regulations; the G8 Summit held in Genoa in July 2001 agreed the creation of the Global Fund to Fight HIV/AIDS, Tuberculosis and Malaria; and WHO's adoption of the first international health treaty, the Framework Convention on Tobacco Control, in May 2003. The driving force behind this shift originated largely within the public health sector, motivated by a desire to secure greater political attention to global public health needs. Key players included WHO Director-General Gro Harlem Brundtland, President of the US Institute of Medicine Ken Shine, former World Bank economist Jeffrey Sachs, and former US Ambassador to the UN and President of the Global Business Coalition on HIV/AIDS, Richard Holbrooke. The target was both the foreign and security policy communities. From the perspective of public health advocates, differences between the two communities have so far not been deeply explored, and the two are broadly (though not always) seen in the same light. For the purposes of analysing public health engagement with these policy communities, this lack of distinction is taken as given.

4 See for example George W. Bush, 'President speaks on fighting global and domestic HIV/AIDS', 31 January 2003, available at: <http://www.state.gov>, accessed on 16 January 2004; Paula J. Dobriansky, 'The fight against HIV/AIDS' and 'The emerging security threat of HIV/AIDS: Russia' both available at: <http://www.state. gov>, accessed on 16 January 2004; Colin L. Powell, 'Presentation at HIV/AIDS plenary, September 22, 2003', available at: <http://www.state.gov>, accessed on 16 January 2004. In addition, US President Clinton issued a Presidential Decision Directive in 1996 calling for a more focused US policy on infectious diseases; the US House International Relations Committee passed the Global Access to HIV/ AIDS Prevention, Awareness, Education and Treatment Act in June 2001 authorising large increases for international programmes; and US Office of National AIDS Policy shifted its focus from domestic to international efforts in 2001.

5 See State Department, *United States Strategic Plan for International Affairs*, first revision (Washington, DC: Department of State, 1999), pp. 9 and 41.

6 *Strategic Plan Fiscal Years 2004–2009: Security, Democracy, Prosperity* (Washington, DC: US Department of State and US Agency for International Development, 2004), p. 76.

7 Foreign and Commonwealth Office, *UK International Priorities: A Strategy for the FCO, Cmnd 6052* (London: HMSO, 2003), p. 13.

8 Department for International Development, *Eliminating World Poverty: Making Globalisation Work for the Poor* (London: HMSO, 2000), pp. 21 and 34.

9 Department of Foreign Affairs and Trade [Australia], *Advancing the National Interest: Australia's Foreign and Trade White Paper* available at: <http://www/ dfat.gov.au/ani>, accessed on 20 January 2004.

10 Alexander Downer, 'Why Health Matters in Foreign Policy', available at: <http:// www.foreignminister.gov.au/speeches/2003>, accessed on 16 January 2004.

11 Roy J. Romanow, *Building on Values: The Future of Health Care in Canada*, Final Report of Commission on the Future of Health Care in Canada (the Romanow Commission). Available at <http://www.healthcarecommissoin.ca>, accessed on 20 January 2004.

12 Department of Foreign Affairs and International Trade [Canada], *A Dialogue on Foreign Policy* and *A Dialogue on Foreign Policy: Report to Canadians*, both available at: <http://www.foreign-policy-dialogue.ca>, accessed on 20 January 2004.

13 For a fuller discussion on health and foreign policy see Colin McInnes, 'Background paper: health and foreign policy', available at <http://www.nuffieldtrust. org.uk/global_health/pubs.php>, accessed on 13 May 2004.

14 See for example the comments of President George W. Bush in signing the Public Health Security and Bioterrorism Response Act, that 'Protecting our citizens against bioterrorism is an urgent duty of . . . American governments. We must develop the learning, the technology and the health care delivery systems that will allow us to respond to attacks with state of the art medical care throughout our entire country.' 'Transcript: Bush signs bioterror bill', Office of the Press Secretary, The White House, 12 June 2002, available at <http://japan.usembassy.gov/e/p/tp-se1440.html>, accessed on 13 May 2004. See also Elizabeth Prescott, 'SARS: A Warning', *Survival*, 45:3 (2003) pp. 207–26.

15 UNAIDS, *Global Summary of the AIDS Epidemic, December 2004*, p. 1, available at <http://www.unaids.org/wad2004/report_pdf.html>, accessed on 12 May 2005. Due to the social stigma of HIV/AIDS infection in many societies, as well as weaknesses in capacity to collect health information, data on morbidity and mortality remain estimates, although UNAIDS believes that the accuracy of its estimates is improving. See UNAIDS, *AIDS Epidemic Update: December 2003*, p. 1, at <http://www.unaids.org>, accessed on 13 May 2004.

16 The full text of Resolution 1308 is available at <http://www.reliefweb.int>. See also Security Council Press Release SC/7068, 'Examining implications of HIV/AIDS for UN peacekeeping operations', 28 June 2001, available at <http://www.un.org/News/Press/docs/2001/sc7086.doc.htm>, accessed on 13 May 2004. The Security Council session was followed by a special session of the General Assembly on HIV/AIDS in 2001.

17 See for example International Crisis Group, *HIV/AIDS as a Security Issue*, June 2001, available at: <http://www.crisisweb.org>, accessed on 2 February 2002; Stefan Elbe, 'HIV/AIDS and the Changing Landscape of War in Africa', *International Security*, 27:2 (2002), pp. 159–77 and *Strategic Implications of HIV/AIDS*, Adeplhi Paper 357 (Oxford: IISS/OUP, 2003); R. Ostergard, 'Politics in the Hot Zone: AIDS and National Security in Africa', *Third World Quarterly*, 23:2 (2002), p. 342; P. Chalk, 'Infectious Disease and the Threat to National Security', *Jane's Intelligence Review*, September 2001, pp. 48–50. Much of this literature, however, fails to distinguish between HIV infection and AIDS. Soldiers infected by HIV may not see their health (and therefore operational efficiency) affected for a number of years. Indeed AIDS may not appear until they have left the armed forces. Although this may raise issues over the treatment of those infected (especially the cost and the opportunity cost in terms of military budgets), the operational consequences may not be as severe as initially feared.

18 WHO, *Severe Acute Respiratory Syndrome (SARS): Report by the Secretariat*, EB113/33, 27 November 2003 (Geneva: WHO, 2003), p. 1. For details of the geographic spread of cases see WHO, *Summary of Probable SARS Cases with Onset of Illness 2002 to 31 July 2003*, 31 December 2003, available at <http://www.who.int/csr/sars/country/table2004_04_21/en/>, accessed on 13 May 2004. See also Kelley Lee, 'Decision making in the face of public health emergencies of international concern' in R. Smith and N. Drager, *Rapid Assessment of the Economic Impact of Public Health Emergencies of International Concern: The Case of SARS* (Geneva: WHO, in press); and Prescott, pp. 211–3.

19 G. F. Zhou and G. Y. Yan, 'Severe Acute Respiratory Syndrome Epidemic in Asia', *Emerging Infectious Diseases*, 9:12 (2003).

20 For example Downer, 'Why Health Matters in Foreign Policy'.

21 National Intelligence Council, *SARS: Down But Still a Threat*, Intelligence Community Assessment ICA 2003–09 (Washington, DC: National Intelligence Council, 2003).

22 Reports from the Commission and details of its work can be found at its homepage: <http://www.cmhealth.org/cmh_papers&reports.htm>.

23 See, for example, Peter Spiro, 'The Legal Challenges SARS Poses', available at <http://www.cnn.com/2003/LAW/04/29/findlaw.analysis.spiro.sars/>, accessed on 14 May 2004. Concerns over the spread of SARS from Toronto led the United States' Centers for Disease Control and Prevention (CDC) to issue health alerts to travellers, including those from Toronto. CDC, 'Update: Severe Acute Respiratory Syndrome – United States, 2003', available at: <http://www.cdc.gov/mmwr/preview/mmwrhtml/mm5217a4.htm>, accessed on 13 May 2004.

24 US National Intelligence Council, *The Global Infectious Disease Threat and Its Implications for the United States*, National Intelligence Estimate NIE99-17D (2000), available at: <http://www.cia.gov/cia/publications/nie/report/nie99-17d.html>, accessed 5 August 2002.

25 Quoted in J. Gow, 'The HIV/AIDS Epidemic in Africa: Implications for US Policy', *Health Affairs*, 21:3 (2002), p. 57.

26 Quoted in J. Lobe, 'Spread of AIDS Seen as a Security Threat', Third World Network, available at: <http://www.twnside.org.sg/title/threat.htm>, accessed 5 August 2002.

27 World Health Assembly Resolution 54.14, *Global Health Security: Epidemic Alert and Response* (Geneva: WHO, 2001).

28 H. Brand et al., *An Evaluation of the Arrangements for Managing an Epidemiological Emergency Involving More than One EU Member State* (Bielefeld: LOGD, 2000).

29 The report remains unpublished by the UK Department of Health. The UK Conservative Party announced plans to control immigration to prevent the spread of HIV and TB in the run-up to the 2005 General Election. See BBC News, 'Tories plan migrant health checks', <http://news.bbc.co.uk/1/hi/uk_politics/4265461.stm>, accessed on 15 May 2005; and politics.co.uk, 'Conservatives would turn away immigrants with TB', <http://www.politics.co.uk/election-2005/conservatives-would-turn-away-immigrants-with-tb-$13008625.htm>, accessed on 15 May 2005.

30 Jeff Collin and Kelley Lee, *Globalisation and Public Health: A Review and Assessment of Public Health Measures in the UK Concerned with Transborder Health Risks* (London: The Nuffield Trust, 2002).

31 J. Gerard Power and Theresa Byrd, *US-Mexico Border Health: Issues for Regional and Migrant Populations* (London: Sage, 1998). Australia, Department of Immigration and Multicultural and Indigenous Affairs, 'The Health Requirement', Fact Sheet, Canberra, 2004. At the Japan/ASEAN Summit held in November 2001, the Japan-ASEAN Information and Human Network for Infectious Disease Control was formed.

32 Richard Coker and K. Lambregts van Weezenbeek, 'Mandatory Screening and Treatment of Immigrants for Latent Tuberculosis in the USA: Just Resistant?' *The Lancet*, 1 November 2001, pp. 270–6.

33 A crucial report setting this agenda came from the Board on International Health of the US Institute of Medicine. See Institute of Medicine, *America's Vital Interest in Global Health: Protecting Our People, Enhancing our Economy and Advancing our National Interests* (Washington, DC: National Academy Press, 1997). See also for example Jennifer Bower and Peter Chalk, *The Global Threat of New and Reemerging Infectious Diseases: Reconciling US National Security and Public Health Policy* (Santa Monica, CA: RAND, 2003), pp. 61–74. Although the major theme is that disease may spread to the United States and elsewhere in the West, an important sub-theme is of concern that the economic burden of disease elsewhere may harm economic growth globally, thus affecting Western economies. See also A. M. Kimball and K. Taneda, 'Emerging Infections and Global Trade: A New Method for Gauging Impact', paper presented at Workshop on the Rapid Assessment of the

Economic Impacts of Public Health Emergencies of International Concern, University of Toronto, January 2004.

34 WHO, 'Facts and Figures: Water, Sanitation and Hygiene Links to Health', Geneva, 2004. Available at <http://www.who.int/water_sanitation_health/publications/factsfigures04/en/print.html> (accessed 31 March 2005).

35 C. Murray and A. Lopez, *Global Burden of Disease* (Cambridge, MA: Harvard University Press, 1994), and 'Progress and Directions in Refining the Global Burden of Disease Approach: A Response to Williams' Discussion Paper' (Geneva: WHO, 2000).

36 Institute of Medicine, *Ending Neglect: The Elimination of Tuberculosis in the United States* (Washington, DC: Division of Health Promotion and Disease Prevention, 2004).

37 Coker and van Weezenbeek, 'Mandatory Screening and Treatment of Immigrants'.

38 In his 2003 evidence to Congress, for example, the Director of the CIA referred to this as a matter of 'grave concern'. See CIA. 'DCI's Worldwide Threat Briefing: The Worldwide Threat in 2003: Evolving Dangers in a Complex World', 11 February 2003, p. 4, available at: <http://www.cia.gov/public_affairs/speeches/2003/dci_speech_02112003.html>, accessed on 14 May 2004. See also The White House, 'Biodefense for the 21st century', 30 April 2004, available at: <http://www.whitehouse.gov/homeland/20040430.html>, accessed on 14 May 2004. The link between public health and bio-terrorism in the US is apparent, for example, in the 2002 Public Health Security and Bioterrorism Preparedness and Response Act and in the work of the CDC. See CDC *Terrorism and Preparedness and Response Strategy*, version March 2004, available at: <http://www.bt.cdc.gov/planning/tprstrategy/index.asp>, accessed on 14 May 2004. The so-called Bioterrorism Act is available at: <http://www.fda.gov/oc/bioterrorism/PL107–188.pdf>.

39 On the problem of Russian biological weapons 'leakage', see Jonathan Tucker, 'Biological Weapons Proliferation from Russia: How Great a Threat', paper presented at the 7th Carnegie International Non-Proliferation Conference, 11–12 January 1999, Washington DC, available at <http://www.ceip.org/programs/npp/tucker.htm>, accessed on 2 February 2004. See also G. Christopher, T. Cieslak, J. Pavlin and E. Eitzen, 'Biological Warfare: A Historical Perspective', *Journal of the American Medical Association* (hereafter *JAMA*), 278:5 (1997), pp. 412–17.

40 David Fidler, 'Facing the Global Challenges Posed by Biological Weapons', *Microbes and Infection*, 1999:1, pp. 1059–66: D. Leigh, Iraq Stockpiled Anthrax in Run-up to Gulf War', *The Guardian*, 15 October 2001. Evidence has recently emerged that the strain of anthrax found in Iraq – anthrax 14578 – may have originated in US labs. See comments by Senator Riegle, Congressional Record (Senate), 9 February 1994, available at: <http://www.svsu.edu/≈boles/index/iraq/ussuppliesiraqgas.htm>, accessed on 15 May 2005.

41 For example, CIA, 'DCI's Worldwide Threat Briefing', p. 4.

42 J. Simon, 'Biological Terrorism: Preparing to Meet the Threat', *JAMA*, 278:5 (1997), p. 428.

43 R. L. Shapiro, C. Hatheway, J. Becher and D. L. Swerdlow, 'Botulism Surveillance and Emergency Response', *JAMA*, 278:5 (1997), pp. 433–5.

44 J. B. Tucker, 'National Health and Medical Services Response to Incidents of Chemical and Biological Terrorism', *JAMA*, 278:5 (1997), pp. 362–8.

45 D. R. Franz, P. B. Jahrling, A. M. Friedlander et al., 'Clinical Recognition and Management of Patients Exposed to Biological Warfare Agents', *JAMA*, 278:5 (1997), pp. 399–411. On 2 December 2002 the UK government announced its intention to inoculate a limited number of key health personnel with the smallpox vaccine in order to create strategically available emergency health personnel in

the event of a biological attack. See CDR Weekly, *Interim Guidelines for Smallpox Response and Management published by the Department of Health*, 5 December 2002, available at <http://www.hpa.org.uk/cdr/PDFfiles/2002/cdr4902.pdf>, accessed on 15 May 2005.

46 G. Pearson, 'The Complementary Role of Environmental and Security Biological Control Regimes in the 21st Century', *JAMA*, 278:5 (1997), pp. 369–72.

47 WHO, 'Countries Need to Plan Effectively for "Deliberate Infections" – WHO Leader Urges Health Ministers', *WHO Press Release*, 24 September 2001. The Global Outbreak Alert and Response Network is a system of 72 global and regional networks of laboratories, public health experts, and internet-based information systems that continually monitor reports and rumours of disease events around the world. The system is backed by WHO and expertise from more than 250 laboratories, and is linked to the International Health Regulations.

48 See, for example, Health Canada, 'Ministerial Statement', Fourth ministerial meeting on health security and bioterrorism, Berlin, 7 November 2003. Available at <www.hc-sc.gc.ca/english/media/releases/2003/ministerial_statement.htm>.

49 Linda D. Kozaryn, 'Bush Signs Health Security, Bioterrorism Act' American Forces Press Service 13 June 2002, available at: <http://www.defenselink.mil/news/Jun2002/n06132002_200206133.html>, accessed on 14 May 2004. The Bioterrorism Act is available at: <http://www.fda.gov/oc/bioterrorism/PL107–188.pdf>.

50 H. C. Lane and A. Fauci, 'Bioterrorism on the Home Front: A New Challenge for American Medicine', *JAMA*, 286:20 (2001), pp. 2595–7.

51 J. Barbera et al., 'Large-Scale Quarantine Following Biological Terrorism in the United States', *JAMA*, 286:21 (2001), pp. 2711–17.

52 These efforts are detailed on the Biological and Toxic Weapons Convention website at: <http://www.opbw.org/>. See also the resource page on strengthening the BWC held by the Department of Peace Studies, University of Bradford: <http://www.bradford.ac.uk/acad/sbtwc/>.

53 J. Laurance, 'US on Alert for Smallpox Terror Attack', *Independent on Sunday*, 22 April 2001.

54 The UK Department of Health holds pre-11 September stocks for 3 million people which could be diluted to cover 15 million people. J. Meikle, 'Wanted: More Smallpox Vaccine', *The Guardian*, 28 October 2002.

55 K. Singh, 'War Profiteering: Anthrax, Drug Transnationals and TRIPS', paper prepared for the Asia-Europe Dialogue Project (2001), available at <http://www.ased.org>.

56 For example, the UK Public Health Laboratory Service (PHLS), now the Health Protection Agency, issued guidelines for action in the event of an anthrax attack. UK PHLS, *Anthrax: Provisional PHLS Guidelines for Action in the Event of a Deliberate Release* (London: CDSC, 2001).

57 See, for example, information on measures promoted or endorsed by the US Department of Health and Human Services at <http://www.hhs.gov/disasters/index.shtml#bioterrorism>.

58 Typical of this is UK Prime Minister Tony Blair's comment on intervention in Kosovo, that 'We must act . . . to save the stability of the Balkan region, where we know chaos can engulf all of Europe'. Statement by the Prime Minister in the House of Commons, 23 March 1999, available at <http://www.fco.gov.uk/news/newstext.asp?2149> accessed on 20 June 1999.

59 See, in particular, Nicholas J. Wheeler, *Saving Strangers: Humanitarian Intervention in International Society* (Oxford: Oxford University Press, 2000).

60 The White House, *National Security Strategy of the United States*, p. 9. Available at <http://www.whitehouse.gov/nsc/nss.html>, accessed on 16 January 2004.

61 Ministry of Defence, *Delivering Security in a Changing World: Defence White Paper*, Cmnd 6041–I (London: HMSO, 2003), p. 5.

62 Stefan Elbe for example has examined the impact of HIV/AIDS on stability. See his *Strategic Implications of HIV/AIDS*.

63 US National Intelligence Council, *The Global Infectious Disease Threat*.

64 See, for example, ibid. and R. Ostergard, 'Politics in the Hot Zone', p. 344.

65 See, for example, P. Chalk, 'Infectious Disease and the Threat to National Security', p. 49; J. Lobe, 'Spread of AIDS Seen as a Security Threat'.

66 D. C. Esty et al., 'State Failure Task Force Report: Phase II Findings', *Environmental Change and Security Project Report* Issue 5 (1999), available at <http://ecsp-si-edu/pdf/Report5–Sect2.pdf>, accessed 8 August 2002. Other studies of state failure exist which may similarly be used to demonstrate this link; our use of the CIA study is simply to demonstrate the potential links rather than to prioritise one set of findings over another.

67 For example, US National Intelligence Council, *The Global Infectious Disease Threat*.

68 US National Intelligence Council, *The Global Infectious Disease Threat*.

69 *The National Security Strategy of the United States*, pp. 21–3 and especially p. 23.

70 Department of Emergency and Humanitarian Action, *Conflict and Health*, Working Paper (Geneva: WHO, 2000). See also WHO, 'From Health Relief to Health Reconstruction: WHO Brief for Afghan Support Group Meeting, 5–7 December 2001', available at: <http://www.reliefweb.int>, accessed on 5 August 2002.

71 WHO, *Peace through Health: Summary of WHO peace building experiences, principles and strategies in Bosnia and Herzegovina* (WHO/EUR/PAR, November 1999).

72 WHO, 'Peacebuilding through Health', *Health in Emergencies* (8), available at: <http://www.reliefweb.int/w/Rwb.nsf/s/CF7700C552584AE2C12569CF0065A20A>, accessed on 5 August 2002.

73 A. Vass, 'Editorial: Peace through Health', *British Medical Journal*, 323, 3 November 2002, p. 1020; WHO Europe, *WHO/DFID Peace Through Health Programme: A Case Study Prepared by the WHO Field Team in Bosnia and Herzegovina* (Copenhagen: WHO, 1998); Graeme MacQueen and Joanna Santa Barbara, 'Peacebuilding through Health Initiatives', *British Medical Journal*, 321, 29 July 2000, pp. 293–6.

74 A. Manenti, *Health as a Potential Contribution to Peace. Realities from the Field: What WHO has learned in the 1990s* (Geneva: WHO, 2001), p. 1. Available at <http://www.who.int/disasters/hbp/developing/HBP_WHOlearned_1990s.pdf>, accessed 1 November 2004.

75 *The National Security Strategy of the United States*, especially p. 23.

76 R. Horton, 'Public Health: A Neglected Counterterrorist Measure', *The Lancet*, 358 (2001), p. 1112. G. MacQueen, 'Iraq: Harm Reduction through Health', *The Lancet*, 360 (2002), p. 1031.

77 For example, Vass, 'Editorial', p. 1020.

78 Vass, 'Editorial', p. 1020.

79 This point might be made more generally about the links between health and stability. Although there are good reasons to believe that such links might exist, the empirical evidence remains patchy.

80 A good contemporary account is A. Nicaso and L. Lamothe, *Global Mafia: The New World Order of Organized Crime* (Toronto: Macmillan Canada, 1995).

81 Other forms of illicit activity with health implications are arms smuggling, illegal dumping of pollutants such as toxic substances, and the unregulated collection and use of biologicals including organs and blood products.

82 Paul Stares, *Global Habit: The Drug Problem in a Borderless World* (Washington, DC: Brookings Institution, 1996); and UN Office on Drugs and Crime, *Global*

Drugs Report 2000 (New York: United Nations, 2001). See also UN Office on Drugs and Crime, *Drugs and Crime Trends in Europe and Beyond*, 29 April 2004, available at: <http://www.unodc.org/pdf/factsheets/unodc_factsheet_eu_29–04–2004.pdf>, *Global Illicit Drug Trends 2003* available at: <http://www.unodc.org/pdf/trends2003_www_E.pdf>, both accessed on 13 April 2005.

83 Interpol, *People Smuggling: Challenge and Response*, Interpol Fact Sheet (2004), available at <www.interpol.int>.

84 USAID, 'Women as Chattel: The Emerging Global Market in Trafficking', *Gender Matters Quarterly*, 1 February 1999.

85 S. Camarota, *Immigration from Mexico: Assessing the Impact on the United States* (Washington, DC: Center for Immigration Studies, 2001); P. Stalker, *Workers without Frontiers: The Impact of Globalization on International Migration* (Boulder, CO: Lynne Rienner, 2000).

86 Collin and Lee, *Globalisation and Public Health*.

87 While the health risks arising from undocumented migration are real, the authors do not support policy proposals that target all migrants for testing, underpinned by threats of deportation or exclusion. Rather, such measures will discourage at risk populations from identifying themselves, putting the host population at further risk. See Collin and Lee, *Globalisation and Public Health* for a discussion of this issue.

88 F. Abrams, 'Tobacco firm may face inquiry over "smuggling"', *The Guardian*, 17 February 2000; and L. Joosens, *Tobacco Smuggling*, Tobacco Control Factsheets, International Union Against Cancer, 2002, available at <http://factsheets.globalink.org/en/smuggling.html>.

89 P. Jha and F. Chaloupka (eds.), *Tobacco Control in Developing Countries* (Oxford: Oxford University Press, 2000).

90 This includes the illegal production and consumption of narcotics, the growing manufacture and distribution of counterfeit pharmaceuticals, and the poorly regulated use of legal drugs such as their sale on the black market. The latter two raise concerns about the undermining of therapeutic effectiveness of existing drugs, resulting for instance in the spread of drug-resistant infections.

91 See for example Jeff Collin, Eric LeGresley, Ross MacKenzie, Sue Lawrence and Kelley Lee, 'Complicity in Contraband: British American Tobacco and Cigarette Smuggling in Asia', *Tobacco Control*, 2004, 13 (Supp. II): ii 104–ii 111; Joanna Busza, Sarah Castle and Aisse Diarra, 'Trafficking and health', *British Medical Journal*, 328 (2004), pp. 1369–71; and Guilhem Fabre and Michel Schiray, *Globalisation, Drugs and Criminalisation* (Paris: UNESCO, 2002).

92 The notable exception to this is the FCTC, though as noted above this proved an uphill task for the public health community. See Collin and Lee, *Globalisation and Public Health*.

93 Downer, 'Why Health Matters in Foreign Policy'.

94 We attempt to address these questions in Colin McInnes and Kelley Lee, 'Health and Security', *Politik* 8:1 (2005), pp. 33–45.

Part 4

CONFLICTS AND INTERVENTIONS

19

CONFLICT AND HEALTH

Public health and humanitarian interventions:
developing the evidence base

Nicholas Banatvala and Anthony B. Zwi

Source: *British Medical Journal*, 321:7253 (2000), 101–5.

Worldwide, millions of people are annually affected by conflict and over
$2bn was spent on non-food emergency aid each year between 1991 and
1997.[1] Recently, 30 million people were estimated to be internally displaced
and 23 million to be refugees (seeking refuge across international borders),
the vast majority of whom were fleeing conflict zones.[2] More agencies than
ever are working in relief activities; over 200 humanitarian agencies responded
to the Rwandan genocide and population displacement.[3]

Populations affected by armed conflict experience severe public health
consequences as a result of food insecurity, population displacement, the
effects of weapons, and the collapse of basic health services.[4][5] Though most
conflicts after the second world war took place in Africa, the Middle East,
Asia, and Latin America, since the end of the Cold War and break up of
the Soviet Union we have also witnessed conflicts in Europe and the former
Soviet Union, notably in Tajikistan, Chechnya, former Yugoslavia, and
Nagorno-Karabakh.[6] Increasingly, with relatively few exceptions, conflicts
are internal rather than waged between states.

This article argues that the evidence base for humanitarian health interventions should be actively developed and explores mechanisms for its
promotion.

Why is evidence on the agenda?

Current debates regarding evidence based medicine[7][8] and evidence based
policy[9] have permeated all spheres of health care, including those associated
with humanitarian health. Basing policies and practice on the best available
evidence is essential to maximising the value of available resources. Key

355

questions regarding the nature of evidence remain: in addition to evidence of effectiveness and efficiency, evidence related to other dimensions of health interventions, such as their humanity, equity, local ownership, and political and financial feasibility, is important. How these relate to humanitarian principles of independence, impartiality, and neutrality warrants further analysis and debate.

Magnitude of the problem

A wealth of evidence has accumulated over the past 25 years on the massive effect of war on public health.[3][10] Refugees and internally displaced people typically experience high mortality immediately after being displaced[10]; the most common causes of death are diarrhoeal diseases (including cholera and dysentery), measles, acute respiratory infections, and malaria, often exacerbated by malnutrition.[10][11] Morbidity from communicable diseases and psychological distress is common,[12][13] and injuries from firearms, antipersonnel landmines, interpersonal violence, and other causes have not been adequately explored and documented. Disabilities related to injury are likely to require long term health care, and providing such care may be costly.[10][14] Food insecurity, crowding, poor access to water and sanitation, and stress increase susceptibility to illness. The damage and breakdown of infrastructures increases exposure to disease and

---

Summary points

Humanitarian interventions are increasingly complex and are difficult and costly to resource

Research to identify effective and efficient approaches to the delivery of aid warrants additional investment

Data on the public health effects of war and on delivery of public health in settings affected by conflict are increasingly being assembled, but the effectiveness of many humanitarian initiatives has not been adequately evaluated

Evaluation of the effectiveness of intervention in conflict settings needs to make explicit the humanitarian principles on which interventions are based

Generating knowledge and promoting an evidence based culture will require collaborative initiatives between implementing agencies, academics, and donors

Incentives to reward lesson learning and derivation of good practice should be explicitly identified

---

diminishes opportunities for health.[5 15] Recent data on the negative consequences of sanctions and embargoes further illustrate these points.[16] Excess mortality occurs especially in children,[11] and unaccompanied and orphaned children and pregnant women are especially vulnerable to a variety of diseases.[17 18]

Increasing knowledge

Although there is a wealth of technical knowledge on which to base effective programmes, there are many constraints to implementing timely, efficient, and effective relief programmes. Conditions that are common in the area affected by disaster are often exacerbated, and displaced people may introduce novel infections into a host community or may become susceptible to conditions present within the area to which they have fled.[19 20] Lack of resistance to infection, immaturity of the immune system in very young children, and immunosuppression associated with malnutrition make children especially vulnerable. Despite dramatic improvements in emergency relief, the American Public Health Association concluded that "a large body of information documents the inability of the international community to prevent high rates of suffering and death in virtually all refugee situations . . . major failings in logistics, administration and an inability to establish sustainable programs are serious barriers to providing effective emergency relief."[21] These problems can be compounded by reactive and often ineffective practices sometimes carried out by inexperienced field teams.[22 23] In one study, experienced logisticians

---

Findings of the joint evaluation of emergency assistance to Rwanda[3]

- Lack of policy coherence
- Lack of prior investment in disaster preparedness measures
- Lack of humanitarian early warning and contingency planning
- Lack of coordination between UN and humanitarian agencies as well as government teams and military contingents
- Poor quality healthcare delivery from many non-governmental organisations
- Inadequate accountability of agencies and inability of agencies to assess their impact
- Poor security in camps
- Inadequate food distribution practices and poorly coordinated registration of refugees
- Importance of the media in developing the international response
- International community slow to provide compensation to communities negatively affected by the displaced population, and as a consequence the host community resentful of the presence of refugees

---

from a variety of non-governmental organisations, given a hypothetical crisis, were in little agreement about how best to provide essential emergency provisions, such as blankets, water, and fuel: "such a lack of consensus among experienced crises operators is both surprising and of concern."[24] These and other reports suggest that relief programmes tend to be ad hoc and would be more effective if they were based on the most up to date and valid knowledge bases, drew on a cadre of more rigorously trained professionals, and assured earlier and more effective programme planning and coordination.[25]

Accountability

There is increasing recognition that relief efforts must be accountable both to the affected populations (potential "beneficiaries") and to their donors. However, there are often few data regarding how potential recipients value or prioritise the aid response. Clearer conceptualisation of what affected populations seek from the international humanitarian response to their needs would be valuable. The UK Department for International Development has indicated a commitment to promoting good practice in humanitarian relief[26] through support to efforts such as the Sphere Project,[27] which aims to establish minimum standards for good practice in the humanitarian field, and the Ombudsman Project,[28 29] which seeks to develop an accountability structure to ensure that the views of beneficiaries can be heard and that humanitarian agencies are more accountable to the populations they seek to serve. Governments, in turn, must expect to be challenged on their initiatives to reduce or manage conflict, as should donors in relation to their humanitarian and development assistance policies and practices.

Value for money

The large sums of money disbursed in response to complex emergencies, and the high costs of providing health care in these settings, has led to donors' concerns with "value for money." Research to identify more effective and efficient approaches to the delivery of aid should therefore be promoted. Indeed, there has been little study to examine the effect of aid on the duration, magnitude, or outcome of war.

A detailed critique of the international response to the 1994 Rwanda crisis concluded that in the face of massive resources from governments and the general public (in the order of $1.4bn between April and December 1994),[3] several factors, notably an enhanced level of policy coherence (see box), would have increased effectiveness and value for money.[3] There is a dearth of relevant literature on the cost effectiveness of humanitarian interventions, with few exceptions,[30] highlighting a major gap in the existing evidence base.

Risk-benefit

Inappropriate or poor quality health care has serious negative effects: increased morbidity, mortality, and disability; further spread of communicable diseases; emergence of resistant organisms: community dissatisfaction and distress. Individuals may experience considerable personal risk and costs to reach health services; if quality is poor this is a net disbenefit to all involved.

Increasingly, humanitarian aid workers may be targets of violence,[31] and the risks of undertaking operational, evaluation, or research activities merits careful deliberation. While it is difficult to justify operating a programme where the impact is impossible to determine and the project cannot be evaluated, a slavish reliance on quantitative indicators of impact may obscure intended and unintended effects.

Principles of research and evaluation in conflict: generating the evidence

The logistic, safety, and practical difficulties of undertaking research during wars and political violence are considerable.[32] Current data are often lacking and historical data have often been destroyed. There are often additional political and resource constraints on undertaking research. In the relief setting, research on health services and systems, programme operation, and health problems is more feasible and usually more appropriate than intervention and aetiological research. Nevertheless, both observational and intervention research is possible, and careful evaluation of ongoing practice and the lessons learned is valuable; such evaluation has been promoted actively by some organisations.

Priorities for health services and systems research are numerous and include understanding how best to upgrade health services for the host population along-side those available to refugees and how to most humanely and efficiently provide good quality services, and identifying key determinants for inter-agency and intersectoral cooperation and coordination (see box).

Ethics and evidence

People caught up in complex emergencies are often highly vulnerable and may have been severely abused. Though conventions and guidelines have been developed to promote the rights of refugee and internally displaced populations, little specific protection is offered to these populations in relation to participating in research. This is especially important given their lack of power and control over their environment. The key elements of an ethical approach are maximising benefit and minimising harm, obtaining informed consent, ensuring confidentiality, and treating individuals with appropriate clinical care and dignity. Humanitarian agencies and their sponsors will need to adopt explicit principles in relation to research and evaluation activity. The promotion of equitable access to services and ensuring that communities have opportunities to benefit from available interventions should also underlie research undertaken in these complex settings. Recent initiatives to establish ethical guidelines for research related to populations affected by conflict, and to ensure that well established ethical guidelines are applied in these settings (J Leaning, personal communication), deserve support. Mechanisms for ensuring the protection of affected populations in relation to research initiatives, some of which may be sponsored by groups with other agendas (for example, development of new drugs or technologies), warrant attention.

Developing evidence: opportunities for partnership

Improving the evidence base requires partnerships between non-governmental organisations, academic units, United Nations and government agencies, donors, and affected communities. New initiatives in evaluation, and in operational and policy research, require an interdisciplinary, transparent, and process oriented approach. The generation of knowledge and the methods used to undertake research must be relevant and appropriate if research findings and recommendations are to be implemented and a cycle of continuous development of good practice and improved standards is to be sustained.

Research questions in complex emergencies

Nutrition

Food security—evaluate methods for determining food security and needs during different stages of an emergency

Caring capacity—determine the effect of humanitarian relief on the caring capacity of households and communities

Micronutrition—develop practical approaches to preventing micronutrient deficiencies

Feeding programmes—identify the reasons for low coverage of, or ineffective, feeding programmes

Reproductive health and women's hea lth

Violence—determine strategies to prevent and respond to gender based violence

Basic care—identify core aspects of essential obstetrics care

Sexually transmitted infections—develop cost effective strategies to decrease sexually transmitted infections, including HIV, in displaced populations

Reproductive health packages—assess the value and limitations of the package of reproductive health services in emergencies promoted by UNHCR and partners

---

Communicable diseases

Water—determine affordable and efficacious distribution strategies; better determine quality and quantity standards

Cholera—assess research opportunities and feasibility for cholera vaccine

Malaria—undertake research on rapid diagnostic tests and the use of mosquito nets impregnated with insecticide in populations on the move

Acute respiratory infections—improve strategies for case finding and case management

Gender—consider gendered impact of conflict on communicable diseases and on ability to access appropriate services

Health service management

Assessment and resource mobilisation—identify mechanisms to improve the decision making process and the involvement of affected communities

Organisation—develop methods to ensure a rapidly established optimal and coordinated health service

Evaluation and impact—set up approaches for managers to establish or adapt evaluation methods and measures of impact

Information management

Data collection—improve tools for population estimation, such as mapping and satellite photographs

Data analysis and use—develop standardised systems for rapid assessment and surveillance; develop manuals, user friendly software, and practice oriented guidelines

Data interpretation—refine evidence-based standards and guidelines

New technologies—define the role of new technologies in collecting, making available, and reporting information

Mental health

Assessment—develop methods for rapid assessment of health needs and resources required

Service delivery—develop affordable, effective, acceptable, and culturally valid interventions at community level

Violence—determine how to provide appropriate and effective population based care

Ethics

Ethical guidelines to underpin research and response to complex emergencies need to be explicitly stated and debated among displaced populations

(Adapted from WHO[33] and Bok[34])

Improved collaboration between individuals in the field and those in the academic environment can help promote an appropriate blend of operational expertise with the collection, analysis, critical interpretation, and dissemination of data. A 1995 *Lancet* editorial argued that "academics may well be the best people to survey and audit the efforts of humanitarian agencies, mediate their interactions, and help them achieve their common purpose."[35] Whether one agrees or not, it is clear that research institutions could do more by establishing effective partnerships with field-based organisations, and contributing actively to policy formulation, intervention evaluation, good practice dissemination, and training.

Examples of collaborative projects include the Sphere Project, a programme involving a range of non-governmental agencies across the globe in developing and promoting standards of good practice,[27] and the Steering Committee for Humanitarian Response (an alliance of several international humanitarian agencies). Both projects aim to develop minimum standards for the delivery of health care in emergencies. However, setting of standards will not necessarily improve the quality of humanitarian response and the accountability of humanitarian agencies to beneficiaries. Ensuring that donor funding to agencies depends in part on their application of the standards of good practice and includes a publicly stated commitment to critical review of their performance, to making available data and assessments of their activities, and to instituting measures to improve practice may be helpful. However, good practice standards have not yet been adequately tested and validated.

Encouraging evidence based practice

Promoting the uptake of good practice is difficult in the emergency aid sector, which is characterised by rapid staff turnover, the perception that there is little time to learn lessons given that there is always another emergency, and the scarcity of resources available for encouraging evidence based practice.

Traditional methods of continuing professional development through printed media, conferences and workshops, and training courses are of value but have inherent limitations.[36] Electronic technologies, including the new wireless applications, offer unique mechanisms for keeping practitioners informed of developments and debates and may help to ensure that current practice is increasingly based on evidence. The aid community generates valuable evaluations and critiques of current practice, but more can be done to develop effective and efficient means of disseminating and generalising from field experience. Improving opportunities and funding to facilitate linkages of academic institutions and non-governmental organisations and to establish mechanisms for disseminating and debating key findings with relevant stakeholders—donors, host governments, service providers, and, wherever possible, representatives of affected communities—will increase the likelihood of benefits being derived from earlier investments in research and evaluation.

More formal methods of audit and review of relief programmes may help in developing improved standards of care and in documenting successes and failures, in considering the equity implications of interventions, and in deriving good practice. Project management tools such as the logical framework and other related approaches, such as use of agreed measures of effectiveness, could become helpful disaster management tools in complex emergencies.[27 37]

Reporting programme activities and outputs is a basic requirement of donors. Robust evaluation methods can facilitate objective assessment of practice through monitoring indicators of achievement. Donors can encourage good practice not only by determining what has been achieved but by rewarding organisations willing to declare their failures and institute robust corrective measures. Though promoting agency membership of the Code of Conduct for the International Red Cross and Red Crescent Movement and Non-Governmental Organisations[38] is valuable, this alone will not assure good practice. The British government has affirmed its will to seek the best possible assessment of needs and a clear framework of standards and accountability from those delivering aid.[26] Agencies that continually underperform can expect to receive less support from institutional donors; pressure to demonstrate effectiveness and efficiency is increasingly present.

A tension exists between saving lives by instituting short term, resource intensive humanitarian interventions and promoting longer term health and systems development. In some circumstances, short term aid may impede the identification of political solutions or may fuel ongoing conflict. There are also legitimate concerns regarding the extent to which humanitarian assistance bypasses other health service structures, thus undermining them and reducing their longer term sustainability. Finally, evidence is required on how best to combine the essential professionalism required to manage the public health of populations in such complex settings while maintaining the humanitarian ethos.[39] Two of the greatest challenges to humanitarian organisations are to institutionalise a sensitive and inclusive culture informed by evidence and to build sustainable mechanisms of crystallising policy advice from the vast and valuable foundation of field experience.[40]

Competing interests: Both authors have been involved in actively promoting an innovative linkage between the London School of Hygiene and Tropical Medicine and MERLIN.

Notes

1 International Federation of Red Cross and Red Crescent Societies. *World disasters report, 1998*. Geneva: International Federation of Red Cross and Red Crescent Societies, 1999.
2 Reed H., Haaga J., Keely C. The demography of forced migration. Summary of a workshop. Washington, DC: National Academy Press, 1998.
3 Joint Evaluation of Emergency Assistance to Rwanda. *The international response to conflict and genocide: lessons from the Rwanda experience. Study 3: Humanitarian*

Aid and efforts. Odense: Steering Committee of the Joint Evaluation of Emergency Assistance to Rwanda, 1996.

4 Toole M. J., Galson S., Brady W. Are war and public health compatible? *Lancet* 1993;341:1193–6.

5 Zwi A. B., Ugalde A. Towards an epidemiology of political violence in the third world. *Soc Sci Med* 1989;7:633–42.

6 Médecins sans Frontières. *World in crisis. The politics of survival at the end of the twentieth century.* New York: Routledge, 1997.

7 Smith R. The scientific basis of health services. *BMJ* 1995;311:961–2.

8 Dean K., Hunter D. New directions for health: towards a knowledge base for public health action. *Soc Sci Med* 1996;42:745–50.

9 Ham C., Hunter D. J., Robinson R. Evidence based policy making. *BMJ* 1995;310:71–2.

10 Levy B. S., Sidel V. W. *War and public health.* Oxford: Oxford University Press, 1997.

11 Centers for Disease Control and Prevention. Famine-affected, refugee, and displaced populations: recommendations for public health issues. *MMWR Morb Mortal Wkly Rep* 1992;41(RR-13).

12 Ressler E. M., Tortorici J. M., Marcelino A. *Children in war: a guide to the provision of services.* New York: Unicef, 1993.

13 United Nations High Commission for Refugees. *Sexual violence against refugees.* Geneva: UNHCR, 1995.

14 International Committee of the Red Cross. *Mines: a perverse use of technology.* Geneva: International Committee of the Red Cross, 1992.

15 Toole M. J., Waldman R. J. Prevention of excess mortality in refugees and displaced populations in developing countries. *JAMA* 1990;263:3296–302.

16 Garfield R. The impact of economic sanctions on health and well-being. London: Overseas Development Institute, 1999. (Relief and Rehabilitation Network paper No 31.)

17 United Nations High Commission for Refugees. *Refugee children–guidelines on protection and care.* Geneva: UNHCR, 1994.

18 Mears C. *Health care for refugees and displaced people.* Oxford: Oxfam, 1994.

19 Prothero R. M. Forced movements of population and health hazards in tropical Africa. *Int J Epidemiol* 1994;23:657–64.

20 Prothero R. M. Disease and mobility: a neglected factor in epidemiology. *Int J Epidemiol* 1977;6:259–67.

21 American Public Health Association. The health of refugees and displaced persons: a public health priority. *Am J Public Health* 1993;83:463–8.

22 Siddique A. K., Salam A., Islam M. S., Akram K., Majumdar R. N., Zaman K., et al. Why treatment centres failed to prevent cholera deaths among Rwandan refugees in Goma, Zaire. *Lancet* 1995;345:359–61.

23 Vis H. L., Goyens P., Brasseur D. Rwanda: the case for research in developing countries. *Lancet* 1991;344:957.

24 LaMont-Gregory E. Cooking fuel and the Rwanda crisis. *Lancet* 1994;344:546.

25 Siddique A. K. Failure of treatment centres to prevent cholera deaths in Goma. *Lancet* 1995;346:379.

26 Short C. *Principles for a new humanitarianism.* London: Department for International Development, 1998.

27 Steering Committee for Humanitarian Response, InterAction. *The Sphere Project: humanitarian charter and minimum standards in disaster response.* Geneva: Sphere Project, 1998.

28 International Programme Advisory and Development Department BR. World Disasters Forum 1998. *An ombudsman for humanitarian assistance? Report on the proceedings.* London: British Red Cross, 1998.

29 Ombudsman Project Working Group. *An ombudsman for humanitarian assistance?* London: Ombudsman Project Working Group, 1998.

30 Van Damme W., De Brouwere V., Boelaert M., Van Lerberghe W. Effects of a refugee-assistance programme on host population in Guinea as measured by obstetric interventions. *Lancet* 1998;351:1609–13.

31 Talbot D. *Summary report of health, safety and field personnel workshop, 29th January 1998.* London: People in Aid, 1998;

32 Armenian H. K. Perceptions from epidemiologic research in an endemic war. *Soc Sci Med* 1989;28:643–7.

33 Division of Emergency and Humanitarian Action. *Consultation on applied health research in complex emergencies 28–29 October 1997.* Geneva: World Health Organization, 1998.

34 Bok S. The new ethical boundaries. In: Leaning J., ed. *Humanitarian crises. The medical and public health response.* Cambridge, MA: Harvard University Press, 1999:179–94.

35 Humanitarian olympics: Solferino to Goma. *Lancet* 1995;345:529–30.

36 Oxman A. D., Thomson M. A., Davis D. A., Haynes B. No magic bullets: a systematic review of 102 trials of interventions to improve professional practice. *Can Med Assoc J* 1995;153:1423–31.

37 Burkle F. M., McGrady K. A. W., Newett S. L., Nelson J. J., Dworken J. T., Lyerly W. H., et al. Complex humanitarian emergencies: III. Measures of effectiveness. *Prehospital and Disaster Medicine* 1995;10:48–56.

38 International Federation of Red Cross and Red Crescent Societies. *Code of conduct for the International Red Cross and Red Crescent Movement and nongovernmental organisations (NGOs).* Geneva: International Red Cross and Red Crescent Movement, 1996.

39 Slim H. The continuing metamorphosis of the humanitarian practitioner: some new colours for an endangered chameleon. *Disasters* 1995;19:110–26.

40 People in Aid. *Code of best practice in the management and support of aid personnel.* London: Overseas Development Institute, 1998.

20

BALANCING NATIONAL SECURITY WITH HUMAN SECURITY – A CALL FOR COMPREHENSIVE PRE-EVENT PUBLIC HEALTH ANALYSIS OF WAR AND DEFENCE POLICY

John Grundy, Peter Leslie Annear and Seema Mihrshahi

Source: *Journal of Peace, Conflict and Development*, 12 (2008), 17 pp.

Abstract

Concepts of national security and human security can be tenuously balanced in any assessment of the risks and benefits of defence development. In order to ensure an effective balance is maintained in the interests of both human and national security, new paradigms and research agendas for pre-event public health analysis of war and defence policy should be applied. This paper discusses traditional approaches to war and public health, and considers the benefits of a shift in public health focus from post-event emergency relief to pre-event analysis of war and defence policy. Three concepts of public health are applied to the analysis of defence policy – injury epidemiology, public health surveillance and social epidemiology. We conclude that a refocus on pre-event analysis will strengthen the role of public health in contributing to prevention of war and in the reorientation of defence planning towards the protection of human security and not only the state.

Introduction

Deaths rates in war reached unprecedented levels in the 20th century, with the increase in deaths far out of proportion to increases in population. There were twice as many civilian deaths (34 million) as military deaths (17 million) in World War II.[1] A large proportion of these deaths were due to indirect causes related to conflict, including insufficient and unsafe water supplies, non-functional sewerage and restricted electricity supplies, deteriorating health services with insecure access, and the flight of health professionals. In absolute terms, the major causes of mortality during complex emergencies such as war are diarrhoeal diseases, acute respiratory infections, neonatal causes and malaria.[2,3,4] Yet typically it is Ministries of Defence and not Ministries of Health that make assessments (necessarily inadequate) of the likely social and population-health outcomes of war.

Defence ministries document the physical causes of morbidity and mortality in wars, but little or no research or public policy debate is oriented toward reducing the impact of war on civilian populations. Analyses of war and defence policy are typically applied from a national security perspective. In contrast, a human security perspective on war and defence policy is less commonly articulated. Recent attention has been focussed on the concept of 'human security' as a distinct but complementary concept to that of national security. Human security can be defined either as the absence of conflict, or more broadly as encompassing human rights, good governance and access to health and education.[5] Human security thus distinguishes the concerns of individuals and communities from the broader concerns of the state. The objective of this paper is to identify the role of public health in the analysis of pre-event scenarios of conflict. We argue that one of the main reasons for the marginalization of public health in war planning and national security assessments has been the failure to develop effective methods of pre-event analysis which focus on human security, resulting in the inability to adequately forecast the long term impacts of conflict on the health of populations.

The changing nature of war and its impact on population health and development

Historians have highlighted the role of modern technology in reshaping the character of warfare, particularly its changing impact on military personnel and civilians. The increasingly destructive capacity of war-making technology is extending the reach of traditional warfare and the level of destruction caused to the economic and social infrastructure of societies in conflict is increasing. In terms of scope and impact, wars are becoming both more intra-state and more civilian. Between 1946 and 1991, there was a twelve fold increase in the number of civil wars.[6] As societies become more urbanised, distinctions between military targets and civilians have been blurred, leading to the modern phenomenon of the so called 'infrastructure war' where urban power and water systems, as well as civilian populations, are strategic military targets.[7]

As a result the rate of civilian deaths in war increased dramatically throughout the twentieth century. In the First World War, 14% of war deaths were civilians. This increased to 67% in the Second World War.[8] The first Gulf War and its aftermath provide an illustration of the size of the effect of conflict on civilian mortality rates. A comprehensive assessment of the impact of the January–February 1991 Gulf War on mortality rates estimated that there were 111,000 civilian deaths from 'post-war adverse health effects', the largest number of casualties caused by the war.[9] Of these deaths, 70,000 were children under the age of 15. Similarly, a national survey conducted in 2004 following conflict in the Democratic Republic of Congo found that the crude mortality rate of the population was 67% higher than pre-conflict measurements.[10] In Iraq, pre-invasion mortality rates were 5.5 per 1000 people per year (95% CI 4.3–7.1), compared with 13.3 per 1000 people per year in the 40 month post-invasion (95% CI 10.9–16.1). It has been estimated that 654,965 people (or 2.5% of the Iraqi population) died as a consequence of the war.[11]

This changing nature of war has recently generated a literature that investigates and analyses the impact of conflict on population health and development. This collective, preventable violence practiced under the banner of national security produces health effects long after the war has ceased. Mortality rates remain high for many years after conflict has ended. The World Health Organisation Global Burden of Disease Study indicates that war will be the eighth leading cause of death by the year 2020.[12]

UNICEF statistical tables clearly document the impact of conflict on the most vulnerable targets of war, women and children. Of the countries with the ten highest under 5 mortality rates seven (Sierra Leone, Angola, Afghanistan, Liberia, Somalia, Guinea Bissau and the Democratic Republic of Congo) are all conflict or immediate post-conflict societies.[13,14] Women are equally as exposed to risk as children at times of conflict, both directly as victims of war and indirectly as a consequence of the conditions created by war. Women and children comprise up to 80% of refugees worldwide.[15] While the use of female rape as a weapon in war is often hidden, estimates of the number of women raped in the recent Bosnian conflict, where rape was consciously used as an instrument of warfare, range from 10,000 to 60,000. Meanwhile, the destruction of transport systems, communications and hospitals due to conflict, and associated increases in poverty and insecurity, undermine the health referral systems on which women depend for their own and their children's survival.[16] Often, women of child bearing age die in village homes from post-partum bleeding, denied access to essential health care services. In the final period of hostilities against the remnant Khmer Rouge in the mid-1990s in Cambodia, the mortality rate on the battlefield was equalled by the number of deaths of mothers in Cambodian villages from pregnancy related causes.[17]

Current public health approaches to war and defence policy

The escalating rate of civilian casualties in war makes a re-examination of the role of the public health professions and public health in relation to war more urgent. Traditionally, public health has played a significant role in military medicine and refugee health. Most public health planning is concerned with the management of post-event situations, typified by field emergency medicine in conflicts and disease control programs in refugee camps. Until recently, both the pre-event public health surveillance of at-risk populations and conflict decision-making or resolution have generally been considered to be outside the sphere of public health.

There are some signs that the public health community is making progress in contributing to the prevention and minimisation of the effects of war, in particular the role of International Physicians for Prevention of Nuclear War (IPPNW) in advocacy for arms control. UNICEF has taken a lead role in pursuing the protection of children's rights, ending the use of child soldiers and protection of children from landmines. Recent data indicates there has been a decline in armed conflicts around the world by nearly 40% since the 1990s and this decline has been attributed to the extensive efforts of UN agencies and NGOs in conflict prevention and peacemaking activities.[18] *The International Crisis Group* has been established to assist with conflict monitoring.[19] WHO has established a *Health Information Network* for Advanced Planning based in Geneva, with the primary purpose of developing an information system for effective contingency planning for health relief in complex emergencies.[20] *The Sphere project* was launched in 1997 and entailed an extensive and broad-based consultation across the humanitarian community. Those involved were drawn from national and international NGOs, UN agencies and academic institutions. The project was responsible for the development of a Humanitarian Charter and identified Minimum Standards to be attained in disaster assistance in each of five key sectors (water supply and sanitation, nutrition, food aid, shelter and health services). Taken together, the Humanitarian Charter and the Minimum Standards contributed to an operational framework for accountability in disaster assistance efforts.[21]

Despite these initiatives, the public health community remains on the margins of conflict awareness-raising, decision-making and mitigation while political, technocratic, legal and military representatives occupy the centre stage. In fact, the decision to go to war is generally made without any regard for the threat to public health. Human security as a concern of warring states has been relegated to the domain of the post-event response (attempted treatment of mass injury, management of refugees, and long term reconstruction). New methods are needed to provide a role for public health in pre-event prevention or alleviation of the effects of war.

Can public health analysis be used to predict the effects of war and defence policy on populations?

A pre-event public health analysis of war and defence policy should include at least three key approaches based on the paradigms of public health – injury epidemiology, public health surveillance and social epidemiology.

1. Injury epidemiology and collective violence

Injury epidemiologists divide analysis of health outcomes into the temporal domains of pre-event, event, and post-event, and further analyse outcomes according to the exposure variables of host, environment, and vehicle of injury (or type of force). This framework can also be applied conceptually to the analysis of war and defence policy. That is, the scientific methodology used to estimate post-war excess deaths can also be used to inform pre-event conflict analysis in newly emerging conflict zones.

Figure 1 illustrates a proposed conceptual framework of public health analysis of conflict, based on the temporal division of events that is characteristic of the approach of injury epidemiologists.

Currently, most public health interventions in conflict focus on periods B and C (conflict and emergency). Period A (the pre-event early warning) is an area of significantly less focus. Within this framework the main exposure variables – the character of the community hosting the conflict, the elements of the social and political environment that contribute most significantly to the conflict event, and the methods, strategies or vehicles of war employed – are considered. Using these methods both the features of the pre-conflict situation and predicated outcomes of unmitigated conflict can be estimated. A recent study which analysed data from conflicts in Sudan, Somalia, the

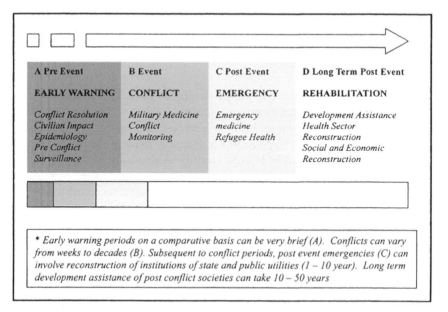

Figure 1 A Conceptual Approach for Public Health Analysis of War and Defence Policy *.

Demographic Republic of Congo and Afghanistan suggested that high rates of civilian mortality are determined more by pre-existing fragility of the effected population than the intensity of the conflict. In many instances a high rate of civilian deaths during conflict shows that international development aid before the conflict was inadequate.[22, 23] Pre-event analysis would allow a longer time frame to prepare plans and interventions that could include conflict resolution, predicting civilian impact, epidemiological assessments on vulnerable populations, mortality and morbidity projections, preventive and preparatory activities for maintenance and restoration of public utilities, and ongoing mechanisms for public health surveillance and response.

2. Public health surveillance and political surveillance

One of the difficulties in conducting accurate public health assessments in pre conflict and conflict situations is the control and manipulation of public information by warring states. In addition, little or no public health information in vulnerable states and conflict situations provides ideal conditions for this information manipulation. Currently, global assessments indicate that there is insufficient available data with which to make accurate pre-event public health estimates. A review of human security in 2005 concluded: 'there is inadequacy of available data [on conflict], especially comparable year on year data that can be used to document and measure national, regional and global trends. In some cases, data are simply non-existent'.[24] Other analysts have observed that, given the enormous cost of military intervention and subsequent rehabilitation of societies and economies, it is surprising there has been so little invested in complex emergency early-warning, detection, preparedness and mitigation projects.[25] Even so, given the significant extent of political surveillance that informs defence policy and notions of national security (protection of the state), an equivalent focus on public health surveillance in the pre-event scenario would provide a more balanced assessment of the potential impact of conflict on human security (the protection of individuals). Similar rigorous and systematic public health techniques to those used in the prevention and control of such social catastrophes as influenza epidemics, TB, HIV/AIDS and tobacco-related disease could be applied to planning for the impact of national and civil conflict. In these cases, public health planners establish criteria for high priority events that include assessments of the frequency, severity, cost, preventability, communicability and public interest of the health events under question. Scientific study in the pre-conflict period could include several themes that are guided by these principles of public health surveillance. Figure 2 outlines potential key analytical questions to be used in association with an analytical framework, along with a proposed research agenda for public health analysis of war and defence policy.

Based on the answers to some of these research questions, the framework shown in Figure 3 outlines a scenario whereby public health and defence

Research Questions for Pre Event Analysis of the Impact of Conflict on Public Health

1. What is the *magnitude* of the population at risk, and the *current distribution and frequency of collective violence* against civilian populations?
2. What are the main *social and demographic characteristics* of populations most at *future risk* from collective violence?
3. What are feasible options for instituting *monitoring systems* to warn and detect of collective violence against civilian populations?
4. What are the main *aetiologies* of conflict?
5. How can conflict strategies be *evaluated*?
6. What is the likely impact of a range of conflict scenarios on the *immediate post conflict situation* in terms of food scarcity, population displacement and destruction of public utilities?
7. Are there case studies that can inform *projections of mortality* and *socio-economic impacts*?
8. Based on historical and social analysis, what are the likely impacts of conflict on longer term *social cohesion* and institutions of state?

A Research Agenda to inform Pre Event Analysis of the Impact of Conflict on Public Health

1. Research and development of a rapid assessment methodology by Ministries of Health, in partnership with Ministries of Defence, of the potential impact of conflict on populations according to a range of conflict scenarios. This could also include the development of guidelines recognised internationally through WHO or other UN agency for MOH country assessments of impact of conflict in populations – short, medium and long term.

Figure 2 Research Questions and a Research Agenda for Guiding Public Health Surveillance of Potential Conflict.

planners can feasibly develop prevention or harm minimization plans and strategies through careful analysis of pre event epidemiological data, social scientific profiles and public health surveillance.

3. Social epidemiology and social pathology

There is an increasing recognition of the social origins of ill-health and of social and economic inequalities in generating conflict. Pathologies derived from conflict logically have their origins in social and political circumstances.

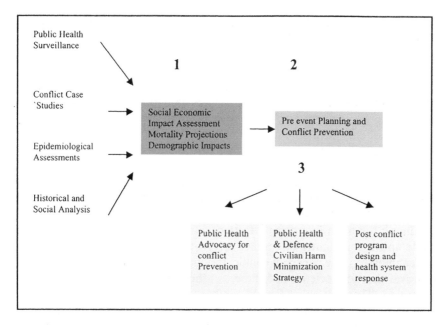

Figure 3 Implementation Framework Based on Public Health Analysis of Early Warning Period.

The public health science of social epidemiology (the analysis of health outcomes based on social exposures such as place and class) can therefore shed some light on our understanding of the impact of conflict on human security. Social epidemiology began with the observation that suicide is not just a characteristic of individuals it is also a characteristic of societies, generating therefore a social rate of suicide.[26] More recent analyses have elucidated concepts of 'unhealthy societies'[27] and 'the social determinants of health'.[28] Social epidemiology thus provides a scientific basis for accurate prediction of the immediate and longer-term health effects of potential conflict. Recent Western defence terminology such as 'regime change', 'surgical strike' and 'pre-emption' are meant to imply that military interventions are time-bound and geographically contained. The use of such terms reflects a lack of aware-ness by political leaders and defence planners of the long term impact of conflict on the health and survival of societies.

The most immediate observation derived from the techniques of social epidemiology is that war is generally inflicted by wealthier societies upon poorer ones. A common characteristic of recent inter-state conflicts has been the unequal technological power of these warring states. The interests of dominant states also prevail frequently in intra-state conflicts in which larger powers have a strategic interest. Between 1946 and 1991, the number of armed conflicts around the world trebled, almost exclusively occurring within economically poor countries. Inequalities are therefore both a cause and an outcome of mass conflict, and the probability of war decreases as national income and state capacity rises.[29]

Perhaps the concept most pertinent to a new concept of public health conflict analysis is that of social capital, which is often defined as the level of trust and cohesion in communities, and has been identified in a wide body of research to be strongly associated with positive health outcomes.[30,31] War destroys not only infrastructure and physical capital (which itself has adverse health effects as already seen) but it also destroys social capital – the essential ingredient for the maintenance and development of communities, social institutions, human security and the state. Notably absent in pre-event defence assessments of conflict is any sense of the likely impact of conflict on the immediate destruction and the longer-term erosion of social capital.

Among the main long-term effects of conflict is the creation of societies made up predominantly of conflict survivors, as in Cambodia or Rwanda. In her analysis of the impact of conflict trauma on its survivors, Judith Herman observes that for societies like these '... there is only one story – the story of atrocity. There are only a limited number of roles. One can be a perpetrator, a passive witness, an ally, or a rescuer. Every new or old relationship is approached with an implicit question: Which side are you on?'[32] Under such conditions the re-development of social capital is long delayed. In some cases, the ongoing prevalence of social trauma from conflict may mean that the process of social rehabilitation becomes inter-generational. Thirty-seven years after the end of the genocidal Pol Pot regime, the Cambodian state and society is still undergoing economic, political and social re-construction. Even today, half the national budget is internationally funded, and until very recently infant and maternal mortality rates were among the highest in the region.[33]

The inclusion of broader sociological and historical analysis into epidemiological assessments of conflict and conflict prevention will position public health planners more strongly to make meaningful projections of the impact of conflict on populations over the immediate and longer term. Combining the skills and perspectives of injury epidemiology (population health), public health surveillance and social epidemiology (social health) will lead to a more critical understanding of the health status of populations threatened by or exposed to episodes of collective violence.

Conclusion: balancing national security and human security in war and defence policy development

Recent assessments that 'lack of post conflict planning' in states such as Timor Leste and Iraq has been a major contributing factor to the current social collapse and turmoil in those countries increases the need for more rigorous pre event public health and social analysis of conflict zones. In depth case studies of these recent conflicts areas and planning failures are required, in order to refine and develop the pre event methodological approaches to conflict prevention and harm minimization.

Scientific analysis can provide informed projections about the impact of war on the health and wellbeing of individuals and communities. Such an analysis also has the potential to equip health planners with the information on which to base preparatory and preventive interventions in the face of conflict. This approach requires an inter-disciplinary dialogue between public health, social scientists and defence planners, shifting the agenda from the role of public health in the post-event emergency and development assistance period to the role of informing pre-event public health analyses of defence policy. In doing so, public health planners have the potential to shift defence and war policy thinking from an exclusive focus on the protection of the state towards the more broad and longer term objective of protecting human security.

Notes

1 Holdstock D., 'Morbidity and Mortality among Soldiers and Civilians' in Taipale I, *War or Health* ed. (London, Zed Books, 2002).
2 Burnham, G., et al., Mortality after the 2003 invasion of Iraq: a cross-sectional cluster sample survey. *Lancet*, (2006). 368(9545): p. 1421–8.
3 Burnham, G. and L. Roberts, A debate over Iraqi death estimates. *Science*, (2006). 314(5803): p. 1241; author reply 1241.
4 Black, R. E., S. S. Morris, and J. Bryce, Where and why are 10 million children dying every year? *Lancet*, 2003. 361(9376): p. 2226–34.
5 Human Security Centre, *Human Security Report 2005*, Oxford University Press, 2005.
6 Human Security Centre, *Human Security Report 2005*, Oxford University Press, 2005.
7 Nokkala A., 'The Changing Character of War', in Taipale (ed.), op. cit.
8 Sidel V., 'The International Arms Trade and its Impact on Health', *BMJ* Vol 311 pp. 1677–1680, 1995.
9 Daponte B., 'A Case Study in Estimating Casualties from War and Its Aftermath: The 1991 Persian Gulf War', *Medicine and Global Survival/The PSR Quarterly* (International Physicians for the Prevention of Nuclear War) Vol. 3 No. 2, 1993.
10 Coghlan B., Brennan R. and Ngoy P., *Mortality in the Democratic Republic of Congo*, International Rescue Committee, New York, 2004.
11 Burnham, G., et al., 2006, op. cit.
12 Murray C. and Lopez D., 'The Global Burden of Disease', WHO/Harvard School of Public Health, www.who.int/chd/images/deaths.gif, accessed May 2000.
13 Salama, P., et al., Lessons learned from complex emergencies over past decade. *Lancet*, 2004. 364(9447): p. 1801–13.
14 UNICEF, *State of the Worlds Children Report 2005*, New York, 2005.
15 Ashford M. and Huet-Vaughn, 'The Impact of War on Women', in Levy B., op. cit., 1997, p. 188.
16 Grundy J. J., The impact of health system reform on remote health in Cambodia and the Philippines, *Rural and Remote Health*, http://rrh.deakin.edu.au, 2001.
17 Grundy J. J., The impact of health system reform on remote health in Cambodia and the Philippines, *Rural and Remote Health*, http://rrh.deakin.edu.au, 2001.

18 Human Security Centre, op. cit.
19 International Crisis Group, www.crisisgroup.org, accessed May 2006.
20 WHO, Health Information Network for Advanced Planning, www.who.org.
21 The Sphere Project, *Ten years in of Sphere in action: enhancing the quality and accountability of humanitarian action* 1997–2007, 2007, Bangalore: Books for Change.
22 Guha-Sapir, D. and W. G. Panhuis, Conflict-related mortality: an analysis of 37 datasets. *Disasters*, 2004. 28(4): p. 418–28.
23 Guha-Sapir, D. and W. G. van Panhuis, The importance of conflict-related mortality in civilian populations. *Lancet*, 2003. 361(9375): p. 2126–8.
24 Human Security Centre, op. cit.
25 Toole M., Waldman R. and Zwi A., 'Complex Emergencies', in Merson M., Black R., and Mills A., (ed.), *International Public Health*, Jones & Bartlett, 2006.
26 Durkhiem E., *Suicide*, Free Press, 1997.
27 Wilkinson R., *Unhealthy Societies*, Routledge, 1997.
28 Marmot R., *Social Determinants of Health*, Oxford University Press, 1999.
29 Human Security Centre, op. cit.
30 Bourdieu P., 'The Forms of Capital', in Richardson (ed.), *Handbook of Theory and Research for the Sociology of Education*, 1986.
31 Putnam R. D., *Bowling Alone – The Collapse and Revival of American Community*, Simon & Schuster, New York, 2000.
32 Herman J., *Trauma and Recovery*, Basic Books, 1997.
33 Ministry of Health Cambodia, *Health Sector Strategic Plan 2003–2007*, MOH, Phnom Penh, 2004.

21

FUTURE HUMANITARIAN CRISES

Challenges for practice, policy, and public health

Frederick M. Burkle, Jr.

Source: *Prehospital and Disaster Medicine*, 25:3 (2010), 191–9.

Abstract

After more than three decades of preoccupation with wars and internal political conflicts, the humanitarian community has the opportunity to re-evaluate what humanitarian crises will dominate both policy and practice in the future. In reality, these crises are already active and some are over the tipping point of recovery. These crises share the common thread of being major public health emergencies which, with a preponderance of excess or indirect mortality and morbidity dominating the consequences, requires new approaches, including unprecedented improvements and alterations in education, training, research, strategic planning, and policy and treaty agendas. Unfortunately, political solutions offered up to date are nation-state centric and miss opportunities to provide what must be global solutions. Public health, redefined as the infrastructure and systems necessary to allow communities, urban settings, and nation-states to provide physical and social protections to their populations has become an essential element of all disciplines from medicine, engineering, law, social sciences, and economics. Public health, which must be recognized as a strategic and security issue should take precedence over politics at every level, not be driven by political motives, and be globally monitored.

The rise of public health emergencies

Public health emergencies (PHE) are defined as crises that "adversely impact the public health system and its protective infrastructure that includes water, sanitation, shelter, food, and health."[1] An increasingly common thread of PHEs have permeated and often dominated the consequences brought on by wars, conflicts, and large-scale disasters in the last third of the 20th century. Public health emergencies occur when the public health protective threshold

377

is destroyed as it is during war; overwhelmed, as it was for the citizens of New Orleans after Hurricane Katrina; not recovered or maintained, as it was when Shia' public health infrastructures south of Baghdad were destroyed by the first Persian Gulf War and purposely ignored by the Saddam regime causing the worst health indices in all of Iraq; or denied, as they were to select ethnic and religious groups during the Post-Cold War internal conflicts and persist for many in the decades long smoldering conflicts of Sudan, Haiti, and Palestine.[2]

In the developed world, public health protections are literally invisible to populations where they are taken for granted. The lack of public health protections is what distinguishes many of the 'have and have not populations' of the world. Wars and large-scale disasters, such as earthquakes and hurricanes, are defined by the direct deaths and injuries they produce. Yet, in a very short time, indirect or preventable deaths from the loss of and failure to recover the public health protections can rapidly eclipse the number of direct mortalities.

There has been little investment in public health infrastructures in all parts of the world. Traditionally, public health systems get the short-end of the stick in funding and human resources, especially in those departments concerned with disaster prevention and preparedness. Post 9/11, Federal funding greatly improved the capacity of the 2,800 local and state health departments in the United States to investigate and control pandemics and the consequences of terrorist events. With recent fiscal constraints both State and Federal funding has declined, leaving many States with considerable gaps in their ability to respond to PHEs. A recent study completed by the Centers for Disease Control and Prevention found that epidemiological capacity, critical to outbreak surveillance and control, decreased between 2006 and 2009.[3]

Public health infrastructures and systems globally have declined, disappeared, or failed to keep pace with the demands of population growth and density. We have entered the 21st century with deficient dwellings, aged and inadequate infrastructure, and insufficient capacity to respond to crises, especially in ensuring access to safe water, food, sanitation, and energy. Ecological and environmental preservations must be considered as essential public health protections. Haiti is an example where decade's long deforestation decimated the protective root structure to an alarming 1%.[4,5] When a hurricane hits Haiti, Cuba, and then Florida . . . the direct deaths are similar in number. However, in the absence of normal protective root structures from trees, the torrential rains led to massive flooding and mudslides in Haiti, resulting in an additional 2,500 or more indirect deaths. When a major disaster hits the island of Hispaniola, the impacts are decidedly worse for the deforested Haiti than the forested Dominican Republic.

Indirect mortality and morbidity is considered preventable. At first glance, all of the "future" humanitarian crises addressed in this paper may seem distinct, but they have in common, a propensity to result in major PHEs. In fact, it is a dominant characteristic in all. However, neither policy nor public health are prepared to address the root causes or the consequences of PHEs— especially at the local operational or community level.

Future crises

For the last three decades, conventional cross-border, internal complex, and asymmetrical wars have dominated our will and diverted attention away from more subtle and slowly emerging crises—all of which have an even greater impact on public health. Governments always have been uncomfortable with public health data. Political parties in power own the public health leadership, budgets, and the agendas that are deemed important and those that are tabled. In the last two decades, there has been a deliberate effort by governments to influence, control, and interpret public health data in a favorable light for political gains. The scientific community, often reticent to enter political disputes, has not been stellar in its capacity to interpret public health consequences in a manner easily understood by the citizenry or decision-makers.

War and conflict

There is no reason to expect that wars, especially asymmetrical warring, will show a decline. The Democratic Republic of the Congo, Somalia, and the Occupied Palestinian Territories will remain chronic and smoldering. Nigeria has every reason to be the next Muslim/Christian hotspot. The Western world, at least the United States, will remain mired in many asymmetrical conflicts that have no easy solution, certainly no conventional one. The internal complex wars of the last three decades were post-Cold War battles over territory and resources. Asymmetrical wars, such as Iraq and Afghanistan, focus on controlling a population bringing all ethnic, religious, and tribal factions into the fray. Territory and resources are a side benefit that is not necessarily an immediate priority of insurgent movements. Asymmetrical warfare has three components that deserve equal attention: the asymmetrical warfare itself, the pervasive insecurity that impacts all elements of society, especially the civilians and aid community, and the emergence, over time, of an unprecedented, prolonged, and catastrophic PHE (Figure 1).[6]

During 2003 Iraq, the humanitarian community warned the coalition military of the danger of not recognizing the impact of asymmetrical war on civilians. This was several years before the "troop surge" became the *soup de jure* solution, in 2007 to protect and "win the hearts and minds" of the populace. In the interim, public health indices, including chronic malnutrition, infant mortality rates, and preventable mortality and morbidity all severely worsened, and which remain even today. Often lost among the attention given to direct violence, social, ethnic, religious disparities and inequities, poverty, injustices, cultural incompatibilities, ignorance, racism, oppression,

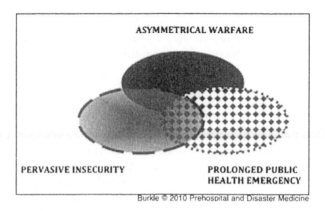

Figure 1 Three equally critical and integrated characteristics of asymmetrical warfare. Reproduced from: Burkle F. M. Jr. Measuring humanitarian assistance in conflicts. *Lancet* 2008;19(371)(9608):189–190, with permission from Elsevier.

and religious fundamentalism all will adversely impact the public health and prevent or slow its recovery. In an early 2010 report, nearly 80% of the already 300,000 conflict-related deaths in Darfur were due to preventable infectious diseases, not violence.[7] In a 2001 Congo study, this figure was 90%.[8]

Post-conflict nation-states

History will show that a shameful chapter in humanitarian assistance is the failure of the international community to recover and rehabilitate post-conflict nation-states. The transition phase from war, before sustainable development is realized, is the most dangerous. Social and political scientists have shown that the number of victims of preventable mortality and morbidity predictably rise once the war has been declared over. These indirect mortalities usually represent 70 to 90% of all the deaths during the war itself, yet markedly increase after the "shooting has stopped."[9] Those indirect deaths remain high for years and do not reach the pre-war baseline for a decade or more. With a declaration of peace, tentative or not, the humanitarian community, including donors, withdraw as funding and media attention disappears. The developed world is quite receptive at responding to emergencies with finding donors and available humanitarian staff to "save lives." However, interest in the hard work of sustainable recovery and rehabilitation seems to be more risky, less receptive, and poorly understood. Indeed, decision-makers are less clear as to what needs to be done and by whom. What is agreed upon is that it takes unprecedented degrees of collaboration, coordination, and communication, a level that is not initially required during the war's humanitarian effort.

Whereas deaths from wars have declined, the number of people exposed to conflict has increased.[10] A major mistake is to assume that once there is some semblance of a declaration of peace, violent conflict ceases. The term "post-conflict" is somewhat of a myth. It does not necessarily mean there is peace. The difference between populations at war and during the post-conflict phase gets blurred with continued varying levels of conflict intensity. Many of the same violent events continue, but now are termed "criminality or banditry", thus speaking to both the urge to affirm that peace has finally arrived and a certain degree of collective denial. For example, security level decision-makers may categorize the post-conflict environment through their own 'language-lens' viewed simply as being 'permissive, non-permissive, or semi-permissive'. Among the confounding variables that make current post-conflict environments different than the celebrated post-World War II recovery, is the massive proliferation and easy availability of weaponry, factors that intimidate the debate toward lasting peace and civility.

Unfortunately 47% of countries return to conflict within a decade, with a rate that is 60% in Africa.[11] It must be remembered that the post-conflict infrastructure and system is usually 10% of what it was before the war. Predictors of a return to war include stagnation of economic recovery and worsening of the infant mortality rate (IMR), a composite index which has less to do with the availability of prenatal, antenatal, and postnatal care than it has to do with combined capacities to organize such services through good governance. Additionally, if the mortality rate remains at the wartime emergency threshold level of 2.0 deaths/10,000/day and the fledgling government lacks the public health infrastructure and healthcare resources to adequately manage it—inevitably, warring will restart.

Post-conflict failures are tragic and increasingly add to the list of "fragile states". Successful progress requires a coordinated mix of military, government, health, education, economic, and other resources—all patiently working together from an agreed upon strategic plan. Humanitarian assistance should not cease, rather it may need to be escalated for the short term so that the population can witness an improvement of quality health care, education, and employment. The post-conflict players must recognize that the transition period remains dangerous for the most vulnerable populations of women, children, and those with mental health problems.

Despite an overall weak track record, successes helped by strategic planning do exist in East Timor, Liberia, Rwanda, and others. Despite the desperation, the complex post-conflict environment and the basic public health needs has captured little attention among governments, donors, and practitioners alike. The knowledge base is scant. Where epidemiological studies proliferated in the war and conflict literature, few studies of the post-conflict environment are available or funded; if it is not being measured, then it does not exist.

Biodiversity crises

Biodiversity systems are areas throughout the world where the major life forms that sustain our global 'biology' are found. It is in these areas where the large majority of the crucial 1,500 vascular plant species, and at least 70% of original vertebrates, reside and define the foundation for sustaining the 'public health' of the planet.[12] Biodiversity hotspots, of which there are 34, are regions with a uniquely rich level of endemic species that also are most threatened.[13] Understandably, dense human habitation tends to occur near biodiversity hotspots, most of which are large forests or located in the tropics.

Tragically, 80% of the major conflicts and wars of the last three decades occurred in 23 of the 34 most biologically diverse and threatened places.[12] Iraq is just one example, where only 6% of land is arable, packed between and sustained by the Tigris and Euphrates rivers. The ongoing war, drought, and increasing dust storms have severely degraded the once fertile soil. Ambitious plans by Turkey and Syria to divert the rivers from their origins with dams and hydroelectric plants may prove to be the final blow to Iraq's agricultural economy. Iraq's Minister of the Environment, Narmin Othman, claimed in January 2010, that environmental degradation is being intensified by an acute drought and water shortage across the country that has seen a 70% decrease in the volume of water flowing through the two rivers as they enter the country from the north. Othman emphasized, "We can no longer in good conscience call ourselves the land between the rivers. A lot of the water we are getting has first been used by Turkey and Syria for power generation. When it reaches us, it is poor quality. That water which is used for agriculture is often contaminated. We are in the midst of an unmatched environmental disaster."[14]

Worldwide overpopulation, deforestation, pollution, and global warming have produced a negative cumulative effect on these sensitive ecosystems that some studies warn is destined for collapse. For the United States, the south-coastal area of California is the only robust biodiversity system in America and a major contributor to its sustainable food supply. Other countries' biodiversity assets have endowed war funding, most notably in the Congo and Cambodia from timber harvesting and the over-production of illicit drug crops that have dominated and scavenged agricultural lands in Afghanistan, South East Asia, and Latin America.[15] Even after the wars, the lingering level of fighting in many post-conflict environments has stymied the recovery of their once robust biodiversity systems. Additionally, the wide availability of weapons provides easy means to kill small animals for bush meat, severely depleting the remaining vertebrate populations.[16]

The resources focused in these unique biodiversity areas of the world must be recognized as "global resources," not a commodity that can be owned by any one nation-state. The nation-states in which they reside are their protectorates and have a duty to ensure their lasting viability. In the coming decades, we will hear more of resource wars, climate change threats, and eminent domain debates, especially in diminishing biodiversity areas, as countries sell or lease off land and other resources to the highest bidder.

Climate change

A recent Editorial in the journal *Nature* cautioned readers that "climate science, like any active field of research, has major gaps in understanding. Yet the political stakes have grown so high in this field, and the public discourse has become so heated, that climate researchers find it hard to talk openly about these gaps" . . . suggesting that those "who deny humanity's influence on climate will try to use any perceived flaw in the evidence to discredit the entire picture. So how can researchers honestly describe the uncertainty in their work without it being misconstrued?"[17]

I share similar anxieties, but like most of my colleagues, I believe the evidence clearly shows both natural climate trends, which have shown increasing influence over many decades, along with man's hand in spawning carbon dioxide emissions equally contribute to the predicament we face today. The undisputed accumulation of carbon emissions never will be absorbed or disappear from our environment. This must be curtailed and hopefully the same science that discovered it can also find a way to eliminate it.

The environmental indicators that will remain under heated debate are climate warming, biodiversity, global cycles of nitrogen and phosphorus, freshwater availability, ocean acidification, stratospheric ozone depletion, and land-use change, which are inter-related. Freshwater availability use is almost at the tipping point. Yemen, as one example, will run out of all water in four years. Ocean acidification impacts anyone who resides on or close to an island nation. The challenges are different with each island, but most serious is general sea level rise, the detrimental effects of increased acidification of sea water on coral reefs, and the eventual collapse of the reef ecosystem. Over several decades, millions of islanders will be forced to relocate. Interestingly, current studies suggest that this migration will be regional migration rather than international, mostly driven by drought, soil degradation, disappearing islands, and loss of food security. It is claimed that Africans will move north to Mediterranean countries.[18-20] Polynesians, at least in today's world, will be welcome in New Zealand and Australia. Kiribati, a Polynesian paradise that straddles the equator, will be the first island to be totally evacuated. President Tong, in testimony to the UN General Assembly, emphatically declared that "when people migrate they will migrate on merit and with dignity" hoping for what he calls a "global distribution" of the population. The process is already happening with groups numbering a thousand receiving skilled job training as nurses in New Zealand. Once work is obtained, they will facilitate the continual and orderly exit of others.[21]

Climate changes directly impact the public health. The water quality and supply on the Polynesian Islands is a major health issue. Rapid urbanization results from relocating coastal families where population growth, density, and the mounting economic challenges stress the fragile public health infrastructure. Public health risks are being posed by contaminated and polluted home rainwater storage, wells, and lagoons showing elevated bacterial contamination. In landlocked areas like China, severe drought, lack of potable water, and 'super dust storms' have resulted in >150 million people that authorities openly admit need to be relocated. Mainly from water shortages and over irrigation, 240 out of 291 major springs have dried up.[22] Africa, where it is now common to see dried up river beds, has lost many of their deeper aquifers. With rising temperatures and diminishing rains, Lake Victoria has dropped six feet in three years.[23]

China's answer is unique in that it has the capacity to build and populate new cities (such as Shenzhen) that are marketed as modern economic free zones. The major motive however, is to provide the public health infrastructure protections that were severely compromised in cities like Shanghai. This novel approach has merits, but it is not a viable option for most of the world's megacities suffering similar PHEs.

Large-scale natural disasters

It is important to remind readers, almost five years after Hurricane Katrina, that indirect public health mortality and morbidity continue to plague New Orleans. The breach of the levees caused much chaos and exposed large gaps in sacrosanct preparedness plans. Waters rapidly flooded emergency generators in the basements of hospitals ceasing their capacity to function and forced the permanent closing of Charity Hospital that once served the indigent population for over 250 years. Never financed enough to invest in an electronic surveillance system, all the New Orleans' Department of Health warehoused paper turned to pulp. The public health system and much of its infrastructure came to a halt. With presses out of commission, a small staff of the *Times Picayune*, a New Orleans newspaper icon, remained behind to post electronic stories.[24] Over the ensuing months, their readers, alarmed at what appeared to be an unexpected increase in published obituaries, contacted the barebones remnants of the Public Health Department which launched a study that confirmed a 47% increase in mortality one year post-Katrina. The excess deaths, attributable to loss of a number of social and physical protections, almost five years later, slowly are being recovered.[25] Immediately there were 38% fewer hospital and 56% fewer psychiatric beds. Despite post-Katrina increases in suicides and mental health problems, psychiatric services continued to suffer with the last inpatient psychiatric bed closing in New Orleans in September 2009. Although funding was requested, as of 2010, a non-paper surveillance system for New Orleans was not budgeted. Experts estimate that it will take 20–25 years to rebuild the city at the current pace.[26]

The Indian Ocean Tsunami has had a similar history. Despite what arguably is, the most robust voluntary donation program ever, almost six years after the Indian Ocean Tsunami, large gaps in shelter, sanitation, potable water, health facilities, and workers have been reported in countries affected by the disaster.[27]

Globalization & urbanization

Being a constructive critic of the economically driven definition of globalization that has dominated our thinking over the last 15 years, I have concerns over its impact on public health. During the 1950s, studies showed severe health indices, especially among women and children in the developing world. This prompted the world health leadership to gather in Alma-Ata in central Asia with plans to provide by the year 2000, equity of health worldwide. The Alma-Ata Declaration assumed that health and education were human rights.[28] Although major progress was made, the initiative eventually stagnated under political pressures and major internal conflicts especially in Africa.[29] In contrast, globalization, dominated by World Bank initiatives, took hold in promoting outsourcing opportunities, new industries, and the development of megacity resources that promised employment to many of the world's poor. Many cities grew at the rate of one million people every six months. The mantra of the World Bank initiatives, "improve the economy and everything else will follow," included health, not as a right, but a "responsibility" that those benefiting from a strong economy would buy. Many areas under World Bank development, historically depended on public healthcare hospitals and other facilities for care. During financial growth, some were maintained from the coffers of the developing industries; but in reality, an overall net reduction in expenditures for public health, health, education, and development occurred. Among the employed and unemployed, a widening gap occurred between the new "have and have not" populations. Health inequities of the 1950s Alma-Ata era returned and worsened among the poor. Urban leadership faced with these disparities admits that "health for many has become a major security issue."[30]

Urbanzation *per se* is not problematic when public health infrastructure precedes population expansion, where outside sources can provide essentials, such as food, and when the urban economy remains an economic advantage to the country. On the other hand, "rapid urbanization" is an unsustainable process. The public health infrastructure cannot keep up and often collapses, and the failing economy drains the nation-state. Mumbai, the most densely populated city worldwide has >30,000 people/km^2, and in some areas, this exceeds one million/km^2. And yet, >1,600 new families move into Mumbai every day.

Rapid urbanization has produced an 'invisible population' with unknown demographics or knowledge of their access to basic health. With little or no representation by the humanitarian community, no one could guarantee basic social and physical protections. This situation worsened with the financial crisis, one example being China, where authorities admit to >26 million newly unemployed. Most of the young adult unemployed males, who sent money home to support their rural families, are unable to return 'home' where the local communities fear they will take the few available jobs away. Authorities admit to increasing criminality and "mass incidents".[31]

The rural poor, as they did during the 1850s Industrial Revolution, flock to urban centers. A poverty-ridden family earning $2/day will gladly welcome $4/day despite remaining locked in extreme poverty. In the developed world, 4–6% of the populations are urban squatters, whereas up to 70% are in the developing world.[32,33] Currently, 59 million new urban dwellers are added annually worldwide, 89% in developing countries.[34] Megacities like Mumbai reveal blatant evidence of the contradictions of globalization, where multiple modern buildings front miles of decrepit shanty towns.

Goldstone in quoting both *The Economist* and UN data suggests that "... most of the world's expected population growth will increasingly be concentrated in today's poorest, youngest, and most heavily Muslim countries, which have a dangerous lack of quality education, capital, and employment opportunities; and, for the first time in history, most of the world's population will become urbanized, with the largest urban centers being in the world's poorest countries, where policing, sanitation, and health care are often scarce."[35] Projections of the UN forecasts (Figure 2), "might even understate the reality because they reflect the 'medium growth' rates."[36]

New occupants tend to move to resource poor and disaster prone areas (i.e., earthquake, flooding) of the cities where sanitation is ignored and infectious diseases more prevalent. Currently, urban settings have the highest

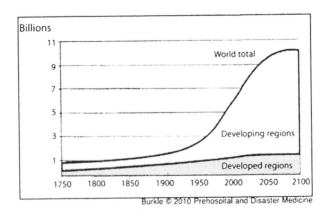

Figure 2 Population growth: 1750–2100. The global population doubled between 1950 and 1987, from 2.5 billion to 5 billion. Reaching the first 2.5 billion took the human species from its beginnings up to 1950; the second 2.5 billion took less than 40 years.
Reproduced from: Merrick T. W., *et al*: World Population in Transition. *Population Bulletin* 1986;41(2):44–45.

worldwide <5 years of age IMR. Dense growth, worsening health indices, poverty, and social tensions are a recipe for increasing disruptive tensions.

A *megacity* usually is defined as a metropolitan area with a population in excess of 10 million.[37] Port-au-Prince, Haiti with a severely dense population of three million did not fit this definition, yet, shared the same problems of abject poverty. It is the density of populations, not the total number, which are the major driver influencing disease, poor sanitation, shelter, unsafe water, and food quality and distribution. If geographic density of populations was used, many more urban settings would be among the growing list of those at great risk. Today, there are over one billion people without "basic food for health," meaning that while they obtain some food, it is not of the quantity or quality (lack of essential micronutrients) to ward off disease. International food programs only feed about 10% of this population.

Epidemics and pandemics

There have been >70 new or re-emerging diseases during this past decade. For viruses and other microorganisms that depend on human transmission to survive, it is a wonderful time to propagate. Dense populations and uninhibited air travel are fertile soil for transmission from one human host to another. Severe acute respiratory syndrome (SARS) was the name given to the coronavirus, a relative of the common cold, which began in Guangdong Province, China and spread to 37 countries in 10 days. Guangdong Province, one of the most densely populated areas of the world, is highly vulnerable to the emergence and re-emergence of common and rare viral pathogens. But it is not just about viruses. In January 2010, one of the smallest yet dense island nations, the Marshall's, was declared a "public health emergency". This happened following an outbreak of drug-resistant tuberculosis (TB), a large mycobacterium, when government authorities considered calling upon special powers of quarantine for people who were not complying with TB prevention requirements.[38] Little known is that between 1969 and today, bubonic plague cases which number only 10–15 per year have spread from northern New Mexico to all states west of the Mississippi.[39] The difference between these cases and those in Africa and India, for example, is the capacity of public health surveillance and management systems in the United States to deal with these threats on a daily basis.

Both SARS and the recent H1N1 can be seen as dry runs for what eventually is predicted to be a pandemic of a more lethal viral pathogen. Viruses mutate incessantly in order to remain viable pathogens. Avian influenza, which to date has not mutated in the one genomic area that would ensure easy human to human spread, has a mortality rate between 40–60%. The poorer the country, the higher the mortality rate. Surveillance systems that are critical to the discovery, investigation, and control of infectious diseases have markedly improved in the developed world out of fear to protect their populations and economies. These systems, though, remain inadequate in developing countries where the emergence and spread of pathogens is most likely.

The SARS experience prompted a modernization of the International Health Regulations (IHR) which legally binds countries to work together to prevent, protect, and control the spread of infectious disease. With SARS, the IHR became a Treaty in 2007 and, to date, has proven to be a successful model for global cooperation to protect the public health.[40,41] However, even with impressive advances in the science of pandemics and in strategic and tactical preparedness, local community operational level plans and capacity remain deficient. Western models of care are individual and hospital-centric. Epidemics and pandemics are by definition PHEs that demand a population-based approach requiring unprecedented coordination and cooperation between the clinical workforce and public health authorities. Operational requirements for communities call for robust tele-healthline systems, surge allocation of scarce resources, system-wide integrated triage-management, citizen-supported self or self-assisted care, and alternative health facilities, to name but a few.

Emergencies of scarcity

Alex Evans, a Fellow at the Center on International Cooperation at New York University, has been at the forefront of alerting society about the need to see energy, food, climate, and water security as "different facets of the same underlying issue of resource scarcity, rather than as separate issues that happen to share a few attributes." The driver of these emergencies is the increasing worldwide demand: energy rise of 45% and food 50% by 2030, and water 25% by 2025. He cautions that the pattern of trying to manage one scarcity at a time without taking the others into consideration creates a "major risk of unintended consequences".[42] Distributional conflicts are already emerging. Resource wars, called complex internal wars, that began among emerging post-Cold War countries in the 1990s were the first hint of problems to come.

These emergencies are inextricably linked to biodiversity hotspots, climate threats, and the scarcity of remaining forests and arable lands, most of which lie in the least developed countries. Import dependent countries, such as China, Japan, South Korea, and many in the Middle East claim the right to purchase farmland in foreign countries to meet national food security needs at home. For almost two years, South Korea negotiated a no-cost, 100-year lease of half of all arable land in Madagascar; a country suffering severe unemployment and poverty. Local farmers had no political voice in the negotiations. South Korea's plan was to exclusively grow corn for their countries' food staple and claim ownership of the land's massive water reserves. When details of this arrangement reached the populace, a political coup abruptly ended the contract. The South Korean government response,

"We want to plant corn there to ensure our food security. Food can be a weapon in this world," reveals much to worry about.[43] Curiously, the fact that this event did not make even a ripple in the world's press or psyche is equally alarming. Similar purchases of energy from Africa, and the Artic, South China, and Caspian Seas by individual countries now are commonplace.

For many decades, the public health of a country was revealed by disasters that kept governments honest by immediately defining the public health and exposing its vulnerabilities.[44] Not surprisingly, governments in power were either replaced post-disaster by election or by coup. Hurricane Katrina and the Haiti earthquake proved the capstone events that exposed the state of public health protections, not that they were very well hidden. Scarcity of energy, water, and food already defines the public health in many countries, but in the near future, these capacities will be the indices to measure the public health country by country.

Evans suggests key agendas to build resilience to scarcity among "poor people and fragile states".[42]

1. Improve surveillance and early warning and cites the G20 Global Impact and Vulnerability Alert System of April 2009 that integrates data about conflict risk, human vulnerability, and political economy dynamics.
2. Mitigate unsustainable population growth. Any reduction requires the empowerment of women, a status not acceptable in most countries that have dense populations.
3. Focus on and support agriculture, especially small farms with technological know-how and micro-credit programs.
4. Initiate social protection systems and safety nets to reduce vulnerability.
5. International effort to scale-up capacity of natural resource governance.
6. Connect conflict prevention resolution with natural resource scarcity in mediation and prevention.
7. Upgrade emergency capacity to deal with scarcity crises.

Impact on policy and public health

The way in which we perceived and defined public health began to change several decades ago. Environmental and public health professionals no longer are defined by a "narrow sanitary engineering approach".[45] Current public health reflects governance, transportation, communication, public safety, the judiciary, and other civil sectors that allow a village, town, city, and nation-state to functionally integrate in providing social and physical protections. This also defines the new public health system and its infrastructure. Many of the younger generation already are chest-deep into globalization as a planned career. New global public health programs at the undergraduate level in 137 universities and colleges have tripled their enrollment in the last three years.[46] Increasingly, physicians, nurses, lawyers, engineers, and economists, just to name a few, are seeking a combined degree with public health. For the most part, this has been their own decision; correctly derived from awareness that public health greatly impacts every discipline. Global health concentrations in schools of public health at the graduate and undergraduate levels are increasingly being launched and refined. Suffering from a post-Sputnik era that favored more vertical concentrations in the sciences to win the Cold War, there is realization now that global health studies require a highly integrative approach that is multidisciplinary, multi-sectoral, and supports the multi-ministerial levels of decisions that are necessary.[47] Science and the humanities must again be equal partners in education.

Whereas politically sensitive issues have been restricted from US public education for decades, there must be a re-evaluation of this shortsighted decision, with global health taking center stage from elementary school on. Other countries are not so impeded. Academia, starting at the grade school level must be the honest broker for accountability and transparency between what is being viewed on television and the younger generation's quest for knowledge.

Humanitarian assistance began to move from rural to urban areas two decades ago, as rural wars forced women and their children to flee to escape rape, murder, and the total absence of social protections. Many of us spent the early decades training the nascent humanitarian community in building rural refugee camps, wells, pit latrines, defecation fields, and learning basic field epidemiology. Now, many of these same women find themselves trapped in urban settings with few social protections and scant opportunities for work except prostitution. The state of health for women and children is worse now than when I began my humanitarian career >45 years ago. Those who define themselves as humanitarian professionals have doubled from a decade ago to almost 200,000 today. They are eager and well traveled. But like us all, they do not know what they don't know. Much of the education and training remains outdated. The humanitarian community, policy works, and the military have entered the 21st century unprepared to protect the urban public health or handle emergencies of scarcity.

When it comes to emergencies of scarcity, no developing or developed country alike should be excluded in meeting Evans' key agendas. Land grabbing and the failure of a concerted "cry of foul" by the rest of the world defines the power and influence that rich countries believe they are entitled to. If it was not for media attention, the Madagascar case would not be known. Land grabbing will continue to severely impact poor people and fragile states which lack the social protections and political and institutional means to resolve access to resources. What is most troublesome is that power brokers do not see this as a major problem, but as a right of countries with means to protect themselves. The answer to our future crises must be a global solution, not one dictated by any one individual nation-state.

We know that the world has the food to feed the existing population, yet >1 billion starve. Can the global community make what works for the IHR treaty and infectious disease control, for water, food, energy, and climate threats? The global community currently has only two very restrictive choices in managing climate threats. One, 'mitigation' defines the legal and diplomatic efforts of the G20 negotiations that call for reduction in population growth rates, ensuring broad social protections and decreasing carbon emissions. So far, they have failed. The second choice is for populations, impacted directly by these threats, to identify their own vulnerabilities, reduce them through their own means, and learn how to "adapt," defined as the "new resilience." In Polynesia, if adaptation does not work, then governments must have strong migration policies in place to emigrate their populations.[21]

The question that will be hotly debated at every level over the next decade is "what responsibilities apply in human relationships on a global or trans-national level." Will "global justice" mature enough to demand of the global community, remediation of past injustices, the establishment of fair terms of cooperation between nations, and willingness to address the basic facts of poverty?[48] As in Haiti today, will the "collective charity" still be based on "feeling sorry," or strive to understand and reverse the political and economic institutional causes.

The global economy will be judged by the capacity of public health infra-structure and systems, both within individual nation-states, and the willingness of the global community to be a partner in ownership. Shared ownership would set priorities, fund strategic recovery and rehabilitation, and support micro- and macro-financing that gives priority to public health protections, both physical and social. If given the political responsibility, the younger generation will in the next two decades, redefine 'globalization' not from economics alone, but from a foundation of health, education, and human rights. Arguably, this will only be realized if water, energy, food, health, sanitation, and shelter are universally protected. In 2002, world governments agreed to significantly slow the rate of biodiversity loss by 2010. This initiative has failed. In part, this is due to the fact that policy-makers at the international level do not have "any single consolidated and robust source of science on biodiversity and ecosystem services to turn to".[49] A proposed Intergovern-mental Platform on Biodiversity and Ecosystem Services (IPBES) is designed not only to improve links between science and policy, but to invest highly in training —opening unprecedented opportunities for burgeoning scientists worldwide.[49]

What to propose for rapid urbanization is equally troublesome, but Paul Romer, the growth economist, does see a silver lining in China's special economic zones. He suggests that hundreds of these "greener" and better planned "high density charter cities" might provide millions of "desperately poor people their first formal sector jobs" lifting themselves out of poverty faster.[50] Whatever the solutions, they will be multidisciplinary with a public health core.

There is nothing in this prediction that should limit sovereignty or threaten cultures or religions. The "grand experiment," which the IHR Treaty represents, must be analyzed to see if its principles can do for future crises what it already has accomplished in controlling infectious disease outbreaks.[51] Whereas, the WHO is the rightful home for threatening diseases, a heavily resourced Office for the Coordination of Humanitarian Affairs (OCHA) under a similar Treaty, could become equally responsible for emergencies such as large-scale natural disasters, and emergencies of scarcity. The OCHA would be expected to have a strong public health presence, authority, and capacity to monitor, prevent, prepare, and manage. Yet, both the IHR treaty and any movement in the same direction through OCHA are "top-down" approaches. What the world fails miserably at is the definitive "bottom-up" remediation of the causes of poverty, public health protections, and war. The latter requires a rewritten and reformed UN Charter and a Security Council that "operationalizes" the Responsibility to Protect (R2P)[52] initiative which is the best hope forward for legitimating "preventive force".[53] The Western world should support a standing task force for the UN, an idea first proposed and tabled as Article 43 in the 1945 UN Charter.

Lastly, public health must take precedence over politics and not be driven by political motives. We talk of a populist movement in the US. Important, yes, but only when the same issues, such as the "empowerment of women", become a "populist global issue" will measurable results occur. Public health must be seen as a "strategic and security" issue that deserves an international monitoring system, something that the G20's Global Impact and Vulnerability Act must strive to do.

References

1. Altevogt B. M., Pope A. M., Hill M. N., Shine K. I. (Eds.). *Research Priorities in Emergency Preparedness and Response for Public Health Systems: A Letter Report*. Washington, DC: Institute of Medicine, Board on Health Sciences Policy, 2008, p 13.

2. Burkle F. M. Jr. Complex Public Health Emergencies. In Koenig K. L., Schultz C. H. (eds): *Disaster Medicine: Comprehensive Principles and Practices*. Cambridge University Press, New York, NY. 2010:361–376.

3. Centers for Disease Control and Prevention (CDC): Assessment of epidemiology capacity in State Health Departments: United States, 2009. *MMWR* 2009;58(49):1373–1377.

4. ReliefWeb. Haiti: Deforestation and disasters: Humanitarian snapshot 2008. Aug 10, 2009. Available at http://ocha-gwapps1.unog.ch/rw/rwb.nsf/db900SID/AHAA-7USLXD?OpenDocument&emid=TC-2008-000143-DOM. Accessed 20 January 2010.

5. ReforestHaiti: International Conference on Reforestation and Environmental Regeneration of Haiti. Honduras, 14–17 Feburary 2007.

6. Burkle F. M. Jr: Measuring humanitarian assistance in conflicts. *Lancet* 2008;371(9608):189–190.

7. Degomme O., Guha-Sapir D.: Patterns of mortality rates in Darfur conflict. *Lancet* 2010;375(9711):294–300.

8. Roberts L., Despines M.: Mortality in the Democratic Republic of the Congo. *Lancet* 1999;353(9171):2249–2250.

9. Ghobarah H. A., Huth P., Russett B.: Civil wars kill and maim people—Long after the shooting stops. *American Political Science Review* 2003;97(2):189–202.

10. Garfield R. M., Polonsky J., Burkle F. M. Jr: Populations exposed to war since World War II. Submitted for publication, January 2010.

11. United Nations Development Group: Report of the UNDG/ECHA Working Group on Transition Issues, Feb, 2004. Available at http://www.google.com/search?client=firefox-a&rls=org.mozilla%3Aen-US%3Aofficial&channel=s&hl=en&q=report+of+the+undg%2Fecha+working+group+on+transiton+issues&btnG=Google+Search. Accessed 24 May 2009.

12. Biodiversity Hotspot Project: Biodiversity hotspots. Available at http://www.uwsp.edu/cnr/wcee/envsci/Framework/pdf/LivingResources/BiodiversityHotspots.doc. Accessed 30 January 2010.

13. Mittermeier C., Hanson T., Machlis G.: Warfare in biodiversity hotspots. *Conservation Biology* 2009;10(1111):1523–1739.

14. Chulov M.: Iraq littered with high levels of nuclear and dioxin contamination, study finds. Available at http://www.guardian.co.uk/world/2010/jan/22/iraq-nuclear-contaminated-sites. Accessed 27 January 2010.

15. Vital Signs 2003. Part Two: Environment Features. VS03, part 2:81–149. Available at http://www.worldwatch.org/system/files/EVS302.pdf. Accessed 28 January 2010.

16. The Bushmeat Trade. Available at http://www.gorilla-haven.org/ghbushmeat.htm. Accessed 27 January 2010.

17. Schiermeier Q.: The real holes in climate science. *Nature* 2010;463:284–287.

18. Baldwin-Edwards M.: Migration in the Middle East and Mediterranean: A regional study prepared for the Global Commission on International Migration. January 2005. Available at http://www.childtrafficking.com/Docs/bald-win_05_mig_mid_med_0408.pdf. Accessed 30 January 2010.

19. de Haas H.: North African migration systems: Evolution, transformations and development linkages. International Migration Institute, University of Oxford. Working Paper 6, 2007.

20. IntelliBriefs. North Africa a transit region for international migration. Available at http://intellibriefs.blogspot.com/2010/01/north-africa-transit-region-for.html. Accessed 29 January 2010.

21. Risse M.: The right to relocation: Disappearing island nations and common ownership of the Earth. *Ethics & International Affairs* 2009;23(3):281–299.

22. Watt J.: China at the crossroads. Available at http://www.guardian.co.uk/world/2009/may/18/china-ecorefugees-farming. Accessed 05 January 2010.

23. Hanley C. J.: Water levels in Lake Victoria dropping fast. Available at http://water-is-life.blogspot.com/2006/12/water-levels-in-lake-victoria-dropping.html. Accessed 05 January 2010.

24. Folkenflik D.: Katrina marked turning point for 'Time Picayune.' Available at http://www.npr.org/templates/story/story.php?storyId=13984564. Accessed 12 January 2010.

25. Stephens K. U. Sr, Grew D., Chin K., Kadetz P., Greenough P. G., Burkle F. M. Jr, Robinson S. L., Franklin E. R.: Excess mortality in the aftermath of Hurricane Katrina: A preliminary report. *Disaster Med Public Health Prep* 2007;1(1):15–20.

26. Quigley B., Finger D.: Katrina Pain Index: 2009. The Louisiana Weekly, News Report. Available at http://news.newamericamedia.org/news/view_article.html?article_id=8a04df63b3b926c80645c8cb2303a1a2. Accessed 10 January 2010.

27. Chang M. H.: Health and housing after the Indian Ocean tsunami. *Lancet* 2007;369(9579):2066–2068.

28. Rohde J., Cousens S., Chopra M., *et al*: Declaration of Alma Ata: International conference on primary health care. Alma-Ata, USSR, 6112 September 1978. Available at http://www.who.int/hpr/NPH/docs/declaration_almaata.pdf. Accessed 30 December 2009.

29. Schneider K., Garrett L.: The end of the era of generosity? Global health amid economic crisis. *Philosophy, Ethics, and Humanities in Medicine* 2009;4:1–7.

30. Owen J. W., Roberts O. Globalization, health and foreign policy: Emerging linkages and interests. *Globalization and Health* 200;1:12–17.

31. Branigan T. Downturn in China leaves 26 million out of work. Available at http://www.guardian.co.uk/business/2009/feb/02/china-unemployment-unrest. Accessed 30 December 2009.

32. Onyango E.: Unplanned settlements, a growing phenomenon in most towns and cities. *Knowledge Matters: Tanzania*. Posted 23 January 2010.

33. Tanzania Information Brief: Cities without slums: Sub-regional programme for eastern and southern Africa. Available at http://ww2.unhabitat.org/campaigns/tenure/documents/Tanzania.doc. Accessed 14 January 2010.

34. Brennan E. M.: Population, urbanization, environment, and security: A summary of the issues. *Environmental Change & Security Project Report*, Woodrow Wilson Center for International Scholars, Washington, DC. Issue 5, No.22, Summer 1999:4–14.

35. Goldstone J. A.: The new population bomb: The four megatrends that will change the world. *Foreign Affairs* 2010;89(1):31–43.

36. Merrick T. W.: World population in transition. *Population Bulletin* 1986;41(2):44–45.

37. How big can cities get? *New Scientist Magazine* 17 June 2006:41.

38. Pro-MED-mail Post: Tuberculosis, drug resistance: Marshall Islands. Available at: http://topnews.us/content/210458-tb-health-emergency-marshall-islands. Accessed 31 January 2010.

39. US Centers for Disease Control and Prevention: Questions and answers about plague. Available at http://www.cdc.gov/ncidod/dvbid/plague/qa.htm. Accessed 03 December 2009.

40. Burkle F. M. Jr: Pandemics: State Fragility's Most Telling Gap. In Cronin P. (Ed.), *Global Strategic Assessment 2009: America's Security Role in a Changing World*. Washington, DC: Institute for National Strategic Studies, National Defense University, US Government Printing Office, 2009, pp 105–108.

41. Baker M. G., Fidler D. P.: Global public health surveillance under new international health regulations. *Emerg Inf Dis* 2006;12(7):1058–1065.

42. Evans A.: Managing scarcity: The institutional dimensions. Available at http://www.globalpolicy.org/security-council/dark-side-of-natural-resources/other-articles-analysis-and-general-debate/48191.html. Accessed 21 September 2009.

43. Jung-a S., Oliver C., Burgis T.: Daewoo to pay nothing for vast land acquisition. Available at http://www.ft.com/cms/s/0/b0099666-b6a4-11dd-89dd-0000779fd18c.html?nclick_check=1. Accessed 12 November 2010.

44. Burkle F. M. Jr, Rupp G.: Hurricane Katrina: Disasters keep us honest. (Commentary). *Monday Developments* 2005;23(17):5.
45. Burkle F. M., Jr.: Globalization and disasters: Issues of public health, state capacity and political action. *Journal of International Affairs* 2006:241–265.
46. Howland K., Kirkwood B. A., Ward C., *et al.* Liberal education and public health: Surveying the landscape. *Peer Review* 2009;11(3):5–8.
47. MacLachlan M.: Rethinking global health research: Towards integrative expertise. *Globalization and Health* 2009;5:6.
48. Miller D.: *National Responsibility and Global Justice.* New York: Oxford University Press, 2007, p 264.
49. Hoag H.: Confronting the biodiversity crisis. *Nature Reports* May 2010;4:51–54.
50. Gunn D.: Can Charter Cities change the world? A Q&A with paul Romer. *The New York Times* 05 May 2010.
51. Burkle F. M. Jr: The grand experiment: International health regulations, pandemics, and future emergencies of scarcity. Presented at the US-CHINA Symposium on Comparative Governance, 14–16 October 2009 co-sponsored by the Kissinger Institute on China and the United States, Woodrow Wilson International Center for Scholars, Washington DC, and the Counselor's Office, State Council, People's Republic of China. pp 1–7.
52. Evans G., Sahnoun M.: The responsibility to protect. *Foreign Affairs* 2002:81(6).
53. Sofaer A. D.: The best defense? *Preventive Force and International Security Foreign Affairs* 2010;89(1):109–118.

22

THE PUBLIC HEALTH ASPECTS OF COMPLEX EMERGENCIES AND REFUGEE SITUATIONS*

M. J. Toole and R. J. Waldman

Source: *Annual Review of Public Health*, 18 (1997), 283–312.

Abstract

Populations affected by armed conflict have experienced severe public health consequences mediated by population displacement, food scarcity, and the collapse of basic health services, giving rise to the term *complex humanitarian emergencies*. These public health effects have been most severe in underdeveloped countries in Africa, Asia, and Latin America. Refugees and internally displaced persons have experienced high mortality rates during the period immediately following their migration. In Africa, crude mortality rates have been as high as 80 times baseline rates. The most common causes of death have been diarrheal diseases, measles, acute respiratory infections, and malaria. High prevalences of acute malnutrition have contributed to high case fatality rates. In conflict-affected European countries, such as the former Yugoslavia, Georgia, Azerbaijan, and Chechnya, war-related injuries have been the most common cause of death among civilian populations; however, increased incidence of communicable diseases, neonatal health problems, and nutritional deficiencies (especially among the elderly) have been documented. The most effective measures to prevent mortality and morbidity in complex emergencies include protection from violence; the provision of adequate food rations, clean water and sanitation; diarrheal disease control; measles immunization; maternal and child health care, including the case management of common endemic communicable diseases; and selective feeding programs, when indicated.

Introduction

Disasters may quickly reverse the substantial gains made during the past two decades by primary health care initiatives in developing countries. A disaster may be defined as a relatively acute situation created by man-made, geophysical, weather-related, or biological events that adversely impacts on the health and economic well-being of a community to an extent that exceeds the local coping capacity. In the case of acute natural disasters such as earthquakes and hurricanes, the direct public health effects are immediate and often devastating. Most deaths and injuries occur during the first few hours following impact and any secondary public health effects are related to displacement of the affected population, destruction of public utilities, and disruption of basic health services. Following the acute response phase of search and rescue, surgical triage, and management of injuries, the public health priorities consist of infrastructure repair, restoration of health services, and rehabilitation of public utilities, especially water supplies. Long-term public health consequences have only occurred following those natural disasters – such as floods – that have destroyed food crops or led to prolonged population displacement in unsanitary camps or settlements. Outbreaks of communicable diseases are rare following acute natural disasters. These problems have not been documented in industrialized countries such as the United States; however, outbreaks of diarrheal disease, hepatitis, and malaria have occurred following some acute natural disasters in developing countries, such as devastating floods in the Sudanese capital of Khartoum in 1988 (58). In this paper, we focus on the public health issues related to populations affected by armed conflicts.

Armed conflict

Severe public health consequences have been documented following most emergencies related to armed conflict, especially in developing countries. Since 1980, approximately 130 armed conflicts have occurred worldwide; 32 have each caused more than 1000 battlefield deaths (15). Between 1975 and 1989, civil conflicts were estimated to have caused approximately 750,000 deaths in Africa, 150,000 in Latin America, 3,400,000 in Asia, and 800,000 in the Middle East (61). Since the end of the cold war in 1991, the toll has increased as new wars have flared or old conflicts reignited in Angola, Somalia, Burundi, Rwanda, Afghanistan, Tajikistan, Sudan, Sierra Leone, Liberia, Sri Lanka, the former Yugoslavia, Azerbaijan, Georgia, and Chechnya. In 1993 alone, 47 conflicts were active, of which 43 were internal wars (55). Armed conflicts have increasingly targeted civilian populations, resulting in high casualty rates, widespread human rights abuses, forced migration, and in some countries the total collapse of governance. This trend is demonstrated by UNICEF's estimate that 1.5 million children have been killed in wars since 1980 (49).

The indirect, or secondary, public health effects of conflicts have been caused by population displacement, food shortages, and collapsed basic health services. Recent examples of mass population movements that attracted widespread media attention have included the Kurdish exodus from northern Iraq in 1991; widespread internal displacement and migration to neighboring countries by Somalis in 1992–93; the displacement of several million persons in the former Yugoslavia between 1992 and 1995; and the migration of up to two million Rwandans in 1994. A new term – *complex emergency* – has been coined to describe situations affecting large civilian populations that usually involve a combination of factors including war or civil strife, food shortages, and population displacement, resulting in significant excess mortality.

Complex emergencies

The evolution of complex humanitarian emergencies follows a relatively consistent sequence: domination of government by one political faction, discrimination against minority ethnic or religious groups or against majority groups by ruling minorities (e.g. Burundi), widespread human rights abuses, leading to civil unrest, violence, and open armed conflict. The destruction of infrastructure, diversion of resources away from social services, and general economic collapse lead to a deterioration in primary health care services, especially prevention programs such as child immunization and antenatal care. Hospitals and surgical facilities may be overwhelmed by the needs of war wounded and general medical services suffer from lack of staff and shortages in essential medical supplies. For example, the major hospital in the central Bosnian city of Zenica reported that the proportion of all surgical cases associated with trauma steadily increased from 22% in April 1992, at the beginning of the war, reaching 78% in November of the same year (13).

Deliberate diversion of food supplies by various armed factions, disruption of transport and marketing, and economic hardship often cause severe food deficits. Farmers may be unable or unwilling to plant or harvest crops in the midst of a war; the supply of seeds and fertilizer may be disrupted; irrigation systems may be damaged by the fighting; and crops, food stores, or animal herds may be intentionally destroyed or looted by armed soldiers. In countries that do not normally produce agricultural surpluses, the impact of these factors on the nutritional status of populations may be severe, particularly in sub-Saharan Africa. When adverse climatic factors have intervened, as in drought-prone countries such as Sudan, Somalia, Mozambique, and Ethiopia, the outcome has been catastrophic. Food shortages and hunger are usually complicating factors rather than primary causes of population migration. For example, a severe drought in Somalia during 1992 exacerbated rather than initiated the flow of refugees fleeing the civil war across the border into Kenya.

Population displacement

Mass migration and food shortages have been responsible for most deaths following civil conflicts in Africa and Asia. *Refugees* are defined under several international conventions as persons who flee their country of origin through a well-founded fear of persecution for reasons of race, religion, social class, or political beliefs (51). The number of dependent refugees under the protection and care of the United Nations High Commissioner for Refugees (UNHCR) steadily increased from approximately 5 million in 1980 to more than 20 million in late 1994 (Table 1) (53). Several of the world's largest ever mass migrations have taken place in recent years; for example, more than 600,000 refugees fled Burundi for Rwanda, Tanzania, and Zaire during a two-week period in late October and early November 1993. Between April and July 1994, an estimated two million Rwandan refugees fled into Tanzania, eastern Zaire, and Burundi provoking the most serious refugee crisis in 20 years. In addition to those persons who meet the international definition

Table 1 Refugee populations of greater than 100,000, December 1994.

Country of asylum	Countries of origin	Estimated number
Iran	Afghanistan, Iraq	2,220,000
Zaire	Rwanda, Angola, Burundi, Sudan	1,527,000
Jordan	Palestinians	1,232,000
Pakistan	Afghanistan	1,200,000
Tanzania	Rwanda, Burundi, Mozambique	752,000
Gaza Strip	Palestinians	644,000
Guinea	Liberia, Sierra Leone	580,000
Sudan	Eritrea, Ethiopia, Chad	550,000
West Bank	Palestinians	504,000
Russian Federation	Tajikistan, Georgia, Azerbaijan	451,000
Lebanon	Palestinians	338,000
Syria	Palestinians	332,000
India	China, Sri Lanka, Bangladesh, Bhutan	327,000
Uganda	Sudan, Zaire, Rwanda	323,000
Cote d'Ivoire	Liberia	320,000
Yugoslavia	Croatia, Bosnia and Herzegovina	300,000
China	Vietnam, Burma	297,000
Armenia	Azerbaijan, Georgia	296,000
Azerbaijan	Armenia, Uzbekistan	279,000
Kenya	Somalia, Sudan, Ethiopia	257,000
Ethiopia	Somalia, Sudan, Eritrea	250,000
South Africa	Mozambique	200,000
Croatia	Bosnia and Herzegovina	188,000
Burundi	Rwanda	165,000
Algeria	Western Sahara, Mali, Niger	130,000
Iraq	Iran, Palestinians	120,000
Bangladesh	Burma	116,000
Ghana	Togo, Liberia	110,000
Nepal	Bhutan, China	104,000
Liberia	Sierra Leone	100,000

Source: United States Committee for Refugees (53).

of refugees, an estimated 25 million people have fled their homes for the same reasons as refugees but remain *internally displaced* in their countries of origin. Most internally displaced persons are found in sub-Saharan Africa, the Middle East, the former Yugoslavia, and in the republics of the former Soviet Union. The reasons for the flight of refugees and internally displaced persons are generally the same: war, civil strife, persecution, and the search for security.

Public health consequences of population displacement

In general, the major health problems of refugees and internally displaced persons are similar in nature. However, the health status of the internally displaced may be worse because access to these populations by international relief agencies is often difficult and dangerous. Also, internally displaced persons may suffer more injuries because they are usually located closer to zones of conflict than are refugees; however, both refugees and internally displaced persons are often victims of landmines, particularly as they cross international borders.

Mortality

The crude mortality rate (CMR) most accurately represents the health status of emergency-affected populations. Mortality rates have been estimated from burial site surveillance, hospital and burial records, community-based reporting systems, and population surveys. The many problems in estimating mortality under emergency conditions include: (*a*) poorly representative population sample surveys; (*b*) failure of families to report all deaths for fear of losing food ration entitlements; (*c*) inaccurate estimates of affected populations for the purpose of calculating mortality rates; and (*d*) lack of standard reporting procedures. In general, however, mortality rates have tended to be under-estimated because deaths are usually underreported or undercounted, and population size is often exaggerated (9). The most reliable estimates of mortality rates have come from well-defined and secure refugee camps where there is a reasonable level of camp organization and a designated agency has had responsibility for the collection of data. The most difficult situations have been those where internally displaced persons have been scattered over a wide area and where surveys could take place only in relatively secure zones. These safe zones may have sometimes acted as magnets for the most severely affected elements of a populations; for example, the Somali town of Baidoa was the site for the storage and distribution of massive amounts of relief food in 1992 and became known as the "famine epicenter" (28). On the other hand, it is possible that the worst-affected communities have been in areas that have been inaccessible by those performing the surveys. In either case, it has proved difficult to extrapolate the findings of surveys on mortality conducted in specific locations to broader populations in conflict-affected countries. Extensive differences in mortality survey methods have been identified; for example, an evaluation of 23 field surveys performed in Somalia between 1991 and 1993 found wide variation in the target populations, sampling strategies, units of measurement, methods of rate calculation, and statistical analysis (3).

Early in an emergency, when mortality rates are elevated, it is useful to express the CMR as deaths per 10,000 population per day. In most developing countries, the baseline annual CMR in nonrefugee populations has been reported between 12–20 per 1000, corresponding to a daily rate of approximately 0.3–0.6 per 10,000 (49). A threshold of 1 per 10,000 per day has been used commonly to define an elevated CMR and to characterize a situation as an emergency (9). During the past 20 years, crude mortality rates as high as 30 times baseline rates have not been unusual during the first month or two following an acute movement of refugees (Table 2). While the situation appeared to improve among refugees during the first few years of the current decade, mortality rates among Rwandan refugees in 1994 were among the highest ever documented. Following the massive influx of Rwandan refugees into the North Kivu region of eastern Zaire in July 1994, the daily CMR based on body counts ranged between 25 and 50 per 10,000 per day (20). The difficulty in estimating the size of the refugee population (the denominator for rate calculations) accounted for the wide range of estimates. Population surveys conducted in the refugee camps, which provided mortality estimates independent of population size, found that between 7% and 9% of the refugees died during the first month after the influx.

Refugees are usually at highest risk of mortality during the period immediately after their arrival in the country of asylum, reflecting long periods of

Table 2 Estimated crude mortality rates (deaths per 1000 per month) in selected refugee populations, 1990–1994.

Date (reference)	Country of asylum	Country of origin	Crude mortality rate
July 1900 (42)	Ethiopia	Sudan	6.9
June 1991 (42)	Ethiopia	Somalia	14.0
March–May 1991 (8)	Turkey	Iraq	12.6
March–May 1991 (2)	Iran	Iraq	6.0
March 1992 (42)	Kenya	Somalia	22.2
March 1992 (24)	Nepal	Bhutan	9.0
June 1992 (9)	Bangladesh	Burma	4.8
June 1992 (11)	Malawi	Mozambique	3.5
August 1992 (11)	Zimbabwe	Mozambique	10.5
December 1993 (14)	Rwanda	Burundi	9.0
August 1994 (44)	Tanzania	Rwanda	9.0
July 1994 (20)	Zaire	Rwanda	59–94

inadequate food and medical care prior to, or during, their flight. For example, the severe deprivation suffered by Mozambican refugees prior to fleeing their country is illustrated by death rates in Zimbabwean refugee camps. During July and August 1992, the daily CMR among Mozambican refugees who had been in Chambuta camp for less than one month was 8 per 10,000 population. This was four times the death rate of refugees who had been in the camp between 1 and 3 months, and 16 times the death rate normally reported for nondisplaced populations in Mozambique (11). The rate at which mortality rates have declined among refugee populations has varied significantly. For example, high initial death rates among Cambodian refugees in Thailand declined to almost baseline levels within one month (9). Even among Rwandan refugees in Goma, the extremely high mortality rate recorded during the first month decreased relatively quickly (Figure 1). On the other hand, the crude and under-five death rates among Somali refugees in Ethiopia in 1988 actually increased over time and remained high for almost 18 months after the initial influx (Figure 2) (38). The different rate of improvement has been associated with the adequacy and promptness of the international assistance program. An apparent stabilization of mortality rates may be due to extremely high mortality rates among the most vulnerable. For example, a survey in Baidoa, Somalia, found that approximately 75% of displaced children under 5 years died within a six-month period and the proportion of children under 5 in the displaced population fell from 18.3% to 7.8% during this period (28).

Rwandan Refugees, North Kivu Camps, Zaire

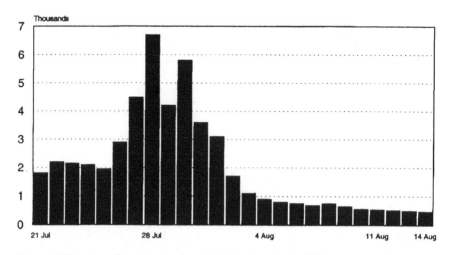

Figure 1 Number of deaths per day, July 21–August 14, 1994.
Source: UNCHR (Reference 20).

Hartisheik A Camp, Ethiopia, 1988-1989

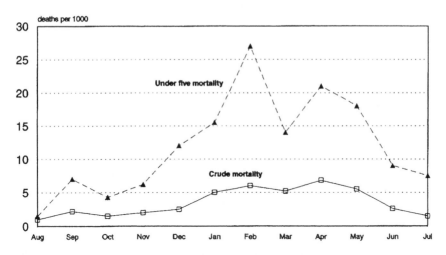

Figure 2 Crude and under-five mortality rates, Somali refugees.
Source: Save the Children Fund; UNCHR; Ethiopian Ministry of Health (Reference 38).

The limited data available suggest that death rates have been extremely high among internally displaced populations. Mortality rates among populations displaced inside Somalia in 1992 and southern Sudan in 1993 were particularly high (Table 3). During the period 1991–1993, the excess mortality due to fighting and famine in Somalia has been estimated at 240,000 deaths in a population of approximately 6 million (21). However, it is not known how many of these deaths occurred among the internally displaced. In Bosnia, CMRs

Table 3 Estimated monthly crude mortality rates (deaths per 1000 per month) among internally displaced persons, 1990–1994.

Date (reference)	Country	Crude Mortality Rate
January–December 1990 (9)	Liberia	7.1
April 1991–March 1992 (23)	Somalia (Merca)	13.8
April–November 1992 (28)	Somalia (Baidoa)	50.7
April–December 1992 (28)	Somalia (Afgoi)	16.5
April 1992–March 1993 (12)	Sudan (Ayod)	23.0
April 1992–March 1993 (12)	Sudan (Akon)	13.7
April 1992–March 1993 (39)	Bosnia (Zepa)	3.0
April 1993 (13)	Bosnia (Sarajevo)	2.9
May 1995 (45)	Angola (Cafunfo)	24.9
February 1996 (48)	Liberia (Bong)	16.5

reported in Muslim enclaves during the height of the war in 1993 were approximately four times prewar rates (39).

Demographic risk factors

Most deaths in refugee populations have occurred among children under 5 years of age; for example, 65% of deaths among Kurdish refugees on the Turkish border occurred in the 17% of the population less than 5 years of age (8). Among newly arrived Mozambican refugees in Malawi in 1992, the age-specific death rate for children under 5 years of age was 4 to 5 times the CMR, suggesting that most refugee deaths were occurring in this age group (11). An exception to this trend was documented in the Rwandan refugee camps of eastern Zaire where under-5 death rates were no higher than CMRs during the first 4 weeks after the influx – probably because most deaths in this population were caused by cholera, which has high attack rates and high case-fatality rates among all age groups (32). Nevertheless, the risk of mortality in the Rwandan refugee population was highest among the more than 10,000 unaccompanied children, mostly orphans, who were registered in North Kivu. Daily death rates in this group during the first six weeks after the influx were 20 to 80 times higher than Rwandan estimates for under-five mortality before the crisis (18). In most emergency situations, gender-specific mortality data has not been collected. However, in the Gundhum II camp in Bangladesh, the death rate among Burmese refugee girls less than 1 year of age was almost twice the rate for boys; among refugees older than 5 years, the female-specific death rate was 3.5 times that for males (9). Among Kurdish refugees on the Turkey-Iraq border in 1991, however, the death rate among males and females was approximately equal (8). Despite the lack of data on women's health in emergency situations, a number of authors have described increased risk of both morbidity and mortality among women in refugee and displaced populations (59).

Causes of mortality and morbidity

The most common reported causes of death among refugees during the early influx phase have been diarrheal diseases, measles, acute respiratory infections, malaria, and other infectious diseases (41). These diseases have been the most critical causes of morbidity and the focus of most public health interventions. The major causes of morbidity among Rwandan refugees in the Zaire camps in August 1994 are typical of those conditions commonly reported in the acute phase of a refugee emergency (Figure 3). High prevalences of acute protein-energy malnutrition have contributed to elevated case-fatality rates for communicable diseases and to overall high mortality rates. In some settings, most deaths could be attributed to one or two communicable diseases. In the Goma camps of eastern Zaire, for example, more than 90% of the estimated

Rwandan Refugees, North Kivu Camps, Zaire, August 8-14, 1994

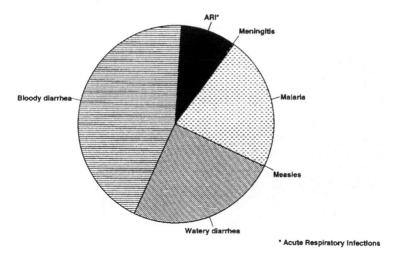

Figure 3 Reported causes of morbidity, outpatient clinics.
Source: UNCHR (Reference 20).

50,000 deaths in the first month after the refugee influx were caused by either watery or bloody diarrhea (20).

DIARRHEAL DISEASES   Epidemics of severe diarrheal disease have been increasingly common among refugee populations. When approximately 400,000 Kurdish refugees fled Iraqi cities in 1991 and found refuge in squalid camps on the Turkish border, more than 70% of deaths were associated with diarrhea, including cholera (8). Cholera epidemics have occurred in refugee camps in Malawi, Zimbabwe, Swaziland, Nepal, Bangladesh, Turkey, Afghanistan, Burundi, and Zaire (9, 20). In the Goma area of eastern Zaire, an explosive cholera outbreak occurred within the first week of the arrival of refugees. This outbreak was associated with rapid fecal contamination of the alkaline water of Lake Kivu, which was the primary source of drinking water for the refugees. As the cholera outbreak subsided, an equally lethal epidemic of dysentery occurred. Consequently, over 90% of deaths in the first month after the influx were attributed to diarrheal disease (Figure 4). Cholera case-fatality rates in refugee camps have ranged between 3% and 30%, depending on the degree of preparedness. Outbreaks of dysentery caused by *Shigella dysenteriae type I* have been reported since 1991 in Malawi, Nepal, Kenya, Bangladesh, Burundi, Rwanda, Tanzania, and Zaire (9, 20). Dysentery case-fatality rates have been as high as 10% in young children and the elderly (14).

Mugunga Camp, Zaire, July–August 1994

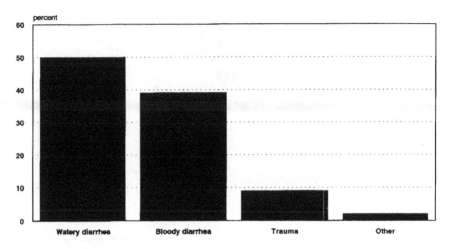

Figure 4 Major causes of death among Rwandan refugees, all ages.
Source: CDC/UNCHR survey (Reference 20).

MEASLES   Outbreaks of measles within refugee camps were common prior to 1990 and caused many deaths. Low levels of immunization coverage, coupled with high rates of undernutrition and vitamin A deficiency, played a critical role in the spread of measles and the subsequent mortality within some refugee camps. Measles has been one of the leading causes of death among children in refugee camps; in addition, measles has contributed to high malnutrition rates among those who have survived the initial illness. Measles infection may lead to or exacerbate vitamin A deficiency, compromising immunity and leaving the patient susceptible to xerophthalmia, blindness, and premature death. In early 1985, the measles-specific death rate among children under 5 in one eastern Sudan camp was 30 per 1000/month; the case-fatality rate (CFR) based on reported cases was almost 30% (35). Large numbers of measles deaths have been reported in camps in Somalia, Bangladesh, Sudan, and Ethiopia (40). Since 1990, mass immunization campaigns have been effective in reducing the measles morbidity and mortality rates in refugee camps; for example, in Kenya, Tanzania, Burundi, and Malawi. In other large refugee populations (e.g. Somalis in Ethiopia in 1989; Iraqis in Turkey in 1991; Rwandans in Zaire and Tanzania in 1994), measles outbreaks did not occur probably because immunization coverage rates were already high in the countries of origin of the refugees (42, 20).

Since 1990, high measles-associated death rates have been reported more commonly in internally displaced populations (e.g. Somalia and Sudan) than among refugees. Population surveys conducted at four different sites in southern

Somalia in 1992–93 found that between 50% and 84% of all deaths were associated with either measles or diarrhea (3). One example of a measles outbreak following an acute natural disaster occurred following the eruption of Mt. Pinatubo in the Philippines in 1991. Among the more than 100,000 people displaced into evacuation camps, more than 18,000 cases of measles were reported. Measles was associated with 22% of deaths reported during the three months following the eruption among this displaced population, most of whom were members of a tribal group that resisted efforts to vaccinate children against measles (10).

MALARIA   Malaria has caused high rates of morbidity and mortality among refugees and displaced persons in countries where malaria is endemic, such as Thailand, eastern Sudan, Somalia, Kenya, Malawi, Zimbabwe, Burundi, Rwanda, and Zaire (9, 20). Malaria-specific mortality rates have been especially high when refugees from areas of low malaria endemicity have fled through, or into, areas of high endemicity. Recent examples include the movement of Cambodian refugees through highly endemic areas into Thailand in 1979, the influx of highland Ethiopians into eastern Sudan in 1985, and the exodus of highland Rwandans into Zaire in 1994. The severity of malaria outbreaks in Africa has been exacerbated by the rapid spread of chloroquine resistance during the 1980s; in addition, resistance to sulfadoxine-pyrimethamine (Fansidar[R]) has also been reported among Rwandan refugees in eastern Zaire since 1994 (Médecins sans Frontières, Holland, unpublished data).

ACUTE RESPIRATORY INFECTIONS   Acute respiratory infections (ARIs) have been consistently reported among the leading causes of death in refugee populations. In Thailand (1979), Somalia (1980), Sudan (1985), Honduras (1986), and Malawi (1989), ARIs were cited among the three main causes of mortality in refugee camps, particularly among children (9). The crowding, poor ventilation, inadequate shelter, and prolonged exposure that refugees and internally displaced persons often experience are common risk factors for respiratory infections with poor outcomes.

MENINGITIS   The crowding associated with refugee camps places refugees at high risk of meningococcal meningitis in endemic areas, particularly in countries within or near the traditionally described "meningitis belt" of sub-Saharan Africa (29). Based on experience elsewhere in Africa, a threshold incidence of 15 cases per 100,000 population per week in two successive weeks has been used to predict a full-blown epidemic. Outbreaks have been reported in Malawi, Ethiopia, Burundi, and Zaire; however, mass immunization has proved to be an effective epidemic control measure in these situations and meningococcal morbidity and mortality rates have been relatively low. In the Zairian camp of Kibumba, the incidence reached 19 per 100,000 during the week of August 8–14, 1994, resulting in a mass vaccination campaign that successfully averted a wider epidemic (20).

HEPATITIS   Outbreaks of hepatitis E infection among refugees in Somalia (1986), Ethiopia (1989), and Kenya (1991) have led to high attack rates and CFRs among pregnant women as high as 17% (5, 25). This disease has only recently been introduced to Africa; therefore, most adults have not been exposed to the disease. Since previous exposure to hepatitis A and B is relatively common in this region, any epidemic of hepatitis-like illness in Africa with high attack rates among adults is likely to be caused by infection with the hepatitis E virus. The virus is enterically transmitted and is often associated with contamination of water supplies; the role of person-to-person spread is not yet clear, but may not be an important mode of transmission.

TUBERCULOSIS   In complex emergencies when basic health services have been disrupted, treatment of patients with active tuberculosis may be inadequate or incomplete, leading potentially to increased transmission in affected communities. Since the war began in Bosnia and Herzegovina in 1991, the incidence of new cases of tuberculosis has reportedly increased fourfold (39). Likewise, in Somalia during the civil war and famine of 1991–1992, routine case-finding, treatment, and follow-up of tuberculosis patients almost ceased. Consequently, there was a marked increase in both the incidence of new cases and the tuberculosis-related CFR (37). Tuberculosis is well recognized as a health problem among refugee and displaced populations. The crowded living conditions and underlying poor nutritional status of refugee populations may foster the spread of the disease. Although not a leading cause of mortality during the emergency phase, tuberculosis often emerges as a critical problem once measles and diarrheal diseases have been adequately controlled. For example, among adult refugees in Somalia and eastern Sudan in 1985, 26% and 38%, respectively, of deaths were attributed to tuberculosis (9). The high prevalence of HIV infection among many African refugee populations may contribute to the high rate of transmission.

HIV INFECTION AND OTHER SEXUALLY TRANSMITTED DISEASES   Although there is no reason to believe that refugees are at higher risk of HIV infection than nonrefugee populations, several recent mass population migrations have taken place in areas where HIV infection prevalence rates are high; for example, in Burundi, Rwanda, Malawi, Ethiopia, and Zaire. In one of the few refugee populations studied for this infection, the HIV prevalence among adult male Sudanese refugees in western Ethiopia in 1992 was 7%; the prevalence of infection among commercial sex workers living in the vicinity of the camp was greater than 40% (CDC, unpublished data, 1992). Serological surveys in this population also revealed high rates of previous infection with syphilis and chancroid. The contribution of HIV infection to morbidity and mortality among refugees has not been documented, but may be significant. In the former Yugoslavia, there have been many reports of sexual assault and increasing prostitution; in addition, high rates of violence-related trauma have increased the rate of blood transfusions (39). In this setting, where shortages of laboratory reagents to test blood for HIV are widespread, the risk of increased transmission of HIV is high, though this trend has not yet been confirmed by studies.

Nutritional deficiencies

PROTEIN-ENERGY MALNUTRITION   The prevalence of moderate to severe acute malnutrition in a random sample of children less than 5 years of age is generally a reliable indicator of this condition in a population. Since weight is more sensitive to sudden changes in food availability than height, nutritional assessments during emergencies focus on measuring weight-for-height. Also, weight-for-height is a more appropriate measurement for ongoing monitoring of the effectiveness of feeding programs. Moderate to severe acute malnutrition is defined as either a weight-for-height more than 2 standard deviations below the mean of the CDC/NCHS/WHO reference population (Z-score less than –2) or weight-for-height less than 80% of the reference population median (9). Severe acute malnutrition is defined as weight-for-height more than 3 standard deviations below the reference mean (Z-score less than –3) or less than 70% of the reference median. All children with edema are classified as having severe acute malnutrition.

As a screening measurement, the mid-upper arm circumference (MUAC) may also be used to assess acute undernutrition, although there is not complete agreement on which cutoff values should be used as indicators. Field studies indicate that a MUAC between 12.0 cm and 12.5 cm correlates with a weight-for-height Z-score of –2; the lower figure (12.0 cm) is more appropriate in children less than 2 years of age (57).

Prevalence rates of acute malnutrition among children less than 5 years of age in various refugee populations have been as high as 50% among Ethiopian refugees in eastern Sudan (1985), 45% among Sudanese refugees arriving in Ethiopia during 1990, 29% among Somali refugees in Kenya in 1991, and 48% among Mozambicans in Zimbabwe (1992) (42). In some settings, refugee children who were adequately nourished upon arrival in camps have developed acute malnutrition due either to inadequate food rations or to severe epidemics of diarrheal disease. In the Hartisheik refugee camp in eastern Ethiopia, for example, the prevalence of acute malnutrition increased from less than 10% to almost 25% during a six-month period in late 1988 and early 1989 due to inadequate food rations (38). Although the prevalence decreased in mid-1989 following improvements in the ration distribution system and supplementary rations for all children under 5 years, six years later the situation again deteriorated. Surveys in March 1995 in Hartisheik found an acute malnutrition prevalence of 13.7% (45).

In early 1991, the prevalence of acute malnutrition among Kurdish refugee children aged 12 to 23 months increased from less than 5% to 13% during a two-month period following a severe outbreak of diarrheal disease (60). Surprisingly, the malnutrition prevalence among children less than 12 months of age was less than 4%; however, a survey revealed that the diarrhea-associated death rate in this age group was three times higher than the death rate among children 12–23 months of age. Thus, it is likely that most malnourished infants died, resulting in a deceptively low malnutrition prevalence among the survivors (60).

The prevalence of acute malnutrition was between 18% and 23% in Rwandan refugee camps in eastern Zaire, following the severe cholera and dysentery epidemics during the first month after the influx (20). Children with a history of dysentery within three days prior to the survey were three times more likely to be malnourished than those with no history of recent dysentery. Also, children in families with no adult male present were at significantly higher risk of malnutrition than those children in households headed by an adult male (20). Prevalence rates of acute malnutrition among the internally displaced have tended to be extremely high. In southern Somalia during 1992, the prevalence of acute malnutrition among children less than 5 years in displaced persons camps in Marka and Qorioley was 75%, compared with 43% among town residents (23). In March 1993, approximately 70% of internally displaced children in several sites in southern Sudan were acutely malnourished (12). Acute malnutrition prevalences documented by sample surveys among various internally displaced populations are presented in Table 4.

MICRONUTRIENT DEFICIENCY DISEASES   High incidence rates of several micronutrient deficiency diseases have been reported in many refugee camps, especially in Africa. Frequently, famine-affected and displaced populations have already experienced low levels of dietary vitamin A intake and, therefore, may have very low vitamin A reserves. Furthermore, the typical rations provided in large-scale relief operations lack vitamin A, putting these populations at high risk. In addition, those communicable diseases that are highly incident in refugee camps, such as measles and diarrhea, are known to rapidly deplete vitamin A stores. Consequently, young refugee and displaced children are at high risk of developing vitamin A deficiency. In 1990, more than 18,000 cases of pellagra, caused by food rations deficient in niacin, were reported among Mozambican refugees in Malawi (7). Numerous outbreaks of scurvy (vitamin C deficiency) were documented in refugee camps in Somalia, Ethiopia, and Sudan between 1982 and 1991. Cross-sectional surveys performed in 1986–1987 reported prevalence rates as high as 45% among females and 36% among males; prevalence increased with age (17). The prevalence of scurvy was highly associated with

Table 4 Prevalence of acute malnutrition* among children <5 years of age in internally displaced and conflict-affected populations, 1988–1995.

Date (reference)	Country (region)	Population affected	Prevalence of acute malnutrition
1988 (9)	Sudan (South Darfur)	80,000	36%
1992 (42)	Southern Somalia	3,000,000	47%–75%
1993 (12)	Sudan (Ame)	47,000	81%
1994 (43)	Sudan (Bahr el Ghazal)[1]	345,000	36.1%
1994 (43)	Ethiopia (Gode)[1]	35,000	35.6%
1994 (44)	Afghanistan (Sarashahi)[2]	163,000	18.6%
1995 (45)	Angola (Cafunfo)[3]	10,000	29.2%
1995 (45)	Liberia (Goba town, Margibi)[2]	N/A	11.7%
1995 (46)	Sierra Leone (Bo)[3]	250,000	19.8%
1995 (46)	Sudan (Labone)[3]	38,000	22.6%
1996 (48)	Zaire (Masisi)[2]	100,000	31.0%

* Acute malnutrition defined either as weight-for-height 2 standard deviations below the reference mean or less than 80% of the reference median.
[1] Survey conducted by Médecins sans Frontières (Belgium).
[2] Survey conducted by Médecins sans Frontières (Holland).
[3] Survey conducted by Action Internationale contre la Faim.

the period of residence in camps, a reflection of the time exposed to rations lacking in vitamin C. Outbreaks of scurvy and beriberi were also reported among Bhutanese refugees in Nepal during 1993 (46). Iron deficiency anemia has been reported in many refugee populations, affecting particularly women of childbearing age and young children (47).

Other health effects

In addition to high prevalence of nutritional deficiencies and a high incidence of communicable diseases, injuries related to war trauma and landmines have been common, especially among internally displaced persons and those who have been trapped in zones of conflict. In Bosnia, excess mortality reported among the displaced or in besieged Muslim enclaves has been associated mainly with war-related trauma. In the capital of Sarajevo, for example, an estimated 6800 deaths (57% of all mortality) and 16,000 injuries were attributed to war trauma between April 1992 and March 1993 (13). The CMR in the city increased almost fourfold between 1991 (prewar) and 1993. Population surveys in southern and central Somalia determined that between 4% and 11% of deaths during April 1992–January 1993 were caused by war-related trauma (3). Sexual assault of displaced women has been increasingly common; for example, reports from the former Yugoslavia estimate that at least 20,000 Bosnian, Serbian, and Croatian displaced women have been raped (1). The Office of the United Nations High Commissioner for

Refugees (UNHCR) documented 192 cases of rape of Somali refugee women in Kenyan camps during a seven-month period during 1993; in addition, several thousand rapes were estimated to have been unreported (52). The psychosocial problems of refugees have not been extensively documented, except for several studies conducted on refugees who have been resettled in industrialized countries. One review of such studies conducted in Canada, the United States, and Sweden found that between 30% and 75% of refugee children and adolescents demonstrated symptoms and signs of posttraumatic stress disorder (26). Increases in neonatal mortality rates and in deaths associated with inadequately treated chronic diseases have also been reported in the former Yugoslavia, where basic medical services have been severely disrupted by the war and related economic collapse (39).

Prevention of public health effects of complex disasters

The prevention of the public health consequences of complex disasters can be classified into three categories: primary, secondary, and tertiary.

Primary prevention

Primary prevention is the basic strategy of public health, and epidemiology is one of its essential tools. In situations of armed conflict, however, epidemiology can be practiced safely and reliably in very few areas. Hence, the traditional documentation, monitoring, and evaluation elements of disease prevention may be ineffective in these situations. The provision of adequate food, shelter, potable water, sanitation, and immunization has proved problematic in countries disrupted by war. Primary prevention in such circumstances, therefore, means stopping the violence.

More effective diplomatic and political mechanisms need to be developed that might resolve conflicts early in their evolution prior to the stage when food shortages occur, health services collapse, populations migrate, and significant adverse public health outcomes emerge. The notion of national sovereignty embodied in the United Nations Charter has sometimes forced the international community to stand by and watch extreme examples of human rights abuses until a certain threshold of tolerance has been crossed and strong action has been taken, as in the case of Somalia. By the time such action has been taken, however, the conflict has often advanced to a stage where any involvement by outside forces is costly and dangerous. Cautious, neutral, but determined diplomacy of the kind practiced by the Atlanta-based Carter Center in Ethiopia, Sudan, Haiti, and Bosnia-Herzegovina might serve as a model for future conflict resolution efforts. Epidemiologists and behavioral scientists might play a role in this process by systematically studying the dynamics and characteristic behaviors that sustain conflict situations and by seeking to identify measures that might reduce the level of tension between opposing sides.

Secondary prevention

Secondary prevention involves the early detection of evolving conflict-related food scarcity and population movements, preparedness for interventions that mitigate their public health impact, and the development of appropriate public health skills to enable relief workers to work effectively in emergency settings.

EARLY DETECTION   Disaster detection activities in the form of early warning systems have existed for some time; however, these systems have tended to focus on monitoring natural rather than man-made hazards. Such systems, implemented by a range of United Nations agencies and US Government-supported programs, routinely monitor crop yields, food availability, staple cereal prices, rainfall, and household income in a number of African countries, as well as conducting periodic vulnerability assessments. The information generated is published and disseminated widely in periodic bulletins and has proven useful in predicting natural disasters, such as drought throughout southern Africa in 1992. Nevertheless, these systems have generally not developed early indicators related to human rights abuses, ethnic conflict, political instability, and migration. Other groups such as Africa Watch, Physicians for Human Rights, Amnesty International, and African Rights have conducted assessments of vulnerability in countries, such as Burundi, relatively early in the evolution of civil conflict. The problem with such assessments is that the results are often ignored by the governments of those nations able to intervene unless their security interests are perceived to be threatened. Early in 1992, for example, reports by several nongovernmental organizations (NGO) on the deteriorating situation in Somalia were largely ignored by the international community. Epidemiologists might play an important role in developing and field testing the sensitivity and predictive value of a broad range of early public health emergency indicators.

CONTINGENCY PLANNING   The inability of the world to promptly address the explosive epidemic of cholera among Rwandan refugees in eastern Zaire, in July 1994, underscored the lack of emergency preparedness planning at a global level. This epidemic highlighted the inadequate reserves of essential medical supplies and equipment for establishing and distributing safe water, as well as revealing a lack of technical consensus on the most appropriate interventions. Agencies that did have the appropriate skills and experience, such as Oxfam and MSF, lacked the necessary resources, and those agencies with the resources and logistics, such as the United States military, lacked the technical experience in emergency relief. Preparedness planning needs to take place both at a coordinated international level and at the level of countries where complex emergencies might occur. Relief agencies need resources to implement early warning systems, maintain technical expertise, train personnel, build reserves of relief supplies, and develop their logistic capacity. At the country level, all health development programs should have an emergency preparedness component that should include the establishment of standard public health policies (e.g. immunization and management of epidemics), treatment protocols, staff training, and the maintenance of reserves of essential drugs and vaccines for use in disasters.

PERSONNEL TRAINING Front-line relief workers in complex emergencies are often volunteers recruited by NGOs who sometimes lack specific training and experience in emergency relief. They require knowledge and practical experience in a broad range of subjects, including food and nutrition, water and sanitation, disease surveillance, immunization, communicable disease control, epidemic management, and maternal and child health care. They should be able to conduct rapid needs assessments, establish public health program priorities, work closely with affected communities, train local workers, coordinate with a complex array of relief organizations, monitor and evaluate the impact of their programs, and efficiently manage scarce resources. In addition, they need to function effectively in an often hostile and dangerous environment; such skills are specific to emergencies and are not necessarily present in the average graduate of a medical or nursing school. Therefore, relief agencies need to allocate more resources to relevant training and orientation of their staff, as well as providing adequate support in the field. Indigenous health workers in emergency-prone countries, while often familiar with the management of common endemic diseases, also need training in the particular skills required to work effectively under emergency conditions.

Tertiary prevention

Tertiary prevention involves prevention of excess mortality and morbidity once a disaster has occurred. The health problems that consistently cause most deaths and severe morbidity as well as those demographic groups most at risk have been identified. Most deaths in refugee and displaced populations are preventable using currently available and affordable technology. Relief programs, therefore, must channel all available resources toward addressing measles, diarrheal diseases, malnutrition, acute respiratory infections, and, in some cases, malaria, especially among women and young children. The challenge is to institutionalize this knowledge within the major relief organizations and to ensure that relief management and logistical systems provide the necessary resources to implement key interventions in a timely manner.

Initially, both refugees and displaced persons often find themselves in crowded, unsanitary camps in remote regions where the provision of basic needs is highly difficult. Prolonged exposure to the violence of war and the deprivations of long journeys by refugees cause severe stress. Upon arrival at their destination, refugees – most of whom tend to be women and children – may suffer severe anxiety or depression, compounded by the loss of dignity associated with complete dependence on the generosity of others for their survival. If refugee camps are located near borders or close to areas of continuing armed conflict, the desire for security is an overriding concern. Therefore, the first priority of any relief operation is to ensure adequate protection and camps should be placed sufficiently distant from borders to reassure refugees that they are safe.

To diminish the sense of helplessness and dependency, refugees should be given an active role in the planning and implementation of relief programs. Nevertheless, giving total control of the distribution of relief items to so-called refugee "leaders" may be dangerous. For example, leaders of the former Hutu-controlled Rwandan government took control of the distribution system in Zairian refugee camps in July 1994, resulting in relief supplies being diverted to young male members of the former Rwandan Army. Surveys indicated that households headed by single women had diminished access to food and shelter material, leading to elevated malnutrition rates among children in those households (20).

In the absence of conflict resolution, those communities that are totally dependent on external aid for their survival because they have either been displaced from their homes or are living under a state of siege must be provided the basic minimum resources necessary to maintain health and well-being. The provision of adequate food, clean water, shelter, sanitation, and warmth will prevent the most severe public health consequences of complex emergencies. It would seem that the temporary location of refugees in small settlements or villages in the host country would have fewer adverse public health consequences than their placement in crowded, often unsanitary camps. Although studies to compare health outcomes among refugees in camps and in free settlements have not been possible, surveillance data from Guinea and Malawi indicate that refugees in local villages have fared better than those in camps (54).

Relief measures

The following measures represent the basic elements of emergency response:

PROVISION OF ADEQUATE FOOD RATIONS   General food rations should contain at least 2000 kilocalories of energy per person per day (more in cold climates), as well as the minimum daily allowances of protein and micronutrients recommended by the United Nations (47). Food should be distributed regularly to family units, taking care that socially vulnerable groups such as female-headed households, unaccompanied minors, and the elderly receive their fair share. In addition, adequate cooking fuel, utensils, and facilities to grind whole-grain cereals need to be distributed. In children less than 2 years of age, breastfeeding will provide considerable protection against communicable diseases, including diarrhea; attempts to introduce or distribute breastmilk substitutes and infant feeding bottles should be strongly opposed in an emergency situation. The evidence that vitamin A deficiency is associated with increased childhood mortality and disabling blindness is now so convincing that supplements of vitamin A should be provided routinely to all refugee children under 5 years of age at first contact and every 3–6 months thereafter (30).

Although *supplementary feeding programs* are often popular with relief agencies, their effectiveness in refugee camps in the absence of adequate general rations has been questioned (19). When the family ration is insufficient to provide adequate energy to all family members, then the supplementary ration (usually 400–600 kilocalories per day) may be the only food source for young children. This is not enough to maintain nutrition. If adequate general rations are provided, children who are clinically undernourished may benefit from daily food supplements, but only if efforts are made to identify them in the community and to ensure their attendance at feeding centers. *Therapeutic feeding programs* should be established to provide total nutritional rehabilitation of severely malnourished children (31).

PROVISION OF ADEQUATE QUANTITIES OF CLEAN WATER AND SANITATION FACILITIES   UNHCR recommends that a minimum of 15 liters of clean water be provided per person per day for domestic needs – cooking, drinking, and bathing (50). In general, ensuring access to adequate quantities of relatively clean water is probably more effective in preventing diarrheal disease, especially bacterial dysentery, than providing small quantities of pure microbe-free water. When refugee camps are unavoidable, the proximity to safe water sources needs to be recognized as the most important criterion for site selection. In addition, measures to prevent post-source contamination need to be implemented, including chlorination, sufficient storage containers, and – if available – containers with narrow openings. Adequate sanitation is an essential component of diarrheal disease prevention. While the eventual goal of sanitation programs should be the construction of one latrine per family, interim measures may include the designation of separate defecation areas and the temporary provision of neighborhood latrines (one for 20 families). To achieve maximal impact, these measures should be complemented by community hygiene education and regular distribution of soap. The objective of postemergency sanitation measures should be to restore the predisaster levels of environmental services rather than attempting to improve on the original levels.

PROGRAMS FOR THE PREVENTION OF SPECIFIC COMMUNICABLE DISEASES   Public pressure for action to control communicable disease following a disaster often focuses on the perceived need for mass vaccination, in particular against cholera and typhoid, diseases commonly associated in the public mind with disasters.

In the case of refugees and displaced persons living in camps where water and sanitation facilities are inadequate, the elevated risk has been well documented. However, mass vaccination against cholera and typhoid fever are not usually indicated for the following reasons:

- If the organism is not present in the area and has not been introduced after the disaster, the disease poses no threat, regardless of environmental conditions. Thus, where the organism is not present, it is highly unlikely to pose a problem even if water supplies are contaminated. At present, cholera may be a threat following disasters in Africa, Asia, much of Latin America, and parts of the former Soviet Union, such as the Central Asian republics and the Caucasus.
- The most practical and effective strategy to prevent waterborne cholera and typhoid is to provide clean water in adequate quantities and adequate sanitation. Sufficient soap and hygiene education will further prevent the transmission of waterborne diseases. Receiving a dose of vaccine may give communities a false sense of security and lead them to fail to take elementary precautions such as boiling water or adequately reheating leftover food.
- A mass vaccination campaign cannot provide protection against typhoid at the time of greatest risk from contaminated water because multiple doses are required to achieve adequate immunity. Currently, the most afford-able vaccine for developing countries (parenteral, heat-phenol-inactivated vaccine) has relatively low efficacy, requires two serial doses 1–4 weeks apart, and has severe side-effects. The newer oral, live-attenuated vaccine (Ty21) has higher efficacy; however, it is expensive and requires that four serial doses be administered (6).
- The traditional parenteral cholera vaccine often used in epidemic settings in the past was only 50% effective in preventing cholera and is no longer recommended by WHO (56). Of the two newer and potentially effective vaccines currently available, one requires two doses and does not induce immunity until 7–10 days after the second dose; the other, a single-dose, oral, live vaccine, has never been subjected to testing under field conditions, and its use in refugee populations would be controversial.

On the other hand, disasters that cause significant displacement of populations into crowded camps create a high risk of *measles* transmission, especially in areas where immunization coverage rates are low. Immunization of children against measles is probably the single most important (and cost-effective) preventive measure in emergency-affected populations, particularly those housed in camps. Since infants as young as 6 months of age frequently contract measles in refugee camp outbreaks and are at greater risk of dying owing to impaired nutrition, it is recommended that measles immunization programs in emergency settings target all children between the age of 6 months and

5 years (40). When undernutrition affects the entire population, and when previous exposure to measles is questionable, it may be prudent to extend the coverage to children 6–14 years of age. Immunization programs should eventually include all antigens recommended by WHO's Expanded Programme on Immunization.

Malaria control in refugee camps is more difficult. Under the transient circumstances that characterize most refugee camps, vector control techniques have generally been impractical and expensive. Prompt identification and treatment of symptomatic individuals is a more effective measure to reduce malaria mortality, although the spread of chloroquine and sulfadoxine-pyrimethamine resistance means that effective case management will become more expensive and technically more challenging in the future.

In areas where epidemics of *meningococcal meningitis* are known to occur, such as in Africa's "meningitis belt," surveillance for meningitis should be established. In the event of an outbreak, vaccination should be considered if the following criteria are met: 1. the presence of meningococcal disease is laboratory confirmed; 2. serogrouping indicates the presence of group A or group C organisms. If it is logistically feasible, the household contacts of identified cases should be checked for vaccination status and then immunized if necessary. It may be simpler to organize a mass immunization program. Because cases of meningococcal meningitis are likely to cluster geographically within a refugee camp, it may be most efficient to focus the vaccination campaign on the affected area(s) first. Vaccination of children and young adults aged between 1 and 25 years will generally cover the at-risk population (29).

EPIDEMIC PREPAREDNESS   Epidemic preparedness is a critical element of an emergency relief program and consists of the establishment of surveillance, including standard case definitions; development of standard case management protocols; agreement on policies for prevention (including vaccination and prophylaxis); identification of a laboratory to confirm index cases of epidemic diseases; identification of sources of relevant vaccines; establishment of reserves of essential medical supplies (ORT, intravenous solutions, and antibiotics); identification of treatment sites, triage systems, and training needs; identification of expert assistance for epidemic investigation; development of environmental management plans; and implementation of community education and prevention programs.

APPROPRIATE CURATIVE PROGRAMS STRESSING MATERNAL AND CHILD HEALTH CARE   An essential drug list and standardized treatment protocols are necessary elements of a curative program. It is not necessary to develop totally new guidelines in each refugee situation: Several excellent manuals already exist, from which guidelines can be adapted to suit local conditions (16, 27). WHO has also developed guidelines for the clinical management of dehydration from diarrhea and for acute respiratory infections that can be used by trained community health workers (CHWs). Curative services should be decentralized in a camp system of CHWs, health posts, central outpatient referral clinics, and a small inpatient facility to treat severe emergency cases. Patients requiring surgery or prolonged hospitalization should be referred to a local district or provincial hospital that will require assistance with drugs and other medical supplies to cope with the extra patient load. Some relief programs, such as those in Somalia, Sudan, and Malawi, have successfully trained large numbers of refugees as CHWs to detect cases of diarrhea, malaria, and acute respiratory infections; provide primary treatment; and refer severely ill patients to a clinic, thereby increasing coverage by health services and diminishing reliance on expatriate workers. Camp medical services need to ensure that women and children have preferential access, and specific programs need to provide an integrated package of growth monitoring, immunization, antenatal and post-natal care, the treatment of common ailments, and health promotion.

MANAGEMENT OF DIARRHEAL DISEASES   The most effective management of acute watery diarrhea, including cholera, is oral rehydration therapy (ORT) supported by adequate nutrition, including continued breastfeeding. The initial high CFR among cholera patients treated in clinics in Goma, Zaire, was found to be due to a slow rate of rehydration, inadequate use of ORT, use of inappropriate intravenous fluids, and the inexperience of many relief workers in the management of severe diarrheal illness (36). Health workers need to be well trained in the clinical assessment of dehydration, the provision of ORT in supervised settings, and the treatment of severe diarrheal illness with intravenous therapy and/or appropriate antibiotics. In the event of an outbreak of *cholera*, early case finding will allow for rapid initiation of treatment. Aggressive case-finding by trained CHWs should be coupled with community education to prevent panic and to promote good domestic hygiene. Treatment centers should be easily accessible. If the attack rate for cholera is high, it may be necessary to establish temporary cholera wards to handle the patient load. Health centers should be adequately stocked with ORS, IV fluids, and appropriate antibiotics. Rehydration needs to be aggressive, but carefully supervised, especially when children are rehydrated with intravenous fluids, in order to prevent fluid overload. Antibiotics have been shown to reduce the volume and duration of diarrhea in cholera patients. Antibiotics should be administered orally; tetracycline is the antibiotic of choice if the pathogen is sensitive. Single-dose doxycycline can be used when available. In recent outbreaks in emergency settings, *Vibrio cholerae* 01 has been resistant to multiple antibiotics; in such situations, especially in developing countries, the use of more expensive antibiotics may not be indicated, and treatment efforts should focus on rehydration.

Dysentery caused by *Shigella dysenteriae* type 1 has become increasingly common in African disaster settings. Appropriate treatment with antimicrobial drugs decreases the severity and duration of dysentery caused by all species and serotypes of *Shigella*, as well as reducing the duration of pathogen excretion. The choice of a first-line drug should be based on knowledge of local susceptibility patterns. If there is no response within 2 days, the antibiotic should be changed to another recommended for shigellosis in the area. Case management of dysentery has been complicated by increasing resistance of *S. dysenteriae* type 1 to common, affordable antibiotics. In the Zaire outbreak, the organism was resistant to all antibiotics except ciprofloxacin, which was used to treat those patients at high risk of mortality (young children, pregnant women, the elderly, and severely ill) (20). The emergence of dysentery caused by antibiotic-resistant strains of *Shigella dysenteriae* type 1 as a major public health problem among refugee populations in central Africa indicates the need for operational research to develop more effective prevention and case management strategies.

During the early phase of any emergency relief operation, *tuberculosis* control activities should be limited to the treatment of patients who present themselves to the health care system and in whom tubercle bacilli have been demonstrated. Although it may be theoretically easier to ensure patient compliance with protracted chemotherapy in the confined space of a refugee camp, the personnel needed to supervise treatment may not be available. In addition, the uncertain duration of stay, frequent changes of camp locations, and poor camp organization may hinder tuberculosis treatment programs. Therefore, tuberculosis control programs should not be established until other more critical priorities have been adequately addressed (33).

HEALTH INFORMATION SYSTEM A surveillance system is an essential part of the relief program and should be established immediately (9). Only information of public health importance should be collected. Mortality surveillance is critical and may require creative data collection methods such as 24-h graveyard surveillance. In addition, surveillance of nutritional status and important epidemic diseases such as measles, cholera, and dysentery should be instituted. Information on program coverage and effectiveness should also be systematically collected; such data should include the average quantity of food rations distributed, per capita clean water available, ratio of families to latrines, immunization coverage, and supplementary feeding program attendance. Information collected by the surveillance system needs to be analyzed and widely disseminated in timely bulletins.

OTHER PROGRAMS Recent wars have consciously targeted civilian populations; refugees from Somalia, Sudan, Mozambique, Angola, and Bosnia-Herzegovina have fled intensely traumatic situations. Many have been severely injured; others have been violently and sexually abused, such as women in the former Yugoslavia, Burmese refugees in Bangladesh, and Somali refugees in Kenya. Increasing numbers of refugees have been severely disabled by landmine injuries. Innovative and culturally appropriate programs of counseling, support, and rehabilitation are urgently needed for these people. Also, there is a need to develop specialized approaches to caring for unaccompanied children, such as those Rwandan children in the camps of eastern Zaire and Tanzania during 1994.

Once the emergency relief phase is over, new challenges arise. Many refugees, such as the Palestinians in the Middle East and the Afghans in Pakistan and Iran, remain in camps for decades. Public health programs need to be community-based and integrated with other development programs (such as education, agriculture, and income generation) that aim to minimize dependency on the outside world, restore dignity to stressed communities, and prepare for eventual repatriation to their homelands. Training of community health workers, particularly women, should be the cornerstone of these longer-term programs. New, and sometimes sensitive, issues such as family spacing and the prevention of infection with the human immunodeficiency virus (HIV) need to be addressed through community development processes (4).

Although existing technical knowledge is sufficient to prevent much of the mortality associated with mass displacement, refugees and internally displaced persons will continue to find refuge in remote regions where the provision of basic needs requires creative approaches. Therefore, there is a need for systematic operational and evaluation research in certain areas of nutrition (for example, effective methods of preventing micronutrient deficiency diseases), water supply, and disease control.

Recent and future trends

During the past decade, much progress has been made among the major relief agencies in standardizing approaches and procedures in public health emergencies. Training courses designed specifically for public health in emergency settings have been developed in Europe, the United States, and Australia. Standard guidelines and essential drugs lists have been developed and are routinely used in emergencies. The role of military forces in providing security and in directly providing emergency assistance has grown rapidly in recent years (34). Military forces have played a prominent role in relief operations in northern Iraq, Somalia, the former Yugoslavia, Zaire, Rwanda, and Haiti. The involvement of the military is often ambiguous, confusing the various tasks of peace-keeping, peace-enforcing, and providing relief. No one would doubt the logistical advantages of the military; however, this is not always matched with appropriate experience in the technical aspects of a relief operation. Furthermore, military assistance is expensive and because it depends on political decisions by national governments, it cannot always be integrated into disaster preparedness planning.

Relief management decisions need to be based on sound technical information, and assistance programs need to be systematically evaluated – not merely for their quantity and content, but also for their impact and effectiveness. Responsibilities for technical coordination and implementation of relief programs should increasingly be shared with proven, competent, and experienced NGOs. Greater resources need to be allocated to personnel training, emergency preparedness planning, and the maintenance of regional reserves of essential relief supplies. These activities need to include government and nongovernment agencies in countries where emergencies are likely to occur.

Recent emergencies have followed a predictable pattern of political unrest, civil war, human rights abuses, food shortages, and, finally, mass population displacement. There has been almost no preparedness for these emergencies within the public health community. Agencies involved in health development projects need to be aware of political realities in certain regions of the world and should integrate preparedness planning into all aspects of public health programs. Health information systems should incorporate plans to simplify and focus on major health problems in the event of emergencies. Immunization, diarrheal disease control, and community health worker training programs should likewise incorporate emergency contingency plans. Finally, increased attention needs to be given to the challenges of rehabilitation of national health services following the cessation of armed conflict and the repatriation of large numbers of refugees to their country of origin (22).

Note

* The US Government has the right to retain a nonexclusive, royalty-free license in and to any copyright covering this paper.

Literature cited

1. Amnesty Int. 1993. Bosnia and Herzegovina: rape and sexual abuse by armed forces. *Amnesty Int. Rep. EUR 63/01/93.* New York: Amnesty Int.
2. Babille M., de Colombani P., Guerra R., Zagaria N., Zanetti C., et al. 1994. Post-emergency epidemiological surveillance in Iraqi-Kurdish refugee camps in Iran. *Disasters* 18:58–75
3. Boss L. P., Toole M. J., Yip R. 1994. Assessments of mortality, morbidity, and nutritional status in Somalia during the 1991–1992 famine. *JAMA* 272:371–76
4. Burkholder B. T., Toole M. J. 1995. Evolution of complex disasters. *Lancet* 346:1012–15
5. Cent. Dis. Control Prev. 1987. Enterically transmitted, non-A, non-B hepatitis – East Africa. *MMWR* 36:241–44
6. Cent. Dis. Control Prev. 1990. Typhoid immunization. Recommendations of the Immunization Practices Advisory Committee. *MMWR* 39(RR-10):1–5
7. Cent. Dis. Control Prev. 1991. Outbreak of pellagra among Mozambican refugees – Malawi, 1990. *MMWR* 40:209–13
8. Cent. Dis. Control Prev. 1991. Public health consequences of acute displacement of Iraqi citizens: March–May 1991. *MMWR* 40:443–46
9. Cent. Dis. Control Prev. 1992. Famine affected, refugee, and displaced populations: Recommendations for Public Health Issues. *MMWR* 41:RR-13

10. Cent. Dis. Control Prev. 1992. Surveillance in evacuation camps after the eruption of Mt. Pinatubo, Philippines. *MMWR* 41/SS-4:9–12

11. Cent. Dis. Control Prev. 1993. Mortality among newly arrived Mozambican refugees, Zimbabwe and Malawi, 1992. *MMWR* 42:468–69, 475–77

12. Cent. Dis. Control Prev. 1993. Nutrition and mortality assessment – Southern Sudan, March 1993. *MMWR* 42:304–8

13. Cent. Dis. Control Prev. 1993. Status of Public Health – Bosnia and Herzegovina, August–September 1993. *MMWR* 42:973, 979–82

14. Cent. Dis. Control Prev. 1994. Health status of displaced persons following civil war – Burundi, December 1993–January 1994. *MMWR* 43:701–3

15. Cobey J., Flanigin A., Foege W. 1993. Effective humanitarian aid: our only hope for intervention in civil war. *JAMA* 270:632–34

16. Desenclos J. C., Berry A. M., Padt R., Farah B., Segala C., Nabil A. M. 1989. Epidemiologic patterns of scurvy among Ethiopian refugees. *Bull. WHO* 67:309–16

17. Desenclos J. C., ed. 1992. *Clinical Guidelines. Diagnostic and Treatment Manual.* Paris: Med. Front. 2nd ed.

18. Dowell S. F., Toko A., Sita C., Piarroux R., Duerr A., Woodruff B. A. 1995. Health and nutrition in centers for unaccompanied children. Experience from the 1994 Rwandan refugee crisis. *JAMA* 273:1802–6

19. Gibb C. 1986. A review of feeding programmes in refugee reception centres in Eastern Sudan, October 1985. *Disasters* 10:17–24

20. Goma Epidemiol. Group. 1995. Public health impact of Rwandan refugee crisis. What happened in Goma, Zaire, in July 1994? *Lancet* 345:339–44

21. Hansch S., Lillibridge S. R., Egeland G., Teller C., Toole M. J. 1994. Lives lost, lives saved: excess mortality and the impact of health interventions in the Somalia emergency. Washington, DC: Refug. Policy Group

22. Macrae J., Zwi A., Forsythe V. 1995. Post-conflict rehabilitation: preliminary issues for consideration by the health sector. London: London Sch. Hyg. Trop. Med. London

23. Manoncourt S., Doppler B., Enten F., Nur A. E., Mohamed A. O., et al. 1992. Public health consequences of civil war in Somalia, April 1992. *Lancet* 340:176–77

24. Marfin A. A., Moore J., Collins C., Biellik R., Kattel U., et al. 1994. Infectious disease surveillance during emergency relief to Bhutanese refugees in Nepal. *JAMA* 272:377–81

25. Mast E. E., Polish L. B., Favorov M. O., Khudyakov Y. E., Khudyakova N. S., Margolis H. 1994. Hepatitis E among refugees in Kenya: minimal apparent person-to-person transmission, evidence for age-dependent disease expression, and new serological assays. In *Viral Hepatitis and Liver Disease*, ed. K. Kishioka, H. Suzuki, S. Mishiro, T. Oda, pp. 375–78. Tokyo: Springer-Verlag

26. McCloskey L. A., Southwick K. 1996. Psychosocial problems in refugee children exposed to war. *Pediatrics* 97:394–97

27. Mears C., Chowdhury S., eds. 1994. *Health Care for Refugees and Displaced People.* Oxford, UK: Oxfam

28. Moore P. S., Marfin A. A., Quenemoen L. E., Gessner B. D., Ayub Y. S., et al. 1993. Mortality rates in displaced and resident populations of Central Somalia during the famine of 1992. *Lancet* 341:935–38

29. Moore P. S., Toole M. J., Nieburg P., Waldman R. J., Broome C. V. 1990. Surveillance and control of meningococcal meningitis epidemics in refugee populations. *Bull. WHO* 68:587–96

30. Nieburg P., Waldman R. J., Leavell R., Sommer A., DeMaeyer E. M. 1988. Vitamin A supplementation for refugees and famine victims. *Bull. WHO* 66:689–97
31. *Nutrition Guidelines*. 1995. Paris: Med. Front. 1st ed.
32. Paquet C., van Soest M. 1994. Mortality and malnutrition among Rwandan refugees in Zaire. *Lancet* 344:823–24
33. Rieder H. L., Snider D. E., Toole M. J., Waldman R. J., Leowski J., et al. 1989. Tuberculosis control in refugee settlements. *Tubercle* 70:127–34
34. Sharp T. W., Yip R., Malone J. D. 1994. US military forces and emergency international humanitarian assistance: observations and recommendations from three recent missions. *JAMA* 272:386–90
35. Shears P., Berry A. M., Murphy R., Nabil M. A. 1987. Epidemiological assessment of the health and nutrition of Ethiopian refugees in emergency camps in Sudan, 1985. *Br. Med. J.* 295:314–18
36. Siddique A. K., Salam A., Islam M. S., Akram K., Majumdar R. N., et al. 1995. Why treatment centers failed to prevent cholera deaths among Rwandan refugees in Goma, Zaire. *Lancet* 345:359–61
37. Sudre P. 1993. Tuberculosis control in Somalia. *EM/TUB/180/E/R/5.93*. Geneva: WHO
38. Toole M. J., Bhatia R. 1992. A case study of Somali refugees in Hartisheik A camp, eastern Ethiopia: health and nutrition profile, July 1988–June 1989. *J. Refug. Stud.* 5:313–26
39. Toole M. J., Galson S., Brady W. 1993. Are war and public health compatible? *Lancet* 341:935–38
40. Toole M. J., Steketee R. J., Waldman R. J., Nieburg P. 1989. Measles prevention and control in emergency settings. *Bull. WHO* 67:381–88
41. Toole M. J., Waldman R. J. 1990. Prevention of excess mortality in refugee and displaced populations in developing countries. *JAMA* 263:3296–302
42. Toole M. J., Waldman R. J. 1993. Refugees and displaced persons: war, hunger, and public health. *JAMA* 270:600–5
43. UN Adm. Comm. Coord. Sub-Comm. Nutr. 1994. *Refug. Nutr. Inf. Syst.* 6:31
44. UN Adm. Comm. Coord. Sub-Comm. Nutr. 1994. *Refug. Nutr. Inf. Syst.* 7:30
45. UN Adm. Comm. Coord. Sub-Comm. Nutr. 1995. *Refug. Nutr. Inf. Syst.* 11:30
46. UN Adm. Comm. Coord. Sub-Comm. Nutr. 1995. *Refug. Nutr. Inf. Syst.* 13:29
47. UN Adm. Comm. Coord. Sub-Comm. Nutr. 1995. *Rep. Workshop Improvement Nutr. Refug. Displaced People in Africa, Machakos, Kenya*, Dec. 5–7. Geneva, Switz: UN
48. UN Adm. Comm. Coord. Sub-Comm. Nutr. 1996. *Refug. Nutr. Inf. Syst.* 15:33
49. UN Children's Fund. 1994. *The State of the World's Children*. New York: UN
50. UN High Comm. Refug. 1992. *Water Manual for Refugee Situations*. Geneva, Switz: UN
51. UN High Comm. Refug. 1992. *Convention and Protocol Relating to the Status of Refugees*. HCR/INF/29/Rev 3. Geneva, Switz
52. US Comm. Refug. 1994. *World Refugee Survey*. Washington, DC: GPO
53. US Comm. Refug. World Refugee Survey. 1995. Washington, DC: GPO
54. Van Damme W. 1995. Do refugees belong in camps? Experiences from Goma and Guinea. *Lancet* 346:360–62
55. Wallensteen P., Axell K. 1994. Conflict resolution and the end of the Cold War, 1989–93. *J. Peace Res.* 31:333–49

56. WHO. 1990. *Guidelines for Cholera Control.* WHO/CDD/SER/80.4 Rev. 2. Geneva: WHO

57. WHO Work. Group. 1986. Use and interpretation of anthropometric indicators of nutritional status. *Bull. WHO* 64:929–41

58. Woodruff B. A., Toole M. J., Rodrigue D. C., Brink E. W., et al. 1988. Disease surveillance and control after a flood: Khartoum, Sudan. *Disasters* 1990(14): 151–62

59. Wulf D., ed. 1994. *Refugee Women and Reproductive Health Care: Reassessing Priorities.* New York: Women's Comm. Refug. Women Child.

60. Yip R., Sharp T. W. 1993. Acute malnutrition and high childhood mortality related to diarrhea. *JAMA* 270:587–90

61. Zwi A., Ugalde A. 1991. Political violence in the Third World: a public health issue. *Health Policy Plan.* 6:203–17

23

COMMUNICABLE DISEASES IN COMPLEX EMERGENCIES

Impact and challenges

Máire A. Connolly, Michelle Gayer, Michael J. Ryan,
Peter Salama, Paul Spiegel and David L. Heymann

Source: *Lancet* 364 (2004), 1974–83.

Communicable diseases, alone or in combination with malnutrition, account for most deaths in complex emergencies. Factors promoting disease transmission interact synergistically leading to high incidence rates of diarrhoea, respiratory infection, malaria, and measles. This excess morbidity and mortality is avoidable as effective interventions are available. Adequate shelter, water, food, and sanitation linked to effective case management, immunisation, health education, and disease surveillance are crucial. However, delivery mechanisms are often compromised by loss of health staff, damage to infrastructure, insecurity, and poor co-ordination. Although progress has been made in the control of specific communicable diseases in camp settings, complex emergencies affecting large geographical areas or entire countries pose a greater challenge. Available interventions need to be implemented more systematically in complex emergencies with higher levels of coordination between governments, UN agencies, and non-governmental organisations. In addition, further research is needed to adapt and simplify interventions, and to explore novel diagnostics, vaccines, and therapies.

Search strategy

The authors undertook full searches of original research reports and reviews, using MEDLINE, PubMed, EMBASE, and WHO databases. Keywords were communicable disease, refugees, population displacement, epidemics, emergencies, immunisation, vector control, shelter, and specific diseases. The authors also used unpublished data from several WHO programmes and

426

from their own expertise and experiences with communicable disease control in complex emergencies.

More than 200 million people live in countries in which complex emergencies affect not only refugees and internally displaced people, but the entire population. Although 10 million refugees are under the protection of the UN High Commissioner for Refugees and can benefit from health interventions, internally displaced people and the conflict-affected population are often dependent on weakened governments (or anti-government forces), UN agencies such as WHO and UNICEF, and non-governmental organisations for delivery of health services. In most complex emergencies, communicable diseases alone, or more commonly in combination with malnutrition, are the major cause of illness and death (see table). Notable exceptions to this rule are the complex emergencies that took place in the former Yugoslavia, Chechnya, and Georgia.

The highest excess morbidity and mortality often occurs during the acute phase of the emergency. Death rates of over 60-fold the baseline have been recorded in refugees and displaced people, with over three-quarters of these deaths caused by communicable diseases.[1] The main causes of morbidity and mortality are diarrhoeal disease—including cholera and dysentery—acute respiratory infection, measles, and malaria, with HIV/AIDS and tuberculosis becoming increasingly important.[2] Children are at particular risk; of the ten countries with the worst mortality rates for children aged under 5 years, seven are affected by complex emergencies.[3]

Table Diseases targeted by preventive measures.

Preventive measure	Impact on spread of
Site planning	Diarrhoeal diseases, acute respiratory infections
Clean water	Diarrhoeal diseases, typhoid fever, guinea worm
Good sanitation	Diarrhoeal diseases, vector-borne diseases, scabies
Adequate nutrition	Tuberculous, measles, acute respiratory infections
Vaccination	Measles, meningitis, yellow fever, Japanese encephalitis, diphtheria
Vector control	Malaria, leishmaniasis, plague, dengue, Japanese encephalitis, yellow fever, other viral haemorrhagic fevers
Personal protection (insecticide-treated nets)	Malaria, leishmaniasis
Personal hygiene	Louse-borne diseases: typhus, relapsing fever, trench fever
Health education	Sexually transmitted infections, HIV/AIDS, diarrhoeal diseases
Case-management	Cholera, stigellosis, tuberculosis, acute respiratory infections, malaria, dengue, haemorhagic fever, meningitis, typhus, relapsing fever

The excess morbidity and mortality caused by communicable diseases during complex emergencies is largely avoidable, as appropriate interventions are available. Experience has shown that, when these interventions are implemented in a timely and coordinated manner, deaths and disease are substantially reduced.

Risk factors

Many factors promoting communicable disease transmission interact synergistically in complex emergencies. These factors include mass population movement and resettlement in temporary locations, overcrowding, economic and environmental degradation, impoverishment, scarcity of safe water, poor sanitation and waste management, absence of shelter, poor nutritional status as a result of food shortages, and poor access to health care. Additionally, the collapse or overwhelming of public health infrastructure and absence of health services hamper prevention and control programmes, with a consequent rise in vector-borne diseases such as malaria, trypanosomiasis, and yellow fever, and vaccine-preventable diseases such as measles and pertussis. The control of tuberculosis and HIV/AIDS is similarly disrupted. These factors are further compounded by absent or unstable governments, ongoing conflict and insecurity limiting access to the affected populations, dearth of drugs and supplies, and multiple agencies providing health care with poor coordination.

In addition to the humanitarian imperative to protect the health of populations in complex emergencies, there are several other justifications for communicable disease intervention in such emergencies. First, there might be a resurgence of old or previously controlled diseases (eg, malaria, trypanosomiasis), and the emergence of drug resistance driven by improper and incomplete use of drugs and the absence of regulatory controls (eg, bacillary dysentery and multidrug-resistant tuberculosis). Second, delays in detection, response, and containment of epidemics in conflict-affected countries represent a constant threat to surrounding countries and to the world. In 2002, 207 outbreak events of international public health importance were verified and 29% of them were recorded in countries affected by complex emergencies (WHO Outbreak, Alert and Response, unpublished). Third, countries affected by conflict represent important potential zones of new disease emergence because of delays in detection and characterisation of new pathogens and their widespread transmission before control measures can be implemented (eg, monkeypox in Democratic Republic of the Congo). Fourth, the continued presence in countries affected by conflict of diseases targeted for eradication (eg, poliomyelitis, Guinea-worm, and leprosy) represents a major threat to these goals and to the huge monetary investment in such initiatives.

Epidemiology

Diarrhoeal diseases

Diarrhoeal diseases are a major cause of morbidity and mortality in complex emergencies. These diseases mainly result from inadequate quality and quantity of water, substandard and insufficient sanitation facilities, overcrowding, poor hygiene, and scarcity of soap. In camp situations, diarrhoeal diseases have accounted for more than 40% of these deaths in the acute phase of an emergency, with over 80% of these deaths occurring in children aged under 2 years. Outbreak investigations have shown that common sources of infections include polluted water sources (by faecal contamination of surface water entering incompletely sealed wells), contamination of water during transport and storage (through contact with hands soiled by faeces), shared water containers and cooking pots, scarcity of soap, and contaminated foods.

After the influx of 800 000 Rwandan refugees into North Kivu, Democratic Republic of the Congo, in 1994, 85% of the 50 000 deaths that were recorded in the first month were caused by diarrhoeal diseases, of which 60% were a result of cholera and 40% were caused by shigella dysentery.[4] The most important cause was scarcity of water; the mean water allowance provided by agencies per person per day in the first week of the crisis was 200 mL.[5] 55 cholera epidemics were reported in Democratic Republic of the Congo between March, 2001 and October, 2002, with a total of 38 000 cases including 2129 deaths affecting 51 health zones in seven provinces, with a case fatality rate of 5.6% (range: 0–33.7%) (WHO Alert and Response, unpublished data). Effective cholera preparedness and control measures should keep case fatality rates below 1%. In a camp situation, in which outbreaks are more easily propagated, a cholera outbreak can last between 3 and 12 weeks;[6] in non-camp settings in Democratic Republic of the Congo, the median duration was 16 weeks (range: 3–59 weeks). In more stable settings, increased frequency of diarrhoeal disease was associated with increased crude and under-5 mortality rates in an investigation of 51 post-emergency camps in seven countries from 1998 to 2000.[7]

Acute respiratory infections

Acute respiratory infections also account for a large proportion of the morbidity and mortality burden in complex emergencies. Conditions such as overcrowding, indoor fires, and inadequate shelter and blankets, especially in cold climates, provide favourable conditions for respiratory droplet transmission. Acute respiratory infections likewise amplify the transmission risk for meningococcal disease through aerosol transmission of respiratory secretions during coughing and sneezing.

429

Acute respiratory infections caused 63% of the morbidity in Nicaraguan refugees in Costa Rica in 1989.[8] In 1993, 30% of the under-5 deaths in residents of Kabul, Afghanistan and 23% of those in displaced people were a result of acute respiratory infections.[9] Pneumonia together with malaria and diarrhoea caused 80% of deaths in Congolese refugee children in Tanzania in 1999.[10] Most data on acute respiratory infections in complex emergencies are limited to mortality; few studies have been done on morbidity rates and even fewer on the specific pathogens causing these infections.

Some interventions in complex emergencies such as vaccination for measles, diphtheria, and pertussis have the added value of reducing the risk of acute respiratory infections, as these vaccine-preventable diseases not only cause acute respiratory infections but also diminish host defences and increase vulnerability to secondary bacterial infections. Vitamin A supplementation during measles vaccination campaigns also acts as a protective factor for acute respiratory infections independently of measles.[11,12]

Measles

Epidemics of measles have been a major cause of mortality in camp settings. Measles accounted for 53% and 42% of deaths in refugees in eastern Sudan and Somalia in 1985, respectively.[13] However, such epidemics were not reported as frequently in the 1990s compared with the 1980s[14] and this trend seems to be continuing. A major factor has been the heightened awareness of the importance of mass measles vaccination campaigns by international agencies and the rapid implementation of an expanded programme on immunisation vaccination programmes in post-emergency settings and camps.[7,15] Of major concern, however, are reports of large-scale epidemics in countries affected by complex emergencies. Of the 15 countries that reported a national measles vaccination coverage of less than 50% in 1999, at least seven were affected by complex emergencies.[16]

Widespread measles epidemics have been reported in Ethiopia,[17] Democratic Republic of the Congo (WHO Alert and Response, unpublished data), and Afghanistan.[18] In Afghanistan alone, before a national campaign, an estimated 30000–35000 deaths caused by measles were recorded annually.[19] The proportion of cases in children older than 5 years in such settings can be substantial. More than two-thirds of measles cases in southern Iraq occur in children 5 years and older as a result of absence of immunisation during the early 1990s after the first Gulf War. In fact, substantial mortality could occur in older children and adults, especially in remote rural settings in which populations might not have been exposed to natural measles virus infection and routine childhood immunisation does not happen.[17] In stable populations, the case fatality rates generally range from 1–5% during the acute phase of the illness.[20] Although epidemics can be well controlled in camps in both the acute and post-emergency phases, this might not be the case in general complex emergency settings, with reported case fatality rates as high as 33%.

Overcrowding is associated with the transmission of a higher infectious dose of measles virus resulting in more severe clinical disease.[21] The frequency of severe measles is also higher in malnourished children, with results from one study showing a dose-response relation between the degree of wasting and cumulative frequency of measles in the preceding 2 weeks.[17] In addition to its association with wasting, measles also rapidly depletes vitamin A stores resulting in eye disease such as xerophthalmia and blindness. Because of poor diversity in diet, vitamin A deficiency might already be common in countries affected by complex emergencies.

Malaria

At least 90% of the 1 million annual deaths from malaria worldwide occur in sub-Saharan Africa and about 30% of malaria deaths in Africa happen in countries affected by complex emergencies.[22] People moving from areas of low endemicity (including non-immune people) to hyperendemic areas are exposed to high malarial transmission. Conversely, movement from hyperendemic to lower endemic areas also heightens epidemic risk in the local communities, especially if there are favourable conditions for the mosquito vector such as stagnant water, flooding, and changes in environment and weather patterns.

Overcrowded conditions and temporary shelters, which increase bite frequency, also promote the transmission cycle. Inadequate access to health care services, which prevents early and appropriate treatment, protracts the time parasites remain in the blood. A massive malaria epidemic happened in Burundi between October, 2000 and March, 2001, affecting seven of 17 provinces; there were over 2.8 million cases in a country with a population of 7 million. A combination of population movement, long-term breakdown in control efforts since the war started in 1993, and high levels of *Plasmodium falciparum* resistance to chloroquine were suggested to be the cause.[23]

Interruption of vector control programmes might not only lead to epidemics but might also cause reemergence of disease. In Afghanistan, malaria was almost eliminated with aggressive vector control programmes in the 1960s and 1970s, before civil unrest began in 1979. However, during the past 30 years the disease has returned, with over 12 of 21 million people now living in malaria-endemic areas and an estimated 2–3 million cases in 1999, mainly caused by *Plasmodium vivax*, but increasingly caused by *P falciparum*.[24]

Meningitis

Large outbreaks of meningococcal meningitis have been reported in complex emergencies. Serogroup A and C of *Neisseria meningitidis* are the main causes of epidemic meningococcal meningitis in most countries, although serogroup W135 is becoming increasingly prevalent in sub-Saharan Africa. Epidemics are happening beyond the traditional meningitis belt to include east, southern, and central Africa (eg, Burundi, Rwanda, and Tanzania from June to October, 2002). Dry season, dust storms, overcrowding, and high rates of acute respiratory infections also amplify the risk of epidemic meningococcal disease.

There were six epidemics of meningococcal meningitis in Democratic Republic of the Congo in the first half of 2002 alone, affecting six health zones in four provinces (WHO Alert and Response, unpublished data). An outbreak in February, 1994, in a Sudanese refugee camp in northern Uganda lasted for over 1 year, and was reported to have begun in the camp's reception centre.[25] A meningococcal outbreak in 2003 affected eight of 12 provinces in Rwanda, seven of 17 provinces in northeastern Burundi, and refugee camps in neighbouring Kibondo province, Tanzania.

Tuberculosis

Tuberculosis is becoming an important problem in complex emergencies. Population mobility and scarcity of access to health services and drugs interrupt tuberculosis control programmes, and transmission is increased as a result of overcrowding and malnutrition. Additionally, complex emergencies might encourage the development of chronic cases and multidrug resistance because of low case detection, high defaulter, and low cure rates, further heightening transmission.[26] Over 85% of refugees originate from, and stay within, countries with high tuberculosis burdens.[27]

Tuberculosis is also a leading cause of death in HIV-infected people. Co-infection with HIV increases the risk of a latent infection progressing to active tuberculosis from 10% to 60–80%.[28] HIV-infected people are also at greater risk of developing severe side-effects from tuberculosis drugs. Additionally, the combination of antiretrovirals and antituberculosis drugs might temporarily worsen the immune status as in the immune reconstitution inflammatory syndrome, and also lead to adverse drug interactions.[29] For example, rifampicin, an antituberculosis drug, induces liver enzymes to break down antiretrovirals, thereby reducing their levels in the blood and potentially leading to drug resistance.

HIV/AIDS

There is a large overlap between countries affected by complex emergencies and those with high HIV prevalance, especially in sub-Saharan Africa. Conflict and displacement could amplify the risk of contracting HIV through use of unsafe blood, poor universal precautions in health care facilities, absence of treatment of sexually transmitted infections, which facilitates HIV transmission, behavioural changes including risk-taking behaviour and contractual sex, scarcity of condoms, and sexual violence.[30] However, these issues should be weighed against the reduction in accessibility and mobility of populations affected by long-standing crises and the pre-conflict baseline HIV prevalence. For example, Sierra Leone, which experienced war from 1991 to 2002, has a low HIV infection rate compared with neighbouring countries.[31] Conversely, the conflict in Côte d'Ivoire, a country with a higher HIV prevalence than its neighbours, raised concern that displaced people might actually exacerbate the HIV situation in surrounding countries. A similar concern surrounds the repatriation of refugees living in Namibia and Zambia, countries with high HIV prevalence, to Angola, a country with low HIV prevalence despite more than two decades of civil war.[32]

Humanitarian agencies have only recently recognised the importance of HIV/AIDS in complex emergencies, believing it was mainly a development issue.[33] However, some of the early HIV/AIDS programmes in complex emergencies were undertaken in Sudanese refugees in Ethiopia in 1992,[34] and Rwandan refugees in Tanzania in 1994.[35] The Interagency Standing Reference Group on HIV/AIDS in Emergency Settings has revised the emergency guidelines and added a matrix of interventions to be undertaken during a complex emergency.[36,37]

Viral haemorrhagic fevers

Outbreaks of viral haemorrhagic fevers are becoming increasingly frequent in complex emergencies. This is partly attributable to better surveillance but also shows changes in human behaviour that potentiate the risk of viral introduction and amplification in human populations. The major viral haemorrhagic fever threats to human populations in complex emergency settings are Ebola haemorrhagic fever, yellow fever, Lassa fever, and Crimean-Congo haemorrhagic fever.[38] Although viral haemorrhagic fevers cause fewer cases and deaths in people in complex emergencies than other communicable diseases, their high case fatality rate and massive psychological effects in the affected communities can be devastating.

Trypanosomiasis and leishmaniasis

Democratic Republic of the Congo had a striking resurgence of trypanosomiasis or sleeping sickness as a direct consequence of conflict. In 1930, over 33 000 cases were recorded, falling to less than 1000 in 1959 after active case finding and treatment.[39] Conflict in the 1960s led to the collapse of the control programme, and, in 2001, the number of cases of trypanosomiasis was estimated to be 40 000 with a prevalence of over 70% in some villages (WHO Communicable Disease Control, Prevention Eradication, unpublished data).

A major outbreak of cutaneous leishmaniasis was reported for the first time in the North-West Frontier province of Pakistan in 1997 in an Afghan refugee camp established for 17 years; the outbreak was probably a result of cross-border movement of infected migrants from Kabul, as the Afghan capital was undergoing a similar outbreak at the time.[40] An epidemic of visceral leishmaniasis (kala azar) in western Upper Nile in Sudan was estimated to have caused 100000 deaths between 1984 and 1994.[41]

Diseases targeted for eradication

Countries affected by complex emergencies present major challenges in the drive to achieve global eradication of diseases. Guinea-worm eradication has been very successful, with the 3.5 million cases of less than 20 years ago now reduced by 98%. 20 formerly endemic countries have eliminated the disease. However, southern Sudan, which had more than 50% of the world's cases in 1995, reported more than 78% of the world's cases in 2001, despite several interventions to stop transmission in the continuing conflict.[42]

Similarly, the WHO Polio Eradication Initiative is focusing on several west African countries, and Afghanistan and Pakistan, where progress has been hampered by conflict. Efforts to achieve eradication during conflict have led to the establishment of more effective immunisation and disease surveillance systems, and poliomyelitis transmission has been interrupted in complex emergency countries such as Cambodia, El Salvador, the Philippines, and Sri Lanka.[43]

Interventions

Prevention and control of communicable diseases, case management, and surveillance are three key components of humanitarian response that provide major opportunities to reduce suffering and death in war-affected populations. Prevention and control interventions exist for the major high mortality communicable diseases. These interventions need to be widely implemented but might need simplification and standardisation according to the context of the situation.

The combination of malnutrition and infection causes most of the preventable deaths in complex emergencies, especially in young children. Malnourished people have compromised immunity and are not only more likely to contract communicable diseases, but also suffer from more frequent, severe, and prolonged episodes of these diseases.

Prevention and control

Site planning and shelter

Site planning at the beginning of an emergency can reduce the frequency of diarrhoeal diseases, acute respiratory infections, measles, meningitis, tuberculosis, and vector-borne diseases. There should be adequate space within and between shelters, and sites should have ready access to water, fuel, and transport, have fertile soil, and be secure. Environmental care, solid waste management, and protection of food stores can prevent explosions in rodent populations and outbreaks of diseases such as tularaemia that took place in post-war Kosovo in 1999–2000[44] and the rise in reported Lassa fever cases in Sierra Leone in 2003. International guidelines for the ideal size of refugee camps are now accepted,[7,45] but refugees increasingly tend to live in the host population so planning can be difficult.[46–49]

Water and sanitation

Aggressive public health preventive measures should augment traditional food and medical relief efforts during a complex emergency. Provision of sufficient clean water (for which minimum agreed standards exist),[50] adequate sanitation for excreta disposal, and management of medical and other solid waste can reduce diarrhoeal disease, typhoid fever, vector-borne disease, and scabies. Public education and sensitisation on issues of water, latrine use, and hygiene are vital in any water and sanitation programme. During the 1991 Kurdish refugee crisis, despite prompt relief efforts and good health status of the population, high rates of malnutrition and mortality were recorded because sufficient preventive interventions were not implemented in a timely way.[51] The provision of appropriate and sufficient water containers,[50] cooking pots, and fuel early in the relief response can reduce the risk of cholera by ensuring that water storage is protected and that food is cooked. Chlorination of water is essential but supplementary home chlorination might be necessary if acceptable, as is provision of soap and sufficient fuel or firewood for cooking.[52] Even the presence of soap used mainly for bathing and washing clothes (200 g per person per month) without education regarding hand-washing was associated with 27% fewer episodes of diarrhoea.[53] A minimum of 250 g of soap should be available per person per month.[50] The combination of malnutrition and infection causes most of the preventable deaths in complex emergencies, particularly in young children. Malnourished individuals have compromised immunity and are not only more likely to contract communicable diseases, but also suffer from more frequent, severe, and prolonged episodes of these diseases. In complex emergencies, it is essential that the food needs of the population are satisfied through the provision of an adequate general ration, and in some situations, through selective feeding programmes.

Immunisation

The major vaccines used in emergency situations are against measles, meningococcal meningitis, poliomyelitis, and yellow fever. Measles immunisation should be implemented immediately in all complex emergency situations if vaccine coverage rates are less than 90% and should not await a single case. Measles campaigns are one of the most cost-effective interventions in public health.[54] Recommendations have concentrated on the need to extend the upper age limit of measles campaigns from 4 years to 12 or 14 years;[55] however, the upper age limit for vaccination should be decided after a thorough review of the epidemiology of measles in the particular setting, and vaccine availability and resources. Furthermore, because case fatality rates might be very common in children aged 6–9 months as protection from maternal antibody wanes, this group should also be included in campaigns. These children, however, need to be revaccinated when they reach 12 months of age. Additionally, unless vitamin A is being delivered through another mechanism— for example, as part of national immunisation days for poliomyelitis—its administration should always be combined with measles campaigns.

Immunisation is the only means of protecting against yellow fever and is the key intervention in an outbreak. Poliomyelitis is not a disease that kills during complex emergencies, but it is associated with poor water and sanitation. The fact that these conditions are common during complex emergencies impedes global plans for its eradication.

Vector control

Important diseases commonly spread by vectors are malaria, dengue, Japanese encephalitis, yellow fever, typhus, and trypanosomiasis. Examples of vector control interventions that have been implemented in complex emergencies include insecticide-treated nets, indoor residual spraying for malaria, and traps for tsetse flies that transmit trypanosomiasis.

The choice of intervention is not prescriptive and depends on effectiveness, feasibility, cost, and speed of supply. The type of shelter available, human behaviour (cultural practices, mobility), and vector behaviour (biting cycle, indoor or outdoor resting vectors) are key local factors in making a decision. Insecticide-treated nets are effective against mosquitoes if properly used by the target population and if the nets can be supported or hung. In malaria-endemic areas of Africa, insecticide-treated nets are the most effective intervention, especially in young children, substantially reducing mortality by up to 60% and morbidity by 45% in trials in The Gambia.[56–58]

Indoor residual spraying of insecticide is commonly used in chronic emergency situations and is appropriate for populations that live in more permanent housing structures and in which the vector rests indoors. The programme should treat all houses and, although effective in west and south Asia when sprayed at the beginning of the transmission season, insecticide spraying is less effective in southeast Asia and of restricted use in the highly endemic parts of Africa. In chronic complex emergencies, repeated application can become very expensive. Environmental control is generally difficult and ineffective in an emergency except on a local scale. Draining water around water tap stands, larviciding breeding sites if these are few in number, and draining ponds if these are not used for washing can all reduce vector breeding sites. Aerial spraying, scrub clearance, and outdoor spraying with residual insecticide are inappropriate interventions at any stage of an emergency.

Epidemic preparedness and response

Epidemic preparedness and the ability to detect and verify the existence of epidemics from the onset of a complex emergency are crucial for early containment of outbreaks and reduction in mortality. There are often delays in detection resulting from an absence of appropriate surveillance and communications infrastructure, staff with no technical knowledge, and insufficient resources to analyse, investigate, and respond adequately to alerts. These delays often occur when populations affected by conflicts are widely dispersed and living in an area with a collapsed public health infrastructure. Early warning necessitates a much broader notion of surveillance using rumours of epidemics generated from early warning networks, involving, for example, non-governmental organisations (both health and non-health) and community workers. This should be combined with the capacity to verify rumours and undertake field investigations to confirm outbreaks through simple descriptive epidemiology and targeted clinical sampling for laboratory diagnosis. Similarly, an effective outbreak response often needs the same networks to be the engine of the response. Planning for such events is vital and should be done with a broad set of partners and adequate provision made to ensure availability of drugs, vaccines, and other supplies such as personal protective equipment that might be needed.

Provisions for appropriate collection, processing, and transport of clinical specimens to designated laboratories, either in or outside the country, should be instituted. Laboratory services are often seen as a low priority in emergency situations and although syndromic diagnosis can be useful in screening because it is sensitive, it is not very disease-specific. Improvement of clinical skills and also the use of simple laboratory tests (malaria rapid diagnostic tests and smears, stool, and urine microscopy) can help to improve diagnosis and therefore management of the patient.

Infection control in health-care settings is a major issue as the scarcity of even the most basic precautions can drive epidemics that are spread easily. Diarrhoeal diseases such as cholera and viral haemorrhagic fevers like Ebola can be amplified in settings with poor infection control. Planning for case management in complex emergencies should address basic infection control such as universal precautions, injection safety, medical waste management, and the planning for and provision of safe and simple isolation facilities.

Specific health education messages can help prevent many diseases including diarrhoeal disease, sexually transmitted infections, and HIV/AIDS. Understanding of personal hygiene can help to prevent diarrhoeal disease, scabies, and louse-borne diseases such as typhus, and relapsing fever. Understanding of local practices and participation of the community is key in implementing these interventions. An investigation in a Malawian refugee camp that underwent repeated cholera outbreaks showed that an improved water bucket with cover and spout to prevent household contamination was more acceptable to the population, despite the existence of a less familiar but more cost-effective method of chlorinating water.[59]

Community education and mobilisation is particularly important for case management of sexually transmitted infections in terms of contact tracing, and for directly observed therapy for TB to ensure treatment completion. At the community level, one home visitor for every 500–1000 people and one traditional birth attendant for 2000 people can be used as a guide. Activities and interaction between refugees and local communities, and culturally appropriate interventions and education need to be considered in any health education programme for disease prevention and control.

Case management

A high standard of care and treatment interventions is crucial in reducing mortality from communicable diseases. Inadequate community outreach, underuse of oral rehydration treatment, a slow rate of rehydration, use of inappropriate intravenous fluids, and inadequate experience of health workers in management of severe cases were some of the factors causing high mortality rates during the 1994 cholera outbreak in Goma, Democratic Republic of the Congo. The highest reported case fatality rate for a single day was 48%.[60] Heightened provision of qualified or local health care workers or both has been associated with reduced crude mortality rates and under-5 mortality rates.[7]

The use of standard treatment protocols in health facilities with agreed upon first-line drugs is also crucial to ensure effective diagnosis and treatment. For acute respiratory infections, empirical treatment with antibiotics is commonly used in complex emergencies based on WHO and national protocols, individual non-governmental organisation guidelines, and occasionally integrated management of childhood illness guidelines. These guidelines need standardisation and adaptation for adults, especially adults with HIV/AIDS, as there are additional pathogens causing acute respiratory infections in these individuals, and the management of the pathogens needs to be more aggressive to prevent complications.

In malaria management, the first priority is the prevention of mortality through early diagnosis and effective treatment. However, increased resistance of *P falciparum* to older antimalarials such as chloroquine and sulfadoxine-pyrimethamine means these drugs have lost effectiveness in most countries. WHO recommends a change in protocol to artemesinin-based combination treatments in countries where resistance levels to older antimalarials have reached 15%; these treatments are recommended by WHO for vulnerable populations affected by complex emergencies because they are highly efficacious, safe, and offer good patient compliance. However, standards for intermittent preventive treatment for pregnant women in complex emergency situations need to be developed.

A simplified and efficient drug regimen is especially important in complex emergencies. Effective, short-course antibiotics need to be identified for pneumonia, shigella dysentery, and sexually transmitted infections, with appropriate education about compliance and treatment. A 3-day regimen of amoxicillin in treating childhood pneumonia is as effective as a 5-day course, which is commonly used in developing countries.[61] A single dose 2-day course of ciprofloxacin could be used for treatment of *Shigella dysenteriae* type 1 rather than the twice-daily 5-day course.[62] Although single-dose formulations are available for the treatment of sexually transmitted infections (azithromycin, ceftriaxone sodium, cefixime, ciprofloxacin), the cheaper but longer (7-day) regimens of doxycycline and erythromycin are commonly used.

Implementation of tuberculosis control programmes in complex emergencies is feasible using the WHO tuberculosis control strategy, Directly Observed Therapy, Short-course (DOTS). Guidelines for refugee camps exist and are being revised and expanded to cover complex emergencies.[27] Local community education and a reliable drug supply are essential in any tuberculosis control programme, as is convenient and acceptable dosing such as thrice-weekly combination treatment rather than daily administration. Use of outreach workers from each ethnic group is important for compliance, as is reducing the distance travelled to seek drugs. An income-generation component could be incorporated to encourage people to stay on the programme after resolution of conflict. In the past, tuberculosis programmes in displaced populations were discouraged as their high mobility made treatment completion difficult, and were judged temporary. However, many complex emergencies are chronic and successful tuberculosis programmes using directly observed therapy in displaced people have been reported in northern India,[63] in Cambodian refugees in Thailand,[64] and in Rwandan and Burundian refugees in Tanzania.[65]

The syndromic management of sexually transmitted infections, which is necessary because of poor diagnostic facilities, might further facilitate antibiotic resistance. Additionally, the high rate of asymptomatic gonococcal and chlamydial infection, particularly in women, not only causes complications, but also facilitates the transmission of HIV. A rapid diagnostic test to detect symptomless infection and allow targeted treatment is warranted. At this stage, most countries affected by complex emergencies, although not providing antiretroviral drugs, should at least provide treatment for opportunistic infections in people living with HIV/AIDS. However, as the drugs become more affordable and voluntary testing and counselling becomes more commonplace, antiretroviral treatment will become a component of humanitarian aid. There are closely similar considerations to tuberculosis treatment in such situations, such as compliance and drug resistance.

439

Surveillance and surveys

Appropriate and effective response to and management of complex emergencies need timely and accurate data obtained from health information systems.[66] Data are obtained to identify and plan for the initial and evolving needs of the affected population and subgroups, to detect epidemics and to prioritise interventions, and to investigate the quality, coverage, and effectiveness of response and programmes. Generally three types of data are obtained: (1) rapid health assessments, consisting of an initial overview of the immediate effect and needs; (2) surveys, defined as intermittent, focused assessments that gather population-based health data; and (3) surveillance, defined as the ongoing, systematic gathering, analysis, and interpretation of health data. Baseline information and trends over time are essential for interpretation.

The four main areas included in a health information system are: (1) mortality; (2) morbidity; (3) nutritional status; and (4) programme indicators. The magnitude of mortality is often used to determine the stage of an emergency, with a crude mortality rate of ≥ 1 death per 10 000 people per day defining the acute emergency phase.[50,67] However, this arbitrary cutoff might not be appropriate in many circumstances (eg, in developed country crises) and thus a doubling of the baseline crude mortality rate is a more appropriate definition if the data are available.[68] Crude mortality rate and under-5 mortality rate are the most commonly reported mortality rates in complex emergencies; however, in developed countries undergoing conflict, other age-specific mortality rates, such as those in elderly people, might be as important.[69] During epidemics, attack rates and case fatality rates need to be calculated.

Research needs

New instruments for complex emergencies are needed, such as rapid diagnostics, insecticide-treated material (eg, blankets and plastic sheeting), new heat stable vaccines, improved geographic information systems and mapping, and improved surveillance and learning instruments (see panel).

Pre-emptive vaccination strategies with oral cholera vaccine are possible only in stable refugee settings, chronic complex emergencies, or in chronic situations with recurrent or seasonal outbreaks where populations are believed to be at risk of an epidemic within 6 months (and not during an ongoing outbreak). Two cholera 01 vaccines are available (a two-dose killed vaccine, and a one-dose live vaccine which is not recommended in African settings in view of the high HIV seroprevalence). Mass vaccination with the two-dose oral cholera vaccine was proved feasible in a refugee camp of 45 000 people in Uganda with 87% coverage after the second round.[70] However, there are many limitations to the use of the vaccines such as the high cost per dose, the chaotic nature of an acute phase of an emergency, restricted accessibility because of security and infrastructure, difficult logistics requiring cold chain

---

***Panel*: Areas where further research is needed include**

Rapid field diagnostics

Use of artemisinin derivatives for malaria, especially in pregnancy, and new antimalarials for intermittent preventive treatment in zones of *P falciparum* resistance to Fansidar

New, short-course therapies for acute respiratory infections, tuberculosis, and typhoid fever

Vaccines—heat-stability, pentavalent vaccines, rotavirus vaccine for infants

Zinc supplementation (with oral rehydration solution)

Survey methodologies for complex emergencies

Mapping and instruments for calculating size of affected populations

---

and shipping, and the minimum 4–5 weeks needed to achieve protection. A cost-effectiveness analysis of strategies for cholera control showed that vaccination and pre-emptive treatment would become more cost-effective than treatment alone if the cost of vaccine, now over US$4, fell to less than $0.12 per dose.[71]

Simple, effective, and affordable methods are needed to treat and safely store non-piped, gathered household water. Point-of-use chlorination and storage in special plastic containers of gathered household water reduced diarrhoeal illness in consumers living in poor sanitation and hygiene conditions in different countries.[72] In Bolivia, monthly episodes of household diarrhoeal illness were 1.25 and 2.2 in intervention and control families, respectively, indicating that 43% of community diarrhoea was preventable by use of the intervention. In Bangladesh, mean episodes of childhood diarrhoea per 1000 days were 19.6 and 24.8 in intervention and control groups, respectively, indicating that about 24% of recorded diarrhoea was preventable by using the intervention. Chlorine disinfection and storage in an appropriate container substantially improved the microbiological quality of non-piped household drinking water and reduced community diarrhoeal disease. Widespread use of this simple treatment and storage system for non-piped domestic water has the potential to greatly reduce the global burden of waterborne diarrhoeal disease.

Insecticide-treated nets are very effective in preventing malaria, however, in complex emergency situations, not everyone is able to afford or obtain a net, and sleeping in tents and under plastic sheeting needs novel and more convenient means of protection. Treated plastic sheeting and bedding have been tested in complex emergencies in Asia and Africa and are a promising option. Permethrin-treated outer clothing worn in the evening or in bed is effective in South Asia but has not been tested in Africa. Insecticide-treated top-sheets, blankets, and cloth wraps (chaddars) in Islamic countries could be used as protection in complex emergency situations. A randomised controlled trial in an Afghan refugee camp in Pakistan of permethrin-treated chaddars used for sleeping and top-sheets showed the chance of a malaria episode was reduced by 64% in children under 10 years and by 38% in people under 20 years.[73] A community-based trial of impregnated bed sheets in Kenya suggest that permethrin-impregnated bed sheets might be protective against malaria in individuals over 5 years old. No protective effect was seen in under-5 year olds; however, the trial had few participants and was done during a malaria epidemic in 1997–98 after El Niño rains.[74]

Plastic sheeting of polyethylene tarpaulins has replaced canvas tents previously used in camp settings. Insecticide-sprayed or impregnated plastic tarpaulins have the potential to prevent malaria transmission and reduce the fly population and factory-impregnated tarpaulins are being field-tested in phase III trials. Outdoor testing of deltramethrin sprayed or factory-impregnated tarpaulins in a refugee camp in Pakistan resulted in 86%–100% mosquito mortality whereas non-treated tarpaulin produced only a 5% mosquito mortality.[75] Although they do not provide a physical barrier to mosquitoes and thus do not protect the individual directly, treated plastic sheeting, if used by most inhabitants, can potentially control malaria by killing high proportions of mosquitoes, thereby reducing their transmission capacity. Complex emergencies are increasingly being characterised by dwellings with a combination of mud, thatch, and plastic, and further investigation into present and new vector control methods are needed.

Some studies suggest that the effectiveness of measles vaccine might be poorer than expected in some warmer, rural settings.[76] More studies are urgently needed to formally document breakdown in vaccine supply and logistics and to develop a more thermostable measles vaccine for developing countries with poor cold chain infrastructure including complex emergencies.

Much of the high excess morbidity and mortality due to communicable diseases that occur in populations in complex emergencies is avoidable. Effective interventions are available but are often poorly implemented, especially in non-camp settings where large geographical areas or entire countries are affected. Available interventions need to be implemented in a more systematic and coordinated manner by governments, UN agencies, and non-governmental agencies. Additionally, further research is needed to adapt and simplify interventions as well as exploring new ones.

References

1 Paquet C., Hanquet G. Control of infectious diseases in refugee and displaced populations in developing countries. *Bull Inst Pasteur* 1998; **96**: 3–14.

2 Connolly M. A., Heymann D. L. Deadly comrades: war and infectious diseases. *Lancet* 2002; **360** (suppl): s23–s24.

3 Black R. E., Morris S. S., Bryce J. Where and why are 10 million children dying every year? *Lancet* 2003; **361**: 2226–34.

4 Goma Epidemiology Group. Public health impact of Rwandan refugee crisis: what happened in Goma, Zaire, in July, 1994? *Lancet* 1995; **345**: 339–44.

5 Bioforce. Cholera in Goma, July 1994. *Rev Epidemio Sante Publique* 1996; **44**: 358–63.

6 World Health Organization. The potential role of new cholera vaccines and control of outbreaks during emergencies. Report of a meeting, 13–14 February 1995. Geneva. Geneva: WHO, 1995. CDR/GPV/95.1

7 Spiegel P., Sheik M., Gotway-Crawford C., Salama P. Health programmes and policies associated with decreased mortality in displaced people in postemergency phase camps: a retrospective study. *Lancet* 2002; **360**: 1927–34.

8 Diaz T., Achi R. Infectious diseases in a Nicaraguan refugee camp in Costa Rica. *Trop Doct* 1989; **19**: 14–17.

9 Gessner B. D. Mortality rates, causes of death, and health status among displaced and resident populations of Kabul, Afghanistan. *JAMA* 1994; **272**: 382–85.

10 Talley L., Spiegel P. B., Girgis M. An investigation of increasing mortality among Congolese refugees in Lugufu camp, Tanzania. May–June 1999. *J Refug Stud* 2001; **14**: 412–27.

11 Julien M. R., Gomes A., Varandas L., et al. A randomized, double-blind, placebo-controlled clinical trial of vitamin A in Mozambican children hospitalized with non measles acute lower respiratory tract infections. *Trop Med Int Health* 1999; **4**: 794–800.

12 Fawzi W. W., Mbise R., Spiegelman D., Fataki M., Hertzmark E., Ndossi G. Vitamin A supplements and diarrheal and respiratory tract infections among children in Dar es Salaam, Tanzania. *J Pediatr* 2000; **137**: 660–67.

13 Toole M. J., Waldman R. J. An analysis of mortality trends among refugee populations in Somalia, Sudan, and Thailand. *Bull World Health Organ* 1988; **66**: 237–47.

14 Toole M. J., Waldman R. J. Refugees and displaced persons. War, hunger and public health. *JAMA* 1993; **270**: 600–05.

15 Toole M. J., Steketee R. W., Waldman R. J., Neiburg P. Measles prevention and control in emergency settings.
Bull World Health Organ 1989; **67**: 381–88.

16 WHO/UNICEF. Measles; mortality reduction and regional elimination strategic plan 2001–5. WHO/VB/01.13 Geneva: WHO, 2001.

17 Salama P., Assefa F., Talley L., et al. Malnutrition, measles, mortality and the humanitarian response during a famine in Ethiopia. *JAMA* 2001; **286**: 563–71.

18 Ahmad K. Measles epidemic sweeps through Afghanistan. *Lancet* 2000; **355**: 1439.

19 Centers for Disease Control and Prevention. National campaign against measles in Afghanistan targeting children 6 months to 12 years of age. *MMWR Morb Mortal Wkly Rep* 2003; **52**: 363–66.

20 World Health Organization. Guidelines for epidemic preparedness and response to measles outbreaks. Geneva: WHO, 1999. WHO/CDS/CSR/ISR/99.1.

21 Aaby P. Malnutrition and overcrowding/intensive exposure in severe measles infection: review of community studies. *Rev Infect Dis* 1988; **10**: 478–91.

22 WHO. Roll Back Malaria. http://mosquito.who.int/cmc_upload/0/000/015/366/RBMInfosheet_7.pdf (accessed July 21, 2003).

23 WHO. Prevention and control of malaria epidemics. 3rd meeting of the Technical Support Network. Geneva: WHO, 2002. WHO/CDS/RBM/2002.40.

24 WHO. Communicable disease profile: Afghanistan and neighbouring countries. WHO/CDS 2002. Geneva: WHO, 2002.

25 Santaniello-Newton A., Hunter P. R. Management of an outbreak of meningococcal meningitis in a Sudanese refugee camp in Northern Uganda. *Epidemiol Infect* 2000; **124**: 75–81.

26 Kessler C., Connolly M., Levy M., Chaulet P. Tuberculosis control in refugees and displaced persons, www.crid.or.cr/digitalizacion/pdf/eng/doc8955/doc8955.htm (accessed July 22, 2003).

27 World Health Organization. Tuberculosis control in refugee situations: an inter-agency field manual. Geneva: WHO, 1997.

28 American Public Health Association. Control of communicable diseases manual. 17th edn. James Chin, ed. Washington DC: American Public Health Association, 2000: 525.

29 Colebunders R., Lambert M. L. Management of co-infection with HIV and TB. *BMJ* 2002; **324**: 802–03.

30 Khaw A. J., Salama P., Burkholder B., Dondero T. J. HIV risk and prevention in emergency-affected populations: a review. *Disasters* 2000; **24**: 181–97.

31 Kaiser R., Spiegel P., Salama P., et al. HIV sero-prevalence and behavioral risk factor survey in Sierra Leone, April 2002. Atlanta: Centers for Disease Control and Prevention, 2002.

32 Spiegel P., De Jong E. HIV/AIDS and refugees/returnees: mission to Angola. Luanda: United Nations High Commissioner for Refugees, 2003.

33 Guidelines for HIV interventions in emergency settings. Geneva: UNHCR, WHO, UNAIDS, 1995.

34 Holt B. Y., Effler P., Brady W., et al. Planning STI/HIV prevention among refugees and mobile populations: situation assessment of Sudanese refugees. *Disasters* 2003; **27**: 1–15.

35 HIV/AIDS and STI prevention and care in Rwandan refugee camps in the United Republic of Tanzania: Best practice collection. Geneva: UNHCR, UNAIDS, 2003.

36 Interagency standing committee (IASC) on HIV/AIDS in emergency settings. Matrix of HIV/AIDS interventions in emergencies. Geneva: IASC, 2002: 12.

37 Interagency standing committee (IASC) on HIV/AIDS in emergency settings. Guidelines for HIV/AIDS interventions in emergencies. Geneva: IASC, 2004.

38 LeDuc J. W. Epidemiology of hemorrhagic fever viruses. *Rev Infect Dis* 1989; **11** (suppl 4): S730–35.

39 Van Nieuwenhove S., Betu-Ku-Mesu V. K., Diabakana P. M., Declercq J., Bilenge C. M. Sleeping sickness resurgence in the DRC: the past decade. *Trop Med Int Health* 2001; **6**: 335–41.

40 Rowland M., Munir A., Durrani N., Noyes H., Reyburn H. An outbreak of cutaneous leishmaniasis in an Afghan refugee settlement in north/west Pakistan. *Trans R Soc Trop Med Hyg* 1999; **93**: 133–36.

41 Seaman J., Mercer A. J., Sondorp E. The epidemic of visceral leishmaniasis in western Upper Nile, southern Sudan: course and impact from 1984 to 1994. *Int J Epidemiol* 1996; **25**: 862–71.

42 Hopkins D. R., Withers P. C. Jr. Sudan's war and eradication of dracunculiasis. *Lancet* 2002; **360** (suppl): s21–s22.

43 Tangermann R. H., Hull H. F., Jafari H., Nkowane B., Everts H., Aylward R. B. Eradication of poliomyelitis in countries affected by conflict. *Bull World Health Organ* 2000; **78**: 330–38.

44 Reintjes R., Dedushaj I., Gjini A., et al. Tularemia outbreak investigation in Kosovo: case control and environmental studies. *Emerg Infra Dis* 2002; **8**: 69–73.

45 Mercer A. Mortality and morbidity in refugee camps in eastern Sudan: 1985–90. *Disasters* 1992; **16**: 28–42.

46 Aaby P., Gomes J., Fernandes M., Djana Q., Lisse I., Jensen H. Nutritional status and mortality of refugee and resident children in a non-camp setting during conflict: follow up study in Guinea-Bissau. *BMJ* 1999; **319**: 878–81.

47 Dualeh M. W. Do refugees belong in camps? *Lancet* 1995; **346**: 1369–70.

48 Harrell-Bond B. Camps: literature review. *Forced Migration Rev* 1998; **2**: 22–23.

49 Van Damme W. Do refugees belong in camps? Experiences from Goma and Guinea. *Lancet* 1995; **346**: 360–62.

50 Steering Committee for Humanitarian Response. The Sphere project: humanitarian charter and minimum standards in disaster response. Oxford: Oxford Publishing, 2004.

51 Yip R., Sharp T. W. Acute malnutrition and high childhood mortality related to diarrhoea. Lessons from the 1991 Kurdish refugee crisis. *JAMA* 1993; **270**: 587–90.

52 Hatch D. L., Waldman R. J., Lungu G. W., Piri C. Epidemic cholera during refugee resettlement in Malawi. *Int J Epidemiol* 1994; **23**: 1292–99.

53 Peterson E. A., Roberts L., Toole M. J., Peterson D. E. The effect of soap distribution on diarrhoea: Nyamithuthu refugee camp. *Int J Epidemiol* 1998; **27**: 520–24.

54 Jamison D. T., Mosley W. H., Measham A. R., Bobadilla J. L. Disease control priorities in developing countries. Oxford: Oxford University Press, 1993.

55 Médecins Sans Frontières. Refugee health: an approach to emergency situations. London: Macmillan Education, 1997.

56 Alonso P. L., Lindsay S. W., Armstrong Schellenberg J. R., et al. A malaria control trial using insecticide-treated bed nets and targeted chemoprophylaxis in a rural area of The Gambia, west Africa. 6. The impact of the interventions on mortality and morbidity from malaria. *Trans R Soc Trop Med Hyg* 1993; **87** (suppl 2): 37–44.

57 Graves P. M., Brabin B. J., Charlwood J. D., et al. Reduction in incidence and prevalence of *Plasmodium falciparum* in under-5-year-old children by permethrin impregnation of mosquito nets. *Bull World Health Organ* 1987; **65**: 869–77.

58 Alonso P. L., Lindsay S. W., Armstrong J. R., et al. The effect of insecticide-treated bed nets on mortality of Gambian children. *Lancet* 1991; **337**: 1499–502.

59 Roberts L., Chartier Y., Chartier O., Malenga G., Toole M., Rodka H. Keeping clean water clean in a Malawi refugee camp: a randomized intervention trial. *Bull World Health Organ* 2001; **79**: 280–87.

60 Siddique A. K., Salam A., Islam M. S., et al. Why treatment centres failed to prevent cholera death among Rwandan refugees in Goma, Zaire. *Lancet* 1995; **345**: 359–61.

61 Pakistan Multicentre Amoxicillin Short Course Therapy (MASCOT) pneumonia study group. Clinical efficacy of 3 days versus 5 days of oral amoxicillin for treatment of childhood pneumonia: a multicentre double-blind trial. *Lancet* 2002; **360**: 835–41.

62 Soares J. L., Arendt V., Coue J. C., et al. Short-term ciprofloxacin treatment of bacillary dysentery due to Shigella dysenteriae type 1 in Rwandan refugees. *Med Trop* 1994; **54**: 319–23.

63 Rodger A. J., Toole M., Lalnuntluangi B., Muana V., Deutschmann P. DOTS-based tuberculosis treatment and control during civil conflict and an HIV epidemic, Churachandpur District, India. *Bull World Health Organ* 2002; **80**: 451–56.

64 Sukrakanchana-Trikham P., Puechal X., Rigal J., Rieder H. L. 10-year assessment of treatment outcome among Cambodian refugees with sputum smear-positive tuberculosis in Khao-I-Dang, Thailand. *Tuber Lung Dis* 1992; **73**: 384–87.

65 Rutta E., Kipingili R., Lukonge H., Assefa S., Mitsilale E., Rwechungura S. Treatment outcome among Rwandan and Burundian refugees with sputum smear-positive tuberculosis in Ngara, Tanzania. *Int J Tuberc Lung Dis* 2001; **5**: 628–32.

66 Marfin A. A., Moore J., Collins C., et al. Infectious disease surveillance during emergency relief to Bhutanese refugees in Nepal. *JAMA* 1994; **272**: 377–81.

67 Centers for Disease Control and Prevention. Famine-affected, refugee, and displaced populations: recommendations for public health issues. *MMWR Morb Mortal Wkly Rep* 1992; **41** (RR-13): 1–76.

68 Spiegel P., Salama P. Emergencies in developed countries: are aid organisations ready to adapt? *Lancet* 2001; **357**: 714.

69 Spiegel P. B., Salama P. War and mortality in Kosovo, 1998–99: an epidemiological testimony. *Lancet* 2000; **355**: 2204–09.

70 Legros D., Paquet C., Perea W., et al. Mass vaccination with a two-dose oral cholera vaccine in a refugee camp.
Bull World Health Organ 1999; **77**: 837–42.

71 Naficy A., Rao M. R., Paquet C., Antona D., Sorkin A., Clemens J. D. Treatment and vaccination strategies to control cholera in sub-Saharan refugee settings: a cost-effectiveness analysis. *JAMA* 1998; **279**: 521–25.

72 Sobsey M. D., Handzel T., Venczel L. Chlorination and safe storage of household drinking water in developing countries to reduce waterborne disease. *Water Sci Technol* 2003; **47**: 221–28.

73 Rowland M., Durrani N., Hewitt S., et al. Permethrin-treated chaddars and top-sheets. Appropriate technology for protection against malaria in Afghanistan and other complex emergencies. *Trans R Soc Trop Hyg* 1999; **93**: 465–72.

74 Macintyre K., Sosler S., Letipila F., et al. A new tool for malaria prevention?: results of a trial of permethrin-impregnated bedsheets (shukas) in an area of unstable transmission. *Int J Epidemiol* 2003; **32**: 157–60.

75 Graham K., Mohammad N., Rehman H., et al. Insecticide-treated plastic tarpaulins for control of malaria vectors in refugee camps. *Med Vet Entomol* 2002; **16**: 404–08.

76 Chen R. T., Weierbach R., Bisoffi Z., et al. A 'Post-honeymoon period' measles outbreak in Muyinga Sector, Burundi. *Int J Epidemiol* 1994; **23**: 185–93.

24

THE THREAT OF COMMUNICABLE DISEASES FOLLOWING NATURAL DISASTERS

A public health response

Stephen C. Waring and Bruce J. Brown

Source: *Disaster Management & Response*, 3:2 (2005), 41–7.

Natural disasters, such as the recent Indian Ocean tsunami, can have a rapid onset, broad impact, and produce many factors that work synergistically to increase the risk of morbidity and mortality caused by communicable diseases. The primary goal of emergency health interventions is to prevent epidemics and improve deteriorating health conditions among the population affected. Morbidity and mortality due to infectious diseases can be minimized providing these intervention efforts are implemented in a timely and coordinated fashion. This article presents a review of some of the major issues relevant to preparedness and response for natural disasters.

On December 26, 2004, an earthquake off the coast of Sumatra in the Indian Ocean triggered a widespread tsunami that resulted in one of the worst natural disasters in modern history (see Web site *http://www.usaid.gov*). Massive casualties that occurred were the result of the direct impact of the tsunami and were mostly a result of drowning or severe trauma from debris. Numerous people were injured and in need of medical or surgical attention, and many survivors were displaced because of damage or destruction of dwellings and massive disruption of infrastructure throughout the affected region.*

---

* According to the WHO report of February 1, 2005, there were 148,724 confirmed deaths, 142,123 missing, 34,410 injured (requiring immediate medical attention), and more than 1.5 million displaced (see Web site *www.who.int.en*).

In the days and weeks following such a devastating disaster, the threat of infectious disease outbreaks is high. The goal of emergency health is to prevent epidemics and improve deteriorating health conditions among the population affected. The highest priority is directed toward diseases that could potentially cause excess mortality and morbidity as a result of the disaster.[1] Immediately following the tsunami disaster, the World Health Organization (WHO) Health Action in Crisis Network was activated to support disease surveillance, advise on outbreak situations, support needs assessments and restoration of public health infrastructure, and mobilize resources and supplies such as drugs and water purification tablets (see Web site *http://www.who.int*). Because public health provides critical services to support clinical care activities, this article provides a timely review of issues relevant to preparation, response, and successful completion of the challenging missions associated with public health disaster relief.

Risk for communicable diseases

Natural disasters that have a rapid onset and broad impact can produce many factors that work synergistically to increase the risk of morbidity and mortality resulting from communicable diseases.[2] Large numbers of people are forced to seek temporary shelter in crowded conditions with inadequate sanitation and waste management, compromised sources of water, potential food shortages, malnutrition, and a low level of immunity, all factors that play a key role in compounding the devastation.[3,4]

The social environment can add further compromise for relief and recovery efforts. Although disease outbreaks are more likely to occur when disasters hit poor and developing regions,[2] an outbreak may occur any time conditions and circumstances favor such an event regardless of where the disaster strikes. Areas that are affected by armed conflicts may experience significant outbreaks.

Providing emergency responses

Pre-event preparation

The morbidity and mortality resulting from infectious diseases can be minimized if public health intervention efforts are implemented in a timely and coordinated fashion. Disaster response is a complex process that requires continual review and revision of preparedness missions at the local, national, and international level. Such efforts are greatly facilitated by ongoing government, academic, and private organizations that have programs designed to provide up-to-date training and education. The public health workforce can take advantage of these services to ensure preparedness planning and responding to complex emergencies and disasters (Tables 1 and 2).

Table 1 Education and training.

- Association of Schools of Public Health, Centers for Public Health Preparedness
  http://www.asph.org/acphp/index.cfm
- Centers for Disease Control and Prevention, Public Health Training Network
  http://www.phppo.cdc.gov/phtn/default.asp
- World Health Organization Health Action in Crisis
  http://www.who.int/hac/techguidance/training/en/
- Federal Emergency Management Agency, Education and Training
  http://www.fema.gov/tab_education.shtm
- American Red Cross Community Disaster Education Materials
  http://www.redcross.org/pubs/dspubs/cde.html#target
- National Disaster Medical System, Response Team Training Program
  http://ndms.umbc.edu/information.asp
- United Nations Disaster Management Training Program
  http://www.undmtp.org/
- American Medical Association, National Disaster Life Support
  http://www.ama-assn.org/ama/pub/category/12606.html

Table 2 Sources for a more in-depth review on emergency preparedness and response.

- Centers for Disease Control and Prevention
  http://www.bt.cdc.gov/
- World Health Organization
  General Information: *http://www.who.int/en/*
  Communicable Disease Control Field Manual: *http://www.who.int/csr/don/en/*
- Federal Emergency Management Agency
  http://www.fema.gov/
- American Red Cross
  http://www.redcross.org/index.html
- Sphere Organization
  http://www.sphereproject.org/

Post-event epidemiology and surveillance

Baseline information. A crucial initial step for a public health emergency response is to establish adequate disease surveillance systems that take into account the inherent disruption of the public health infrastructure. Outbreaks are prevented when public health can detect increases in diarrheal, respiratory, and other communicable diseases early and rapidly. Therefore, responders will need to use pre-impact epidemiologic information, such as baseline (expected) frequencies and distributions of disease (ie, incidence, prevalence, and mortality), known risks, immunization coverage for vaccine preventable diseases, and awareness (education) among the community to plan and implement the response.[5-7]

Rapid assessments. Responders should conduct a health assessment of the community as soon as possible within the first week following a disaster. The primary purpose is to identify the immediate impact and health needs in order to enhance timely decision making and direct planning. Rapid health assessments use all available pre-impact information on baseline health, as well as other characteristics of the region (eg, demographic, geographic, environmental, health facilities and services, transportation routes, and security), information from key informants, and visual inspection of the affected area.[8]

Rapid epidemiologic assessments can provide more detailed analysis of ongoing threats and facilitate monitoring of response and recovery. These assessments should be planned and completed as soon as possible following the initial health assessments and build on the information already acquired. While rapid epidemiologic assessments require additional resources and multiple skills and expertise, they have been used in a number of postdisaster settings to assess immediate health needs and facilitate ongoing response efforts.[9–15]

Surveillance and assessment systems need to be tailored to whatever means are available during the immediate period after the impact. In a disaster setting with widespread disruption and displacement, information networks could include a variety of sources, ranging from rumors from untrained observers to communications with local health care providers. The goal is to have the capacity to initiate field investigations immediately to verify all potential outbreaks.

Details such as laboratory protocols, case definitions, and case management protocols for all catchment areas need to be addressed during the initial phase of the response. The frequency and method of reporting (usually a telephone alert system) also should be established as a matter of protocol at the outset with the necessary resources and personnel in place to ensure effective monitoring. Thresholds for every disease with epidemic potential should be established, and it should be determined at what point above that level that a response must be initiated (ie, epidemic threshold).[8]

The actual implementation of surveillance and rapid needs assessments under field conditions is not without substantial challenges. The goal is timely and accurate delivery of information on the health status of an affected population, which needs to be adequately understood and communicated to ensure the effort will meet expectations. Issues such as compromises between what is collected and how it is to be analyzed, competing priorities for the same information, limitations of resources, lack of available information required to produce meaningful estimates, and lack of standardization of collection and reporting protocols are all considerations for planning and implementing such an endeavor.[16]

Anticipated diseases following disasters

Diarrheal diseases

Diarrheal diseases may be a major contributor to overall morbidity and mortality rates following a disaster. After a disaster there is a large scale disruption of infrastructure, water quality becomes compromised, there is poor sanitation, and massive numbers of the population are displaced into temporary crowded shelters. Common sources of infection are contaminated water supplies and contaminated foods. One of the leading causes of diarrhea in such crowded conditions is cholera, which can spread rapidly and lead to very high mortality rates across all age groups. According to the WHO, cholera continues to be a major global threat in many developing regions of the world, and the threat of an epidemic is constant throughout any given year.[17,18] Cholera must be rapidly recognized and treated in the acute post-disaster phase to prevent an epidemic (see Table 3). The emergence of antibiotic-resistant strains of *Vibrio cholera* complicate control efforts in some regions and also should be taken into consideration when treating patients who do not respond to conventional therapy. Other causes of diarrheal disease are also capable of contributing to a high incidence of morbidity and mortality following a disaster (Table 3). More than 350,000 cases of diarrhea resulted from the July 2004 flood in Bangladesh, many resulting from *Escherichia coli*, particularly in children; dysentery (*Shigella*); and cholera.[19] Cholera and dysentery warrant particular concern because of their ease of transmission, rapid spread in crowded conditions, and immediate life-threatening conditions. Guidelines on managing an outbreak of acute diarrhea in emergency settings are available from the WHO (see Web site *http://w3.whosea.org*). Other foodborne and waterborne diseases such as typhoid fever, hepatitis, and leptospirosis also are capable of producing severe illness and high case fatalities.

Acute respiratory infections

Acute respiratory infections can be a major cause of morbidity and mortality in emergency settings. The combination of overcrowding, susceptibility, malnourishment, and poor ventilation in temporary shelters increase the risk for pneumonia. Many acute infections involve only the upper respiratory system and may be mild and self-limiting. Lower respiratory infections, such as bronchitis and pneumonia, generally are more severe and require medical attention and even hospitalization. According to the WHO, acute respiratory infections account for up to 20% of all deaths in children younger than 5 years, with the majority of deaths resulting from pneumonia. Therefore, depending on the region affected and the characteristics of the displaced population and temporary dwellings, acute respiratory infections may account for a major portion of the overall morbidity.[3] Acute-care clinicians should be aware of the potential for exposure resulting from aspiration of contaminated flood water. Early recognition and management are keys to avoiding an outbreak.

Measles

While measles epidemics are an expected threat in some complex emergency settings, few outbreaks have been associated with acute natural disasters.[2,3]

Table 3 Communicable diseases with epidemic potential (all except tetanus) in natural disasters.

Disease	Transmission	Agent	Clinical features	Incubation period
Waterborne				
Cholera	Fecal/oral, ontaminated water or food	*Vibrio cholerae* serogroups O1 or O139	Profuse watery diarrhea, vomiting	2 hours to 5 days
Lepto-spirosis	Fecal/oral, contaminated water	*Leptospira* spp	Sudden onset fever, headache, chills, vomiting, severe myalgia	2–28 days
Hepatitis	Fecal/oral, contaminated water or food	Hepatitis A, E virus	Jaundice, abdominal pain, nausea, diarrhea, fever, fatigue and loss of appetite	15–50 days
Bacillary dysentery	Fecal/oral, contaminated water or food	*Shigella dysenteriae* type 1	Malaise, fever, vomiting, blood and mucous in stool	12–96 hours
Typhoid fever	Fecal/oral, contaminated water or food	*Salmonella typhi*	Sustained fever, headache, constipation	3–14 days
Acute respiratory				
Pneumonia	Person to person by airborne respiratory droplets	*Streptococcus pneumoniae, Haemophilus influenzae*, or viral	Cough, difficulty breathing, fast breathing, chest indrawing	1–3 days
Direct contact				
Measles	Person to person by airborne respiratory droplets	Measles virus (*Morbillivirus*)	Rash, high fever, cough, runny nose, red and watery eyes; serious postmeasles complications (5%–10% of cases)—diarrhea, pneumonia, croup	10–12 days
Bacterial Meningitis (meningococcal meningitis)	Person to person by airborne respiratory droplets	*Neisseria meningitides*— serogroups A, C, W135	Sudden onset fever, rash, neck stiffness; altered consciousness; bulging fontanelle in <1 year of age	2–10 days
Wound-related				
Tetanus	Soil	*Clostridium tetani*	Difficulty swallowing, lockjaw, muscle rigidity, spasms	3–21 days
Vectorborne				
Malaria	Mosquito (*Anopheles* spp)	*Plasmodium falciparum, P vivax*	Fever, chills, sweats, head and body aches, nausea and vomiting	7–30 days
Dengue fever	Mosquito (*Aedes aegypti*)	Dengue virus-1, -2, -3, -4 (*Flavivirus*)	Sudden onset severe flu-like illness, high fever, severe headache, pain behind the eyes, and rash	4–7 days
Japanese encephalitis	Mosquito (*Culex* spp)	Japanese encephalitis virus (*Flavivirus*)	Quick onset, headache, high fever, neck stiffness, stupor, disorientation, tremors	5–15 days
Yellow fever	Mosquito (*Aedes, Haemogogus*)	Yellow fever virus (*Flavivirus*)	Fever, backache, headache, nausea, vomiting; toxic phase-jaundice, abdominal pain, kidney failure	3–6 days

CSF, Cerebrospinal fluid; *ELISA*, enzyme-linked immunosorbent assay; *HAV*, Hepatitis A virus; *HEV*, hepato-encephalomyelitis virus; *JE*, Japanese encephalitis; *WCC*, white blood cell count.

Table 3 (cont'd)

Diagnosis	Treatment	Prevention/control
Direct microscopic observation of *V cholerae* in stool	Intensive rehydration therapy; antimicrobials based on sensitivity testing	Hand washing, proper handling of water/food and sewage disposal
Leptospira-specific IgM serologic assay	Penicillin, amoxicillin, doxycycline, erythromycin, cephalosporins	Avoid entering contaminated water; safe water source
Serologic assay detecting anti-HAV of anti-HEV IgM antibodies	Supportive care; hospitalization and barrier nursing for severe cases; close monitoring of pregnant women	Hand washing, proper handling of water/food and sewage disposal; Hepatitis A vaccine
Suspect if bloody diarrhea; confirmation requires isolation of organism from stool	Nalidixic acid, ampicillin; hospitalization of seriously ill or malnourished; rehydration	Hand washing, proper handling of water/food and sewage disposal
Culture from blood, bone marrow, bowel fluids; rapid antibody tests	Ampicillin, trimethoprim-sulfamethoxazole, ciprofloxacin	Hand washing, proper handling of water/food and sewage disposal; mass vaccination in some settings
Clinical presentation; culture respiratory secretions	Co-trimoxazole, chloramphenicol, ampicillin	Isolation; proper nutrition; if cause is *Streptococcus*, polyvalent vaccine to high-risk populations
Generally made by clinical observation	Supportive care; proper nutrition and hydration; vitamin A; control fever; antimicrobials in complicated cases with pneumonia, dysentery; treat conjunctivitis, keratitis	Rapid mass vaccination within 72 hours of initial case report (priority to high risk groups if limited supply); Vitamin A in children 6 mo to 5 years of age to prevent complications and reduce mortality
Examination of CSF—elevated WCC, protein; gram-negative diplococci	Penicillin, chloramphenicol, ampicillin, ceftriaxone, cefotaxime, co-trimoxazole; supportive therapy; diazepam for seizures	Rapid mass vaccination
Entirely clinical	Tetanus immune globulin	Thorough wound cleaning, tetanus vaccine
Parasites on blood smear observed using a microscope; rapid diagnostic assays if available	Chloroquine, sulfadoxine-pyrimethamine	Mosquito control, insecticide-treated nets, bedding, clothing
Serum antibody testing with ELISA or rapid dot-blot technique	Intensive supportive therapy	Mosquito control, isolation of cases, mass vaccination
Serologic assay for JE virus IgM specific antibodies in CSF or blood (acute phase)	Intensive supportive therapy	Mosquito control, isolation of cases, mass vaccination
Serologic assay for yellow fever virus antibodies	Intensive supportive therapy	Mosquito control, isolation of cases, mass vaccination

Global awareness and rapid implementation of post-emergency immunization campaigns have contributed to a trend of decreasing frequency of reports of measles epidemics during the past couple of decades.[20] However, following the eruption of Mount Pinatubo in the Philippines in 1991, measles accounted for 25% of the cases of morbidity and 22% of the cases of mortality among the more than 100,000 people displaced. The high morbidity and mortality rates were attributed to the indigenous tribe who were the majority of the displaced population and who had a very low immunization coverage and cultural barriers to care.[21] Therefore, the possibility of a measles epidemic following a natural disaster remains high and can only be prevented through an effective early warning system and rapid response to suspicious reports. Indeed, in the ongoing post-tsunami relief efforts throughout Indonesia and other regions, the WHO early warning system has been integral in preventing a measles epidemic (see Web site *http://www.who/int/en*).

Tetanus

The likelihood of tetanus also should be a consideration in any disaster situations, such as a tsunami. The inherent chaos from collapsing structures and swirling debris inflicts numerous crush injuries, fractures, and serious contaminated wounds. Tetanus is an expected complication when disasters strike in regions where tetanus immunization coverage is low or nonexistent. It is essential that injured people receive prompt surgical and medical care of contaminated open wounds as well as appropriate tetanus immunization and immunoglobulin, depending on vaccination history and seriousness of the wound infection (see Web site *http://www.who/int/en*).

Vectorborne diseases

The risk of acquiring a vectorborne disease, such as malaria and dengue fever, is usually higher following a disaster such as a hurricane (typhoon), flood, or tsunami because of an increase in the number and range of vector habitats. Whereas the initial force may actually flush out mosquito breeding sites, the insects return shortly after waters begin to recede. The changing dynamics of vector breeding, coupled with the displacement of large numbers of people into temporary crowded shelters, favor vectorborne outbreaks even in areas where normal transmission risk is low. There generally is a lag time of up to 8 weeks before the onset of vectorborne diseases.[22]

Malaria. Malaria epidemics represent serious public health emergencies that occur with little warning. When disasters occur in malaria-endemic areas where the public health infrastructure is disrupted and highly vulnerable populations exist, the likelihood of an epidemic is high. An epidemic of malaria in a disaster setting usually occurs 4 to 8 weeks after initial impact and is characterized by several weeks duration before it peaks.

It is possible to control malaria in the early stages when cases are diagnosed early and treated. If laboratory diagnosis is limited or delayed, treatment can be based solely on clinical history without demonstration of parasites.[23] Vectors of malaria are exclusively from the mosquito genus *Anopheles*, which breed in stagnant fresh or brackish water. Transmission efficiency depends on species of mosquito, preferred breeding habitats, and prevalence of the parasite. In some endemic areas, the disruptions caused by flooding may change what would otherwise be poor breeding conditions, such as primarily salt water, into those more favorable for increased breeding. This can occur when water is diluted by rain or other sources of fresh water. Malaria is becoming more difficult to control because of an emergence of antimalarial resistance to medications over the years and an increased transmission potential. The vector habitats may have an expanding range as a result of climatic changes associated with global warming.[24] Malaria control is important for diverse regions like that affected with the Indian Ocean tsunami.

Dengue. Dengue spreads rapidly and may affect large numbers of people during an epidemic. Dengue Hemorrhagic Fever is associated with high mortality, particularly in children. There has been a dramatic increase in the incidence of disease during the past 20 years, with up to an estimated 100 million cases occurring annually.[25] The virus is endemic throughout all tropical regions of the world and is transmitted by *Aedes* mosquitoes, primarily *Ae aegypti*. The vector is particularly suited for an urban cycle of transmission because it breeds primarily in containers and other sources of standing water in and around human dwellings rather than groundwater pools and swamps.

Similar to malaria, conditions following a disaster increase the likelihood of a dengue epidemic, and only through adequate early warning and rapid response can outbreaks be contained. Effective prevention and control for both diseases requires vector control, which may prove challenging during recovery periods depending on availability of adequate resources and appropriate access to breeding habitats.

Closing comments

Emergency health relief workers are concerned with the rapid detection and response to immediate health needs. The role of public health is to prevent epidemics with interventions such as proper placement of shelters, adequate sanitation and personal hygiene, provision of clean water and adequate nutrition, vaccinations, vector control, and health education.[8] Any emergency response designed to mitigate adverse health effects resulting from natural disasters requires a multidisciplinary approach that employs a broad range of expertise to help minimize exposure to known health threats while identifying and attending to those in need of immediate treatment. This multidisciplinary effort also forms the framework for postdisaster recovery, which will require extensive ongoing preparedness planning, education, and training efforts.

We are hopeful for continued progress toward complete recovery from the Indian Ocean tsunami disaster and other disasters that occurred before or since December 26, 2004. The ultimate goal is to translate lessons learned from these devastating events into better preparedness and response for another natural disaster or other complex emergency certain to follow, if not already here.

References

1. US Agency for International Development (USAID). Disaster reduction: a practitioner's guide. Office of US Foreign Disaster Assistance; Washington, DC: 2002.
2. Toole M. J. Communicable diseases and disease control. In: Noji E., editor. The public health consequences of disasters. New York: Oxford University Press; 1997. pp. 79–100.
3. Connolly M. A., Gayer M., Ryan M. J., Salama P., Spiegel P., Heymann D. L. Communicable diseases in complex emergencies: impact and challenges. Lancet 2004;364:1974–83.
4. World Health Organization. Tsunamis: technical hazard sheet and natural disaster profile. WHO; Geneva: 2005.
5. Noji E. K. Disaster epidemiology and disease monitoring. J Med Systems 1995;19:171–4.
6. Noji E. K. Disaster epidemiology. Emerg Med Clin North Am 1996;14:289–300.
7. Noji E. K. The public health consequences of disasters. Prehosp Disaster Med 2000;15:147–57.
8. Connolly M. A. Communicable disease control in emergencies: a field manual. WHO; Geneva: 2005.
9. Centers for Disease Control and Prevention. Rapid assessment of injuries among survivors of the terrorist attack on the World Trade Center—New York City, September 2001. JAMA 2002;287:835–8.
10. Centers for Disease Control and Prevention. Rapid assessment of vectorborne diseases during the Midwest flood—United States, 1993. MMWR 1994;43:481–3.
11. World Health Organization. Expanded programme on immunization. Rapid assessment of serological response to oral polio vaccine. Weekly Epidemiol Record 1990;65:34–5.
12. Glass R. I., Cates W. Jr, Nieburg P., Davis C., Russbach R., Nothdurft H., et al. Rapid assessment of health status and preventive-medicine needs of newly arrived Kampuchean refugees, Sa Kaeo, Thailand. Lancet 1980;1:868–72.
13. Henderson R. H., Sundaresan T. Cluster sampling to assess immunization coverage: a review of experience with a simplified sampling method. Bull World Health Org 1982;60:253–60.
14. Malilay J., Flanders W. D., Brogan D. A modified cluster-sampling method for post-disaster rapid assessment of needs. Bull World Health Org 1996;74:399–405.
15. Waring S. C., Reynolds K. M., D'Souza G., Arafat R. R. Rapid assessment of household needs in the Houston area after Tropical Storm Allison. Disaster Manage Response 2002;Sep:3–9.
16. Wetterhall S. F., Noji E. K. Surveillance and epidemiology. In: Noji E., editor. The public health consequences of disasters. New York: Oxford University Press; 1997. pp. 37–64.

17. Goma Epidemiology Group. Public health impact of Rwandan refugee crisis: what happened in Goma, Zaire, in July, 1994? Goma Epidemiology Group [see comment]. Lancet 1995;345:339–44.
18. World Health Organization. Cholera, 2003. Weekly Epidemiology Record. WHO; Geneva: 2004.
19. Akram K., Zamman K. Floods Situation Report 13 October 2004. In: WHO-SEA, editor. Emergency and humanitarian action. Geneva: WHO; 2004.
20. Spiegel P., Sheik M., Gotway-Crawford C., Salama P. Health programmes and policies associated with decreased mortality in displaced people in post emergency phase camps: a retrospective study. Lancet 2002;360:1927–34.
21. Centers for Disease Control and Prevention. Surveillance in evacuation camps after the eruption of Mt. Pinatubo, Philippines. MMWR 1992;41:9–12.
22. World Health Organization. Flooding and communicable diseases fact sheet: risk assessment and preventive measures. Available from: *http://who.int/hac/ techguidance/ems/flood_cds*.
23. Trigg P. Malaria epidemics: forecasting, prevention, early detection and control: from policy to practice. Roll Back Malaria Department. Leysin, Switzerland. 2004.
24. Saker L., Lee K., Cannito B., Gilmore A., Campbell-Lendrum D. Globalization and infectious diseases: a review of the linkages. Special Programme for Research and Training in Tropical Diseases. WHO; Geneva: 2004.
25. World Health Organization. SEARO regional guidelines on dengue/DHF prevention and control (updated 2004). WHO Regional Publication 1997. Available from: *http://w3.whosea.org*.